# The Complete Four Sport Stadium Guide

By The Sports Staff of USA Today

Edited by Balliett & Fitzgerald

Tom Dyja, Project Editor

**ACKNOWLEDGEMENTS:** Buzzy Albert, Kevin Allen, Mel Antonen, Hrayr Avakian, Steve Ballard, Rod Beaton, Jarrett Bell, Susan Bokern, Jerry Bonkowski, Erik Brady, Mike Brehm, Reid Cherner, Dan Denton, Mike Dodd, Eric Duhatschek, David DuPree, Gordon Forbes, Barbara Geehan, Chuck Johnson, Gabe Labao, Rick Lawes, Ford Levy, Michelle Mattox, Wayne McKnight, Silvia Molina, Claire Moran, Carrie Muskat, Gene Policinski, Robert Robinson, Jack Rux, Ted Ryan, Walter Rykiel, Claude Saindon, Jon Saraceno, Pohla Smith, Mark Spector, Bob Velin, Larry Weisman.

**A Balliett & Fitzgerald Book**

for

**Fodor's Travel Publications, Inc.**

New York ∗Toronto ∗ London ∗ Sydney ∗ Auckland

First Edition

ISBN: 0-679-02849-8

Special thanks to the staff at Balliett & Fitzgerald Inc., including managing editor Duncan Bock; design consultant Steven Johnson; graphic artists Eric Liftin, Phil Chin and Rachel Florman; editorial assistants Milly Hui, Stephanie Schwartz and Philip Hood; and contributing editor for basketball and baseball, Bruce Adelson;also to Chelsea Mauldin at Fodor's and especially to John Shostrom.

Cover Design: John Olenyik

Book Design: High Falls Design

Cover Photographs: Mike Powell/AllSport (baseball player); Stephen Parker/ Syracuse Univ. S.I.D. (basketball player); Brian Drake/Sportschrome (hockey player); Robert Tringali, Jr./Sportschrome (football player)

**Special Sales**

Fodor's Travel Publications are available at special discounts for bulk purchases (100 copies or more) for sales promotions or premiums. Special editions, including personalized covers, excerpts of existing guides, and corporate imprints, can be created in large quantities for special needs. For more information, write to Special Marketing, Fodor's Travel Publications, 201 East 50th St., New York, NY 10022. Inquiries from Canada should be sent to Random House of Canada Ltd., Marketing Department, 1265 Aerowood Drive, Mississauga, Ontario L4W 1B9.

MANUFACTURED IN THE UNITED STATES OF AMERICA

10 9 8 7 6 5 4 3 2 1

# How to use the Four Sport Stadium Guide

THE USA TODAY FOUR SPORT STADIUM GUIDE IS designed to give fans at home and on the road a detailed, insider's view into every Major League Baseball, National Football League, National Basketball Association and National Hockey League venue in the USA and Canada. This unique volume delivers team trivia and strategic tips for those following a game at home and up-to-date, direct and savvy practical information for those visiting the park. Each stadium includes a color illustration and seating diagram. By using the USA TODAY Four Sport Stadium Guide, your knowledge about the ins and outs of each stadium and arena will match that of longtime fans at those venues.

The Guide is divided into four sections: baseball, football, basketball and hockey. Each league's section covers the primary venue for every team (listed alphabetically by city). We have chosen the venue for the current or upcoming season, with the exception of expansion teams that have yet to begin play. If a venue is used for two sports, it is covered in each sport's section. Venue chapters are 1 to 3 pages long, depending on the sport and the length and eventfulness of a team's stay in its current home, with as much information about each team as space will allow. Topics covered differ only slightly from sport to sport (for instance, information about training camps is included only for baseball and football, because access is less available to basketball and hockey fans).

In the baseball chapter the first page for every team has an introduction to the history and character of that park, a sidebar with "Stadium Stats" (address, dimensions, age, etc.), "Stadium Firsts" (first game, first pitcher, etc.) and "Ground Rules" (those unique to that stadium, as provided by the leagues), plus detailed information in "Parking," "Weather," "Media Bites" (local media outlets) and "Cuisine" (in and out of the stadium). These categories continue on the third page of each team section, with "Lodging near the Stadium," "Minor Leagues," "Spring Training," "Getting to the Stadium" and a timeline of memorable moments. Also on page 3 of each team section are "Home-Field Advantage" (specific aspects that give the home team the edge) and "Team Notebook" (listing franchise history, Hall of Famers, retired numbers and more). The second page of each section is devoted to a color-coded stadium illustration and seating diagram, with ticket prices keyed to the chart, plus ticket sales information and

"In the Hot Seats," a wrap-up of the best and worst seats. Ticket scalping, although a common practice, is illegal in some cities. While we have included information about it, that is in no way an endorsement of the practice. Check local ordinances if you plan to obtain tickets from sources other than the team or its ticket agency.

The only exceptions to the three-page format in the baseball section are the Kansas City Royals' Kauffman Stadium (2 pages), and the Colorado Rockies' new Coors Field (1 page).

The football chapter features two-page sections for all but five teams (which each have one page). The "Team Notebook" and the timeline move to the first page, and "Home-Field Advantage" and "Getting to the Stadium" go to the second page to accompany the stadium diagram.

The basketball and hockey chapters follow, with each team given either 1 or 2 pages.

The stadium and arena illustrations, while as realistic as possible, are by necessity not to scale because they must also function as seating diagrams. Prices provided are primarily for the single-game, rather than season, ticket buyer. *Note: All prices, contacts and programs listed in the book, as well as our stadium illustrations and seating diagrams, are current as of our closing editorial date in the summer of 1994. Minor league baseball affiliations change frequently. Call before you make your plans.*

# Table of contents

# BASEBALL

**Continued on next page**

Continued from previous page

# FOOTBALL

# BASKETBALL

# HOCKEY

# BASEBALL

Photo by Russell Beeker, *Baseball Weekly*

## American League

## National League

## STADIUM STATS

**Location:** 521 Capital Ave. SW, Atlanta, GA 30312
**Opened:** April 12, 1966
**Surface:** Prescription Athletic Turf (PAT grass)
**Capacity:** 52,710
**Outfield dimensions:** LF 330, LC 385, CF 402, RC: 385, RF 330.
**Services for fans with disabilities:** Seating available in row 27 of the field section.

## STADIUM FIRSTS

**Regular-season game:** April 12, 1966, 3–2 loss to the Pittsburgh Pirates in 13 innings.
**Pitcher:** Tony Cloninger of the Braves.
**Batter:** Matty Alou of the Pirates.
**Hit:** Rico Carty of the Braves.
**Home run:** Joe Torre of the Braves.

## GROUND RULES

• Dugouts: Any ball hitting the guard rails, the netting on the home-plate side of either dugout, the facing on or over either dugout, or the front ledge of the lip in front of the dugout is in play.
• Backstop: A ball lodging in the padding or on top of the camera booth is dead; it counts as one base on a pitch and two bases on a throw by a fielder. A ball thrown into the stands under the fence going from dugout to dugout is one base on a pitch and two bases on a throw by a fielder.
• Canvas: A catch may be made off of the canvas. A ball lodged behind or under the canvas is dead; it counts as one base on a pitch and two bases on a throw by a

*(Continued on page 8)*

# Atlanta–Fulton County Stadium

Until the Braves were wooed away from Milwaukee in 1966, Atlanta's baseball tradition was linked mostly to a Southern Association team called the Crackers. Since then, no small share of the sport's recent great moments has taken place in this rather undistinctive stadium in downtown Atlanta. One moment, though, stands out above all: April 8, 1974.

Los Angeles Dodgers pitcher Al Downing was on the mound; Henry Aaron, No. 44, was at the plate. Aaron's drive arched deep to left center where it cleared the wall and set a record that might very well stand forever. Reliever Tom House chased down Aaron's 715th home-run ball as the 53,775 in attendance cheered.

While Aaron hit maybe the most famous home run ever here, many others have gone deep, too—so many, in fact, that during the '70s, Fulton County Stadium came to be known as "the Launching Pad." The real reason for its reputation, though, had less to do with the nature of the ballpark and more with power hitters like Bob Horner and Earl Williams, and bad pitchers. It did make a difference, however, when the left-field power alley was moved from 375 feet to 385.

Aside from the home runs, the Stadium once was known primarily for having the worst field in the majors. The grass was choppy, dangerously loose and unstable, and the infield dirt was hard and prone to yielding unnatural bounces. The Braves hired a new groundskeeper, planted more resilient grass, touched up the infield dirt and *voilà*—a much better field was born.

Anyone looking for Chief Nok-A-Homa or Homer-the-Brave—men in American Indian regalia who carried on, mostly after a Braves home run—will be disappointed, but most fans were not sorry to see them go. Of course, the tomahawk chop lives on and probably will continue to when the Braves move permanently into the stadium being built next door for the 1996 Olympic Games.

## HOT TIPS FOR VISITING FANS

**Parking**
The Braves have parking for approximately 6,000 cars. The exact figure is not available because it changes almost weekly while construction of the Braves' future home, the Olympic stadium, goes on just south of Atlanta–Fulton County Stadium. Parking is $7.

Gypsy lots farther out run from $5 to $10, but beware: They sometimes park cars so tightly that you have to wait well after the game for stragglers blocking you in. Plus, the area around the stadium is not very well lighted or very safe. Three freeways converge around the ballpark, so traffic isn't a problem.

**Weather**
Often steamy, and be prepared for rain, too. The Braves might lead the majors in rain delays from all the early-evening thunderstorms that race through.

**Media bites**
**Radio:** WGST (640 AM, 105.7 FM), WPCH (FM 95).
**TV:** Superstation WTBS (Channel 17) and SportSouth (cable). The Braves' broadcasters on WTBS are Skip Caray, Pete Van Wieren, Joe Simpson and Don Sutton. Ernie Johnson and Ernie Johnson Jr. work strictly on SportsSouth.

**Cuisine**
The Braves have two food courts, one in the upper level and one in the lower. The fare is mostly standard: fried chicken, French fries, hot dogs and hamburgers, along with a few specialty items such as turkey hot dogs, smoked sausage, Italian sausage, rotisserie chicken, fried chicken, Jamaican beer and deli sandwiches. Little is worth pursuing, and the hot dogs are notoriously bad. Fulton County Stadium features several Budweiser and Miller beer products, plus such imports as Heineken, Foster's, Molson, Corona, Tecate and Beck's.

Fitzgerald's (404-659-7900), in the mall near the Marriott, and Manuel's (404-525-3447) are the best spots for after the game, but plenty of young fans prefer the Hard Rock Cafe (404-688-7625). Jocks 'n' Jills (404-873-5405) on Peachtree and Champions (404-521-0000) in the Marriott are two sports-oriented places that also draw big crowds. If you want a wider selection, go to Underground Atlanta, which features many bars and restaurants.

# IN THE HOT SEATS AT FULTON COUNTY STADIUM

Tickets are hard to come by. The Braves at one point in the spring of 1994 thought they would sell out the entire season before the first game. They didn't, but they are not one of the franchises that holds back tickets for game-day sales. This makes it more likely you're going to have to visit a scalper.

• **Bad seats:** The worst seats are the upper level in the outfield, especially back a few rows. You can't see the warning track below, so if an outfielder makes a great catch against the wall, you'll find out second hand. The seats in the area behind home plate and along each foul line to the base, normally coveted, are not exceptional values because there is more foul ground here than in most ballparks. That means you are farther from the action.

The sun covers the first-base side of the Stadium longest, but this is one stadium in which you might want to avoid the sunny side. In other towns, those seats might be perfect for tanning, but in steamy Atlanta, you'll cook way before you'll brown.

 **Ticket scalping:** Scalpers are not hard to find. They line Capitol Avenue along the east side of the Stadium, and Fulton Street along the north side, ready to bargain.

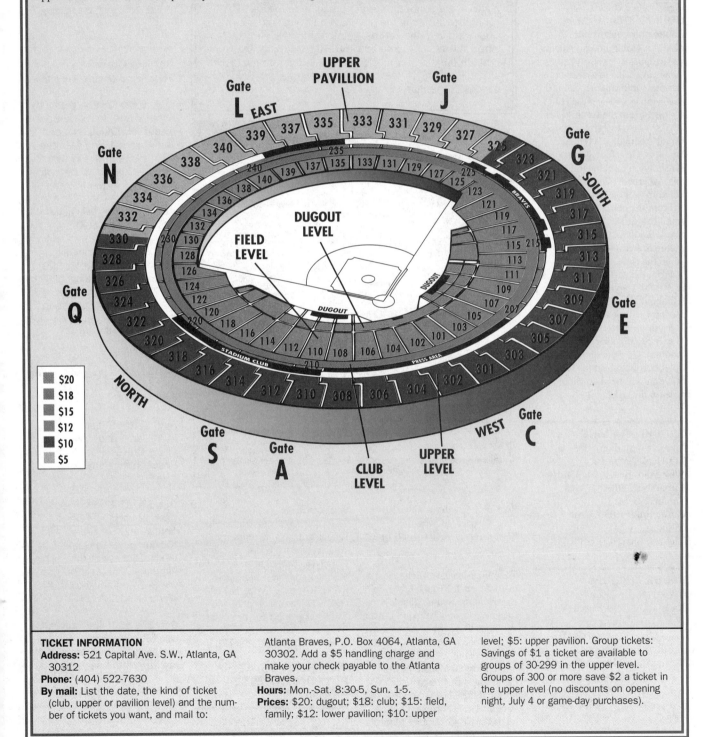

**TICKET INFORMATION**
**Address:** 521 Capital Ave. S.W., Atlanta, GA 30312
**Phone:** (404) 522-7630
**By mail:** List the date, the kind of ticket (club, upper or pavilion level) and the number of tickets you want, and mail to:

Atlanta Braves, P.O. Box 4064, Atlanta, GA 30302. Add a $5 handling charge and make your check payable to the Atlanta Braves.
**Hours:** Mon.-Sat. 8:30-5, Sun. 1-5.
**Prices:** $20: dugout; $18: club; $15: field, family; $12: lower pavilion; $10: upper

level; $5: upper pavilion. Group tickets: Savings of $1 a ticket are available to groups of 30-299 in the upper level. Groups of 300 or more save $2 a ticket in the upper level (no discounts on opening night, July 4 or game-day purchases).

## LODGING NEAR THE STADIUM

**Ritz Carlton**
181 Peachtree St. N.E.
Atlanta, GA 30303
(404) 659-0400/(800) 241-3333
2 miles from the stadium.

**Hyatt Regency**
265 Peachtree St. N.E.
Atlanta, GA 30303
(404) 577-1234/(800) 233-1234
About 2½ miles from the stadium.

## GETTING TO FULTON COUNTY STADIUM

**Public transportation:**
MARTA (Metropolitan Atlanta Rapid Transit Authority) bus service is available to the stadium. For more information, call (404) 848-3456 or (404) 848-4711.
**By car:** From the south, take I-75/85 north to exit 90, Ralph-David Abernathy Avenue/ Stadium. Go left at stop sign on Washington Street and then right onto Abernathy Avenue. The Stadium will be on the left.

From the north, take I-75/85 south to exit 91, Fulton Street/Stadium. Go left onto Fulton Street; the Stadium will be on the right.

From the east, take I-20 west to exit 24, Capitol Avenue. Go left about ¼ of a mile; the Stadium will be on the right.

From the west, take I-20 east to exit 22, Windsor Street/ Stadium. Go right about ¼ of a mile. Left onto Fulton. The Stadium will be about ¾ of a mile on the right.

## SPRING TRAINING

Municipal Stadium
715 Hank Aaron Dr.
West Palm Beach, FL 33401
**Capacity:** 7,200
**Surface:** Grass
**Game time:** 1:05 P.M. or 7:05 P.M.
**Tickets:** (407) 471-6100

## MINOR LEAGUES

| Class | Team |
|---|---|
| AAA | Richmond (VA) Braves |
| AA | Greenville (SC) Braves |
| A | Durham (NC) Bulls |
| A | Macon (GA) Braves |
| Rookie | Danville (VA) Braves |

## HOME-FIELD ADVANTAGE

At 1,000 feet above sea level, Fulton County Stadium is one of the highest parks in the league. Though the altitude doesn't have the same effect on players that it can have in Denver, it has contributed to the Stadium's reputation as a launching pad. A number of great long-ball hitters—including Hank Aaron, Dale Murphy, David Justice and Fred McGriff—have taken advantage of the conditions to post some impressive power numbers.

On the field, the Braves know to beware the bullpen mounds down the right- and left-field lines. These can be high-risk elements for players pursuing foul flies.

Another advantage is the change in atmosphere. In 1991, the year the Braves won their first NL pennant since moving to Atlanta in 1966, Fulton County Stadium turned from a rather placid ballpark into an enthusiastic one, full of tomahawk-chopping fans whose excitement can infect the home team.

### BRAVES TEAM NOTEBOOK

**Franchise history**
Boston Red Stockings, Reds or Red Caps, 1876–82; Boston Beaneaters, 1883–1906; Boston Doves, 1907–10; Boston Rustlers, 1911; Boston Braves, 1912–1935; Boston Bees, 1936–40; Boston Braves, 1941–52; Milwaukee Braves, 1953–65; Atlanta Braves, 1966–present

**World Series titles**
1914, 1957

**National League pennants**
1877, 1878, 1883, 1891, 1892, 1893, 1897, 1898, 1914, 1948, 1957, 1958, 1991, 1992

**Division titles**
1969, 1982, 1991, 1992, 1993

**Most Valuable Players**
John Evers, 1914
Bob Elliott, 1947
Henry Aaron, 1957
Dale Murphy, 1982, 1983
Terry Pendleton, 1991

**Rookies of the Year**
Alvin Dark, 1948
Sam Jethroe, 1950
Earl Williams, 1971
Bob Horner, 1978
David Justice, 1990

**Cy Young Awards**
Warren Spahn, 1957
Tom Glavine, 1991
Greg Maddux, 1993

**Hall of Fame**
Babe Ruth, 1936
George Wright, 1937
Cy Young, 1937
Hoss Radbourne, 1939
George Sisler, 1939
Rogers Hornsby, 1942
Dan Brouthers, 1945
James Collins, 1945
Hugh Duffy, 1945
King Kelly, 1945
Jim O'Rourke, 1945
Johnny Evers, 1946
Tommy McCarthy, 1946
Ed Walsh, 1946
Kid Nichols, 1949
Paul Waner, 1952
Al Simmons, 1953
Harry Wright, 1953
Rabbit Maranville, 1954
Billy Hamilton, 1961
Bill McKechnie, 1962
John Clarkson, 1963
Burleigh Grimes, 1964
Casey Stengel, 1966
Lloyd Waner, 1967
Joe "Ducky" Medwick, 1968
Dave Bancroft, 1971
Rube Marquard, 1971
Joe Kelley, 1971
Warren Spahn, 1973
Earl Averill, 1975
Billy Herman, 1975
Al Lopez, 1977
Eddie Mathews, 1978
Henry Aaron, 1982
Enos Slaughter, 1985
Hoyt Wilhelm, 1985
Ernie Lombardi, 1986
Red Schoendienst, 1989
Gaylord Perry, 1991

**Retired numbers**
21 Warren Spahn
35 Phil Niekro
41 Eddie Mathews
44 Hank Aaron

| | | |
|---|---|---|
| Rookie | Idaho Falls (ID) Braves | |
| Rookie | Gulf Coast (FL) Braves | |

The minor-league affiliate closest to Atlanta is the Class A Macon Braves of the South Atlantic League. Macon's ballpark, Luther Williams Field, which opened in 1929, is one of baseball's oldest. Not surprisingly, baseball has a long history in Macon; in 1904, the league's first season, the team captured the Class C South Atlantic League pennant with a record of 67-45. Among Macon's famous alumni are Tony Perez and Pete Rose.

To reach Williams Field, which is approximately 80 miles from Atlanta, take the Coliseum exit from I-16. Turn right at the foot of the exit ramp. Go 1 block and turn left on Riverside Drive. The ballpark is ½ block in front of you.

**Ticket prices:** $5: box seats; $4: general admission. For information, call (912) 745-8943.

## THE BRAVES AT FULTON COUNTY STADIUM

**July 14, 1968:** Henry Aaron hits his 500th home run. Mike

## GROUND RULES

**(Continued from page 6)**

fielder. A batted ball lodging behind or under the canvas is two bases.
• Foul poles: A ball hitting any part of the screen area supported by the foul poles down left- or right-field line is a home run. A ball going over the outfield fence into the open space directly below the screen area is a home run.

McCormick of the San Francisco Giants is the pitcher.

**Aug. 1, 1972:** San Diego's Nate Colbert sets an RBI record for a doubleheader, knocking in 13 runs as the Padres sweep the Braves 9–0 and 11–7. Colbert slugs five home runs in the two games.

**Aug. 5, 1973:** Phil Niekro no-hits the Padres 9–0.

**April 8, 1974:** Henry Aaron becomes the major leagues' all-time home-run king, hitting his 715th in a game against the Los Angeles Dodgers to surpass Babe Ruth. The Braves go on to a 7–4 victory.

**June 30, 1978:** Willie McCovey hits his 500th home run, served up by Jamie Easterly of the Braves.

**Aug. 1, 1978:** Larry McWilliams and Gene Garber of the Braves stop Pete Rose's hitting streak at 44 games.

**Oct. 14, 1992:** Francisco Cabrera knocks in David Justice and Sid Bream with a two-out single in Game 7 of the NLCS against the Pittsburgh Pirates. The Braves win 3–2 and advance to the World Series.

**Oct. 3, 1993:** The Braves clinch their division with a 5–3 win over the Rockies on the last day of the season.

## STADIUM STATS

**Location:** 333 W. Camden St., Baltimore, MD 21201
**Opened:** April 6, 1992
**Surface:** Grass
**Capacity:** 48,079
**Outfield dimensions:** LF 333, LC 410, CF 400, RC 373, RF 318
**Services for fans with disabilities:** Seating available throughout the stadium.

## STADIUM FIRSTS

**Regular-season game:** April 6, 1992, 2–0 loss to the Cleveland Indians.
**Pitcher:** Rick Sutcliffe of the Orioles.
**Batter:** Kenny Lofton of the Indians.
**Hit:** Paul Sorrento of the Indians.

## GROUND RULES

• Foul poles with screens attached are judged outside of playing field.
• Thrown or fairly batted ball that remains behind or under the canvas or canvas holder is two bases. Ball rebounding in playing field is in play.
• Ball striking surfaces, pillars or facings surrounding the dugout is ruled in dugout.
• Ball striking railing around photographers' booths is in play.

# Oriole Park at Camden Yards

O pened in 1992 with the idea that nostalgia would take priority over the flashy technology that's usually associated with new sports facilities, Oriole Park, 2 blocks from where the legendary Babe Ruth was born, is a ballpark that honors its elder counterparts—Chicago's Wrigley Field, Boston's Fenway Park, and New York's Polo Grounds. And while the new stadium was built to look like old-time parks, its architecture has a local flavor. The park gives new life to the B&O Warehouse, a turn-of-the-century building 1,016 feet long and 51 feet wide.

The warehouse, which has restaurants, sports bars and the Orioles' offices, towers above right field, framing the scene and serving as an inviting target for home-run hitters, although it has never been hit during a game. The warehouse gives the park a unique coziness while enabling the city to stay in touch with its industrial past.

Camden Yards has an out-of-town scoreboard, another revived feature of the old-fashioned parks, that spews out up-to-the-minute scores, pitching changes and assorted details from other games.

The stadium is double-decked. There are outfield bleacher seats that soak up the sun. Fans enter the stadium through wrought-iron gates and arched portals.

Walkways are spacious, and concessions stands provide excellent service. The new stadium has become *the* place to be, which often results in die-hard fans being shut out. The suit-and-tie crowd also tends to be quieter.

## HOT TIPS FOR VISITING FANS

**Parking**
If you want to get one of the 5,000 spaces in the parking lots, make sure to arrive at least 45 minutes before the first pitch.

If you miss out, don't fret: another 30,000 spaces are available in lots and garages throughout downtown, all within a mile's walk of Oriole Park. Actually, it's not all bad to park outside the stadium site.

A bracingly short 10- to 15-minute walk will get fans quickly out of the most congested areas, allowing them to hit the road ahead of traffic.

**Weather**
April and September are unpredictable: Temperatures can swing to either extreme, but those months may also offer gorgeous weather. The one sure bet is the heavy humidity during the summer months, particularly in July and August. For those games, wear loose clothing and prepare for oven like temperatures, even in the late innings of a night game.

Rain delays—the biggest headache in baseball—are shorter than at most parks, once precipitation stops. The park has a drainage system that can remove 75,000 gallons of water from the field in one hour. Club seats are a good deal in hot weather because they are air-conditioned. For weather info, call (410) 936-1212.

**Media bites**
**Radio:** WBAL (1090 AM) with Jon Miller, Fred Manfra and Chuck Thompson.

**TV:** WMAR (Channel 2) with Jon Miller, Scott Garceau and Brooks Robinson; and Home Team Sports (cable) with Mel Proctor, John Lowenstein, Jim Palmer and Tom Davis. Orioles' broadcaster Jon Miller is nationally known from his work on ESPN. His voice is soothing, his descriptions are crisp, and the best part is that he can do imitations of legendary broadcasters from other teams. However, if you're listening to a broadcasted game on radio or TV, you'll miss the highly entertaining public-address announcing of Rex Barney, a flame-throwing pitcher for the Brooklyn Dodgers in 1943–50. When a fan catches a foul ball, Barney says, "Give that fan a contract." At the end of announcements, his "thank youu-uuuu" has become a Baltimore staple.

**Cuisine**
The fabulous taste of Maryland's Chesapeake Bay crab cakes are as much a part of Baltimore baseball as bats and balls. They are served with tartar or cocktail sauce, and lemon wedges. Stands at Oriole Park sell a dozen different imported beers to wash down the crab cakes. Most popular: Corona with a slice of lime.

After the game, try Boog's Pit Beef, where former first baseman Boog Powell cooks up beef sandwiches and talks baseball at his barbecue pit. Sandwiches are $4.75. To find the pit? Follow the clouds of smoke that billow behind center field. If you're into football memories, check out Tom Matte's setup, called Matte's Ribs, 60 feet from Boog's. For $5.50, the former Colts running back serves up a plate of ribs, cole slaw, corn bread and a wet towel.

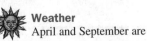

# IN THE HOT SEATS AT CAMDEN YARDS

Tickets for Orioles games at Camden Yards are extremely difficult to come by for fans who just show up hoping to buy a ticket. Most games are near sellouts. There's competition and long lines for any individual tickets that go on sale. It is best to plan ahead—as early as December. The Orioles cut off season-ticket sales at 27,500 to make sure there is an ample supply of single-game tickets, but with a season-ticket waiting list of 8,000, it's easy to imagine how fast tickets get gobbled up.

• **Midnight sales:** Every December, the Orioles put 1 million tickets on sale at Moonlight Madness, a carnival-style event that, in addition to ticket sales, allows fans to tour the park, get players' autographs, visit Santa Claus and buy memorabilia.

There's no admission charge, but fans are encouraged to bring toys for charity.

• **Extra view:** Seats down the third-base line in the first deck are the best for getting a view of Baltimore's skyline.

• **Bad seats:** Word is, there isn't a bad seat in the house, but that's not true. The seats that wrap around the corner in left field and a couple of sections down the right-field line are not pointed in the proper direction for baseball, making for awkward and uncomfortable viewing. Also, several rows of seats at the back of the lower deck have an obstructed view: Fans can't see outfielders because of the second deck's overhang.

• **Special program:** For a $15 membership fee, fans 16 and under can join the Cal Ripken Junior Orioles, a program that allows them to buy two reserve tickets to three games. The membership also includes a chance to meet Ripken, clinics, pregame prizes and a chance to be a bat-girl/batboy or a broadcaster.

• **Bargain dates:** There are eight dates in which upper-reserve tickets are available at half-price, $4. Call (410) 685-9800 for dates.

 **Scalping:** The ballpark is a chic place to be, a social event in which a good chunk of those who show up have only a fleeting interest in baseball. That leaves the hard-core fans—true baseball lovers—on the outside, dealing with scalpers for tickets. The market can be competitive, and for big regular-season games, ticket prices can double.

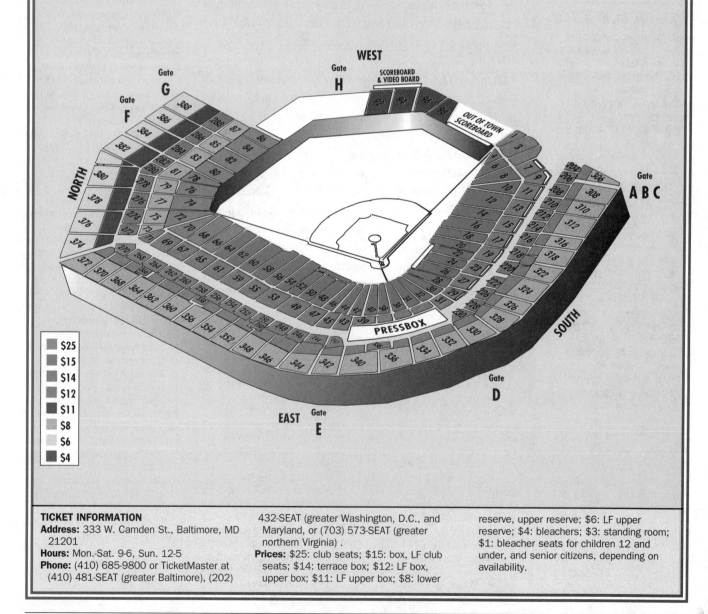

**Legend:**
- $25
- $15
- $14
- $12
- $11
- $8
- $6
- $4

## TICKET INFORMATION

**Address:** 333 W. Camden St., Baltimore, MD 21201
**Hours:** Mon.-Sat. 9-6, Sun. 12-5
**Phone:** (410) 685-9800 or TicketMaster at (410) 481-SEAT (greater Baltimore), (202) 432-SEAT (greater Washington, D.C., and Maryland, or (703) 573-SEAT (greater northern Virginia) .
**Prices:** $25: club seats; $15: box, LF club seats; $14: terrace box; $12: LF box, upper box; $11: LF upper box; $8: lower reserve, upper reserve; $6: LF upper reserve; $4: bleachers; $3: standing room; $1: bleacher seats for children 12 and under, and senior citizens, depending on availability.

## LODGING NEAR THE STADIUM

**Stouffer Harborplace Hotel**
202 E. Pratt St.
Baltimore, MD 21201
(410) 547-1200/(800) 535-1201
A few blocks from the stadium.

**Baltimore Marriott Inner Harbor**
110 S. Eutaw St.
Baltimore, MD 21201
(410) 962-0202/(800) 228-9290
Across the street from the stadium.

## GETTING TO THE YARDS

**Public transportation:** More than 20 bus lines go within 4 blocks of the stadium. The Baltimore Metro is speedy, and it provides more than 8,000 free parking spots. Take the metro to Lexington Market or Charles Center Stations, and pick up a shuttle to the park. MTA information: (410) 539-5000.
**By car:** Take MD 295 or U.S. 40 to downtown Baltimore, or I-95 to exit 53, 52 or 51.

## MINOR LEAGUES

| Class | Team |
|---|---|
| AAA | Rochester (NY) Redwings |
| AA | Bowie (MD) Baysox |
| A | Frederick (MD) Keys |
| A | Albany (CA) Polecats |
| Rookie | Bluefield (WV) Orioles |
| Rookie | Sarasota (FL) Orioles |

The Frederick Keys compete in the Carolina League. To get to Frederick from Baltimore, take I-70 west and go 40 miles. Harry Grove Stadium (seating 5,500) is at exit 54.

   **Ticket prices:** $7: box seats; $5: general admission; $3: GA for children. Call (301) 662-0013 for information.
   The Class AA Bowie Baysox play at the Prince George Stadium, located 40 miles south of Oriole Park and 25 minutes east of Washington, D.C. The stadium, which seats 10,000, is surrounded by woods.
   **Ticket prices:** $7: box seats; $5: general admission; $3: children 5-14, senior citizens and

active military. Free for kids in Little League uniforms and children under 5. Call (301) 805-6000 for more information.

### SPRING TRAINING
Al Lang Stadium
180 2nd Ave., S.E.
St. Petersburg, FL 33701
**Capacity:** 7,004
**Game time:** 1:05 P.M. or 7:05 P.M.
**Tickets:** (813) 893-7490
Huggins-Stengel Complex

---

## HOME-FIELD ADVANTAGE

With a close right field—the corner is 318 feet from home plate—you'd think there would be baseballs banging off the 25-foot wall every night. That's not the case. In 1993, for example, only 21 hits bounced off the right-field scoreboard. The theory: There's a wind that blows over the scoreboard toward center field. It's not strong enough to hold in a well-hit ball that goes for a home run, but it can take an average line drive destined for the wall and turn it into a fly-ball out.

The left- and center-field fence is 7 feet high, so the home-run-robbing catch is back. There's usually about a dozen heists a year, and more than half belong to Orioles outfielders.

Players love playing in Oriole Park, because for the most part they enjoy small stadiums that are full of fans. They say it adds to the electricity of the game.

They also like the real conditions: Fresh air, green grass and the views out from the stadium. And they appreciate Oriole Park for the state-of-the-art facilities: Roomy clubhouses, comfortable lounges, well-lighted indoor batting cages and plenty of exercise equipment.

And the Orioles are the lucky ones who call this stadium home.

---

## ORIOLES TEAM NOTEBOOK

| | | |
|---|---|---|
| **Franchise history**<br>Milwaukee Brewers, 1901; St. Louis Browns, 1902-53; Baltimore Orioles, 1954–present | **Rookies of the Year**<br>Roy Sievers, 1949<br>Ron Hansen, 1960<br>Curt Blefary, 1965<br>Al Bumbry, 1973<br>Eddie Murray, 1977<br>Cal Ripken Jr., 1982<br>Gregg Olson, 1989 | Heinie Manush, 1964<br>Branch Rickey, 1967<br>Goose Goslin, 1968<br>Satchel Paige, 1971<br>Jim Bottomley, 1974<br>Robin Roberts, 1976<br>Frank Robinson, 1982<br>Brooks Robinson, 1983<br>George Kell, 1983<br>Luis Aparicio, 1984<br>Rick Ferrell, 1984<br>Hoyt Wilhelm, 1985<br>Jim Palmer, 1990<br>Bill Veeck, 1991<br>Reggie Jackson 1993 |
| **World Series titles**<br>1966, 1970, 1983 | | |
| **American League pennants**<br>1944, 1966, 1969, 1970, 1971, 1979, 1983 | **Cy Young Awards**<br>Mike Cuellar, 1969 (tie)<br>Jim Palmer, 1973, 1975, 1976<br>Mike Flanagan, 1979<br>Steve Stone, 1980 | |
| **Division titles**<br>1969, 1970, 1971, 1973, 1974, 1979, 1983 | **Hall of Fame**<br>George Sisler, 1939<br>Rogers Hornsby, 1942<br>Hugh Duffy, 1945<br>Jessie Burkett, 1946<br>Eddie Plank, 1946<br>Rube Waddell, 1946<br>Dizzy Dean, 1953<br>Bobby Wallace, 1953 | **Retired numbers**<br>4 Earl Weaver<br>5 Brooks Robinson<br>20 Frank Robinson<br>22 Jim Palmer<br>33 Eddie Murray |
| **Most Valuable Players**<br>Brooks Robinson, 1964<br>Frank Robinson, 1966<br>Boog Powell, 1970<br>Cal Ripken Jr., 1983, '91 | | |

1320 Fifth St. N.
St. Petersburg, FL 33701
(813) 892-5971
**Game time:** 1:05 P.M.

## THE ORIOLES AT CAMDEN YARDS

**June 28, 1989:** Razing of the 85-acre parcel (on which Baltimore's new stadium will be constructed) begins.

**Oct. 6, 1991:** The Orioles

---

play their last game in Memorial Stadium, which has been home to the Orioles for 38 years (and 3,036 games). On this final day, more than 100 past and present Orioles return to the field in an emotional postgame tribute. Bringing tears to the eyes of players and fans alike, Orioles management brings back scores of ex-Orioles, puts them in their old uniforms and has them return to their positions on the field. No introductions are necessary.

**April 6, 1992:** Oriole Park at Camden Yards becomes the official home of the Orioles.

**1992:** The Orioles bring their magic with them to their new stadium in their first season at Oriole Park at Camden Yards. The O's 22-game improvement is second only to the record-breaking 32½-game improvement in 1989.

**June 22, 1992:** The game at Camden Yards draws 45,156 spectators, giving the Orioles their 12th consecutive sellout and their 20th full house of 1992.

**Sept. 2, 1992:** The Orioles and the Maryland Stadium Authority agree on a lease that will make Oriole Park at Camden Yards the Orioles' home for the next 30 years—doubling the length of the original agreement.

**Jan. 4, 1993:** *Time* magazine names Oriole Park at Camden Yards among the Top 10 Best Designs of '92.

**Aug. 7, 1993:** Cal Ripken hits two homers for the first time at Camden Yards and drives in four runs as the Orioles beat Cleveland 8–6. It is the 12th two-homer game of Ripken's career.

# Fenway Park

A warm, sunny afternoon at Fenway Park is baseball's version of a religious experience.

Except for the electronic scoreboard in center field, the park has changed little since it was built in 1912. The two-story red-brick facade still goes well with Boston's worn-down urban setting. Inside, you'll find baseball's only single-deck park and certainly its coziest, given that some of the seats are closer to home plate than the dugouts are. However, the most distinctive feature of Fenway is the Green Monster, the intimidating 37-foot wall in left field. It was created to keep cheap home runs from flying out of the stadium. At its base is a hand-operated scoreboard that shows scores and pitching changes from games around the American League. Completing the scene are the famous Citgo sign looming over the Green Monster and the Prudential Building over the right-field fence.

Even through a long championship drought—the last time the Red Sox won the World Series was 1918, before they sold Babe Ruth to the New York Yankees—and the painful teases of 1975 and 1986, New England fans love their team. The traditions of the Red Sox and the beauty of the park outweigh any of the inconveniences of a small, old-fashioned stadium. Just go with a mitt and be ready to talk baseball—that's how Red Sox fans pass the time while waiting in long lines at the hot-dog stands, ticket windows and bathrooms.

Do not wear a Yankees shirt. Or a Mets shirt, for that matter. Legend has it that the sale of the Babe to the Yankees put a curse on Boston baseball, a curse that felt all too real when the ball rolled between Bill Buckner's legs in 1986 at the other New York ballpark. Curse or not, an eerie reminder is posted on the green facade above the right-field grandstand. The Red Sox have retired only four numbers—Ted Williams' No. 9, Joe Cronin's No. 4, Bobby Doerr's No. 1 and Carl Yastrzemski's No. 8. As Boston author Dan Shaughnessy points out, the numbers are arranged 9-4-1-8, or 9/4/18—the eve of the 1918 World Series.

## STADIUM STATS

**Location:** 4 Yawkey Way, Boston, MA 02215
**Opened:** April 20, 1912
**Surface:** Grass
**Capacity:** 33,871
**Outfield dimensions:** LF 315, LC 379, CF 390, Deep CF 420, Deep RC 380, RF 302.
**Services for fans with disabilities:** Seating available in grandstand.

## STADIUM FIRSTS

**Regular-season game:** April 20, 1912, 7–6 over the New York Highlanders.
**Pitcher:** Buck O'Brien of the Red Sox.
**Batter:** Guy Zinn of the Highlanders.

## GROUND RULES

• Foul poles, screen poles and screen on top of left-field fence are outside playing field.
• A ball going through scoreboard, either on the bound or fly, is two bases.
• A fly ball striking left-center-field wall to right of line behind flag-pole is a home run.
• A fly ball striking wall or flag-pole and bounding into bleachers is a home run.
• A fly ball striking line or right of same on wall in right center is a home run.
• A fly ball striking wall left of line and bounding into bullpen is a home run.
• A ball sticking in the bullpen screen or bouncing into the bullpen is two bases.
• A batted or thrown ball remaining behind or under canvas or in tarp cylinder is two bases.
• A ball striking the top of the scoreboard in left field in the ladder below top of wall and bounding out of the park is two bases.

## HOT TIPS FOR VISITING FANS

**Parking**
Some limited parking is available at the Prudential Center Garage a few blocks away and at the Riverside MBTA Station. A number of private lots are around the park at Kenmore Square and at Boston University. All these lots can be pretty inconvenient, though. If you know you have to leave early, park where you can get out, because getting blocked in is common. Parking in and around Fenway costs $5-$15.

**Weather**
April and September can be cool. Summer months can be hot.

**Media bites**
**Radio:** WRKO (680 AM). Joe Castiglione and Jerry Trupiano are the announcers.
**TV:** WSBK (Channel 38) and NESN (cable). Sean McDonough and Bob Montgomery do the games on WSBK, and Bob Kurtz and Jerry Remy handle the NESN games.

**Cuisine**
In a city of tradition, what else would be the most popular concessions item but the Fenway frank? The Fenway frank is a legend—you can even buy them in supermarkets, where they're marked with a Red Sox logo. But the supermarket frank has a different taste from the ballpark's frank, which is all beef and has more spice. Locals add mustard, ketchup, onions and relish. At $2, the Fenway Frank is a steal. They are eaten for the nostalgia, not necessarily the taste. Specialty foods at Fenway are for show only.

After the game, try the Cask N' Flagon (617-536-4840) on the corner of Landsdowne and Brookline. Loaded with Red Sox memorabilia going back to the days of Babe Ruth, even Yankee fans say it's a must-stop when they come to town. Two wide-screen and six 20-inch TVs mean you won't miss a play while enjoying your Green Monster burger, piled with green peppers and onions. In fact, it's close enough to the park that the original Green Monster can be seen from the bar's front door. Two or three home runs a year land on the roof, and employees see them on TV and then climb up to get the baseballs.

## LODGING NEAR THE STADIUM
**Sheraton Boston Hotel and Towers**
39 Dalton St.
Boston, MA 02199
(617) 236-2000/(800) 648-3838
About 5 blocks from the stadium.

**(Continued on page 14)**

# IN THE HOT SEATS AT FENWAY PARK

Tickets go on sale Dec. 1 at Fenway Park. Usually, tickets are difficult to get on game day, but you might get lucky late in the season if the Sox aren't in a pennant race.

• **Good seats:** Outside of the pole seats, virtually any seat in the grandstand is good, but some are better than others. For example, several sections of seats down the right-field line point toward center field, not the infield. The advantage of sitting in right field is that both bullpens are in front of the bleachers. Opposing relievers sometimes have to warm up with soda cups bouncing off their heads. Fans can get rowdy, but Fenway's crowd-control personnel keep things under control.

All bleachers seats have excellent views. They're great for getting sun, and they're the same price as the seats down the right-field line. Bleacher fans usually start the wave. The best seat in the bleachers is the red one in row 33. It's easy to find because all the other seats are green. It marks the longest home run hit to right field, by Ted Williams. The ball went 502 feet and broke the straw hat of a sun-blinded fan.

• **Bad seats:** Pole seats are a fact of life at every old-fashioned ballpark, and while they can be a pain, they're better than nothing at Fenway. Ticket sellers will warn fans before they sell a seat with an obstructed view. Locals say pole seats aren't ideal, but if fans can bend their heads to the left and right, the game can be seen.

• **Family sections:** Sections 32 and 33, located down the left-field line, are good for families because they're nondrinking, nonsmoking sections. Also, the overhang protects children in case of rain.

**Scalping:** You'd think that with less than 34,000 seats, scalpers would have a field day, but tickets usually go on the scalp market with minimal inflation.

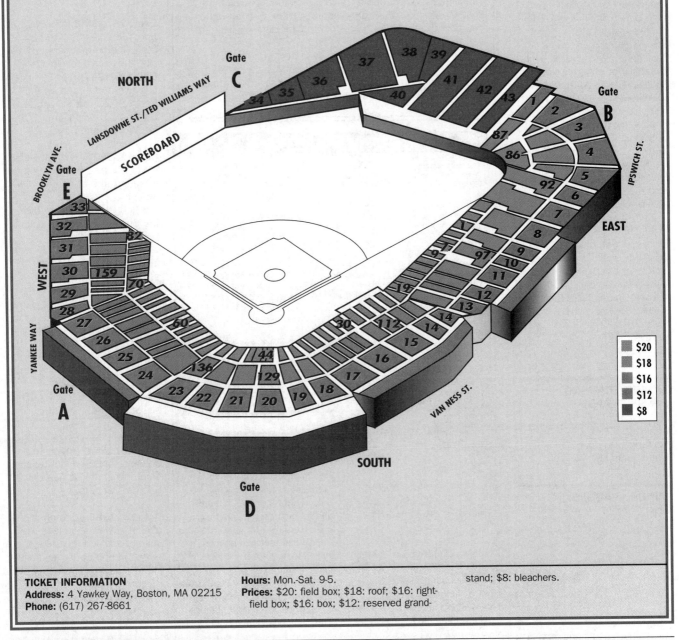

**TICKET INFORMATION**
**Address:** 4 Yawkey Way, Boston, MA 02215
**Phone:** (617) 267-8661

**Hours:** Mon.-Sat. 9-5.
**Prices:** $20: field box; $18: roof; $16: right-field box; $16: box; $12: reserved grandstand; $8: bleachers.

(Continued from page 12)

**Boston Marriott Copley Place**
110 Huntington Ave.
Boston, MA 02116
(800) 228-9292/(617) 236-5800
About ½ mile from the stadium.

## GETTING TO FENWAY PARK

**Public transportation:** The Nos. 8, 60 and 65 buses go to Kenmore Square, which is about 3 blocks north of the Park, as does the Green line on the T. Commuter trains from the western suburbs stop at Yawkey Station, 2 blocks west of Fenway. For more information, call (617) 722-3200 or (800) 392-6100.
**By car:** From the west, take the Massachusetts Turnpike to the Prudential exit. Make a right onto Dalton Street, then a left at the light onto Boylston Street. At the second set of lights, turn right onto Ipswich Street. Continue for a ¼ mile (Ipswich becomes Van Ness Street) and make a right onto Yawkey Way. The stadium is on the left.

From the north, take Route 93 South and follow signs to Storrow Drive. Take Storrow to the Kenway/Kenmore Square exit. At the top of the exit ramp, bear right onto Boylston Street, then proceed as above.

From the south, take I-95 North. Follow the Dedham Maine/New Hampshire split. Take Exit 20A/Route 9 East off I-95. Continue on Route 9 East about 10 or 12 miles, past the Chestnut Hill Reservoir. Turn left onto Brookline Avenue, continue on to Boylston Street and take a right. Go ¼ mile and make a left onto Yawkey Way. The stadium will be on your right.

## SPRING TRAINING

City of Palms Park
Fort Myers, FL 33901
**Capacity:** 6,850
**Surface:** Grass
**Game time:** 1:05 P.M.

## MINOR LEAGUES

| Class | Team |
|---|---|
| AAA | Pawtucket (RI) Red Sox |
| AA | New Britain (CT) Red Sox |
| A | Lynchburg (VA) Red Sox |
| A | Sarasota (FL) Red Sox |

| | |
|---|---|
| Short Season A | Utica (NY) Blue Sox |
| Rookie | Fort Myers (FL) Red Sox |

The Pawtucket Red Sox are the closest minor-league team. McCoy Stadium has been the Pawsox' home since 1942. This is where, on April 18, 1981, Pawtucket and the Rochester

## HOME-FIELD ADVANTAGE

Fenway Park's outfield is a maze of difficulties for opposing outfielders, which gives the Red Sox the biggest home-field advantage in the American League.

The outfield wall's height starts with the 37-foot Green Monster in left and then, as the fence zigzags its way to right field, it drops to 17, 5 and then 3 feet. Opposing outfielders reserve an extra 20 minutes a day to practice catching line drives off the wall.

The grandstand rises along a few feet from the foul line. Players who chase baseballs toward the line fear smashing into the grandstand wall that intersects with the Green Monster.

The right-field fence is waist-high. The trick here is to shut out the verbal abuse from the bleachers fans and concentrate on trying to make a catch while falling over the fence and into the bullpen. Nobody did that better than Dwight Evans.

The proximity of the fans to the field can be distracting. Hitters, not pitchers, have the advantage because infielders have little room—and outfielders have none—to catch foul pop-ups. Unfortunately for pitchers, cheap outs are rare.

But pitchers, at least some, take advantage of how the Green Monster looms in left field. Many a batter has left Fenway with an inflated strikeout total, a few meager pop-ups and an out-of-sync swing.

### RED SOX TEAM NOTEBOOK

**Franchise history**
Boston Americans or Pilgrims, 1901–1907; Boston Red Sox, 1907–present

**World Series titles**
1903, 1912, 1915, 1916, 1918

**American League pennants**
1903, 1904, 1912, 1915, 1916, 1918, 1946, 1967, 1975, 1986

**Division titles**
1975, 1986, 1988, 1990

**Most Valuable Players**
Tris Speaker, 1912
Jimmie Foxx, 1938
Ted Williams, 1946, 1949
Jackie Jensen, 1958
Carl Yastrzemski, 1967

Fred Lynn, 1975
Jim Rice, 1978
Roger Clemens, 1986

**Rookies of the Year**
Walt Dropo, 1950
Don Schwall, 1961
Carlton Fisk, 1972
Fred Lynn, 1975

**Cy Young Awards**
Jim Lonborg, 1967
Roger Clemens, 1986, 1987, 1991

**Hall of Fame**
Babe Ruth, 1936
Tris Speaker, 1937
Cy Young, 1937
Eddie Collins, 1939
Jimmy Collins, 1945
Hugh Duffy, 1945
Jesse Burkett, 1946
Frank Chance, 1946
Jack Chesbro, 1946
Lefty Grove, 1947
Herb Pennock, 1948
Jimmie Foxx, 1951

Ed Barrow, 1953
Al Simmons, 1953
Joe Cronin, 1956
Joe McCarthy, 1957
Heinie Manush, 1964
Ted Williams, 1966
Red Ruffing, 1967
Waite Hoyt, 1969
Lou Boudreau, 1970
Harry Hooper, 1971
Bucky Harris, 1975
Billy Herman, 1975
Tom Yawkey, 1980
George Kell, 1983
Juan Marichal, 1983
Luis Aparicio, 1984
Rick Ferrell, 1984
Bobby Doerr, 1986
Carl Yastrzemski, 1989
Ferguson Jenkins, 1991
Tom Seaver, 1992

**Retired numbers**
1 Bobby Doerr
4 Joe Cronin
8 Carl Yastrzemski
9 Ted Williams

Red Wings played the longest game in organized baseball history. After 8 hours, 7 minutes and 32 innings, the game was called at 4:09 A.M. with the score 2–2. When play resumed on June 23, Pawtucket won 3–2 in the 33rd inning.

To get to McCoy Stadium from I-95 South, take exit 2A, then go on Newport Avenue for 2 miles. Turn right on Columbus and follow for about 1 mile. McCoy Stadium will be on the right.

## THE RED SOX AT FENWAY PARK

**June 23, 1917:** After the starting pitcher, Babe Ruth, walks the first batter and is ejected for arguing, Ernie Shore comes on in relief and retires 27 Washington Senators in a row. The Red Sox win 4–0.

**July 9, 1946:** Ted Williams hits two home runs and drives in five runs, going 4-for-4 in the All Star Game.

**June 8, 1950:** The Red Sox tie an American League record for most runs when they beat the St. Louis Browns 29–4.

**Sept. 28, 1960:** In his last at-bat, Ted Williams hits his 521st home run.

**Oct. 11, 1967:** Rico Petrocelli hits two home runs as the Red Sox top the St. Louis Cardinals 8–4 in Game 6 of the World Series.

**Oct. 21, 1975:** Carlton Fisk leads off the 12th inning with a home run that barely curves around the foul pole, giving the Red Sox a 7–6 win over the Cincinnati Reds in Game 6 of the World Series.

**Oct. 2, 1978:** Tied in the standings after regular-season play, the New York Yankees and Red Sox play a one-game playoff to decide the AL East. Home runs by Bucky Dent and Reggie Jackson give the Yankees a 5–4 win.

**Sept. 12, 1979:** Carl Yastrzemski gets his 3,000th hit, off Jim Beattie of the Yankees.

**April 29, 1986:** Roger Clemens sets a major league record when he strikes out 20 Seattle Mariners.

**Oct. 15, 1986:** Clemens pitches seven scoreless innings and Jim Rice hits a three-run home run, leading the Sox to a 8–1 win over the California Angels and the American League pennant.

# Anaheim Stadium

Anaheim Stadium is nicknamed "the Big A" for the giant A-frame scoreboard that rises 230 feet. The three-level stadium has been home to the California Angels since its opening and was renovated in 1979 to provide additional seats for football's Los Angeles Rams.

As befitting its mellow southern California setting, Anaheim Stadium stresses friendliness and helpfulness, and as ballparks go, the Big A gets an A for cleanliness, too. Most Big A crowds are typically laid-back, but because of the heavy influx of Easterners to southern California, fans become more lively whenever the Angels play the Boston Red Sox or the New York Yankees.

The stadium sustained earthquake damage before the 1993 season, but no games were canceled. The JumboTron scoreboard tipped over into the left-field seating area, destroying hundreds of seats as well as the scoreboard. A temporary scoreboard was used during the 1994 season, and part of the left-field seating area was out of use through the middle of August. The repairs are expected to run into the millions but should be completed in time for the 1995 season.

## HOT TIPS FOR VISITING FANS

### Parking
On-site parking for 16,000 automobiles provides adequate space. Parking costs $5. Even at sellouts, the lot is rarely full. A number of private lots charge about $3, and many fans park on nearby side streets. Traffic flow is smooth in and out the stadium; the three main entrances are off major freeways.

### Weather
The temperature is normally mild year-round in southern California. The average weather conditions are sunny and 75 degrees.

### Media bites
**Radio:** KMPC (710 AM). Bob Starr and Billy Sample are the announcers.
**TV:** KTLA (Channel 5) and Prime Ticket Cable. Ken Wilson and former major-league pitcher Ken Brett are the announcers.

### Cuisine

Kosher and regular hot dogs are the biggest sellers, along with peanuts and beer. Mexican, sushi, Italian, fish and chips, and a potato bar are also available. You must try the cinnamon rolls sold near Gate 1 on the field level—just follow the line, which is usually long at any point before or during the game. Busch, Budweiser and Miller are available, as are several specialty beers.

Popular postgame hangouts are the National Sports Grill (714-549-3630) on State College Boulevard, T.G.I. Friday's (714-978-3308), El Torito's (714-956-4880), The Catch (714-634-1829) and Charlie Brown's (714-634-2211), all located across the street from the stadium.

## LODGING NEAR THE STADIUM
**Doubletree Hotel**
100 The City Dr.
Anaheim, CA 92668
(714) 634-4500/(800) 222-8733
1½ miles from the stadium.

**The Anaheim Ramada Inn**
1331 E. Katella Ave.
Anaheim, CA 92805
(714) 978-8088/(800) 228-0586
1½ blocks from the stadium.

## GETTING TO ANAHEIM STADIUM
**Public transportation:** The No. 49 and No. 50 buses run to Anaheim Stadium. For more information, call Orange County Transit District at (714) 636-7433.
**By car:** From the northwest, drive south on I-5 toward Anaheim, and exit at Katella Avenue. Turn left and continue on Katella about 1½ miles to State College Boulevard. Turn right and continue about ¼ mile to the Stadium.

From the south, drive north on I-5, and exit to Highway 57 (called Orange Freeway) North. Exit at Orangewood. Continue about 2 miles and turn left onto Orangewood. Proceed 1 block to the entrance to the Stadium.

From points north, take Highway 57 south, get off at Orangewood, turn right and continue 1 block to the Stadium entrance, which is on the right.

From Long Beach, go east on Highway 22 to City Centre Drive and turn left. After about a mile it becomes State College Boulevard. Continue north to the Stadium entrance, 6 blocks up on the right side.

## SPRING TRAINING
Tempe Diablo Stadium
2200 W. Alameda
Tempe, AZ 85282
**Capacity:** 9,785
**Surface:** Bermuda grass
**Game time:** 12:05 P.M.
**Tickets:** (602) 350-5200

## MINOR LEAGUES

| Class | Team |
|---|---|
| AAA | Vancouver Canadians |
| AA | Midland (TX) Angels |
| A | Lake Elsinore (CA) Storm |

**(Continued on page 17)**

## STADIUM STATS
**Location:** 2000 Gene Autry Way, Anaheim, CA 92806
**Opened:** April 19, 1966
**Surface:** Bluegrass
**Capacity:** 64,593
**Outfield dimensions:** LF 370, CF 404, RF 370.
**Services for fans with disabilities:** Seating available in sections 1-6, 47 and 49. Fans with disabilities should request that parking attendants point out a space in the reserved parking lot closest to their entry gate.

## STADIUM FIRSTS
**Regular-season game:** April 19, 1966, 3–1 loss to the Chicago White Sox.
**Pitcher:** Marcelino Lopez of the Angels.
**Batter:** Tommie Agee of the White Sox.
**Hit:** Jim Fregosi of the Angels.
**Home run:** Rick Reichardt of the Angels.

## GROUND RULES
• The foul poles and attached screen are in fair territory. A fly ball striking either one is a home run.
• A ball that enters the dugout is out of play (a ball going in, through or over all television and photography booths is considered the same as in the dugout). A pitched ball is one base, and a thrown ball is two bases.
• A batted ball striking the guy wires supporting the backstop is dead, but a pitched ball is one base and a thrown ball is two bases.
• A ball that lodges in the outfield fence is dead and counts for two bases.

# In the Hot Seats at Anaheim Stadium

The Angels sell approximately 13,000 season tickets, so tickets are usually available for every game at every price level. Big games generally sell out level by level. Season ticketholders generally fill the seats between the bases. After that, tickets are sold on a "best available" basis.

• **Good seats:** Sun lovers should try to get a seat on the first-base side or in right and center field. The best tickets are field-level MVP seats located between the bases.

• **Bad seats:** The stadium's sightlines are good, but avoid the upper level in dead center, which is too far from the field. Obstructed-view seats are sold last and only at the customer's request.

**Scalping:** Tickets are pretty easy to come by, so it's not necessary to resort to scalpers. A local ordinance against scalping on city property is strictly enforced. Still, some scalpers can be found outside, generally in the parking lot.

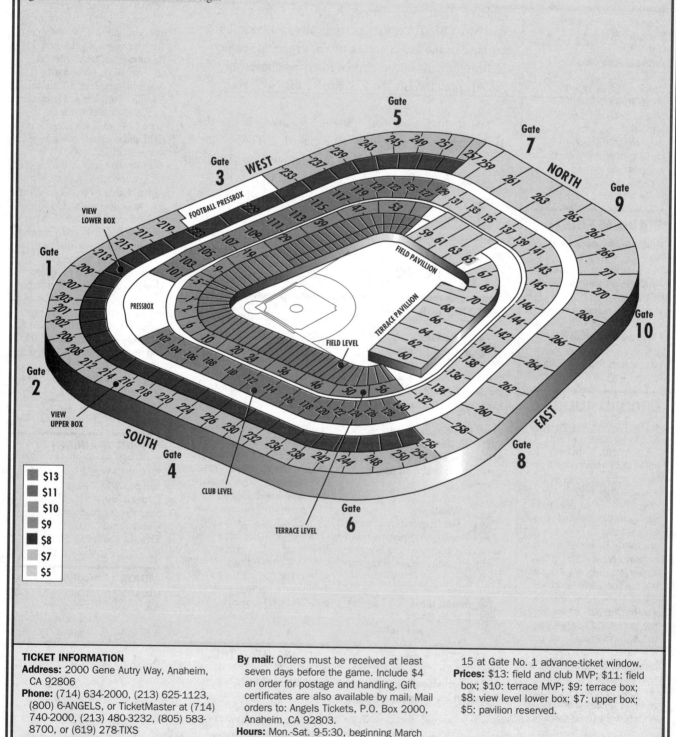

**Price Legend:**
- $13
- $11
- $10
- $9
- $8
- $7
- $5

## TICKET INFORMATION

**Address:** 2000 Gene Autry Way, Anaheim, CA 92806

**Phone:** (714) 634-2000, (213) 625-1123, (800) 6-ANGELS, or TicketMaster at (714) 740-2000, (213) 480-3232, (805) 583-8700, or (619) 278-TIXS

**By mail:** Orders must be received at least seven days before the game. Include $4 an order for postage and handling. Gift certificates are also available by mail. Mail orders to: Angels Tickets, P.O. Box 2000, Anaheim, CA 92803.

**Hours:** Mon.-Sat. 9-5:30, beginning March 15 at Gate No. 1 advance-ticket window.

**Prices:** $13: field and club MVP; $11: field box; $10: terrace MVP; $9: terrace box; $8: view level lower box; $7: upper box; $5: pavilion reserved.

(Continued from page 15)

| A | Cedar Rapids (IA) Kernels |
| Short Season A | Boise (ID) Hawks |
| Rookie | Mesa (AZ) Angels |

The Angels' nearest minor-league affiliate is the Class A Lake Elsinore Storm of the California League. The Storm's nickname was selected by team owner Ken Stickney who, as owner of the Storm's league rival, the Rancho Cucamonga Quakes, as well as the Las Vegas Thunder of the International Hockey League, has expressed a decided preference for weather-related monikers. 1994 marked the first season of pro baseball in Lake Elsinore.

To reach the Storm's stadium from Anaheim, which is only 50 miles away, take I-15 south and exit at Diamond Drive/Railroad Canyon Road. Turn right on Diamond and follow it straight to the stadium.

**Ticket prices:** $5: box seats; $4: reserved seats; $3: general admission. For more information, call (909) 245-4487.

## HOME-FIELD ADVANTAGE

Two low fences in the right- and left-field corners make it possible for outfielders to pull homers out of the stands, but they also make it possible for fans to pull long fly outs into the stands for home runs.

Anaheim Stadium has been known to be favorable to long-ball hitters, even if the Angels have not always stocked their teams with them. Reggie Jackson, Wally Joyner and Brian Downing all took advantage of the situation. Overall, though, it's a strong pitchers' park, with a lower batting average than most, as well as fewer walks, doubles and triples.

### ANGELS TEAM NOTEBOOK

**Franchise history**
Los Angeles Angels, 1961–1965; California Angels, 1966-present

**Division titles**
1979, 1982, 1986

**Most Valuable Player**
Don Baylor, 1979

**Rookie of the Year**
Tim Salmon, 1993

**Cy Young Award**
Dean Chance, 1964

**Hall of Fame**
Frank Robinson, 1982
Hoyt Wilhelm, 1985
Rod Carew, 1991

Reggie Jackson, 1993

**Retired numbers**
26 Gene Autry
29 Rod Carew
30 Nolan Ryan

## THE ANGELS AT ANAHEIM STADIUM

**Sept. 27, 1973:** Nolan Ryan strikes out 16 Minnesota Twins, setting the major-league record for most strike-outs in a season with 383.

**Aug. 12, 1974:** Ryan sets a team record when he strikes out 19 Boston Red Sox.

**Sept. 28, 1974:** Ryan no-hits the Twins 4–0, his third no-hitter as an Angel.

**Sept. 12, 1976:** 53-year-old Minnie Minoso of the Chicago White Sox singles off Sid Monge to become the oldest player to get a hit in a major-league game.

**Sept. 17, 1984:** Reggie Jackson hits his 500th home run, off Bud Black of the Kansas City Royals.

**Aug. 4, 1985:** Rod Carew gets his 3,000th hit, against the Twins.

**April 11, 1990:** Mark Langston and Mike Witt combine to no-hit the Seattle Mariners 1–0.

**Sept. 30, 1992:** George Brett of the Kansas City Royals gets his 3,000th hit, off Tim Fortugno of the Angels.

# Wrigley Field

## STADIUM STATS

**Location:** 1060 W. Addison St., Chicago, IL 60613
**Opened:** 1914
**Surface:** Grass.
**Capacity:** 38,765
**Outfield dimensions:** LF 355, LC 368, CF 400, RC 368, RF 353.
**Services for fans with disabilities:** Call (312) 404-4107 for information.

## STADIUM FIRSTS

**Regular-season game:** April 20, 1916, 7–6 over the Cincinnati Reds in 11 innings.
**Pitcher:** C. Hendrix, Cubs.
**Batter:** R. Killefer, Reds.
**Home run:** J. Beall, Reds.

## GROUND RULES

• If the ball hits the railing or screen above the bleacher wall and bounces back onto the playing field, it is in play.
• If the ball hits the top of the screen and drops between the screen and wall, or hits the screen and bounces into the bleachers, it's a home run.
• If the ball sticks in the screen or in the vines, it's a double.
• If the ball hits foul markers above the painted mark, it's a home run.
• If the ball goes under the grates in left field or right field and remains there, it's a double.
• If the ball hits the foul markers below the painted mark and bounces back on playing field, it is in play.
• If the ball goes in or under the grates on either side of home plate and remains there, it's one base on a pitched ball and two bases on a thrown ball.

Known as "the Friendly Confines" and tucked into a neighborhood of vintage brownstones on Chicago's north side, Wrigley Field is the ballpark down the street and feels like home the minute you walk in. Wrigley has kept up with modern times at its own pace, not adding lights until 1988 or sky boxes until 1989.

But even those changes do little to alter the nostalgic feel one has here. Wrigley is one of the few ballparks that can sell out even if the home team is in last place. This is the park with the best bleachers in baseball, the only place where Harry Caray sings "Take Me Out to the Ballgame" and the stadium where there are more day games than anywhere else.

The ivy vines clinging to the outfield walls were planted in 1938 by Bill Veeck, but you have to wait until May for them to turn green against the 11-foot-high brick wall. The scoreboard, constructed in 1937, presides over the park from center field and is still operated manually. It was built before expansion and lacks room for all the games played. The only ball hit off the scoreboard was a golf ball, teed up by pro Sam Snead in 1951; Roberto Clemente homered just left, Bill Nicholson missed just to the right.

Originally known as Weeghman Park, the park was renamed for team owner William Wrigley Jr. in 1920. The current owners, the Tribune Company, bought the team in 1981. The ballpark is one of the few where players have fun interacting with fans. Get there early, especially if pitchers Roger McDowell and Orel Hershiser are in town. They play catch with the bleacher fans during batting practice and usually right up until game time.

### HOT TIPS FOR VISITING FANS

**Parking**
Parking is almost non-existent, with no single main lot and several small vendors along Clark Street. The Cubs offer prepaid parking through their ticket office and through TicketMaster. Wrigleyville and Lake View residents have special stickers that allow them to park in the neighborhood, and regulations are strictly enforced. Tow trucks do good business at Cubs night games, so pay to park somewhere legitimate. The vendors know that. They raise parking prices for night games.

**Weather**
Former Cubs manager Don Zimmer used to call the ballpark, "Wrigley Field I" and "Wrigley Field II," depending on which way the breeze was blowing off Lake Michigan. If the wind is from the west or southwest, you want a seat in the bleachers because balls will usually be flying out of the ballpark. If the wind is from the east or northeast, bring a jacket. The meteorologists are correct when they say it's cooler by the lake; April, May and September can be significantly colder because of gusts off the water.

**Media bites**
**Radio:** WGN (720 AM); Cubs great Ron Santo is color commentator.
**TV:** WGN (Channel 9); all games, home and away, are carried on superstation WGN, which also is owned by the Tribune Company. Cubs fans around the country come to Wrigley Field to see if the ivy is really as green as it looks on television (it is) and to sing along with Harry Caray. You *must* sing along with Harry.

**Cuisine**
Wrigley Field has three restaurants—the Stadium Club, the Friendly Confines Cafe and the Sheffield Grill. Inside the ballpark, concessions offer everything from Italian beef sandwiches to traditional fare such as hot dogs, hamburgers, popcorn, pretzels and peanuts. New in 1994 were stands offering imported beers.

Across the street, The Cubby Bear is usually jammed for both pre- and postgame refreshments, along with nearby Sluggers and Murphy's Bleachers, on Waveland and Sheffield. Many different ethnic restaurants have popped up in the neighborhood along Clark Street, including ones serving Ethiopian, Mexican, Japanese, Thai and Italian food. For those less adventurous, McDonald's and Taco Bell are across Clark from the ballpark. If you skipped breakfast, check out the Yum-Yum Donut store on Clark and pick up a bag while waiting for the gates to open.

After the game, fans usually head to one of the above sports bars to discuss the game or wait out rush-hour traffic on the expressways. El Jardin (312-528-6775), a Mexican restaurant on Clark south of the ballpark, is popular for its postgame nachos. Some flock to Hi-Tops, another sports bar, located on Sheffield and Addison.

## LODGING NEAR THE STADIUM
**Hyatt Regency**
151 E. Wacker Dr.
Chicago, IL 60601

**(Continued on page 20)**

# In the Hot Seats at Wrigley Field

The Cubs have a season-ticket base of about 11,000 for weekday games, 19,000 for weekends, but you usually can get a ticket unless it's opening day. Tickets are also tough to get for night games, which always feel like a Saturday night no matter what day of the week it is. Because of an agreement with the city of Chicago, only 18 night games are played out of the 81 home dates. Day games on Friday usually start one hour later than the regular 1:20 P.M. first pitch.

The most difficult series for tickets are those against the St. Louis Cardinals, which are among the best series to see. Busloads of folks from Peoria have bought seats well in advance, and the ballpark is always loud and red. Plan far ahead for the Cards as well as for summer weekends. A three-game series against Cincinnati in July 1994 drew a record 120,000 people—

and the Cubs were in last place at the time.

• **Good seats:** The sun-drenched bleachers are the prime location and are still general admission. Although bleacher seats can be bought in advance, some are held back each day for that game. The bleachers have their regulars, and the left-field and the right-field sections have a friendly rivalry. One rule is observed by both—any home run hit into the seating area by the opposing team is thrown back onto the field.

If you want sunshine and can't get in the bleachers, the terrace, or lower section, along the first-base line is the warm side of the ballpark. The third-base side is usually in the shade midway through the game.

• **Bad seats:** The back rows of the terrace reserved area are the few bad seats

because of the claustrophobic upper-deck overhang. When sky boxes were added, they reduced the visibility for those seats. You will be able to see the field, and television screens provide instant replays. But you can't see the scoreboard, there are a few obstructing posts, and the seats are always in the shade.

• **Special programs:** Wrigley offers a non-alcoholic family section in the left-field corner of the bleachers, and a group section in the right-field corner.

 **Scalping:** Scalpers are plentiful, especially across from the main entrance at Clark and Addison, and near the El tracks on Addison and Sheffield. Police and stadium security do monitor them.

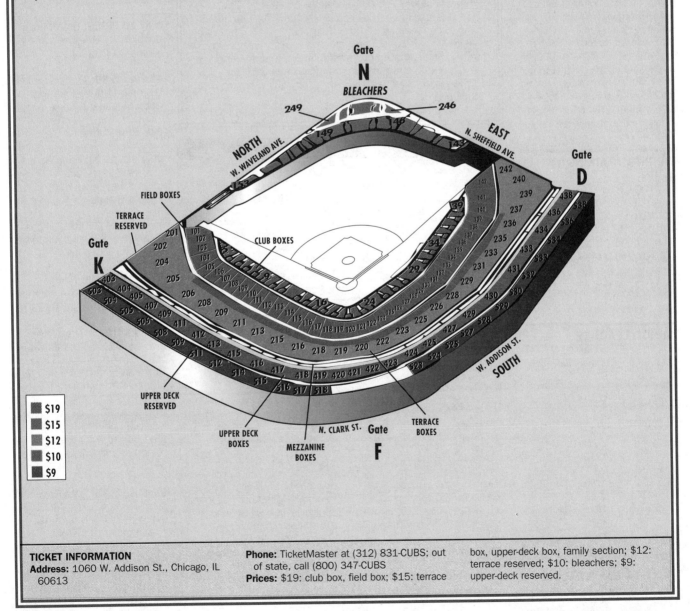

$19
$15
$12
$10
$9

**TICKET INFORMATION**
**Address:** 1060 W. Addison St., Chicago, IL 60613

**Phone:** TicketMaster at (312) 831-CUBS; out of state, call (800) 347-CUBS
**Prices:** $19: club box, field box; $15: terrace

box, upper-deck box, family section; $12: terrace reserved; $10: bleachers; $9: upper-deck reserved.

(Continued from page 18)

(312) 565-1234/(800) 233-1234
About 5 miles from the stadium.

**Westin Hotel**
909 N. Michigan Ave.
Chicago, IL 60611
(312) 943-7200/(800) 228-3000
About 4 miles from the stadium.

## GETTING TO WRIGLEY FIELD

**Public transportation:** The Howard–Dan Ryan (Red Line) El line stops at the Addison Street station next to the stadium. The No.152 Addison Street bus and the No.22 Clark Street bus stop at the park. For more information, call (312) 836-7000.

**By car:** From the south, head north on Lake Shore Drive, exit at Belmont (3200 North) to Clark Street. Turn right and continue to Addison Street. The stadium is on the corner of Clark and Addison streets.

From the north, head south on Lake Shore Drive. Exit at Irving Park (4000 North), take a left on Clark and continue to Addison. The stadium is on the corner of Clark and Addison.

## SPRING TRAINING

HoHoKam Park
1235 N. Center St.
Mesa, AZ 85201
**Capacity:** 8,963
**Surface:** Grass
**Game time:** 1:05 P.M.
**Tickets:** (602) 678-2222
**Training facility:** Fitch Park
655 N. Center St.
Mesa, AZ 85201

## MINOR LEAGUES

| Class | Team |
|---|---|
| AAA | Des Moines Cubs |
| AA | Orlando Cubs |
| A | Daytona (FL) Cubs |
| A | Peoria (IL) Chiefs |
| Short Season A | Williamsport (PA) Cubs |
| Rookie | Huntington (WV) Cubs |
| Rookie | Osceola (FL) Cubs |

The closest minor-league team to Chicago is the Class A Kane

County Cougars of the Midwest League. The Cougars' opponents include the Peoria Chiefs and the South Bend (IN) Silver Hawks, the Midwest League affiliates of the Cubs and the White Sox respectively. Since Kane County made its debut in 1991, the franchise has set league records for highest attendance in 1992 and 1993.

To reach Kane County's Elfstrom Stadium in suburban Geneva, approximately 35 miles from Chicago, take I-290 West to I-88 South. Exit at Farnsworth Road and stay on Farnsworth until Cherry Lane. Go west on Cherry until you reach the ballpark.

---

## HOME-FIELD ADVANTAGE

Check the flags on top of the scoreboard when you enter. That will tell you what kind of day it'll be at Wrigley Field. Many a pitcher is left shaking his head after a game because of the unexpected wind currents that turn routine fly-ball outs into home runs.

The small foul territory benefits fans and hitters. Foul balls end up souvenirs, giving batters another pitch. The groundskeepers tend to keep the grass long, which slows any bunt attempts.

Day baseball might be great for out-of-town fans but is a tough adjustment for visiting ballplayers, who are used to starts at 7 P.M., not 1:20 P.M.

The home dugout is along the third-base line, and Cubs managers say it gives them the worst view of the game. The infield is slightly sloped, and from their ground-level perch, they can barely see a close play at first base. Forget about trying to track a fly ball into the left-field corner.

Bullpens are next to the seats down the left- and right-field lines, and relievers, being who they are, will talk to the crowd before the game or between innings. The pens also provide a little obstacle course for outfielders trying to chase balls into foul territory.

The ivy-covered outfield walls are lovely, but not very friendly. Nothing but brick sits behind the lush green leaves, and many a rookie outfielder finds that out quickly and painfully. Balls lost in the ivy are ground-rule doubles.

---

## CUBS TEAM NOTEBOOK

**Franchise history**
Various names, 1876–1904; Chicago Cubs, 1905–present

**World Series titles**
1907, 1908

**National League pennants**
1876, 1880, 1881, 1882, 1885, 1886, 1906, 1907, 1908, 1910, 1918, 1929, 1932, 1935, 1938, 1945

**Division titles** 1984, 1989

**Most Valuable Players**
Frank Schulte, 1911
Rogers Hornsby, 1929
Gabby Hartnett, 1935
Phil Cavarretta, 1945
Hank Sauer, 1952
Ernie Banks, 1958, 1959
Ryne Sandberg, 1984

Andre Dawson, 1987

**Rookies of the Year**
Billy Williams, 1961
Ken Hubbs, 1962
Jerome Walton, 1989

**Cy Young Awards**
Ferguson Jenkins, 1971
Bruce Sutter, 1979
Rick Sutcliffe, 1984
Greg Maddux, 1992

**Hall of Fame**
Grover Cleveland Alexander, 1938
Cap Anson, 1939
A.G. Spalding, 1939
Rogers Hornsby, 1942
Roger Bresnahan, 1945
Hugh Duffy, 1945
King Kelly, 1945
Frank Chance, 1946
Johnny Evers, 1946
Clark C. Griffith, 1946
Joe Tinker, 1946
Rube Waddell, 1946
Frankie Frisch, 1947
Mordecai Brown, 1949

Jimmie Foxx, 1951
Dizzy Dean, 1953
Rabbit Maranville, 1954
Gabby Hartnett, 1955
Joe McCarthy, 1957
John Clarkson, 1963
Burleigh Grimes, 1964
Kiki Cuyler, 1968
Lou Boudreau, 1970
Monte Irvin, 1973
George Kelly, 1973
Billy Herman, 1975
Ralph Kiner, 1975
Fred Lindstrom, 1976
Robin Roberts, 1976
Ernie Banks, 1977
Hack Wilson, 1979
Chuck Klein, 1980
Lou Brock, 1985
Hoyt Wilhelm, 1985
Billy Williams, 1987
Ferguson Jenkins, 1991
Tony Lazzeri, 1991
Leo Durocher, 1994

**Retired numbers**
14 Ernie Banks
26 Billy Williams

---

Ticket prices: $6: box seats; $5: reserved; $4: bleachers; $3: lawn general admission. For more information, call (7089) 232-8811.

## THE CUBS AT WRIGLEY FIELD

**May 2, 1917:** Jim "Hippo" Vaughn of the Cubs and Fred Toney of the Cincinnati Reds both throw no-hitters through nine innings until Olympian Jim Thorpe, then playing with the Reds, singles in the winning run in the 10th.

**Oct. 1, 1932:** After an exchange between Babe Ruth and Cubs pitcher Charlie Root during Game 3 of the World Series, Ruth allegedly points to the bleachers and proceeds to hit a home run to that spot.

**May 13, 1958:** Stan Musial doubles off Moe Drabowsky for his 3,000th hit.

**May 4, 1960:** Announcer Lou Boudreau trades jobs with Cubs manager Charlie Grimm. The Cubs win 5–1 over the Pittsburgh Pirates.

**May 12, 1970:** Ernie Banks hits his 500th career home run, off Pat Jarvis of the Atlanta Braves.

**Sept. 2, 1972:** Milt Pappas no-hits the San Diego Padres 8–0.

**Sept. 16, 1975:** Rennie Stennett goes 7-for-7 as the Pirates beat the Cubs 22–0.

**May 17, 1979:** The Phillies give up a 21–9 lead but win 23–22 in 10 innings. Dave Kingman has three home runs and six RBI batted in.

**Oct. 2, 1984:** Gary Matthews hits two home runs, leading the Cubs to a 13–0 romp over the Padres in Game 1 of the NLCS.

**Sept. 8, 1985:** Pete Rose singles for his 4,191st hit, tying him with Ty Cobb for most hits in baseball history.

**Aug. 9, 1988:** The Cubs beat the New York Mets 6–4 in the first official night game at Wrigley.

# Comiskey Park

## STADIUM STATS

**Location:** 333 W. 35th St., Chicago, IL 60616
**Opened:** April 18, 1991
**Surface:** Bluegrass sod with eight types of grass
**Capacity:** 44,321
**Outfield dimensions:** LF 347, LC 375, CF 400, RC 375, RF 347.
**Services for fans with disabilities:** 400 wheel-chair-accessible seats. Call ticket office for more information.

## STADIUM FIRSTS

**Regular-season game:** April 18, 1991, 16–0 loss to the Detroit Tigers
**Pitcher:** Jack McDowell of the White Sox.
**Batter:** Tony Phillips of the Tigers.
**Hit:** Alan Trammell of the Tigers.
**Home run:** Cecil Fielder of the Tigers.

## GROUND RULES

• Foul poles and attached screens are outside the playing field.
• A ball remaining under or behind the tarpaulin is deemed out-of-play.
• The top step of the dugout is considered the dugout; a ball landing there is considered dead.
• A ball striking the railing in front of the camera pit is in play.

On April 18, 1991, Comiskey Park became the first new sports facility to open in the Windy City since Chicago Stadium in 1929. It was also the first baseball-only stadium to debut since Royals Stadium opened in Kansas City in 1972. The White Sox didn't go far when they decided to build a second Comiskey. The $137 million ballpark is on Chicago's south side, across the street from the old park, which was razed and replaced by a parking lot.

The architecture firm HOK—which also designed Oriole Park at Camden Yards, Cleveland's Jacobs Field and Coors Field in Denver—took pains to capture old Comiskey's charm. The rose-colored, precast-concrete exterior reflects the original look. The brick arches are emulated with arched windows. But unlike old Comiskey, which had beams that obstructed views, the new Comiskey is column-free.

Among other notable features of the ballpark are a Sony JumboTron video screen, a 140- by 30-foot center-field scoreboard and an exploding scoreboard with huge pinwheels that can been seen from outside the stadium after White Sox home runs. Eight kinds of grass make up the lush playing field, and the infield uses dirt from the original park. The team clubhouses are spacious and plush, and there are 90 sky boxes for corporate spectators. Fan amenities include a picnic patio area for pregame parties and six kennels for pets.

Comiskey Park fans are family-oriented, and their loyalty runs deep. Few White Sox fans share the same sentiment for the Cubs, considered the north side's team. Crowds are generally into the game, knowledgeable and well-behaved.

Along with all of the food and off-field entertainment to be found at Comiskey, the White Sox have kept the spirit of late, legendary owner Bill Veeck alive in a way that he would truly appreciate.

## HOT TIPS FOR VISITING FANS

**Parking**
The stadium has a little more than 7,000 parking spaces at $8 a space, including a big lot where old Comiskey Park used to be. The old park's home plate and batters' box are marked in the parking lot. A few private lots are around; a lot at the school across the railroad tracks charges $6. The park is in a residential neighborhood, so side-street parking is limited.

**Weather**
They don't call Chicago the Windy City for nothing. The wind shifts wreak havoc with the ball, benefiting hitters. Summer average temperatures can range from the mid-60s at night to 85 in the daytime, so bring a jacket. Rain has no lasting effect on the quick-draining field.

**Media bites**
**Radio:** WMAQ (670 AM—English); WIND (560AM—Spanish). John Rooney and Ed Farmer announce on WMAQ; Hector Molina and former White Sox shortstop Chico Carrasquel are on WIND.
**TV:** WGN-TV (Channel 9) and SportsChannel (cable). Ken Harrelson and Tom Paciorek are the announcers. Every game is televised by one of the two stations or ESPN or The Baseball Network.

**Cuisine**
Concessions stands, decorated with ceramic-tile fronts and neon signs, are dispersed throughout the main and upper concourses. The stands feature ethnic dishes that reflect the city's diversity, including Tex-Mex, pizza and various desserts. Most of the stands have adjacent seating areas. Comiskey favorites are the grilled chicken-breast sandwich, chicken fajitas and Maxwell Street–style pork chops and fried onions. Several Shortstop ministands offer a limited menu of hot dogs, bratwurst, beer and sodas. The Kids Corner is a pint-sized concessions stand with pint-sized meals (hot dogs and soda, peanut butter and jelly sandwiches) for pint-sized prices. Adults must be accompanied by children.

The south side has several popular postgame spots, including Jimbo's, a couple of blocks from the stadium, and Connie's Pizzeria, at 26th Street and Archer. If you're interested in heading back towards the Loop and the north side, Pizzeria Uno (312-321-1000) is the home of the deep-dish pizza, and Ed Debevic's (312-664-1707) offers a retro-diner experience. In a town that loves its meat, Carson's, The Place for Ribs (312-280-9200), has some of the very best.

## LODGING NEAR THE STADIUM
**Days Inn**
520 S. Michigan Ave.
Chicago, IL 60605
(312) 786-0000/(800) 942-7543
1 mile from the stadium.

**(Continued on page 23)**

# IN THE HOT SEATS AT COMISKEY PARK

The White Sox have become one of the American League's top draws since moving into their new ballpark, averaging more than 30,000 fans a game. Season-ticket sales are usually between 17,000 and 25,000, so walk-up sales are brisk.

• **Good seats:** With a capacity of more than 44,000, Comiskey Park has an abundance of good seats. In addition to the traditionally good lower boxes between the bases, the club level also has good views. The upper-deck boxes are worth a look if you can't get anything lower down. The bleachers get the most sun.

• **Bad seats:** A couple dozen seats are just behind the foul pole. These obstructed-view seats are sold last and marked as such on the ticket.

• **Special programs:** On Mondays all seats in the park are half-price, and there are half-price upper-reserve seats for selected games.

 **Scalping:** Scalpers are hard to miss along 35th Street, towards the Dan Ryan Expressway, even though good seats are usually available at the box office.

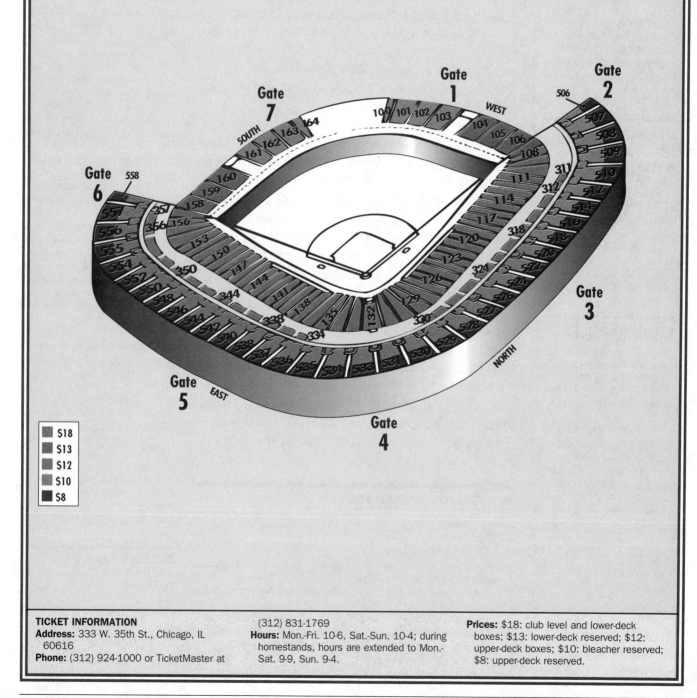

$18
$13
$12
$10
$8

**TICKET INFORMATION**
**Address:** 333 W. 35th St., Chicago, IL 60616
**Phone:** (312) 924-1000 or TicketMaster at

(312) 831-1769
**Hours:** Mon.-Fri. 10-6, Sat.-Sun. 10-4; during homestands, hours are extended to Mon.-Sat. 9-9, Sun. 9-4.

**Prices:** $18: club level and lower-deck boxes; $13: lower-deck reserved; $12: upper-deck boxes; $10: bleacher reserved; $8: upper-deck reserved.

**(Continued from page 21)**

**Hyatt Regency**
151 E. Wacker Dr.
Chicago, IL 60601
(312) 565-1234/(800) 233-1234
About 5 miles from the stadium.

## GETTING TO COMISKEY PARK

**Public transportation:** Take the Dan Ryan El to 35th Street or the No. 24 Wentworth, No. 44 Wallace/Racine or No. 35 35th Street bus to the park. Call (312) 836-7000 for more information.
**By car:** From the south, drive north on I-94 and exit at 35th Street.

From the north, head south on Lake Shore Drive and get off at 31st Street.

From the west, head east on I-290 to I-94. Proceed south and exit at 31st Street.

## SPRING TRAINING

Ed Smith Stadium
12th St. and Tuttle Ave.
Sarasota, FL 34237.
**Ticket office:** (813) 953-3388
**Capacity:** 7,500
**Surface:** Grass
**Game time:** 1:05 P.M. or 7:05 P.M.

## MINOR LEAGUES

| Class | Team |
|---|---|
| AAA | Nashville Sounds |
| AA | Birmingham (AL) Barons |
| A | Prince William (VA) Cannons |
| A | South Bend (IN) Silver Hawks |
| A | Hickory (NC) Crawdads |
| Rookie | Sarasota (FL) White Sox |

## HOME-FIELD ADVANTAGE

Fans have responded enthusiastically to the new Comiskey Park since it opened in 1991. Starting with a franchise-record attendance of 2,934,154 in 1991, the team has experienced similar success in subsequent seasons, although the total yearly attendance has not matched that of 1991. In 1993 Chicago area fans, still excited about their new ballpark, plus a team which ranks among the league's best, flocked to the park to see Frank "the Big Hurt" Thomas, one of baseball's top players, as well as a White Sox team that was involved in postseason play for the first time since 1983.

Fan support is about the only clear advantage that Comiskey Park gives the White Sox. Whereas the centerfield wall at the old Comiskey was moved in and out in various seasons, depending on the power of the team, the new Comiskey is not quite as adaptable.

### WHITE SOX TEAM NOTEBOOK

**Franchise history**
Chicago White Sox, 1901–present

**World Series titles**
1906, 1917

**American League pennants**
1900, 1901, 1906, 1917, 1919, 1959

**Division titles**
1983, 1993

**Most Valuable Players**
Nellie Fox, 1959
Dick Allen, 1972
Frank Thomas, 1993

**Rookies of the Year**
Luis Aparicio, 1956
Gary Peters, 1963
Tommie Agee, 1966

Ron Kittle, 1983
Ozzie Guillen, 1985

**Cy Young Awards**
Early Wynn, 1959
LaMarr Hoyt, 1983
Jack McDowell, 1993

**Hall of Fame**
Eddie Collins, 1939
Charles Comiskey, 1939
Hugh Duffy, 1945
Frank Chance, 1946
Johnny Evers, 1946
Clark Griffith, 1946
Ed Walsh, 1946
Chief Bender, 1953
Al Simmons, 1953
Ted Lyons, 1955
Ray Schalk, 1955
Hank Greenberg, 1956
Edd Roush, 1962
Red Faber, 1964
Luke Appling, 1964

Charles "Red" Ruffing, 1967
Harry Hooper, 1971
Early Wynn, 1972
John "Jocko" Conlan, 1974
Bob Lemon, 1976
Al Lopez, 1977
George Kell, 1983
Luis Aparicio, 1984
Hoyt Wilhelm, 1985
Bill Veeck, 1991
Tom Seaver, 1992
Steve Carlton, 1994

**Retired numbers**
2 Nellie Fox
3 Harold Baines
4 Luke Appling
9 Minnie Minoso
11 Luis Aparicio
16 Ted Lyons
19 Billy Pierce

The minor-league team nearest to Chicago is the Class A Kane County Cougars of the Midwest League. The Cougars' opponents include the Peoria Chiefs and the South Bend Silver Hawks, Midwest League affiliates of the Cubs and the White Sox, respectively. Since Kane County made its debut in 1991, the franchise has set league records for highest total attendance in 1992 (323,769) and 1993 (354,327). In '93, the Cougars drew more fans to the ballpark than any other Class A team.

To reach Kane County's Elfstorm Stadium in suburban Geneva, approximately 35 miles from Chicago, take I-290 West to I-88 West. Exit at Farnsworth Road, then at Cherry Lane, go west until you reach the ballpark.

**Ticket prices:** $6: box seats; $5: reserved seats; $4: bleachers; $3: lawn general admission; For more information, call (708) 232-8811.

## THE WHITE SOX AT COMISKEY PARK

**April 22, 1991:** Frank Thomas hits the Sox' first homer at the new Comiskey Park during the stadium's first night game. The Sox beat the Baltimore Orioles 8–7.

**April 9, 1993:** Bo Jackson, playing with an artificial hip, hits a home run with his first swing on opening day.

**June 22, 1993:** Carlton Fisk catches his 2,226th game, putting him past Bob Boone for most games caught.

**Sept. 27, 1993:** The White Sox win the West with a 4–2 victory over the Seattle Mariners on a three-run homer by Bo Jackson.

**Oct. 5, 1993:** The Toronto Blue Jays beat the White Sox in Game 1 of the ALCS 7–3, but rumors of Michael Jordan's retirement steal the show.

# Riverfront Stadium

## STADIUM STATS

**Location:** 100 Riverfront Stadium, Cincinnati, OH 45202
**Opened:** June 30, 1970
**Surface:** AstroTurf 8
**Capacity:** 52,952
**Outfield dimensions:** LF 330, LC 375, CF 404, RC 375, RF 330.
**Services for fans with disabilities:** Seating available on the Green Level. Call (513) 421-4510 for more information.

## STADIUM FIRSTS

**Regular-season game:** June 30, 1970, 8–2 loss to the Atlanta Braves.
**Pitcher:** Jim McGlothlin of the Reds.
**Batter:** Sonny Jackson of the Braves.
**Hit:** Felix Millan of the Braves.
**Home run:** Hank Aaron of the Braves.

## GROUND RULES

• Any ball hitting foul screen in left or right field is a home run.
• Any ball bouncing over fence is a two-base hit.
• Any ball hit down right-field or left-field line and bouncing into box seats in stands is a two-base hit.
• Ball remaining behind or underneath canvas is one base on pitch and two bases on throw by fielder and two bases on a batted ball. Fielder may make catch standing on canvas.
• Everything else in play unless the ball goes into the dugout.

W hat a shame that a ballclub with such a rich baseball tradition has to play its games in such a sterile environment. The Reds, the oldest professional baseball team, are housed in a facility with all the charm and tradition of a six-lane highway.

The city opened the Stadium in 1970, and while it's pleasant and clean, it lacks any feel of a ballpark. Like its cousins in Pittsburgh and Philadelphia, the circular stadium has artificial turf, sliding pits, no view of downtown and no sense of the city.

Outside the park, it's quite nice. The Stadium is set on the banks of the Ohio River next to the historic John A. Roebling Suspension Bridge; Roebling, the architect, used it as a prototype for his next project, the Brooklyn Bridge. The plaza outside the Stadium overlooks the Ohio River on one side and offers a marvelous view of the downtown skyline on the other. Pedestrian bridges cross an interstate highway and connect the site to downtown, which is clean and safe.

The atmosphere in the ballpark will never be described as circuslike, but descriptions of it as a morgue are a bit harsh. Unlike some of the newer parks in which corporate America has bought up the box seats, Cincy's regulars are baseball fans. They're just not rowdy.

The ballclub is the most conservative in baseball. Reds players are not permitted to grow facial hair, and owner Marge Schott has made news with (among other things) her dislike of players wearing jewelry. The Reds were the last team in the big leagues to allow players to wear spikes with commercial logos (they relented in the early 1980s), and the team once banned male fans from going bare-chested in the stands (it's OK now).

## HOT TIPS FOR VISITING FANS

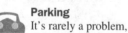

**Parking**
It's rarely a problem, and traffic clears out quickly after the games. A three-level city garage surrounds the Stadium, but that's sold out on a season-subscription basis. Open-air city lots adjacent to the Stadium can handle about 1,800 cars and charge $3.50. Within a 12-block radius, facilities can handle about 20,000 cars. Garages and open lots are easy to find—if you look hard enough, you often can find a free spot on the street after business hours. Or you can park across the river in Covington, Ky., and walk across the Roebling Bridge to the stadium.

**Weather**
From snow delays on opening day to blistering heat in August, you can expect almost anything in Cincinnati. Night games in April can be chilly, but spring and fall in the Queen City are usually very pleasant. Heat and humidity can be oppressive in the middle of summer, especially in the blue seats near the artificial turf.

**Media bites**
**Radio:** WLW (700 AM) is the radio flagship. Marty Brennaman, who joined the team in 1974, is a solid pro and one of the best announcers in baseball. His distinctive voice and tell-it-like-it-is approach make him one of the city's most treasured assets. He does both radio and television. Radio sidekick Joe Nuxhall, a former Reds pitcher who has been in the booth since 1967, is an acquired taste. Cincinnati natives love his folksy style and his unabashed partisanship. Don't knock Joe to a native. Marty and Joe are a Cincinnati institution, having worked as a team for more than 20 years.

**TV:** WLWT-TV (Channel 5) and SportsChannel Cincinnati (cable). George Grande and ex-Red Chris Welsh handle the announcing.

**Cuisine**
Reds owner Marge Schott is the champion of the $1 hot dog. She consistently lobbies the concessions service to keep the price of the basic frank at a buck. The dog is nothing special, but Cincinnati's culinary traditions are in evidence in other menu items. Metts and brats (German sausages) by Hillshire Farms are at several stands, and that local delicacy, Cincinnati chili, is represented. You can buy a cheese coney (a hot dog with Cincinnati chili and shredded cheese) at eight Gold Star Chili stands. Cincinnati, with its German roots, has a glorious tradition in beer brewing. Unfortunately, only one local beermaker, Hudepohl-Schoenling, remains, but it makes several fine brews. Try Hudepohl's Christian Moerlein or Little King's Bruin Pale Ale. Also recommended are any of the brews from the local microbrewery, Oldenburg. Other premium and imported beers are available at the bar on the blue level behind home plate and four auxiliary locations.

Several popular pregame and postgame spots can be found on Pete Rose Way (formerly Second Street), a five-minute walk from the stadium. Caddy's (513-721-3636) and Flanagan's Landing (513-421-4055) are the

**(Continued on page 26)**

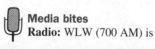

# IN THE HOT SEATS AT RIVERFRONT STADIUM

The Reds don't often sell out, but the bulk of the 10,400 field boxes are sold on a season-ticket basis. Ditto the green (second-level) seats on the infield. Many of the attractive weekend dates have brisk advance sales, as fans from Kentucky, Indiana and central Ohio make their annual weekend trips to catch the Reds.

• **Good seats:** If you're not afraid of heights and haven't planned ahead, try the "top six" seats — one of the best bargains in baseball. The top six rows of the entire stadium are sold only on game days (unless all other tickets are sold in advance). You can walk up to the box office the day of the game and, for $3.50,

buy a ticket behind home plate — albeit at the top of the upper deck. The seats are high, but for real fans who like to be in the infield, they're a bonus.

• **Bad seats:** The green seats in the outfield are very popular, but if you sit in them, you might wonder why. You get a fine view of outfielders' backs, but you're a long way from the plate. The same goes for the limited number of blue seats in the outfield.

 **Scalping:** Ticket brokers, a. k. a. scalpers, are legal in Cincinnati as long as they have vendor licenses issued by the city.

However, they aren't permitted to sell Reds tickets for more than face value on the Stadium grounds or Pete Rose Way. Legally, they should be north of Fourth Street (about 3 blocks from the stadium), but they are frequently found by the entrance to the pedestrian walkway, a block closer. The city's policy also has spawned brokerages, some with offices downtown, that sell tickets to all games. For an average game, buyers can pay about $20 for blues (face value: $11.50). For weekend series against a team battling the Reds in a pennant race, though, that can go up to $50-$75. Fans selling extra tickets at face value or below are permitted on the plaza, so buyers sometimes try there first.

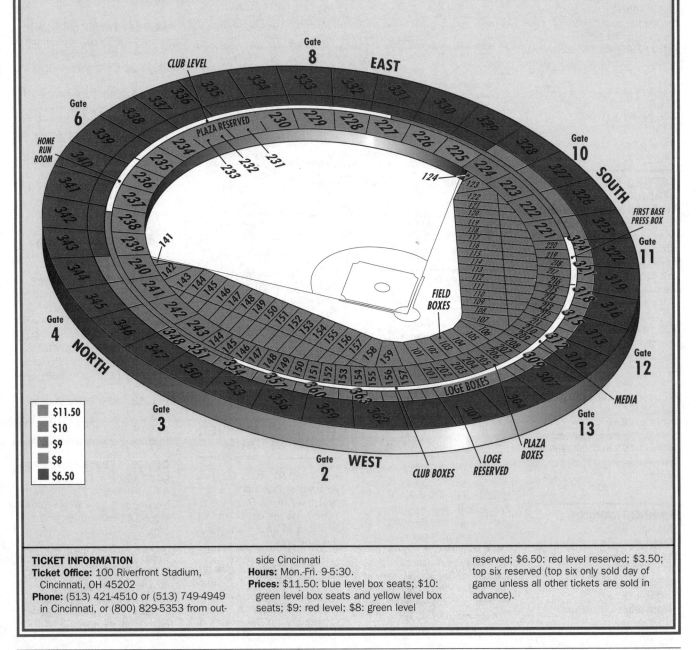

$11.50
$10
$9
$8
$6.50

---

**TICKET INFORMATION**
**Ticket Office:** 100 Riverfront Stadium, Cincinnati, OH 45202
**Phone:** (513) 421-4510 or (513) 749-4949 in Cincinnati, or (800) 829-5353 from out-side Cincinnati
**Hours:** Mon.-Fri. 9-5:30.
**Prices:** $11.50: blue level box seats; $10: green level box seats and yellow level box seats; $9: red level; $8: green level reserved; $6.50: red level reserved; $3.50; top six reserved (top six only sold day of game unless all other tickets are sold in advance).

---

(Continued from page 24)

standbys. The waterfront features several popular places, including Covington Landing (606-291-9992) on the Kentucky side and the Montgomery Inn Boathouse (renowned for its ribs) on the Cincinnati side (513-721-7427). Chili parlors serving the traditional Cincinnati fare are all over downtown; the two top chains are Skyline and Gold Star. Izzy's has great corned-beef sandwiches and two downtown locations. Ice cream lovers must sample Graeter's creamy ice cream, with chips the size of a Hershey bar.

## LODGING NEAR THE STADIUM

**Westin Hotel**
21 E. Fifth St. (corner of Vine St. and Fountain Square)
Cincinnati, OH 45202
(513) 621-7700/(800) 228-3000
About 5 blocks from the stadium.

**Hyatt Regency**
151 W. Fifth St.
Cincinnati, OH 45202
(513) 579-1234/(800) 233-1234
About 5 blocks from the stadium.

## GETTING TO RIVERFRONT STADIUM

**Public Transportation:** Metro Center's Nos. 28 and 49 buses go to Fourth Street and Broadway, 1½ blocks from the . Stadium. For more information, call (513) 621-4455.
**By car:** From points north in Ohio, go south on I-75, get over onto the right and exit at Pete Rose Way. Take Pete Rose Way less than 1½ miles to the Stadium, which will be on the left.
From the south, head north on I-75, stay right and exit at Pete Rose Way. Take Pete Rose Way to the Stadium.
From the west, head east on I-74 to I-75 South, then follow instructions above from the north.

## SPRING TRAINING

Plant City Stadium
1900 S. Park Rd.
Plant City, FL 33564
(813) 752-1878
**Capacity:** 6,700
**Surface:** Grass
**Game time:** 1:05 P.M. or 7:05 P.M.

## HOME-FIELD ADVANTAGE

In keeping with the city's reputation as a polite town, Riverfront Stadium is perfectly fair: symmetrical, average dimensions (330 feet down the lines, 404 to center), favoring neither the hitter or pitcher. The Stadium is not the kind you can build a team for, but as on all artificial surfaces, the home team needs speed. The Reds have a better record at home than on the road, but in seven of the last 10 years, that advantage has been fewer than five games a year.

## REDS TEAM NOTEBOOK

**Franchise history**
Cincinnati Reds (AA), 1882–1889; merged w/ Washington Senators in 1889; Cincinnati Reds, 1890–1943 (NL); Cincinnati Redlegs, 1944–1945; Cincinnati Reds, 1946–present

**World Series titles**
1919, 1940, 1975, 1976, 1990

**National League pennants**
1919, 1939, 1940, 1961, 1970, 1972, 1975, 1976, 1990

**Division titles**
1970, 1972, 1973, 1975–76, 1979, 1990

**Most Valuable Players**
Ernie Lombardi, 1938
Bucky Walters, 1939
Frank McCormick, 1940
Frank Robinson, 1961
Johnny Bench, 1970,
1972
Pete Rose, 1973
Joe Morgan, 1975, 1976
George Foster, 1977

**Rookies of the Year**
Frank Robinson, 1956
Pete Rose, 1963
Tommy Helms, 1966
Johnny Bench, 1968
Pat Zachry, 1976 (tie)
Chris Sabo, 1988

**Hall of Fame**
Christy Mathewson, 1936
George Wright, 1937
Candy Cummings, 1939
Buck Ewing, 1939
Charles "Hoss" Radbourne, 1939
Rogers Hornsby, 1942
King Kelly, 1945
Clark Griffith, 1946
Joe Tinker, 1946
Mordecai Brown, 1949
Harry Heilmann, 1952
Al Simmons, 1953
Rhoderick "Bobby"
Wallace, 1953
Harry Wright, 1953
Arthur "Dazzy" Vance, 1955
Sam Crawford, 1957
Bill McKechnie, 1962
Edd Roush, 1962
Eppa Rixey, 1963
Miller Huggins, 1964
Lloyd Waner, 1967
Kiki Cuyler, 1968
Jesse Haynes, 1970
Jake Beckley, 1971
Chick Hafey, 1971
Joe Kelley, 1971
Rube Marquard, 1971
George Kelly, 1973
Jim Bottomley, 1974
Amos Rusie, 1977
Larry MacPhail, 1978
Warren Giles, 1979
Frank Robinson, 1982
Ernie Lombardi, 1986
Johnny Bench, 1989
Joe Morgan, 1990
Tom Seaver, 1992

**Retired numbers**
1 Fred Hutchinson
5 Johnny Bench

## MINOR LEAGUES

| Class | Team |
|---|---|
| AAA | Indianapolis Indians |
| AA | Chattanooga (TN) Lookouts |
| A | Winston-Salem (NC) Spirits |
| A | Charleston (WV) Wheelers |
| Rookie | Billings (MT) Mustangs |
| Rookie | Princeton (WV) Reds |

The Red's closest minor-league affiliate is the Class AAA Indianapolis Indians of the American Association. Baseball first came to this city in 1903 when Indianapolis was one of the American Association's charter franchises. The Indians play in Bush Stadium, the oldest ballpark in the Association, having opened in 1931. The Stadium was the setting for the film *Eight Men Out*, which told the story of the Black Sox World Series scandal of 1919.
To reach Indianapolis' Bush Stadium, approximately 110 miles from Cincinnati, take the Meridian Street exit from I-65. Turn right and head to 16th Street, then turn left onto 16th Street. The stadium is 1½ miles ahead on the left.

## THE REDS AT RIVERFRONT STADIUM

**July 1, 1970:** Reds get their first win at Riverfront, 9–2 over the Atlanta Braves. Tommy Helms becomes the first Red to hit a home run at the new park.

**Oct. 5, 1970:** Reds sink the Pittsburgh Pirates 3–2 to complete a three-game sweep of the National League Championship Series and win their first league pennant

since 1961.

**Oct. 11, 1972:** Reds score two in the bottom of the ninth inning to beat the Pirates 4–3 in the fifth and deciding game of the NLCS.

**Oct. 15, 1972:** Oakland's Joe Rudi makes a leaping, back-handed catch against the wall to stop a two-run homer in the ninth inning of Game 2 in the World Series. The A's win the game 2–1, and the series.

**April 4, 1974:** Hank Aaron ties Babe Ruth's all-time home-run record on opening day.

**May 5, 1978:** Pete Rose gets his 3,000th hit, a single off the Montreal Expo's Steve Rogers.

**June 16, 1978:** Tom Seaver throws the Reds' first no-hitter at Riverfront, beating the St. Louis Cardinals 4–0.

**July 15, 1980:** Johnny Bench breaks Yogi Berra's major league record for catchers with a homer off the Expos' David Palmer.

**April 18, 1981:** Tom Seaver records strikeout No. 3,000, getting St. Louis' Keith Hernandez.

**Sept. 11, 1985:** Pete Rose becomes baseball's all-time hit leader at 4,192, with a single to left-center field off San Diego Padre Eric Show.

**Sept. 16, 1988:** Tom Browning becomes the first pitcher in Reds history to throw a perfect game, beating the Los Angeles Dodgers 1–0.

**Oct. 12, 1990:** Reds sink the Pirates 2–1 in the sixth and final game of the 1990 NLCS for their first pennant since 1976.

**Oct. 16, 1990:** Billy Hatcher goes 3-for-3 in Game 1 and 4-for-4 in Game 2 of the World Series, setting a World Series record with seven consecutive hits.

**Sept. 7, 1993:** Cardinal Mark Whiten hits four homers and drives in 12 runs (both of which tie major-league records) in the second game of a doubleheader.

# Jacobs Field

## STADIUM STATS

**Location:** 2401 Ontario St., Cleveland, OH 44115
**Opened:** April 4, 1994
**Surface:** Grass
**Capacity:** 42,400
**Outfield dimensions:** LF 325, LC 370, CF 405, RC 375, RF 325.
**Services for fans with disabilities:** Seating available throughout the stadium. For information, call (216) 241-8888.

## STADIUM FIRSTS

**Regular-season game:** April 4, 1994, a 4–3 win over the Seattle Mariners in 11 innings.
**Pitcher:** Dennis Martinez of the Indians.
**Batter:** Rich Amaral of the Mariners.
**Hit:** Rich Amaral.
**Home run:** Eric Anthony of the Mariners.

## GROUND RULES

• A batted ball hitting the foul pole or attached screen is a fair ball.
• A thrown or fair batted ball that goes behind or under the field tarp or drum covers and remains there is two bases. A ball that rebounds into the playing field is in play.
• A ball striking the roof or the color facing of the dugout, camera pits or diamond suites is considered in the dugout and equals two bases.
• A thrown ball that enters the camera pits, dugouts, or diamond suites and remains is two bases.
• A pitched ball that strikes the roof or facing,

*(Continued on page 29)*

Downtown Cleveland has not been the same since Jacobs Field opened in 1994. Part of the Gateway Sports Complex, which includes a multipurpose arena for the NBA's Cleveland Cavaliers, the new home of the Cleveland Indians is viewed by city officials as more than a sports facility. In its first year, Jacobs Field already has helped to revitalize a neighborhood that had been condemned.

Though it has been just as successful, Jacobs Field was designed as the antithesis of Oriole Park at Camden Yards in Baltimore. Cleveland didn't want its ballpark to be a throwback to yesteryear, opting instead for a contemporary marvel. The urban setting and brick give the stadium some traditional feel, but Jacobs Field is modern in every sense, from its white color to its steel beams, which were purposely left exposed to blend with the architecture of Cleveland's bridges and to foster the city's steeltown image. The ballpark's vertical light towers, unlike any in North America, echo the smokestacks and skyscrapers visible from the stands.

The Indians' past has not been forgotten, however. Bob Feller's statue sits outside the stadium in Indian Square, where 3-foot-high granite blocks spell out WHO'S ON FIRST? People sit on the blocks and have lunch. Inside, huge full-color and backlighted murals of current players line the walls. The park has 25 "great moment" signs throughout park, one of which depicts Len Barker's perfect game.

The Indians are trying to create a family-style atmosphere, although the huge number of sellout crowds sometimes makes this hard to maintain. All in all, the park combines the modern features of baseball with the best of its traditions.

## HOT TIPS FOR VISITING FANS

**Parking**
With 34,000 spaces within a 15-minute walk, including 17,000 within a 10-minute walk, parking is not a concern. Parking is $10 at the stadium, $8-$10 in surrounding lots. The parking was intentionally dispersed to create business in different parts of the downtown area.

**Media bites**
**Radio:** WKNR (1220 AM) is the flagship station.
**TV:** WUAV (Channel 43) and SportsChannel Ohio (cable).

**Weather**
The former stadium was on Lake Erie, so the move to the heart of downtown has provided the Indians with a somewhat warmer climate. Still, on any given night, temperatures can dip, and fans are recommended to bring a jacket or sweater.

Stangely enough, despite the move away from the lake, Jacobs Field is more prone to winds than old Municipal Stadium. The open spaces in the outfield help the breezes come through, creating a swirling effect on the play-

ing field, 18 feet below street level. During the first few weeks after Jacobs Field opened, officials thought they were in another Wrigley Field because every other inning, the wind changed directions. Preliminary wind studies had suggested the ball would travel straight to right field, but that hasn't been the case. Only one home run was hit to right in the first few months of the 1994 season.

**Cuisine**
The Indians have doubled the number of food items on sale, from 40 in the old park to 80 at Jacobs Field, with the menu ranging from Caesar salads to Evian water. You can get standard fare such as hot dogs and beer, but Jacobs Field also includes a bakery where goods are baked on the premises and a delicatessen that offers a choice of breads. Fans can eat in Picnic Plaza areas throughout the ballpark, the largest in center field.

Although the park is in one of the poorer sections of the city, development of Cleveland Flats and Jacobs Field had enhanced the economic status of the area. Businesses and restaurants are investing more heavily because of the volume of people now visiting the area. Popular after-game spots include Mel's Grill (216-781-1771) and Alvie's (216-273-7351), both within walking distance.

## LODGING NEAR THE STADIUM

**Cleveland Marriott Society Center**
127 Public Square
Cleveland, OH 44114
(216) 696-9200/(800) 228-9290
10 blocks from the stadium.

**The Stouffer Tower City Plaza**
24 Public Square
Cleveland, OH 44113
(216) 696-5600/(800) 468-3571
Less than a mile to the stadium via an indoor walkway in the mall at Tower City Plaza.

# IN THE HOT SEATS AT JACOBS FIELD

The capacity is 42,400, including a standing-room-only section in left field. People arrive up to an hour before the game to get good standing space. When a home run is hit into the area, some people scramble for the ball, but others don't want to leave their spots.

• **Good seats:** The obvious choices are between home plate and the bases in the lower deck, but better bargains exist. A $6 bleacher seat is the toughest ticket in town—understandable when you consider that the bleachers are patterned after Wrigley Field's, and the 19-foot left-field wall, just 370 feet from home plate, is a mini-version of Fenway Park's Green Monster. Another good buy, at $12, are the middle-level mezzanine seats in right field.

• **Bad seats:** A few obstructed-view seats are in the upper corners of left and right field. Those seats are sold last, and fans buying them are told they might have problems seeing certain parts of the field. The Indians, with a contending team for the first time in years, haven't had any problems selling the handful of not-so-good seats.

• **Special programs:** Jacobs Field has no family section, arguing that the whole ballpark caters to families. However, a designated area for youngsters, Kidsland, is in the lower deck in right field.

 **Ticket scalping:** This is a seller's market, with a markup of up to 10 times the face value. In 1994, the Indians were involved in their first pennant race since 1959, and the surge stirred the city. Officials now crack down on scalpers, whereas before they would look the other way.

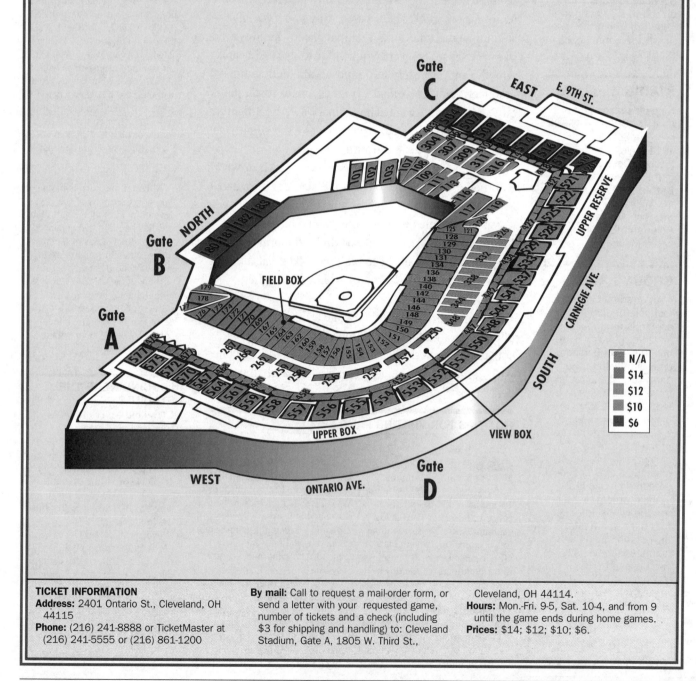

**Legend:**
- N/A
- $14
- $12
- $10
- $6

## TICKET INFORMATION

**Address:** 2401 Ontario St., Cleveland, OH 44115
**Phone:** (216) 241-8888 or TicketMaster at (216) 241-5555 or (216) 861-1200

**By mail:** Call to request a mail-order form, or send a letter with your requested game, number of tickets and a check (including $3 for shipping and handling) to: Cleveland Stadium, Gate A, 1805 W. Third St., Cleveland, OH 44114.
**Hours:** Mon.-Fri. 9-5, Sat. 10-4, and from 9 until the game ends during home games.
**Prices:** $14; $12; $10; $6.

## GETTING TO JACOBS FIELD

**Public transportation:** All RTA (Regional Transit Authority) trains go to Tower City. Then either take the RTA bus from Public Square and Tower City Center/Prospect Avenue to the stadium or walk (approximately 10 minutes) via the the walkway at Tower Center. For more bus and rail routes, contact the Regional Transit Authority at (216) 621-9500.

**By car:** From the south, take I-77 North to the East Ninth Street exit. Continue south on East Ninth a little less then a mile to Gateway area parking.

From the southwest, take I-90 or I-71 North to the Inner Belt merge. Continue on I-90 to the Ontario Street Exit. Take Ontario to Gateway parking.

From the west, take West Shoreway from Lakewood and continue across the Main Avenue Bridge. Continue ½ mile and exit right onto West Sixth Street. Continue on West Sixth to area parking.

From the east, take I-90 West/Route 2 to Ohio. Continue on Route 2 when I-90 curves to the left and exit off of Route 2 onto East Ninth Street. Make a left onto East Ninth and continue south to Gateway parking.

## SPRING TRAINING

Chain of Lakes Stadium
Winter Haven, FL 33880
**Capacity:** 7,042
**Surface:** Grass
**Game time:** 1:05 P.M. or 7:05 P.M.

## MINOR LEAGUES

| Class | Team |
|---|---|
| AAA | Charlotte Knights |
| AA | Canton/Akron (OH) Indians |
| A | Kinston (NC) Indians |
| A | Columbus (GA) Redstixx |
| Short Season A | Watertown (NY) |
| Rookie | Burlington (NC) Indians |

The Indians' closest minor-league affiliate is the Class AA Canton/Akron Indians of the Eastern League. Canton/Akron plays in Thurman Munson Memorial Stadium, named after the New York Yankees catcher and Canton native who was killed in a plane crash in 1979. Before heading to the park for an evening of baseball, fans can relive their favorite gridiron memories by stopping at the nearby Pro Football Hall of Fame in Canton.

To reach Thurman Munson Memorial Stadium, which is approximately 60 miles from Cleveland, take the Cleveland Avenue exit from I-77. From Cleveland Avenue, turn left on Mills and then left on Allen Avenue.

**Ticket prices:** $5: reserved seats; $4: general admission. For information call (216) 456-5100.

## HOME-FIELD ADVANTAGE

The biggest advantage comes in playing before packed crowds in a cozy, first-class ballpark after years of playing before small audiences in an old, dank, sprawling stadium. Players are in love with the park's plush grass field. Five different strands of Kentucky bluegrass make the turf durable enough to deal with Cleveland's harsh winters. A top-of-the-line drainage system allows the field to dry quickly. Other than a couple of symphonic concerts, few other events are deemed suitable for Jacobs Field. Tractor pulls? Not. Jacobs Field is intended to be a shrine to baseball.

Home-run shots into the left-field porch are also creating a furor at the new ballpark, although Jacobs Field is not an easy park in which to hit doubles. Balls hit down the lines, especially in left field, where the ball bounces back quickly, have made easy outs of base runners trying to stretch a single.

### INDIANS TEAM NOTEBOOK

**Franchise history**
Cleveland Broncos, 1901; Cleveland Blues, 1902–1904; Cleveland Naps, 1905–1911; Cleveland Molly McGuires, 1912–1914; Cleveland Indians, 1915–present

**World Series titles**
1920, 1948

**American League pennants**
1920, 1948, 1954

**Most Valuable Players**
George Burns, 1926
Lou Boudreau, 1948

Al Rosen, 1953

**Rookies of the Year**
Herb Score, 1955
Chris Chambliss, 1971
Joe Charboneau, 1980
Sandy Alomar Jr., 1990

**Cy Young Award**
Gaylord Perry, 1972

**Hall of Fame**
Nap Lajoie, 1937
Tris Speaker, 1937
Cy Young, 1937
Jesse Burkett, 1946
Bob Feller, 1962
Elmer Flick, 1963
Sam Rice, 1963
Stan Coveleski, 1969

Lou Boudreau, 1970
Satchel Paige, 1971
Early Wynn, 1972
Earl Averill, 1975
Ralph Kiner, 1975
Bob Lemon, 1976
Joe Sewell, 1977
Al Lopez, 1977
Addie Joss, 1978
Frank Robinson, 1982
Hoyt Wilhelm, 1985
Gaylord Perry, 1991
Bill Veeck, 1991

**Retired numbers**
3 Earl Averill
5 Lou Boudreau
18 Mel Harder
19 Bob Feller

## GROUND RULES

*(Continued from page 27)*

or enters the camera pits, dugouts or diamond suites is one base.
• A ball passing through or under the outfield fence is two bases.
• A fair batted ball that travels over the yellow line on the top of the outfield wall (on the fly) is a home run.
• A thrown ball that strikes the fence rails in front of the third- or first-base camera pits and returns to the field is in play.
• A thrown or fair batted ball that goes over or between the fence rails from the dugout to the foul poles equals two bases.
• A fair batted ball bouncing on the outfield wall is two bases.

## THE INDIANS AT JACOBS FIELD

**June 13, 1994:** The Indians beat the Toronto Blue Jays 7–3 and go into a tie for first place in the AL Central Division.

**June 25, 1994:** Cleveland's team-record 18-game home winning streak is stopped by the New York Yankees, who win 9–5 in a rain-shortened contest.

**June 25, 1994:** Cleveland opens a home stand in first place by four games, the latest in the season they have had a lead that large since their pennant-winning season in 1954.

**July 3, 1994:** Paul Sorrento has four hits and four runs batted in, including a game-winning single, as the Indians defeat the Minnesota Twins 10–9 in 11 innings.

**STADIUM STATS**

**Location:** 20th and Blake Sts., Denver, CO 80204
**Opens:** Spring 1995
**Surface:** Grass
**Capacity:** 50,000
**Outfield dimensions:** RF 350, CF 415, LF 347.
**Services for fans with disabilities:** Seating available for 450 wheelchair users.

**TEAM NOTEBOOK**

**Franchise history:**
Colorado Rockies, 1993–present.

**TICKET INFORMATION**
**Address:** 1700 Broadway, Suite 2100, Denver, CO 80290
**Phone:** (303) ROCKIES or (800) 388-ROCK
**Hours:** Mon.-Sat. 9-6

**LODGING NEAR THE STADIUM**

**Westin Hotel**
1672 Lawrence St.
Denver, CO 80202
(303) 572-9100/(800) 228-3000
About 1 mile from the stadium.

**Hyatt Regency**
1750 Welton St.
Denver, CO 80202
(303) 295-1234/(800) 233-1234
About 1½ miles from the stadium.

**GETTING TO COORS FIELD**
**Public transportation:** The RTD provides 16 buses to the downtown area. Call (303) 299-6000 for more information.
**By car:** Coors Field is at 20th and Blake streets. From I-25, take the 22nd Street Viaduct, which leads into the parking lot.

# Coors Field

Coors Field, the Rockies' new ballpark, is a perfect fit—both with Denver's long baseball tradition and with the trend of building new stadiums that recall the game's early days. Coors Field, located in a 25-square-block historic district known as lower downtown, or LoDo to locals, was built on the site of the Denver Union Railroad Depot, which opened in 1876. As if to emphasize the historic quality of the ballpark, a 66-million-year-old dinosaur bone was unearthed as the field was being built.

With its steel design and intimate dimensions, Coors Field will have the look and feel of an old-time ballpark. It will feature the majors' smallest foul territory between the seats and the infield corners, and other than the right-field wall, the outfield fence will be only 8 feet high. (The right-field wall is higher to accommodate a manually operated out-of-town scoreboard.) Fans also will be afforded one of the most spectacular views in baseball: the Rocky Mountains loom beyond the left-field fence.

Local artists have added further touches with two huge murals. Combined with the setting and the park's handsome and evocative design, they will help to make Coors Field a memorable place in which to watch a baseball game.

## HOT TIPS FOR VISITING FANS

**Parking**
Approximately 6,000 parking spaces are at Coors Field, as well as limited parking in the area.

**Weather**
Anyone who has watched the Rockies or Denver Broncos on television knows early spring and fall can be cold. Snow can occur in April, so be sure to dress warmly if you decide to visit any time other than in the summer.

**Media bites**
**Radio:** KOA (850 AM).
**TV:** KWGN (Channel 2). Charlie Jones, who has broadcast NFL games since 1959, and Dave Campbell, an ESPN baseball analyst and a former big-league player, share television duties on Rockies telecasts.

**Cuisine**
After the game, try Wynkoop Brewing Co. or The Wahzee Supper Club (303-623-9518), a trendy restaurant/club, considered among the best in Denver and known for its jazz and pizza.

**SPRING TRAINING**
Hi Corbett Field
3400 E. Camino Campestre
Tucson, AZ 85716
**Capacity:** 7,726
**Surface:** Grass
**Times:** 12:05 P.M., 1:05 P.M. or 7:05 P.M.

**MINOR LEAGUES**

| Class | Team |
|---|---|
| AAA | Colorado Springs Sky Sox |
| AA | New Haven (CT) Ravens |
| A | Central Valley (CA) Rockies |
| A | Asheville (NC) Tourists |
| Short Season A | Bend (OR) Rockies |
| Rookie | Chandler (AZ) Rockies |

The Rockies' closest minor-league affiliate is the Class AAA Colorado Springs Sky Sox of the Pacific Coast League. Sky Sox Stadium, 6,500-plus feet above sea level, roughly 1,300 feet higher than Denver's Mile High Stadium, touts itself as the highest ballpark in North America. The team's nickname comes from Colorado Springs' high altitude and the franchise's former affiliation with the Chicago White Sox in the 1950s.

To reach Colorado Springs' Sky Sox Stadium, approximately 70 miles from Denver, take the Woodman Road exit from I-25 South. Turn left and go through several traffic lights until you reach Powers Boulevard. Turn right. To reach the ballpark, visible on your left, turn left on Barns Road.

**Ticket prices:** $6: box seats; $5: children under 13 and senior citizens 60 and over.

**HOME-FIELD ADVANTAGE**
As at Mile High Stadium, the Rockies have a built-in advantage because of Denver's high altitude, cool temperatures and sudden snow squalls. All can be quite unsettling. The small size of Coors Field compared to Mile High should accentuate noise from the stands.

**IN THE HOT SEATS**

During their first two seasons, the Rockies averaged nearly 57,000 fans a game. Mile High Stadium, with a capacity in excess of 76,000, could easily accommodate whoever wanted to come. Coors Field, which holds 50,000, will be another story.

 **Scalping:** Given the size of Mile High Stadium and a very visible police presence there, scalping was not common. With fewer tickets available for Coors Field, though, the situation may change.

# Tiger Stadium

The grand playground at the corner of Michigan and Trumbull in Detroit is one of the most fabled sites in professional sports. In an era of mass marketing, Tiger Stadium remains remarkably free of fan gimmickry. Detroit fans are intelligent about baseball and don't have to be egged on by a phony applause machine to cheer for their team.

Baseball at the Tiger Stadium site dates to 1896 and the Western League. Although there have been several names changes—Bennett Park, Navin Field, Briggs Stadium and, finally, Tiger Stadium—little else has changed about one of the last remaining classic ballparks.

A Motor City fixture since its concrete-and-steel grandstand was built in 1912, Tiger Stadium underwent an $8 million face lift in 1993. Nonetheless, it faces an uncertain future. Several studies are examining whether to refurbish the venerable ballpark or build a new one. If a new ballpark is built, it will only be to add revenue with frills such as sky boxes; everyday fans are so loyal that they formed a human chain around the stadium a few years ago to show their support. Tiger Stadium remains a great place to see a game not in spite of its age, but because of it.

## HOT TIPS FOR VISITING FANS

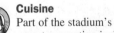

**Parking**
Tiger Stadium has no on-site parking, but the number of private lots in the vicinity is more than adequate. The freedom of choice benefits consumers, with the closer lots charging $5 or $6 and the lots 2 or 3 blocks farther away charging $2 or $3. The surface streets and extensive freeway system have been developed to accommodate easy movement of traffic before and after games.

**Weather**
Temperatures rise and fall in the course of a summer day in Detroit, generally ranging from the mid-60s to the high 70s. But it can get colder or hotter.

**Media bites**
**Radio:** WJR (760 AM).
**TV:** WDIV (Channel 4) and the PASS (Pro-Am Sports System) cable network.

**Cuisine**
Part of the stadium's recent renovation included Tiger Plaza, a food court outside the stadium. It offers 208 menu items, including standard ballpark fare and, of course, pizza, which has become the local favorite. The brand has changed, though, from previous owner Tom Monaghan's Domino's to current owner Mike Illitch's Little Caesars.

The Lindell A.C. (313-964-1122) remains one of the Stadium area's most popular watering holes. Nemo's (313-965-3180), Hoot Robinson's (313-965-7772), and Reedy's Saloon (313-961-1722) are also good haunts for fans. The Greektown area, about a mile away, is a good stopping-off point for dining before and after the game.

## STADIUM STATS

**Location:** 2121 Trumbull Ave., Detroit, MI 48216
**Opened:** April 20, 1912
**Surface:** Grass
**Capacity:** 52,416
**Outfield dimensions:** LF 340, LC 365, CF 440, RC 370, RF 325.
**Services for fans with disabilities:** Seating available in the Tiger Den behind home plate, the reserve section along the third-base line and in the left-field grandstand.

## STADIUM FIRSTS

**Regular-season game:** April 20, 1912, 6-5 over the Cleveland Indians.
**Pitcher** George Mullin of the Tigers.
**Batter:** Jack Graney of the Indians.

## GROUND RULES

• Foul poles are outside the playing field.
• A batted ball striking the facing or any part of the upper stands in fair territory and bouncing back onto field is a home run.
• Fly balls that strike lights underneath the upper stands from right-field to centerfield in fair territory and bounce back onto the field are home runs.
• Balls striking the yellow line of the flagpole or below it and caroming into stands count for two bases.
• Balls striking the yellow line of the flagpole or below it and bouncing back onto the field are in play.
• Balls striking above the yellow line on the flagpole: home run.
• A fair bounding ball going onto the roof of

*(Continued on page 33)*

## LODGING NEAR THE STADIUM

**Ritz-Carlton Dearborn**
Fairlane Plaza
300 Town Center Dr.
Dearborn, MI 48126
(313) 441-2000
About 15 miles from the stadium.

**Hyatt Regency Dearborn**
Fairlane Town Ctr.
Dearborn, MI 48126
(313) 593-1234/(800) 233-1234
About 20 miles from the stadium.

## GETTING TO TIGER STADIUM

**Public transportation:** The Linwood bus line runs to Tiger Stadium. For more information, call (313) 935-4910.
**By car:** From the north, take the Lodge Freeway (Highway 10) south to the I-75/Flint-Toledo exit. Stay in the right lane while exiting. Then, almost immediately, exit I-75 at Trumbull Avenue. The Stadium is on your right.

From the south, take I-75 north to exit 49A, Rosa Parks Boulevard. Continue on Rosa Parks to the Stadium, which is on the left.

From the west, take I-96, the Jeffries Freeway. Stay in the left lane and exit at Lodge Freeway. Continue 1 mile on the Lodge Freeway to the Rosa Parks Boulevard and Civic Center exit. The Stadium will be straight ahead.

From the east, take I-94 west. Stay to the left, and take exit 215A, the Lodge Freeway (Highway 10 South). Continue about 1½ miles to I-75, the Fisher Freeway to Flint-Toledo. Continue on I-75, and exit at Trumbull Avenue. The Stadium will be directly ahead.

## SPRING TRAINING

Marchant Stadium
P.O. Box 90187
Lakeland, FL 33804
**Capacity:** 7,027
**Surface:** Grass
**Game time:** 7 P.M.
**Tickets:** (813) 688-7911

# In the Hot Seats at Tiger Stadium

The Tigers' attendance is directly related to their success on the field. Give the fans a winner, and they will come. Give them a loser, and, well, the last couple of seasons have not been box-office smashes. Given the team's mediocre state, tickets are easy to get for almost any game. The exception is the season opener, which is virtually always sold out way ahead of time. The Tigers sold about 8,000 season tickets in 1994 and do most of their business with single-game advance and walk-up sales.

• **Good seats:** Tiger Stadium's seating is closer to the field than any other ballpark. The upper deck sits right on top of the lower deck, meaning even the higher seats have an excellent viewpoint. Despite its capacity of 52,416, Tiger Stadium is fan-friendly. It also boasts a center-field bleacher section of 10,000 seats priced at $5, one of the best buys in baseball. Except for a few seats along the lines and the bleachers, the Stadium's roof provides refuge from the rain.

• **Bad seats:** The one drawback of Tiger Stadium is the number of obstructed-view seats, about 5,000. The beams that obstruct the view of the field are reminiscent of those of the Polo Grounds and Ebbets Field.

**Scalping:** Though scalping is illegal in Michigan, there is plenty around the ballpark. Fans rarely need them, however.
    A few years back, a scandal erupted when club officials held back good tickets for scalping purposes, rather than selling them at the box office.

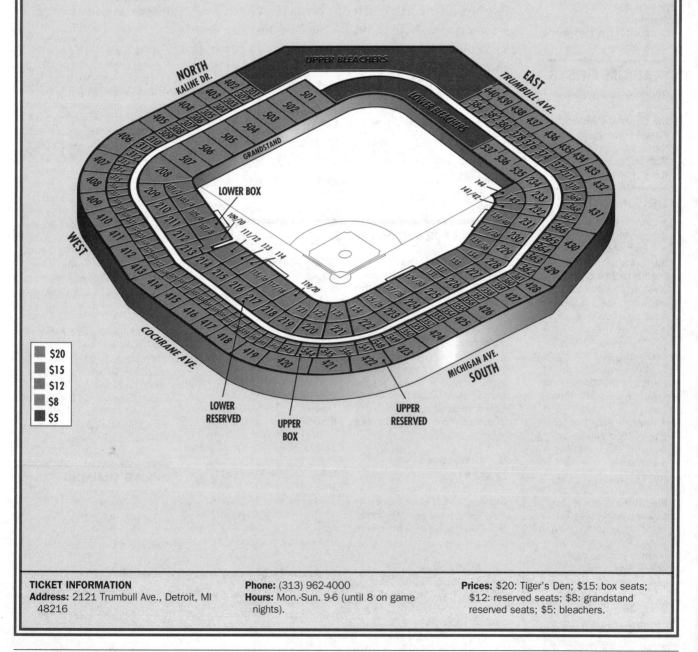

| | |
|---|---|
| ■ | $20 |
| ■ | $15 |
| ■ | $12 |
| ■ | $8 |
| ■ | $5 |

---

**TICKET INFORMATION**
**Address:** 2121 Trumbull Ave., Detroit, MI 48216

**Phone:** (313) 962-4000
**Hours:** Mon.-Sun. 9-6 (until 8 on game nights).

**Prices:** $20: Tiger's Den; $15: box seats; $12: reserved seats; $8: grandstand reserved seats; $5: bleachers.

## MINOR LEAGUES

| Class | Team |
|-------|------|
| AAA | Toledo (OH) Mudhens |
| AA | Trenton (NJ) Thunder |
| A | Lakeland (FL) Tigers |
| A | Fayetteville (NC) Generals |
| Short Season A | Jamestown (NY) Jammers |
| Rookie | Bristol (VA) Tigers |

The Tiger's closest minor-league affiliate is the Class AAA Toledo Mudhens of the International League. Pro baseball came to Toledo in 1883. The next season, Moses "Fleet" Walker and his brother, Welday, became the first African-American ballplayers in major league history; 43 years later, Casey Stengel, who later became the New York Yankees' manager, led Toledo to a Junior World Series title as that team's skipper.

To reach Toledo's Ned Skeldon Stadium, approximately 60 miles from Detroit, take exit 4 from the I-475 bypass and follow U.S. 24 for 2 miles. Turn left onto Key Street; the park will be on your right.

**Ticket prices:** $5: box seats; $4: reserved seats; $3: general admission; children 14 and under and senior citizens over 60 receive a $1 discount on all seats.

## THE TIGERS AT TIGER STADIUM

**Oct. 9, 1934:** Commissioner Kenesaw Mountain Landis removes St. Louis Cardinal Ducky Medwick from Game 7

## HOME-FIELD ADVANTAGE

Traditionally, the Tigers have emphasized power hitting over speed. The short right-field line, with an overhanging upper deck, is a left-handed power hitter's dream. The limited foul territory, also gives hitters an advantage. All told, Tiger Stadium is considered a hitter's park, although the wasteland in centerfield—440 feet to dead center, the deepest outfield in baseball—can help a smart pitcher.

The Tigers grounds crew has been accused of doing all kinds of things, from watering down the base paths to growing really thick infield grass, to accentuate the home-field advantage.

### TIGERS TEAM NOTEBOOK

**Franchise history**
Detroit Tigers, 1901–present

**World Series titles**
1935, 1945, 1968, 1984

**American League pennants**
1907, 1908, 1909, 1934, 1935, 1940, 1945, 1968, 1984

**Division titles**
1972, 1984, 1987

**Most Valuable Players**
Mickey Cochrane, 1934
Hank Greenberg, 1935, 1940
Charlie Gehringer, 1937

Hal Newhouser, 1944, 1945
Denny McLain, 1968
Willie Hernandez, 1984

**Rookies of the Year**
Harvey Kuenn, 1953
Mark Fidrych, 1976
Lou Whitaker, 1978

**Cy Young Awards**
Denny McLain, 1968, 1969 (tie)
Willie Hernandez, 1984

**Hall of Fame**
Ty Cobb, 1936
Dan Brouthers, 1945
Hughie Jennings, 1945
Mickey Cochrane, 1947
Al Simmons, 1953
Charlie Gehringer, 1956

Edward G. Barrow, 1956
Hank Greenberg, 1956
Sam Crawford, 1957
Heinie Manush, 1964
Goose Goslin, 1968
Waite Hoyt, 1969
Billy Evans, 1973
Sam Thompson, 1974
Earl Averill, 1975
Bucky Harris, 1975
Eddie Mathews, 1978
Al Kaline, 1980
George Kell, 1983
Rick Ferrell, 1984

**Retired numbers**
2 Charlie Gehringer
5 Hank Greenberg
6 Al Kaline

of the World Series as Tigers fans shower Medwick with fruit and vegetables in left field. St. Louis wins 11–0.

**Oct. 7, 1935:** The Tigers beat the Chicago Cubs 4–3 in the sixth game of the World Series to win the title.

**May 15, 1937:** Tigers great Mickey Cochrane is hit in the head with a pitch by New York

Yankee Bump Hadley, ending Cochrane's career.

**Sept. 30, 1945:** Hank Greenberg returns from World War II to hit a pennant-clinching home run in the last game of the season.

**June 15, 1948:** The Tigers play their first night game at Tiger Stadium. The gates open at 6, but management

## GROUND RULES
### (Continued from page 31)

either bullpen dugout counts for two bases.
• A ball going through or sticking in the screen on fair ground is two bases.
• A pitched ball sticking or remaining on the backstop screen is one base, while a thrown ball doing the same is two bases.

doesn't start the game until 9:30, thinking that the lights won't take effect until it is dark.

**May 15, 1952:** Virgil Trucks wins his no-hitter 1–0 when Vic Wertz homers off the Washington Senators with two outs in the bottom of the ninth.

**Sept. 14, 1968:** Denny McLain wins his 30th of the season, against the Oakland A's.

**Sept. 17, 1968:** The Tigers clinch the pennant with a 2–1 win over the Yankees.

**June 18, 1975:** Fred Lynn of the Boston Red Sox enjoys one of the best days in big-league history, hitting three home runs and driving in 10 runs in a 15–1 victory.

**June 1, 1976:** Mark "the Bird" Fidrych makes his debut at Tiger Stadium.

**Oct. 4, 1984:** Kirk Gibson's two home runs lead the Tigers to an 8–4 win over the San Diego Padres in Game 5, clinching the World Series title.

## STADIUM STATS

**Location:** 8400 Kirby Dr., Houston, TX 77054
**Opened:** April 9, 1965
**Surface:** Artificial turf (Magic Carpet)
**Capacity:** 54,313
**Outfield dimensions:** LF 325, LC 375, CF 400, RC 375, RF 325.
**Services for fans with disabilities:** Seating available on the third level behind home plate, and on the mezzanine level in right and left fields.

## STADIUM FIRSTS

**Regular-season game:** April 12, 1965, 2–0 loss to the Philadelphia Phillies.
**Pitcher:** Bob Bruce of the Astros.
**Batter:** Tony Taylor of the Phillies.
**Hit:** Tony Taylor.
**Home run:** Dick Allen of the Phillies.

## GROUND RULES

• Dugouts: The ball remains in play unless it enters the dugout or crosses the yellow line therein. If it enters the dugout, it counts for one base on a throw by a pitcher or two bases on a throw by a fielder.
• Behind home plate: Any thrown ball hitting above, on or below the padding or screen behind the home-plate area remains in play if it rebounds onto field; if the ball lodges in the padding or behind the plexiglass camera shield, it counts for one base on a pitch or two bases on throw by a fielder.
• Hitting roof or speakers: A ball hitting the roof or speakers in fair territory is playable if caught by fielder. The batter is then out.

(**Continued on page 36**)

# Astrodome

Few people would call it the Eighth Wonder of the World now, but the Astrodome was the first major-league ballpark to be enclosed.

Houston's first ballclub, the Colt 45s, played in Colt Stadium in 1962–64, and all the near-tropical pleasures of the city became part of the fan experience: the periodic torrential rains, usually just before game time, the Amazonian rain-forest humidity and, especially, the mosquitos almost as big as the ball in play. The Astrodome was eagerly anticipated—if not for its new inhabitants, then for the air conditioning it promised.

The stadium was built for $31.6 million, and the roof went up with 4,796 panes of glass. But the architects forgot that players must peer up to follow the flight of a batted ball. The panes made that nearly impossible, so they were painted, and everyone thought the problem was solved.

Then the grass died. To remedy the situation, the Monsanto Corporation developed a short, plush carpet called AstroTurf. The game was never the same again.

Visiting players soon had another surprise: The still air had a chilling effect on home runs. Power hitters were punished by the ball's not carrying. The Astrodome quickly gained a reputation as one of the long-ball hitters' least favorite parks.

As well as changing the height of the outfield walls, the Astros have tried to liven things up over the years with such embellishments as a Wild West scoreboard extravaganza that went off whenever an Astros player homered. That was dropped after the 1987 season. For a short time, ushers wore space outfits. Thankfully, that too was dropped.

With a long line of imitators and a history as rich as the oil men and tycoons who put it in Texas, the Astrodome is a unique—and pleasantly cool—repository of great baseball moments.

## HOT TIPS FOR VISITING FANS

**Parking**
The huge Astrodome lots have room for 24,600 cars, which makes private lots unnecessary. Parking is $4. The Astros have an early-bird lot for $1 in the northwest corner of the property, a decent walk from the ballpark. It opens at 5 P.M. and closes at 6 P.M. for night games.

**Weather**
You can get rained out at the Astrodome. It happened once. You could look it up. On June 15, 1976, 10 inches of rain fell, and the flooding was too bad to hold a game. Count on real relief from Houston's humidity when you go inside the Astrodome. The AC has 6,600 tons of cooling capacity, and the temperature hovers around 72.

 **Media bites**
**Radio:** KPRC (950 AM) is the flagship station, with Milo Hamilton and Larry Dierker as the primary announcers. Bill Brown, Vince Cotroneo, Bill Worrell and Enos Cabell also broadcast for the Astros. KXYZ (1320 AM) does the Spanish-language broadcasts, with Francisco Ernesto Ruiz announcing.
**TV:** KTXH (Channel 20) and the Home Sports Entertainment channel do telecasts. Brown does play-by-play for TV, with Dierker and Worrell helping.

**Cuisine**
The Astrodome features several items with a distinctive Texas flair. Luther's Barbecue Stand, run by a popular local chain, sells beef barbecue and a gigantic barbecued potato, with a variety of toppings. You can get nachos with chili, cheese and plenty of jalapeño peppers. Other foods include oversized Dome Dogs, grilled burgers, and grilled Italian sausages. A variety of beers, including Heineken and Mexican brews, are sold.

Pappasito's (713-784-5253) is about 10 minutes from the Astrodome and is a good choice for a postgame Tex-Mex meal; check out the athlete-autographed menus on the ceiling over the bar. Astros and visiting players are occasional customers. Willie G's (713-840-7190) is also nearby. This New Orleans–style restaurant serves Cajun dishes and specializes in fresh seafood; it also features Shiner's, a popular Texas brew. The Yucatan Liquor Stand, Dave & Busters, and other spots on Richmond Avenue are standard postgame hangouts, but they're geared more to the singles scene than to sports fans.

# IN THE HOT SEATS AT THE ASTRODOME

The capacity for baseball is 54,313. The Astros, even in their best seasons and even when they had Nolan Ryan, were rarely a threat to sell out. Walk-up tickets are no problem. Those who buy them in the early afternoon at the stadium can take the Astrodome tour to kill time. It is fascinating, and fans are allowed to stand on the field.

• **Bad seats:** Outfield seats are far from the action. Avoid the general-admission seats in left and right field on either side of the pavilion; some of these are obstructed by supports. Once you get in, don't plan to move down to better seats, especially the Diamond Level boxes (ex-president George Bush's section). The ushers vigorously enforce the sit-in-your-seat edict.

**Scalping:** Though it's legal, it's unknown around the Astrodome. Longtime fans don't even recall seeing them in 1986, when the Astros were in the playoffs.

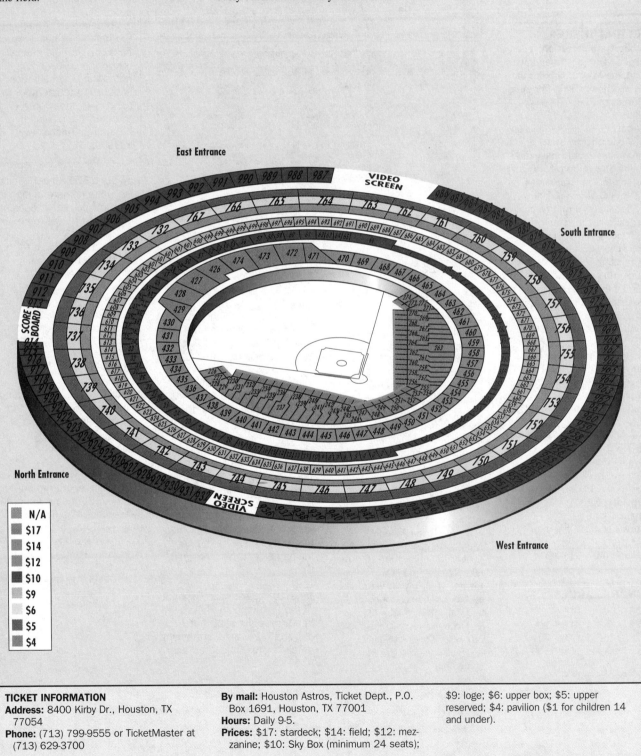

Legend:
- N/A
- $17
- $14
- $12
- $10
- $9
- $6
- $5
- $4

**TICKET INFORMATION**
**Address:** 8400 Kirby Dr., Houston, TX 77054
**Phone:** (713) 799-9555 or TicketMaster at (713) 629-3700

**By mail:** Houston Astros, Ticket Dept., P.O. Box 1691, Houston, TX 77001
**Hours:** Daily 9-5.
**Prices:** $17: stardeck; $14: field; $12: mezzanine; $10: Sky Box (minimum 24 seats);

$9: loge; $6: upper box; $5: upper reserved; $4: pavilion ($1 for children 14 and under).

## LODGING NEAR THE STADIUM

**Sheraton Astrodome**
8686 Kirby Dr.
Houston, TX 77054
(713) 748-3221/(800) 325-3635
1 block from the stadium.

**Holiday Inn Astrodome**
8111 Kirby Dr.
Houston, TX 77054
(713) 790-1900/(800) 552-0942
¾ mile from the stadium.

## GETTING THERE

**Public transportation:** You can catch a Metro bus from downtown: the No. 18 Kirby or the No. 15 Hiram-Clark. For more information, call (713) 635-4000.
**By car:** From the South Loop 610, exit at Kirby Street or continue about ½ mile and exit at Fannin Street. From Kirby, the parking-lot entrances are at Westridge, Murworth and McNee streets. From Fannin, the entrances are at Naomi, Holly Hall and Northwest Drive. Or take Main Street north and approach from either McNee, Murworth or Westridge streets.
From the east, take Old Spanish trail to North Stadium Drive. Make a left and use the North Stadium Drive entrance.
From the north, go south on I-45 to North Sheridan Drive, which turns into GreenBriar Drive, then Fannin Street. Use the parking entrances off Naomi, Holly Hall and Northwest Drive.

## SPRING TRAINING

Osceola County Stadium
1000 Bill Beck Blvd.
Kissimmee, FL 34744
**Capacity:** 5,100
**Surface:** Grass
**Game time:** 12:05 P.M. or 6:35 P.M.
**Tickets:** (407) 933-2520

## MINOR LEAGUES

| Class | Team |
|---|---|
| AAA | Tucson (AZ) Toros |
| AA | Jackson (MS) Generals |
| A | Osceola (FL) Astros |
| A | Quad City (IA) River Bandits |
| Short Season A | Auburn (NY) Astros |
| Rookie | Osceola (FL) Astros |

The closest minor-league team to Houston is the Class AA San Antonio Missions of the Texas League. One of the Missions' opponents is the Jackson Generals, Houston's Texas League affiliate. 1994 marked the Missions' first season in their new ballpark, Municipal Stadium, designed by the architects of Cleveland's Jacobs Field. Except for five years (1943–45, 1965–66), pro baseball has been played in this city since 1903.
To reach San Antonio's Municipal Stadium, approximately 200 miles from Houston, take Route 35 south from downtown to Highway 90 West. The park is at the intersection of 90 and Callaghan Road.
**Ticket prices:** $7: executive box seats; $6: box seats; $5: reserved seats; $4: general admission.

## HOME-FIELD ADVANTAGE

Most visiting teams hate the Astrodome, especially hitters daunted by its reputation as a Death Valley for home runs. The city also has a history of pro athletes getting arrested by police who are allegedly gunning for them. Gary Sheffield was the most recent victim, in 1993, but four New York Mets were arrested several years ago, as was Roger Clemens of Boston. In almost every case, the players were cleared. Though the Houston police deny that they look for athletes, this puts players in a bad frame of mind.

### ASTROS TEAM NOTEBOOK

**Franchise history**
Houston Colt .45s, 1962–64; Houston Astros, 1965–present.

**Division titles**
1980, 1986

**Rookie of the Year**
Jeff Bagwell, 1991

**Cy Young Award**
Mike Scott, 1986

**Hall of Fame**
Robin Roberts, 1976

Eddie Mathews, 1978
Joe Morgan, 1990

**Retired numbers**
25 Jose Cruz
32 Jim Umbricht
33 Mike Scott
40 Don Wilson

## THE ASTROS AT THE ASTRODOME

**Sept. 13, 1965:** Willie Mays hits his 500th home run, off the Astros' Don Nottebart.

**June 22, 1966:** The Astrodome attendance record is set as 50,908 see the Los Angeles Dodgers and Sandy Koufax beat the Astros 5–2.

**June 18, 1967:** Don Wilson no-hits the Atlanta Braves 2–0 for the first no-hitter in the Astrodome.

**April 30, 1969:** Jim Maloney of the Cincinnati Reds no-hits the Astros. The next night, Wilson no-hits the Reds.

**April 29, 1974:** Lee May ties a major-league record by hitting two home runs in one inning against the Chicago Cubs.

**June 10, 1974:** Mike Schmidt of the Philadelphia Phillies hits a towering shot that deflects off a speaker hanging in fair territory in center field.

## GROUND RULES

**(Continued from page 34)**

• A ball hitting the roof or speakers in fair territory will be judged fair or foul relative to where it hits the ground or is touched by a fielder.
• Any ball that hits the speaker or roof in foul territory is a foul ball, and the ball is dead.
• Outfield area: A fairly batted ball in left field, center field or right field hitting above the yellow line is a home run. Any ball bouncing above the line from fair territory is considered to have left the playing field and will be ruled a two-base hit.

**July 30, 1975:** Relief pitcher Jose Sosa homers in his first major league at-bat, becoming the first Astro ever to do so.

**July 11, 1985:** Nolan Ryan fans Danny Heep for his 4,000th strikeout.

**Oct. 15, 1986:** In one of the most exciting games ever played, the New York Mets beat the Astros 7–6 in 16 innings to earn a trip to the World Series.

**1992:** The Astros are forced to go on a 26-day road trip because the Astrodome is hosting the Republican National Convention.

**Aug. 5, 1994:** Jeff Bagwell sets team records when he hits his 38th home run of the season and has five RBI, to bring his total to 112, in a 12–4 win against the San Francisco Giants.

# Kauffman Stadium

K nown as one of baseball's most beautiful ballparks, Kauffman Stadium was one of the first baseball-only stadiums built in the last two decades. Its football cousin, the Kansas City Chiefs' Arrowhead Stadium, sits next door, and together the two stadiums make up the Harry S. Truman Sports Complex.

The Stadium's most prominent feature is a 322-foot-wide water spectacular behind the outfield wall. It's the largest privately funded fountain in the world. The Stadium also features a 12-story-high scoreboard built in the shape of the Royals' crest and a state-of-the-art Sony JumboTron color video-display board. The Stadium will switch to natural grass beginning with the '95 season.

The Royals organization is focused on fostering a family-type crowd, which has proved to be very successful for the organization as well as the fans. Kauffman Stadium encourages this atmosphere with features such as a picnic-and-music area, known as the Royal Courtyard, and an amusement area with a pitching booth.

## HOT TIPS FOR VISITING FANS

**Parking**
The stadium has 22,000 parking spaces available for $5 a vehicle, more than enough to handle a sellout crowd. Traffic moves swiftly on and off the nearby freeway.

**Weather**
Kansas City is traditionally hot in August and September. Rain is not much of a threat because the excellent drainage system leaves the field dry in no time, leading to few postponed games. The drainage system will remain in place after grass is installed for 1995.

**Media bites:**
**Radio:** WIBW (580 AM) .
**TV:** KSMO (Channel 62).
Former Royals pitcher Paul Splittorff does color on television.

**Cuisine**
Barbecued pork and beef are favorites. Ice-cream sundaes and deli foods also are very popular. Budweiser, Miller and Coors are among the national brands of beer sold. A local brew, Boulevard Beer, also is popular.
Within walking distance of the Stadium is Saunders, a sports

bar, and Quincy's, located in the Adam's Mark hotel. Westport, an area located about 20 minutes away, has several bars that cater to the upscale younger crowd.

### LODGING NEAR THE STADIUM

**Westin Crown Center**
1 Pershing Rd.
Kansas City, MO 64108
(816) 474-4400/(800) 228-3000
About 10 miles from the stadium.

**Holiday Inn Sports Complex**
4011 Blue Ridge Cutoff
Kansas City, MO 64133
(816) 353-5300/(800) HOLIDAY
Across the street from the stadium.

### SPRING TRAINING

Baseball City Stadium
300 Stadium Way
Davenport, FL 33837
**Capacity:** 7,000
**Surface:** Grass
**Game time:** 1:00 P.M.
**Tickets:** (813) 424-7211

### MINOR LEAGUES

| Class | Team |
|---|---|
| AAA | Omaha Royals |
| AA | Memphis Chicks |
| A | Wilmington (DE) Blue Rocks |
| A | Rockford (IL) Royals |
| Short Season A | Eugene (OR) Emeralds |
| Rookie | Fort Myers (FL) Royals |

The Royals' closest minor-league affiliate is the Class AAA Omaha Royals of the American Association.

To reach Omaha's Rosenblatt Stadium, approximately 190 miles from Kansas City, take the 13th Street exit from I-80. The stadium will be visible.

**Ticket prices:** $6: Field seats; $5: view box; $3: general admission. For more information, call (402) 734-2550.

## THE ROYALS AT KAUFFMAN STADIUM

**May 15, 1973:** Nolan Ryan throws his first no-hitter and the first at the Stadium, striking out 12 as the California Angels win 3–0.

**Oct. 10, 1976:** The Royals get their first playoff win at the Stadium, beating the New York Yankees 7–3.

**Oct. 17, 1980:** The Royals get their first World Series victory, edging the Philadelphia Phillies 4–3 in 10 innings behind homers by George Brett and Amos Otis.

**Oct. 27, 1985:** A five-hitter by Bret Saberhagen and a two-run homer by Daryl Motley key an 11–0 win over the St. Louis Cardinals in Game 7 of the World Series. The Royals also trailed this series 3–1.

**Sept. 29, 1993:** Future Hall-of-Famer Brett singles in his final at-bat, off the Cleveland Indians' Jeremy Hernandez.

# IN THE HOT SEATS AT KAUFFMAN STADIUM

Walk-up sales are very common because games rarely sell out. In addition, 5,000 general-admission seats go on sale one hour before the start of each game. These seats are split between the right and left fields (half in each).

Fireworks nights, typically on holidays, always attract big crowds, and are generally sellouts. The Royals have big rivalries with the Oakland A's, who formerly played in Kansas City, and the Chicago White Sox. A rivalry is also developing

with the Cleveland Indians, but their biggest rival for a number of years has been the New York Yankees.

• **Good seats:** Being a baseball-only stadium, Kauffman Stadium has no bad seats. For sunbathers, the left-field stands are generally the best place to be. Some fans prefer plaza reserved seats or box seats, but any ticket will do.

• **Special programs:** The Royals offer

half-price reserved seats on Mondays and Thursdays. A limited number of standing-room-only tickets are available for most otherwise sold-out games.

**Scalping:** Ticket availability limits scalping activity, but some can be found off the Stadium premises.

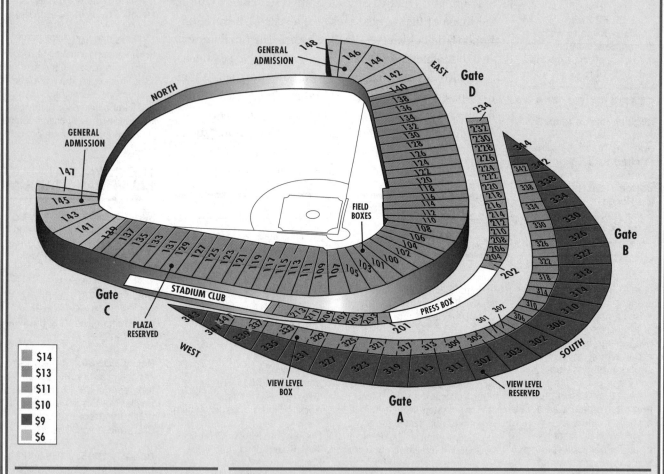

$14
$13
$11
$10
$9
$6

## HOME-FIELD ADVANTAGE

The 1994 season was the last for artificial turf at Kaufman Stadium. A new grass playing surface will be ready for the 1995 season and will take some getting used to. The Royals also plan to modify the outfield walls by moving them in a few feet and lowering them.

## GETTING TO KAUFFMAN STADIUM

**Public transportation:** Stadium Express Bus service runs from downtown, the Crown Center and Country Club Plaza to Kauffman Stadium. Service begins 1 hour and 50 minutes before game time. Call (816) 221-0660 for more information.

**By car:** From the south, take I-435 to the stadium exit at Stadium Drive. The Stadium will be ahead.

From the north, take I-435 to I-70. Take I-70 to the Harry S. Truman Sports Complex exit, then take the Blue Ridge cutoff to the Stadium.

From both east and west, take I-70 to the Harry S. Truman Sports Complex exit, then take the Blue Ridge cutoff to the Stadium.

## TICKET INFORMATION

**Address:** 1 Royal Way, Kansas City, MO 64129
**Phone:** (800) 422-1969 or (816) 921-8000
**By mail:** P.O. Box 419969, Kansas City, MO

64141. Specify dates, number of tickets and preferred location. Include $2 postage and handling.
**Hours:** Daily 9-6.
**Prices:** $14: club-level box; $13: field-level

box; $11: plaza-level reserved; $10: view-level (upper) box; $9: reserved; $6: general admission.

# Dodger Stadium

According to a recent book, Walter O'Malley was riding in a helicopter over Los Angeles, scouting for the Dodgers' new home when he noticed a spot where several freeways converged. "Can I have that?" he asked a government official.

The rest is Dodgers history. O'Malley got what he wanted: As the Dodgers began their West Coast life in 1958 at the Los Angeles Coliseum, construction was under way on Dodger Stadium at Chavez Ravine. Some squatters and goatherds were evicted first, including one family that had to be carted away kicking and screaming and even biting the marshalls who took them. The result was a jewel—a gorgeous, clean, friendly and efficient ballpark on a hilltop overlooking downtown Los Angeles. Between the ushers in their straw boaters, the tasty Dodger dogs, and the great views of the San Gabriel Mountains on one side and the city skyline on the other, this park has as much personality as any of its older cousins off to the east.

The presence of Tommy Lasorda (who, contrary to rumors, does not live here) and Mike Brito (a Dodgers employee who sports a Panama hat, cigar and radar gun in his role as goodwill ambassador, occasional scout and recorder of pitch velocities) lend a sense of tradition to the place that offsets the "come late, leave early" attitude of many fans. If the game is slow, fans will bat beach balls from section to section, playing an elaborate cat-and-mouse game with the ushers. Still, Dodger Stadium was the first ballpark to draw 3 million fans in one season, so even if the fans don't always show it, Dodger blue definitely runs through the veins of Angelenos.

## HOT TIPS FOR VISITING FANS

**Parking**
The stadium has parking for 16,000 cars; the cost is $4. Lots funnel into nearby freeways much more easily than the common perception has it, helped by fans leaving early. No lot empties much faster than the others. If you arrive early by the Elysian Park Road entrance, you can see "Dodger Mom," a rabid fan who's always first in line waiting for the parking gates to open.

**Weather**
The climate is almost never a factor. The Dodgers have not had a rainout since April 21, 1988. You can count on warm weather generally, but ocean breezes and high elevation usually preclude stifling heat. It can get cool in the evenings, especially in April and September, so long sleeves help at those times of the year.

Another, more ominous, natural phenomenon is always in the back of the minds of those attending Dodgers games. Dodger Stadium is built on a fault line, so the earthquake that shook up Candlestick Park could look minor league compared to what could happen if the Big One ever hits southern California.

### Media bites
**Radio:** The Dodgers' flagship radio station is KABC (790 AM), with legendary Vin Scully behind the microphone. Color is handled by Ross Porter and Rick Monday, a former Cub and Dodger famed for the game in which, as a visiting Cub, he tore a U.S. flag away from people who had trotted onto the outfield with intentions of burning the Stars and Stripes. The Spanish broadcasts are on KWKW (1330 AM), with Jaime Jarrin and Rene Cardenas.
**TV:** KTLA (Channel 5) carries the games on television.

### Cuisine
Dodger dogs are required eating. Long, thin and grilled to perfection, it's the best hot dog in baseball. Insiders recommend the "Red Hot" spicy dog. Order it grilled, not steamed. Take the time to find the Gulden's mustard dispensers. Pizza Hut, Carl's Jr. and Taco Bell are on hand to serve less traditional fare, and TCBY draws long lines for its frozen yogurt served in plastic, mini Dodger batting helmets.

Don't miss the loge-level peanut vendor who is renowned for throwing peanuts across sections to customers with accuracy that would shame many NBA guards. Drop the bag and you risk his wrath. He is reportedly available for private functions and carries business cards to give to favored customers.

There are many choices for after the game. The stadium bumps against Chinatown, which has any number of quality spots. On Broadway, an Italian place called Little Joe's (213-489-4900) is highly recommended. Felipe's (213-628-3781) on Alameda just below Chinatown, is where the French-dip sandwich was invented; it has great food and a casual, sawdust-on-the-floor atmosphere. Downtown near the Coliseum is a wonderful barbecue spot, Mr. Jim's. Their slogan is "You Don't Need Teeth to Eat Mr. Jim's Beef."

Those with strong connections and big budgets should head for Spago's or Morton's, where the Hollywood big shots schmooze, dine and do business.

# IN THE HOT SEATS AT DODGER STADIUM

Dodger Stadium is the only ballpark in the majors (excluding new yards for the Baltimore Orioles, the Chicago White Sox and the Texas Rangers) that has never changed capacity. It has always held 56,000. Though architect Emil Praeger designed the ballpark so the outfield could be enclosed and capacity raised to 85,000, that has never been done.

Prime seats can be had for most games on a walk-up basis. Season tickets are $2,700.

• **Good seats:** The seats nearly everyone wants are the dugout-level seats right behind the plate. You get serious air time when you sit there.

• **Bad seats:** Counting the club level, five decks rise from behind the plate. If you are in the top deck, you might as well be trying to spot the waves in Malibu for all the distance you are from the field. Top-deck seats in foul ground down the lines are even more daunting. No wonder people leave early—if they get home before the game ends, they might actually see a player. The pavilion seats (a k a the bleachers) are superior to top-deck spots; they're closer to the action, and no alcohol is sold there.

 **Scalping:** Scalpers line the streets encircling the stadium. Those willing to pay can get premium seats from them, but should have a seating chart for verification and be prepared to pay plenty. After all, this is Los Angeles, and the stadium is just off the Hollywood Freeway. Plenty of high rollers are willing to pay top dollar for a good ticket, so the scalpers have a strong bargaining position.

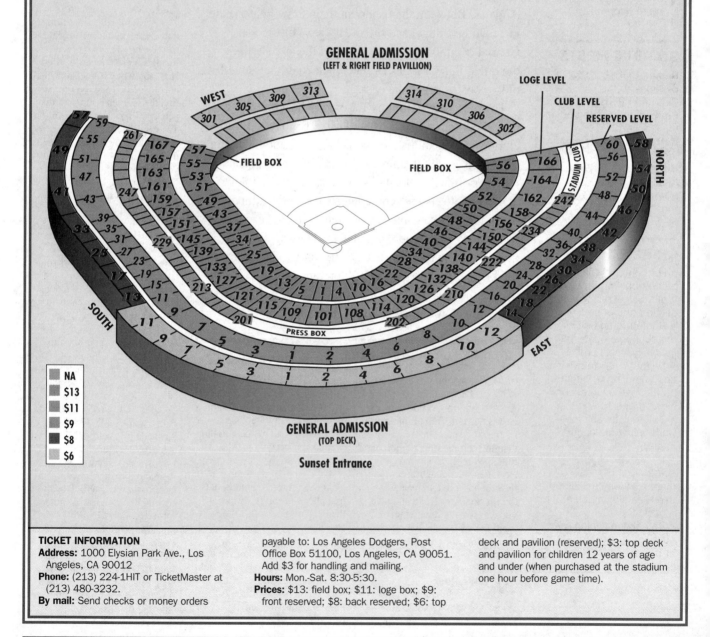

**GENERAL ADMISSION**
**(LEFT & RIGHT FIELD PAVILLION)**

LOGE LEVEL
CLUB LEVEL
RESERVED LEVEL

WEST

NORTH

FIELD BOX

FIELD BOX

STADIUM CLUB

SOUTH

PRESS BOX

EAST

| | NA |
| | $13 |
| | $11 |
| | $9 |
| | $8 |
| | $6 |

**GENERAL ADMISSION**
**(TOP DECK)**

**Sunset Entrance**

**TICKET INFORMATION**
**Address:** 1000 Elysian Park Ave., Los Angeles, CA 90012
**Phone:** (213) 224-1HIT or TicketMaster at (213) 480-3232.
**By mail:** Send checks or money orders payable to: Los Angeles Dodgers, Post Office Box 51100, Los Angeles, CA 90051. Add $3 for handling and mailing.
**Hours:** Mon.-Sat. 8:30-5:30.
**Prices:** $13: field box; $11: loge box; $9: front reserved; $8: back reserved; $6: top deck and pavilion (reserved); $3: top deck and pavilion for children 12 years of age and under (when purchased at the stadium one hour before game time).

## LODGING NEAR THE STADIUM

**Sheraton Grande**
333 S. Figueroa St.
Los Angeles, CA 90017
(800) 325-3535/(213) 617-1133.
About 8 miles from the stadium.

**Inter-Continental**
251 S. Olive St.
Los Angeles, CA 90017
(800) 327 0200/(213) 617-3300
About 2 miles from the stadium.

## GETTING TO DODGER STADIUM

**Public transportation:** The No. 635 runs to all Dodgers games. Buses let fans off between parking lots 8 and 10. Call (213) 937-8920 for more information.
**By car:** From the north, take Freeway 101 South to the Alvarado exit. Turn left and then make a right onto Sunset Boulevard. Continue on Sunset for about 2 miles and make a left onto Elysian Park Avenue. Go 1 mile on Elysian to the stadium.

From the south, take Freeway 101 North to the Alvarado exit. Turn right onto Sunset Boulevard and proceed as above.

## SPRING TRAINING

Holman Stadium
P.O. Box 2887
4001 26th St.
Vero Beach, FL 32961
**Capacity:** 6,500
**Surface:** Grass
**Game time:** 1:05 P.M.

## MINOR LEAGUES

| Class | Team |
|---|---|
| AAA | Albuquerque Dukes |
| AA | San Antonio Missions |
| A | Vero Beach (FL) Dodgers |
| A | Bakersfield (CA) Dodgers |
| Short Season A | Yakima (WA) Bears |
| Rookie | Great Falls (MT) Dodgers |

The closest minor-league team to Los Angeles is the Class A Riverside Pilots of the California League. One of the Pilots' opponents is the Bakersfield Dodgers, Los Angeles' California League affiliate. Although Riverside was a charter member of the league when it debuted in 1941, this

city lost its franchise after that season and did not regain it until 1988. Today, the team plays on the campus of the University of California at Riverside.
To reach Riverside's Sport Center, approximately 60 miles from Los Angeles, take the Blaine Street exit from I-60 and turn left. Turn right on Rustin and the ballpark will be on your left.

## HOME-FIELD ADVANTAGE

Dodger players are used to the rock-hard crushed-brick infield that leads to bad hops. The mound is often alleged to be a little higher than anywhere else, an advantage for pitching, which historically has been a Dodgers strength. The outfield corners are sometimes a challenge because of the waist-level fence right at the line, leading to some strange caroms.

The "come late, leave early" ritual is not something the team boasts about, either. Large segments of fans tend to wander in a few innings into the game, possibly because of the traffic or the fashionably late lifestyle of Lotusland. These same people like to leave two or three innings early. They're trying to beat traffic, but traffic is a 24-hour problem in Los Angeles, so what's the point? A team can't get charged up for a late-inning rally when it sees droves of fans walking out.

## DODGERS TEAM NOTEBOOK

**Franchise history**
Brooklyns, 1884–88 (AA); Brooklyn Bridegrooms, 1889 (AA); Brooklyn Bridegrooms 1890–98; Brooklyn Superbas, 1899–1910; Brooklyn Infants, 1911–13; Brooklyn Robins, 1914–31; Brooklyn Dodgers, 1932–57; Los Angeles Dodgers, 1958–present

**World Series titles**
1955, 1959, 1963, 1965, 1981, 1988

**National League pennants**
1916, 1920, 1941, 1947, 1949, 1952, 1953, 1955, 1956, 1959, 1963, 1965, 1966, 1974, 1977, 1978, 1981, 1988

**Division titles**
1974, 1977, 1978, 1981, 1983, 1985, 1988

**Most Valuable Players**
Jake Daubert, 1913
Dazzy Vance, 1924
Dolph Camilli, 1941
Jackie Robinson, 1949
Roy Campanella, 1951, 1953, 1955
Don Newcombe, 1956
Maury Wills, 1962
Sandy Koufax, 1963
Steve Garvey, 1974

Kirk Gibson, 1988

**Rookies of the Year**
Jackie Robinson, 1947
Don Newcombe, 1949
Joe Black, 1952
Jim Gilliam, 1953
Frank Howard, 1960
Jim Lefebvre, 1965
Ted Sizemore, 1969
Rick Sutcliffe, 1979
Steve Howe, 1980
Fernando Valenzuela, 1981
Steve Sax, 1982
Eric Karros, 1992
Mike Piazza, 1993

**Cy Young Awards**
Don Newcombe, 1956
Don Drysdale, 1962
Sandy Koufax, 1963, 1965, 1966
Mike Marshall, 1974
Fernando Valenzuela, 1981
Orel Hershiser, 1988

**Hall of Fame**
Willie Keeler, 1939
George Sisler, 1939
Dan Brouthers, 1945
Hugh Jennings, 1945
Wilbert Robinson, 1945
Thomas McCarthy, 1946
Joe McGinnity, 1946
Paul Waner, 1952
Rabbit Maranville, 1954
Ted Lyons, 1955
Dazzy Vance, 1955
Zack Wheat, 1959
Max Carey, 1961

Jackie Robinson, 1962
Burleigh Grimes, 1964
Heinie Manush, 1964
Monte Ward, 1964
Casey Stengel, 1966
Branch Rickey, 1967
Lloyd Waner, 1967
Kiki Cuyler, 1968
Joe "Ducky" Medwick, 1968
Roy Campanella, 1969
Waite Hoyt, 1969
Dave Bancroft, 1971
Joe Kelley, 1971
Rube Marquard, 1971
Sandy Koufax, 1972
George Kelly, 1973
Billy Herman, 1975
Fred Lindstrom, 1976
Al Lopez, 1977
Larry MacPhail, 1978
Hack Wilson, 1979
Duke Snider, 1980
Frank Robinson, 1982
Walter Alston, 1983
Juan Marichal, 1983
Don Drysdale, 1984
Pee Wee Reese, 1984
Arky Vaughan, 1985
Hoyt Wilhelm, 1985
Ernie Lombardi, 1986
Tony Lazzeri, 1991
Leo Durocher, 1994

**Retired numbers**
1 Pee Wee Reese
4 Duke Snider
19 Jim Gilliam
24 Walter Alston
32 Sandy Koufax
39 Roy Campanella
42 Jackie Robinson
53 Don Drysdale

**Ticket Prices:** $5: reserved seats; $3: general admission; $2 GA for kids under 12.
For more information, call (909) 276-3352.

**April 11, 1962:** The Dodgers get their first win at Dodger Stadium, beating the Cincinnati Reds 6–2.

**Sept. 23, 1962:** Maury Wills breaks Ty Cobb's single-season record with his 97th stolen base.

**Oct. 6, 1963:** Sandy Koufax six-hits the New York Yankees as the Dodgers sweep the World Series.

**Sept. 9, 1965:** Koufax fires a 1–0 perfect game against the Chicago Cubs, his fourth no-hitter in as many years.

**Oct. 14, 1965:** Koufax shuts out the Minnesota Twins for the second time, as the Dodgers win Game 7, 2–0, for their fourth World Championship.

**June 13, 1973:** Steve Garvey, Davey Lopes, Bill Russell and Ron Cey start together in the Dodgers' infield for the first time, beginning a record 8½ year run.

**Sept. 2, 1979:** Manny Mota cracks his 145th career pinch hit in a 6–2 come-from-behind win over the Pittsburgh Pirates, establishing a major-league record.

**Sept. 6, 1981:** Fernando Valenzuela blanks St. Louis 5–0 for his seventh shutout, tying the record for rookies.

**Oct. 15, 1988:** Kirk Gibson makes his only appearance in the 1988 World Series, pinch-hitting with two out in the bottom of the ninth, and hits a game-winning two-run homer off Oakland Athletics closer Dennis Eckersley.

**June 4, 1990:** Rookie Ramon Martinez fans 18 batters in a victory over the Atlanta Braves, matching Koufax's club high.

**Oct. 3, 1993:** In the season finale, Rookie of the Year Mike Piazza hits his 34th and 35th homers and drives in 4 runs as the Dodgers end the San Francisco Giants' pennant drive.

## STADIUM STATS

**Location:** 2269 N.W. 199th St., Miami, FL 33056
**Opened:** Aug. 16, 1987
**Surface:** Grass
**Capacity:** 47,662
**Outfield dimensions:** LF 330, LC 385, CF 404, RC 385, RF 345.
**Services for fans with disabilities:** Seating available in sections 103, 125, 128, 131, 153 and 156.

## STADIUM FIRSTS

**Regular-season game:** April 5, 1993, 6–3 over the Los Angeles Dodgers.
**Pitcher:** Charlie Hough of the Marlins.
**Batter:** Jose Offerman of the Dodgers.
**Hit:** Benito Santiago of the Marlins.
**Home run:** Tim Wallach of the Dodgers.

## GROUND RULES

• If a ball bounds off any portion of the railing around the photographers' booths, it is in play.
• If a ball strikes any portion of the left-field scoreboard below the uppermost edge, it is in play.
• If a ball strikes any portion of the foul poles in left field above any edge of the scoreboard, or in right field above the top of wall, it is a home run.

# Joe Robbie Stadium

When H. Wayne Huizenga first mentioned adapting Joe Robbie Stadium to house an expansion baseball team, purists howled. Visions of Toronto's old Exhibition Stadium haunted fans. The only way Huizenga could convince the fans (and baseball owners) that it could be done was to build it. And convince them he did.

Constructed as a football-only stadium for the NFL Dolphins in 1987, Huizenga and company spent about $20 million to convert Joe Robbie to dual-purpose in 1990. While the home of the Florida Marlins is no Camden Yards, it's better than purists expected. The capacity for baseball is about 47,500—reduced from the 73,000 for football by both a desire for a more intimate atmosphere and the reality that some of the upper-deck outfield seats would've been awful. Because of the conversion, the outfield configuration is a little unusual in center field, making for some interesting caroms off the nooks and crannies—all the better for baseball flavor.

The 202-foot-long out-of-town scoreboard in left and left-center field also contributes to the nice baseball feel. It's a manually operated board that, like Wrigley Field's, provides an inning-by-inning score of every other major-league game. Nicknamed the Blue Blocker or the Teal Tower, it has 465 openings for numerals and a 5-foot-high clock in the middle, and at its apex rises 33 feet above the playing surface. More than 3,600 numbers were produced to accommodate all the possible combinations of runs. It comes into play quite a bit, sometimes in unlikely ways. Atlanta's Ryan Klesko crashed into the left-field wall beneath it last year and knocked a few numbers out of the scoreboard. The crowd, no longer made up of rookie big-league devotees, adds to the atmosphere. While pretty knowledgeable, many fans are still learning some of the subtleties of the game. Expect more of a family crowd, with less heckling or vulgarity, than at Dolphins games.

### HOT TIPS FOR VISITING FANS

**Parking**
The parking lot was built to accommodate crowds of 70,000-plus for football, so it handles the baseball crowd easily. It's probably the best in the National League. Spaces are available for 14,970 cars, 254 buses and a helicopter (yes, there's a helipad). Cost for cars is $5. On opening day and occasional other dates when huge crowds are expected, alternate lots open. The only drawback: With crowds of 35,000-plus, getting out of the lot can take a long time.

**Weather**
Hot and humid, and then summer comes. In south Florida, early spring is perfect and fall is very nice. But June, July and August get very steamy. The Marlins play very few day games in the summer. From June 1 to mid-September, most Sunday games start at 6:05 P.M. and Saturday games at 7:05 P.M. Nights are rarely uncomfortable. Florida also gets lots of rain in the summer, but the Marlins have had fewer rainouts than expected. In their first 1½ seasons, they've had only two rainouts—one in 1993 and one in the first half of the '94 season. Fans who show up for batting practice are more affected by the weather; late-afternoon thundershowers frequently force players to take hitting in indoor cages. But the drainage system and an excellent grounds crew almost always get the field ready in time for the first pitch.

 **Media bites**
**Radio:** WQAM (560 AM) has English-language broadcasts with Joe Angel and Dave O'Brien; WCMQ (1210 AM), with Felo Ramirez and Manolo Alvarez, broadcasts in Spanish.
**TV:** WBFS (Channel 33) and Sunshine Network (cable), with Jay Randolph and Gary Carter, broadcast in English.

**Cuisine**
Excellent variety, including several tasty dishes that reflect the Latin influence in south Florida. The *arepa*, a South American dish made of two grilled cornbread "pancakes" stuffed with mozzarella cheese, is particularly popular. Try the *medinoche* sandwich (sliced pork, ham, cheese, mustard and pickle served hot on oval-shaped egg bread) and a Cuban sandwich that's similar, but on Cuban bread. Also tasty is the *empanada*, a turnover-like pastry filled with chicken or beef. Cuban coffee is available. Reflecting the New York influence in Miami, a fully kosher concessions stand was opened behind home plate in 1994; it's closed on Friday and Saturday. Carts around the concourses serve Hebrew National hot dogs and Italian sausage with pepper and onion. Domino's

**(Continued on page 44)**

# IN THE HOT SEATS AT JOE ROBBIE STADIUM

The Marlins have about 20,000 season ticketholders, so all box seats on or near the infield are sold out on a season basis. Individual-game tickets are available for boxes down the lines. You can buy a ticket for a future game without leaving your seat at Joe Robbie. In a service called Ticket Express, ticket sellers roam the stadium like vendors, take your order at your seat and return with the ticket.

• **Good seats:** If you don't mind a premium price, buy a seat on the club (200) level, still on the lower deck. It gives you access to luxury-box concessions and wait-

er service at your seat. Tickets are $30 behind the plate, $20 around the bases and $13 out by the foul poles.

• **Bad seats:** Sightlines from the lower-level seats between the infield edge and the foul poles present a problem. Since they were built for football, seats are pointed toward the 50-yard line, which is center field. You have to twist to watch the action at home plate. Some terrace boxes (at the corners in the football configuration) are pointed more toward the infield, but from those you have to look over the bullpen.

• **Family sections:** The park has two no-smoking, no-alcohol sections, one on each level. On the lower level, it's section 134 (down the right-field line near the foul pole); upstairs it's section 403 (down the left-field line).

**Scalping:** Scalpers who work the Dolphins, Heat and Panthers games seem to take the summer off. Scalping is illegal, the club is working to police it, and the market isn't very profitable because good seats are usually available at the gate.

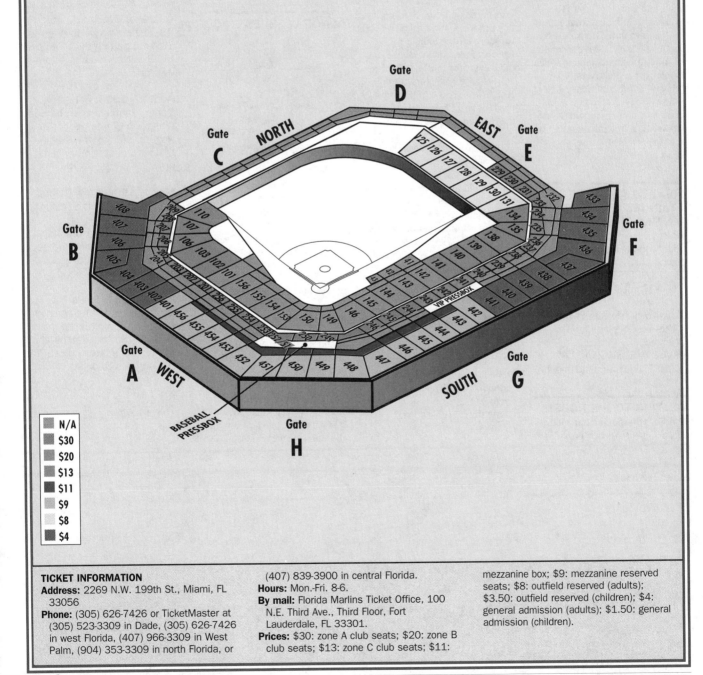

| | |
|---|---|
| ■ | N/A |
| ■ | $30 |
| ■ | $20 |
| ■ | $13 |
| ■ | $11 |
| ■ | $9 |
| ■ | $8 |
| ■ | $4 |

**TICKET INFORMATION**
**Address:** 2269 N.W. 199th St., Miami, FL 33056
**Phone:** (305) 626-7426 or TicketMaster at (305) 523-3309 in Dade, (305) 626-7426 in west Florida, (407) 966-3309 in West Palm, (904) 353-3309 in north Florida, or

(407) 839-3900 in central Florida.
**Hours:** Mon.-Fri. 8-6.
**By mail:** Florida Marlins Ticket Office, 100 N.E. Third Ave., Third Floor, Fort Lauderdale, FL 33301.
**Prices:** $30: zone A club seats; $20: zone B club seats; $13: zone C club seats; $11:

mezzanine box; $9: mezzanine reserved seats; $8: outfield reserved (adults); $3.50: outfield reserved (children); $4: general admission (adults); $1.50: general admission (children).

(Continued from page 42)

vendors sell small pizzas in the stands, and chains like Carvel, Arby's and TCBY have outposts in the concourses. Special stands sell such imported beers as Heineken and Molson Ice, but the most popular drink is 16 ounces of ice-cold bottled water. Marlins owner H. Wayne Huizenga bought the remaining 50% of the Stadium in 1994 (he purchased 50% in 1990) and has promised even better concessions and/or reduced prices.

No popular postgame spots are within walking distance of the Stadium. The neighborhood is sandwiched by interstates and populated with small plazas, supermarkets, fast-food restaurants and a topless joint. The area isn't particularly dangerous, but pedestrian traffic isn't recommended. Fans drive a couple of miles to an area around Pines Boulevard and University Dr., where a number of bar-restaurants (Friday's, Hooters, etc.) cater to a stadium crowd. North Miami Beach, with a number of night-spots, is also a relatively short drive.

## LODGING NEAR THE STADIUM
**Don Shula Hotel and Golf Club**
15255 Bull Run Rd.
Miami Lakes, FL 33014
(305) 821-1150/(800) 247-4852
About 12 miles from the stadium.

**Turnberry Isle Resort**
19999 W. Country Club Dr.
Aventura, FL 33180
(305) 932-6200/(800) 327-7028
About 7 miles from the stadium.

## GETTING TO JOE ROBBIE
**Public transportation:** Metro-Dade Transit Agency provides

transportation to the Stadium via bus service. Call (305) 638-6700 for more information.
**By car:** From south Miami and the Keys, take U.S. 1 to I-95 North. Take I-95 North to the Ives Dairy Road exit. Proceed west on Ives Dairy for 5 miles; the Stadium will be on your right.

From West Palm Beach and Fort Lauderdale, either take I-95 south to the Ives Dairy exit, or take the Florida Turnpike south to the Honey Hill Road Stadium exit. The stadium will be your right.

From Naples and Fort Myers, take I-75 to I-595 east. Get off at the Florida Turnpike south and continue to the Honey Hill Road Stadium exit.

## SPRING TRAINING
Space Coast Stadium and Carl Barger Baseball Complex
5600 Stadium Parkway.
Melbourne, FL 32940
**Capacity:** 7,200
**Surface:** Grass.
**Game time:** 1:05 P.M. or 7:35 P.M.

### HOME-FIELD ADVANTAGE

The layout of the ballpark makes it tough to hit home runs. It's 434 feet to center field, the 22- to 33-foot scoreboard makes the left-field fence tough to clear, and the ball doesn't carry well to right. The outfield gaps are spacious, so the Marlins have placed a priority on stockpiling speedy outfielders like Chuck Carr and Carl Everett. The dimensions probably help the young Marlins by cutting their expansion-caliber pitching some slack.

### MARLINS TEAM NOTEBOOK
**Franchise history** 1993–present.
Florida Marlins,

**Retired number**
5 Carl F. Barger

## MINOR LEAGUES
| Class | Team |
|---|---|
| AAA | Edmonton Trappers |
| AA | Portland (ME) Sea Dogs |
| A | Brevard County (FL) Manatees |
| A | Kane County (IL) Cougars |
| Short Season A | Elmira (NY) Pioneers |
| Rookie | Melbourne (FL) Marlins |

The minor-league team closest to Miami is the Class A West Palm Beach Expos of the Florida State League. One of the Expos' opponents is the Brevard County Manatees, the Marlins' affiliate in the Florida State League. Montreal Expos Manager Felipe Alou rates West Palm Beach as his favorite among the five cities he managed in during his minor-league career. His first season was 1990, when his team captured the FSL regular-season title with 92 wins, best among all minor-league teams.

To reach West Palm Beach's Municipal Stadium, which is about 70 miles from Miami, take exit 53, Palm Beach Lakes Boulevard, from I-95 and head east. The ballpark will be on the right, about ¾ mile from the highway.

**Ticket prices:** $5: general admission; $3: children under 13 and senior citizens 65 and over; For more information, call (407) 684-6801.

## THE MARLINS AT JOE ROBBIE STADIUM

**May 1, 1993:** Jeff Conine hits the first grand slam at Joe Robbie, off Colorado Rockie David Nied.

**Oct. 2, 1993:** A crowd of 43,210 shows up to see the Marlins, putting the team over the 3 million mark in attendance.

**April 17, 1994:** Catcher Benito Santiago charges San Francisco Giants pitcher Kevin Rogers, starting the Marlins' first regular-season on-field brawl.

**May 1, 1994:** Gary Sheffield homers, leading the Marlins to a 9–4 win over the Cincinnati Reds. Florida's 13–12 record marks the second time they are over .500 in their history.

**June 6, 1994:** Jesus Tavarez hits a game-winning pinch-hit single in the bottom of the ninth to give the Marlins an 11–10 comeback win over the Los Angeles Dodgers.

## STADIUM STATS

**Location:** 201 S. 46th St., Milwaukee, WI 53201
**Opened:** April 6, 1953
**Surface:** Grass
**Capacity:** 53,192
**Outfield dimensions:** LF 362, LC 392, CF 402, RC 392, RF 362.
**Services for fans with disabilities:** Seating available in the 35th row of the lower grandstand and in the first row of the bleacher section.

## STADIUM FIRSTS

**Brewers regular-season game:** April, 7, 1970, 12–0 loss to the California Angels.
**Pitcher:** Lew Krausse of the Brewers.
**Batter:** Sandy Alomar of the Angels.

## GROUND RULES

• Foul poles and the screens attached are outside the playing field.
• A ball hitting the bats or bat rack is considered in the dugout.
• A ball hitting the facing of the dugout roof is considered in the dugout.
• A ball hitting the cable or above the break on the screen behind home plate is out of play.
• A ball staying under or behind the tarp is out of play; if it rebounds onto the field, it's in play.
• A ball hitting the top of the outfield padding in fair territory and bouncing into stands is two bases.
• A ball hitting the railings of the photographer's well and rebounding is in play; if it bounces into the well or dugout area of stands, the ball is out of play.

# Milwaukee County Stadium

The Brewers had a tough act to follow when they moved from Seattle in 1970. Milwaukee fans fell in love with baseball by watching the National League Braves, who moved there from Boston in 1953. They had Hall of Famers Henry Aaron, Eddie Mathews and Warren Spahn. The Braves left for Atlanta to start the 1966 season, and Milwaukee fans still miss the team.

If Boston's Fenway Park represents baseball's early days and Toronto's SkyDome the future, then Milwaukee County Stadium is a snapshot of baseball in the 1950s, those days of Aaron, Mathews and Spahn. It sits in the industrial Menomonee River Valley, next to I-94 and several miles from downtown Milwaukee. It has towering light poles, real bleachers and green grass. The city's skyline—church steeples, smokestacks and the Allen Bradley clocktower—can be seen from the two decks of seats, and on clear nights, the clock hovers like a full moon.

For the most part, Beer City fans are loyal blue-collar workers with little sympathy for whining millionaire players. Instead they tend to relate more to Robin Yount's no-nonsense work ethic or stubbly faced Gorman Thomas, crashing into a fence. Just ask Rick Manning. He came to the Brewers in a trade for Thomas, and Brewers fans rode him every time he stepped to the plate. It didn't help when Manning, in August 1987, hit a game-winning single to keep Paul Molitor, now a Blue Jay, from getting another chance to extend his 39-game hitting streak. Manning was booed.

## HOT TIPS FOR VISITING FANS

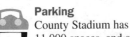

**Parking**
County Stadium has 11,000 spaces, and at $5 a space, the price is a bargain. For those interested in a little exercise before sitting down with an Italian sausage, plenty of spaces beyond the Stadium are cheaper but require a good hike.

**Weather**
Temperatures can take nasty dips in April and May, so be prepared to dress as if you are attending a Green Bay Packers' football game. September afternoons are beautiful. The most relaxing time to

attend is in the sunshine of a weekday afternoon.

**Media bites**
**Radio:** WTMJ (620 AM). On beer commercials he might have the worst seat in the house, but the Brewers' radio voice, Bob Uecker—a local hero who has made a career out of his lack of playing ability—has the best spot in the stadium. His voice is a staple from busy Milwaukee streets to quiet dairy farms across the state.
**TV:** WVTV (Channel 18).

 **Cuisine**
Brats and brewskis.
Before a game, clouds of smoke and the aroma of fired-up grills linger in the Stadium's parking lots as tailgate parties swirl around RVs, pickup trucks and the trunks of cars. The bratwursts are out of this world. First they're browned on a grill for 10 minutes, then put into a mixture of beer, green peppers and onions to cook for a half hour or so. Pop open a beer and experience a true Wisconsin tradition.

Inside, the Brewers feature baseball's best bratwurst—with a secret sauce so popular that it's sold in supermarkets throughout Wisconsin—and Italian and Polish sausages. Other popular items include corned beef, steak, roast-beef sandwiches, fresh-dough pizza, garlic bread and meatball subs. Not surprisingly, County Stadium features Milwaukee's hometown beer, Miller.

Milwaukee means beer, so instead of singing "Take Me Out to the Ball Game" during the seventh-inning stretch, Brewers fans sing "Roll Out the Barrel." It doesn't stop there. "Bernie Brewer" lives in a chalet just above a giant-sized stein of beer beyond the center-field bleachers. Every time the Brewers hit a home run or win a game, Bernie slides down a chute into the beer stein.

Those who want to find Brewers fans to talk baseball with before and after the game should check out Saz's (414-453-2410), a rib restaurant 1 mile north of the stadium. The specialty is a rack of ribs with Saz's own barbecue sauce. Saz's has parking and runs buses to Brewers' games. Luke's Sports Bar (414-223-3210) is popular with the Brewers and opposing players; check out the 50 television sets and three bars with different sports themes.

# IN THE HOT SEATS AT MILWAUKEE COUNTY STADIUM

Good seats are almost always available for a walk-up fan. Normally, the Brewers have two and three times as many seats as fans. That fact, of course, kills the scalping market. The toughest ticket is opening day, no matter how wet, cold and snowy Wisconsin's weather may be.

• **Good seats:** Outfield seats are all bleachers, but the best of the bleachers are in right field. They overlook the action in the bullpen—from relievers loosening up

to sunflower-seed-spitting contests. The left-field bleachers are good too, but they don't have the bullpen view. In the afternoon, both sets of bleachers are great for working on a tan.

The upper deck has no bad seats. You can see the field and the whole city of Milwaukee.

• **Bad seats:** The worst seats in the house are the four or five rows in the back of the first deck. Because of the second deck's

overhang, long fly balls get cut from view. But hey, because the Stadium is virtually empty, just move. Some seats are directly behind a pole, but they're seldom sold.

**Scalping:** Because of ticket availability, not much of a market exists.

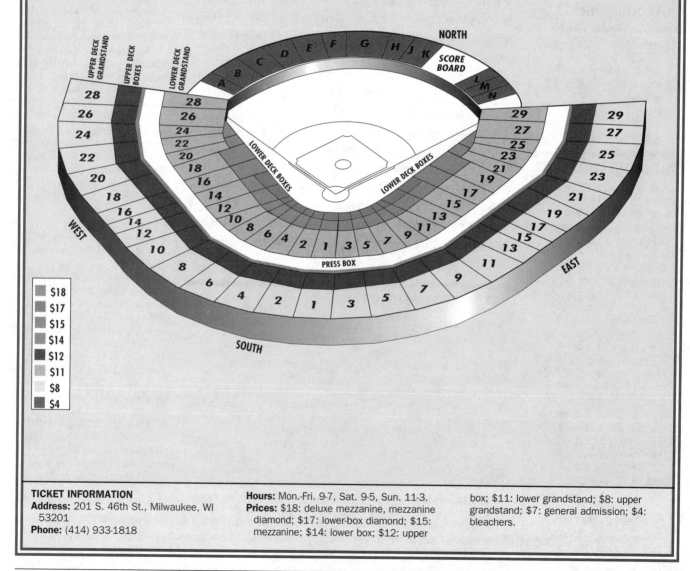

$18
$17
$15
$14
$12
$11
$8
$4

**TICKET INFORMATION**
**Address:** 201 S. 46th St., Milwaukee, WI 53201
**Phone:** (414) 933-1818

**Hours:** Mon.-Fri. 9-7, Sat. 9-5, Sun. 11-3.
**Prices:** $18: deluxe mezzanine, mezzanine diamond; $17: lower-box diamond; $15: mezzanine; $14: lower box; $12: upper

box; $11: lower grandstand; $8: upper grandstand; $7: general admission; $4: bleachers.

## LODGING NEAR THE STADIUM

**Pfister Hotel**
424 E. Wisconsin Ave.
Milwaukee, WI 53201
(414) 273-8222/(800) 558-8222
About 2 miles from the stadium.

**Hyatt Regency**
333 W. Kilbourn Ave.
Milwaukee, WI 53201
(414) 276-1234/(800) 233-1234
About 4 miles from the stadium.

## GETTING TO MILWAUKEE COUNTY STADIUM

**Public transportation:** On game days, a special bus line, No. 99, runs along Wisconsin Avenue directly to County Stadium. For more information, call (414) 344-6711.

**By car:** From the north, go south on U.S. 41 to the County Stadium exit.

From the south, take U.S. 41 north, and enter the Stadium at Gate 6.

From the west, take I-94 east to the County Stadium exit. Enter the Stadium at Gate 1.

From the east, take I-94 west to U.S. 41. Continue south on U.S. 41 and enter the Stadium at Gate 6.

## SPRING TRAINING

Campadre Stadium
4001 S. Alma School Rd.
Chandler, AZ 85248
(602) 895-6000
**Capacity:** More than 10,000
**Surface:** Grass
**Game time:** 1 P.M.

## MINOR LEAGUES

| Class | Team |
| --- | --- |
| AAA | New Orleans Zephyrs |
| AA | El Paso Diablos |
| A | Stockton (CA) Ports |

## HOME-FIELD ADVANTAGE

Except for the temperature, which can turn a baseball crowd into a football crowd as late as June, no stadium is more neutral than County Stadium. The outfield fences are nondescript and the infield grass is level, but ever try to hit a baseball with a wooden bat when it's freezing? Opposing teams dread coming into Milwaukee when it's cold. Brewers players don't care for it either, but they have become used to hot-water bottles in the on-deck circle.

County Stadium, which celebrated its 40th birthday in 1993, might be on the endangered-species list. The Brewers hope to have a new stadium built next to County Stadium by opening day 1996, but they've have been plagued by environmental problems that have delayed groundbreaking. Also, a state lawmaker has proposed using lottery money to build a domed stadium downtown.

### BREWERS TEAM NOTEBOOK

**Franchise history**
Seattle Pilots, 1969;
Milwaukee Brewers,
1970–present.

**American League pennant**
1982

**Division title**
1982

**Most Valuable Players**
Rollie Fingers, 1981
Robin Yount, 1982, 1989

**Cy Young Awards**
Rollie Fingers, 1981

Peter Vuckovich, 1982

**Hall of Fame**
Henry Aaron, 1982
Rollie Fingers, 1992

**Retired numbers**
34 Rollie Fingers
44 Henry Aaron

| | |
| --- | --- |
| A | Beloit (WI) Brewers |
| Rookie | Helena (WA) Brewers |
| Rookie | Chandler (AZ) Brewers |

The Brewers' closest minor-league affiliate is the Class A Beloit Brewers of the Midwest League. After the 1905 season, in which Beloit's entry in the Class D Wisconsin Association won 50 of 109 games and finished 18 games behind first-place La Crosse, the community's team left town. Beloit was without baseball for 75 years, until 1982, when the minor leagues returned.

To reach Beloit's Pohlman Field, approximately 45 miles from Milwaukee, exit at Route 81 west from I-90. Take 81 to Cranston Road. Turn right and head to Pohlman Field.

**Ticket prices:** $4: reserved seats; $3: general admission. For more information, call (608) 362-2272.

## THE BRAVES AND BREWERS AT MILWAUKEE COUNTY STADIUM

**May 26, 1959:** Harvey Haddix of the Pittsburgh Pirates pitches 12 perfect innings against the Milwaukee Braves, but he loses 1–0 in the 13th.

**May 6, 1970:** The Brewers

notch their first home win, behind pitcher Bob Bolin.

**June 19, 1974:** Steve Busby of the Kansas City Royals no-hits the Brewers.

**July 15, 1975:** Bill Madlock drives in two runs in the ninth to win the 46th All-Star Game for the National League.

**July 20, 1976:** Hank Aaron hits his 755th and last home run, off Dick Drago of the California Angels.

**Aug. 27, 1982:** The Oakland A's Rickey Henderson breaks Lou Brock's single-season record when he steals his 119th base. He finishes the season with 130.

**Oct. 10, 1982:** Cecil Cooper singles in two runs in the seventh that put the Brewers ahead for good in Game 5 of the ALCS. The Brewers beat the California Angels 4–3.

**Oct. 16, 1982:** The Brewers get their first home win in the World Series, 10–2 over the St. Louis Cardinals in Game 4.

**July 31, 1990:** Nolan Ryan gets his 300th win, beating the Brewers 11–3.

**Sept. 9, 1992:** Robin Yount gets his 3,000th hit, off the Cleveland Indians' Jose Mesa, becoming the third-youngest player to reach that milestone.

# HHH Metrodome

## STADIUM STATS

**Location:** 501 Chicago Ave. S., Minneapolis, MN 55415
**Opened:** April 3, 1982
**Surface:** AstroTurf
**Capacity:** 56,144
**Outfield dimensions:** LF 343, LC 385, CF 408, RC 367, RF 327.
**Services for fans with disabilities:** Seating available in the upper and lower decks.

## STADIUM FIRSTS

**Regular-season game:** April 6, 1982, 11–7 loss to the Seattle Mariners.
**Pitcher:** Peter Redfern of the Twins.
**Batter:** Julio Cruz of the Mariners.
**Hit:** Dave Engle of the Twins.
**Home run:** Dave Engle.

## GROUND RULES

• Foul poles are in fair territory.
• Balls that hit the roof or speakers in fair territory: If the ball is caught by a fielder, the batter is out and base runners advance at their own risk.
• A ball hitting the roof or speakers in fair territory shall be judged fair or foul in relation to where it hits the ground or is touched by a fielder.
• Any ball that hits the speaker or roof in foul territory is a foul ball; however, if the ball is caught by a fielder, the batter is out and base runners advance at their own risk.
• A ball that hits a speaker in foul territory and ricochets back into fair territory is still a foul ball; if the ball is caught by a fielder, the batter is out and the base runners advance at their own risk.

The billowy roof looks like one of Grandma's lemon-meringue pies against the Minneapolis skyline. Inside, thousands of blue seats rise above the green turf in a cramped stadium that has nothing but basic necessities. No flash, no extra conveniences. Except for a muddy replay board, high technology is nonexistent.

Minnesota's Hubert H. Humphrey Metrodome—named for the state's favorite son, a former U.S. vice president—is everything Minnesota isn't. The state's favorite activities are outdoors. It leads the nation in fishing and snowmobile licenses, and the boundary waters in northern Minnesota offer the most breathtaking recreation scenery in the world. Given their love of fresh air and weather, local baseball fans had trouble parting with Metropolitan Stadium, a classic ballpark from the 1960s.

The Twins, though, belong to more than Minnesota. Twins fever runs high along the country roads of the Dakotas and battles with Cubs fever in Iowa's small towns and Wisconsin's dairy farms. The Dome was built for these out-of-state fans who appreciate the roof because they can make four- and five-hour one-way trips without having to worry about rainouts.

Players don't appreciate the stadium, though. They detest the turf, poor lighting and size. Home runs crash into the 7,600 retractable football seats that hang like vultures in right field. A 16-foot tarp, known as the "trash bag," extends the height of the right-field fence to 23 feet. The seats are better situated for football, and the stadium is remarkably loud.

All this adds up to a less-than-premier baseball viewing experience. But then again, you won't get wet if you drove all the way from Watertown, S.D.

## HOT TIPS FOR VISITING FANS

**Parking**
Arrive early and park a block or two from the Metrodome on the street, using eight-hour meters. The cost is $3, about half of what it costs for a parking lot or garage. If the metered spaces aren't available, park far away from the stadium and enjoy a nice walk in a clean, safe city. In most cases, the closer fans park to the Metrodome, the better chance they have of getting clogged in postgame traffic. Some parking lots are situated so fans can use walkways over the Mississippi River.

**Weather**
Not a problem, unless you park several blocks away and have a long walk in early April or late September. Even with football weather outdoors, inside the Dome is always 68-70 degrees. Even dome games, though, can be postponed because of weather: On April 14, 1983, heavy snowfall caved in the air-inflated roof, causing the Metrodome's only postponement.

**Media bites**
**Radio:** WCCO (830 AM).

Play-by-play man Herb Carneal is as much a part of Twins history as Oliva, Killebrew and Carew.

**TV:** WCCO (Channel 4). Al Newman, Tommy John, Dick Bremer and Bob Carpenter are the announcers.

**Cuisine**
The Metrodome offers basic baseball food: hot dogs, beer, pop, pizza, popcorn and snow cones. The place hasn't been overrun with fast-food franchises. The burger stands behind home plate offer delicious hamburgers and crisp onion rings. Other stands offer a kids specialty—a peanut-butter-and-jelly sandwich, plus chips and a cookie, all in a pail with Twins logo for $1.50.

Though nothing is special about his beer, local fans actually get a charge out of buying their cold ones from Wally the Beerman. He has a deep "beer here" voice, but other than that, he pours his beers like any other beer vendor in the country. Still, Wally has his own baseball card and T-shirt, and he plugs local liquor stores on TV. He serves wedding parties, too.

Once the game is over, try Mississippi Live, an entertainment complex with 15 venues under one roof—a minimall of bars. Nine bars have different themes such as daquiris, country, disco, piano, sports and guitar music. The cover charge is $3-$5, except on Monday and Tuesday, when it's free. Customers can go from one venue to the next while carrying their drinks.

The Mall of America, the nation's largest retail and amusement park, is in Bloomington at the site of the Twins' old park. The mall has 430 stores, roller-coaster rides, and Knott's Camp Snoopy. The location of Metropolitan Stadium's home plate is marked, as is the location of the seat that marks the longest home run hit in Met Stadium, by Hall of Famer Harmon Killebrew.

# IN THE HOT SEATS AT HHH METRODOME

Twins tickets sell well, but walk up to the ticket office on virtually any game day, and tickets will be available. Tickets also are available via computer and credit card at local Rainbow food stores. The computer gives fans the view of the field from the seats they've chosen. If they don't like it, they can make another selection. When fans decide and the credit card is checked, the computer spits out the tickets in a matter of seconds.

• **Good seats:** The best seats for baseball are anywhere between sections 119 and 132 in the first deck and 220-229 in the second deck. These seats offer the best possible view of the diamond. If you can't get a ticket for "the baseball section," the next-best location is left field, particularly sections 141, 100 and 101. Get seats at

least 10 rows up in the middle of the row. They'll give a straight view of the field, and you won't have to stand up every time another fan wants to leave. Also, if you're 10 rows up, you'll be over the plexiglass atop the left-field seats.

For a cheap ticket with a cheap view, try the right-field seats. Arrive early and chase home-run balls from batting practice. But plan on watching the replay of any plays in right on TV—the right fielder can't be seen from these seats.

The Metrodome doesn't have rowdy fans, but section 231, in the second deck just beyond third base, is a no-alcohol family section.

• **Bad seats:** In sections 133-135 or 229-232 down the left-field line or sections 116-118 or 218-220 down the right-field

line, make sure not to get an aisle seat. Vendors and fans constantly block the view by walking in front of the seats.

• **Special plans:** Ten knot-hole days are sponsored by SuperAmerica. An adult who buys a $4 general admission ticket gets two free tickets to be used by kids 14 and under.

 **Scalping:** Scalpers are plentiful but, because of competition, are usually not much of a factor. Perhaps because of the low-key, hard-working honesty of the Midwest, season ticketholders sell their extra tickets at cost outside the door.

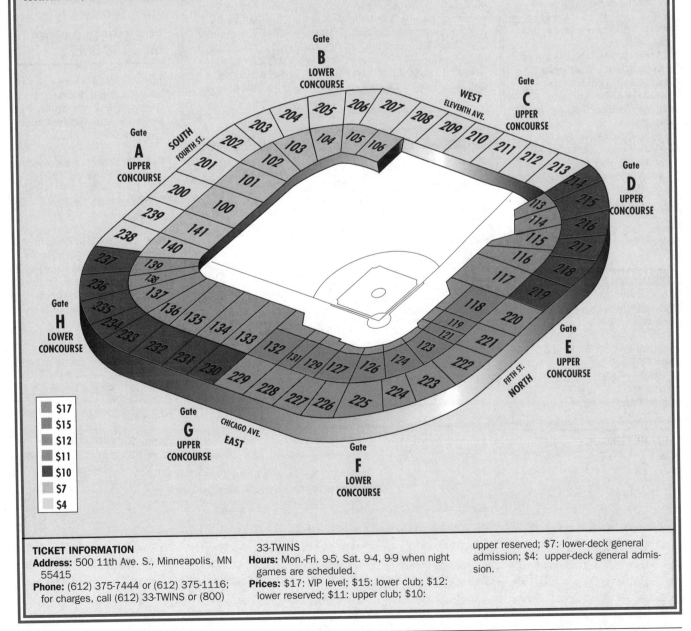

| | |
|---|---|
| ■ | $17 |
| ■ | $15 |
| ■ | $12 |
| ■ | $11 |
| ■ | $10 |
| ■ | $7 |
| □ | $4 |

**TICKET INFORMATION**
**Address:** 500 11th Ave. S., Minneapolis, MN 55415
**Phone:** (612) 375-7444 or (612) 375-1116; for charges, call (612) 33-TWINS or (800) 33-TWINS
**Hours:** Mon.-Fri. 9-5, Sat. 9-4, 9-9 when night games are scheduled.
**Prices:** $17: VIP level; $15: lower club; $12: lower reserved; $11: upper club; $10: upper reserved; $7: lower-deck general admission; $4: upper-deck general admission.

## LODGING NEAR THE STADIUM
**Hyatt Regency**
1300 Nicollet Mall
Minneapolis, MN 55403
(612) 730-1234/(800) 233-1234
15 blocks from the stadium.

**The Minneapolis City Center**
30 S. Seventh St.
Minneapolis, MN 55402
(612) 349-4000/(800) 228-9290
2 miles from the stadium.

## GETTING TO THE METRODOME
**Public transportation:** A shuttle bus operates from downtown Minneapolis one hour before and one hour after well-attended games. Stops are marked with shuttle bus signs. To check the schedule, call (612) 349-7000.
**By car:** From the south, drive north on I-35 West to the Third Street exit. Continue on Third to stadium lots.

From the north, head south on I-35 West to the Washington Avenue exit. Turn left onto Washington, then left onto Chicago Avenue. Continue to stadium.

From the east, go west on I-94. Exit onto Fifth Street. The stadium is visible.

From the west, take I-394 East to the Fourth Street exit. Head east and turn on any street west of the Metrodome for parking. Or go east on I-94 and follow Fourth Street North signs.

## SPRING TRAINING
Lee County Sports Complex
14200 Six Mile Cypress Parkway
Fort Myers, FL 33912
(813) 768-4280
South of Fort Myers, Florida, near I-75
**Capacity:** 7,500
**Surface:** Grass
**Game time:** Noon

## MINOR LEAGUES
| Class | Team |
| --- | --- |
| AAA | Salt Lake City Buzz |
| AA | Nashville Xpress |
| A | Fort Myers (FL) Miracle |
| A | Fort Wayne (IN) Wizards |
| Rookie | Elizabethton (TN) Twins |
| Rookie | Fort Myers (FL) Twins |

The nearest minor-league affiliate to Minneapolis is the Class A

## HOME-FIELD ADVANTAGE

Four factors give the Twins a definite advantage.

The noise: The Metrodome can be deafening. During the 1987 and 1991 World Series, some St. Louis and Atlanta players wore earplugs to try to block thundering sounds that rivaled an airplane's decibel level. The Twins, by the way, took both World Series, winning all eight games at home.

The ceiling: This is the only stadium where an outfielder can't take his eye off a fly ball. General rule: At least one Twins fly ball each series is lost in the roof by opposing outfielders. The roof is white, but the lights cast eerie shadows that demand major adjustments by outfielders.

The center-field fence: The outfield fence in center field is 7 feet high, and that makes for the acrobatic, home-run-robbing catches that Kirby Puckett has made famous.

Weird ground rules: The speakers are in play. So is the roof, 195 feet at its highest point above the playing field. Dave Kingman once hit a ball into the roof while he was with the A's. The ball never came down so it was ruled a ground-rule double. On the other hand, Twins DH Chili Davis hit a ball that would have been a home run to right until it hit a speaker and was caught by Baltimore second baseman Mark McLemore, proving that the Metrodome doesn't always play favorites.

### TWINS TEAM NOTEBOOK

**Franchise history**
Washington Senators, 1901–60; Minnesota Twins, 1961–present

**World Series titles**
1924, 1987, 1991

**American League pennants**
1924, 1925, 1933, 1965, 1987, 1991

**Division titles**
1969, 1970, 1987, 1991

**Most Valuable Players**
Walter Johnson, 1913, 1924
Roger Peckinpaugh, 1925

Zoilo Versalles, 1965
Harmon Killebrew, 1969
Rod Carew, 1977

**Rookies of the Year**
Albie Pearson, 1958
Bob Allison, 1959
Tony Oliva, 1964
Rod Carew, 1967
John Castino, 1979 (tie)
Chuck Knoblauch, 1991

**Cy Young Awards**
Jim Perry, 1971
Frank Viola, 1988

**Hall of Fame**
Walter Johnson, 1936
Tris Speaker, 1937
George Sisler, 1939
Ed Delahanty, 1945

Clark Griffith, 1946
Al Simmons, 1953
Joe Cronin, 1956
Sam Rice, 1963
Heinie Manush, 1964
Goose Goslin, 1968
Stan Coveleski, 1969
Lefty Gomez, 1972
Early Wynn, 1972
Bucky Harris, 1975
Harmon Killebrew, 1984
Rick Ferrell, 1984
Rod Carew, 1991
Steve Carlton, 1994

**Retired numbers**
3 Harmon Killebrew
6 Tony Oliva
29 Rod Carew

Madison (WI) Hatters of the Midwest League. 1994 marked the first year Madison was affiliated with the St. Louis Cardinals, following the franchise's 11-year relationship with the Oakland A's. Madison's first pro team, the Senators, debuted in 1907, nearly 50 years before Warner Park was built.

To reach Warner Park, 250 miles from Minneapolis, take the Highway 30 exit off I-90. Stay on 30 until the Aberg Avenue/STH/Airport exit. Take Aberg Avenue ½ mile to Packers Drive. Turn left, stay in the left lane and turn onto Northport Avenue. Go to the second traffic light and turn left on Sherman. Take the first right into the ballpark.

**Ticket prices:** $5: box seats; $4: reserved; $3: general admission; $2: children under 16 or people 60 and over.

## THE TWINS AT THE METRODOME

**July 27, 1983:** Ben Oglivie of the Milwaukee Brewers hits the longest homer at the Metrodome, a 481-foot shot to the second deck.

**Oct. 25, 1987:** Frank Viola gets the win as the Twins take Game 7 and the World Series against the St. Louis Cardinals.

**Oct. 27, 1991:** In what has been called the greatest World Series game, the Twins break a scoreless tie in the bottom of the 10th to win Game 7 against the Atlanta Braves.

**Aug. 31, 1993:** The Twins play the longest game at the Metrodome, beating the Indians 5–4 on a Pedro Munoz homer in the bottom of the 22nd inning.

**Sept. 16, 1993:** Dave Winfield gets his 3,000th hit off Dennis Eckersley, in an 8–3 loss to the Oakland A's.

# Olympic Stadium

A Montreal Expos game is the closest thing you'll find to overseas baseball. The French-speaking city has a distinctly European flavor that is apparent even in the sterile confines of Olympic Stadium. Pitchers are *lanceurs,* the shortstop is the *arrêt-court,* and a balk is a *feinte irregulière.*

Over the last few years, the club and the Stadium authorities have made significant improvements to the ambience. At the suggestion of an usher, they moved home plate 40 feet closer to the backstop to improve sightlines and bring fans closer to the action. The outfield bleachers also were moved and brought behind the fences in left and right fields. A far-away section in center field was closed, and a new, larger scoreboard with a state-of-the-art video board was installed. No one will call this huge park homey, but it's a vast improvement.

Other improvements remain to be made. The Stadium was designed for the 1976 Olympics, and the plan included a retractable fabric roof. The Stadium was strictly open-air the first several years, as the tower and roof weren't completed until 1987. Since then, retracting the roof has proved expensive and troublesome—the canvas-like surface was torn a couple of times in the process. The dome is now on virtually all the time. Plans are not finalized, but it's expected to be replaced with a permanent roof in time for the 1996 season. Some of that construction could interfere with the ballclub's 1995 schedule.

Such problems aren't new here. In September 1991, a 55-ton block of concrete dropped from the side of the Stadium, forcing its closure for safety reasons. The Expos were forced to play the final 13 games of their home schedule on the road.

The stadium is a marvel from the outside—you have to get a couple of blocks away to appreciate the view. With its lights on at night, it looks like a huge flying saucer. Public tours are available, and a cable car whisks you to the top of the world's largest inclined tower for an excellent view of the city.

---

## HOT TIPS FOR VISITING FANS

**Parking**
Olympic Stadium brags it has Canada's largest indoor parking garage under the stadium—space for 4,000 vehicles, at $8 for games. You can also park in street lots for $7, and there's plenty of outdoor parking on steets and lots within ½ mile of the park.

**Weather**
Summers are generally cool and pleasant in Montreal, but early or late in the season, pack a sweater at least. The park itself is domed and climate-controlled.

**Media bites**
**Radio:** CIQC (600 AM), with Dave Van Horne, Ken Singleton, Elliott Price and Richard Griffin, is the English-language flagship station. CKAC (730 AM) is the French-language flagship, with Jacques Doucet, Rodger Brulotte and Alain Chantelois.
**TV:** The Sports Network (TSN, national cable) with Van Horne, Singleton and Bruce Perrin, is in English. CBFT (Channel 2) and RDS (cable) broadcast in French.

**Cuisine**
*C'est magnifique!* OK, that might be a slight exaggeration, but it's very good. You won't find authentic French cooking at the Big O, but an excellent variety of ballpark food is available. The main food court is on the 100 level behind home plate. Smoked meat, a Montreal specialty that (according to one New Yorker) is a cross between corned beef and pastrami, is available at Briskets. Another tasty dish is Kojax Souflaki; it's souvlaki, but that's not the French spelling—they say that's the way people pronounce it. It's served as a sandwich or plate, in chicken or beef, and is a favorite of the ballpark employees, which says something. Also popular are the Expos Burger and Poulet Frix Kentucky (Kentucky Fried Chicken). Ice cream, pastries, hot dogs, and Cordero wine from Chile are also available at individual stands.

Rusty 10, a sit-down restaurant/bar, is located on the 100 level between home and third base. The bar area is decorated with dozens of old photos of the team. The place is named after Rusty Staub, one of the most popular players in team history, who also happens to be a gourmet chef.

For the kids, a baseball amusement area is on the 100 level down the left-field line. *Le cage des frappeurs* (batting cage), a radar gun pitching cage and video games are featured.

Olympic Stadium is just outside downtown Montreal, and the size of the complex doesn't

**(Continued on page 53)**

# In the Hot Seats at Olympic Stadium

Expos tickets are rarely in great demand, so you usually can walk up and obtain a seat in a decent location. Field-level box seats on the infield between home and third base or between home and first are called the VIP section and feature wait service at your seat. The new seats (complete with cupholders) are bigger and much more comfortable than the rest and provide an excellent view of the game. They cost C$25 a pop. Most, but not all, are bought by season ticketholders. Sit in one of the "regular" seats and you half expect to see Captain Kirk next to you. Made in the futuristic mode of the 1970s, they're small, made of molded plastic in pastel colors and have a single armrest. Still, they're much more comfortable than they look.

• **Bad seats:** Even with the restructuring of the playing field, many seats are a *looong* way from the action. Avoid the higher rows in the $17 seats on the 100 level. Technically they're boxes, but think of them as lower reserve. The upper deck is also quite high, so when you get to the top rows there, you might feel closer to the roof than to the batter's box.

Montreal is a hockey town, something you're reminded of on the 100 level. A walkway separates lower boxes from mid-level boxes. In front of the first row of the mid-level seats, a pane of Plexiglas protects fans (presumably from foul balls). If you don't like sitting behind the glass at hockey games, avoid these seats. Also, some of the lower rows in the upper reserve have a view obstructed by safety crossbars.

 **Scalping:** Though technically a no-no, scalping is out in the open, and the bigger the game, the more visible the hawkers. They greet fans on the walk from the subway to the stadium and in the lobby area by the souvenir shop. For a big regular-season game, they command C$40 and up for a box seat (about double face value), depending on the location.

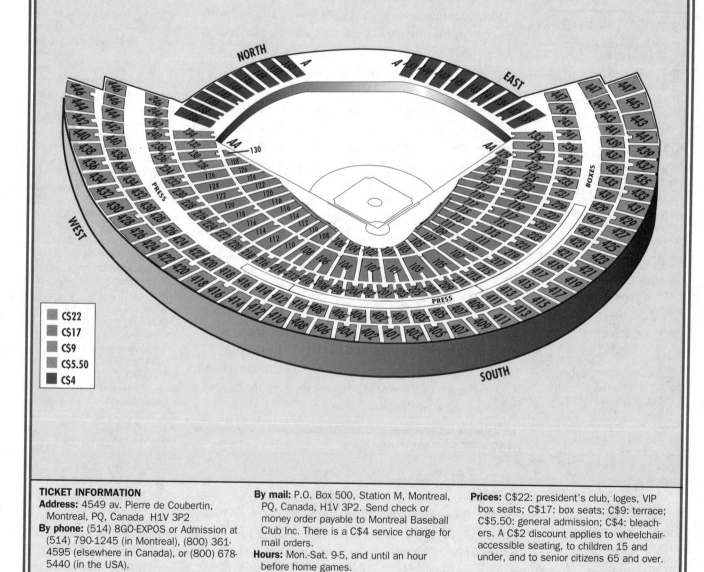

**Legend:**
- C$22
- C$17
- C$9
- C$5.50
- C$4

**TICKET INFORMATION**
**Address:** 4549 av. Pierre de Coubertin, Montreal, PQ, Canada H1V 3P2
**By phone:** (514) 8GO-EXPOS or Admission at (514) 790-1245 (in Montreal), (800) 361-4595 (elsewhere in Canada), or (800) 678-5440 (in the USA).

**By mail:** P.O. Box 500, Station M, Montreal, PQ, Canada, H1V 3P2. Send check or money order payable to Montreal Baseball Club Inc. There is a C$4 service charge for mail orders.
**Hours:** Mon.-Sat. 9-5, and until an hour before home games.

**Prices:** C$22: president's club, loges, VIP box seats; C$17: box seats; C$9: terrace; C$5.50: general admission; C$4: bleachers. A C$2 discount applies to wheelchair-accessible seating, to children 15 and under, and to senior citizens 65 and over.

**(Continued from page 51)**

lend itself to sports bars nearby. Most fans ready for entertainment head downtown, a 10-15 minute Metro ride or a $10-$15 cab ride. Crescent Street has several excellent spots, from the distinguished Les Halles (514-844-2328) restaurant for a late dinner to the Hard Rock Cafe (514-987-1420). And of course, sightseers will want to visit Old Montreal and the Port. For deli fare, Dunn's (514-866-4377) downtown is popular. A reminder: many of the nicer spots require gentlemen to wear a jacket.

## LODGING NEAR THE STADIUM

**Le Centre Sheraton**
1201 blvd. René-Lévesque
Montreal, PQ
Canada P3H 2L7
(514) 878-2000/(800) 325 3535
About 3 miles from the stadium.

**Ramada Centre-Ville**
1005 rue Guy
Montreal, PQ
Canada H3A 2K4
(514) 938-4611/(800) 272-6232
About 8 miles from the stadium.

## GETTING TO OLYMPIC STADIUM

**Public transportation:** Metro trains run daily from downtown Montreal to the Olympic Stadium's Pie IX station.
**By car:** From New England, take I-87 north from New York to Quebec Highway 15. Take Highway 15 through Montreal to the Jacques Cartier Bridge. Stay left as you exit. Continue to the first stop light and turn right onto Sherbrooke Street. Continue on Sherbrooke to the Stadium.

From further west, take I-81 north to the Canadian Highway 401. Take 401 east to Quebec

Highway 20. Go north to Highway 40. Take Highway 40 to the boulevard Pie IX exit south. Proceed to the Stadium.

From Ontario, take Highway 417 East to Quebec Highway 40 North. Take 40 North to the boulevard Pie IX exit south. Proceed to the Stadium.

## TRAINING CAMP

Municipal Stadium
715 Hank Aaron Dr.,
West Palm Beach, FL 33401
(407) 684-6801
**Capacity:** 7,500
**Surface:** Grass
**Game time:** 1:05 P.M. or 7:05 P.M.

## MINOR LEAGUES

| Class | Team |
|---|---|
| AAA | Ottawa Lynx |
| AA | Harrisburg (PA) Senators |
| A | West Palm Beach (FL) Expos |
| A | Burlington (IA) Bees |
| Short Season A | Vermont Expos |
| Rookie | West Palm Beach (FL) Expos |

The Expos' closest minor-league affiliate is the Class AAA Ottawa Lynx of the International League. After a 38-year absence, pro baseball received a big reception upon its return to Ottawa in 1993. That season, the Lynx were second among all minor league teams in attendance, attracting 663,926 fans. The team's nickname was selected for a uniquely Canadian reason: lynx, the name for a type of cat found in northern Canada, is spelled the same in English and French.

To reach Ottawa's Stadium, approximately 130 miles from

## HOME-FIELD ADVANTAGE:

While the ball carries well in the dome in the summer months, Olympic Stadium is not a home-run hitters' park. As such, the Expos generally build a ballclub around speed and moderate power; the team often has several players with 15 home runs and 15 stolen bases a year. Marquis Grissom is following in the stolen-base tradition of Ron LeFlore and Tim Raines. Generally, the crowd is small but loud. The dome, of course, is a major factor. For big games with good attendance, the crowd noise is a definite advantage and, as vast as it is, the place can rock. The Expos usually are about five games a year better at Olympic Stadium, but four times since 1982 (not counting 1994), they've had a better record on the road than at home.

### EXPOS TEAM NOTEBOOK

| Franchise history | Division title | Andre Dawson, 1977 |
|---|---|---|
| Montreal Expos, 1969–present | 1981 | **Retired numbers** |
| | **Rookies of the Year** | 8 Gary Carter |
| | Carl Morton, 1970 | 10 Rusty Staub |

Montreal, take route 417 to the Vanier Parkway. Go over a bridge and turn right on Coventry Road. The ballpark will be on your right.

**Ticket prices:** $8.45 and $6.35: field box seats; $4.25: reserved seats. For more information, call (613) 747-5969.

## THE EXPOS AT OLYMPIC STADIUM

**May 20, 1978:** Willie Stargell of the Pittsburgh Pirates hits a 535-foot home run into the second deck of right field.

**May 10, 1981:** Charlie Lea no-hits the San Francisco Giants 4–0.

**Oct. 19, 1981:** Rick Monday of the Los Angeles Dodgers hits a two-out home run in the ninth to give the Dodgers a 2–1 win over the Expos in the deciding Game 5 of the NLCS.

**July 13, 1982:** Olympic Stadium hosts the first All-Star Game to be played outside the USA.

**April 4, 1988:** The New York Mets' Darryl Strawberry hits a 525-foot home run off the lip of the roof in right field.

**Aug. 23, 1989:** The Expos lose the longest game in their history to the Dodgers 1–0. The game lasts 22 innings and includes the ejection of Expos mascot Youppi! in the 11th.

**May 23, 1991:** Tommy Greene of the Philadelphia Phillies no-hits the Expos 2–0.

# Shea Stadium

## STADIUM STATS

**Location:** 126th St. and Roosevelt Ave., Flushing, Queens, NY 11368
**Opened:** April 17, 1964
**Surface:** Grass
**Capacity:** 55,601
**Outfield dimensions:** LF 338, LC 371, CF 410, RC 371, RF 338.
**Services for fans with disabilities:** Seating available behind home plate and near third base at the field level.

## STADIUM FIRSTS

**Regular-season game:** April 17, 1964, 4–3 loss to the Pittsburgh Pirates.
**Pitcher:** Jack Fisher of the Mets.
**Batter:** Dick Schofield of the Pirates.
**Hit:** A single by Tim Harkness of the Pirates.
**Home run:** April 23, 1964, by Ron Hunt of the Mets, against the Cubs.

## GROUND RULES

• A ball rolling under any part of the field boxes and staying out of sight is one base on a throw by a pitcher from the rubber, or two bases on throw by a fielder.
• A ball hitting the side of the facing of the dugout is considered in the dugout.
• A ball going into the dugout is one base on a throw by a pitcher from the rubber and two bases from field.
• A fair ball bouncing over the fence is two bases.
• A fair ball bouncing over the temporary fence in foul territory in left and right field is two bases.
• A ball caught in the padding of the outfield fence is two bases.

O K, this isn't The House that Stengel built. The only monument in the outfield is a giant top hat with an apple inside. Shea Stadium will never have the history and tradition of its crosstown neighbor in the Bronx, and at 30-plus years old it's showing some age, but overall it's a fine ballpark. Built as a dual-purpose facility (and home to the NFL Jets until 1984), Shea is now a baseball-only stadium and is better for it.

Named after New York lawyer William A. Shea, who helped bring the National League back to the city after the Dodgers and the Giants left, it was one of the first dual-purpose stadiums with moveable box seats to rotate between football and baseball configurations. The Mets moved to the new park in the third year of their existence; the 1969 World Series upset of Baltimore and the dramatic come-from-behind victory over Boston in Game 6 of the 1986 Series have helped create a lore for the park, if not a strong sense of history.

Shea's main landmark is the huge scoreboard in right-center field. The 86-foot-high, 175-foot-long structure was originally called the Stadiarama Scoreboard (it was the '60s, folks). On the top was a rear–projection screen that was used to display full-color slides of players at night games—a breakthrough at the time. But the screen was used only sporadically and was eventually replaced by a display depicting the New York skyline. The large part of the old matrix board is now a beer ad. A Diamond Vision video replay board is in left-center field, and the top hat (from which the "Big Apple" pops up when a Met homers) is in center.

Watching baseball in New York is an interactive experience—the fans are part of the show. The local faithful are extremely knowledgeable and are not shy about sharing their insights. For the most part, the play-by-play from the stands is funny and relatively good-natured. The vocabulary is not always PG, however. Overall, the atmosphere is pure baseball—the smell of hot dogs permeates the park, and the chatter centers on the game, not that day's Dow Jones.

## HOT TIPS FOR VISITING FANS

 **Parking**
About 7,000 spaces are available in stadium parking, at $5. For heavy crowds, secondary lots are opened across Roosevelt Avenue. Very limited on-street parking is within walking distance, but vandalism makes it inadvisable.

Check the dates of the U.S. Tennis Open next door at Flushing Meadows, and proceed on those days with fair warning: It's a logjam. Some New Yorkers avoid going to Shea during tennis time. If you have to be there, consider taking public transportation, because you might end up being routed to alternate parking several blocks from the park.

If you're visiting New York and driving to Shea, get a map and plan the route. New York's expressways can be a maze to the uninitiated, but they're well marked if you know where you're going. (It also helps to know which bridge or tunnel is located in the direction you want to head, because signs are frequently marked that way). Crime on New York subways is publicized worldwide, but most New Yorkers feel that if you come and go with the ballpark crowd, you shouldn't have any problem.

 **Weather**
Like the rest of the Northeast, New York can have wet, chilly springs, and day games in the summer can be scorchers. Shea usually doesn't get as hot as midtown, however, and a breeze occurs often.

**Media bites**
**Radio:** WFAN (660 AM) is the radio flagship with Hall of Fame announcer Bob Murphy, along with Gary Cohen and Howie Rose.
**TV:** WWOR (Channel 9) and SportsChannel (cable). Former slugger Ralph Kiner does play-by-play, and Tim McCarver is nationally known for his insightful color commentary. Gary Thorne, Rusty Staub and Fran Healy also contribute.

 **Cuisine**
Specialty stands offer deli sandwiches and the like. But if you want a real taste of New York, try one of the knishes and the Hebrew National kosher hot dogs. Vendors sell pizzas in the stands, and you can get Carvel ice cream, a popular soft-serve brand. Premium beers such as Beck's, Molson and New Amsterdam are available at a number of concessions stands. There's a lot to do before the game if scouting out food isn't a priority. The gates at Shea open two hours before game time, so autograph hunting is possible by

**(Continued on page 56)**

# IN THE HOT SEATS AT SHEA STADIUM

Shea was originally designed with the option to enclose it into a circular stadium (like Anaheim Stadium), but because that was never done, outfield seating is nearly nonexistent. About 95% of the seats are in foul territory. The design has one drawback. When you put 50,000 seats between the left-field and right-field lines, something has to give, so the upper deck is *up*. Seats there still have good sightlines, but they are high and set back. The loge and mezzanine provide excellent seats in the infield. A small bleacher area is set up in left-center field, but it's strictly for picnic groups. With the team rebuilding, ticket availability is not a problem.

• **Bad seats:** Avoid the last two or three rows of the loge (blue) and mezzanine (green) levels (rows K and L in loge and N, O, and P in the mezzanine). The deck above creates an overhang that blocks all or part of the scoreboards and leaves you guessing on high fly balls. The last row is awful, third-from-the-top passable but still a distraction for serious fans. The club discounts these tickets sharply (from $12 to $6.50), but most fans would be happier taking a seat in the upper deck for the same price.

No-alcohol sections are set aside in the upper deck, but at least they're not in sections that are a long-distance call to home plate. They're sections 10-16, between home and third base. Smoking in the seating areas was permitted in 1994. The sun sets behind home plate, but fans on the third-base side get a few more rays than first-base fans.

**Scalping:** There aren't many scalpers these days. With the Mets near the basement, good seats are usually available. When the market is there, so are the scalpers, and they are hard to miss.

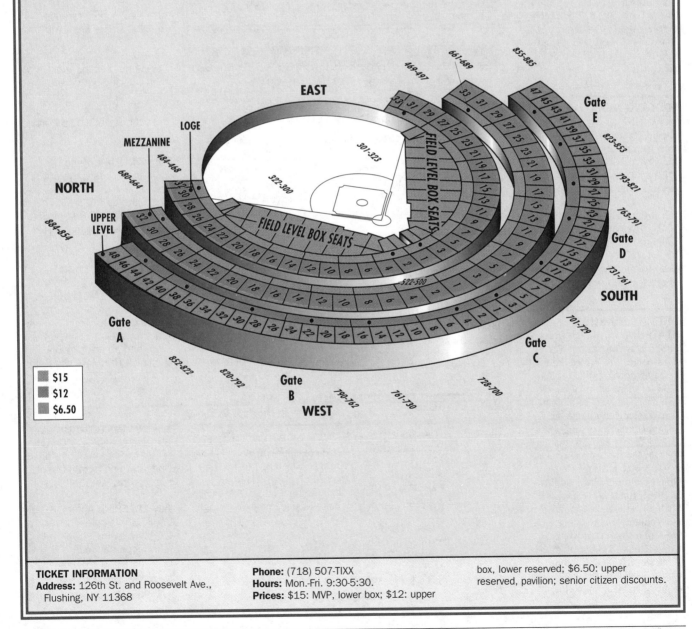

$15
$12
$6.50

**TICKET INFORMATION**
**Address:** 126th St. and Roosevelt Ave., Flushing, NY 11368

**Phone:** (718) 507-TIXX
**Hours:** Mon.-Fri. 9:30-5:30.
**Prices:** $15: MVP, lower box; $12: upper

box, lower reserved; $6.50: upper reserved, pavilion; senior citizen discounts.

(Continued from page 54)

the field. Also, an interactive theme park, Nickelodeon Extreme Baseball, was built by the club and the cable network during the summer of '94. It's beyond the right-field scoreboard and adapts Nickelodeon's participatory games to a baseball theme. It's open from two hours before first pitch until the game is over; cost is $5 with a game ticket. It's also open when the team is on the road and during the day when the team plays at night.

After the game, go to Manhattan. A city as diverse as New York doesn't have any one or two spots that qualify as the postgame hangouts, but you will find sports fans in Mickey Mantle's (212-688-7777) on Central Park South and in Lee Mazzilli's new place, Mazzilli's Sports Cafe (212-877-6787) on the west side. Sportswriters like Runyon's (212-223-9592) and P.J. Clarke's (212-759-1650) on the east side.

## LODGING NEAR THE STADIUM

**Grand Hyatt**
Park Ave. at Grand Central
New York, NY 10017
(212) 883-1234/(800) 233-1234
About 7 miles from the stadium.

**Doral Park Hotel**
70 Park Ave. (corner of E. 38th St.)
New York, NY 10016
(212) 687-7050/(800) 22 DORAL
About 7 miles from the stadium.

## GETTING TO SHEA STADIUM

**Public transportation:** Take subway No. 7 to Willets Point (Shea Stadium); call (718) 330-1234 for more information. Or take the Long Island Railroad Port Washington Line to the Shea Stadium stop; call (718) 217-5477 for more information.
**By car:** From Manhattan, take the Triborough Bridge to the Grand Central Parkway to the Northern Boulevard (Shea Stadium) exit. Follow signs to the Stadium.

From the north, take the Cross-Bronx Expressway to the Whitestone Bridge. Continue onto the Whitestone Expressway to the Shea Stadium/Northern Boulevard exit.

## HOME-FIELD ADVANTAGE

When the Mets win and fans pack Shea, the crowd is a big plus. In the championship (mostly near-championship) days of the 1980s, the atmosphere was electric and pumped up the team. The crowd would cheer for players to make a curtain call from the dugout after a big home run, which led to the team's reputation for being arrogant showboaters. In the lean days of the '90s, the crowd is more subdued. Those wearing a jersey or the colors of the opposing team should still expect some comment on their wardrobe, though. It's usually good-natured but can be persistent. If you don't want to take any lip, restrict your logo emblems to alligators, penguins and polo ponies. Some players are bothered by the low-flying planes landing or taking off at nearby LaGuardia Airport. The jets generally buzz the stadium beyond left field, and some players opt to step out of the batter's box when they hear 'em coming. Mets slugger Bobby Bonilla admitted wearing earplugs at Shea to block out the plane noise in his first year in New York, but skeptics thought it was to muffle the boos he was getting from disgruntled fans.

### METS TEAM NOTEBOOK

**Franchise history**
New York Mets, 1962–present.

**World Series titles**
1969, 1986

**League pennants**
1969, 1973, 1986

**Division titles**
1969, 1973, 1986, 1988

**Rookies of the Year**
Tom Seaver, 1967
Jon Matlack, 1972
Darryl Strawberry, 1983
Dwight Gooden, 1984

**Cy Young Awards**
Tom Seaver, 1969, 1973, 1975
Dwight Gooden, 1985

**Hall of Fame**
Casey Stengel, 1966
George Weiss, 1971
Yogi Berra, 1972
Warren Spahn, 1973
Willie Mays, 1979
Duke Snider, 1980
Tom Seaver, 1992

**Retired numbers**
14 Gil Hodges
37 Casey Stengel
41 Tom Seaver

## SPRING TRAINING

Thomas J. White Stadium
St. Lucie County Sports Complex
525 N.W. Peacock Blvd.
Port St. Lucie, FL 34986
**Capacity:** 7,400
**Surface:** Grass
**Game time:** 1:10 P.M.
**Tickets:** (407) 871-2115

## MINOR LEAGUES

| Class | Team |
|---|---|
| AAA | Norfolk (VA) Tides |
| AA | Binghamton (NY) Mets |
| A | St. Lucie (FL) Mets |
| A | Capital City (SC) Bombers |
| Short Season A | Pittsfield (MA) Mets |
| Rookie | Kingsport (TN) Mets |
| Rookie | St. Lucie (FL) Mets |

The closest minor-league team to New York City is the Short Season Class A Hudson Valley Renegades of the NY-Penn League. The Renegades' opponents include the Oneonta Yankees and the Pittsfield Mets, the NY-Penn League affiliates of the New York big-league teams. 1994 was Hudson Valley's first season. That was also the first year an organized baseball team was based in Fishkill, a suburban community in Dutchess County, north of N.Y.C.

To reach Fishkill's Dutchess Stadium, approximately 55 miles from N.Y.C, take I-684 to I-84 west. Exit at No. 11, Route 90, and turn right on 90. The ballpark is about a mile on the right.

## THE METS AT SHEA STADIUM

**Sept. 24, 1969:** The Mets beat the St. Louis Cardinals 6–0, clinching their first division title.

**Oct. 16, 1969:** Future Mets manager Davey Johnson makes the final out of Game 5 of the World Series, giving the Mets a 5–3 win over the Baltimore Orioles and the team's first world championship.

**May 14, 1972:** Willie Mays hits a solo home run in his first game as a Met to beat the San Francisco Giants 5–4.

**Oct. 8, 1973:** Cincinnati Red Pete Rose slides hard into second, setting off a brawl with Met Buddy Harrelson in the NLCS. The Mets win 9–2.

**April 5, 1983:** Tom Seaver begins his second tour as a Met, starting before the largest opening-day crowd at Shea since 1968. The Mets beat the Philadelphia Phillies 2–0.

**July 24, 1984:** Keith Hernandez hits a two-out single to beat the Cardinals 9–8. The Mets go 20 games over .500 and are in first place the latest in the season since 1973.

**Oct. 25, 1986:** Down 5–3 with two outs in the bottom of the ninth, the Mets stage a remarkable comeback in Game 6 of the World Series, aided by a Bob Stanley wild pitch and an error by Bill Buckner. The Mets win 6–5 and go on to win Game 7 and their second world championship.

**July 18, 1991:** Darryl Strawberry and Gary Carter return to Shea as Los Angeles Dodgers, and both hit home runs as the Mets fall 10–5.

**July 28, 1993:** Anthony Young breaks a major-league-record 27-game losing streak with a relief appearance in a 5–4 win over the Florida Marlins.

# Yankee Stadium

Few stadiums have thicker history books than Yankee Stadium: just think of 33 American League pennants, 22 World Series championships, Monument Park, pinstripes, Tar Wars and the Yankee Clipper. At "the House that Ruth Built," familiar black-and-white images come to life. Home plate is where Ruth and Lou Gehrig delivered their famous farewells. Fans can stand 15 feet from where the Iron Horse set his consecutive-game record of 2,130. A look down the third-base line brings back memories of Yogi Berra hugging Don Larsen after the perfect game in the '56 World Series, and the ornate facade lacing the top of the outfield calls to mind Reggie Jackson's three-homer Game 6 in 1977.

The atmosphere starts outside. When fans step off the subway platform in Yankee Stadium's left-field corner, the Big Apple sights and sounds immediately hit them. The area is crowded but well-lighted, with newspaper pages blowing in the wind. Softball and basketball games go on across the street, and the smell of fresh pretzels on an open grill lingers in the air. Subway trains rumble by.

Inside, Yankee Stadium is a sea of blue—blue seats with a blue outfield fence. It's a handsome, relaxing baseball site that merges the best of the past and present. After two years of renovation in the mid-'70s, the Stadium reopened in 1976 with escalators to complement the old concrete swirls and a team as colorful as any the Mick ever played on.

As gripping as its baseball history is, the Stadium is also the home of some other great moments in sports. In 1958 the Baltimore Colts beat the New York Giants here, 23–17, for the NFL championship in what has been called the greatest game ever played. And it was here that Knute Rockne urged his team to win one for the Gipper.

Given all that has happened within these walls, Yankee Stadium is not just an important site in sports history—it's a landmark in American history.

## HOT TIPS FOR VISITING FANS

**Parking**
Driving is not recommended, because parking is extremely tight (only 6,900 spaces). But if you must, arrive by 5 P.M. to be assured of a parking place. Or park at Grand Concourse, 3 blocks east of the Stadium on 161st Street. The cost is $8, and you get a jump on postgame traffic congestion.

**Weather**
Cool in April and September; hot in June, July and August. Snow is possible in April.

**Media bites**
Radio: WABC (770 AM).

John Sterling and Michael Kay are the announcers.

**TV:** WPIX (Channel 11) and MSG Network (cable). Dewayne Staats does play-by-play and Tony Kubek does color on MSG; former Yankees Bobby Murcer and Hall of Famer Phil "Scooter" Rizzuto, a New York institution, are on WPIX.

**Cuisine**
The Café Olé Stand serves eight types of international coffee. The Yankees bakery has cookies, pie, cake and rolls. Vanilla cookies are the specialty. The goods are baked up the street and hauled in fresh every day. The food court on the lower level features imported beers and a wide range of food offerings.

For those fans who drive and arrive early, try the Sidewalk Cafe, between the Stadium and Garage No. 8. For ticketholders only, it serves corn on the cob, barbecued ribs, sandwiches, hot dogs, chicken, French fries, imported beers and soft drinks. It opens at 5 P.M. for night games and 11 A.M. for day games. Though the area has an image of blight, a 3-block area on 161st Street near Yankee Stadium is flush with convenience stores and ethnic restaurants, including Indian, Chinese, Irish, Spanish and fried-chicken spots. Another option is to go into Manhattan. Mickey Mantle's Restaurant and Sports Bar (212-688-7777) is a fine choice. It's loaded with sports memorabilia, including jerseys worn by Mantle, DiMaggio and Stan Musial. Mantle's own favorite dish is the chicken-fried steak.

## LODGING NEAR THE STADIUM

**Grand Hyatt**
Park Ave. at Grand Central
New York, NY 10017
(212) 883-1234/(800) 233-1234
About 6 miles from the stadium.

**Doral Park Hotel**
70 Park Ave. (corner of E. 38th St.)
New York, NY 10016
(212) 687-7050/(800) 22-DORAL
About 6 miles from the stadium.

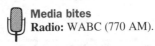

# In the Hot Seats at Yankee Stadium

In 1994, much was made about low attendance figures at Yankee Stadium. Good seats are available on game day. They probably won't be behind home plate, but they'll certainly be good baseball seats. Single-game tickets go on sale Dec. 1.

• **Good seats:** If first-deck box seats are not an option, the tier-level reserved in the second deck are good. The seats are high, but the entire playing field can be seen, and it's good territory for foul balls. And, if you're not afraid of heights, go to the top row and check out the view. The sights include parts of New Jersey, the Hudson River, the Empire State Building and the World Trade Center.

The outfield bleachers are filled mostly with die-hard, blue-collar fans who make at least a dozen trips a season to Yankee Stadium. The regulars in the bleachers feel like family—some only see each other at games, but still send Christmas cards. Bleacher fans are generally rowdy, but the party people sit near the top and they respect those who don't come to party. Newcomers and families sit in the front rows and are not bothered.

The loge seats are good if you don't want to feel the elements. Shielded from the sun and rain, the seats are squeezed in under the second deck, but the view of the field is excellent.

• **Bad seats:** The lower-tier box seats down the left-field line (main boxes 202-350 and field boxes 2-136) are no place for young kids or fans with slow reflexes. The seats are close to the field, and line drives come ripping in at 110 mph. More than a few fans have been hit.

 **Scalping:** Not many fans use scalpers, because the Yankees usually sell only 20,000 to 30,000 tickets a game. Those who buy from scalpers often pay 20% more than the face value.

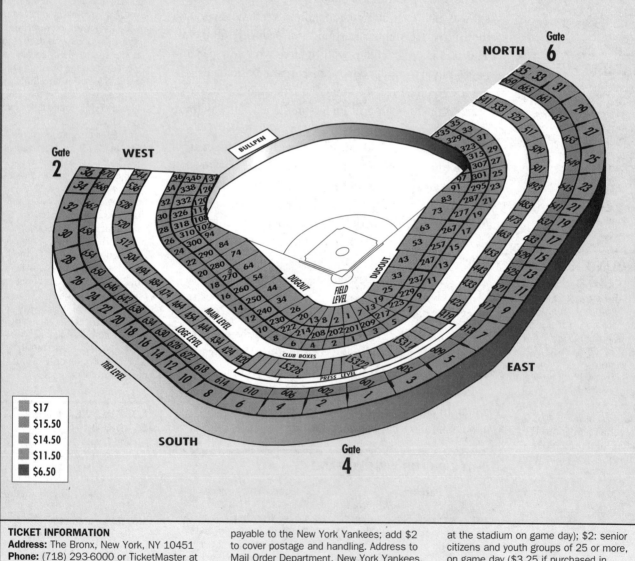

$17
$15.50
$14.50
$11.50
$6.50

**TICKET INFORMATION**
**Address:** The Bronx, New York, NY 10451
**Phone:** (718) 293-6000 or TicketMaster at (212) 307-7171
**Hours:** Mon-Sun. 9-5, and through the conclusion of all night games.
**By mail:** Make check or money orders payable to the New York Yankees; add $2 to cover postage and handling. Address to Mail Order Department, New York Yankees, Yankee Stadium, The Bronx, NY 10451.
**Prices:** $17: lower/loge box seats; $15.50: tier box; $14.50: lower reserved; $11.50: tier reserved; $6.50: bleachers (sold only at the stadium on game day); $2: senior citizens and youth groups of 25 or more, on game day ($3.25 if purchased in advance).

## GETTING TO YANKEE STADIUM

**Public transportation:** Take the No. 4, the C or the D subway train to the 161 Street Station, or take the BX6, BX13 or the BX 35 (free transfer) bus to 161st Street. For more information, call (718) 330-1234.

**By car:** From Manhattan, take the FDR Drive north to Harlem River Drive North. Continue to West 155 Street. Continue east via the Macombs Dam Bridge to Jerome Avenue.

From the north, take I-87 south across the Tappan Zee Bridge. Exit I-87 at exit 6; the Stadium is straight ahead.

## SPRING TRAINING

Fort Lauderdale Stadium
5301 N.W. 12th Ave.
Fort Lauderdale, FL 33309
**Capacity:** 8,340
**Surface:** Grass
**Game time:** 1:05 P.M. or 7:05 P.M.
**Tickets:** (305) 776-1921

## MINOR LEAGUES

| Class | Team |
|---|---|
| AAA | Columbus (OH) Clippers |
| AA | Albany-Colonie (NY) Yankees |
| A | Tampa Yankees |
| A | Greensboro (NC) Bats |
| Short Season A | Oneonta (NY) Yankees |
| Rookie | Tampa Yankees |

The closest minor-league team to New York City is the Short Season Class A Hudson Valley Renegades of the NY-Penn League. The Renegades' opponents include the Oneonta Yankees and the Pittsfield Mets, the NY-Penn League affiliates of New York's big-league teams. 1994 was Hudson Valley's first season. That was also the first year an organized baseball team was based in Fishkill, a suburban community in Dutchess County, north of N.Y.C.

To reach Fishkill's Dutchess Stadium, approximately 55 miles from N.Y.C., take I-684 to I-84 west. Exit at No. 11, Route 90, and turn right on 90. The ballpark is about a mile up on the right.

## HOME-FIELD ADVANTAGE

Yankee Stadium's spacious, sloping outfield is a challenge to visiting outfielders. The fence from right center to the right-field corner takes a drastic curve. Batted balls can bounce like a pinball in the corner, and an outfielder has to work in confined space. A strong arm, though, can nail runners advancing to second or third base.

Death Valley, the left-center-field area, is 399 feet from home plate, and center field is 408 feet away. That means outfielders need speed and a strong arm to patrol the area adequately. Any batted ball that gets away from an outfielder can turn into an inside-the-park home run.

Pitchers despise the short right-field fence as much as they love the space in the other direction. The right-field fence is 314 feet from home plate. The best way to defend against a cheap home run here is to pitch lefties to the outside part of the plate and make batters go the other way.

Foul territory behind home plate is roomy. Foul territory wide of third and first bases is shallow, giving batters a big advantage.

### YANKEES TEAM NOTEBOOK

**Franchise history**
Baltimore Orioles, 1901–02; New York Highlanders, 1903–12; New York Yankees, 1913–present

**World Series titles**
1923, 1927, 1928, 1932, 1936, 1937, 1938, 1939, 1941, 1943, 1947, 1949, 1950, 1951, 1952, 1953, 1956, 1958, 1961, 1962, 1977, 1978

**American League pennants**
1921, 1922, 1923, 1926, 1927, 1928, 1932, 1936, 1937, 1938, 1939, 1941, 1942, 1943, 1947, 1949, 1950, 1951, 1952, 1953, 1955, 1956, 1957, 1958, 1960, 1961, 1962, 1963, 1964, 1976, 1977, 1978, 1981

**Division titles**
1976, 1977, 1978, 1980, 1981

**Most Valuable Players**
Babe Ruth, 1923
Lou Gehrig, 1927, 1936
Joe DiMaggio, 1939, 1941, 1947
Joe Gordon, 1942

Spud Chandler, 1943
Phil Rizzuto, 1950
Yogi Berra, 1951, 1954, 1955
Mickey Mantle, 1956, 1957, 1962
Roger Maris, 1960, 1961
Elston Howard, 1963
Thurman Munson, 1976
Don Mattingly, 1985

**Rookies of the Year**
Gil McDougald, 1951
Bob Grim, 1954
Tony Kubek, 1957
Tom Tresh, 1962
Stan Bahnsen, 1968
Thurman Munson, 1970
Dave Righetti, 1981

**Cy Young Awards**
Bob Turley, 1958
Whitey Ford, 1961
Sparky Lyle, 1977
Ron Guidry, 1978

**Hall of Fame**
Babe Ruth, 1936
Lou Gehrig, 1939
Willie Keeler, 1939
Clark Griffith, 1945
Frank Chance, 1946
Jack Chesbro, 1946
Herb Pennock, 1948
Paul Waner, 1952
Edw. G. Barrow, 1953
Bill Dickey, 1954
Home Run Baker, 1955
Joe DiMaggio, 1955
Dazzy Vance, 1955

Joe McCarthy, 1957
Bill McKechnie, 1962
Burleigh Grimes, 1964
Miller Huggins, 1964
Casey Stengel, 1966
Branch Rickey, 1967
Red Ruffing, 1967
Stan Coveleski, 1967
Waite Hoyt, 1969
Earl Combs, 1970
Geo. M. Weiss, 1970
Yogi Berra, 1971
Lefty Gomez, 1972
Mickey Mantle, 1974
Whitey Ford, 1974
Bucky Harris, 1975
Joe Sewell, 1977
Larry MacPhail, 1978
Johnny Mize, 1981
Enos Slaughter, 1985
Catfish Hunter, 1987
Gaylord Perry, 1991
Tony Lazzeri, 1991
Reggie Jackson, 1993
Phil Rizzuto, 1994

**Retired numbers**
1 Billy Martin
3 Babe Ruth
4 Lou Gehrig
5 Joe DiMaggio
7 Mickey Mantle
8 Bill Dickey and Yogi Berra
9 Roger Maris
10 Phil Rizzuto
15 Thurman Munson
16 Whitey Ford
32 Elston Howard
37 Casey Stengel
44 Reggie Jackson

## THE YANKEES AT YANKEE STADIUM

**June 1, 1925:** Lou Gehrig replaces Wally Pipp at first base.

**Sept. 30, 1927:** Babe Ruth hits his 60th home run of the season, off Washington Senator Tom Zachary.

**April 18, 1929:** The Yankees become the first major-league team to wear numbers on their uniforms.

**May 28, 1946:** The first night game is played at Yankee Stadium.

**Oct. 8, 1956:** Don Larsen pitches a perfect game against the Brooklyn Dodgers in Game 5 of the World Series.

**Oct. 1, 1961:** Roger Maris breaks Ruth's record with his 61st home run of the season, in the last game.

**May 14, 1967:** Mickey Mantle hits his 500th home run, off Baltimore Oriole Stu Miller.

**Aug. 15, 1976:** The remodeled Yankee Stadium opens.

**Oct. 14, 1976:** Chris Chambliss homers in the ninth inning of Game 5 of the ALCS to clinch the Yankees' 30th pennant.

**Oct. 18, 1977:** Reggie Jackson hits three home runs in Game 6 as the Yankees take their 21st World Championship by beating the Los Angeles Dodgers.

**July 4, 1983:** Dave Righetti no-hits the Boston Red Sox.

**July 24, 1983:** George Brett of the Kansas City Royals hits a two-run home run in the ninth inning to put the Royals ahead 5–4, but a check of his bat reveals pine tar past the 18 inch limit. Brett is called out to end the game. The Royals protest successfully and the rest of the game is played August 18, ending in a 5–4 Kansas City win.

**Sept. 29, 1987:** Don Mattingly breaks Ernie Banks' major-league record when he hits his sixth grand slam of the season, off Bruce Hurst of the Red Sox.

**Sept. 4, 1993:** Jim Abbott no-hits the Cleveland Indians 4–0.

# Oakland Coliseum

## STADIUM STATS

**Location:** 7000 Coliseum Way, Oakland, CA 94621
**Opened:** 1966
**Surface:** Bluegrass
**Capacity:** 47,313
**Outfield dimensions:** RF 330, CF 400, LF 330.
**Services for fans with disabilities:** Seating available at field level behind row 38, and in sections 103, 107-109, 125-127 and 131.

## STADIUM FIRSTS

**Regular-season game:** April 17, 1968, 4–1 loss to the Baltimore Orioles.
**Pitcher:** Lew Krausse of the A's.
**Batter:** Curt Blefary of the Orioles.
**Home run:** Boog Powell of the Orioles.

## GROUND RULES

• A fly ball striking the foul poles and/or the screen attached above the fence is a home run.
• A ball that goes into players' and/or photographers' dugouts is out of play.
• A ball that sticks or goes behind the fence padding in the corners and the outfield and remains there is two bases.
• A ball that goes into the bullpen bench and rebounds onto the playing field is in play. If the ball remains on or under the bench, it is two bases.
• A ball hitting any portion of the fence or screen in back of home plate is in play.

Oakland–Alameda County Coliseum made its debut as home of the Oakland Athletics in 1968. The bowl-shaped Coliseum was built in 1965 and began hosting major-league baseball after then-owner Charlie Finley moved the team to the Bay Area from Kansas City.

Flamboyance was the A's calling card during the Finley era. Games featured such oddities as a mascot mule named Charlie O that paraded the field before games; colorful green-and-gold sleeveless uniforms that looked more suitable for a softball team; an innovative jackrabbit device behind home plate that served balls for the umpires; and, in 1974, world-class sprinter Herb Washington as baseball's first, and to date only, "designated runner" devoted solely to that function.

After Finley's departure, the laid-back California atmosphere along with the comparative calm left by his absence gave the Coliseum the nickname "the Mausoleum." It took the Bash Brothers—Jose Canseco and Mark McGwire—to put the energy back into the stadium. While the A's have fallen from those World Series days of the late '80s, the excitement remains, as does the comfortable, family-oriented atmosphere fostered by the Haas family, which owns the team.

Given the generally good sightlines and the circular configuration, the Coliseum appears intended solely for baseball. In fact, it was originally built for football's Oakland Raiders. The A's are one of the few teams without luxury boxes. In the early years, the Coliseum's scoreboard was notorious for not working, but after the Haas family bought the team in 1980, a manually operated out-of-town scoreboard was installed and has become a much-copied addition.

## HOT TIPS FOR VISITING FANS

**Parking**
The stadium has 10,000 spaces at $6 each. If the game is sold out, free overflow parking is across the freeway, a 10-minute walk away. Try to arrive at least half an hour to an hour before the game.

**Weather**
The Bay Area rarely gets too cold or too hot or too windy, and Oakland is a few degrees warmer than San Francisco, but you should dress for the summer like the locals

do—in layers. The fog sometimes moves in at night, making the air heavy and home runs harder to hit. But rainouts are rare, and conditions are most often ideal.

**Media bites**
**Radio:** KFRC (610 AM—English), KNTA (1430 AM—Spanish). Lon Simmons, Bill King and Ray Fosse do the English broadcasts, and Amaury Pi-Gonzales and Erwin Higueros announce the games in Spanish.
**TV:** KRON (Channel 4) and

SportsChannel (cable). Dick Stockton and Ray Fosse are the broadcasters on Channel 4.

 **Cuisine**
The Coliseum offers a wide variety of food, from basic hot dogs, all sorts of barbecued meats, pastas, soft-serve ice cream, Chinese food, Roundtable pizza and Subway sandwiches, to health-conscious foods like veggie burgers and salads. The popular microbrewery stand offers brands from Seattle and California. Name brands like Miller and Budweiser also are sold.

Pregame tailgating is very popular, but most people go home after the games. Near the stadium, the Hyatt hotel is a popular haunt for visiting and hometown players, as is the Hilton Sports Bar across the street. Francesco's (510-569-0653) is also nearby. Downtown, try the Pacific Coast Brewing Co. (510-836-2739), and Mac's Bar and Grill, and the Old Spaghetti Factory (510-893-0222) in Jack London Square.

## LODGING NEAR THE STADIUM

**Oakland Airport Hilton**
1 Hegenberger Rd.
Oakland, CA 94621
(510) 635-5000/(800) 445-8667
7 blocks from the stadium.

**Waterfront Plaza**
10 Washington St.
Oakland, CA 94607
(510) 836 3800/(800) 836-3800
About 5 miles from the stadium.

## GETTING TO OAKLAND COLISEUM

**Public transportation:** Bay Area Rapid Transit (BART) trains go from San Francisco and other adjacent areas to the Coliseum BART station. From there, you walk over a bridge to the stadium. For more information, call (510) 465-2278 or (415) 788-2278.
**By car:** The Coliseum is adjacent to I-880 on Coliseum Way, about 6 miles south of downtown Oakland. Take the 66th

**(Continued on page 62)**

# IN THE HOT SEATS AT OAKLAND COLISEUM

**B**ecause the stadium holds 47,200 and season-ticket sales usually number about 15,000, tickets are available on a walk-up basis for almost every game. Generally some good seats are available on all levels, except during rare sellouts.

• **Good seats:** The $17.50 MVP seats, in the lower level along the baselines, are considered the best. The lowest-priced ticket is a $4.50 bleacher seat behind the outfield fence. If you enjoy sun and a more involved atmosphere, these seats are a great deal.

• **Bad seats:** There are no obstructed views or peculiarities that make any seats very bad, nor is the stadium so large that distance is a serious factor. Foul poles are in sections 103 and 131 in the field level, so avoid these, if possible. Also, the foul ground is one of the largest in the major leagues, so anyone who sits in the boxes hoping to get a close look at their favorite players might be disappointed. This is especially true of the seats directly behind the plate; a notch in the backstop wall places them farther back than at other parks.

 **Scalping:** Scalpers surround the ballpark but aren't allowed on stadium property. With good seats available, fans don't need to use them.

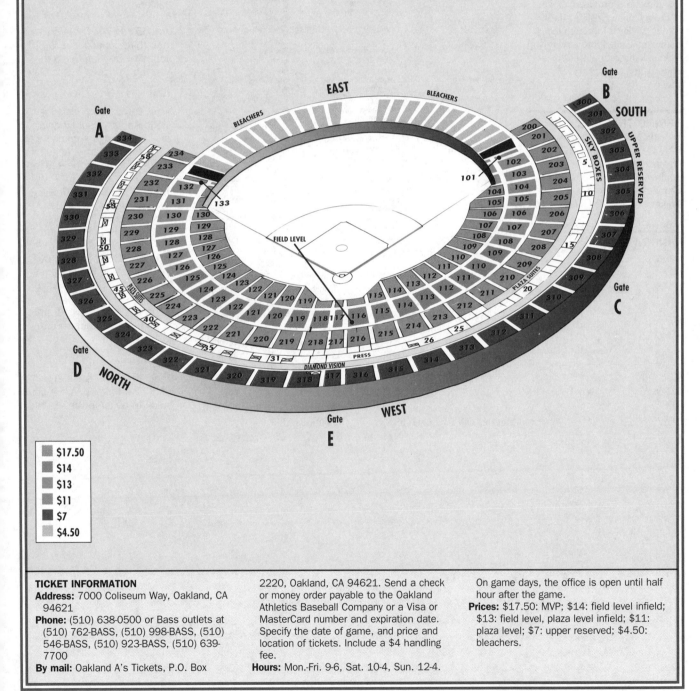

Legend:
- $17.50
- $14
- $13
- $11
- $7
- $4.50

**TICKET INFORMATION**
**Address:** 7000 Coliseum Way, Oakland, CA 94621
**Phone:** (510) 638-0500 or Bass outlets at (510) 762-BASS, (510) 998-BASS, (510) 546-BASS, (510) 923-BASS, (510) 639-7700
**By mail:** Oakland A's Tickets, P.O. Box 2220, Oakland, CA 94621. Send a check or money order payable to the Oakland Athletics Baseball Company or a Visa or MasterCard number and expiration date. Specify the date of game, and price and location of tickets. Include a $4 handling fee.
**Hours:** Mon.-Fri. 9-6, Sat. 10-4, Sun. 12-4.

On game days, the office is open until half hour after the game.
**Prices:** $17.50: MVP; $14: field level infield; $13: field level, plaza level infield; $11: plaza level; $7: upper reserved; $4.50: bleachers.

**(Continued from page 60)**

Avenue or Hegenberger Road exit off I-880.

From San Francisco, drive east over the Bay Bridge to I-580 toward Hayward. Take I-980 to Oakland and get on I-880 south. Get off at 66th Avenue and follow signs to the Coliseum.

From Marin County, take I-580 over the San Rafael Bridge to I-80. Take I-80 to I-580 toward Hayward and follow above directions.

From Sacramento, take I-80 west toward Oakland. Get on I-580 toward Hayward and follow directions provided above.

From Contra Costa County, take Highway 24 through the Caldecott Tunnel into downtown Oakland and get onto I-980. Follow directions provided above.

## SPRING TRAINING

Phoenix Municipal Stadium
5999 E. Van Buren
Phoenix, AZ 85008
**Surface:** Grass
**Game time:** 1:05 P.M.
**Tickets:** (602) 392-0074

## MINOR LEAGUE

| Class | Team |
|---|---|
| AAA | Tacoma (WA) Tigers |
| AA | Huntsville (AL) Stars |
| A | Modesto (CA) A's |
| A | West Michigan Whitecaps |
| Short Season A | Southern Oregon A's |
| Rookie | Scottsdale (AZ) A's |

## HOME-FIELD ADVANTAGE

The Coliseum's natural-grass field is arguably the best in baseball. A noteworthy trait of the field is the large foul territory, making the park pitcher-friendly. The stadium has always had tall outfield grass, making triples in the alleys few and far between.

## A'S TEAM NOTEBOOK

**Franchise history**
Philadelphia Athletics, 1901–54; Kansas City Athletics, 1955–67; Oakland Athletics, 1968–present

**World Series titles**
1910, 1911, 1913, 1929, 1930, 1972, 1973, 1974, 1989

**American League pennants**
1902, 1905, 1910, 1911, 1913, 1914, 1929, 1930, 1931, 1972, 1973, 1974, 1988, 1989, 1990

**Division titles**
1971, 1972, 1973, 1974, 1975, 1981, 1988, 1989, 1990, 1992

**Most Valuable Players**
Eddie Collins, 1914
Mickey Cochrane, 1928
Lefty Grove, 1931
Jimmie Foxx, 1932, 1933
Bobby Shantz, 1952
Vida Blue, 1971
Reggie Jackson, 1973
Jose Canesco, 1988
Rickey Henderson, 1990
Dennis Eckersley, 1992

**Rookies of the Year**
Harry Byrd, 1952
Jose Canesco, 1986
Mark McGwire, 1987
Walt Weiss, 1988

**Cy Young Awards**
Vida Blue, 1971
Jim "Catfish" Hunter, 1974
Bob Welch, 1990
Dennis Eckersley, 1992

**Hall of Fame**
Ty Cobb, 1936
Nap Lajoie, 1937
Connie Mack, 1937
Tris Speaker, 1937
Eddie Collins, 1939
Jimmy Collins, 1945
Eddie Plank, 1946
Rube Waddell, 1946
Mickey Cochrane, 1947
Lefty Grove, 1947
Herb Pennock, 1948
Jimmie Foxx, 1951
Chief Bender, 1951
Al Simmons, 1953
Frank "Home Run" Baker, 1955
Zack Wheat, 1959
Elmer Flick, 1963
Luke Appling, 1964
Stan Coveleski, 1969
Waite Hoyt, 1969
Lou Boudreau, 1970
Satchel Paige, 1971
George Kell, 1983
Enos Slaughter, 1985
Willie McCovey, 1986
Jim "Catfish" Hunter, 1987
Billy Williams, 1987
Joe Morgan, 1990
Rollie Fingers, 1992
Reggie Jackson, 1993

**Retired numbers**
27 Jim "Catfish" Hunter
34 Rollie Fingers

The closest minor-league team to Oakland is the Class A San Jose Giants of the California League. San Jose (one of San Francisco's minor-league teams) frequently plays the Modesto A's, Oakland's California League affiliate. With the exception of five years—1959–61 and 1977–78—pro baseball has been played in San Jose since 1947. But this city's baseball history goes back even farther, to 1896, when San Jose was a charter franchise in the California State League, which folded after the '96 season ended.

To reach San Jose from the Bay Area, less than 45 miles away, take I-880 south to I-280 south. Exit at 10th Street. Turn right on 10th and then left on Alma; Municipal Stadium will be on the right.

**Ticket prices:** $6: box seats; $5: adults; $2: children under 10 (children under 4 are free); $2: senior citizens 65 and over. For more information, call (408) 297-1435.

## THE A'S AT OAKLAND COLISEUM

**May 8, 1968:** Catfish Hunter throws a perfect game against the Minnesota Twins.

**Oct. 21, 1973:** A 5–2 win over the New York Mets in Game 7 of the World Series gives the A's their second world championship in Oakland.

**Oct. 17, 1974:** The A's take their third consecutive World Series by beating the Los Angeles Dodgers 3–2 in Game 5.

**Sept. 28, 1975:** Vida Blue, Glenn Abbott, Paul Lindblad and Rollie Fingers combine to no-hit the California Angels in the final game of the season.

**Oct. 15, 1981:** Fan "Crazy" George Henderson creates "the wave," at least for the first time in a baseball stadium.

**Oct. 14, 1989:** The A's win Game 2 of the World Series 5–1 over the San Francisco Giants. Game 3 in San Francisco is postponed after a 7.1 earthquake hits the Bay Area.

**May 1, 1991:** Rickey Henderson of the A's steals his 939th base, passing Lou Brock to become the all-time leader.

# Veterans Stadium

## STADIUM STATS

**Location:** Pattison Ave. and Broad St., Philadelphia, PA 19101
**Opened:** April 10, 1971
**Surface:** AstroTurf
**Capacity:** 62,382
**Outfield Dimensions:** LF 330, CF 408, RF 330.
**Services for fans with disabilities:** Seating available behind sections 205, 251, 328, 346 and 347.

## STADIUM FIRSTS

**Regular-season game:** April 10, 1971, 4–1 over the Montreal Expos.
**Pitcher:** Jim Bunning of the Phillies.
**Batter:** Boots Day of the Expos.
**Hit:** Larry Bowa of the Phillies.
**Home run:** Don Money of the Phillies.

## GROUND RULES

• Dugout: A ball has to enter the dugout or hit the yellow bars or yellow line to be considered out of play. A ball entering the open area above the end of dugout inside the yellow line is considered out of play.
• Fences: Glass area has openings at top. If a ball sticks in the opening, it is a ground-rule double. A ball sticking under the padding in the outfield fence is in play. In left and right field the stands protrude to a point near the foul lines. If a ball lands in fair territory and bounces over the points and lands in the playing area, it is considered to be in the stands and is a ground-rule double.
• A ball off the screen behind home plate is in play. A ball hitting the pipe to the right of the right-field foul pole is in play.

Veteran Stadium often is used as an example of all that is wrong with the ballparks of the 1970s. Carpeted with an artificial surface, fully enclosed but with no roof, heavy on the concrete and impersonal, the ballpark is part of the sprawling sports complex in South Philadelphia that includes the Spectrum. The Vet is a concrete structure, roundish, marked by huge vertical pillars. The highest seats are as elevated as those in any ballpark in North America.

Phillies' owner Bill Giles has been looking to arrange a baseball-only stadium for his team on the model of Oriole Park at Camden Yards or Jacobs Field. His motivation is obvious. For one thing, the upkeep at Veterans Stadium is handled mostly by Giles, and the Vet needs plenty of it. No matter how the Phillies fare, no matter how much the Phillie Phanatic distracts fans' attention, those who visit the Vet can't help but notice that it's not a good ballpark.

The artificial surface is reviled by players as the worst in the National League. There are worn and bare spots, and it is hard almost everywhere. There's even a myth that the Stadium is crumbling. The rumor is false, but the yard still feels a bit as though it is decaying; Mike Schmidt even complained of a "cat-stink" smell in the dugouts and runways in the late '80s.

At least some good things have happened here. The Phillies won their first World Series championship in 1980. They got back to the World Series and lost in 1983 and '93 and reached the NL playoffs in 1976-78. Given the sorry history of the Phillies, this was a real turnaround. The Phillies reached the Series in 1915 (and won one game) and in 1950 (and won none). They previously had played in the Baker Bowl, the ultimate hitters park, where the stands once collapsed, killing 12. They played in Shibe Park, later named Connie Mack Stadium, through the 1970 season.

## HOT TIPS FOR VISITING FANS

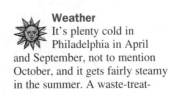

**Parking**
The lots surrounding the stadium charge $5 and have spaces for 14,000 cars. Don't be afraid to pull into the Spectrum lot next door. In fact, it might be a smart move because you can walk briskly to your car after the game and get out faster. This tactic is especially effective if you are driving onto southbound I-95.

Another main artery is the Schuylkill Expressway. It is nicknamed "Sure-kill" for a reason. Also avoid Broad Street—too many lights.

**Weather**
It's plenty cold in Philadelphia in April and September, not to mention October, and it gets fairly steamy in the summer. A waste-treatment center sits a few miles from the stadium, and every now and then breezes waft that aroma to the ballpark.

 **Media bites**
**Radio:** WOGL (1210 AM).
**TV:** WPHL (Channel 17) and PRISM (cable). Richie Ashburn, Harry Kalas, Andy Musser, Chris Wheeler and Garry Maddox are the broadcasters.

 **Cuisine**
The Phillies have upgraded their concessions, but the cheese steaks are still not as good as those found in stands outside the ballpark, and more expensive to boot. The Italian water ices in the stadium have the same problems. Pennsylvania funnel cake, a local pastry specialty, is available, and there's the usual stuff—Pizza Hut, grilled chicken, etc.

South Street is nice for pregame dining or postgame revelry. Cafe Nola (215-627-2590) serves excellent Cajun fare that visiting ballplayers love. Susanna Foo (215-545-2666) has first-rate Chinese food. Better yet, go to the Italian Market in south Philadelphia and find your way to Pat's King of Steaks (215-339-9872) for that Philadelphia specialty, the cheese steak. Yummy, but tell your arteries to expect heavy traffic. Get an Italian water ice if you can find room after the cheese steak. There's a stand near Pat's. Lemon water ice is the best.

For those interested in more action, the happening place is Legends at the Holiday Inn, Stadium. One of the owners is Ron Jaworski, a former Philadelphia Eagles quarterback.

## LODGING NEAR THE STADIUM
**Sheraton Society Hill**
1 Dock St. (corner of Second and Walnut)
Philadelphia, PA 19103
(215) 238-6000/(800) 325-3535
3 miles from the stadium.

(Continued on page 65)

# IN THE HOT SEATS AT VETERANS STADIUM

Y ou can walk up and get seats—the ballpark has plenty of room—but getting great ones is another matter. Forget about the field boxes; they go as season tickets.

• **Good seats:** The best bargain is a general admission ($5) seat at the 700 (top) level. Arrive early and you can claim a seat right behind home plate. You'll be in nosebleed territory (no, concessionaires do not stroll aisles selling oxygen), but behind the plate is a great spot, regardless. The seats in left and center field get the most sun during day games; the deluxe seats (200 level) get it almost all through the game.

• **Bad seats:** Try to avoid seats in the 700 level down the foul lines. The angles make it difficult to follow the ball off the bat. You're better off at the 500 level or 600 level in the outfield.

 **Scalping:** Tickets for good seats are peddled outside the stadium. The demand is not great for marked-up seats, so you can take a tough negotiating stance.

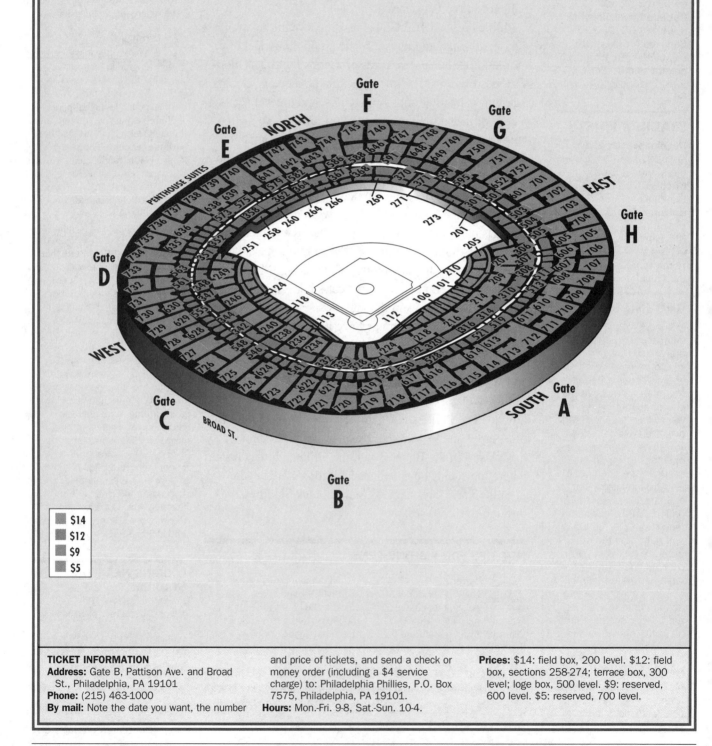

$14
$12
$9
$5

**TICKET INFORMATION**
**Address:** Gate B, Pattison Ave. and Broad St., Philadelphia, PA 19101
**Phone:** (215) 463-1000
**By mail:** Note the date you want, the number and price of tickets, and send a check or money order (including a $4 service charge) to: Philadelphia Phillies, P.O. Box 7575, Philadelphia, PA 19101.
**Hours:** Mon.-Fri. 9-8, Sat.-Sun. 10-4.

**Prices:** $14: field box, 200 level. $12: field box, sections 258-274; terrace box, 300 level; loge box, 500 level. $9: reserved, 600 level. $5: reserved, 700 level.

(Continued from page 63)

**The Ritz Carlton**
17th and Chestnut St. at Liberty
Place
Philadelphia, PA 19106
(215) 563-1600/(800) 241-3333
7 miles from the stadium.

## GETTING TO VETERANS STADIUM

**Public transportation:** By sub-way, take the Broad Street line from 15th and Market south-bound to the last stop, Broad and Pattison. The Stadium is 1 block away. Call (215) 580-7800 for more information.

**By car:** From the north, take I-95 south to the Broad Street exit. Go to the first light (Zinkoff Boulevard) and turn right. The Stadium is on your left.

From the south, take I-95 north to the Broad Street exit and proceed as above.

From the west, take I-76 east. At Century City, stay to the right and follow signs for New Jersey and the Sports Complex, heading toward the Walt Whitman Bridge. Take the Broad Street exit, No. 45 (Sports Complex), and go right at the bottom of the ramp onto Broad Street. Stay to the far left, to Pattison Avenue. Stadium is on the left.

From the east, cross Walt Whitman Bridge to I-76 West through the tolls, to exit 46B, South Seventh Street. Go through one traffic light to Pattison Avenue. Right to the first traffic light. Go left onto 11th Street. Stadium on your right.

## SPRING TRAINING

Jack Russell Memorial Stadium
800 Phillies Dr.
Clearwater, FL 34615
**Capacity:** 7,195
**Surface:** Grass
**Game time:** 1:05 P.M. or
7:05 P.M.
**Tickets:** (215) 463-6000

## MINOR LEAGUES

| Class | Team |
|---|---|
| AAA | Scranton/Wilkes-Barre (PA) Red Barons |
| AA | Reading (PA) Phillies |
| A | Clearwater (FL) Phillies |
| A | Spartanburg (SC) Phillies |
| Short Season A | Batavia (NY) Clippers |
| Rookie | Martinsville (VA) Phillies |

The Phillies' closest minor-league affiliate is the Class AA Reading Phillies of the Eastern League. Since Reading became one of Philadelphia's farm teams in 1967, this team has sent more than 130 players to the big leagues. Among the alumni: Phillies Mike Schmidt, Greg Luzinski, Bob Boone, and Larry Bowa, plus such other stars as Ryne Sandberg and Julio Franco.

To reach Reading Municipal Memorial Stadium, which is approximately 60 miles from Philadelphia, take U.S. 422 west to Route 222 north. Exit at Route 61 south. The ballpark is 1 block past the exit on your right.

**Ticket prices:** $5: reserved seats; $3.50: general admission; $2: children between ages 5 and 14. For more information, call (610) 375-8469.

## THE PHILLIES AT VETERANS STADIUM

**Aug. 17, 1972:** Steve Carlton gets his 20th win of the season and his 15th in a row, as the Phillies beat the Cincinnati Reds 9–4.

## HOME-FIELD ADVANTAGE

Veterans Stadium, like its nearly identical twins in Pittsburgh and Cincinnati, has a large, cavernous feel. Fans in the upper-deck sections really do have "Bob Uecker" seats, far from the field. But this distance does not prevent the Phillies or opposing players from hearing the boos that rain down from the stands with a regularity and ferocity that might surprise those unaccustomed to watching pro sports in Philadelphia. Even Hall of Fame third baseman Mike Schmidt was not spared from receiving the occasional wrath of the hometown fans during his 15-year career.

As tough as the fans can be with the Phillies, opposing players, especially those from such archrivals as the Mets, the Pirates and the Braves, can get even harsher treatment. The Vet, as this ballpark is known to Philadelphians, can be a surprise to unexpecting rookies and other uninitiated souls.

Veterans Stadium is a good hitters park with a hard, fast, artificial surface that the Phillies' fielders cope with better than visitors.

### PHILLIES TEAM NOTEBOOK

**Franchise history**
Worcester Brown Stockings, 1880–1882; Philadelphia Phillies, 1883–present

**World Series title**
1980

**National League pennants**
1915, 1950, 1980, 1983, 1993

**Division titles**
1976, 1977, 1978, 1980, 1983, 1993

**Most Valuable Players**
Chuck Klein, 1932
Jim Konstanty, 1950
Mike Schmidt, 1980, 1981, 1986

**Rookies of the Year**
Jack Sanford, 1957
Dick Allen, 1964

**Cy Young Awards**
Steve Carlton, 1972, 1977, 1980, 1982
John Denny, 1983
Steve Bedrosian, 1987

**Hall of Fame**
Nap Lajoie, 1937
Grover Cleveland Alexander, 1938
Dan Brouthers, 1945
Ed Delahanty, 1945
Hugh Duffy, 1945
Hughie Jennings, 1945
Johnny Evers, 1946
Tommy McCarthy, 1946
Kid Nichols, 1949
Jimmie Foxx, 1951
Chief Bender, 1953
Harry Wright, 1953

Billy Hamilton, 1961
John Clarkson, 1963
Elmer Flick, 1963
Eppa Rixey, 1963
Tim Keefe, 1964
Casey Stengel, 1966
Lloyd Waner, 1967
Dave Bancroft, 1971
Sam Thompson, 1974
Bucky Harris, 1975
Roger Connor, 1976
Robin Roberts, 1976
Hack Wilson, 1979
Chuck Klein, 1980
Joe Morgan, 1990
Ferguson Jenkins, 1991
Steve Carlton, 1994

**Retired numbers**
1 Richie Ashburn
20 Mike Schmidt
32 Steve Carlton

**May 4, 1973:** The Phillies play their longest game since 1919 when they beat the Atlanta Braves 5–4 in 20 innings.

**Oct. 7, 1980:** Greg Luzinski hits a two-run homer, bringing the Phillies a 3–1 win over the Houston Astros in the opening game of the League Championship Series.

**Oct. 14, 1980:** The Phillies win Game 1 of the World Series against the Kansas City Royals 7–6, with the help of Bake McBride's three-run homer.

**Oct. 21, 1980:** The Phillies win their only world championship when Tug McGraw strikes out the Royals' Willie Wilson at 11:29 P.M.

**April 29, 1981:** Steve Carlton strikes out the Montreal Expos' Tim Wallach to reach 3,000 strikeouts.

**Aug. 10, 1981:** Pete Rose singles to break Stan Musial's NL record for hits.

**June 7, 1983:** Steve Carlton passes Nolan Ryan on the all-time strikeout list by striking out the St. Louis Cardinals' Lonnie Smith, victim number 3,552.

**Oct. 8, 1983:** The Phillies take the pennant, with Gary Matthews' three-run homer leading a 7–2 win over the Los Angeles Dodgers.

**June 11, 1985:** Von Hayes homers twice in the first inning as the Phillies bomb the New York Mets 26–7.

**June 29, 1989:** The Phillies retire Steve Carlton's No. 32, then go on to defeat the Pittsburgh Pirates, 6–2.

**May 26, 1990:** The Phillies retire Mike Schmidt's No. 20.

**Aug. 15, 1990:** Terry Mullholland pitches the first no-hitter in Veterans Stadium history and the Phillies' first no-hitter this century, beating the San Francisco Giants, 6–0.

# STADIUM STATS

**Location:** 600 Stadium Circle, Pittsburgh, PA 15212
**Opened:** July 16, 1970
**Surface:** AstroTurf
**Capacity:** 47,972
**Outfield dimensions:** LF 335, LC 375, CF 400, RC 375, RF 335.
**Services for fans with disabilities:** Seating available in right field.

# STADIUM FIRSTS

**Regular-season game:** July 16, 1970, a 3–2 loss to the Cincinnati Reds.
**Pitcher:** Dock Ellis, Pirates.
**Batter:** Ty Cline, Reds.
**Hit:** Richie Hebner, Pirates.
**Home run:** Tony Perez, Reds.

# GROUND RULES

• The photographers' benches are considered to be part of players' bench. A ball crossing the line in front of the players' bench, or going over the screen on the railing of the photographers' bench, is considered to have gone into the bench.
• A ball that hits the posts in the dugout and remains on the playing field is in play.
• A fair hit ball striking the screen in front of either bullpen is in play.
• A fair hit ball sticking in the screen in front of either bullpen is two bases.
• A fair hit ball going through or under the screen in front of either bullpen is two bases.
• A ball hitting any part of the foul-line screen above the top of the outfield fence is a home run.

# Three Rivers Stadium

When Three Rivers Stadium opened in 1970, the master plan called for a sprawling complex of office buildings and businesses to sprout around it on the north side of the Allegheny River by the year 2000. Today, city planners are hoping the Pirates will be out of the Stadium and into a new park downtown shortly after the turn of the century. It's still *very* early in the process, but there's talk of a Camden Yards clone or Forbes Field reincarnation. The problem? Though Three Rivers is still in good shape and perfectly functional, it's difficult to love. It's the quintessential cookie-cutter stadium of the early 1970s.

The Pirates, the city and the Stadium Authority are trying hard to recraft the atmosphere. They covered the upper-deck outfield seats with decorative tarps in 1993 to add baseball flavor and a sense of intimacy to the park. They installed a statue honoring Hall of Famer Roberto Clemente to the plaza. They added a baseball boardwalk of distinctive concessions and banners on the lower-level concourse. They put in a new $4.3 million Sony Jumbotron video board in 1994 and added two out-of-town scoreboards just over the outfield walls. All these measures help, but you can't make Fenway Park out of a cereal bowl.

The Clemente statue is the latest nod to the rich history of the 108-year-old club. At the base of the statue is a baseball diamond etched in the stone. At each base is a patch of "hallowed ground" (enclosed but visible) from fields where Clemente played—Santurce Field in Puerto Rico, Forbes Field and Three Rivers.

The Pirates have been one of baseball's most successful teams since they moved into Three Rivers. In their first 24 years in the park (through 1993), they won nine NL East Division titles and two World Series and had 16 winning seasons. Clemente played there for 2½ seasons before his death in a plane crash, and Willie Stargell thrilled fans with his titanic home runs. He reached the upper deck four times—no one else has done it more than once.

## HOT TIPS FOR VISITING FANS

**Parking**
Stadium lots can handle 4,000 cars, which is OK for your average game but a problem with a big crowd. Cost is $4. Signs around the stadium will direct you to alternate lots east and north of the park. You'll also find a few lots on or near Allegheny Avenue (northwest), an easy walk through an underpass to the park. Count on paying $4-$5.

**Weather**
Bundle up in April, as the nights can be downright cold. (Stadium veterans report having seen a fire or two in the bullpens over the years.) Pittsburgh summers are usually quite pleasant. Temperatures hit 90 degrees on occasion in July and August, but that's not the norm, and evenings are cooler. September days and evenings are mild, making for fine baseball weather.

**Media bites**
**Radio:** KDKA (1020 AM).
**TV:** KDKA (Channel 2) and KBL Sports Network (cable). The announcers on both are Larry Frattare, Steve Blass and Greg Brown.

**Cuisine**
In the last few years, the stadium has put some Pittsburgh flavor into its concessions, a move that has proved to be a hit. Dagwood would love Primanti Bros. on the lower level; their specialty sandwiches ($4.75) come piled with meat, cheese, cole slaw, tomatoes, and french fries—all stuffed between fresh slices of bread. The standby is cheese steak, but you can also get pastrami, corned beef, sausage and more. Fish lovers head around the corner to Benkovitz's stand for lightly breaded fresh fish fillets; the sandwich comes with two fillets on a kaiser roll with fixings. Imported beers—Beck's, Beck's Dark, Molson Golden and Amstel Light—are available at two Beers of the World stands. The local brew, Iron City, is also available. Parents might want to check out the Kidcession on the lower level, where $1.75 buys a hot dog, soda, chips and a coloring book for younger fans.

Tailgate parties are a Pittsburgh tradition that started at Steelers football games but carried over to Pirates outings. Throw a small grill and some dogs in the trunk, and you'll fit right in. If concrete with yellow stripes isn't your idea of ambience, the Clark Bar & Grill Restaurant (412-231-3720) is the best option. Located in the Clark Building on Martindale Street across the parking lot from Gate B, it's popular with players and

**(Continued on page 68)**

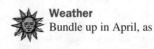

# In the Hot Seats at Three Rivers Stadium

With the upper-deck outfield seats now covered (the tarps would be removed for World Series games), capacity is reduced from 58,729 to 47,972. But tickets still are no problem. The team averages about 25,000 in its best seasons. You can almost always walk up the day of the game and buy a good seat. Opening day and playoffs, of course, are exceptions.

• **Good seats:** Getting a very good box seat with little notice is possible, particularly if you're seeking a single seat. The stands are close to the action, so anything in the club boxes on the infield is a treat. The terrace boxes in the upper deck also are excellent and not too high. Upper reserves are about the same as with any of the cookie-cutter stadiums—excellent sightlines but too high. The sunny side of the stadium is down the third-base line out to left field. It gets plenty of sun and can get hot on July afternoons.

• **Bad seats:** During day games, it can be difficult to pick up the ball off the bat from the club boxes down the lines. The angle and the light-green color of the artificial surface contribute to the problem. If you're down the left-field line, the problem is with balls hit to the right side of the infield (away from you) and vice versa. This problem can take a couple of innings to get used to and seems to be more of a problem on bright days.

• **Family sections:** Sections 177-183, the lower-deck left field, are no smoking, and one section is no-smoking/no-drinking.

**Scalping:** Because ticket demand is rarely overwhelming, scalping isn't big business. It's illegal, and the club says the stadium grounds are policed. Still, scalpers can be found near the gate ramps. Tickets to the 1994 All-Star Game were selling for two to three times face value, but on most nights, it is a buyer's market.

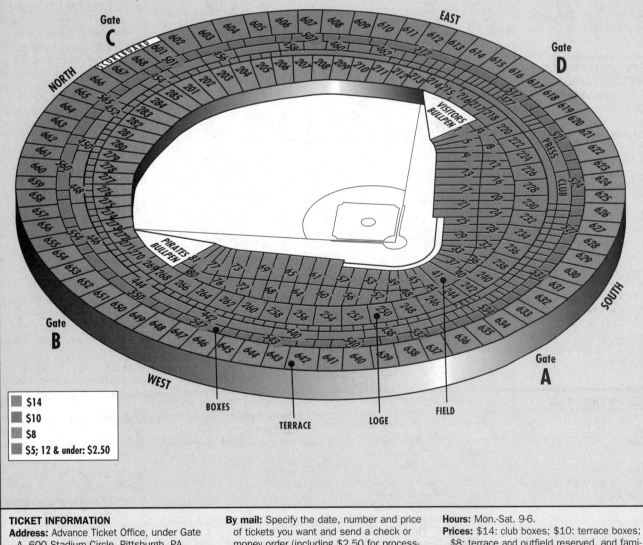

Legend:
- $14
- $10
- $8
- $5; 12 & under: $2.50

---

**TICKET INFORMATION**
**Address:** Advance Ticket Office, under Gate A, 600 Stadium Circle, Pittsburgh, PA 15212
**Phone:** (412) 323-5000 or TicketMaster at (412) 323-1919 or (800) 366-1212

**By mail:** Specify the date, number and price of tickets you want and send a check or money order (including $2.50 for processing charges) to: Pittsburgh Pirates, Three Rivers Stadium, P.O. Box 7000, Pittsburgh, PA 15212.

**Hours:** Mon.-Sat. 9-6.
**Prices:** $14: club boxes; $10: terrace boxes; $8: terrace and outfield reserved, and family sections; $5: general admission (adults); $2.50: general admission (children under 13).

**(Continued from page 66)**

fans alike. Former Pirates' Mike LaValliere (now with the White Sox) and John Smiley (now a Cincinnati Red) are part owners. The north side by the river is mostly residential or warehouses, so there aren't many other businesses or restaurants nearby. Many fans jump in their cars and cross the Fort Duquesne Bridge to downtown.

## LODGING NEAR THE STADIUM

**Pittsburgh Vista Hotel**
1000 Penn Ave.
Pittsburgh, PA 15222
(412) 281-3700/(800) 367-8478
1 mile from the stadium

**Westin in William Penn**
530 William Penn Place
Pittsburgh, PA 15219
(412) 281-7100/(800) 228-3000
About 3 miles from the stadium.

## GETTING TO THREE RIVERS STADIUM

**Public transportation:** Call Port Authority Transit at (412) 231-5707 for information.
**By car:** From the south, take I-79 North to I-279 North. Go over the Fort Pitt Bridge and the Fort Duquesne Bridge to exit 11B. The stadium lots are directly off I-279.
From the north, take I-79 South to I-279 South to the Stadium exit.
From the east, take the Pennsylvania Turnpike to I-376 West to downtown and the Stadium exit.
From the west, take the Ohio Turnpike to the Pennsylvania Turnpike, then head south on I-79 to I-279 South to the Stadium exit.

## SPRING TRAINING

Pirate City
1701 27th St. E.
Bradenton, FL 34208

McKechnie Field
17th Ave. W. and Ninth St. W
Bradenton, FL 34208
**Capacity:** 6,562
**Surface:** Grass
**Game time:** 1:05 P.M.

## HOME-FIELD ADVANTAGE

Like its dual-purpose, artificial-surface, symmetrical cousins of the late '60s and early '70s, Three Rivers offers little edge to the home team. The stadium has no quirky spots or features worth tailoring a team to suit. In the early 1970s, the team won with big, power-hitting players and was nicknamed "the Lumber Company." In the late '70s, they lost some of that power but added speed and won with the moniker "Lumber 'n' Lightning." In the early 1990s, they used a blend of pitching, power and defense to win three consecutive NL East crowns. All three eras produced solid teams that could have won in any park. Over the years, the Pirates have posted a better record at Three Rivers than on the road, but not unusually so.

### PIRATES TEAM NOTEBOOK

**Franchise history**
Pittsburgh Pirates, 1887–present

**World Series titles**
1909, 1925, 1960, 1971, 1979

**National League pennants**
1901, 1902, 1903, 1909, 1925, 1927, 1960, 1971, 1979

**Division titles**
1970, 1971, 1972, 1974, 1975, 1979, 1990, 1991, 1992

**Most Valuable Players**
Paul Waner, 1927
Dick Groat, 1960
Roberto Clemente, 1966
Dave Parker, 1978
Willie Stargell, 1979 (tie)

Barry Bonds, 1990, 1992

**Cy Young Awards**
Vernon Law, 1960
Doug Drabek, 1990

**Hall of Fame**
Honus Wagner, 1936
Connie Mack, 1945
Fred Clarke, 1945
Jack Chesbro, 1946
Rube Waddell, 1946
Frankie Frisch, 1947
Pie Traynor, 1948
Paul Waner, 1952
Rabbit Maranville, 1954
Arthur "Dazzy" Vance, 1955
Joe Cronin, 1956
Hank Greenberg, 1956
Max Carey, 1961
Bill McKechnie, 1962
Burleigh Grimes, 1964
Heinie Manush, 1964
James "Pud" Galvin, 1965

Casey Stengel, 1966
Branch Rickey, 1967
Lloyd Waner, 1967
Kiki Cuyler, 1968
Waite Hoyt, 1969
Jake Beckley, 1971
Joe Kelley, 1971
Roberto Clemente, 1973
George Kelly, 1973
Billy Herman, 1975
Ralph Kiner, 1975
Fred Lindstrom, 1976
Al Lopez, 1977
Chuck Klein, 1980
Arky Vaughan, 1985
Willie Stargell, 1988

**Retired numbers**
1 Billy Meyer
4 Ralph Kiner
8 Willie Stargell
9 Bill Mazeroski
20 Pie Traynor
21 Roberto Clemente
33 Honus Wagner
40 Danny Murtaugh

## MINOR LEAGUES

| Class | Team |
| --- | --- |
| AAA | Buffalo Bisons |
| AA | Carolina (NC) Mudcats |
| A | Salem (VA) Buccaneers |
| A | Augusta (GA) Green Jackets |
| Short Season A | Welland (ON) Pirates |
| Rookie | Bradenton (FL) Pirates |

The Pirates' closest minor league affiliate is the Class AAA Buffalo Bisons of the American Association. The Bisons have drawn more than 1 million fans to Pilot Field for six consecutive seasons. In 1993, the team's attendance was 1,058,620. In 1992, the attendance of 1,117,867 was only about 100,000 less than that of the Houston Astros, even though Houston plays more games in a bigger ballpark than Buffalo does.

To reach Buffalo's Pilot Field, which is about 250 miles from Pittsburgh, take the Church Street exit from I-190 and follow signs to the ballpark.

**Ticket prices:** $7.75: special reserved seats; $6.25: reserved seats; $3.75: bleachers. For more information, call (716) 846-2000.

## THE PIRATES AT THREE RIVERS STADIUM

**Aug. 14, 1971:** Bob Gibson no-hits the Pirates in an 11–0 St. Louis Cardinals win.

**Oct. 6, 1971:** Homers by Al Oliver and Richie Hebner lead the Bucs to a 9–5 win in Game 4 of the NLCS over the San Francisco Giants, earning a trip to the World Series.

**Oct. 13, 1971:** The Pirates and Baltimore Orioles play the first night game in World Series history. Pittsburgh wins Game 4, 4–3.

**Aug. 9, 1976:** John Candelaria no-hits the Los Angeles Dodgers 2–0.

**May 11, 1977:** Ted Turner enjoys the shortest managerial career ever as he takes over his Atlanta Braves for one game. The Pirates win 2–1, and Turner is suspended by Commissioner Bowie Kuhn.

**April 18, 1979:** The Philadelphia Phillies' Greg Luzinski hits the longest home run in Three Rivers history, a 483-foot shot off Don Robinson.

**Oct. 5, 1979:** Willie Stargell and Bill Madlock homer, and the Pirates beat the Cincinnati Reds 7–1 to take the National League Pennant in Game 3 of the NLCS.

**Oct. 14, 1979:** Bert Blyleven gets the win as the Pirates take Game 5 of the World Series, 7–1 over the Orioles.

**April 18, 1987:** Philadelphia's Mike Schmidt hits his 500th home run, off Don Robinson.

**Sept. 20, 1992:** Mickey Morandini of the Phillies turns an unassisted triple play.

**July 8, 1994:** The Pirates unveil a statue honoring Roberto Clemente as part of the All-Star Game festivities at Three Rivers.

# San Diego Jack Murphy Stadium

## STADIUM STATS

**Location:** 9449 Friars Rd., San Diego, CA 92108
**Opened:** Aug. 30, 1967
**Surface:** Santa Ana Bermuda Grass
**Capacity:** 46,510
**Outfield dimensions:** LF 327, LC 370, CF 405, RC 370, RF 327.
**Services for fans with disabilities:** Seating in Plaza level, sections 17, 25, 44-46 and 57-59; in loge level, section 31.

## STADIUM FIRSTS

**Regular-season game:** April 8, 1969, 2–1 over the Houston Astros.
**Pitcher:** Dick Selma of the Padres.
**Batter:** Jesus Alou of the Astros.
**Hit:** Jesus Alou.
**Home run:** Ed Spiezio of the Padres.

## GROUND RULES

• Photographers' areas adjacent to first-base and third-base dugouts are considered part of dugouts. Ball in these areas is out of play, same as both dugouts.
• Bullpens are in play.
• Everything else is standard ground rules.

Think San Diego has no baseball tradition? Think again. Ted Williams, one of the greatest hitters of all time, was born in San Diego and started his career there. Tony Gwynn, a five-time National League batting champion, is from San Diego, too, and he has become almost as much of a cultural icon here as the surfboard. There were even Padres before these Padres. They played in Lane Field.

This time around, the Padres play in Jack Murphy Stadium, named after the sportswriter who helped San Diego land major-league franchises in football and baseball. Some longtime baseball observers, stunned by the lack of interest in today's Padres, recall the crowds from the summer of 1984—the year the team reached the World Series—as the loudest they'd ever heard at an open-air stadium.

The silence is deafening now. The Padres are being rebuilt with youngsters to save money. New ownership stripped the club of assets, and fans have stayed away. The biggest event since the Series was probably Roseanne Arnold's unique version of the national anthem before a 1990 game. And once in 1988, the late Chub Feeney, then the Padres president, leaned out of the owner's box and gave the finger to fans who were booing him.

The ballpark is still attractive, even if the team is not. Situated in Mission Valley, between two steep ridges, it's about 8 miles from the Pacific Ocean, near the junction of Interstates 15 and 8. The Murph has an open end in the outfield and five levels (including a club level) stacked in three decks. A large video scoreboard in right-center field shows live telecasts of games in the East while the Padres and their opponents take batting practice.

You're likely to encounter America's finest—uniformed members of the armed forces—taking over a section or two in the outfield seats at a game. Different branches of the service try to outchant the other, and give the fans something to root for.

## HOT TIPS FOR VISITING FANS

**Parking**
Stadium lots have space for 18,751 cars, the second-largest in the major leagues. No street parking is nearby.

Traffic congestion used to be a problem, but now that the club isn't drawing, you can get out to the two interstates.

### Weather

Don't look for rain delays. The weather is divine—that's why San Diego is such a popular vacation destination. The Padres, who have not been rained out since April 20, 1983, don't have a full-time rain-delay squad. Instead, designated concessionaires and cleanup crew members will spring to the field and unroll the tarp, if necessary.

All of which accounts for the skunk who lives inside the tarp. So far, no one has been sprayed, and his annual visits make highlight reels every year, something that few Padres can boast of recently. With the departure of the San Diego Chicken, the skunk might prove to be an appropriate replacement mascot.

### Media bites

**Radio:** KFMB (760 AM); XEXX (1420 AM) in Tijuana does the Spanish-language broadcasts, with Mario T. Zapiain, Eduardo Ortega and Matias Santosas announcing.

**TV:** KUSI-TV (Channel 51) shows road games. The broadcasters are Jerry ("Oh, Doctor") Coleman, Bob Chandler and Ted Leitner, who also do the radio shows.

### Cuisine

Sushi is no longer sold. It was eliminated this season to a few howls of indignation (none from local fish). You can get fish tacos from Rubio's, a local fast-food taco outlet. Consisting of crisp fried fish with lettuce and salsa, they're well worth trying. Other notable options include java from gourmet coffee carts, Rallyburgers for those with more traditional tastes, and deluxe sausages. Randy Jones' barbecue stand has ribs, chicken, hot dogs and corn on the cob, served up and supervised by the former Padres pitcher who won 42 games over the 1975–76 seasons. The Stadium Club is on the third level on the third-base side; it's

**(Continued on page 71)**

# In the Hot Seats at Jack Murphy Stadium

Capacity is 46,510, with maybe one-quarter of the seats used in a typical game. The Padres sell only about 8,000 season tickets, so you can get good seats on a walk-up basis. The top deck is closed from left-center field to the right-field corner. In an attempt to put the best face on things, each closed section is covered by a tarp, but unoccupied seats still abound. However, don't try to move down to a better location—ushers are vigilant about letting customers sit only in their assigned seats.

All seats in the stadium are reserved, including the $5 pavilion seats beyond right field, which aren't as bad as you might think; they get lots of sun during day games, so you can strip down and catch some rays. Some outfield seats are actually prized. The right-field stands, in particular, allow fans to commune with Tony Gwynn, whose popularity exceeds that of any San Diego athlete, even Chargers linebacker Junior Seau.

• **Bad seats:** All seats have unobstructed views of the field, but fans in the pavilion seats can't see the main scoreboard or the Diamond Vision that towers above the section. Beyond center field, many seats are more than 500 feet from home plate. Seats on the field level beyond the dugouts extend close to the playing field down both foul lines, so fans there must be prepared to dodge foul line drives.

• **Special programs:** The junior Padres program for youngsters 14 and under offers tickets to eight games for $6. The knothole gang, a seniors' program, offers tickets to eight games for $6. Also, every Friday night is family night. For $29, families receive four loge-level seats, four hot dogs, four Cokes, a game program and parking. Special nights for Little League and the military are scheduled.

 **Scalping:** Given the state of ticket sales, fans needn't bother. Whatever market there is favors the buyers.

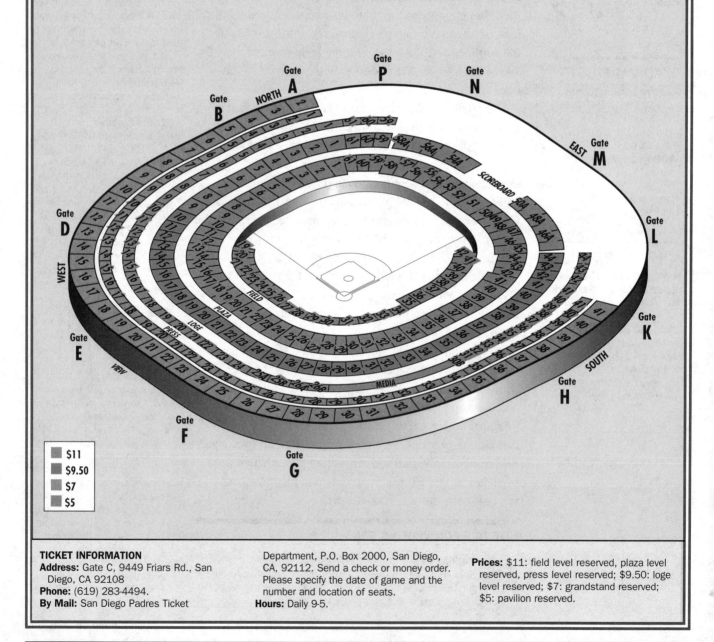

$11
$9.50
$7
$5

**TICKET INFORMATION**
**Address:** Gate C, 9449 Friars Rd., San Diego, CA 92108
**Phone:** (619) 283-4494.
**By Mail:** San Diego Padres Ticket Department, P.O. Box 2000, San Diego, CA, 92112. Send a check or money order. Please specify the date of game and the number and location of seats.
**Hours:** Daily 9-5.

**Prices:** $11: field level reserved, plaza level reserved, press level reserved; $9.50: loge level reserved; $7: grandstand reserved; $5: pavilion reserved.

**(Continued from page 69)**

open to season ticketholders and offers dinner before and during the game. The Sports Club is on the first level on the third-base side. It is open to the public and offers table seating, food, a bar and a dozen imported beers.

After the game, one possible destination is the Gaslamp Quarter, a restored turn-of-the-century section of downtown, about 6 miles from the Stadium. It's known for its nightlife, with numerous restaurants and clubs that range from upscale to funky. The area is adjacent to several new waterfront hotels, the convention center and the Horton Plaza downtown shopping center. Try Kansas City Barbecue (619-231-9680), downtown near the Marriott. Some of the bar scenes from the Tom Cruise movie *Top Gun* were filmed in this popular stop. Order the tasty Hot Links. Closer to the stadium, 2 or so miles away, is Mission Valley's Hotel Circle and Restaurant Row. Padres Pub in the Hilton Mission Valley is a good choice. Also try Trophy's Bar & Grill (619-296-9600) on Friars Road near the ballpark, and Bully's East on Texas Street.

## LODGING NEAR THE STADIUM

**Hyatt Regency**
1 Market Place
San Diego, CA 92101
(619) 232-1234/(800) 233-1234
10 miles from the stadium.

**The Mission Valley Marriott**
8757 Rio San Diego Dr.
San Diego, CA 92108
(619) 692-3800/(800) 228-9290
About 2 miles from the stadium.

## GETTING TO JACK MURPHY STADIUM

**Public transportation:**
Working with the Padres, San Diego transit provides a shuttle bus. For more information call (619) 233-3004. The North County Transit also provides a shuttle bus to the games Thursday through Sunday; call

## HOME-FIELD ADVANTAGE

Wind is rarely a factor, and the stadium has picked up the reputation for being a launching pad since the 8-foot inner fence was added.

Outfielders can steal a home run by leaping and reaching over the fence to catch the ball.

Balls hit down the lines and into foul territory in the left- and right-field corners can cause problems. Veteran Tony Gwynn is adept at playing the right-field foul line. Some fair balls hit the stands that extend close to the field midway down the line, and kick back into right field. Gwynn often plays the carom instead heading for the corner, fields the ball in medium right and throws the runner out at second.

### PADRES TEAM NOTEBOOK

| Franchise history | Rookies of the Year | Hall of Fame |
|---|---|---|
| San Diego Padres, 1969–present | Butch Metzger, 1976 (tied) | Willie McCovey, 1986 |
| | Benito Santiago, 1987 | Gaylord Perry, 1991 |
| **National League pennant** | | Rollie Fingers, 1992 |
| 1984 | **Cy Young Awards** | **Retired number** |
| | Randy Jones, 1976 | 6 Steve Garvey |
| **Division title** | Gaylord Perry, 1978 | |
| 1984 | Mark Davis, 1989 | |

(619) 722-NCTD or (619) 743-NCTD for details.

**By car:** From the north, take I-805 South to I-8 East to I-15 North. Take the Friars Road West and follow it about half a mile to the Stadium.

From the west, take I-8 eastbound and get off at Stadium Way, which leads to Friars Road and the stadium.

From the east, take I-8 West to I-15 North to the Friars Road Exit. Follow Friars Road west ½ mile to the stadium.

From the south, take I-805 North to I-8 and follow the directions provided above from the west.

## SPRING TRAINING

Peoria Stadium
8131 Paradise Lane
Peoria, AZ, 85382
(602) 486-7000
**Capacity:** 7,000 permanent seating, 3,000 in grass seating in outfield.
**Surface:** Grass
**Game time:** 1:05 P.M. or 7:05 p.m.

## MINOR LEAGUES

| Class | Team |
|---|---|
| AAA | Las Vegas Stars |
| AA | Wichita (KS) Wranglers |
| A | Rancho Cucamonga (CA) Quakes |
| A | Waterloo (IA) Diamonds |
| Short Season A | Spokane (WA) Indians |
| Rookie | Peoria (AZ) Padres |

As of 1994, the first season of pro baseball in Lake Elsinore, the closest minor-league team to San Diego is the Class A Lake Elsinore Storm of the California League. Lake Elsinore often plays the Rancho Cucamonga Quakes, the Padres' California League affiliate. The Storm's nickname was selected by team owner Ken Stickney, who, as owner of both the Quakes and the Las Vegas Thunder of the International Hockey League, has expressed a decided prefer-

ence for weather related monikers.

To reach the Diamond from San Diego, which is approximately 50 miles away, take I-15 north and exit at Diamond Drive, the second exit in Lake Elsinore.

**Ticket prices:** $5: box seats; $4: reserved seats; $3: general admission. For more information, call (909) 245-4487.

## THE PADRES AT JACK MURPHY STADIUM

**Sept. 22, 1969:** Willie Mays hits his 600th home run off of Mike Cockins of the Padres.

**June 12, 1970:** Dock Ellis of the Pittsburgh Pirates throws the only no-hitter in stadium history, blanking the Padres 2–0. He later claims to have been on LSD during the game.

**May 25, 1982:** Ferguson Jenkins of the Chicago Cubs gets his 3,000th strikeout.

**Sept. 20, 1984:** The Padres clinch their first division title, beating the San Francisco Giants 5–4.

**Oct. 7, 1984:** An error by Leon Durham of the Cubs allows the Padres to erase a 3–0 deficit and win 8–3 in Game 5 of the NLCS.

**Oct. 10, 1984:** The Padres get the only World Series win in their history, defeating the Detroit Tigers 5–3.

**Aug. 4, 1993:** Tony Gwynn has six hits against the Giants, his career best.

**Aug. 6, 1993:** Gwynn gets his 2,000th hit, a single off of the Colorado Rockies' Bruce Ruffin.

# Candlestick Park

It is loved. It is loathed. In a little more than 30 years, it has been home to both Willie Mays and Barry Bonds, probably the best players of their eras. But Candlestick Park remains best known for its weather conditions. It has been shaken by an earthquake and rattled by wind. Mark Twain is credited for saying the coldest winter he ever spent was a summer in San Francisco, but many a frozen Giants fan has since changed that to "a night at Candlestick."

Developer Charles Harney was the man—the villain, really—who in 1958 offered Candlestick Point, a rocky outcropping into San Francisco Bay, for the Giants' new home. Mayor George Christopher loved the site, as did Giants' owner Horace Stoneham. After two years at Seals Stadium, the Giants moved into Candlestick in 1960; by the time the ballpark was expanded and enclosed in 1971–72 to make room for the NFL 49ers, the Stick had become a meteorological legend. Unfortunately, the mayor and the owner had toured the area during the day. Days at Candlestick are gorgeous—the chill, fog and wind arrive at dusk.

To get around the elements, the Giants play more day games than any team in baseball other than the Chicago Cubs: 57 in 1994, up from 53 in '93 and 44 in '92. Go at night only if you're interested in the bizarre. During night games, hotdog wrappers and other paper products are routinely pushed into the outfield corners and trapped there by gusty winds, occasionally forcing outfielders to sift wildly through several inches of trash to recover a ball still in play. Flocks of birds have dive-bombed players; caps have been blown off the heads of infielders and pinned against the outfield wall.

## HOT TIPS FOR VISITING FANS

**Parking**
There are 8,300 spots for cars and 200 for buses in 77 acres around the stadium. Lots generally charge $10. It helps to arrive early—about an hour ahead—if you want to avoid bottlenecks. Traffic backs up in a particularly frustrating manner at the two exits off U.S. 101, the nearby north-south highway (and one very harrowing drive). Don't park in the surrounding area. The neighborhood can be rough, and your car might be damaged.

**Weather**
The wind and cold aren't the only odd conditions. The field is occasionally enveloped in a dense fog. It tends to stream over the top of the stands like smoke from a major forest fire, then it settles on the field like an apparition. Bundle up for night games, and though the weather is usually pleasant and warm during the day, a sweater or light jacket is never a bad idea.

**Media bites**
**Radio:** KNBR (680 AM) has Hank Greenwald on play-by-play with Ted Robinson and Mike Krukow. There is also a Spanish-language broadcast on KIQI (1010 AM) of all home games and select road games. Julio Gonzalez and Edgar Martinez handle the duties.

**TV:** KTVU-Fox (Channel 2) and SportsChannel (cable). SportsChannel has Mike Krukow and Duane Kuiper, both of whom KTVU also use.

 **Cuisine**
Yum-yum. Polish sausage is regarded by aficionados as one of the better concessions foods anywhere. Other fans contend that the top concessions item is a 12-clove garlic-chicken sandwich provided by The Stinking Rose, a hot spot in North Beach, San Francisco's Little Italy. The Mexican stand offers sensational garlic-chili French fries; if you're partial to hot foods, don't miss them.

Gordon Biersch microbrewery serves cold drafts of its exquisite beer, plus good pub food. As far as anyone knows, this was the first major league ballpark to serve wine (although whine is always served at Fenway Park). Concessions stands were recently widened, which means lines are shorter, but there are more of them.

After the game, head into town. San Francisco is as wonderful as you've heard; the city supports more restaurants per capita than any other in the country. Try Chinese at the nationally renowned (but inexpensive) House of Nanking (415-421-1429) on Kearney Street off Columbus Avenue. Also off Columbus, the Washington Square Bar & Grill (415-982-8123), affectionately known as "The Washbag," is a baseball insider's hangout.

## LODGING NEAR THE STADIUM
**Parc 55 Hotel**
55 Cyril Magnin St.
San Francisco, CA 94102
(415) 392-8000/(800) 338-1338
About 3 miles from the stadium.

**(Continued on page 74)**

---

## STADIUM STATS

**Location:** Candlestick Park, San Francisco, CA 94124
**Opened:** April 12, 1960
**Surface:** Bluegrass
**Capacity:** 62,000
**Outfield dimension:** LF 335, LC 365, CF 400, RC 365, RF 330.
**Services for fans with disabilities:** Call (415) 467-8000 for information.

## STADIUM FIRSTS

**Game:** April 12, 1960, 3–1 over the St. Louis Cardinals.
**Pitcher:** Sam Jones of the Giants.
**Batter:** Joe Cunningham of St. Louis.
**Hit:** Bill White of the Cardinals.
**Home run:** Leon Wagner of the Cardinals.

## GROUND RULES

- A ball hitting either foul pole or the attached screens above the black ring painted on the poles is a home run. A ball that hits either foul pole below the black ring or hits the top of the fence and bounds onto the playing fields is in play.
- A fair ball that bounds into the stands or over the fence is a two-base hit.
- A thrown ball that goes behind the backstop screen is one base, if it was thrown by the pitcher from the rubber. All other overthrows are two bases.
- A ball going over the fence under the screen attached to the foul poles is a home run.
- A ball that hits the fence of the dugouts or the bat rack is in play. A ball that goes into the dugout is out of play.
- A ball that goes into the bullpen is in play.

---

# IN THE HOT SEATS AT CANDLESTICK PARK

The Giants have a small season-ticket base. You can get good walk-up seats. The Mets and the Dodgers are the leading draws.

• **Good seats:** There are some nights when it gets so cold, there are no good seats, save the super boxes on the mezzanine level. They have heat. The rows in the lower stands rise gradually, so your view is limited if you sit behind anyone tall.

• **Bad Seats:** The left-field bleachers once stopped 20 to 30 feet from the fence, prompting fans to scramble from their seats and fight wildly over home-run balls that fell into the demilitarized zone. One reason the Giants moved their bleachers right to the wall before the 1993 season was to eliminate that kind of scramble. They are still not great seats, but at least you won't get stepped on anymore. The JumboTron scoreboard in right center pro-

vides a clear picture, but those sitting in the center- or right-field upper deck can't see it.

**Scalping:** There's not much of a market, because buyers can always walk up to the window and get a seat.

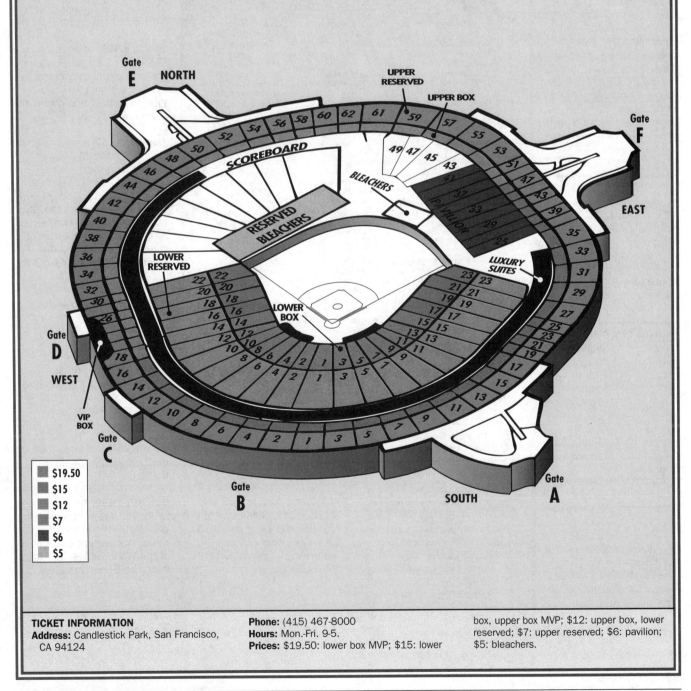

**TICKET INFORMATION**
**Address:** Candlestick Park, San Francisco, CA 94124

**Phone:** (415) 467-8000
**Hours:** Mon.-Fri. 9-5.
**Prices:** $19.50: lower box MVP; $15: lower

box, upper box MVP; $12: upper box, lower reserved; $7: upper reserved; $6: pavilion; $5: bleachers.

(Continued from page 72)

**Westin St. Francis**
335 Powell St.
San Francisco, CA 94102
(415) 397-7000/(800) 228-3000
About 7 miles from the stadium.

## GETTING TO CANDLESTICK PARK

**Public transportation:** The Municipal Railway (MUNI) and the San Mateo County Transit District (SamTrans) provide bus service to the stadium. For schedule information, call (415) 673-MUNI or SamTrans at (800) 660-4287.

**By car:** From San Francisco and points north, take U.S. 101 to the Cow Palace–Brisbane exit, not the Candlestick Park exit. Continue to Third and turn left over the freeway, continuing on Third Street, about ¼ mile, then make a right onto Jamestown Avenue. Go about 1¼ miles to the main lot.

From the south, exit from 101 onto Third. Then follow the directions above.

## SPRING TRAINING

Scottsdale Stadium
7408 E. Osborn Rd.
Scottsdale, AR 85251
**Capacity:** 10,000 (7,000 fixed seats and 3,000 lawn seating)
**Surface:** Material grass
**Game time:** 1:05 P.M. or 7:05 P.M.

## MINOR LEAGUES

| Class | Team |
|---|---|
| AAA | Phoenix Firebirds |
| AA | Shreveport (LA) Captains |
| A | San Jose (CA) Giants |
| A | Clinton (IA) Lumber Kings |
| Short Season A | Everett (WA) Giants |
| Rookie | Scottsdale (AZ) Giants |

The closest minor-league team to San Francisco is the Class A San Jose Giants of the California League. San Jose (one of the Giants' minor-league teams) frequently plays the Modesto A's, Oakland's California League affiliate. With the exception of only five years, 1959–61 and 1977–78, pro baseball has been played continuously in San Jose since 1947. But this city's baseball history goes back even further, to 1896, when San Jose was a charter franchise in the California State League, which folded after the '96 season ended.

To reach San Jose from the Bay Area, which is less than 45 miles away, take I-880 South to I-280 South. Exit at 10th Street. Turn right on 10th and then left on Alma; Municipal Stadium will be on the right.

**Ticket prices:** $6: box seats; $5: adults; $2: children under 10 (children under 4 are free) and $2: senior citizens 65 and over. For more information, call (408) 297-1435.

---

## HOME-FIELD ADVANTAGE

When Roger Craig managed the Giants, he ordered players not to complain about conditions. He knew the opposition would be unhappy and eager to leave, and figured the Giants would hold a home-field advantage.

Visiting clubs have a good deal to complain about. Only the home dugout has runway access to the clubhouse, so a visiting player has to walk from the left field dugout, across the field, and up the right-field line to reach the visitor's clubhouse. Until 1994, only the Giants' dugout had a heater, and the home team is still in sole possession of a little heated hut for a bullpen.

---

### GIANTS TEAM NOTEBOOK

**Franchise history**
Troy Trojans, 1879–82; New York Gothams, 1883–84; New York Giants, 1885–1957; San Francisco Giants, 1958–present.

**World Series titles**
1905, 1921, 1922, 1933, 1954

**National League pennants**
1905, 1911, 1912, 1913, 1917, 1921, 1922, 1923, 1924, 1933, 1936, 1937, 1951, 1954, 1962, 1989

**Division titles**
1971, 1987, 1989

**Most Valuable Players**
Larry Doyle, 1912
Bill Terry, 1930
Carl Hubbell, 1933, 1936
Willie Mays, 1954, 1965
Willie McCovey, 1969
Kevin Mitchell, 1989
Barry Bonds, 1993

**Rookies of the Year**
Willie Mays, 1951

Orlando Cepeda, 1958
Willie McCovey, 1959
Gary Matthews, 1973
John Montefusco, 1975

**Cy Young Award**
Mike McCormick, 1967

**Hall of Fame**
Christy Mathewson, 1936
John McGraw, 1937
William "Buck" Ewing, 1939
Willie Keeler 1939
Rogers Hornsby, 1942
Roger Bresnahan, 1945
Dan Brouthers, 1945
King Kelly, 1945
James O'Rourke, 1945
Jesse Burkett, 1946
Joe McGinnity, 1946
Frankie Frisch, 1947
Carl Hubbell, 1947
Mel Ott, 1951
Bill Terry, 1954
Gabby Hartnett, 1955
Ray Schalk, 1955
Bill McKechnie, 1962
Edd Roush, 1962
Burleigh Grimes, 1964
Tim Keefe, 1964
Monte Ward, 1964
Casey Stengel, 1966
Joe "Ducky" Medwick, 1968
Waite Hoyt, 1969

Dave Bancroft, 1971
Jake Beckley, 1971
Rube Marquard, 1971
Ross Youngs, 1972
Monte Irvin, 1973
George Kelly, 1973
Warren Spahn, 1973
Mickey Welch, 1973
Roger Conner, 1976
Fred Lindstrom, 1976
Amos Rusie, 1977
Willie Mays, 1979
Hack Wilson, 1979
Duke Snider, 1980
Johnny Mize, 1981
Travis Jackson, 1982
Juan Marichal, 1983
Hoyt Wilhelm, 1985
Ernie Lombardi, 1986
Willie McCovey, 1986
Joe Morgan, 1990
Gaylord Perry, 1991
Steve Carlton, 1994

**Retired numbers**
Christy Mattewson (Did not wear a number during career)
John McGraw (Did not wear a number during career)
3 Bill Terry
11 Carl Hubbell
14 Mel Ott
24 Willie Mays
27 Juan Marichal
44 Willie McCovey

---

## THE GIANTS AT CANDLESTICK PARK

**Oct. 5, 1962:** The Giants win their first World Series game at Candlestick, 2–0 over the New York Yankees.

**Oct. 15, 1962:** Billy Pierce holds the Yankees in a 5–2 win in Game 6 of the World Series.

**Sept. 22, 1963:** Willie McCovey hits three consecutive home runs against the New York Mets.

**Aug. 22, 1965:** Juan Marichal attacks Los Angeles Dodgers catcher John Roseboro with his bat.

**July 3, 1966:** Atlanta's Tony Cloninger, a pitcher, becomes the only player in National League history to hit two grand slams in one game. The Braves win 17–3.

**July 14, 1967:** Marichal is the victim of Eddie Mathews' 500th home run.

**Sept. 17, 1968:** Gaylord Perry of the Giants no-hits the St. Louis Cardinals 1–0. The next afternoon, Ray Washburn of the Cardinals returns the favor, no-hitting the Giants for a 2–0 win.

**July 10, 1984:** Fernando Valenzuela strikes out Dave Winfield, Reggie Jackson and George Brett in order. The next inning, Doc Gooden strikes out three more American Leaguers, and the National League wins the All-Star Game 3–1.

**Oct. 10, 1987:** The Giants hit three homers to edge past the Cardinals in Game 4 of the NLCS 4–2.

**Oct. 17, 1989:** An earthquake rocks the Bay Area, damaging Candlestick Park and causing the postponement of Game 3 of the World Series. Ten days later, the Series resumes.

---

# Kingdome

## STADIUM STATS

**Location:** 201 S. King St., Seattle WA 98104
**Opened:** 1976
**Surface:** AstroTurf
**Capacity:** 59,702
**Outfield dimensions:** LF 331, LCF 376, CF 405, RCF 352, RF 413.
**Services for fans with disabilities:** Seating available in sections 102-103, 136-139, 201-206, 212, 214, 220, 222, 238 and 240. For more information, call the ticket office.

## STADIUM FIRSTS

**Regular-season game:** April 6, 1977, 7–0 loss to the California Angels.
**Pitcher:** Diego Segui of the Mariners.
**Batter:** Jerry Remy of the Angels.

## GROUND RULES

**Photographers' area**
• The ball is in play if it hits the retaining fence and bounces back into the playing field.
**Hitting suspended objects**
• A batted ball hitting any suspended object, such as speakers, wires, streamers, etc., in fair territory shall be judged fair or foul in relation to where it lands or is touched by a fielder. If caught by a fielder, the batter is out and baserunners advance at their own risk.
• A batted ball hitting any suspended object in foul territory is a foul ball, regardless of where it lands or is touched by a fielder. If the ball is caught by a fielder, the batter is out and the baserunners advance at their own risk.

**(Continued on page 77)**

The Kingdome, home of the Seattle Mariners, isn't as regal as it once was—unless the subject is Ken Griffey Jr., heir apparent to the throne of baseball's best all-around player. The $67 million multipurpose facility, which also houses the NFL's Seahawks, was fittingly named when it opened in March 1976, but 18 years have left the Kingdome weather-beaten, turning the exterior of its gray roof to an unsightly rusty red.

The stadium covers more than nine acres and measures 250 feet at its apex. The constant threat of rain is the main reason an indoor baseball facility was deemed necessary; rain or shine, fans know a game will be played. Unfortunately, the concrete-base roof, unlike the translucent Teflon that drapes Minnesota's Metrodome, makes for a dim atmosphere that's not much different than outdoors in Seattle, where cloudy, rainy days are the norm.

The Mariners' 1994 home schedule was interrupted when ceiling tiles began falling, forcing games to be played in the opposition's stadiums until safety could be guaranteed. It was the first time in the Dome's 18-year history that any sporting event was called off. A $4 million contract was awarded in 1993 to strip the entire roof and resurface it, but the work won't be completed until 1995.

A typical Kingdome crowd can be heard as an echoing scream. The stadium is rarely full for a Mariners game, and sounds reverberate. Baseball has not yet been accepted in Seattle as the "in" thing to do, but a change in the team's losing fortunes would probably turn that around.

## HOT TIPS FOR VISITING FANS

**Parking**
The Kingdome has three lots—one to the north and two to the south—with a combined 4,000 spaces that are adequate for the crowds the Mariners draw. Parking is $5, but car pools of three or more persons receive a $1 discount. Fans with car problems (lost keys, a dead battery, etc.) should contact a Kingdome lot attendant for assistance.

**Weather**
Rain is not uncommon, so a light jacket and an umbrella are always good to have as you make your way to the Kingdome. As long as there's a roof there, you don't have to worry about the weather once you're inside.

**Media bites**
**Radio:** KIRO (710 AM).
**TV:** KSTW (Channel 11). Dave Niehaus, Ron Fairly, Chip Caray and Ken Levine, who was one of the writers of the television show M*A*S*H, announce the games.

**Cuisine**
The Mariners offer a variety of brand-name foods at concessions stands and portable carts throughout the Kingdome. The offerings include Coca-Cola products, Dreyer's ice cream, Ezell's fried chicken, Jana's cookies, Nalley's nachos, Starbucks coffee, Espresso beverages, TCBY frozen yogurt, Ballpark franks, Pure Water natural mineral waters and Seattle smoked barbecue.

Opportunites for shopping, eating and entertainment are plentiful in nearby Pioneer Square, where the city was started in the late 19th century. Sneakers, a sports bar, is a popular pregame and postgame hangout. For more formal dining, there's F.X. McRory's Chop House (206-623-4800), New Orleans Creole Restaurant (206-622-2563) and Larry's (206-624-7665).

Visitors also can take advantage of the waterfront, which is a short walk northwest of the Kingdome and features several seafood eateries. The waterfront also affords a great view of the sprawling Olympic Mountains and Puget Sound.

## LODGING NEAR THE STADIUM

**Westin Hotel Seattle**
1900 Fifth Ave.
Seattle, WA 98101
(800) 228-3000/(206) 728-1000
2 miles from the stadium.

**Holiday Inn Crown Plaza**
1113 Sixth Ave.
Seattle, WA 98101
(206) 464-1980/(800) HOLIDAY
About 1 mile from the stadium.

## GETTING TO THE KINGDOME

**Public transportation:** Catch a southbound bus on Third Avenue. Get off at Third and Jackson, about 2 blocks from the Kingdome. For more information, call Metro Transit at (206) 553-3000.
**By car:** From the north, I-5 to the Airport Way exit, No. 164. Right onto Dearborn Street to Airport Way South. Go left and then left again onto Fourth Avenue South. Go ¼ mile to South Royal Brougham Way. Right to Kingdome Lot B or C.

From the south, Spokane Street exit (No. 163) on I-5 North. Follow Spokane (lower

**(Continued on page 77)**

# In the Hot Seats at the Kingdome

The Mariners sell anywhere from 8,000 to 15,000 season tickets. It is usually possible to walk up and get good tickets.

• **Bad seats:** The worst seats are in the upper deck. They're quite a distance from the field. You still can see the game, but it's a miniature version.

• **Special programs:** Every Sunday home game is seniors day, which allows fans 62 or older to buy seats on a two-for-one basis. Also offered are a $20 birthday package and a $25 anniversary package, with ticket costs extra. Paid "will call" tickets can be picked up at the courtesy window outside Gate D.

**Scalping:** Games rarely sell out, so there's not much market for scalpers.

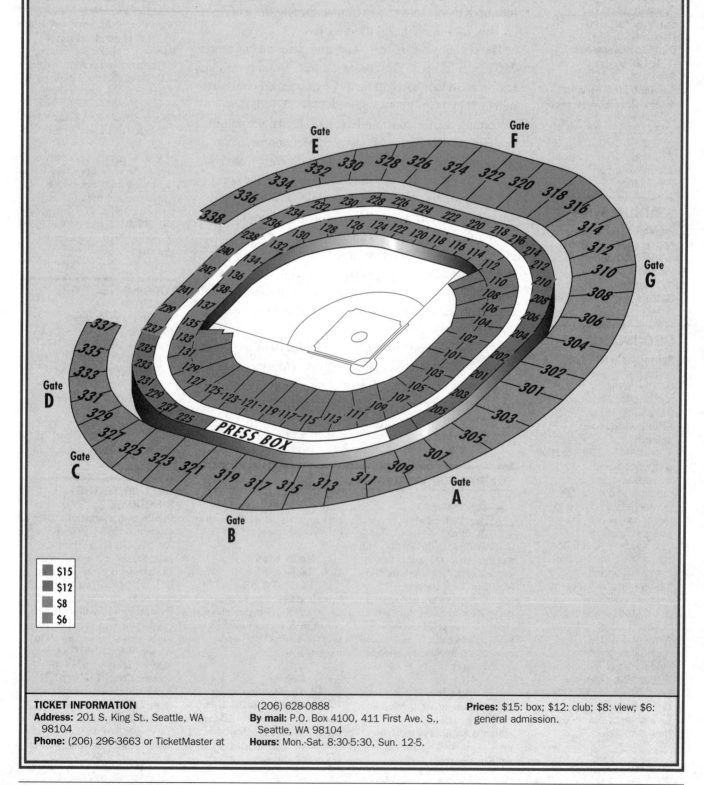

- ■ $15
- ■ $12
- ■ $8
- ■ $6

**TICKET INFORMATION**
**Address:** 201 S. King St., Seattle, WA 98104
**Phone:** (206) 296-3663 or TicketMaster at

(206) 628-0888
**By mail:** P.O. Box 4100, 411 First Ave. S., Seattle, WA 98104
**Hours:** Mon.-Sat. 8:30-5:30, Sun. 12-5.

**Prices:** $15: box; $12: club; $8: view; $6: general admission.

**(Continued from page 75)**
level) to Fourth Avenue South, to South Royal Brougham and proceed to Lot B or C.

From the east, I-90 to the Dearborn Street exit. Left on Fourth Avenue South to South Royal Brougham. Right to Lot B or C.

## SPRING TRAINING
Peoria Sports Complex
8131 West Paradise Lane
Peoria, AZ 85382
(602) 412-3061
**Capacity:** 10,000 (7,000 seats and 3,000 on lawn)
**Surface:** Grass
**Game time:** 1:05 P.M.
**Ticket information:** (602) 784-4444

## MINOR LEAGUES

| Class | Team |
|---|---|
| AAA | Calgary Cannons |
| AA | Jacksonville (FL) Suns |
| A | Riverside (CA) Pilots |
| A | Appleton (WI) Foxes |
| Short Season A | Bellingham (WA) Mariners |
| Rookie | Peoria (AZ) Mariners |

The closest minor-league team to Seattle is the short-season Class A Everett Giants of the Northwest League. The Giants frequently play the Bellingham Mariners, Seattle's Northwest League affiliate. Everett's first pro team, the Smokestackers, disbanded after only one season in 1905. Baseball did not return until 1984, when the current franchise made its debut. The Giants play in Everett Memorial Stadium, where Ken Griffey Jr. hit his first professional home run, in 1987.

## HOME-FIELD ADVANTAGE

It's hard to say there's any advantage to playing in a stadium where the roof is collapsing and the fans are lukewarm. The Mariners played an extended road trip in '94 because of the Kingdome's problem with falling ceiling tiles. Stadium problems are nothing new to Seattle, where an NBA basketball game was once rained out because of roof problems at the arena. The good news: The Kingdome's roof revived talk of a new park in Seattle.

### MARINERS TEAM NOTEBOOK

| Franchise history | Rookie of the Year | Hall of Fame |
|---|---|---|
| Seattle Mariners, 1977–present | Alvin Davis, 1984 | Gaylord Perry, 1991 |

To reach Everett Stadium from Seattle, which is 28 miles away, take I-5 north to the Broadway exit, No. 192. The ballpark is ¼ mile down Broadway.

**Ticket prices:** $6.50: adult reserved seats; $4.50: reserved seats for children 14 and under; $4.50: adult general admission; $3.50: general admission for children 14 and under. For more information call (206) 258-3673.

## THE MARINERS AT THE KINGDOME

**June 9, 1979:** "Willie Horton Night" sees Horton hit his 300th home run.

**May 6, 1982:** Gaylord Perry gets his 300th win, beating the New York Yankees 7–3.

**April 2, 1990:** Brian Holman sets down the first 26 Oakland A's before Ken Phelps homers. The Mariners win 6–1.

**June 2, 1990:** Randy Johnson throws the first no-hitter in Mariners history, beating the Detroit Tigers 2–0.

**Aug. 31, 1990:** Ken Griffey and Ken Griffey Jr. became the first father and son to play in the same game.

**April 22, 1993:** Chris Bosio no-hits the Boston Red Sox 7–0.

**July 28, 1993:** Ken Griffey Jr. homers in his eighth consecutive game, but the Mariners lose 5-1 to the Minnesota Twins.

**Sept. 22, 1993:** Nolan Ryan's last appearance: He pitches to six batters and is unable to retire any.

**May 23, 1994:** Ken Griffey Jr. breaks Mickey Mantle's record for most home runs in the first two months of the season, hitting his 21st in a 7–5 loss to the Oakland A's.

## GROUND RULES
**(Continued from page 75)**

• A batted ball sticking in any supended object in foul territory will be called a strike. A batted ball sticking in any suspended object in fair territory will be a ground-rule double.

**Outfield area**
• A fair batted ball clearing the wall is a home run. A fair batted ball bouncing over the wall is a ground-rule double.

**Dugouts**
• A ball will be considered thrown into the dugout only if it hits an object or person within the dugout. A thrown ball hitting the lip at the base of the dugout or the frame around the dugout and bouncing back into the playing field is in play.
• A thrown ball hitting any player's equipment that is left on or in front of the lip at the base of the dugout will be considered in the dugout.

**Bullpen areas**
• A ball will be considered in play going into the bullpen area and coming back out onto the playing field. A ball going into the bullpen area and obstructed by a player, equipment or bench will be called dead.

# Busch Stadium

## STADIUM STATS

**Location:** 250 Stadium Plaza, St. Louis, MO 63102
**Opened:** May 12, 1966
**Surface:** AstroTurf
**Capacity:** 56,627
**Outfield dimensions:** LF 350, LC 378, CF 402, RC 378, RF 350.
**Services for fans with disabilities:** Seating available behind home plate in the field-box and loge-reserve sections.

## STADIUM FIRSTS

**Regular season game:** May 12, 1966, 4–3 over the Atlanta Braves in 12 innings.
**Pitcher:** Ray Washburn of the Cardinals.
**Batter:** Felipe Alou of the Braves.
**Hit:** Gary Geiger of the Braves.
**Home Run:** May 13, 1966, by Julian Javier of the Cardinals.

## GROUND RULES

• A fly ball hitting above yellow line on the outfield wall is a home run.
• A fair ball bounding into field boxes, bleachers, over the fence in the outfield or enclosed area in left- or right-field corners or going through or under fences is a double.
• A ball rolling onto top step of dugouts is in play. The photographer's area is part of the dugout.
• A pitch, thrown or batted ball that hits anyone on the field, except as otherwise provided for in the Official Rules, is in play.
• Any batted ball hitting tarpaulin is a foul ball.
• A ball going through the wire behind plate or lodging in it is one base on a throw by pitcher and two bases if thrown by a fielder.

Busch Stadium was the second of the oval, dual-purpose cookie-cutter stadiums, and among its genre, Busch is considered a cut above the average (which isn't saying much). But the reasons for this advantage rest more with the fans and surrounding area than with the ballpark.

St. Louis is a baseball town, and the game's traditions run deep here. The park is splashed with red as fans wear apparel in the team colors. The crowd isn't rowdy, but it's always into the game. The franchise has a rich history of colorful teams and winning—from the Gashouse Gang of the 1930s and early '40s to Whitey Herzog's base-stealing ballclubs of the 1980s. A statue of Hall of Famer Stan "the Man" Musial greets visitors by the prime entrance.

The park was part of a huge urban-renewal project that included construction of the Gateway Arch on the banks of the Mississippi River. Small arches are built into the rim of the stadium in the upper deck, and the Arch (about 8 blocks away) is visible from the stands beyond the left-field foul pole. If only the field were grass. The park had a natural surface the first four years but converted to AstroTurf because the heat and conversion to football took its toll. The football team is gone, but the artificial surface stays.

The ballclub is owned by the Anheuser-Busch brewery, and the connection is in evidence in more than just the beer selection. A giant scoreboard with the company logo sits in left-center, and when a Cardinal hits a home run, the A-B eagle in the logo "flies" around the scoreboard. Instead of "Take Me Out to the Ballgame" for the seventh-inning stretch, the club plays the Budweiser theme and the crowd claps along. (Traditionalists can breathe easy: "Take Me Out to the Ballgame" is played in the eighth inning). Even the brewery's Clydesdales make appearances on special occasions.

## HOT TIPS FOR VISITING FANS

**Parking**
Unless you are in a great rush to leave after the game, use the two stadium garages ($5) across the street on the east and west sides. They're convenient—connected to the park by a pedestrian bridge. Together, they offer room for 5,000 cars, and while they fill close to capacity most every game, you usually can get in.

Several other lots and garages are within a few blocks of the park, charging from $2 to $10-plus.

**Weather**
If you've never been to St. Louis in summer, brace yourself. The summer months are hot and very humid. And nights aren't necessarily cooler in July and August—90 degrees at 6 P.M. isn't news. You have to take your chances—you could find a perfect day for baseball, or an afternoon in a 50,000-seat sauna. April nights can be chilly, but September is usually very pleasant.

**Media bites**
**Radio:** KMOX (1120 AM). Hall of Famer Jack Buck, his son Joe and ex-Cardinals player Mike Shannon handle the announcing chores on radio and on Channel 11.
**TV:** KPLR-TV (Channel 11) and Prime Network (cable), which has commentary by Joe Buck and ex-Cards reliever Al "the Mad Hungarian" Hrabosky.

**Cuisine**
OK, but nothing special. St. Louis is basically a hot-dog-and-beer town at the park. The dogs are pretty tasty, and the bratwurst is definitely a cut above normal. The beer is Anheuser-Busch in all its glory, and don't look for anything other than its products. A food court on the lower concourse offers a nice selection of burgers, brats, etc. A kids area on the lower concourse features a play area and kids menu at concessions.

Because the park is downtown, fans have an excellent choice of pre- and postgame spots. Charlie Gitto's Pasta House on North Sixth Street and Mike Shannon's (314-421-1540) on North Seventh Street, which has steaks and seafood and lots of sports memorabilia, are very popular spots within a couple of blocks of the stadium. Umpires and writers frequent the Missouri Bar & Grill (314-231-2234) on North Tucker Boulevard, across from the St. Louis Post Dispatch. Players will pop in Alligator Alley Bar & Broiler (314-231-4287) on South Seventh after games. Before Sunday afternoon games, head for the Adams Mark Hotel (314-241-7400) for its wonderful brunch. It's just a 3-block walk from the stadium. One of the best steakhouses in the midwest is Dierdorf & Hart's restaurant (ex-football-Cardinals Dan Dierdorf and Jim Hart are part owners) in Union Station (314-421-1772)—a five-minute cab ride out Market Street.

# IN THE HOT SEATS AT BUSCH STADIUM

The Cardinals attract 2 million fans a year—they have a season-ticket base of more than 17,000 and draw from all over Missouri and four neighboring states, so advance sales are brisk and start in the offseason. The Cards begin to receive mail orders for the coming season in September, four months before they begin processing them. All the field boxes are sold on a season-ticket basis (except for disabled-accessible seating), as are loge boxes and reserves on the infield. You can still get behind home plate in the upper deck—terrace boxes, reserve and general admission. On the lower levels, you have to go down the lines, but the sightlines in the park are pretty good.

• **Good seats:** Upper decks in the circular stadiums of the 1970s are high, no getting around it. But the Busch top level is not as steep as some of its cousins, so it's not a bad seat. The terrace boxes (at $12, not exactly a bargain) are a fine seat if you can get on the infield. The bleachers in left-center and right-center fields are also popular. They're sold on the day of game only, for just $5. But one word of warning: You're in the sun during day games, and the heat can be oppressive.

• **Bad seats:** Be careful of the back rows in the loge reserve. Like most of the parks in Busch's mold, an overhang problem exists under the second deck. And they tuck you back a fair piece at Busch. You won't get wet during rain delays, but you'll miss high flies and the gorgeous view of the Arch.

**Scalping:** Scalpers will work the bridge connecting the Stadium to the parking garage, and sometimes you'll find them in front of the main gates. Demand is high for Cubs games. Fans sometimes buy from season ticketholders selling an extra or two at face value in front of the park.

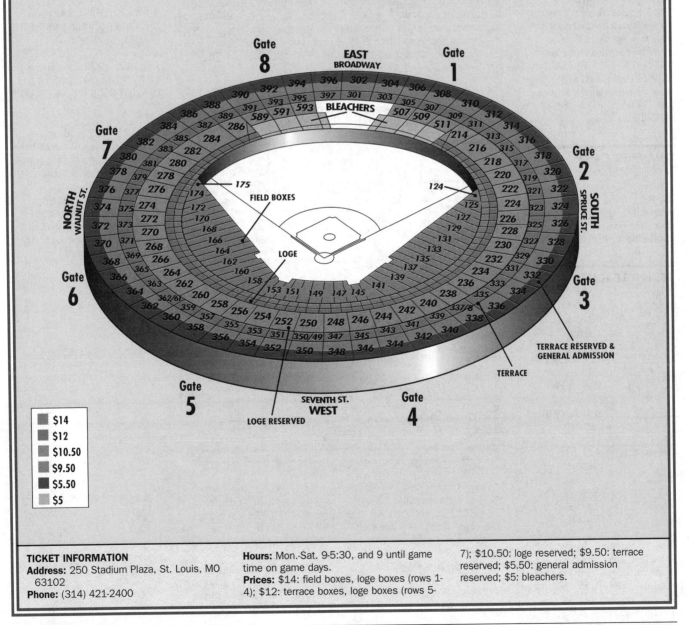

**TICKET INFORMATION**
**Address:** 250 Stadium Plaza, St. Louis, MO 63102
**Phone:** (314) 421-2400

**Hours:** Mon.-Sat. 9-5:30, and 9 until game time on game days.
**Prices:** $14: field boxes, loge boxes (rows 1-4); $12: terrace boxes, loge boxes (rows 5-7); $10.50: loge reserved; $9.50: terrace reserved; $5.50: general admission reserved; $5: bleachers.

## LODGING NEAR THE STADIUM

**Adams Mark Hotel**
Fourth and Chestnut
St. Louis, MO 63102
(314) 241-7400/(800) 444-2326
3 blocks from the stadium.

**The St. Louis Marriott Pavilion**
1 S. Broadway
St. Louis, MO 63102
(314)421-1776/(800) 228-9290
Across the street from the stadium.

## GETTING TO BUSCH STADIUM

**Public transportation:** Bi-State Development buses go to the stadium. For more information, call (314) 231-2345.
**By car:** From the north, take I-55 South, I-64 West. Then I-70 West or U.S. 40 West to the Poplar Street Bridge. Continue to the Busch Stadium exit and follow signs to the Stadium.

From the west or the south, use I-55 North, I-70 East, I-44 East or US 40 East to St. Louis, then go to the Busch Stadium exit. Follow signs to the Stadium.

## TRAINING CAMP

Al Lang Stadium
180 Second Ave. S.E.
St. Petersburg, FL 33701
**Capacity:** 7,600
**Surface:** Grass
**Game time:** 1:05 P.M.

## MINOR LEAGUES

| Class | Team |
|---|---|
| AAA | Louisville Redbirds |
| AA | Arkansas Travelers |
| A | St. Petersburg (FL) Cardinals |
| A | Madison (WI) Hatters |
| A | Savannah (GA) Cardinals |
| Short Season A | New Jersey Cardinals |
| Rookie | Johnson City (TN) Cardinals |
| Rookie | Chandler (AZ) Cardinals |

The closest minor-league team is the Class A Peoria Chiefs of the Midwest League. Pro baseball returned to Peoria in 1983 after a 26 year absence. One of the Chiefs' opponents is the Madison Hatters, the Cardinals' Midwest League affiliate. The Chiefs, a Chicago Cubs farm team since 1985, have sent such prominent players as Greg Maddux, Mark Grace and Derrick May on to Wrigley Field.

To reach Peoria's Pete Vonachen Stadium, approximately 170 miles from St. Louis, take the North University exit from I-74. Turn left on North University and then left on Nebraska. The ballpark will be on your left.

**Ticket prices:** $5: box seats; $4: reserved seats; $3: general admission. For more information, call (309) 688-1622.

## HOME-FIELD ADVANTAGE

Busch Stadium is not a home-run hitters' park. It traditionally has been considered a big park geared to line-drive hitters who could sting the ball into the gaps of a spacious AstroTurf outfield. Over the years, outfield speed was as much a tradmark of the club as the traditional Cardinal-on-a-bat logo. Lou Brock, Lonnie Smith, Willie McGee and Vince Coleman patrolled the plastic grass in the '70s and '80s, and the Cards finished with the best record in the NL East Division four times and appeared in three World Series in the '80s. (They were often contenders but never won the division in the '70s). The Cardinals haven't ranked higher than eighth in the National League in home runs since 1967. Between 1982 and '91, they finished last every year but one.

The reputation of the park is still true, but not to the extent it was in the '80s. The walls have been lowered from 10 feet to 8 feet, and the centerfield fence is 402–feet—12 feet shorter than previously. The power alleys also are about 10 feet closer than they once were. Still, the Cards tend to be a club built around line-drive hitters (center fielder Ray Lankford represents the speed and power combination they seek), and they remain much tougher at home than on the road. In 1993 they were 17 games over .500 at Busch, five games under .500 elsewhere.

### CARDINALS TEAM NOTEBOOK

**Franchise history**
St. Louis Cardinals, 1892-present

**World Series titles**
1926, 1931, 1934, (tie)
1942, 1944, 1946, 1964, 1967, 1982

**National League pennants**
1926, 1928, 1930, 1931, 1934, 1942, 1943, 1944, 1946, 1964, 1967, 1968, 1982, 1985, 1987

**Division titles**
1982, 1985, 1987

**Most Valuable Players**
Roger Hornsby, 1925
Bob O' Farrell, 1926
Jim Bottomley, 1928
Frankie Frisch, 1931
Dizzy Dean, 1934
Joe "Ducky" Medwick, 1937
Mort Cooper, 1942
Stan Musial, 1943, 1946, 1948
Marty Marion, 1944

Ken Boyer, 1964
Orlando Cepeda, 1967
Bob Gibson, 1968
Joe Torre, 1971
Keith Hernandez, 1979 (tie)
Willie McGee, 1985

**Rookie of the Year**
Wally Moon, 1954
Bill Virdon, 1955
Bake McBride, 1974
Vince Coleman, 1985
Todd Worrell, 1986

**Cy Young Award**
Bob Gibson, 1968, 1970

**Hall of Fame**
John McGraw, 1937
Cy Young, 1937
Grover Cleveland Alexander, 1938
Rogers Hornsby, 1942
Roger Bresnahan, 1945
Wilbert Robinson, 1945
Frankie Frisch, 1947
Jesse Burkett, 1948
Mordecai Brown, 1949
Kid Nichols, 1949
Dizzy Dean, 1953

Bobby Wallace, 1953
Rabbit Maranville, 1954
Dazzy Vance, 1955
Bill McKechnie, 1962
Burleigh Grimes, 1964
Miller Huggins, 1964
Pud Galvin, 1965
Branch Rickey, 1967
Joe "Ducky" Medwick, 1968
Stan Musial, 1969
Jesse Haines, 1970
Jake Beckley, 1971
Chick Hafey, 1971
Jim Bottomley, 1974
Roger Connor, 1976
Bob Gibson, 1981
John Mize, 1981
Walter Alson, 1983
Lou Brock, 1985
Enos Slaughter, 1985
Hoyt Wilhelm, 1985
Red Schoendienst, 1989
Steve Carlton, 1994

**Retired numbers**
6 Stan Musial
14 Ken Boyer
17 Dizzy Dean
20 Lou Brock
45 Bob Gibson
85 August A. Busch Jr.

## THE CARDINALS AT BUSCH STADIUM

**Oct. 8, 1967:** Bob Gibson wins his second game of the World Series, beating the Boston Red Sox 6–0.

**Oct. 2, 1968:** In Game 1 of the 1968 fall classic, Gibson strikes out a World Series-record 17 batters in the Cardinals' 4–0 victory over the Detroit Tigers.

**Set. 15, 1969:** Steve Carlton strikes out 19 New York Mets in a 4–3 loss.

**Sept. 10, 1974:** Lou Brock breaks Maury Wills' record for steals in a season, getting his 105th against the Philadelphia Phillies.

**April 16, 1978:** Bob Forsch throws a no-hitter against the Phillies, winning 5–0.

**Aug. 13, 1979:** Lou Brock singles off Dennis Lamp of the Chicago Cubs for his 3,000th hit.

**Sept. 23, 1979:** Brock steals his 938th base, establishing an all-time record not broken until Rickey Henderson.

**Oct. 20, 1982:** Joaquin Andujar and Bruce Sutter team up to win Game 7 of the World Series, 6–3 over the Milwaukee Brewers.

# The Ballpark in Arlington

## STADIUM STATS

**Location:** 1000 Ballpark Way, Arlington, TX 76011
**Opened:** April 1, 1994
**Surface:** Grass
**Capacity:** 43,521
**Outfield dimensions:** LF 334, LC 388, CF 400, RC 377-407, RF 325.
**Services for fans with disabilities:** Call (817) 273-5222 for information.

## STADIUM FIRSTS

**Regular-season game:** April 11, 1994, 4–3 loss to the Milwaukee Brewers.
**Pitcher:** Kenny Rogers of the Rangers.
**Batter:** Pat Listach of the Brewers.
**Hit:** Pat Listach of the Brewers.
**Home run:** Dave Nilsson of the Brewers.

## GROUND RULES

• Ball striking railing separating photographers bench or facing of dugout roof and rebounding to field is considered in the dugout.

• A fly ball hitting the foul poles or screens above the fence line is a home run.

• A ball lodging in the outfield-fence padding or in the manually operated scoreboard in the left-field fence is a ground-rule double.

Is anything done on a small scale in Texas? Of course not. That's why The Ballpark in Arlington—even the name is gigantic—is definitely Texas. It's the tallest building in an area where one- and two-story buildings spread across the Texas plains and flatlands. It takes up 1.4 million square feet. Even the grass reflects the grand scale of the Lone Star State—it was grown on a farm in "nearby" Combine, three hours away.

While the exterior facade is all Texas—granite from Texas quarries, Texas-style cast-stone carvings, 35 Longhorn steer heads and 21 Lone Star emblems—its arches bring memories of the original Comiskey Park in Chicago. Inside, the ballpark continues its salute to baseball's most-treasured scenes. In left field, a 14-foot wall and a hand-operated scoreboard bring a touch of Fenway Park. The foul poles made the trip across the street from old Arlington Stadium. In right field, the two-deck porch recalls Detroit's Tiger Stadium; atop sits a sign that reads "Hit It Here and Win a Free Suit," à la Brooklyn's Ebbets Field. If you begin to forget where you are, the Lone Star emblems on the aisle seats (which have cup holders) should bring you back to Texas.

The Ballpark is in the suburbs, so there's no downtown view. No matter: The Rangers built one, and what they built looks like a block of buildings out of New Orleans. The main structure is a four-story office building with floor-to-ceiling glass walls and steel trusses. Those who work in it can watch the game from their balconies. One complaint fans have is that the replay board is on top of the right-field porch, but designers planned it that way. They didn't want the board to detract from the game.

The Ballpark in Arlington is enclosed, with one small tunnel that runs between the right-field porch and the foul pole. It lets in a tad of light, an idiosyncrasy that makes it unique. On the right day, a left-handed batter might get just the right pitch and crash a baseball completely out of the stadium. It's a once-in-a-century shot. But that's Texas for you.

## HOT TIPS FOR VISITING FANS

**Parking**
Nine lots are available, each costing $5. Each lot is color-coded and is named for a Texas historical figure from the era of the Republic of Texas, in the 1830s and 1840s. Check out the Walk of Fame on your way in. It's a brick walk, ranging from 18 to 70 feet wide,

which rings the perimeter of the park. It's divided into panels featuring each year the Rangers have been in the American League (their first season was 1972), with the entire roster from each season included on the bricks. Fans can buy bricks and make their own inscriptions.

**Weather**
With the exception of the occasional gully-washer, Texas weather in baseball season is always hot.

**Media bites**
**Radio:** WBAP (820 AM—English), KXEB (910 AM—Spanish) .
**TV:** KTVT (Channel 11) and Home Sports Entertainment (cable). Former major leaguers Steve Busby and Jim Sundberg are the KTVT announcers.

**Cuisine**
Aside from the traditional stadium food of hot dogs and pizza, the Ballpark in Arlington serves smoked meats made in the team's own smokehouse. Also, a sports grill run by T.G.I. Friday's behind the upper home-run porch in right field draws a crowd because of its full view of the playing field. The Ballpark also houses its own bakery, which supplies fresh-baked cookies and other desserts. The concessions stands sell Miller, Coors and Budweiser beers. For more formal dining, the private Diamond Club is open to members before and after games. The club seats about 500 on four tiers and provides a full view of the field.

After the game, some fans head to Bobby Valentine's Sports Gallery Cafe (817-261-1000), a five-minute drive from the ballpark. The walls are filled with sports memorabilia, including mementos from Valentine's career; the Nolan Ryan Room features baseball cards from each of Ryan's 5,217 strikeout victims. If you don't want to watch one of the 25 televisions, there is

(Continued on page 83)

# IN THE HOT SEATS AT THE BALLPARK IN ARLINGTON

Though the Ballpark has been drawing large crowds, it hasn't been selling out as consistently as some other new parks. Tickets are available for all games on a walk-up basis.

• **Good seats:** There are 1,500 bleacher seats. Always a ballpark delight, the benches were moved from old Arlington Stadium, and they are sun-drenched. For a real old-time, knothole-gang feel, ask for tickets in the right-field porch that allow you to view the game through an opening in the fence.

• **Bad seats:** The terrace club boxes in the last few rows of the lower deck can be blocked by railings and the overhang, and the grandstand reserved seats on the upper deck give you as good a view of the traffic pattern at the Dallas–Fort Worth airport as of the ballgame.

**Scalping:** The new stadium is drawing big crowds, but plenty of ticketholders are willing to sell for face value.

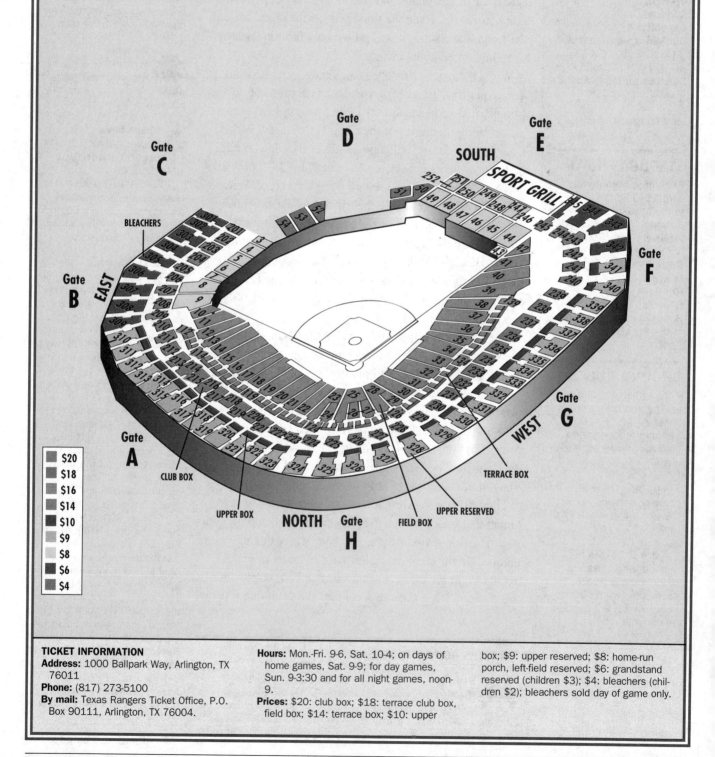

$20
$18
$16
$14
$10
$9
$8
$6
$4

## TICKET INFORMATION

**Address:** 1000 Ballpark Way, Arlington, TX 76011
**Phone:** (817) 273-5100
**By mail:** Texas Rangers Ticket Office, P.O. Box 90111, Arlington, TX 76004.

**Hours:** Mon.-Fri. 9-6, Sat. 10-4; on days of home games, Sat. 9-9; for day games, Sun. 9-3:30 and for all night games, noon-9.
**Prices:** $20: club box; $18: terrace club box, field box; $14: terrace box; $10: upper box; $9: upper reserved; $8: home-run porch, left-field reserved; $6: grandstand reserved (children $3); $4: bleachers (children $2); bleachers sold day of game only.

(Continued from page 81)

free shuttle service to and from every home game.

## LODGING NEAR THE STADIUM

**Arlington Marriott**
1500 Convention Center Dr.
Arlington, TX 76011
(817) 261-8200/(800) 228-9290
Across the street from the park.

**Hyatt Regency Dallas (at Reunion Tower)**
300 Reunion Blvd.
Dallas, TX 75207
(214) 651-1234/(800) 233-1234
Approximately 20 miles from the park.

## GETTING TO THE BALL-PARK IN ARLINGTON

**Public transportation:** Shuttle buses go to the stadium from the Six Flags Mall. For more information, call (817) 640-3251.
**By car:** From Dallas, take I-30 west to the Ballpark Way exit. Go left on Stadium Drive East to parking lots.
From Fort Worth, take I-30 east to the Cooper Street exit. Go south to Randol Mill Road, then left to parking lots.
From South Arlington, take Highway 360 north to Division Street. Go left to Stadium Drive, then right to parking lots.

## SPRING TRAINING

Charlotte County Stadium
Rangers Complex
2300 El Jobean Rd.
Port Charlotte, FL 33948
**Capacity:** 6,026
**Surface:** Bermuda grass

## HOME-FIELD ADVANTAGE

It pays to be a left-handed batter at The Ballpark in Arlington. The right-field foul pole is 325 feet from home plate, and the fence is only 8 feet high.

Other than that, home runs aren't easy to get. The fence moves out to 407 feet in right-center field, its deepest point. The power alley goes from 381 to 377 feet at one corner of the bullpen. That quirk can make life difficult for opponents' outfielders. Playing the indentation is one more thing they have to be aware of when they come to town.

While the hitters don't get a break with the outfield fence, they do get a break with the limited foul territory. The distance between home plate and the screen is 60 feet, meaning the fans are closer to the batter than the pitcher is. Down the lines, the first row of seats is only 9½ feet from the foul poles.

### RANGERS TEAM NOTEBOOK

| Franchise history | Most Valuable Player | Hall of Fame |
|---|---|---|
| Washington Senators, 1961–71; Texas Rangers, 1972–present | Jeff Burroughs, 1974 | Ted Williams, 1966 Ferguson Jenkins, 1991 Gaylord Perry, 1991 |
| | **Rookie of the Year** Mike Hargrove, 1974 | |

**Game time:** 1:30 P.M.
**Tickets:** (813) 625-9500

## MINOR LEAGUES

| Class | Team |
|---|---|
| AAA | Oklahoma 89ers |
| AA | Tulsa Drillers |
| A | Port Charlotte (FL) Rangers |
| A | Charleston (SC) Riverdogs |
| Short Season A (NY) | Hudson Valley Renegades |
| Rookie | Port Charlotte (FL) Rangers |

The Rangers' closest minor-league affiliate is the AAA Oklahoma City 89ers of the American Association. The team's nickname was selected by a local schoolteacher in honor of the land rush of 1889 and the western pioneers from that era. Such prominent players as Rusty Staub, Ryne Sandberg, Ruben Sierra and Juan Gonzalez have been 89ers since the team played its first game in 1961.

To reach Oklahoma City's All-Sports Stadium, approximately 210 miles from Arlington, take the State Fairgrounds/10th Street exit from I-44 at the intersection of I-44 and I-40. Go right onto 19th Street. Go right at the first light, 89ers Drive. The ballpark will be in front of you.

**Ticket prices:** $6.50: box seats; $5.50: reserved seats. $4.50: general admission. For more information, call (405) 946-8989.

## THE RANGERS AT THE BALLPARK IN ARLINGTON

**April 27, 1994:** Joe Carter of the Toronto Blue Jays drives in his 30th run of the month, setting a major-league record for RBIs in April.

**May 14, 1994:** Texas moves into first place with a 5–2 win over the Chicago White Sox.

**June 13, 1994:** Jose Canseco hits three home runs and knocks in a career-high eight runs as Texas beats Seattle, 17–9.

**July 5, 1994:** First-place Texas beats the first-place Cleveland Indians and goes on to take the series, two games to one.

**July 28, 1994:** Kenny Rogers of the Rangers pitches the 12th perfect game in major-league history, beating the California Angels 4–0.

## STADIUM STATS

**Location:** 300 Bremner Blvd., Toronto, ON, Canada M5V 3B3
**Opened:** June 5, 1989
**Surface:** AstroTurf 8
**Capacity:** 51,000
**Outfield dimensions:** LF 328, LC 375, CF 400, RC 375, RF 328.
**Services for fans with disabilities:** Seating available in the first and second level between home plate and the bases in sections 115-128. Additional seating is in sections 109-112 and 131-134 in the outfield first level, and in sections 207-208 and 240-241 in outfield second level.

## STADIUM FIRSTS

**Regular-season game:** June 5, 1989, 5–3 loss to the Milwaukee Brewers.
**Pitcher:** Jimmy Key of the Blue Jays.
**Batter:** Paul Molitor of the Brewers.
**Hit:** Paul Molitor.
**Home run:** Fred McGriff of the Blue Jays.

## GROUND RULES

• A ball hitting the fence or screen in back of home plate is in play.
• Ball going into camera booth behind home plate, one base if thrown by pitcher from rubber; other thrown balls, two bases.
• A ball hitting the padding and bouncing over the fence is two bases.
• A fair batted or thrown ball lodged in the padding is worth two bases.
• A fair batted or thrown ball that is on the steps of the dugout is considered in the dugout.
• Ball hitting padding on outfield fence in foul territory is dead.

# SkyDome

SkyDome, the only stadium in the world with a retractable roof, brings a set of numbers to baseball that is even more impressive than the numbers the Blue Jays have posted inside it during the last few years. The roof covers 8 acres and weighs 11,000 tons, the equivalent of 3,372 automobiles. When closed, a 31-story building could fit inside. The field is large enough to store eight Boeing 747s, or 516 African and 743 Indian elephants. SkyDome—Canadians don't use "the" in its name—is made of enough concrete to build a sidewalk from St. Louis to Toronto. It looks like a giant turtle on the Toronto skyline and sits under the CN Tower, the tallest free-standing structure in the world. A 348-room hotel is integrated into the facility, as well as seven restaurants and bars.

And they even play baseball in it! If you have never seen a baseball game in Canada, you are in for some surprises. Fans here tend to be somewhat more sedate than their counterparts in the States. They can also be as inclined to applaud an opponent's noteworthy play as to cheer for the home team. But don't be fooled: SkyDome fans are doggedly loyal to their team. Only one thing can divert attention from the Blue Jays in Toronto—hockey. Though the Jays have won two World Series, the Maple Leafs are still the favorites here.

## HOT TIPS FOR VISITING FANS

**Parking**
If you drive, be prepared to pay. There are 5,000 spaces within a 20-minute walk, but parking-lot owners usually jack up the parking rates to more than double the usual cost. Prices depend on how much time is left before the ballgame starts. The closer it is to game time, the higher the price. Prices usually start at $8 and can run as high as $20 by the first pitch. Also, be aware that Toronto has strict laws about illegal on-street parking during morning (7 A.M.-9 A.M.) and afternoon (3:30 P.M.-6:30 P.M.) rush hours, so cars parked illegally have a great chance of being towed.

**Weather**
SkyDome combines the best of both worlds: when the weather's nice, games are played under blue skies and sun, but in the cold of April and September and on rainy days, the roof closes.

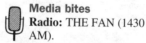
**Media bites**
**Radio:** THE FAN (1430 AM).
**TV:** CFTO and the Total Sports Network (cable). Tommy Hutton, who announces on CFTO, and Buck Martinez, who's on cable, played in the big leagues for a combined total of nearly 30 seasons, including the six seasons that Martinez caught for the Blue Jays.

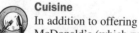
**Cuisine**
In addition to offering McDonald's (which runs SkyDome concessions), SkyDome features such popular items as Italian sausages, corned beef, and Country Style Donuts. Molson and Labatt's beers are available on tap and in bottles.
The closest postgame restau-

rant is in the CN Tower next door. The Tower has a mind-warp theater, laser-beam games, miniature golf, a revolving restaurant and Horizon's Bar. Call (416) 868-6937 for more information. Alice Fazooli's (416-979-1910) is 2 blocks south of SkyDome and is well known for its large collection of baseball art and memorabilia. Blue Jays players are frequent customers. Al Frisco's, about 5 blocks away, has four home-brewed beers on tap and 12 other, mostly Canadian, varieties. Downtown is Eaton Centre, a large mall with 340 shops and services, and many restaurants.

## LODGING NEAR THE STADIUM

**Westin Harbour Castle**
1 Harbour Square
Toronto, ON Canada, M5J 1A6
(416) 869-1600/(800) 228-3000
About 1¼ miles from the stadium.

**Toronto Hilton**
145 Richmond St. W.
Toronto, ON Canada, M5H 2L2
(416) 869-3456/(800) 445-8667
5 blocks south of the stadium.

## GETTING TO SKYDOME

**Public transportation:** Take the Yonge-University-Spadina subway line to Union Station at Front and Bay streets. For more information, call the Toronto Transit Commission at (416) 393-4636.
**By car:** From the south, take the Queen Elizabeth Expressway east toward Toronto. Exit at the Gardener Expressway exit. Take the Gardener Expressway to the Spadina Avenue exit. Take Spadina north and make a right on Blue Jay Way; the stadium will be on your left.
From the east, take the Gardener Expressway and follow the directions given above.
From the west, take the Dun Valley Parkway to the Gardener Expressway and continue as directed above.

# IN THE HOT SEATS AT SKYDOME

$P$lan, then write. Now that the Jays have moved into SkyDome, tickets can be incredibly difficult to get. The Blue Jays have attracted more than 4 million fans in each of the last three seasons. The team operates a charge line, but it can take forever to get through. To avoid potentially fruitless dialing, write several weeks in advance for tickets. Also check the ticket windows at Gate 9 on game day, since there are often unused season tickets and players' tickets.

• **Good seats:** Like all new parks, SkyDome was planned so virtually all

seats are good for baseball. The 200-level seats are probably the best. The sections are smaller, the seats are padded, and most fans believe sitting a level up makes for better angles on the game. First-deck seats are nice too, but those behind home plate have to contend with the safety net. If all that's left is the outfield, don't fret. Any of the lower-deck outfield seats are good. Fans can see the pitches and the flight of the ball, and unlike in other parks across both leagues, the fans aren't known to be rowdy.

• **Bad seats:** The seats in the 500 level

put the "Sky" in SkyDome. The view and the angles are excellent, but the seats are candidates for the steepest in the league. Try not to get dizzy, and watch your step. Use the rail between the aisles on your way up.

 **Scalping:** Large numbers of scalpers can be found outside SkyDome. The Blue Jays do not own the property surrounding the ballpark, and they can't prevent scalpers from congregating as close as possible to the ticket windows.

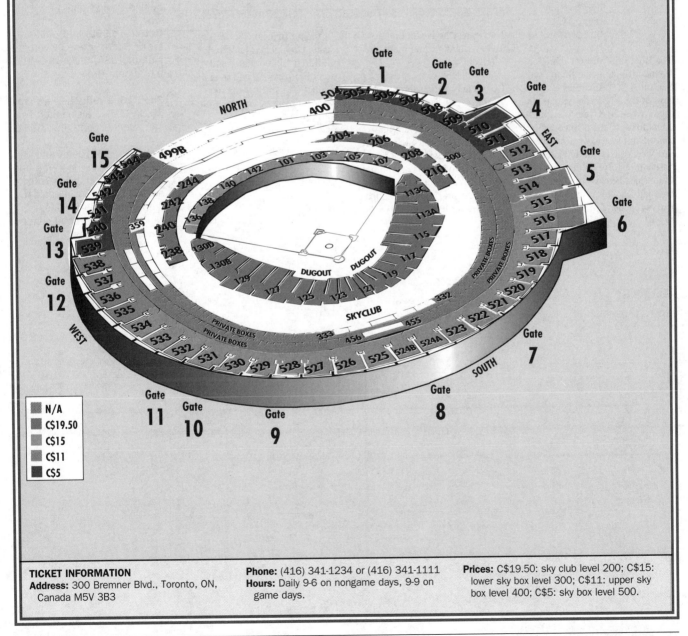

| Legend | |
|---|---|
| | N/A |
| | C$19.50 |
| | C$15 |
| | C$11 |
| | C$5 |

---

**TICKET INFORMATION**
**Address:** 300 Bremner Blvd., Toronto, ON, Canada M5V 3B3

**Phone:** (416) 341-1234 or (416) 341-1111
**Hours:** Daily 9-6 on nongame days, 9-9 on game days.

**Prices:** C$19.50: sky club level 200; C$15: lower sky box level 300; C$11: upper sky box level 400; C$5: sky box level 500.

## SPRING TRAINING

Dunedin Stadium at Grant Field
311 Douglas Ave.
Dunedin, FL 34698
**Capacity:** 6,218
**Game time:** 1:05 P.M., 1:35 P.M.
or 7:35 P.M.
**Tickets:** (813) 733-0429

## MINOR LEAGUES

| Class | Team |
| --- | --- |
| AAA | Syracuse (NY) Chiefs |
| AA | Knoxville (TN) Smokies |
| A | Dunedin (FL) Blue Jays |
| A | Hagerstown (MD) Suns |
| Short Season A | St. Catherines (ON) Blue Jays |
| Rookie | Medicine Hat (AL) Blue Jays |
| Rookie | Dunedin (FL) Blue Jays |

The Blue Jays' closest minor-league affiliate is the Short Season A St. Catherines Blue Jays of the NY-Penn League. In 1986, when St. Catherines fielded its first pro team since 1930, this small Ontario community just west of Niagara Falls made baseball history. At that time, St. Catherines became the first pro baseball franchise run by women, namely, general manager Ellen

## HOME-FIELD ADVANTAGE

SkyDome is spacious and uses artificial turf. Nothing is unusual about the outfield fence and its distance from home plate. The park's size makes it feel like a National League stadium, in that it favors batters who have speed and who can hit the ball into gaps. A good example: When Paul Molitor left the cold weather and thick grass of Milwaukee, he couldn't wait to see how well he could hit in SkyDome. In 1993, his batting average was 64 points higher in Toronto than on the road.

### BLUE JAYS TEAM NOTEBOOK

**Franchise history**
Toronto Blue Jays,
1977–present

**World Series titles**
1992, 1993

**Division titles**
1985, 1989, 1991,
1992, 1993

**American League pennants**
1992, 1993

**Most Valuable Player**
George Bell, 1987

**Rookie of the Year**
Alfredo Griffin, 1979
(tie)

Harrigan (who is still on the job) and assistant general manager Marilyn Finn.

To reach St. Catherines' Community Park, approximately 70 miles from Toronto, take the QEW to Route 406 South. Exit at Glendale and turn left. Stay on Glendale to the end and turn left on Merritt. Stay in the left lane, cross a railroad bridge and turn right on Weymour. The ballpark will be on your right, across the street from Merritton High School.

**Ticket prices:** C$5: reserve seats; C$4: general admission. Children 13 and under and senior citizens 60 and over can deduct C$1 from the above prices. For more information, call (905) 641-5297.

## THE BLUE JAYS AT SKYDOME

**June 29, 1990:** The Oakland A's Dave Stewart pitches the first no-hitter at SkyDome.

**Oct. 2, 1991:** Toronto clinches the American League East with a 6–5 win over the California Angels in the last game of the season.

**Sept. 24, 1992:** Dave Winfield sets a team single-season record for homers by a DH with his 23rd. He also becomes the oldest player in major-league history to get more than 100 RBIs.

**Oct. 8, 1992:** The Jays win their first postseason game at SkyDome, beating the A's 3–1 behind David Cone.

**Oct. 20, 1992:** In the first World Series game played outside the USA, the Jays beat the Atlanta Braves 1–0.

**Sept. 26, 1993:** The Jays draw 50,518 fans, raising their season attendance to 4,057,947.

**Oct. 23, 1993:** Joe Carter's three-run home run in the bottom of the ninth gives Toronto an 8–6 Game 6 win against the Philadelphia Phillies, clinching their second consecutive World Series title.

# FOOTBALL

Courtesy of Lambeau Field

## American Conference

## National Conference

# The Georgia Dome

TM

## STADIUM STATS

**Location:** 1 Georgia Dome Dr. N.W., Atlanta, GA 30313
**Opened:** Aug. 12, 1992
**Surface:** AstroTurf
**Capacity:** 71,594
**Services for fans with disabilities:** Besides 700 wheelchair-accessible seats, text phones (TTY) and hearing-amplification devices are available. Guide dogs for sight-impaired guests are welcome.

## STADIUM FIRSTS

**Regular-season game:** Sept. 6, 1992, 20–17 over the New York Jets.
**Points scored:** A 25-yard field goal by Norm Johnson of the Falcons.

## TEAM NOTEBOOK

**Franchise history:** Atlanta Falcons, 1966–present.
**Division title:** 1980.
**Pro Football Hall of Fame:** Norm Van Brocklin, 1971.
**Retired numbers:** 31, William Andrews; 57, Jeff Van Note; 60, Tommy Nobis.

The Georgia Dome, not the worst-to-first Braves or the '96 Olympics, began to transform Atlanta's professional-sports image from Losersville USA to Big League—and when you see the Dome, it's easy to understand why. The Falcons have one of the best venues in the NFL, suitable to host the Super Bowl, even if the chances of the host team's playing in one soon appear dim.

Built especially for football, the Dome sparkles and draws applause even from the pundits who said they'd never root for a team in, or even go inside, an enclosed stadium. Unlike most other domes, this one doesn't resemble an erector set. Atlanta's indoor playground has a billowy roof and attractive teal colors on the outside; 150 trees dot the property and mammoth windows allow natural light to fill the interior walkways.

It gets even better inside. Seats, even in the upper-deck corners, are angled so spectators can see the field without having to turn their bodies, and the roof is supported with cables, so no pillars obstruct the view. When the Falcons are on and the run-and-shoot is carving up defenses, the Georgia Dome can be an electric place. Music blares and a 300-pound break-dancer in the east end zone revs up his engine and gyrates.

## HOT TIPS FOR VISITING FANS

 **Parking**
Traffic is not a huge hassle, even an hour before game time, because city officials discourage fans from driving to the Dome. But if you want to drive, the Georgia Dome advertises 17,000 spaces available in the vicinity of the Dome. However, unless you're a luxury-suite owner with a parking pass to the Gold and Green lots, or you want to arrive three hours early and pay $10 or $15 at a private lot, don't try parking at the Dome.

If you want to pay $3 and don't mind a 15-minute walk, you can leave your car in the parking decks at Underground Atlanta (see Cuisine).

**Weather**
Because of the dome, football fans can't enjoy the splendid fall Sunday afternoons, but they also don't have to brave the chill that comes from 9 p.m. starts for Monday night games or the blustery weather that can overtake Atlanta in December.

**Media bites**
**Radio:** WSB (750 AM). 18-year Falcon veteran Jeff Van Note is the analyst. Van Note is the club leader in games played and was a six-time Pro Bowl performer.
**TV:** Preseason games are televised on WSB-TV (Channel 2), the ABC affiliate. WATL (Channel 36) is the Fox affiliate.

 **Cuisine**
You are not allowed to bring food and beverages into the Dome, but the Food Court is well stocked. Whatever you want, you can probably find: Mexican and deli food, pizza, ice cream, salads and so on.

A variety of imported beers is available on the Executive Club level, and Club level ticketholders can have a cold one brought to their seat. The Kickers Bar on the lower level concourse offers the same selection and is open to all ticketholders.

A five-minute walk from the Dome is the CNN Center, which features five restaurants, including a sports bar, and a variety of fast-food eateries.

Underground Atlanta, with 150 stores and pushcarts, as well as 12 restaurants and clubs, is 15 minutes away. Many of these spots, such as Hooters (404-688-0062), offer brunch-and-ticket packages for Falcons games. Lombardi's (404-522-6568) is an after-game stop that opens at 5 on Sundays. Or drop by Jocks 'n' Jills at the corner of 10th Street and Peachtree Road.

## LODGING NEAR THE STADIUM

**Omni Hotel at CNN Center**
100 CNN Center
Atlanta, GA 30335
(404) 659-0000/(800) 843-6664
2 blocks from the stadium.

**Atlanta Airport Hilton and Towers**
1031 Virginia Ave.
Atlanta, GA 30354
(404) 767-9000/(800) 455-8667
7 miles from the stadium.

## THE FALCONS AT THE GEORGIA DOME

**Aug. 23, 1992:** A sellout crowd watches the Falcons win the first football game in the Georgia Dome, 20–10 over the Philadelphia Eagles.

**Sept. 6, 1992:** The Falcons win their first regular-season game, against the New York Jets 20–17.

**Nov. 1, 1992:** Billy Joe Tolliver comes off the bench to throw a 13-yard touchdown to Michael Haynes, leading the Falcons to a 30–28 victory over the Los Angeles Rams.

**Nov. 29, 1992:** The Falcons beat the New England Patriots 34–0 in their first shutout since 1988. Atlanta gives up just 15 passing yards, and Deion Sanders has two interceptions.

# IN THE HOT SEATS AT THE GEORGIA DOME

This isn't Broadway, where you pay for the privilege of sitting close to the stars. Every seat in the house is $27, whether you are up close or in the rafters. The hardest tickets to find are against the Saints and 49ers. The Falcons have 53,000 season ticketholders, so that leaves 18,594 seats for walk-up and sale by phone. Single-game tickets go on sale in mid-July.

Of course, toward the end of the 1993 season, with the Falcons faring poorly, you could find a good seat close to the field without much difficulty.

• **Bad seats:** Decent seats are available in the thinner air of the upper deck between the 20-yard lines. But like any major football stadium, when you get upper-deck seats outside the 20s (behind the end zone, for instance) the view can be remote, to say the least.

• **Scalping:** Fans can easily find tickets from brokers on the street. CNN Center, which is five minutes away, usually is a gathering spot for people unloading tickets.

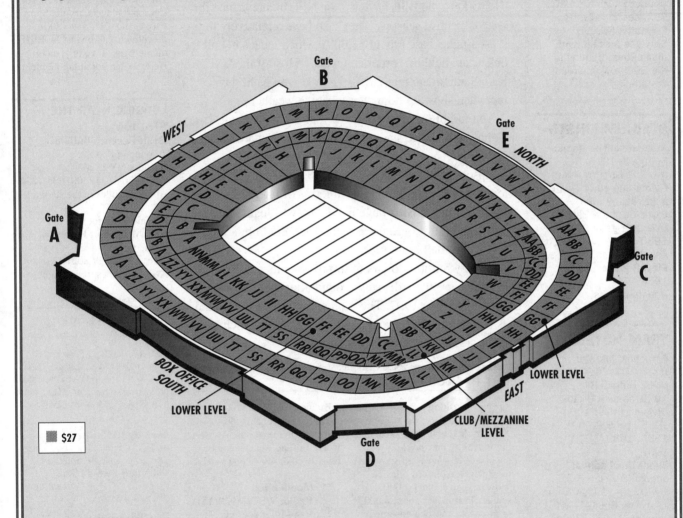

$27

## HOME-FIELD ADVANTAGE

Though the Falcons had two below-average teams (combined record 12-20) in their first two years in the Dome, they were 9-7 at home. The team has been built for the Dome's racetrack rug: small, speedy receivers Andre Rison, Mark Haynes and Bert Emanuel, who are extra fast inside on artificial surface, were drafted for the pass-first offense the Falcons have been using.

## GETTING TO THE GEORGIA DOME

**Public transportation:** The Omni/Dome/GWCC and Vine City MARTA stations are within close proximity. Use the former if your ticket tells you to enter at Gate C or D; the latter for Gate A, B or E. Bus service is available from the airport. Call (404) 848-4711 for more information.

**By car:** From Hartsfield Atlanta International Airport, take I-75/85 North about 11 miles to Exit 96 (Georgia World Congress Center/International Boulevard). At the end of the exit ramp, make a left onto International, and continue 10 blocks to the Georgia World Congress Center. Left at the fork to Magnum Street, where you can make a right into the stadium parking lot.

### TICKET INFORMATION
**Address:** 1 Georgia Dome Dr. NW, Atlanta, GA 30313
**Phone:** (404) 223-8000 or TicketMaster at

(404) 429-6400 or (800) 326-4000
**Hours:** Mon.-Fri. 9-5.
**Prices:** All seats are $27.

**Training camp:** 2745 Burnette Rd., Suwanee, GA

# Rich Stadium

The Buffalo Bills of recent vintage have had one of the most distinct home-field advantages in the NFL. The reasons are Rich Stadium and those who fill its seats. Bills fans are so rabid that games at Rich Stadium sometimes feel more like college games. Even though Buffalo has one of the NFL's biggest stadiums in one of its smallest markets, the Bills have led the NFL in attendance for six consecutive seasons. They also have a relatively low season-ticket base (about 53,000), which means not all the tickets are held by corporate fat cats. Most of those at Rich Stadium are real fans—the kind who paint their faces and show up no matter what the weather.

You might say it's the House that Simpson Built. Erie County put up the stadium in suburban Orchard Park largely because of the excitement stirred by O.J. Simpson during his playing days. Some lean years followed O.J.'s departure, both in terms of talent and fan support, but the Bills have been a playoff team since 1988, and they continue to make Rich Stadium a repository of football memories.

Twenty million dollars in improvements are planned to make sure the Bills stay around after their 25-year lease expires in 1997. The money will go for such items as new luxury boxes and a new scoreboard, which the Bills say will be the nation's largest.

## HOT TIPS FOR VISITING FANS

**Parking**
In theory, the stadium lots hold 15,000 cars, but in reality, they hold only about 11,000—unless it snows, in which case plowed piles of snow take up another 1,000 spaces. That means about 8,000 or more cars must be absorbed by the lot at the college across the street, at nearby restaurants and bars, and in the yards of local residents ready to make a quick buck. If you really want to park in a stadium lot, arrive at least two hours before the game. Many fans arrive early for elaborate tailgate parties anyway.

**Weather**
An old joke has it that there are two seasons in Buffalo: winter and the Fourth of July. That may not seem so funny in the fourth quarter of a January playoff game. The truth is, the NFL loads up the Bills' home schedule early so that most years they play only one regular-season game late in the season. At its worst, Buffalo weather can be brutally cold, snowy and windy.

**Media bites**
**Radio:** WBEN (930 AM). Van Miller does play-by-play, which he's been doing for all but a few seasons since they began play in 1960.
**TV:** WGRZ (Channel 2) is the NBC affiliate.

**Cuisine**
Only the usual stadium fare—no Buffalo specialities like chicken wings or roast beef on kümmelweck rolls. Your best bet is the Italian sausage with peppers and onions. The hot dogs are made by Sahlen's (which is good), but they're steamed instead of grilled (which isn't). You can get Polish sausage, but for real kielbasa try the Broadway Market near downtown. There are two kinds of beer for sale: reduced alcohol (3.2%) and no alcohol. For real beer and better food, try restaurants near the stadium such as Salfranco's (716-649-7644), Rettig's (716-649-9673) and Ilio DiPaulo's (716-825-3675). To see some players, try the Sport City Grille (716-849-1200) downtown. It's owned by Bills quarterback Jim Kelly, as is Network, an adjoining nightclub.

## LODGING NEAR THE STADIUM
**Hyatt Regency Buffalo**
2 Fountain Plaza
Buffalo, NY 14202
(716) 856-1234/(800) 233-1234
About 15 miles to the stadium.

**Buffalo Marriot**
1340 Millersport Highway
Amherst, NY 14221
(716) 689-6900/(800) 228-9290
About 15 miles to the stadium.

## THE BILLS AT RICH STADIUM

**Dec. 16, 1973:** O.J. Simpson runs for 200 yards, bringing his total to 2,003 and becoming the first player to rush for 2,000 yards in a single season. The Bills beat the New York Jets 34–14.

**Sept. 7, 1980:** The Bills stop an NFL-record, 20-game losing streak to a single opponent when they beat the Miami Dolphins 17–7. Fans tear down the goal posts.

**Dec. 23, 1990:** A crowd of 80,235 at Rich Stadium watches the Bills clinch their fourth AFC Eastern Division title by defeating the Dolphins 24–14.

**Jan. 27, 1991:** The Bills rack up 502 yards in total offense and destroy the Los Angeles Raiders 51–3 for their first AFC championship.

**Sept. 6, 1992:** James Lofton breaks Steve Largent's career record for receiving yards (13,089) in a 40–7 win over the Rams.

**Jan. 3, 1993:** Down by 32 points in the third quarter of an AFC wild-card game, the Bills, led by quarterback Frank Reich, beat the Houston Oilers 41–38.

# IN THE HOT SEATS AT RICH STADIUM

Single-game tickets go on sale July 9. Tickets for the hottest games sell out early. For other games—say, the Indianapolis Colts—tickets are sometimes available at the stadium on game day.

• **Bad seats:** The beauty of this football-only stadium is that it affords arguably the best sightlines in the NFL. The closest thing to bad seats are the first several rows of the lower-level end zone, which are sometimes obstructed by personnel on the field, and the last several rows on the home-side upper level, which take the brunt of the northwest wind in bad weather.

• **Special programs:** There is a Family Section with no alcohol in the Upper Level at the end-zone corner near Gate 1.

**Scalping:** Because the stadium is so big, scalpers don't often get big prices, but for the best games—the playoffs, the Dolphins, glamour NFC visitors—scalpers may get as much as double a ticket's face value.

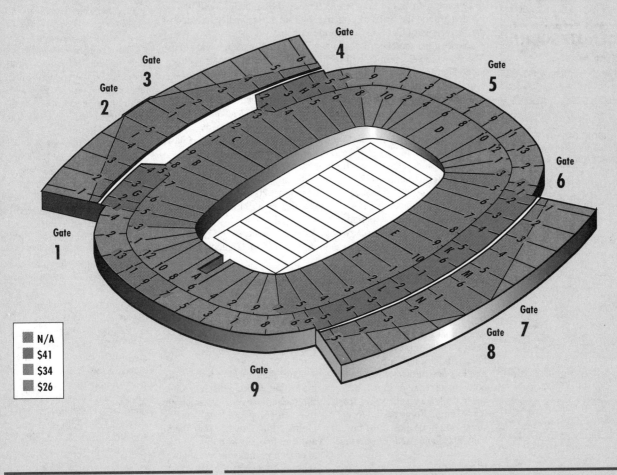

Gate 4

Gate 3

Gate 2

Gate 5

Gate 6

Gate 1

Gate 7

Gate 8

Gate 9

■ N/A
■ $41
■ $34
■ $26

## HOME-FIELD ADVANTAGE

It comes from two things. One is loud, rowdy fans. And the second? The answer, my friend, is blowing in the wind—usually out of the northwest. About 70% of the points at Rich Stadium are scored in the end zone nearest the tunnel—because that's the way the wind blows. How pronounced is Buffalo's home-field advantage? The Bills have played eight playoff games at Rich Stadium and won all of them. Too bad for the Bills that they can't play Super Bowls here.

## GETTING TO RICH STADIUM

**Public transportation:** Metro buses Nos. 14B and 14C stop at the stadium. Call (716) 855-7300 for more information.

**By car:** From either downtown or the Greater Buffalo International Airport, take the Kensington Expressway to the southbound New York State Thruway (Route 90). Go approximately 8 miles, then exit at Orchard Park (exit 55). From exit 55, follow Route 219 south toward Orchard Park. Exit on Milestrip Road West and continue to the first traffic light, at Abbott Road. Take a left onto Abbott and continue straight through traffic light. Stadium is on the left.

## TICKET INFORMATION
**Address:** 1 Bills Dr., Orchard Park, NY 14217
**Phone number:** (716) 649-0015

**Hours:** Mon.-Thurs. 8-6, Fri. 8-7, Sat. 8-4 (Mon.-Fri. 9-5 during the offseason).
**Prices:** $41: club level; $34: sidelines, corners and club-level end zone; $26: lower-level end zone.

**Training camp:** Fredonia State University, Fredonia, NY

# Carolinas Stadium

## STADIUM STATS

**Opens:** June 1996
**Surface:** Grass
**Capacity:** 72,350
**Services for fans with disabilites:** Seating available in all sections.

## TEAM NOTEBOOK

**Franchise history:**
Carolina Panthers, 1995.

## TICKET INFORMATION

**Address:** Carolinas Stadium, P.O. Box 3411, Charlotte, NC 28234
**Phone:** (704) 358-7800
**Hours:** Mon.-Fri. 8:30-5:30

Bold, colorful, unique. That's the kind of stadium that owner Jerry Richardson had in mind when Charlotte was awarded an NFL expansion franchise.

Built on 31 parcels of land in a barren end of downtown Charlotte, the Panthers' NFL stadium will feature three 75-foot-tall, black-granite entry portals, each to be flanked by two 18-foot statues of fierce-looking panthers. The stadium colors—royal blue and silver inside, black outside—will reflect the team colors. Instead of the usual parking lots, the Stadium will be surrounded by a nature lover's promenade. The parklike setting will include spacious grass lawns, as well as 150 oak trees and other regional plants sure to delight picnickers. In keeping with an old Southern college tradition, hedges will be planted around the walls to give the stadium a personality like that of the University of Georgia Stadium in Athens.

Inside, huge scoreboard displays will tower above each end zone. The showtime electronics will include a 24-by-32-foot color replay video board, a 17-by-32-foot animation board, and a 10-by-50-foot scoreboard and game-in-progress statistics board.

The man who put it all together is Richardson, who used to catch passes from Baltimore Colts legend Johnny Unitas. Richardson is president of Flagstar, the USA's fourth-largest food company (Denny's, Hardee's). Richardson follows George (Papa Bear) Halas as only the second NFL player to become a majority owner. Richardson hopes the "powerful look" of the stadium will be memorable and intimidating to rival teams. The proximity of the seats to the field—60 feet to the first sideline row and just 20 feet to the end zone—means a favorable noise factor and is sure to make a game in Charlotte an exciting experience.

The stadium won't be ready until 1996, however, so the Panthers' home in 1995 will be Clemson Stadium (81,473 seats), about 100 miles southwest of Charlotte.

## HOT TIPS FOR VISITING FANS

### Parking
A minimal number of spaces will be available for players and staff. Fans will park in nearby corporate lots downtown, which can hold 36,000 cars, or in a 1,200-space deck across the street from the Stadium. Some main feeder streets might be closed off on game days and used for parking.

### Weather
Charlotte enjoys a moderate climate, with short, mild winters and cool summer nights. The average temperature in July is 79 degrees; in December, 42 degrees. Carolinians wear lightweight summer clothes into late October. After that, bring a sweater or light jacket. The first frost usually doesn't arrive until Thanksgiving.

### Cuisine
Given Richardson's corporation, stadium service will reflect the fast-food business. More than 200 concessions stands will offer eight kinds of hot dogs, hamburgers, bratwursts, salads and other Denny's or Hardee's products. Plans are to sell beer inside the stadium. Sales are permitted starting at 11:45 A.M. on Sundays.

After the game, 52 restaurants are within walking distance of the stadium, several of which are in hotels (Marriott, Raddison, Holiday Inn, Omni). Sports bars are sure to open with the approach of the team's inaugural season. Two spots that survived the inner-city decay of the '60s and '70s are the Open Kitchen (704-375-7449), a nostalgic Italian bistro on Morehead Street, and the Foundry Pub (704-347-1841), a trendy bar on Cedar Street.

## HOME-FIELD ADVANTAGE
Carolinas Stadium is supposed to reflect strength and power. The euphoria that's sure to sweep the Stadium could help the home team. But remember, Tampa Bay fans were euphoric, too, and the Buccaneers lost their first 26 games.

## IN THE HOT SEATS

Considering the frenzy for tickets even before Charlotte was awarded an expansion franchise, the Panthers expect early sell-outs. However, about 8,000 single-game tickets will go on sale in the summer of 1996. As of May 1994, a few season tickets were available. The cost: $320 (end zone) and $350 (sideline) for a 10-game package.

The Panthers' ticket plan, like the Stadium, is certainly bold. So bold that it won expansion votes from a number of NFL owners. Before buying season tickets, you have to pay up to $5,400 for a PSL, or Permanent Seat License, revenues from which go toward building the Stadium. To purchase season tickets for the Panthers' inaugural season, fans had to plunk down $600 (corner end zone) to $5,400 (lower level, inside the 20-yard lines) for seat licenses, plus another $190-$600 for the ticket. Season ticketholders will be given preference for tickets to games at Clemson Stadium in 1995.

There won't be a bad seat anywhere. Club seats go for $1,237-$2,237 (plus an annual fee of $975-$2,975) and include access to a full-service lounge. If you hurry, a few season tickets might be available in sections C (lower-level end zone) and E (upper-level sideline). They'll cost $2,700-$3,000 (remember the one-time PSL fee, plus $320-$350 for the ticket).

**Scalping:** The Panthers expect a lot of it. As one official noted, "This is a hotbed down here, where people are going crazy over the team. Anytime you get that kind of demand . . ."

## STADIUM STATS

**Location:** 425 McFetridge Pl., Chicago, IL 60605
**Opened:** Oct. 9, 1924
**Surface:** Grass
**Capacity:** 66,950
**Services for fans with disabilities:** Seating available in sections 14-17.

## STADIUM FIRSTS

**Regular-season game:** Sept. 19, 1971, 17–15 over the Pittsburgh Steelers.
**Points scored:** P. Pearson of the Steelers recovered a fumble in the end zone for a touchdown.
**Overtime game:** Oct. 1, '78, 25–19 loss to the Oakland Raiders.
**Playoff game:** Jan. 5, '86, 21–0 over the New York Giants.

## TEAM NOTEBOOK

**Franchise history:** Decatur Staleys, 1920; Chicago Staleys, '21; Chicago Bears, '22–present.
**Division titles:** 1921, '32–34, '37, '40–43, '46, '56, '63, '84–88, '90.
**Super Bowl appearance:** XX, Jan. 26, '86, 46-10 over the N.E. Patriots.
**Pro Football Hall of Fame:** Halas, '63; Grange, '63; Nagurski, '63; Healy, '64; Lyman, '64; Trafton, '64; Driscoll, '65; Fortmann, '65; Luckman, '65; Kiesling, '66; McAfee, '66; Turner, '66; Layne, '67; Stydahar, '67; Hewitt, '71; George, '74; Connor, '75; Sayers, '77; Butkus, '79; Blanda, '81; Atkins, '82; Musso, '82; Ditka, '88; Page, '88; Jones, '91; Payton, '93.
**Retired numbers:** 3, Nagurski; 5, McAfee; 7, Halas; 28, Galimore; 34, Payton; 41, Piccolo; 42, Luckman; 56, Hewitt; 61, George; 66, Turner; 77, Grange.

# Soldier Field

Even after 70 years, people still have a hard time getting its name right: It's Soldier Field, not Soldier's Field. Opened in 1926 as a memorial to the men and women who served in World War I, Soldier Field faithfully has served the Windy City by hosting everything from boxing matches to religious conventions. Its best-known tenants, the Bears, have called the place home since 1971. Before then, the Bears shared the Cubs' den at Wrigley Field, but the Mike Ditka years—all played in the shadows of Soldier Field's majestic columns—have made this stadium as much a hallowed place as the "friendly confines" of Wrigley Field.

With Lake Michigan to the east and the downtown skyline serving as an impressive backdrop to the north, Soldier Field's location is awe-inspiring. As befits the Windy City, breezes that range from comfortably cool in September to downright arctic in December often blow across the stadium. Still, on a Monday night game with the skyline lighted, the view is magical enough to make fans forget they're frozen stiff.

Despite talk about the Bears building a stadium in the next decade, Soldier Field probably will continue to stand tall and proud for many years to come. An $18 million face lift (the third in 15 years) in preparation for the World Cup helped spruce up this grand old park, one of the elder statesmen of NFL stadiums.

## HOT TIPS FOR VISITING FANS

**Parking**
Only 6,000 spaces are available in the three lots surrounding Soldier Field. Fans lucky enough to get into one of those lots before they reach capacity pay $10. Get there early, at least two or three hours before kickoff. A better option is to park in the downtown Grant Park underground garage and catch a free shuttle. If you're eating downtown, ask if they piggyback a bus ride to the game with the meal; some do. Some fans park for free on nearby streets and walk four to eight blocks, but be warned that the surrounding area is known for car break-ins and vandalism.

**Weather**
Because temperatures along the lakefront can sometimes be 10-15 degrees lower than inland, always wear a warmer jacket or coat than usual.

If you're going to a game in late fall or early winter, be prepared to bring boots, blankets, and gloves or mittens, because the wind chill index is often below zero.

**Media bites**
**Radio:** WGN (720 AM). Wayne Larrivee does play-by-play, and former Bears Gary Fencik and Dick Butkus provide analysis.
**TV:** WMAQ (Channel 5) broadcasts preseason games. For regular-season games, WFLD (Channel 32) is the Fox affiliate.

**Cuisine**
If there's something Chicago fans like just as much as their Bears, it's their food, and Soldier Field has plenty of options. For those who don't do their cooking at pre- and postgame tailgate parties, Ballpark Franks and Kosher Hot

Dogs make good starters. The best dog in the house is the Chicago-style, which comes with tomato, onion, relish, mustard, celery salt, pickle and hot pepper. Also worthy of mention: Connie's thick-crust pizza (a Chicago favorite), Italian beef, chicken-breast and fish sandwiches, and bratwurst and Polish and Italian sausages.

To wash all that down, there's a wide selection of beers, with 14 imported brews, as well as Old Style and the usual American standbys such as Miller and Budweiser.

For later, there are several watering holes within a 5-mile drive or taxi ride of the stadium. Try Red Kerr's, Blackie's, Kitty O'Shea's (in the Hilton Towers hotel), America's Bar, Planet Hollywood (312-266-7827), the Hard Rock Cafe (312-943-2252), and just about any bar in the famed Rush Street and Division Street corridor.

## LODGING NEAR THE STADIUM

**The Westin Hotel Chicago**
909 N. Michigan Ave.
Chicago, IL 60611
(312) 943-7200/(800) 228-3000
3 miles from the stadium.

**The Hyatt Regency**
151 E. Wacker Dr.
Chicago, IL 60601
(312) 565-1234/(800) 233-1234
3 miles from the stadium.

## THE BEARS AT SOLDIER FIELD

**Nov. 20, 1977:** Walter Payton rushes for an NFL-record 275 yards in a 10–7 win over the Minnesota Vikings.

**Dec. 18, 1977:** Bob Thomas kicks a 28-yard field goal with nine seconds left in overtime to give the Bears a 12–9 win over the New York Giants and their first playoff berth in 14 years.

**Dec. 7, 1980:** The Bears beat the Packers 61–7, matching their regular-season team record for points.

**Dec. 20, 1987:** Future Hall of Famer Walter Payton scores two touchdowns in his final regular-season game at Soldier Field.

# IN THE HOT SEATS AT SOLDIER FIELD

Soldier Field has 100,000 seats, but fewer than 67,000 are used for Bears games. With 60,000 season ticketholders and a waiting list of more than 9,000 (the turnover rate is about 1%), your best bet is to buy remaining single-game tickets, which almost always are for end-zone seats. The Bears have a mail-order sale every year, but the request must be postmarked by June 1. Once mail requests are filled, the team usually holds a one-day ticket sale at Soldier Field in July. Any leftovers are often on sale through TicketMaster.

If you have a choice, get a seat on the east side of the stadium, preferably not too high and not too close to the field. That way, you have a clear view of the field and will be less likely to feel the bitter breezes that can blow in from Lake Michigan. Also, the east side of the stadium gets more sun. The seats throughout are relatively comfortable.

• **Bad seats:** Avoid the far corners of the stadium because trying to see the opposite end of the field is next to impossible.

• **Special programs:** The team has 820 tickets in sections 29 and 31 for sale at the ticket office in Lake Forest or, during the season, at the box office at Soldier Field.

Alcohol is not allowed. If you're caught nipping in these sections, you'll be ejected.

• **Scalping:** It's generally possible to buy scattered game-day tickets in front of Gate 0, at the south end of the stadium. Tickets usually can be bought at face value unless they're for a divisional or other high-profile game, when prices can double or even triple. Word of warning: Chicago police launch occasional stings. Those caught scalping are arrested, their tickets are confiscated, and they face a fine.

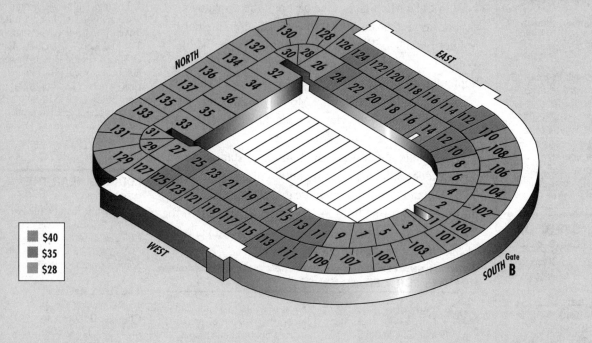

$40
$35
$28

## HOME-FIELD ADVANTAGE

During the mid- to late-'80s, "Bear weather" was the ultimate home advantage. If under 40 degrees and the wind blustery—snow was an added plus—smart money would be on a win for the Bears. In the five seasons from 1984 to '88, they went 36–8 at Soldier Field, but in recent years Chicago's advantage has eroded. Since 1989, the Bears are just 25–17 at home.

One factor that affects play is the wind off Lake Michigan. It swirls from the north one minute and gusts in from the south the next, usually, it seems, just before a field goal or extra-point kick goes up.

## GETTING TO SOLDIER FIELD

**Public transportation:** Two Chicago Transportation Authority bus lines, No. 146 (Marine Drive/Michigan Ave.) and No. 128 (Soldier Field Express), stop at the stadium. Call (312) 836-7000 for more information.

**By Car:** From O'Hare Airport, Kennedy Expressway east to Ohio Street exit. Go east to Columbus Drive. Turn right and follow the signs.

## TICKET INFORMATION
**Address:** 950 N. Western Ave., Lake Forest, IL 60045
**Phone:** (708) 615-BEAR (2327)
**Hours:** Mon.-Fri. 9-4 (8-4 in the offseason).

**Prices:** $40: sections 14-23 and 114-123; $35: sections 10-13, 110-113, 24, 25, 124 and 125; $28: sections 1-9, 100-109, 26-36 and 126-137. Sections 29 and 31 are no-alcohol sections.

**Training Camp:** University of Wisconsin–Platteville, Platteville, WI

# Riverfront Stadium

## STADIUM STATS

**Location:** 200 Riverfront St., Cincinnati, OH 45202
**Opened:** June 30, 1970
**Surface:** AstroTurf
**Capacity:** 60,389
**Services for fans with disabilities:** Seating available in the Plaza Level.

## STADIUM FIRSTS

**Regular-season game:** Sept. 21, 1970, 31–21 over the Oakland Raiders.
**Points scored:** Five-yard touchdown run by Sam Wyche of the Cincinnati Bengals.
**Overtime game:** Oct. 30, 1977, 13–10 over the Houston Oilers.
**Playoff game:** Jan. 3, 1983, 28–21 over the Miami Dolphins.

## TEAM NOTEBOOK

**Franchise history:** Cincinnati Bengals, 1968–69 (AFL); Cincinnati Bengals, 1970–present (NFL).
**Division titles:** 1970, 1973, 1981, 1988, 1990.
**Super Bowl appearances:** XVI, January 24, 1982, 26–21 loss to the 49ers; XXIII, January 22, 1989, 20–16 loss to the 49ers.
**Pro Football Hall of Fame:** Paul Brown, 1967; Forrest Gregg, 1977; Bill Walsh, 1993.
**Retired number:** 54, Bob Johnson.

The no-frills atmosphere in Riverfront Stadium goes with the city's buttoned-down image like a cardigan sweater. The franchise founded by legend Paul Brown believes that fans come to see football and not a circus, so you won't see much to distract you from the action. The field has no logos or marks on it other than the hashmarks and sidelines; there's not even a Bengals logo in the end zone. (In 1985, when the Reds marked the spot of Pete Rose's hit that broke Ty Cobb's record, the Bengals erased it for their next game, even though it wasn't on the field of play.) You won't see mascots, either. Safety concerns benched Benzoo, a white tiger cub that the Cincinnati Zoo brought to the games for years. But the club did bring back the Ben-Gals cheerleaders in 1994 after an absence of several years, and banners in good taste are encouraged.

The city-owned stadium is the typical multi-purpose facility built in the early 1970s, and while it's functional, it has little character. The setting is just fine, on the banks of the Ohio River next to the historic John A. Roebling Suspension Bridge. Fans can walk from the heart of downtown by using pedestrian bridges. Bengal fans do get cranked up when the team is winning. Though New Orleans gets credit for it, the "Who Dey" chant started in Cincinnati in 1981 as the Bengals marched to the Super Bowl. It goes, "Who dey think gonna beat dem bengals? Noooo-body." And it's still used (under appropriate game conditions).

## HOT TIPS FOR VISITING FANS

**Parking**
A three-level garage surrounds the stadium, but that's sold out on a season-subscription basis. Open-air city lots adjacent to the stadium can handle about 1,800 cars and charge $3.50, but a good 50% of those spaces are season subscriptions, so show up a couple of hours early to get in. There are also facilities for about 20,000 cars within 12 blocks of the stadium. Or you can park across the river in Covington and walk across the Roebling Bridge to the stadium. Postgame traffic is rarely a problem.

**Weather**
Fall weather in Cincinnati is generally quite pleasant—it's comfortable past election day. Average temperature in December is 42 degrees, perfect football weather for some. But it also can get very cold—people still talk about the 9-below-zero AFC Championship Game in January 1981.

**Media Bites**
**Radio:** Ken Broo and former Bengal Dave Lapham handle the broadcasts. The flagship station is WLWA (550 AM).
**TV:** Preseason games are telecast on WKRC (Channel 12). For regular-season games, WLWT (Channel 5) is the NBC affiliate.

**Cuisine**
The standard ballpark fare is available, but Cincinnati's culinary traditions also are in evidence. *Metts* and brats (German sausages) are served—they won't be the best you'll eat in Cincy, but they're representative. You can also sample some of that Cincinnati chili at special stands. And try one of the beers from the local brewery, Hudepohl-Schoenling.

Postgame crowds head for Pete Rose Way and the hot spots on the waterfront. Caddy's (513-721-3636) and Flanagan's Landing (513-421-4055) are the standbys. Montgomery Inn Boathouse (513-721-7427), famous for their ribs, and Covington Landing (606-291-9992) across the river in Covington, Ky. And no trip to Cincinnati is complete without a double-dip cone of ice cream with *huge* chocolate chips.

## LODGING NEAR THE STADIUM

**Hyatt Regency of Cincinnati**
151 W. 5th St.
Cincinnati, OH 45202
(513) 579-1234/(800) 233-1234
4 to 5 blocks from the stadium.

**Omni Netherland Plaza Hotel**
35 W. 5th St.
Cincinnati, OH 45202
(513) 421-9100/(800) 843-6664
2 blocks from the stadium.

## THE BENGALS AT RIVERFRONT STADIUM

**Nov. 17, 1975:** Ken Anderson completes 30 of 46 passing attempts for 447 yards. The Bengals win 33–24 over the Buffalo Bills.

**Jan. 10, 1981:** The Bengals brave 9-below-zero temperatures and a minus-59 wind chill to play in their first AFC Championship Game, against the San Diego Chargers, which the Bengals win 27–7.

**Jan. 8, 1988:** The Bengals make it to their second Super Bowl by defeating the Buffalo Bills 27–10 for the AFC Championship.

**Dec. 17, 1989:** Led by Boomer Esiason's four touchdown passes, the Bengals trounce the Houston Oilers 61–7 at Riverfront Stadium.

**Dec. 23, 1990:** James Woods sets a team record by rushing for 201 yards in a 40–20 victory over the Houston Oilers.

# In the Hot Seats at Riverfront Stadium

Riverfront is one of the smaller-capacity NFL stadiums, so tickets are usually in demand. The games against such rivals as Cleveland and Pittsburgh always sell out quickly. The season-ticket base is about 50,000, so there are only 6,000 to 10,000 seats on sale for each individual game. When the Reds' baseball season is finished, 700 seats are added in the lower end zones; most are available for individual games. The Bengals can't sell those tickets until the Reds are officially eliminated, so last-minute buyers sometimes get lucky.

Also, a limited number of seats under cover on the club level are available, with a catch or two. They're portable folding chairs—and they may not be around much longer. The sections are designated for use as a stadium restaurant club, which the city says it will build eventually. But the city has been saying that for years.

• **Bad seats:** The bulk of the tickets not sold on a season basis are in the upper-deck reserve sections, and they're just fine. Some of the most overrated seats are the blue-level field boxes along the sidelines, which are almost all season tickets, anyway. Cincinnati is essentially a baseball town—fans like to sit close to the action and feel that way about football as well. But many of those "prime" boxes are actually poor football seats. The angles are bad, and you have to look over the heads of players walking the bench.

**Scalping:** Ticket scalpers and brokers are legal in Cincinnati. Figure on paying about double the face value for upper-deck seats and about triple the face value for ones closer to the field. You have to go north of 4th Street to find them—scalping is not permitted on the stadium plaza, Pete Rose Way, 3rd Street, or 4th Street. However, you may want to try the plaza first—fans selling extra tickets at face value or below *are* permitted to sell there.

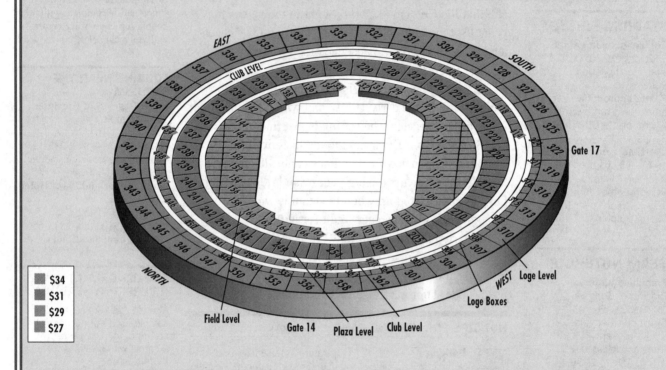

- $34
- $31
- $29
- $27

*Field Level · Gate 14 · Plaza Level · Club Level · Loge Boxes · Loge Level · Gate 17*

## HOME-FIELD ADVANTAGE

Like most stadiums of similar style, Riverfront holds little home-field advantage for the Bengals besides the crowd. But that can be a formidable edge when the team is a contender—Cincinnati was undefeated in 10 games at home (regular season and playoff) in their last Super Bowl season, 1988. The Bengals rarely practice here, so the players don't have the feel for the turf that comes with daily workouts. Certain sections of the turf (especially the southwest corner of the field) don't get much sun in the later part of the season and stay wetter and slicker than the rest of the field. Veteran Bengal receivers know the areas and their characteristics and try to play them during games, though this isn't nearly the factor it was in the early to mid-1980's, when the turf was getting worn. It has since been replaced, and the field has a much better drainage system. Also, the sliding pits for the baseball bases and the mound are covered with artificial-turf inserts for football. A sixth sense for where the inserts are and the difference in the turf (it's much less worn than the rest, so traction is greater) are also a small edge for the home team.

## GETTING TO RIVERFRONT STADIUM

**Public transportation:** Shuttle buses run on game day from various shopping areas in the city. Call (513) 621-4455 for information.

**By car:** From the south, take I-75 North. Stay in the right lane as you cross the Brent Spence Bridge over the Ohio River. Take the first exit after the bridge onto Pete Rose Way. Stadium is on the right.

From the north, take I-75 South. Follow signs for downtown. Exit onto Pete Rose Way. Stadium is on the right.

---

**TICKET INFORMATION**
**Address:** 200 Riverfront St., Cincinnati, OH 45202
**Phone number:** (513) 621-3550

**Hours:** Mon.-Fri. 9-5.
**Prices:** $34: club; $31: plaza; $29: lower field; $27: upper level.

**Training camp:** Wilmington College, Wilmington, OH

# Municipal Stadium

Municipal Stadium—cavernous, creaky, and often dank during the NFL's cold winter months—is one of the league's oldest ballparks. Sitting on a landfill off the sometimes-frigid shores of Lake Erie, it has hosted everything from heavyweight championship bouts to the Beatles. Extensive renovations during a 10-year period (1974–84) helped upgrade the stadium, but it's the unrehabilitated nature of the fans in the "Dawg Pound" that has given football season at Municipal its unique character.

All the woofing started when former Browns cornerback Hanford Dixon began barking at his teammates during the 1985 season. By 1986, the end-zone section had become a full-fledged pound. Though Cleveland native and former late-night-TV host Arsenio Hall never admitted it, team officials believe he cribbed his woofing act from the Dawg Pound. Now, more than 6,000 end-zone tickets are sold. Because the section mostly contains regular Browns fans, they generally police themselves and trouble is kept to a minimum. The best advice for out-of-town fans (particularly those from Pittsburgh, Cincinnati and Houston): don't wear opposing teams' colors—Dawg Pounders don't like getting their noses rubbed in it, so to speak.

## HOT TIPS FOR VISITING FANS

**Parking**
Downtown parking is available. Try to get to the stadium an hour before kickoff for a hassle-free experience. A tip: Take West Third Street to the lot west of Municipal Stadium, which usually has spaces ($5) available up until kickoff because most folks assume the lot is full. The worst place to park: lots on Lake Erie, east of the stadium, where cars get bunched in and the single lane clogs the flow.
Tailgating is very popular and is encouraged. Groups of 50 or more may reserve and arrange a complete tailgate party catered by the Browns (216-891-5000, ext. 5053). Parties include game tickets, a catered meal, private tent, and team souvenirs.

**Weather**
It's often delightful in September and October, but November brings a distinct chill to the air. By December, look out: whipping lake winds, freezing rains and snow are the elements that visiting teams (and fans) must confront. Be prepared. It never hurts to pack a poncho, wear long johns, or don gloves and hats.

**Media bites**
Radio: WMMS (100.7 FM). TV: WKYC (Channel 3, NBC), WAKC (Channel 23, ABC) and pre-season coverage available on WOIO (Channel 19, Fox).

**Cuisine**
The stadium hot dogs are the locals' favorite—and they love to smother 'em with Bertram's mustard, made regionally. Otherwise, the fare is mostly standard and there are no special beers. For sit-down dining, try Alvie's Stadium Cafe (216-861-5055), located on the stadium's fourth floor. Enter through Gate A, section 17, on the lower concourse.
Pregame brunch at Stouffers' Inn On The Square (216-696-5600), 3 blocks from the stadi-um, is recommended on game day. After the game, for moderately priced American cuisine, check out Grand Slam (216-696-4884) on the West Bank of the Flats—an area of bars, restaurants and clubs near the stadium.

## LODGING NEAR THE STADIUM

**Cleveland Marriot Society Center**
127 Public Square
Cleveland, OH 44114
(216) 696-9200/(800) 228-9290
3 blocks from the stadium.

**Sheraton Cleveland City Center Downtown**
777 St. Clair Ave.
Cleveland, OH 44114
(216) 771-7600/(800) 325-3535
2 blocks from the stadium.

## THE BROWNS AT MUNICIPAL STADIUM

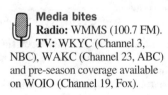

**Dec. 24, 1950:** Otto Graham throws for four touchdowns and Dante Lavelli hauls in 11 receptions, a combined effort that leads the Browns to a 30–28 win over the Los Angeles Rams for the NFL championship in their first season in the league.

**Nov. 24, 1957:** Running back Jim Brown rushes for 237 yards on 31 carries against the Rams. The Browns win 45–31.

**Dec. 27, 1964:** Jim Brown rushes for 114 yards and wide receiver Gary Collins scores three touchdowns as the Browns win the NFL championship 27–0 over the Baltimore Colts.

**Sept. 21, 1970:** The Browns beat the New York Jets 31–21 in the first *Monday Night Football* broadcast.

**Jan. 3, 1987:** Bernie Kosar passes for an NFL post season record 489 yards in a 23–20 double-overtime win over the New York Jets.

**Dec. 18, 1988:** In the last game of the regular season, the Browns come back to beat the Houston Oilers 28–23, after being down 16 points in the third quarter, to clinch a wild-card berth.

---

## STADIUM STATS

**Location:** West 3rd St., Cleveland, OH 44114
**Opened:** July 1, 1931
**Surface:** Grass
**Capacity:** 78,512
**Services for fans with disabilities:** Seating available in lower-level sections 16, 17, 26 and 27 and in second-level sections 14 and 30.

## STADIUM FIRSTS

**Regular-season game:** Sept. 6, 1946, 44–0 over the Miami Seahawks.
**Points scored:** A touchdown pass from Cliff Lewis to Mac Speedie of the Browns.
**Overtime game:** Sept. 26, 1977, 30–27 over the New England Patriots.
**Playoff game:** Dec. 17, 1950, 8–3 over the New York Giants.

## TEAM NOTEBOOK

**Franchise history:** Cleveland Browns, 1946–49 (AAFC); Cleveland Browns, 1950–present.
**Division titles:** 1950, '51, '52, '53, '54, '55, '57, '64, '65, '67, '68, '69, '71, '80, '85, '86, '87, '89.
**Pro Football Hall of Fame:** Otto Graham, 1965; Paul Brown, 1967; Marion Motley, 1968; Jim Brown, 1971; Lou Groza, 1974; Dante Lavelli, 1975; Len Ford, 1976; Bill Willis, 1977; Doug Atkins, 1982; Willie Davis 1981; Bobby Mitchell, 1983; Paul Warfield, 1983; Mike McCormack, 1984; Frank Gatski, 1985; Len Dawson, 1987.
**Retired numbers:** 14, Otto Graham; 32, Jim Brown; 45, Ernie Davis; 46, Don Fleming; 76, Lou Groza.

# IN THE HOT SEATS AT MUNICIPAL STADIUM

Single-game tickets go on sale in June. Because the stadium seats so many, finding tickets—particularly for non-AFC Central games—sometimes isn't difficult a day or two before or even on the day of the game. If a game is not sold out on game day, tickets go on sale at 9 A.M. at the stadium.

If you don't mind sitting next to grown men who wear rubber dog masks and bark, spend $21 and buy a ticket to the Dawg Pound. If you can find one, that is. Those seats are the stadium's hottest sell-

ers and always the first to sell out. Besides the rowdy atmosphere, there's also a practical reason for hunkering down on the bleacher seats. With the stadium's odd, bow-type configuration, you'll be closer to the 50-yard line in the bleachers than if Browns owner Art Modell invited you to sit in his private box.

• **Bad seats:** Lower-deck end-zone seats, $17. Sure, bluebloods and the faint of heart may enjoy sitting in the closed, end-zone portion far away and opposite the

Dawg Pound, but you won't be able to see the top of the scoreboard—or even high punts, especially if you're deep in the section. Network television cameras and vehicles further impede viewing.

 **Scalping:** It's illegal, but it's not policed aggressively. The fact is, given the size of Municipal Stadium, it's not often necessary.

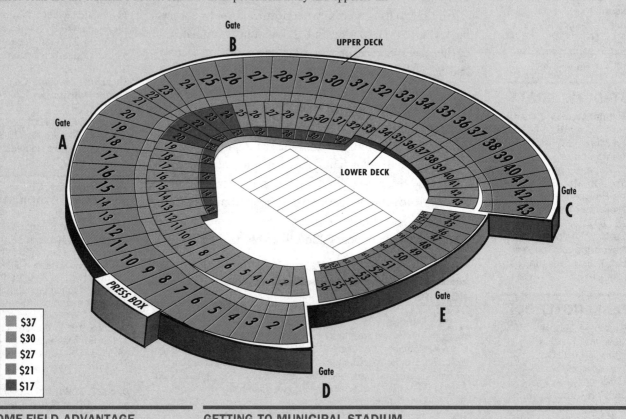

| | |
|---|---|
| ■ | $37 |
| ■ | $30 |
| ■ | $27 |
| ■ | $21 |
| ■ | $17 |

## HOME-FIELD ADVANTAGE

In past years, the Browns have often used a combination of a strong running game (Marion Motley, Jim Brown, Leroy Kelly, Greg Pruitt, Kevin Mack, et al.), and inclement weather to march into the play-offs. Visiting players also sometimes find the Dawg Pound excessively hostile. Before the team cracked down, it was common for fans to throw dog biscuits and, weather permitting, snowballs at the opposing team. One Browns official describes the Dawg Pound as the closest thing you can get to a Duke basketball student section in an NFL stadium.

## GETTING TO MUNICIPAL STADIUM

**Public transportation:** There is no public transportation to the stadium.

**By car:** From the west, take I-90 east to the East Ninth Street exit.
From the east, take I-90 west to Route 2

West. Exit at East Ninth.
From the south, take I-77 north to the East Ninth Street exit. At East Ninth, head northwest towards Lake Erie. Take a left onto North Marginal. Stadium is straight ahead.

## TICKET INFORMATION
**Address:** West 3rd St., Cleveland, OH 44114
**Phone:** (216) 523-8600
**Hours:** Mon.-Fri. 9-5, Sat. 9-5 (Sat. 9-1 in the

offseason).
**Prices:** $37: upper deck rows 1-10; $30: upper deck rows 11 and higher; $27: lower deck sections 1-19 and 25-43; $21: bleachers (sections 44-64); $17: lower

deck sections 20-24 and ground level sections 12-34.

**Training camp:** Cleveland Browns' Training and Administrative Complex, Berea, OH

# Texas Stadium

TM

## STADIUM STATS

**Location:** 2401 E. Airport Freeway, Irving, TX 75062
**Opened:** Oct. 24, 1971
**Surface:** Texas Turf
**Capacity:** 65,846
**Services for fans with disabilities:** Gate 6 is a designated entrance. Seating on the field and in sections 20-21.

## STADIUM FIRSTS

**Regular-season game:** Oct. 24, 1971, 44–21 over the New England Patriots.
**Points scored:** A 56-yard touchdown run by Cowboy Duane Thomas.
**Overtime game:** Sept. 28, 1975, 37–31 over the St. Louis Cardinals.
**Playoff game:** Jan. 2, 1972, 14–3 over the San Francisco 49ers.

## TEAM NOTEBOOK

**Franchise history:** Dallas Cowboys, 1960–present.
**Division titles:** 1966–71, '73, '76, '77–79, '81, '85, '92, '93
**Super Bowl appearances:** V, Jan. 17, 1971, 16–13 loss to the Baltimore Colts; VI, Jan. 16, '72, 24–3 over the Miami Dolphins; X, Jan. 18, '76, 21–17 loss to the Pittsburgh Steelers; XII, Jan. 15, '78, 27–10 over the Denver Broncos; XIII, Jan. 21, '79, 35–31 loss to the Pittsburgh Steelers; XXVII, Jan. 31, '93, 52–17 over the Buffalo Bills; XXVIII, Jan. 30, '94, 30–13 over the Buffalo Bills.
**Pro Football Hall of Fame:** F. Gregg, '77; L. Alworth, '78; H. Adderley, '80; B. Lilly, '80; R. Staubach, '85; M. Ditka, '88; T. Landry, '90; T. Schramm, '91.

Even if you've never been to Texas Stadium, if you follow pro football, this sparkling palace home will feel familiar. The Dallas Cowboys have been one of the NFL's most popular and most-televised teams, frequently beaming their stadium into many of the nation's living rooms.

The hole in the roof is the most striking difference with other NFL facilities. The truth of the old joke that the hole is there "so God can watch his favorite football team play" has not been confirmed, but the partial roof combines an outdoor atmosphere with an indoor environment and does a decent job of protecting fans from inclement conditions. The stadium is clean, well-maintained and plush, with few, if any, bad seats; the proximity of the stands to the field generates intimacy on game days. Meanwhile, the Dallas Cowboys cheerleaders, the Ring of Honor around the facade and the enormous support generated by Cowboys fans all create a bigger-than-life, Lone Star State atmosphere.

Texas Stadium crowds once were criticized because upscale fans in fur coats and three-piece suits seemed to be "too cool" to cheer, but in recent years Cowboys fans have become younger and more boisterous. Since Jerry Jones' purchase of the team in 1989, the Cowboys have gone to great lengths to accommodate this new generation, which explains why the old Cowboys Band has been replaced with blaring, up-tempo music and why Texas Stadium, long distinguished as a "dry" stadium, began selling beer and wine coolers in 1993.

## HOT TIPS FOR VISITING FANS

**Parking**
About 130 acres of parking provide 16,500 spaces on three lots distinguishable by color, as well as another 500 spots for buses. The Blue Lot ($12) is directly outside the stadium, but season ticketholders gobble these up. The Red Lot ($7) also is reserved parking and the waiting list exceeds 500. The Green Lot ($5) is beyond the Red Lot and operates on a cash-only, unreserved basis.

Virtually no options exist beyond the stadium lots. However, the Days Inn across Highway 183 from the stadium is one option that fills up fast. Fans who park in the hotel lot (about $10) still will have to hike across a bridge.

**Weather**
The start of the season generally produces excruciating heat. And when it's hot outside, the humidity inside is even worse because of the half dome/half outdoor configuration. For the rest of the season, though, weather is not a major factor.

**Media bites**
**Radio:** KVIL-FM (103.7) is the flagship station for the Cowboys Network.
**TV:** KDAF (Channel 33, Fox) and WFAA (Channel 8, ABC) carry Cowboys games. KDFW (Channel 4, CBS) has rights to some preseason games.

**Cuisine**
Texas Stadium features

52 full concession stands, 16 specialty stands and 20 vendor stands divided almost evenly between the lower and upper levels. In recent years, Tex-Mex items have become extremely popular, particularly the chicken fajitas and jalapeño hot dogs.

Options abound for after the game. Cowboys Sports Cafe (214-401-3939), owned by ex-Cowboys Tony Dorsett and Everson Walls, is frequented by current players. Former Cowboys receiver Drew Pearson's Sports 88 (214-369-8880) is a very popular restaurant/club/sports bar in North Dallas. Large-screen TVs, live music and a novelty shop are the draws, as is a decor inspired by Cowboys memorabilia.

## LODGING NEAR THE STADIUM
**Holiday North Dallas**
2645 LBJ Freeway
Dallas, TX 75234
(214) 243-3363
6 miles from the stadium.

**Love Field Courtyard**
2383 Stemmons Trail
Dallas, TX 75234
(214) 352-7676
1 mile from the stadium.

## THE COWBOYS AT TEXAS STADIUM
**Dec. 9, 1972:** Calvin Hill rushes for 111 yards in a 34–24 win over the Washington Redskins, becoming the first Cowboy to gain 1,000 yards in a season.

**Sept. 24, 1973:** The Cowboys win 40–3 over the Saints, marking the team's 100th victory, all with Tom Landry as coach.

**Jan. 1, 1978:** The Cowboys slam the Vikings 23–6, taking their fourth NFC championship on the way to a Super Bowl victory over the Denver Broncos.

**Dec. 28, 1980:** Landry's coaching record becomes 200-119-6 when the Cowboys beat the Los Angeles Rams 34–13.

**Dec. 27, 1992:** The Cowboys set a team record for victories in a season (13) by beating the Chicago Bears 27–14.

# IN THE HOT SEATS AT TEXAS STADIUM

If you're not a season ticketholder, the best bet is to get in line the day single-game tickets go on sale in late-June to mid-July. After the 56,000 or so season tickets are accounted for, the entire slate of games goes on sale, starting with fewer than 6,000 tickets per game. The most attractive games—such as those against NFC East rivals or the 49ers—usually sell out within hours, and playoff games are known to sell out within 20 minutes. To cut down on scalping and to offer opportunities for more fans to buy tickets, the Cowboys limit the number of tickets an individual can purchase to a single game—generally 10 for regular-season games and four to six for playoff contests.

On game days, scattered single seats sometimes are available at the Texas Stadium box office. It is extremely rare for two seats to be sold together in these cases, but the quality of seats might surprise you.

• **Scalping:** Although not illegal in Texas,

a city ordinance makes the selling of tickets on Texas Stadium grounds illegal. At one time, this was hardly enforced and scalpers would turn deals outside the gate entrances, but uniformed police officers have cracked down in recent years, and scalpers now work the freeway shoulders and parking lots. Of course, the bigger the game, the higher the price. Bargains usually can be found during the panic period right after kickoff.

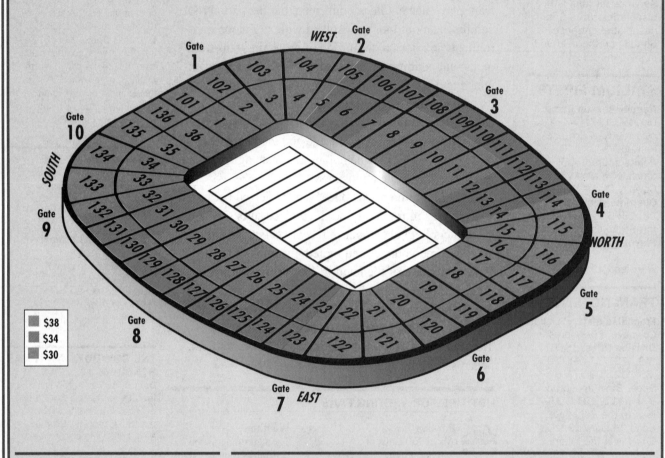

$38
$34
$30

## HOME-FIELD ADVANTAGE

In addition to noise, other nuances at Texas Stadium might favor the Cowboys. The field isn't completely level—it slopes toward the sidelines. Also, during day games, distinct sunny and shaded areas can hamper visibility. And some visiting teams have complained that Texas Stadium has a slower field because crews dampen the artificial turf before games.

## GETTING TO TEXAS STADIUM

**Public transportation:** Special stadium buses provided by Dallas Area Rapid Transit (DART)—"The Cowboy Flyer"—are available on game days from various locations, including downtown. Call (214) 979-1111 for information.

**By car:** Texas Stadium is at the intersection of Loop 12, Highway 114, and Highway 183.

From Dallas–Fort Worth International Airport, take 114 east to the stadium.

From the east and west, follow I-30 to Loop 12 northbound.

### TICKET INFORMATION
**Address:** Texas Stadium, 2401 E. Airport Freeway, Irving TX 75062
**Phone:** (214) 579-5000 or TicketMaster at (214) 373-8000
**Hours:** Mon.-Fri. 9-4.
**Prices:** $38: prime sidelines; $34: sidelines;

$30: corners and end zones.
**Special packages:** Call (800) DABOYS1 for information about packages that include hotel rooms, tickets and transportation to the stadium. These packages offer better seats than you can get from the box office at the stadium. Also, Dallas Cowboys

Travel (214-556-2800) books trips for home and away games; packages include tickets.

**Training camp:** St. Edward's University, Austin, TX

TM

## STADIUM STATS

**Location:** 1200 Featherstone Rd., Pontiac, MI 48342
**Opened:** Aug. 23, 1975
**Surface:** AstroTurf
**Capacity:** 80,368
**Services for fans with disabilities:** Seating available in the bleachers and in sections 106-108 of the 100 level. Tickets go on sale two Mondays before game day.

## STADIUM FIRSTS

**Regular-season game:** Oct. 6, 1975, 36–10 loss to the Dallas Cowboys.
**Points scored:** 21-yard field goal by Toni Fritsch of the Cowboys.
**Overtime game:** Nov. 27, 1980, 23–17 loss to the Chicago Bears.
**Playoff game:** Jan. 5, 1992, 38–6 over the Dallas Cowboys.

## TEAM NOTEBOOK

**Franchise history:** Detroit Lions, 1934–present.
**Division titles:** 1935, '52–54, '57, '83, '91.
**Pro Football Hall of Fame:** Earl (Dutch) Clark, 1963; Bill Dudley, '66; Bobby Layne, '67; Jack Christiansen, 1970; Hugh McElhenny, '70; Ollie Matson, '72; Joe Schmidt, '73; Dick (Night Train) Lane, '74; Yale Lary, '79; Frank Gatski, '86; Doak Walker, '86; Alex Wojciechowicz, '86; John Henry Johnson, '87; Lem Barney, '92.
**Retired Numbers:** 7, Dutch Clark; 22, Bobby Layne; 37, Doak Walker; 56, Joe Schmidt; 85, Chuck Hughes; 88, Charlie Sanders.

# Pontiac Silverdome

The idea for a domed stadium in the Detroit area had been kicked around for years, but it took firm hold in Tiger Stadium on Thanksgiving Day, 1968. The Lions lost to the Philadelphia Eagles in a nationally televised game in which the mud was so deep that 11 pairs of football shoes were lost and not recovered until the spring.

Less than seven years later, the Lions debuted in the Pontiac Metropolitan Stadium, and they haven't lost a football shoe since. The stadium was nicknamed "PonMet," much to the chagrin of Pontiac city officials. It got its current name in 1976 when retired Lions vice president Edwin J. Anderson, viewing the facility from the air, called it "a silver dome."

The Silverdome has had its share of problems. The Teflon roof has collapsed twice, and in 1978 a plan to clean the artificial turf backfired: The Astroturf was shipped to an airport and laid out on a runway in hopes that rain would beat dirt to the surface, where it could be vacuumed off. Unfortunately, it never stopped raining, so the Stadium Authority had to pay to have several tons of excess rainwater shipped back with the turf.

The stadium has several advantages over Detroit's other arenas. Unlike Tiger Stadium, it has no obstructed views in the house, and unlike The Palace and Joe Louis Arena, tickets are generally available and don't require a second mortgage. While the basketball and hockey venues cater to white-collar fans, the Silverdome appeals to the shot-and-beer crowd—and as long as the Lions continue to show signs of life, fans will keep coming.

## HOT TIPS FOR VISITING FANS

**Parking**
Of the 10,000 parking spaces available on-site, several hundred were sacrificed for the grass field used for World Cup soccer matches. The field remained on the parking lot until needed indoors.

The price of parking ($7) is controlled by the Silverdome and must be prepaid. Several private lots are within ½ mile of the arena, most of which cost around $5. Some fans prefer to save a couple of bucks by using the shuttle from the Phoenix Center in downtown Pontiac, about 2 miles from the Silverdome. The fee downtown is $3 per car, and the shuttle bus is free. Traffic generally isn't a problem.

**Weather**
Always 72 degrees inside the stadium, which is great for those chilly December games. However, with 60,000 warm bodies inside, preseason games in August can get toasty.

**Media bites**
**Radio:** WWJ (950 AM).
**TV:** WJBK (Channel 2, Fox); WXYZ (Channel 7, ABC).

**Cuisine**
The best-selling items are hot dogs, foot-long chili dogs, fresh kielbasa and Italian sausage with all the trimmings. The beer, all premium and all draft, comes in 14- and 22-ounce cups for $3.50 and $4.75, respectively.

Before the game, try the Main Event Sports Bar and Grille, at the north end of the Silverdome at club level. The restaurant can handle about 1,000 people at a time, and most come for the 15-entree, pregame buffet at $22.50 per person. Because only 200 people can get window seats, most fans head for their seats by the end of the first quarter.

Few bars or restaurants are around the Silverdome, and Ted's Bar and Grill (810-373-4440) is the only one within walking distance. In downtown Pontiac, Griff's Grill (810-334-9292) offers burgers and a hearty dose of rock 'n' roll.

## LODGING NEAR THE STADIUM

**Troy Warren Auburn Hills Marriott**
200 W. Big Beaver
Troy, MI 48084
(810) 680-9797/(800) 228-9290
10 miles from the stadium.

**Guest Quarters Suite Hotel**
850 Tower Dr.
Troy, MI 48098
(810) 879-7500/(800) 424-2900
10 miles from the stadium.

## THE LIONS AT THE SILVERDOME

**Nov. 12, 1978:** Horace King sprints 75 yards for a touchdown in the longest run ever from scrimmage in the Silverdome. The Lions beat the Tampa Bay Buccaneers 34–23.

**Dec. 18, 1983:** A 23–20 win over the Tampa Bay Buccaneers clinches the Lions' first division title since 1957.

**Oct. 19, 1986:** Eric Hipple throws the longest pass completed in the dome to Leonard Thompson—94 yards, for a touchdown. The Lions win 48–17 over the Chicago Bears.

**Nov. 23, 1989:** Barry Sanders breaks the 1,000-yard mark when he runs for 145 yards in a 13–10 win over the Cleveland Browns.

**Jan. 5, 1992:** The Lions beat Dallas Cowboys 38–6 in their first home playoff game in 35 years, and the first in the Silverdome.

# IN THE HOT SEATS AT THE SILVERDOME

The size of the Silverdome is a double-edged sword. While the large capacity makes it easier for more fans to watch the Lions, it also makes it more difficult to sell out, so almost all home games are blacked out locally. Even the Lions' playoff game against the Packers in 1993—just the second playoff game at the Silverdome—wasn't sold out in time to lift the blackout.

• **Special programs:** Season ticketholders—there are 35,000, 25,000 of whom date from the Silverdome's first year—get a $25 discount by purchasing early. During the preseason, a variety of two-for-one specials are sponsored by various corporations.

The bleachers on the lower level in the corner of the south end zone are a tremendous bargain. The seats are better-situated than many in the house and are cheaper than all the seats in the upper level. They go on sale two weeks before game day.

• **Bad seats:** Although no seats have an obstructed view of the field, the only Diamondvision scoreboard is in the south end zone, so people sitting on south side of the stadium miss out.

• **Scalping:** The size of the stadium limits scalping since good seats usually are available at bargain rates. When demand is high, though, the Pontiac police aggressively monitor ticket scalpers on stadium grounds. The best place to find tickets is near the privately owned parking lots that surround the stadium.

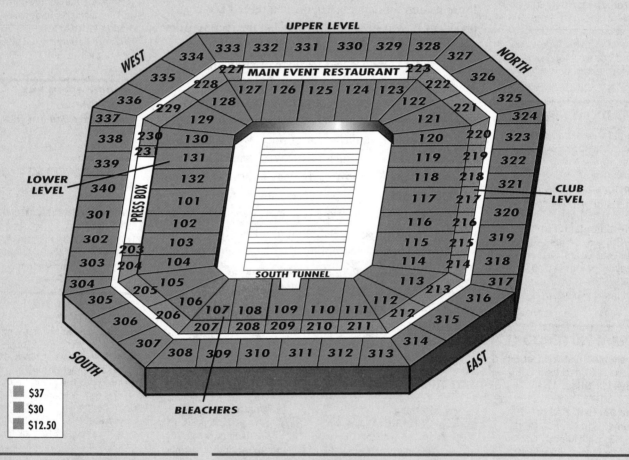

$37
$30
$12.50

---

## HOME-FIELD ADVANTAGE

It doesn't happen often, but when the Silverdome is packed with 80,000 fans, the noise resembles screaming with a metal bucket over your head. The bench area is less than 6 feet from the front row of seats, so opposing players have no place to hide from biting comments from Detroit fans.

## GETTING TO THE SILVERDOME

**Public transportation:** There is no way to reach the Silverdome on public transportation.

**By car:** From Chicago, I-90 East to I-94 East to I-275 North to I-696 East to M-24 North (Telegraph Road) to Square Lake Road. Follow Square Lake Road east to the first exit, Opdyke Road. At the stop sign at the end of the ramp, turn right to the first stoplight, then right onto Opdyke Road. The Silverdome is just less than 3 miles ahead, on the left.

From Detroit, I-75 North to M-59 West. Take the first exit and left onto Opdyke Road. The Silverdome is on the corner of M-59 and Opdyke Road.

From Port Huron, I-94 West to M-59 West, left on Opdyke Road. The Silverdome is on the corner.

---

**TICKET INFORMATION**
**Address:** Pontiac Silverdome, 1200 Featherstone Rd., Pontiac, MI 48342
**Phone:** (313) 335-4151 or TicketMaster at

(810) 645-6666
**Hours:** Mon.-Sat. 10-6 (Sat. 10-2 when game is away; Mon.-Fri. 9-5 in offseason).
**Prices:** $37: club level; $30: upper and

lower deck; $12.50: bleachers.

**Training Camp:** Pontiac Silverdome, Pontiac, MI

TM

## STADIUM STATS

**Location:** 1900 Eliot St., Denver, CO 80204
**Opened:** 1948
**Surface:** Grass
**Capacity:** 76,273
**Services for fans with disabilities:** Seating available in sections 101, 111, 113, 123 and 136.

## STADIUM FIRSTS

**Regular-season game:** Oct. 2, 1960, 31–14 over the Oakland Raiders.
**Points scored:** 17–yard field goal by Eugene Mingo of the Broncos.
**Overtime game:** Nov. 30, 1975, 13–10 over the San Diego Chargers.
**Playoff game:** Dec. 24, 1977, 34–21 over the Pittsburgh Steelers.

## TEAM NOTEBOOK

**Franchise history:** Denver Broncos, 1960–69 (AFL), Denver Broncos 1970-present (NFL).
**Division titles:** 1977, 1978, 1984, 1986, 1987, 1989, 1991.
**Super Bowl appearances:** XII, Jan. 15, 1978, 27–10 loss to the Dallas Cowboys; XXI, Jan. 25, 1987, 39–20 loss to the New York Giants; XXII, Jan. 31, 1988, 42–10 loss to the Washington Redskins; XXIV, Jan. 28, 1990, 55–10 loss to the San Francisco 49ers.
**Pro Football Hall of Fame:** Fred Gehrke, 1972; Willie Brown, 1984; Doak Walker, 1986; Stan Jones, 1991.
**Retired numbers:** 18, Frank Tripucka; 44, Floyd Little.

# Mile High Stadium

Constructed by the Howsam family on a rat-infested city dump west of downtown Denver, Bears Stadium was originally meant for baseball when it opened in August 1948. Not until December 1968 did it become Mile High Stadium, but since the Broncos' first game in 1960, Denver hasn't been the same.

Broncos fans are so devoted that Mile High has been called the loudest outdoor arena in North America, which says something about how deafening a home game can be. For Denver fans, rooting for the Broncos is a religious experience, not a social occasion. If it's snowing, the visiting team might have as much to fear from snowballs thrown from the south stands as from John Elway's passes. Watching over the mayhem is Bucky the Bronco, the signature horse that has stood atop the south-stands scoreboard since 1976; 30 feet tall and made of white fiberglass, Bucky was modeled after Trigger, the Roy Rogers horse of cinema fame. While Bucky might be the only one that doesn't mind Mile High's plumbing problems and too few restrooms, the fans put up with the aging stadium simply because of the electric atmosphere. In their eyes, Sundays at Mile High have no equal in the NFL.

## HOT TIPS FOR VISITING FANS

**Parking**
Space for 9,010 vehicles in city-owned lots at the Denver Sports Complex. However, most of the city-owned lots north of 17th Avenue (closest to Mile High) are by permit only. Parking costs $5-$20, depending on the distance from the stadium. Shuttle service is available from far-flung parking areas. Additional parking is available across I-25 at various Auraria Campus sites.

To beat the traffic, arrive two hours before kickoff and enjoy a tailgate party. Immediately before and after the game, the sellout crowds create massive traffic jams. City police do a consistently remarkable job of getting traffic flowing 30-45 minutes after the game.

**Weather**
The Broncos have played several ice-cold games at home, but Denver's fall and winter weather usually is mild, more so than NFL cities in the Midwest and the Northeast. Only at three Broncos home games has the temperature at kickoff been below 20 degrees, and none since 1978.

**Media bites**
**Radio:** KOA (850 AM) is the flagship station for the Broncos radio network. Larry Zimmer does play-by-play, and Browns and Broncos veteran Dave Logan handles color commentary.
**TV:** KCNC (Channel 4) is the NBC affiliate.

**Cuisine**
Choices are a cut above standard stadium fare. Among the selections are gourmet hot dogs, barbecued meats, tossed salads, deli sandwiches, iced and hot cappuccino, bottled water, fresh-squeezed lemonade, and imported beers. New items include cinnamon rolls and the buffalo-meat burger, a Rocky Mountain specialty that has a considerably lower cholesterol and fat content than a hamburger.

Several sports bars, including Zang Brewing Company (303-455-2500) and Brooklyn's (303-572-3999), are nearby. Zang's, as locals call it, is 3 blocks from Mile High in a brick building that dates from 1871. It has 16 televisions, two satellite systems and sports memorabilia. Broncos safety Steve Atwater often comes by, as do Nuggets Dikembe Mutombo and LaPhonso Ellis, and Charlie Hayes of the Rockies. Brooklyn's is 200 yards south of the stadium, in an area that was known many years ago as "Little Brooklyn." The bar has 30 televisions and four satellite systems. Both spots are wall-to-wall with people before and after Broncos home games.

## LODGING NEAR THE STADIUM
**Westin Hotel Tabor Center**
1672 Lawrence St.
Denver, CO 80202
(303) 572-9100/(800) 228-3000
1 mile from the stadium.

**Denver Marriott City Center**
1701 California St.
Denver, CO 80202
(303) 297-1300/(800) 228-9290
5 miles from the stadium.

## THE BRONCOS AT MILE HIGH STADIUM
**Oct. 22, 1973:** Before a stirred-up Monday-night crowd, the Broncos come back to tie the Oakland Raiders 23–23 with a Jim Turner field goal.

**Jan. 1, 1978:** The Broncos earn a place in the Super Bowl by defeating the Raiders 20–17.

**Jan. 10, 1988:** A 34–10 victory over the Houston Oilers puts the Broncos in the AFC championship game. They make it all the way to the Super Bowl, where they lose to the Washington Redskins.

**Jan. 14, 1990:** The Broncos take their fourth AFC championship by beating the Cleveland Browns 37–21.

**Jan. 4, 1992:** Down 21–6, the Broncos come back to beat the Houston Oilers 26–24 in an AFC divisional playoff game.

# IN THE HOT SEATS AT MILE HIGH STADIUM

Every nonstrike regular-season and post-season game hosted by the Broncos has been sold out since 1970. That streak of 188 sellouts dates to Denver's first NFL season. The Broncos have sold more than 73,000 season tickets every year since 1977. The waiting list for season tickets reached a high of 18,000 in 1987 and is now at 3,500. Sixty percent of the tickets were increased $8 in February 1994, but the team felt no major backlash from fans, perhaps because the last price hike had been before the 1989 season.

The week of a home game, you sometimes can purchase scattered singles from the team, but those occasions are rare. Generally, the only tickets available are those returned by the visiting team.

• **Bad seats:** Though the stadium was built for baseball, it doesn't have a bad seat for football. No seats have obstructed views at Mile High, which has five levels. Among the best seats are those in the third level, sections 301 through 346.

 **Scalping:** There aren't any bargains.

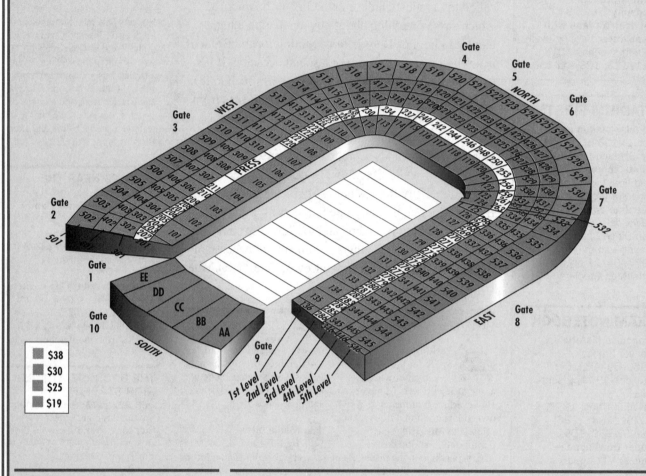

$38
$30
$25
$19

## HOME-FIELD ADVANTAGE

It's no exaggeration to say the Broncos enjoy the biggest advantage in the NFL. Between 1977, their first playoff season, and 1994, the Broncos were the league's winningest home team, with a 99–33 record in regular-season games. Part of the advantage surely comes from being the only team that plays at 5,280 feet. Visiting teams, particularly those outside the AFC West, often place oxygen tanks and masks behind their benches.

## GETTING TO MILE HIGH STADIUM

**Public transportation:** Buses stop on Federal Boulevard, at the southeast corner of the stadium. Call RTD at (303) 299-6000 for more information.

**By car:** From the north or south: I-25 to the Mile High Stadium exit. The Stadium is off 19th Avenue and Federal.

## TICKET INFORMATION
**Address:** 1900 Eliot St., Denver, CO 80204
**Phone:** (303) 433-7466
**Hours:** Mon.-Fri. 8-5 (also open game day during the season).
**Prices:** $38: first-level sections 101-110 and 125-136, third-level sections 301-314 and 334-346, and fourth-level sections 401-414 and 434-445; $30: first-level sections 111-124, third-level sections 315-333, fourth-level sections 415-433, and fifth-level sections 501-514 and 533-546; $25: fifth-level sections 515-533; $19: south end-zone sections AA, BB, CC, DD, EE.

**Training Camp:** Lawrenson Hall, University of Northern Colorado, Greeley, CO

TM

## STADIUM STATS

**Lambeau Field**
**Location:** 1265 Lombardi
Ave., Green Bay, WI 54307
**Opened:** Sept. 29, 1957
**Surface:** Grass
**Capacity:** 59,543
**Services for fans with
disabilities:** Seating in
club sections 90 and 91.

**Milwaukee County
Stadium** (see Milwaukee
Brewers, page 45)

## STADIUM FIRSTS

**Regular-season game:**
Sept. 29, 1957, 21–17
over the Chicago Bears.
**Points scored:** 95-yard
touchdown run by Ed
Brown of Chicago.
**Playoff game:** Dec. 31,
1961, 37–0 over the
New York Giants.

## TEAM NOTEBOOK

**Franchise history:** Green
Bay Packers, 1921–
present.
**Division titles:** 1929–31,
'36, '38, '39, '44,
'60–62, '65–67, '72.
**Super Bowl appearances:**
I, Jan. 15, 1967, 35–10
over the Kansas City
Chiefs; II, Jan. 14, '68,
33–14 over the Oakland
Raiders.
**Pro Football Hall of
Fame:** Hubbard, Hutson,
Lambeau, McNally,
1963; Hinkle, '64;
Michalske, Herber,
Kiesling, '66; Tunnell,
'67; Lombardi, '71;
Canadeo, '74; Ford,
Taylor, '76; Gregg, Starr,
'77; Nitschke, '78;
Adderley, '80; Davis,
Ringo, '81; Hornung, '86;
Wood, '89; Hendricks,
'90; Stenerud, '91.
**Retired numbers:** 3,
Canadeo; 66, Nitschke;
14, Hutson; 15, Starr.

# Lambeau Field

This immaculate, oval-shaped structure (named after Earl L. "Curly" Lambeau, founder and first coach of the Green Bay Packers) in tiny Green Bay, Wisconsin, gives football fans exactly what they want—seats close to the action, no upper decks, terrific sight-lines and a huge parking lot. All these things make Lambeau Field perhaps the best pro football stadium in the country. Never mind that the steel benches do little for the gluteus maximus—the action is so close to the stands that you can almost hear the quarterback call signals and the pads collide. The backs of the end zones aren't more than a few yards from the first row of the stadium, and the sideline benches are close enough that players can hear insults hurled at them from the front row. Fans arrive early and are rabid in their enthusiasm.

Forty years ago, when the Packers were still shaky financially, they started playing games in Milwaukee County Stadium to help attendance. Currently, one pre-season and three regular-season games are played there. One problem in Milwaukee is that the stadium is designed for baseball; it is the only NFL field on which both teams stand on the same sideline, separated by a piece of tape at the 50-yard line. Another problem is that County Stadium holds just 56,051, and several thousand seats have obstructed views. The fans in Milwaukee, perhaps irritated by the poor viewing angles, tend to be more fickle than fans in Green Bay. They don't accept losing very well and are quick to boo the smallest of indiscretions. Still, they can be as loud and boisterous as Lambeau Field fans if things are going right.

## HOT TIPS FOR VISITING FANS

**Parking**
Approximately 5,200
spots are around
Lambeau Field, with an additional 1,000 behind the Brown
County Arena. Fans start filing
into the lots three hours before
the game to get prime tailgating
spots. If the main lots are full,
park in the makeshift lots in the
neighborhood. Most of the major
streets around the stadium don't
allow parking on game day.

Getting to the stadium can be
a time-consuming affair.
Generally all nearby highway
exits are backed up on game day.
One alternative is to overshoot
the Lombardi Avenue exit on
Highway 41 and peel back to the

stadium through the side streets.

**Weather**
Headgear, thick socks,
and heavy shoes or boots
are a must once October rolls
around. Typically, the Packers
play one late-season game at
Lambeau, which is almost
always bitterly cold. The most
common outfit for these occasions is bright-orange hunting
overalls and snow boots.

**Media bites**
**Radio:** WTMJ (620 AM)
is the flagship station of the
Packer Radio Network. Jim
Irwin and Packers great Max
McGee are the announcers.

**TV:** WGBA (Channel 26) is
the Fox station.

**Cuisine**
Lambeau Field offers
standard fare: bratwurst,
hot dogs, popcorn, candy, beer
and soda. Most people bring
their own eats. Tailgaters grill
anything from hot dogs and
bratwurst to steaks and chops.

The most popular eatery is
Kroll's (414-468-4422), which
specializes in hamburgers and
chili. The restaurant is full for
hours after the game. Two local
bars, the 50-Yard Line and the
Stadium View, are pregame and
postgame hangouts.

## LODGING NEAR THE STADIUM
**The Radisson in Green Bay**
2040 Airport Dr.
Green Bay, WI 54313
(414) 494-7300/(800) 333-3333
About 4 miles from the stadium.

**Paper Valley Hotel**
333 W. College Ave.
Appleton, WI 54911
(414) 733-8000/(800) 242-3499
40 miles from the stadium.

## THE PACKERS AT LAMBEAU FIELD
**Dec. 31, 1961:** The Packers
take their seventh NFL championship with a 37–0 win over the
New York Giants.

**Dec. 26, 1965:** Don Chandler
hits a 25-yard field goal in the
second overtime of a playoff
game to beat the Baltimore
Colts 13–10.

**Dec. 31, 1967:** In 16 below-
zero temperatures, Bart Starr
sneaks over from the 1-yard line
in the last minute, leading the
Pack to a 21–17 win over the
Dallas Cowboys and their third
consecutive NFL title.

**Dec. 21, 1969:** Don Horn passes for five touchdowns and 410
yards in a 45–28 rout of the
St. Louis Cardinals.

**Jan. 8, 1983:** Playing their first
playoff game at Lambeau Field
since 1967, the Packers top
the Cardinals 41–16 behind
four Lynn Dickey touchdown
passes.

# IN THE HOT SEATS AT LAMBEAU FIELD

About 15,000 people are on the waiting list for season tickets, and in the last two years, only 18 names moved up. Because the Packers sell out on a season-ticket basis in Green Bay, they don't offer single-game tickets until the week of the game—and even then only a couple of hundred seats turned in by the opposing team are available. In Milwaukee, about 50,000 tickets are reserved for season ticketholders, and the remainder go on sale starting Feb. 1. Once the schedule is determined, orders are filled for Milwaukee tickets and remaining tickets go on sale immediately.

• **Good seats:** Lambeau has no poles, and sightlines are excellent. If you have to sit in the end zones, sit in the south one so you don't have to crane your neck to see the replay board. The Packers plan to put another replay board in the south end zone some day.

**Scalping:** A Green Bay city ordinance prohibits the sale of tickets for more than face value, and undercover agents patrol outside the stadium. The best way to buy a ticket for a single game is to check the local newspapers. But for the most part, the "tickets wanted" ads far outnumber the "tickets for sale" ads.

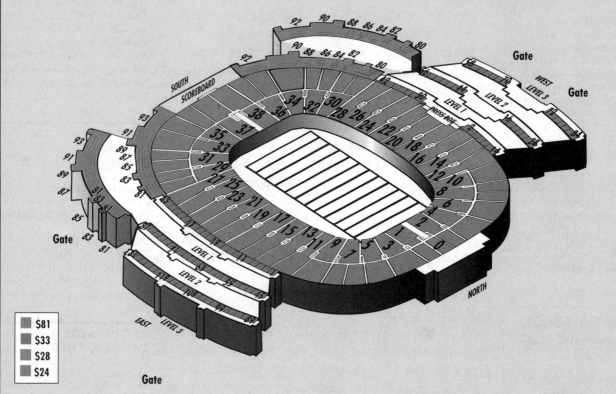

- $81
- $33
- $28
- $24

## HOME-FIELD ADVANTAGE

The locker rooms: The Packers dress in plush surroundings, but visitors dress in a tin can on the opposite side of the stadium.

The cold: The Packers live in the bitter cold day-to-day, and their bodies are used to it. Some players come on the field without sleeves in sub-zero weather.

The field: A heating system used to defrost the ice on the field often creates slick spots outside the hash marks. The Packers can determine which cleats are best in warmups, but opponents usually have to make do with what they brought.

## GETTING TO LAMBEAU FIELD

**Lambeau Field**
**Public transportation:** Lambeau Field can't be reached by public transportation on weekends.

**By car:** From either Highway 41 or Highway 172, take the Lombardi Avenue exit. Go right and follow Lombardi for 1 mile to Lambeau Field.

**Milwaukee County Stadium**
**Public transportation:** The No. 90 bus runs along Wisconsin Avenue to the stadi-um. Call (414) 344-6711 for more information.

**By car:** From the north or south, take I-94 West to the County Stadium exit. The Stadium will be visible from the highway.

From the east, take I-94 to U.S. 41 southbound. The stadium exit is just after the turn onto 41.

From the west, take I-94 to the VA/County Stadium exit. The Stadium will be visible; follow the signs to parking.

**TICKET INFORMATION**
**Lambeau Field**
**Address:** 1265 Lombardi Ave., Green Bay, WI 54303
**Phone:** (414) 496-5719
**Hours:** Mon.-Fri. 9-5.
**Prices:** $81: club (south end-zone sections 90, 92, 88 and 83); $33: luxury boxes.

$28: sideline; $24: other end-zone sections.

**Milwaukee County Stadium**
**Address:** 201 S. 46th St., Milwaukee, WI 53214
**Phone:** (414) 342-2717
**Hours:** Mon.-Fri. 8:30-4.

**Prices:** $30: mezzanine and upper boxes; $27: lower grandstand sidelines and all upper grandstands; $24: lower grand-stands in end zones and bleachers; $20: lower boxes.

**Training camp:** St. Norbert College, West De Pere, WI

# Astrodome

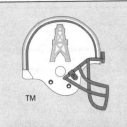

## STADIUM STATS

**Location:** Loop 610, Kirby and Fannin Sts., Houston, TX 77054
**Opened:** April 12, 1965
**Surface:** "Magic Carpet" AstroTurf
**Capacity:** 62,439
**Services for fans with disabilities:** Tickets for accessible seating may be purchased at West Gate B, Mon.-Fri. 9-5, or by calling (713) 799-9555. Also available two hours before kickoff at the Astrodome USA Media Entrance, near W-1 parking.

## STADIUM FIRSTS

**Regular-season game:** Sept. 9, 1968, 26–21 loss to the Kansas City Chiefs.
**Points scored:** 5-yard touchdown run by Hoyle Granger of the Oliers.
**Overtime game:** Oct.28, 1979, 27–24 over the New York Jets.
**Playoff game:** Dec.24, 1979, 13–7 over the Denver Broncos.

## TEAM NOTEBOOK

**Franchise history:** Houston Oilers, 1960–69 (AFL); Houston Oilers, 1970–present (NFL).
**Division titles:** 1960, 1961, 1962, 1967, 1991, 1993.
**Pro Football Hall of Fame:** George Blanda, 1981; Sid Gillman, 1983; Ken Houston, 1986; John Henry Johnson, 1987; Earl Campbell, 1991.
**Retired numbers:** 34, Earl Campbell; 43, Jim Norton; 65, Elvin Bethea.

L ooking for an NFL stadium with an intimate atmosphere, good visibility, and hair-raising crowd noise? Welcome to the Eighth Wonder of the World, the Harris County Domed Stadium—popularly known as the Astrodome. You could also say it's the Mother of All Domes, since it was constructed in 1961, long before the arrival of its closed-top offspring in New Orleans, Pontiac, Seattle, Indianapolis, and Minneapolis. This fact has earned the stadium yet another moniker— "Astrodome. The Original."

Like many elderly NFL venues, the Astrodome has been spruced up in recent seasons to provide better amenities and expanded seating. Most recently, in 1988, 10,000 seats were added to satisfy Texas' football-hungry fans—capacity is now at 62,439. A new football-only AstroTurf system was also installed, making the Astrodome the only artificial-turf stadium in the USA with entirely separate fields for football and baseball. This was the fourth time that the Astrodome has received a new rug.

All Texas football fans are sophisticated when it come to the Science of the Pigskin, and Oilers fans are certainly no different. While the fans go wild when the Oilers "do the right thing" on the field, they can become boo-birds at the drop of a pass. Games at the Astrodome remain a pulsating experience for everyone—players, coaches and fans. Sometimes the place can get so loud that the dome feels about ready to blow off.

## HOT TIPS FOR VISITING FANS

**Parking**
It's excellent, with terrific access. There are more than 24,300 spaces, all at a reasonable $4.

Houston traffic is notoriously bad during rush hour on weekdays, so plan to come at least an hour early for Monday night games to avoid any tie-ups.

Don't bother coming early for tailgating—it's totally prohibited here.

**Weather**
Houston's late-summer and early-fall parking-lot weather can still be sticky with humidity. Generally, falls are gorgeous, and winters are typically moderate.

**Media bites**
**Radio:** KTRH (740 AM). Tom Franklin, Russ Small and former Oilers coach Bum Phillips are the announcers.
**TV:** KPRC (Channel 2, NBC), KTRK (Channel 13, ABC).

**Cuisine**
Stadium fare has been merely okay in recent seasons, but a change in ownership and management has led to upgraded choices. The Astrodome now has more than 120 food and beverage outlets, which offer Texas barbeque, pizza, hot dogs, burgers, deli items, and multiple brands of Dome Foam, a k a beer.

Nearby restaurants include the Hard Rock Cafe (713-520-1134), the Palm (713-977-2544) for steak and Pappasito's (713-668-5756) for Mexican.

## LODGING NEAR THE STADIUM

**Sheraton Astrodome**
8686 Kirby Dr.
Houston, TX 77054
(713) 748-3221/(800) 325-3535
1 block from the stadium.

**Holiday Inn Astrodome**
8111 Kirby Dr.
Houston, TX 77054
(713) 790-1900/(800) 465-4329
About 6 blocks from the stadium.

## THE OILERS AT THE ASTRODOME

**Feb. 10, 1968:** Owner K.S. "Bud" Adams, Jr. announces that the Oilers will move to the Harris County Domed Stadium for the 1968 season.

**Dec. 14, 1969:** The Oilers come from behind to beat the Boston Patriots 27–23 and assure themselves a playoff spot.

**Oct. 1, 1972:** The Oilers stun Joe Namath and the New York Jets 26–20 in the Astrodome for their only 1972 victory.

**Oct. 19, 1975:** The Oilers come from behind to defeat Washington 13–10 in the Astrodome for their first win over an NFC team.

**Dec. 21, 1980:** A 20–16 victory over the Minnesota Vikings in the Astrodome clinches the Oilers' third playoff spot in three years. Earl Campbell sets an NFL record by rushing over 200 yards in a single game for the fourth time that season.

**Dec. 27, 1987:** The Oilers clinch their first playoff berth since 1980 as they defeat the Bengals 21–17.

**Dec. 16, 1990:** Quarterback Warren Moon has the second-best passing performance in NFL history, completing 27 of 45 for 527 yards in a 27–10 win over the Kansas City Chiefs.

**Dec. 29, 1991:** Safety Bubba McDowell intercepts two passes near the Oilers' goal line to nail down a 17-10 wild-card victory over the New York Jets.

# IN THE HOT SEATS AT THE ASTRODOME

Season tickets go on sale in March, and individual-game tickets are available in August. There is no ticket lottery, though mail orders with requests for specific seats can be sent in July. For large groups, mail order is suggested, but only price range can be selected; the Oilers pick the seats.

Tickets are often available, sometimes even on game day; sellouts are rare. In 1993, Randall's, a local supermarket, bought the last couple of thousand tickets each week and sold them at their stores. That same season, the Oilers offered a deal for those buying tickets to purchase the next several games in advance on an installment plan, with the option to buy playoff tickets later or upgrade to a better plan the following season.

• **Bad seats:** The Oilers removed about 2,500 obstructed-view seats in 1993, but there are still some bad ones in the back rows of the upper deck (bring your binoculars!).

**Scalping:** Scalping is legal in Texas, but it's not permitted on stadium grounds. Still, there are scalpers who stand along the roadsides adjoining stadium property. Another option is to look in the Yellow Pages under "Tickets."

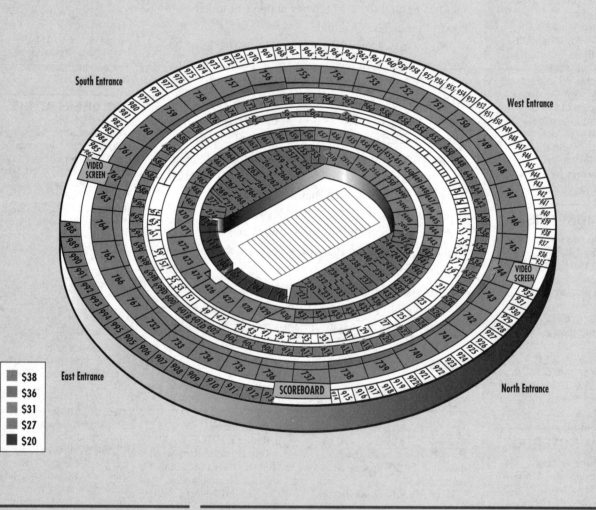

South Entrance

West Entrance

East Entrance

North Entrance

VIDEO SCREEN

VIDEO SCREEN

SCOREBOARD

- $38
- $36
- $31
- $27
- $20

## HOME-FIELD ADVANTAGE

During the rough-and-tumble Jerry Glanville era, the dome was fondly referred to as "The House of Pain" by rabid Oilers fans. Glanville is gone, but visiting teams still find the acoustics deafening and the surface rock-hard. It's a nasty place to play when on the road.

## GETTING TO THE ASTRODOME

**Public transportation:** The No. 15 Hiram-Clark and No. 18 Kirby buses stop at the Astrodome. Call (713) 635-4000 for more information.

**By car:** From Intercontinental Airport, take Highway 59 South to Highway 288 South. Take exit 288 at Holly Hall Street and make a right onto Holly Hall, which dead-ends at the Astrodome parking lot.

From Hobby Airport, take Broadway heading north to I-45 North. On I-45, get into the left lane and exit onto Loop 610. Take Loop 610 to the Kirby Drive exit and make a right onto Kirby. The Astrodome will be on your right.

## TICKET INFORMATION

**Address:** Houston Oilers Ticket Office, P.O. Box 1516, Houston, TX 77251; or go to Astrodome, in lobby of APC Building at 6910 Fannin St.

**Phone number:** (713) 797-1000 or TicketMaster at (713) 629-3700
**Hours:** Mon.-Fri. 8:30-5 plus Sat. 9-5 before a home game.
**Prices:** $38: loge, sky club; $36: field level,

mezzanine, upper boxes (rows 20-38); $31: all other mezzanine and upper boxes; $27: lower west reserved, upper reserved (rows 6-19), pavilion; $20: lower east reserved.

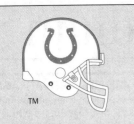

TM

## STADIUM STATS

**Location:** 100 S. Capital Ave., Indianapolis, IN 46225
**Opened:** May 3, 1984
**Surface:** AstroTurf
**Capacity:** 60,129
**Services for fans with disabilities:** Seating available at each gate behind row 40 on level 1.

## STADIUM FIRSTS

**Regular-season game:** Sept. 2, 1984, 23–14 loss to the New York Jets.
**Points scored:** A 3-yard touchdown run by Curtis Dickey of the Colts.
**Regular-season win:** Sept. 30, 1984, 31–17 over the Buffalo Bills.
**Overtime game:** Oct. 29, 1989, 23–20 loss to the New England Patriots.

## TEAM NOTEBOOK

**Franchise history:** Miami Seahawks, 1946; Baltimore Colts, 1947–49 (AAFC); Baltimore Colts, '50–83 (NFL); Indianapolis Colts, 1984–present.
**Division titles:** 1948 (tie), '58, '59, '64, '65 (tie), '67 (tie), '68, '70, '75, '76, '77, '87.
**Super Bowl appearances:** III, Jan. 12, 1969, 16–7 loss to the New York Jets; V, Jan. 17, 1971, 16–13 over the Dallas Cowboys.
**Pro Football Hall of Fame:** A. Donovan, '68; J. Perry, '69; Y.A. Tittle, '71; G. Marchetti, '72; R. Berry, '73; J. Parker, '73; L. Moore, '75; W. Ewbank, '78; J. Unitas, '79; G. Blanda, '81; T. Hendricks, '90; J. Mackey, '92.
**Retired numbers:** 19, J. Unitas; 22, B. Young; 24, L. Moore; 70, A. Donovan; 77, J. Parker; 82, R. Berry; 89, G. Marchetti.

# RCA Dome

Ten years and 159 NFL games haven't changed one fact about the RCA Dome: It's a pleasant place to spend a Sunday. Not provocative. Not exciting. Not loud. Just pleasant.

The RCA Dome sits near the heart of Indianapolis. It has a Teflon-coated fiberglass roof 19 stories high and weighs 257 tons. A day and a half is needed to set up the Dome for a Colts game, because workers have to roll out 28 15-foot rolls of AstroTurf, each weighing two tons.

Given the Colts' recent record, all that work seems for naught. Since their move, the Colts never have approached the kind of success they had in Baltimore, and Indianapolis sports fans have yet to build a bandwagon for the team, let alone jump on it. In fact, many fans seem to view home games as a way to avoid raking the leaves on Sunday afternoons. Typical Midwestern politeness permeates the Dome. This makes for a relaxed and, well, pleasant atmosphere rather than the kind of heart-stopping, ear-ringing drama and noise at many other stadiums. If the Bears, Bengals or Browns are in town, the excitement does ease up and some folks go so far as to paint their faces. Still, the atmosphere on game days rarely—if ever—matches the electricity of the Indiana high school basketball tournament, the state's true sporting passion.

■ $29 ■ $23 ■ $15

## HOT TIPS FOR VISITING FANS

### Parking
Considering the Dome is downtown, parking isn't a problem: 44,300 spaces are within a square mile of the Dome, and 51,000 are in the so-called "regional center." The cost is $5–$15.

### Weather
In September, it's 70 degrees outside. But in November and December, the Dome's Teflon roof offers welcome relief from snow and temperatures in the teens and lower.

### Media bites
**Radio:** The Colts' flagship radio station is WNDE (1240 AM).
**TV:** WTHR-TV (Channel 13) is the local NBC affiliate.

### Cuisine
Like any other stadium, the usual hot dogs, popcorn and pretzels are available. They're also worth avoiding. Smart fans frequent the small stands in the Dome's concourse. Pizza Hut is a favorite, as is one stand that serves shrimp and crab legs, and another that features Bavarian roasted almonds. The choicest eats, however, are at Ma & Pa's Barbecue. The menu includes barbecue sandwiches, ribs, red-hots and sweet-potato pie.

After the game, Union Station, which harbors dozens of shops

and restaurants, is within walking distance. Rick's Cafe Americain (317-634-6666) and Norman's (317-269-2545) are popular with sports crowds.

### LODGING NEAR THE STADIUM
**Indianapolis Westin Hotel**
50 S. Capital Ave.
Indianapolis, IN 46204
(317) 262-8100/(800) 228-3000
Adjacent to the stadium.

**Omni Severin**
40 W. Jackson Place
Indianapolis, IN 46225
(317) 634-6664
1 block from the stadium.

### GETTING TO THE RCA DOME
**Public transportation:** Call (317) 635-3344 for Metro bus information.
**By car:** From Chicago, take 65S to West Street (or Martin Luther King Drive—exit 114) to Maryland Street.

From Indianapolis International Airport, follow 465S to 70E to West Street. Exit left, then north to Maryland.

From Louisville, take 65N to 70W to West Street. Exit and go north.

### HOME-FIELD ADVANTAGE
Since their relocation in 1984, the Colts are 32–48 at home and 27–52 on the road. They have posted a winning record at home only twice, going 6–2 in 1988 and 1989.

### IN THE HOT SEATS
The Colts' season-ticket base has dipped to approximately 40,000. That's in stark contrast to the first year, when well over 100,000 people sent in season-ticket requests. Single-game tickets go on sale in mid-July. Although attendance is down, generally 50,000-plus show up. It isn't difficult to get tickets, even on the day of the game, except perhaps when Chicago, Dallas or San Francisco comes to town.

• **Bad seats:** The $15 tickets are "obstructed seating." Team officials insist that fewer than 1,000 are sold, all in the top row.

 **Scalping:** They're around, but with tickets so easy to come by, little reason exists to patronize them.

### TICKET INFORMATION
**Address:** 7001 W. 56th St., Indianapolis, IN 46254
**Phone:** (317) 297-7000
**Order by mail:** P.O. Box 53200, Indianapolis, IN 46253
**Hours:** Mon.-Fri. 9-5.
**Training camp:** Anderson University, Anderson, IN

# Jacksonville Stadium

## STADIUM STATS

**Location:** 1 Stadium Place, Jacksonville, FL 32202
**Opening:** Aug. 15, 1995 (projected)
**Cost:** $121 million (projected)
**Surface:** PAT/Grass
**Capacity:** 73,000
**Services for fans with disabilities:** Seating available throughout the stadium.

## TEAM NOTEBOOK

**Franchise history:** Jacksonville Jaguars, 1995.

## TICKET INFORMATION
**Basic information:** Call (904) 633-2000.
**Stadium Club programs:** Call (904) 633-6000.

Don't call the expansion Jacksonville Jaguars' sparkling new home a renovated Gator Bowl: It bears only a slight resemblance to its past. All that remains of the old structure is the upper deck and a ramping system. Jacksonville Stadium might be considered a cousin to the Buffalo Bills' home, Rich Stadium: a large bowl with rows extending from the field level to the upper deck, with a partially open south side that in Jacksonville's case faces the St. John's River. No poles obstruct sightlines.

The whole place feels plush. To a large degree, the design was intended to appeal to the club patron. All of the open-air club seats are concentrated between the 30-yard lines, rather than encircling the stadium, as is more common. Another plus to the design is that the bulk of the seats are along the sidelines; while many stadiums have only about 50% of their seating along the sidelines, Jacksonville Stadium has at least 75%.

The facility, which also houses the team's offices and adjacent practice field, is too new to have a personality. But the rousing spirit of having pro football in Jacksonville is already in evidence, from the $50 million the city spent to upgrade infrastructure and landscaping surrounding the Stadium, to the 80-foot glass atrium built at the Stadium's main entrance, to the enthusiasm of the locals. As did its predecessor, the new stadium will continue to host those college football staples, the Gator Bowl and the Florida-Georgia clash.

## HOT TIPS FOR VISITING FANS

### Parking
Adjacent to the stadium are 3,500 spaces. Prices were undetermined at press time. Another estimated 3,500 spaces are available on city-owned lots in outlying areas. Numerous side streets near the stadium may provide parking options for those who don't mind a short walk. The city is trying to acquire additional land in nearby areas for expanded parking facilities.

### Weather
Average temperatures range from the hot-and-humid low-80s in August to the mid-50s in January. Florida is noted for its rainy climate, but Jacksonville's yearly average of 54 inches doesn't keep it as wet as Miami or Pensacola.

### Media bites
**Radio:** At press time, a flagship station for the Jaguars' radio network was undetermined. WNZS (930 AM) is the local 24-hour all-sports station.
**TV:** WTLV (Channel 12, NBC) and WJKS (Channel 17, ABC).

### LODGING NEAR THE STADIUM
**The Omni**
245 Water St.
Jacksonville, FL 32202
(904) 355-6664/(800) 843-6664

About 3 miles from the stadium.

**The Marriott at Sawgrass Resort**
100 TPC Blvd.
Ponte Verde Beach, FL 32082
(904) 285-7777/(800) 457-4653
15 miles from the stadium.

### GETTING TO JACKSONVILLE STADIUM
**Public transportation:** A number of buses pass by Jacksonville Stadium. Call (904) 630-3100 for more information.
**By car:** From Jacksonville International Airport, pick up I-95 South and follow until 20th Street Expressway exit. Follow 20th Street Expressway east, which turns into Haynes Street. Take a right at Victoria Street, follow to Adams Street and make right onto Stadium grounds.

From the south, take I-95 North to Main Street exit. Follow Main over bridge to Forsyth Street, take left at Bay. Bay turns into Florida Avenue; follow to East Duval Street. Take right at East Duval, onto Stadium grounds.

The Fuller-Warren drawbridge about 2-3 miles west of the Stadium on I-95 may cause periodic, unexpected delays.

## HOME-FIELD ADVANTAGE
An expansion team doesn't have many advantages in the NFL. The Tampa Bay Buccaneers and the Seattle Seahawks entered the league as expansion teams in 1976 and still haven't been to the Super Bowl—a dry spell indicative of the long building process most expansion franchises go through. But if there's one area in which the Jaguars believe they can compete, it's in the excitement of their fans: Jacksonville led the USFL in attendance during the mid-1980s, and even before the Jaguars' franchise was granted, it was apparent that rabid fan support would be a given in football-crazed Florida. When Jacksonville finally landed an NFL franchise, celebrations spilled into the streets and Jaguars' merchandise sold at a brisk clip.

## IN THE HOT SEATS

Jaguars Club seats sold out in less than 10 days when Jacksonville was in the final stages of its quest for an expansion team. Between the 30-yard lines are 12,000 club seats valued at $150 a pop.

State-of-the-art luxury suites feature large seating areas, wet bars, catered food and television monitors with satellite feeds for other NFL games. And designers didn't forget the rich finishes and fax machines. There's also a club for suite patrons. Virtually all of the suites were leased within months of the franchise's birth.

Limited single-game tickets are available for each game. Naturally, the more attractive the opponent, the quicker they'll fly.

 **Scalpers:** Selling tickets for more than face value is illegal in Jacksonville, but considering the big events they've had on the site, such as the annual Florida-Georgia clash and the Gator Bowl, seats can probably be found at inflated prices.

# Arrowhead Stadium

Since it was dedicated on Aug. 12, 1972, Kansas City's Arrowhead Stadium has been one of the jewels in the crown of NFL stadiums. It looks even better today than it did when it opened, and the sleek design means there isn't a bad seat in the house. It's hard to imagine in this glittering era of Joe Montana and Marcus Allen that the Chiefs once had a down time.

In those days, as former All-Pro nose tackle Bill Maas remembers, "I went into a gas station and left my car unlocked. I had four tickets on the dash, and I came back out and you'll never believe what happened—there were eight tickets on the dash." Perhaps the lowest day in Chiefs' history came on Jan. 2, 1983, when they drew 11,902 fans to a season-ending 37–13 win over the New York Jets. On that same day, the now-defunct Kansas City Comets of the Major Indoor Soccer League attracted 15,000 to their game at Kemper Arena.

Times have changed. As a waiting list for season tickets grows, fans pack Arrowhead Stadium to cheer a team that has reached the playoffs every year since 1990. They wear red and gold, wave their banners and pound their tom-toms. While they can be rowdy, it's a good-natured rowdiness preserved by Arrowhead's strict policing of drunkenness and obscenity. Arrowhead is one of the league's loudest stadiums and one of the most exciting places to watch a professional football game.

## HOT TIPS FOR VISITING FANS

**Parking**
Arrive early if you don't want to park in Outer Mongolia. Athough the Chiefs offer on-site parking for 26,000 vehicles, the situation has drawn heat from fans who were used to the days when the Chiefs attracted 40,000, not 77,000. Still, it's better than most NFL cities—in fact, only the Meadowlands offers more. The red reserve stadium lots cost $10; gold reserve lots are $12 but are for season ticketholders only. Other lots are $7. The other reason to come early is that Chiefs fans love tailgating parties. Gates open three hours before the game and that's when the tailgaters arrive.

**Weather**
The Chiefs have played very few snowy games at Arrowhead, but be prepared for cold, as the wind often swirls around inside the stadium.

**Media bites**
**Radio:** KCFX (101.1 FM).
**TV:** Channel 4, the NBC affiliate, carries most games, though former Chiefs quarterback Len Dawson is sports director of the competing Channel 9.

**Cuisine**
The best food is outside before the game. Arrive early and sample some of the tailgating fare. Most of those tending pits are happy to share their food with appreciative lovers of barbecue. Inside, it's typical ballpark fare. The Chiefs offer barbecue, hot dogs, hamburgers and the like, but the stadium has no signature food item. Most common U.S. brands of beer are available.

After the game, players hang out in Lot E, where All-Pros Derrick Thomas and Neil Smith have been known to barbecue burgers for fans at their famous smokehouse pit.

Two of the hottest sports spots in Kansas City are within walking distance of Arrowhead. Saunders is a sports bar that features wall after wall of photos and memorabilia, and Quincy's, in the Adam's Mark Hotel, hosts the Chiefs' official postgame party and is the site of the postgame radio program.

In Westport, just south of Kansas City, is the area's most famous watering hole. A trip to see the Chiefs has to include a beer at Kelly's, where you can find any number of professional athletes and sports lovers at the bar.

# IN THE HOT SEATS AT ARROWHEAD

The Chiefs are the hottest ticket in town. The waiting list for season tickets does not bode well, but single-game seats go on sale in mid-July. Tickets were raised an average of $2.22 in 1994, but the Chiefs' still are among the lowest-priced in the NFL. Occasionally tickets are turned back in before games, so seats sometimes are available the week, or even the day, of the game.

**• Bad seats:** Arrowhead has no obstructed- view seats. The Chiefs have jumbo color scoreboards at each end of the field. Many fans ask for tickets in the north stands because they're in the sun for most of the noon games and some of the 3 P.M. starts. The visitors' bench is on the north side as well, so it's also a favorite spot for hecklers.

The no-alcohol, family section was discontinued because of a lack of interest, but the Chiefs strictly enforce stadium rules.

**Ticket scalping:** Those who arrive at Arrowhead and need a ticket should beware. Scalping is not allowed on the premises, and anyone attempting to sell a ticket—even for face value—can be arrested. Still, it seems as if plenty of tickets are available outside: Most scalpers can be found tying up traffic. Markups run between $25 and $50 for regular-season games, with playoff tickets going in the $150-$300 range.

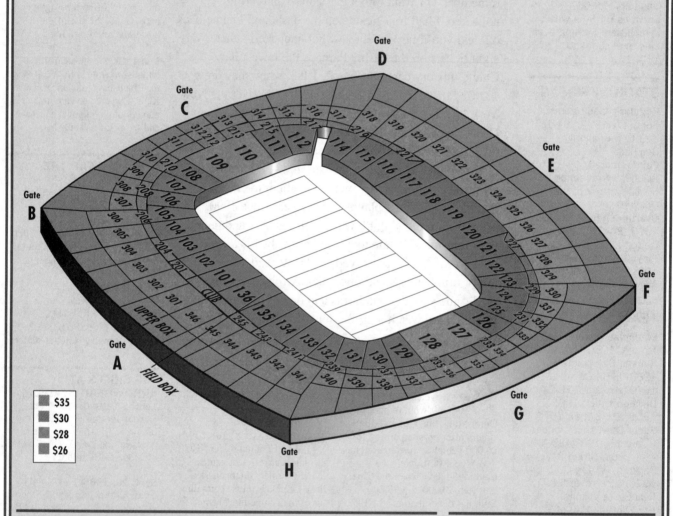

## HOME-FIELD ADVANTAGE

Talk to Denver quarterback John Elway or Buffalo's Jim Kelly about Kansas City fans. Elway calls Arrowhead the toughest stadium in the NFL. The Chiefs make no bones about the importance of playing at home. They lost just one game there in 1993 and the some of the noisiest fans in the NFL were a big reason. Linebacker Derrick Thomas says, "They are so noisy and crazy, I can't believe it. When an opponent gets in the red zone, the fans make it awfully tough. There's no way to audible down there, and that makes our job easier."

## GETTING TO ARROWHEAD

**Public transportation:** Special shuttles run on game day. Call Metro Bus at (816) 221-0660 for information.

**By car:** From Heart Airport, take I-435 South. Follow I-435 to I-70 East. Exit to the left. Take I-70 1/4 mile to the Blue Ridge cutoff. The stadium is on the right.

**TICKET INFORMATION**
**Address:** 1 Arrowhead Dr., Kansas City, MO 64129
**Phone number:** (816) 924-9400

**Hours:** Mon.-Fri. 8:30-5 (also Sat. 9-12 in season).
**Prices:** $35: club level; $30: field box; $28: field reserve and upper box; $26: upper

reserve; $20: youth/senior (season tickets only).
**Training camp:** University of Wisconsin–River Falls, River Falls, WI

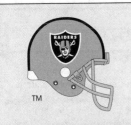

## STADIUM STATS

**Location:** 3911 S. Figueroa St., Los Angeles, CA 90037
**Opened:** Oct. 6, 1923
**Surface:** Grass
**Capacity:** 68,000
**Services for fans with disabilities:** Seats available in the Middle Level. Call (310) 322-5901 for further information.

## STADIUM FIRSTS

**Regular-season game:** Nov. 22, 1982, 28–24 over the San Diego Chargers.
**Points scored:** 20-yard field goal by Rolf Benirschke of the Chargers.
**Overtime game:** Oct. 28, 1984, 22–19 loss to the Denver Broncos
**Playoff game:** Jan. 8, 1983, 27–10 over the Cleveland Browns.

## TEAM NOTEBOOK

**Franchise history:** Oakland Raiders, 1960–1969 (AFL); Oakland Raiders, 1970–1981 (NFL); Los Angeles Raiders, 1982–present.
**Division titles:** 1967–70, '72–76, '78, '82, '83, '85, '90.
**Super Bowl appearances:** II, Jan. 14, 1968, 33–14 loss to the Green Bay Packers; XI, Jan. 9, 1977, 32–14 over the Minnesota Vikings; XV, Jan. 25, 1981, 27–10 over the Philadelphia Eagles; XVIII, Jan. 22, 1984, 38–9 over the Washington Redskins.
**Pro Football Hall of Fame:** R. Mix, 1979; J. Otto, '80; G. Blanda, '81; W. Brown, '84; G. Upshaw, '87; F. Biletnikoff, '88; A. Shell, '89; T. Hendricks, '90; A. Davis, '92.

It came as no surprise when the Coliseum was named a California and U.S. historical landmark in 1984. Home at one time or another for the Los Angeles Rams, Raiders and Dodgers, the Southern Cal Trojans and the UCLA Bruins, as well as the centerpiece for the 1932 and 1984 Summer Olympics, the Coliseum is the oldest NFL stadium and has been the stage for some of the most memorable sporting events of the 20th century.

Still, the Coliseum is close to obsolete. The Northridge earthquake in January 1994 did major, but reparable, structural damage, and more than a few fans—and Raiders' boss Al Davis—probably think it didn't go far enough.

Attempts have been made to upgrade the old lady since the Raiders moved here in 1982, but the Coliseum still has some seats in another area code. And there's not a luxury box in sight—good news for purists, bad news for the NFL. The team's annual attempts at negotiating a sweetheart deal with other cities have yet to succeed, and no one has volunteered to build a stadium in L.A., so the Coliseum remains, for now, the home of the Raiders.

## HOT TIPS FOR VISITING FANS

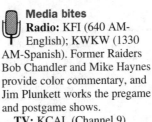

**Parking**
It ain't easy, folks. You're best bet is to arrive early and park in one of the lots adjacent to the Coliseum or Sports Arena for $8. The problem is that only 6,000 spaces are available. Additional parking is on the USC campus directly to the north for $10, which many consider more convenient. Otherwise, you can park at any number of private businesses and homes surrounding the Coliseum. As you approach, you'll see scores of cardboard signs and young entrepreneurs waving you into their driveways or lawns; the closer you get, the more you pay, as much as $20-$25. The area surrounding the Coliseum is not the most dangerous section of south central L.A., but visitors should be cautious, especially after dark. The crime rate in the neighborhood is a factor in the Raiders' low attendance, but you'll usually witness more violence in the stands than outside the stadium.

**Weather**
For sunny days, shades and sun block. Short sleeves and shorts will do early in the fall. After that, bring a sweater.

**Media bites**
**Radio:** KFI (640 AM-English); KWKW (1330 AM-Spanish). Former Raiders Bob Chandler and Mike Haynes provide color commentary, and Jim Plunkett works the pregame and postgame shows.
**TV:** KCAL (Channel 9) broadcasts the Raiders' preseason games. KNBC (Channel 4) is the NBC affiliate for regular-season games.

**Cuisine**
Lines can be long and slow, particularly at a sellout. Pizza and specialty sausages are available, but otherwise, it's mostly hot dogs, nachos and so on.
Although safety around the Coliseum has been an issue in recent years, some people hang out after games at nearby restaurants and bars. Julie's Restaurant (213-747-9266), Julie's Trojan Barrel (213-747-2575) and Margarita Jones (213-747-4400) are all within walking distance. Another possibility is to take a 15 to 20-minute drive up the Pasadena Freeway and hang out for an evening in Old Pasadena, the spectacularly successful redevelopment of downtown Pasadena. The food, drink and music are drawing people from all over southern California.

## LODGING NEAR THE STADIUM

**Los Angeles Hilton and Towers**
930 Wilshire Blvd.
Los Angeles, CA 90017
(213) 629-4321/(800) 445-8667
½ mile from the stadium.

**Westin Hotel at Los Angeles Airport**
5400 W. Century Blvd.
Los Angeles, CA 90045
(310) 216-5858/(800) 228-3000
11 miles from the stadium.

## THE RAIDERS AT THE COLISEUM

**Jan. 15, 1983:** 90,688 tickets are issued for the playoff game between the Raiders and the Jets, an NFL playoff record. New York wins 17–14.

**Jan. 8, 1984:** Before 92,335, the Raiders top the Seattle Seahawks, 30–14, winning their 3rd conference championship.

**Sept. 9, 1990:** The Raiders win 14–9 over the Denver Broncos for the franchise's 150th home victory.

**Dec. 30, 1990:** A 17–12 win over the San Diego Chargers brings the Raiders their 14th division championship.

**Jan. 13, 1991:** The Raiders win the 20th postseason game in franchise history, 20–10 over the Cincinnati Bengals. Raiders running back Bo Jackson suffers the injury which ends his football career.

# IN THE HOT SEATS AT MEMORIAL COLISEUM

The Raiders don't reveal how many season tickets are sold, but individual tickets usually are available. In fact, you generally can walk up and buy as many as you need. Bring a friend; bring 20. One warning: Raiders attendance fluctuates wildly. L.A. fans are notorious bandwagon jumpers, and when the Raiders are on a roll, the crowd grows dramatically.

• **Bad seats:** At the Coliseum, it's defi-

nitely worth a few extra dollars to try to get between the goal lines, which encompasses about 30,000 seats. The upper sections of the vast seating area beyond the west end zone contain some of the worst seats in the NFL. If you're on a budget and want to live dangerously, you might try the $15 grandstand seats in the east end zone. You can see just about anything, maybe even some of the game. One more tip— and we're serious about this—don't wear

shirts and hats of the visiting team. Some hard-core Raiders fans don't appreciate it.

 **Scalping:** Ticket resales at the site are illegal in California. That doesn't mean fans can't get a scalped ticket, however, and scalpers occasionally do business outside the stadium on rare sell-outs. For most games, though, decent tickets are available through conventional out-

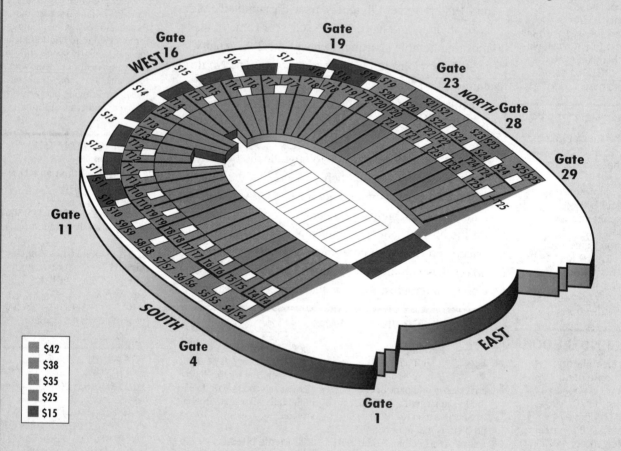

| | |
|---|---|
| ▤ | $42 |
| ▤ | $38 |
| ▤ | $35 |
| ▤ | $25 |
| ■ | $15 |

## HOME-FIELD ADVANTAGE

The Raiders might have more of an advantage than other teams in L.A., where weather is not a factor and crowds are rather blasé. The team is 64–36 at home since moving to the Coliseum in 1982, probably because their fans are a little different from the typical L.A. breed. Raiders crowds can be intimidating when they gang up—vocally, that is—on the Broncos or the Chiefs.

## GETTING TO MEMORIAL COLISEUM

**Public transportation:** Numerous RTD Bus lines serve the Coliseum. Call RTD Bus information at (213) 626-4455 for more details.

**By car:** The Coliseum is just off the Harbor Freeway (110), but you can avoid long lines at Harbor offramps by approaching the stadium from the Santa Monica

Freeway (10) and heading south on Vermont. The University of Southern California will be on your left, then you'll see the Coliseum and parking signs.

From Los Angeles International Airport, take Century Boulevard east to 110 North toward Los Angeles. Exit on Martin Luther King Boulevard to Hoover Street, right into the Coliseum.

## TICKET INFORMATION
**Address:** 332 Center St., El Segundo, CA 90245 or Los Angeles Sports Arena Box Office, 3939 S. Figueroa, Los Angeles, CA 90037
**Phone:** (310) 322-5901 or TicketMaster at (213) 480-3232

**Hours:** El Segundo: Mon.-Fri. 9-6, Sat. 9-4. Sports Arena Office: Mon.-Fri. 10-6.
**Prices:** $42: lower, middle and upper levels in sections 6-8 and 21-23; $38: lower, middle and upper levels in sections 5, 6, 8, 9, 20, 21, 23 and 24; $35: lower and middle levels in sections 4, 5, 9, 10, 19,

20, 24 and 25; $25: lower and middle levels in sections 10-19 and upper levels in sections 4, 5, 9, 10, 19, 20, 24 and 25; $15: upper levels in sections 10-19 and the bleachers.

TM

## STADIUM STATS

**Location:** 1900 State College Blvd., Anaheim, CA 92806
**Opened:** April 19, 1966
**Surface:** Grass
**Capacity:** 69,008
Services for fans with disabilities: Seating behind sections 1, 2, 3, 5, 7, 45, 47 and 49 on the terrace level.

## STADIUM FIRSTS

**Regular-season game:** Sept. 7, 1980, 41–20 loss to the Detroit Lions.
**Points scored:** 98-yard kickoff return by Drew Hill of the Rams.
**Overtime game:** Dec. 21, 1980, 20–17 over the Atlanta Falcons.
**Playoff game:** Jan. 4, 1985, 20–0 over the Dallas Cowboys.

## TEAM NOTEBOOK

**Franchise history:** Cleveland Rams, 1937–45; Los Angeles Rams, 1946–present.
**Division titles:** 1945, '49, '50, '51, '55, '67, '69, '73, '74, '75, '76, '77, '78, '79, '85.
**Super Bowl appearance:** XIV, Jan. 20, 1980, 31–19 loss to the Pittsburgh Steelers.
**Pro Football Hall of Fame:** B. Waterfield, 1965; D. Reeves, 1967; E. Hirsch, 1968; T. Fears, 1970; A. Robustelli, 1971; N. Van Brocklin, 1971; O. Matson, 1972; B. George, 1974; D. Lane, 1974; D. Jones, 1980; M. Olsen, 1982; S. Gillman, 1983; J. Namath, 1985; T. Schramm, 1991.
**Retired numbers:** 7, B. Waterfield; 74, M. Olsen.

# Anaheim Stadium

When the Rams moved from Cleveland in 1946, they were one of the best teams in the NFL, and in 1951 they brought Los Angeles an NFL title. When they left Los Angeles in 1980 to move down the freeway to Orange County's Anaheim Stadium, they once again were one of the league's best, having won seven consecutive division titles and having just appeared in a Super Bowl. But Anaheim Stadium has been no kinder to the Rams than to its original tenant, baseball's California Angels. The Angels have never gone to the World Series and the Rams, since moving to Anaheim, have not gone to the Super Bowl. Recently, they haven't even been close. Attendance and interest have dwindled, and owner Georgia Frontiere is seriously considering moving the franchise to another city. If you want to see NFL football in Anaheim Stadium, now's the time.

Don't worry about too much advance planning—this is one of the easiest tickets in professional sports. As the saying goes, good seats are available. Well, decent seats, anyway. No one is going to accuse Anaheim Stadium of hosting the quintessential football experience. The seats were designed for viewing baseball. The folks at Anaheim do a nice job converting the facility for football, but it just isn't the same as viewing a game at a real football stadium. The crowd's constant booing of the home players, plus angry banners such as "Please, Georgia, Sell The Team," don't add to the ambience.

However sad the play, remember you're just a few blocks from Disneyland, the happiest place on earth. Most people can't afford NFL football and Disneyland on the same day, but it's worth a thought.

## HOT TIPS FOR VISITING FANS

**Parking**
Acres and acres. About 15,000 spaces are available at $6. Convenient access is provided by the Santa Ana (I-5) and Orange (57) freeways, as well as 26 entrance lanes from three surface streets.

**Weather**
Not much. Assume sunshine and warm weather, and adjust to anything else. If it rains, you won't be the only one without an umbrella. If the Boy Scout in you won't let you leave home unprepared, bring a wind breaker or sweat shirt, something you can tie around your waist if you end up not needing it.

**Media bites**
**Radio:** KMPC (710 AM). Bob Starr does play-by-play, and Jack Snow provides analysis.
**TV:** KFOX (Channel 11) is the local Fox affiliate.

**Cuisine**
If the football is uninspiring, the food is worth investigating. Choices include fish and chips, sushi, deli sandwiches, salads, pizza, tacos and burritos. One of the longest lines is for some big, sticky cinnamon rolls worth 10 or 15 minutes out of your life.
Numerous restaurants (with bars) are just minutes from

Anaheim. The Catch (714-634-1829) and Charley Brown's (714-634-2211) draw sports crowds, and Mr. Stox (714-634-2994) is a popular all-around eatery. A few miles away, Mamma Cozza's (714-635-0063) serves good Italian food to a Rams clientele.

## LODGING NEAR THE STADIUM

**The Anaheim Hilton and Towers**
777 Convention Way
Anaheim, CA 92802
(714) 750-4321/(800) 222-9923
3 miles from the stadium.

**The Anaheim Ramada Inn**
1331 E. Katella Ave.
Anaheim, CA 92805
(714) 978-8088/(800) 228-0586
1½ blocks from the stadium.

## THE RAMS AT ANAHEIM STADIUM

**Dec. 26, 1982:** The Chicago Bears win 34–26 despite 509 yards passing by Vince Ferragamo.

**Oct. 6, 1985:** The Rams defense stops the Minnesota Vikings 1 inch from the goal line as time runs out, preserving a 13–10 victory.

**Jan. 4, 1986:** Eric Dickerson rushes for a team- and NFL-playoff-record 248 yards in a 20–0 win over the Dallas Cowboys.

**Nov. 16, 1986:** Rookie Jim Everett throws three touchdown passes in his debut, but the Rams lose 30–28 to the New England Patriots.

**Sept. 24, 1989:** The Rams beat the Green Bay Packers 41-38 behind Greg Bell's 221 yards rushing.

**Dec. 27, 1992:** Todd Kinchen returns two punts for touchdowns, leading the Rams past the Atlanta Falcons 38–27.

# IN THE HOT SEATS AT ANAHEIM STADIUM

The club-level seats go mostly to season ticketholders. Field-level seats are, as the name suggests, level with the field, so some have obstructed views. Terrace-level seats ($23-$30) provide unobstructed views but are a long way from the players. The view-level (upper-deck) seats probably provide the best overall view, provided you're not too high up in a corner. Single-game tickets go on sale in mid-July.

If you're adventurous, you can join a group of loyal fans in the north end zone who call themselves the melonheads because they, well, put a hollowed out watermelon on their heads. No one's exactly sure why, except it has something to do with "keeping cool." Whatever.

 **Scalping:** In Anaheim, they're not sure what this is. The concept of having difficulty getting tickets is foreign. For the record, however, California law and Anaheim ordinances forbid scalping.

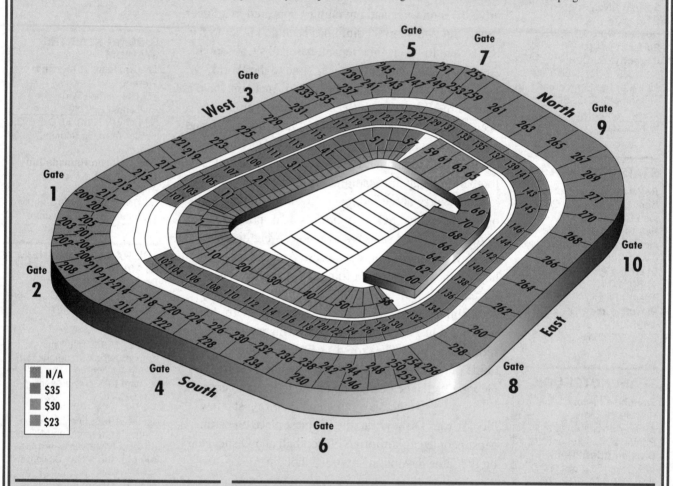

## HOME-FIELD ADVANTAGE

Basically none. Sports crowds in L.A. are among the most transient in the country. Many fans are from somwhere else and often maintain allegiance to teams from their hometowns. Since it's an open-air stadium and the crowd is often split in its loyalty, noise is not a hindrance to visiting teams. Wind, rain, snow . . . none of that, either. Anaheim Stadium is truly a level playing field, although you wouldn't know it by the scores of the past few years. Since 1989, the Rams are 11–21 at home.

## GETTING TO ANAHEIM STADIUM

**Public transportation:** Amtrak trains stop a short walk from the stadium; on Sunday, these trains are nicknamed "Ramtrak." Call (800) 872-7245 for more information.

**By car:** From LAX, take Century Boulevard east to the 405/San Diego Freeway South to the 110/Harbor Freeway East to the 91/Artesia Freeway East. Go left when 91 splits, then south on the 5/Santa Ana Freeway. Exit at State College Boulevard/City Drive and go north to the stadium.

## TICKET INFORMATION

**Address:** 1900 State College Blvd., Anaheim, CA 92806
**Phone:** (714) 937-6767
**Hours:** Mon.-Fri. 9-5.
**Prices:** $35: field level, odd-numbered sections 7-57 (rows L-Z) and sections 60, 62, 64 and 66-70 (rows A-ZZ); terrace level, odd-numbered sections 7-57; club level, sections 101-146. $30: field level, odd-numbered sections 1-5, sections 7-57 (rows A-K); and even-numbered sections 2-42; terrace level, sections 1-6, even-numbered sections 8-40, and sections 59, 61, 63 and 65. $23: field level, even-numbered sections 44-58; terrace level, sections 46-58; view level, sections 201-271.

**Training camp:** California State University at Fullerton, Fullerton, CA

# Joe Robbie Stadium

## STADIUM STATS

**Location:** 2269 N.W. 199th St., Miami, FL 33056
**Opened:** Aug. 16, 1987
**Surface:** Grass
**Capacity:** 74,916
**Services for fans with disabilities:** Seating available in sections 103, 125, 128, 131, 153 and 156.

## STADIUM FIRSTS

**Regular-season game:** Oct. 11, 1987, 42–0 over the Kansas City Chiefs.
**Points scored:** 6-yard touchdown run by Ricky Isam of the Dolphins.
**Overtime game:** Oct. 8, 1989, 13–10 over the Cleveland Browns.
**Playoff game:** Jan. 5, 1991, 17–16 over the Kansas City Chiefs.

## TEAM NOTEBOOK

**Franchise history:** Miami Dolphins, 1966–1969 (AFL); Miami Dolphins, 1970–present (NFL).
**Division titles:** 1971, 1972, 1973, 1974, 1979, 1981, 1983, 1984, 1985, 1992.
**Super Bowl appearances:** VI, Jan. 16, 1972, 24–3 loss to the Dallas Cowboys; VII, Jan. 14, 1973, 14–7 over the Washington Redskins; VIII, Jan. 13, 1974, 24–7 over the Minnesota Vikings; XVII, Jan. 30, 1983, 27–17 loss to the Washington Redskins; XIX, Jan. 20, 1985, 38–16 loss to the San Francisco 49ers.
**Pro Football Hall of Fame:** Paul Warfield, 1983; Larry Csonka, 1987; Jim Langer, 1987; Bob Griese, 1990; Larry Little, 1993.
**Retired number:** 12, Bob Griese.

---

**B**uilt in 1987 with the comfort of the spectator in mind, Joe Robbie Stadium has everything you'd expect from a state-of-the-art facility: grass field, unobstructed views, 19-inch-wide seats with chair backs and armrests, TV monitors at the 40 concessions stands, restrooms aplenty and giant TV screens at either end of the field. It certainly beats the old Orange Bowl in amenities, parking, cleanliness and sightlines, but the old excitement the fans had for their team seems not to have been rekindled in this new, more sterile abode.

In the Orange Bowl, the closed end put a wall of fans on top of the action, where they could (and did) inject themselves into the game by roaring in support of the defense on goal-line stands. At the open end, palm trees and a dolphin tank contributed to the tropical atmosphere. At Joe Robbie Stadium, the fans are more removed and behave that way. Some suggest that the well-stocked concessions stands and plush seats have softened a once-hardy lot.

Game day continues to bring a diverse mix to the stadium, a blend of wealthy and not-so-wealthy, Anglo and Latino, native and snowbird. Tailgating is also popular, but the Dolphins supporters have yet to recapture the spirit they had at the Orange Bowl. Of course, the Dolphins haven't won any Super Bowls in a while, either.

## HOT TIPS FOR VISITING FANS

**Parking**
Spaces next to the stadium are reserved and sold to season ticketholders at $100 for 10 games. Persons holding single-game tickets are steered by parking attendants to auxiliary lots on the east and west sides of the stadium, where parking is $10. Shuttle buses ferry patrons to the stadium. On-street parking is limited.

Overflow situations rarely occur; when they do arise, it's usually on Monday nights, when car-pooling breaks down because of the late start. Smart shoppers arrive about two hours before kickoff. Traffic tends to back up on N.W. 199th Street, which leads to Joe Robbie from I-95.

**Weather**
Sultry and steamy. Fans are encouraged to drink plenty of fluids (not just soft drinks and beer) and wear hats, sunglasses and light-colored clothing. It's also smart to get a fold-up raincoat at novelty stores. Brief downpours are not uncommon.

**Media bites**
**Radio:** WIOD (610 AM—English), WQBA (1140 AM—Spanish).
**TV:** Sold-out regular-season games are on WTVJ (Channel 4, NBC).

**Cuisine**
A person could forget he or she is in a stadium. Mrs. Field's Cookies, Carvel, Domino's, Arby's and Burger King await, as do ethnic specialties such as Cuban sandwiches and kosher cuisine. Choices among the expanded selection of standard fare: hot dogs, sausages, chicken-breast sandwiches and stuffed potatoes.

Grill and deli stands are sprinkled throughout the concourses, plus a Stadium Cafe for more-varied selections. Seats on the club level have automated menu service, so patrons never have to leave their seats. As beers go, teetotalers can enjoy O'Doul's; the regular and light beers of the major brewers are on sale.

South Florida offers many fine restaurants to enjoy after Dolphins games. Longtime coach Don Shula owns Shula's Steakhouse (305-822-2324) in nearby Miami Lakes; huge portions are the hallmark. Joe's Stone Crab (305-673-0365) is probably the busiest and best-known restaurant in Miami.

## LODGING NEAR THE STADIUM

**Marina Marriott Fort Lauderdale**
1881 S.E. 17th St.
Fort Lauderdale, FL 33316
(305) 463-4000/(800) 228-9290
19 miles south of the stadium.

**Don Shula Hotel and Golf Club**
15255 Bullrun Rd.
Miami Lakes, FL 33014
(305) 821-1150
10 miles from the stadium.

## THE DOLPHINS AT JOE ROBBIE STADIUM

**Nov. 1, 1987:** The Dolphins beat Pittsburgh 35–24, giving Don Shula his 250th regular-season victory.

**Oct. 23, 1988:** Dan Marino throws for 521 yards—the second most in NFL history—but the Dolphins lose to the New York Jets 44–30.

**Dec. 12, 1988:** Marino tosses his 193rd touchdown pass and becomes the first NFL quarterback to pass for more than 4,000 yards in four seasons as the Dolphins top the Cleveland Browns 37–31.

**Dec. 9, 1990:** A 23–20 overtime win over the Philadelphia Eagles puts the Dolphins in the playoffs for the first time since 1985.

**Jan. 10, 1993:** Miami wins 31–0 over the San Diego Chargers in an AFC playoff game, their largest postseason margin of victory.

# IN THE HOT SEATS AT JOE ROBBIE STADIUM

Single-game seats usually go on sale in May, but don't worry too much about planning ahead. About 20,000 tickets usually are available on game day. Why do the Dolphins save 20,000 tickets a game? They don't. They want to sell them. They try to sell them. Sometimes, they get lucky.

Since so many tickets are available for most home games—though sellouts have increased recently—folks who want to go on a whim generally are in luck. The least attractive draw over the years has been

Indianapolis, so the Colts could be an out-of-town visitor's best shot.

• **Bad seats:** Because of Joe Robbie Stadium's symmetrical design, no seats are obstructed. There are no poles, the bane of old-time parks. If there's a place to avoid, it's the upper deck on the visitors' side; these seats have no protection from the sun, which can be fierce into late October.

• **Special packages:** The Dolphins offer

a family section that includes an area where alcoholic beverages are forbidden. The 5,000 seats in the family section are a bargain at $20, compared to the top price of $33 elsewhere in the park.

 **Scalping:** With tickets so freely available, scalping has not been a problem. Tickets cannot be resold on stadium grounds.

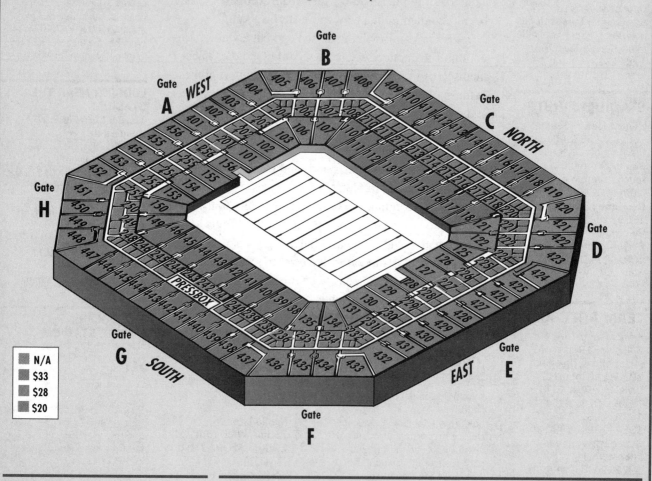

Legend:
- ■ N/A
- ■ $33
- ■ $28
- ■ $20

## HOME-FIELD ADVANTAGE

The weather always has been the Dolphins' friend and the visitors' enemy. With mean daytime temperatures of 82 degrees in September, conditioning is critical. For a team that practices in the cold to come down and play in December is an exercise in physical and mental fitness. The Dolphins have, for years, leaned toward somewhat undersized linemen because the bigger guys wilt too quickly in the heat.

### TICKET INFORMATION
**Address:** 2269 N.W. 199th St., Miami, FL 33056
**Phone:** (305) 620-2578
**Hours:** Mon.-Sat. 10-6.

## GETTING TO JOE ROBBIE STADIUM

**Public transportation:** Special, event-specific transportation is available from Dade, Broward and Palm Beach counties. Call Dade Transit, (305) 638-6700; Broward Transit, (305) 857-8400; and Palm Beach County Transportation Authority, (407) 233-1114, for details. Park and Ride service is available for games. From Miami, call (800) 874-7245 for details.

**Prices:** $33: sections 110-118, 138-146, 410-418 and 438-466; $28: sections 101-107, 121-135, 149-156, 401-409, 419-425, 431-437 and 447-456 (426-430 are designated as family sections for $20;

**By car:** From Fort Lauderdale, take I-595 West to Florida Turnpike South, then 9 miles to exit 2 (N.W. 199th Street/Honey Hill Road). Exit to 199th and make a right.

From Miami Airport, take I-95 North to Ives Dairy Road, then west for 9 miles (during which the road changes to 199th). The stadium is on the right.

three of the five are designated alcohol-free, including section 427, which is non-smoking as well).

**Training camp:** Nova University, Davie, FL

# HHH Metrodome

TM

## STADIUM STATS

**Location:** 500 11th Ave. S., Minneapolis, MN 55415
**Opened:** April 3, 1982
**Surface:** AstroTurf
**Capacity:** 63,000
**Services for fans with disabilities:** Seating available in the first row of the second deck.

## STADIUM FIRSTS

**Regular-season game:** Sept. 12, 1982, 17–10 over the Tampa Bay Buccaneers.
**Points scored:** 51-yard field goal by Bill Capece of the Buccaneers.
**Overtime game:** Dec. 26, 1987, 27–24 loss to the Washington Redskins.
**Playoff game:** Jan. 9, 1982, 30–24 over the Atlanta Falcons.

## TEAM NOTEBOOK

**Franchise history:** Minnesota Vikings, 1961–present.
**Division titles:** 1968, 1969, 1970, 1971, 1973, 1974, 1975, 1976, 1977, 1978, 1980, 1989, 1992.
**Super Bowl appearances:** IV, Jan. 11, 1970, 23–7 loss to the Kansas City Chiefs; VIII, Jan. 13, 1974, 24–7 loss to the Miami Dolphins; IX, Jan. 12, 1975, 16–6 loss to the Pittsburgh Steelers; XI, Jan. 9, 1977, 32–14 loss to the Oakland Raiders.
**Pro Football Hall of Fame:** Hugh McElhenny, 1970; Fran Tarkenton, 1986; Jim Langer, 1987; Alan Page, 1988; Jan Stenerud, 1991.
**Retired numbers:** 10, Fran Tarkenton; 88, Alan Page.

Baseball purists complain about the Hubert H. Humphrey Metrodome, but football fans like it better. The team has done well at home since moving here, and fans have been treated to what, in general, is a comfortable environment. Vikings fans tend to be much older than Twins fans, and sitting indoors on a December day in Minnesota is just fine with most of them. The Vikings crowd is notoriously quiet except during the most exciting moments of the games. In fact, many younger fans who like to get rowdy often are told to sit down and shut up by folks behind them. It's quite a departure from the old days at the Met, where tailgating was allowed and many fans kept warm with flasks.

Despite seats angled for the best football watching, the Metrodome recently has become a somewhat annoying place to watch a game—even for football fans. That's because the huge color replay scoreboards show commercials at least as often as they show replays. And with the roof holding the volume in, the ads are very loud. That might be one big reason that attendance has declined steadily over the last decade, despite the team's success.

Former Bears coach Mike Ditka often criticized the stadium, helping the Metrodome get in the news regularly. He once called it a big livestock hall, and the Vikings responded by putting huge fake cows and other animals on the field. When he called it the "Rollerdome," the Vikings had all their cheerleaders wear in-line skates.

The Vikings miss Ditka.

## HOT TIPS FOR VISITING FANS

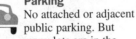

**Parking**
No attached or adjacent public parking. But many lots are in the blocks surrounding the facility. Anyone arriving an hour before kickoff should find fairly clear sailing. The nearest lots charge at least $10 a car, but fans willing to walk—less than 2 blocks in some cases—can find $5 lots.

Chicago Avenue, north of the Metrodome, usually is closed by police from Third to Sixth streets two hours before game time, so fans have to go an extra couple of blocks either north or south to drive around.

**Weather**
Fortunately for the Vikings, the Twins have had to endure the brunt of the weather-caused calamities at the Metrodome. For whatever reason, most of the weather-induced collapses to the Dome's Teflon roof have occurred during baseball season. While coats aren't necessary once inside, earplugs are a must because of the volume of the commercials during time-outs.

**Media bites**
**Radio:** All games can be heard on KFAN (1130 AM), the Twin Cities' all-sports network. Pregame shows start 2 1/2 hours before kickoff, and postgame analysis lasts through the ride home—even if home is Aberdeen, Bismark or Duluth.

**TV:** The Fox affiliate is Channel 29, and the NBC station is KARE (Channel 11).

**Cuisine**
Mediocre, or sometimes worse. Hot dogs, popcorn and the like are just OK; beer is offered in basic domestic brands. The best bet is the ice cream. Both hand-packed and soft-serve are good, and soft-serve sundaes are dished up in edible waffle-cone cups.

After the game, the best-kept secret is the Picked Parrot (612-332-0673), near Target Center. It's more of an upscale bar and grill, but its ribs are tasty and tender with plenty of zing. If you don't like them spicy, go to Market Barbecue (612-872-1111) or Rudolph's (612-623-3671). Sawatee (612-338-6451), just a few blocks east of the Metrodome on Washington Avenue, offers excellent Thai food.

## LODGING NEAR THE STADIUM

**Crown Sterling Suites**
425 S. Seventh St.
Minneapolis, MN 55415
(612) 333-3111/(800) 433-4600
3 blocks from the stadium.

**Holiday Inn Crown Plaza Northstar**
618 Second Ave. S.
Minneapolis, MN 55402
(612) 338-2288/(800) 556-7829
7 blocks from the stadium.

## THE VIKINGS AT THE METRODOME

**Nov. 28, 1982:** Tommy Kramer throws five touchdown passes in a 35–7 win over the Chicago Bears.

**Sept. 16, 1984:** Randy Holloway gets five sacks against the Atlanta Falcons in a 27–20 win.

**Dec. 4, 1988:** With one of their biggest victory margins ever, the Vikings demolish the New Orleans Saints 45–3.

**Dec. 26, 1988:** Wade Wilson throws for 253 yards and Anthony Carter logs 102 receiving yards, as the Vikes beat the Los Angeles Rams 28–17 in the first round of the NFC playoffs.

**Oct. 4, 1992:** Down 20–0 to the Bears after three quarters, the Vikings roar back before a Monday night television audience to win 21–20.

# IN THE HOT SEATS AT THE HHH METRODOME

Most games eventually sell out, but tickets for many games can be purchased the week of the game. Only rarely are walk-up sales available on game days.

The toughest ticket is for the annual game against the NFC Central Division archrival Green Bay Packers. Scalpers can fetch upwards of $300 apiece via agencies and $100 on the street for good seats to Packers games. Many Minnesotans are old Packers fans, and many Wisconsinites cross the border to attend.

• **Good seats:** Metrodome has no obstructed views, and many fans like to sit high, the better to see plays develop. For value, the $19 seats around the top rows of the stadium are hard to beat in the NFL.

**Scalping:** Most locate near the intersection of Chicago Avenue and 6th Street, others near the will-call windows on the 11th Avenue side of the stadium. Purchasers who wait until after kickoff buy for well below face value.

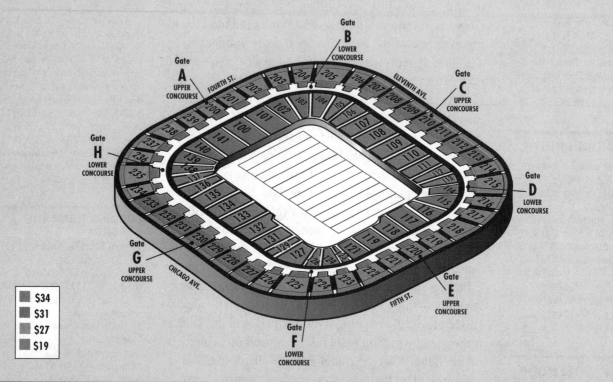

**Legend:**
- $34
- $31
- $27
- $19

## HOME-FIELD ADVANTAGE

Like all other teams that play in domed stadiums, the Vikings have not gone to the Super Bowl since they moved into the Metrodome. Mike Lynn, the former general manager, once said that the Metrodome actually worked against the Vikings because it makes them "soft" when playing tough playoff games outdoors. Moving out of Metropolitan Stadium in 1981, the Vikings lost one of the NFL's best home-field advantages—an icy one that separated snowmen from boys. But still, in 1989 the Vikings won the NFC Central Division despite their 2–6 road record because they went 8–0 at the Metrodome. The previous season they went 11–5, with seven wins at home.

## GETTING TO METRODOME

**Public transportation:** The Metrodome Shuttle has three routes that cover downtown Minneapolis. Service runs one hour before and after games. Call M.T.C. at (612) 373-3333 for additional bus information.

**By car:** From the north, go south on 35W to Washington Avenue and exit right. Go 2 blocks, left onto 11th Avenue, then right onto Fifth Street. The Metrodome is on the right.

From the south, take 35W north to Fifth Street exit. The Metrodome is on the right.

From the east, head west on 94 to Fifth street exit. The Metrodome is on the right.

From the west, follow 394 East to Fourth Street exit. Turn on any street west of the Metrodome for parking. Or, east on 94 and follow Fourth Street North signs.

## TICKET INFORMATION

**Address:** Vikings Ticket Office, 500 11th Ave. S., Minneapolis, MN 55415
**Phone:** (612) 333-8828 or TicketMaster at (612) 989-5151
**Hours:** Mon.-Fri. 8:30-5, plus Sat. 8-12 before home games (Mon.-Fri. 8:30-4 in the offseason).

**Prices:** $34: all rows of lower deck sections 105-113 and 127-137, and rows 1-6 in upper deck sections 207-213 and 227-233; $31: all rows in lower deck sections 100-104, 138-141 and 114-126, rows 1-6 of upper deck sections 200-206, 234-239 and 226, and rows 7-25 in upper deck sections 207-213 and 227-233; $27: rows 7-25 in upper deck sections 200-206, 214-226 and 234-239; $19: rows 26-31 in all upper deck sections.

**Training camp:** Mankato State University, Mankato, MN

# Foxboro Stadium

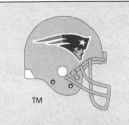

Foxboro Stadium is quintessential New England. The permanent home of the Patriots—thanks to stadium owner Bob Kraft, who purchased the team in 1993 using the lease as a purchasing wedge—is as raw as a New England winter and as chilly as a New England spring, with no frills and seldom many thrills (14–50 record through '93). Being a Patriots fan is like serving on an Atlantic fishing boat: lots of ups and downs, plenty of wet weather and not a lot of excitement.

Billy Sullivan owned the franchise when it played at Boston University. It "graduated" to Fenway Park, then to Boston College and Harvard, before Bay State Raceway owner E. M. Loew offered a piece of land less than an hour from Boston, Worcester and Providence.

A vote was won from the townsfolk of Foxboro—the only town whose selectmen can decide NFL Monday night football schedules—and the first game was played less than a year after groundbreaking.

It's a very basic stadium with one big bonus—great sightlines. There are good seats everywhere. And $10 million has been put into improvements since Kraft bought the stadium, with another $60 million promised.

Coach Bill Parcells said he became convinced of fan support when 42,810 showed up for a Jets game in 1993 with bonechilling winds gusting to 68 mph, accompanied by relentless sheets of rain.

## HOT TIPS FOR VISITING FANS

### Parking

If the coach wants to test how tough his players are, he should send them to the parking lots. If they can take the potholes, they can take NFL hits. The Stadium has 18,500 licensed spaces, some 5,000 of those in private lots, and only controls the surrounding lots. Expect to wrestle with the traffic congestion after the game. Access to and from the Stadium is supposed to be improved with the long-range goal of an offramp to service nearby Route 95.

### Weather

Yes, there's weather, a smorgasbord of it, and stories, too, like the infamous Snowplow Game, a 3–0 win over Miami in '82. A small plow cleared the space from which John Smith kicked the field goal on a day that started in sunshine and ended in a blizzard.

Smith, now retired, calls the Foxboro winds the worst. "They swirl. In Buffalo it comes in one direction; at Foxboro they just swirl."

### Media Bites

**Radio:** WBZ (1030 AM). Gil Santos and Gino Cappelletti have been doing the play-by-play and color together since 1982.

**TV:** WBZ (Channel 4) is the NBC affiliate.

### Cuisine

You can dine New England inn style at the nearby Lafayette House, or visit Demitri's Red Snapper, where the team once held a wildcat strike in the parking lot and dined on a free buffet until Demitri saw how much they could consume. The Red Wing on Route 1 is famous for its fried clams and scallops and for its old-style diner section.

The Stadium has upgraded food offerings to include Philly cheese-steak sandwiches, D'Angelo's Papa Gino's pizza and fried dough as well as the usual fare.

## LODGING NEAR THE STADIUM

**Holiday Inn**
700 Myles Standish Blvd.
Taunton, MA 02780
(508) 823-0430/(800) HOLIDAY
About 17 miles from the stadium.

**Providence Marriott**
Charles at Orms Street
Providence, RI 02904
(401) 272-2400/(800) 228-9290
About 20 miles from the stadium.

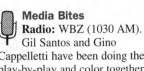

## THE PATRIOTS AT FOXBORO STADIUM

**April 4, 1970:** The city of Foxboro is named the Patriots' new hometown.

**Sept. 23, 1970:** Ground is broken for Schaefer Stadium.

**Dec. 31, 1978:** In the only playoff game in Foxboro, Patriots lose to the Houston Oilers 31–14.

**May 23, 1983:** Schaefer Stadium renamed Sullivan Stadium in honor of Patriots owner and founder William H. "Billy" Sullivan.

**June 29, 1983:** Sullivan Stadium officially rededicated with a free concert by the Boston Pops.

**Sept. 7, 1986:** The 10-foot-wide by 15-foot-long 1985 AFC championship banner is raised at Sullivan Stadium in a pregame ceremony.

**Sept. 21, 1986:** Tony Eason throws for 414 yards for a team record, exceeding Vito "Babe" Parilli's 400 yards. The Pats lose to the Seattle Seahawks, 38–31.

**Dec. 4, 1988:** Veteran wide receiver Stanley Morgan catches his 500th career pass with 26 seconds remaining in the first quarter against the Seahawks.

**May 3, 1991:** Natural grass is installed in what is now Foxboro Stadium.

# IN THE HOT SEATS AT FOXBORO STADIUM

New owner Kraft, who has had season tickets since the Stadium opened, said he wants fans to "come here and know they are going to sit with the same people in the same area. The problems we've had are with the transient crowds. You never knew who would be next to you."

Despite recent price hikes, season-ticket sales have been brisk.

• **Bad seats:** The most expensive sections begin right behind the player benches and in spite of the field's being below the seats, the view here is still obstructed by players.

• **Special programs:** There is a family section for NFL games where security is more visible. Foxboro Stadium hosts approximately six concerts a year.

**Scalping:** Patriots were known as pilgrims the last time anyone saw a scalper in Foxboro.

In 1993 a radio station, trying to promote a big home crowd for the final game against Miami, asked season ticketholders who weren't going to use their tickets to give them to the station to distribute. There were more givers than takers.

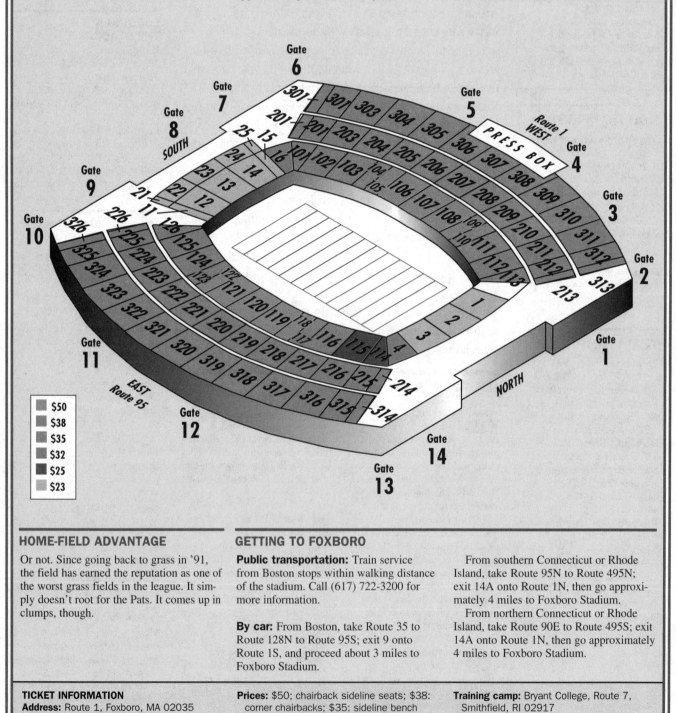

- $50
- $38
- $35
- $32
- $25
- $23

## HOME-FIELD ADVANTAGE

Or not. Since going back to grass in '91, the field has earned the reputation as one of the worst grass fields in the league. It simply doesn't root for the Pats. It comes up in clumps, though.

## GETTING TO FOXBORO

**Public transportation:** Train service from Boston stops within walking distance of the stadium. Call (617) 722-3200 for more information.

**By car:** From Boston, take Route 35 to Route 128N to Route 95S; exit 9 onto Route 1S, and proceed about 3 miles to Foxboro Stadium.

From southern Connecticut or Rhode Island, take Route 95N to Route 495N; exit 14A onto Route 1N, then go approximately 4 miles to Foxboro Stadium.

From northern Connecticut or Rhode Island, take Route 90E to Route 495S; exit 14A onto Route 1N, then go approximately 4 miles to Foxboro Stadium.

**TICKET INFORMATION**
**Address:** Route 1, Foxboro, MA 02035
**Phone:** (800) WIN-PATS
**Hours:** Mon.-Fri. 9-5.

**Prices:** $50; chairback sideline seats; $38: corner chairbacks; $35: sideline bench seats; $32: sideline corner; $25: special family section; $23: end zones.

**Training camp:** Bryant College, Route 7, Smithfield, RI 02917

# Louisiana Superdome

New Orleans Saints linebacker Rickey Jackson has entered the Superdome many times in his NFL career, but never the way he did one Saturday night in mid-February 1994. Jackson rode into the arena on a float. He was the grand marshal of the parade of the Krewe of Endymion, the largest parading organization in the history of New Orleans' Mardi Gras. Located in downtown New Orleans, within walking distance of the French Quarter, a riverboat casino, and many shops and restaurants, the Superdome is the only pro sports stadium in the country that hosts a Carnival parade. And that's only one of the unique uses of this sports palace, which has become the favored destination of everything from Super Bowls to tractor pulls.

Truth is, it's always a party inside the Superdome, especially when the Saints are in town. As the only major league sports franchise in the city, the Saints have enjoyed a love affair with New Orleans fans that has only intensified with the team's recent winning ways. Although the stadium is so big that the Astrodome could fit inside, Saints games have sold out for virtually seven years. The Superdome on game day is a prime example of a city letting the good times roll.

## HOT TIPS FOR VISITING FANS

**Parking**
The Superdome parking garage can hold 5,000 cars. Fans usually begin arriving at the Superdome about 2½ hours before kickoff; the traffic flow into the garages is steady. Parking costs $8.

More than 10,000 additional parking spaces are within easy walking distance. But be careful. During special events, police are quick to tow illegally parked vehicles. Beware of parking scammers. Don't get waved into an area by someone who looks like an attendant and who'll then take your money and laugh while you get towed. If you're staying downtown, your best bet is to walk.

Traffic after the game isn't bad because the stadium is next to an interstate highway.

**Weather**
The temperature inside the dome is 64 or 65 degrees before the game and around 72 once it starts. Outside, fall in New Orleans is warm and usually dry. Inclement weather during football season is more the exception than the rule.

**Media bites**
**Radio:** WQEU (1280 AM) and WYLD (98.5 FM).
**TV:** Preseason games that are not televised nationally are carried on WWL-TV (Channel 4) in New Orleans. Channel 38 is the Fox affiliate.

**Cuisine**
Popeye's Fried Chicken, which originated in New Orleans, is sold here, but the rest of the choices usually run toward standard stadium fare. For something more substantial, try the Dome Cafe, on the Plaza Level by Gate H. It offers a buffet on game day that starts two hours before kickoff and goes until game time. A cafeteria is open the same hours as the Dome Cafe on game days.

You can consume the libation of your choice, including mixed drinks, in your Superdome seat.

This is New Orleans, the Big Easy, remember? The police aren't worried about crowd control; they're used to handling millions during Carnival season. Still, night games can get rowdy.

After the game, you can find virtually any ethnic cuisine in New Orleans, from soul food at the Praline Connection (504-943-3934) to seafood at Ralph and Kacoo's (504-522-5226) and the Acme Oyster House (504-522-5973). Mulates (504-522-1492) has fine Cajun food, and Commander's Palace (504-899-8221) is known for serious gourmet fare—but make sure to call for a reservation. If you're still in a football mood, drive to suburban Metairie, where place-kicker Morten Andersen has a Champions restaurant (504-834-0600) in the Lakeside Mall.

**LODGING NEAR THE STADIUM**
**Hyatt Regency**
Poydras St. at Loyola Ave.
New Orleans, LA 70140
(504) 561-1234/(800) 233-1234
Next to the stadium.

**Hotel Inter-Continental**
444 St. Charles Ave.
New Orleans, LA 70130
(504) 525-5566/(800) 445-6563
About 7 blocks from the stadium.

**THE SAINTS AT THE SUPERDOME**
**Oct. 30, 1977:** Fake field-goal pass from Tom Blanchard to Elois Grooms helps upset the Los Angeles Rams 27–26.

**Dec. 3, 1979:** Though the Saints lose to the Raiders, Chuck Muncie rushes for 128 yards to become the first Saint to gain 1,000 yards in a season.

**Sept. 4, 1983:** George Rogers sets a team record by rushing for 206 yards against the St. Louis Cardinals. The Saints win 28–17.

**Jan. 3, 1988:** The Saints play their first playoff game, losing 44–10 to the Minnesota Vikings.

**Nov. 20, 1988:** The Saints secure their second consecutive winning season, 42–0 over the Denver Broncos.

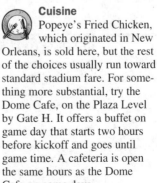

# IN THE HOT SEATS AT THE SUPERDOME

Good luck. The Saints enjoy a season-ticket base of more than 50,000. Still, depending on how well the home team has been playing, game tickets are sometimes available close to game day. Individual-game tickets—usually for the Plaza, padded Terrace, and Terrace levels—go on sale in mid-July, although applications are available in February. Since orders are filled on a first-come, first-served basis, apply early.

• **Bad seats:** Even in the upper levels of the Terrace, seats for football offer excellent viewing with field glasses. If you're trying to get a last-minute ticket, you'll likely sit there, so bring those binoculars.

**Scalping:** Those who don't mind missing kickoff can usually get tickets for face value or less from one of the few scalpers outside.

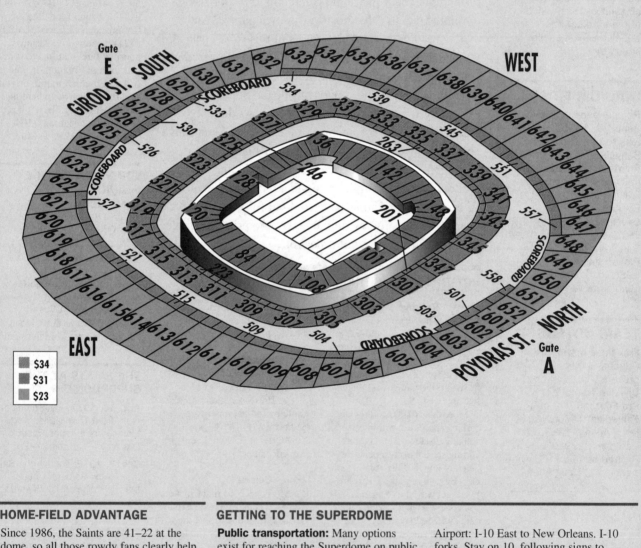

## HOME-FIELD ADVANTAGE

Since 1986, the Saints are 41–22 at the dome, so all those rowdy fans clearly help.

## GETTING TO THE SUPERDOME

**Public transportation:** Many options exist for reaching the Superdome on public transportation. Call RTA at (504) 569-2700 for details.

**By car:** From New Orleans International Airport: I-10 East to New Orleans. I-10 forks. Stay on 10, following signs to Slidell. Take Superdome exit (on left) ⅔ mile past the fork; exit left. Superdome is on the right.

**TICKET INFORMATION**
**Address:** 1500 Poydras St., New Orleans, LA 70112
**Phone:** (504) 522-2600 or TicketMaster at (504) 522-5555

**Hours:** Mon.-Fri. 9-5, plus Sat. 9-5 before home games.
**Prices:** $34: loge (200 and 300 levels), padded terrace (500 level); $31: plaza (100 level); $23: terrace (600 level).

**Training camp:** University of Wisconsin–La Crosse, La Crosse, WI

## STADIUM STATS

**Location:** East Rutherford, NJ 07073
**Opened:** Oct. 10, 1976
**Surface:** AstroTurf
**Capacity:** 78,124
**Services for fans with disabilities:** Seating available in sections 117–125.

## STADIUM FIRSTS

**Regular-season game:** Oct. 10, 1976, 24–14 loss to the Dallas Cowboys.
**Points scored:** 8-yard touchdown by Robert Newhouse of the Cowboys.
**Overtime game:** Dec. 18, 1977, 12–9 loss to the Chicago Bears.
**Playoff game:** Dec. 29, 1985, 17–3 over the San Francisco 49ers.

## TEAM NOTEBOOK

**Franchise history:** New York Giants, 1925–present.
**Division titles:** 1927, '33–35, '38, '39, '41, '44, '46, '56, '58, '59, '61–63, '86, '89, '90.
**Super Bowl appearances:** XXI, Jan. 25, 1987, 39–20 over the Denver Broncos; XXV, Jan. 27, 1991, 20–19 over the Buffalo Bills.
**Pro Football Hall of Fame:** Hein, Henry, Hubbard, Mara, Thorpe, 1963; Guyon, Herber, Owen, '66; Strong, Tunnell, '67; McElhenny, '70; Robustelli, Tittle, '71; Brown, '75; Flaherty, '76; Gifford, '77; Leemans, '78; Badgro, '81; Huff, '82; Weinmeister, '84; Tarkenton, '86; Csonka, '87.
**Retired numbers:** 1, Flaherty; 7, Hein, 14, Tittle; 32, Blozis; 40, Morrison; 42, Conerly; 50, Strong.

# Giants Stadium

Decked in red-white-and-blue team colors, the 78,124-seat Giants Stadium offers terrific sightlines and the magical Manhattan skyline across the Hudson as a backdrop. Before what might be the league's best facility for football was built, this area, known as the Jersey Meadowlands, was a vast swampland filled with rats and abandoned car frames. Maybe the best way to explain why Giants Stadium is so football-fan friendly is to note that you can't fit a baseball field inside.

The Giants are strictly a blue-collar, grind-it-out team that has had only eight winning seasons (but two Super Bowl titles) since the stadium opened. The wind, known to the natives as the Hawk, has helped the Giants win a lot of games, as have their fans, unfairly reputed to be an affluent lot who sit on their hands. Attend an NFL East matchup with, say, the Philadelphia Eagles, and you'll know that the noise can be deafening.

Of course, it might not be only team spirit that drives the Giants when they play at the Meadowlands—it could be a spirit of a different sort. An outrageous but popular theory holds that slain Teamsters boss Jimmy Hoffa is buried underneath the stadium. Cries to excavate each end zone are sure to be heard again in 1996, the 20th anniversary of Hoffa's disappearance.

## HOT TIPS FOR VISITING FANS

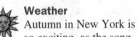

**Parking**
The stadium lot, with 24,800 spots, is among the NFL's largest. Tailgaters arrive four hours before kickoff. The cost is $5. Some fans park at nearby hotels (Sheraton, Hilton, Days Inn) and run car pools to the game. It's not a good idea to walk because you have to cross busy Route 17 and walk a tightrope path along approach roads.

Departing the stadium can tax your patience. The George Washington Bridge backs up routinely, and the addition of a few thousand cars makes the wait a good hour. The Lincoln Tunnel often is a better option for Manhattan. Travelers to Westchester County and Connecticut might prefer the Tappan Zee Bridge, although it also has heavy traffic on Sunday nights, especially in September when vacationers continue to return from the Catskill Mountains and other points north.

**Weather**
Autumn in New York is so exciting, as the song goes. But not late autumn, when the infamous Meadowlands winds begin howling, sometimes accompanied by snow. September games can be played in summerlike heat, accompanied by high humidity, but eight weeks later, heavy sweaters and parkas are in fashion.

**Media bites**
**Radio:** WOR (710 AM) is the club's flagship station.
**TV:** Home and away games are carried on Fox (Channel 5).

**Cuisine**
The Giants have added beer on tap, with 32 portable stands spread about the stadium. Other premium brands include Heineken, Bud Ice, Miller Light and Molson. Cappuccino and espresso also are sold, and if you're really adventurous, you can get a frozen margarita. Harry M.

Stevens operates 40 concessions stands, including two chili stands on the lower level. (See Jets, p. 127.)

The favorite hangout for Giants fans is Manny's (201-939-1244) in nearby Moonachie. You can't beat the ambience and nostalgic mementos of old Giants heroes. Former coach Bill Parcells dined there on Sunday nights . . . if the Giants won. Manny's serves a terrific brunch and runs buses to home games. Two other favorite stops are in Manhattan—Gallagher's Steak House (212-245-5336) and the Dakota Bar and Grill (212-427-8889).

## LODGING NEAR THE STADIUM

**Sheraton Meadowlands**
2 Meadowlands Plaza
East Rutherford, NJ 07073
(201) 896-0500/(800) 325-3535
Across the highway from the stadium.

**Meadowlands Hilton**
2 Harmon Plaza
Secaucus, NJ 07094
(201) 348-6900/(800) 445-8667
1 mile from the stadium.

## THE GIANTS AT GIANTS STADIUM

**Dec. 21, 1985:** Joe Morris gains 202 yards on the ground as the Giants top the Pittsburgh Steelers 28–10.

**Jan. 4, 1987:** Joe Morris runs for 159 yards and defensive tackle Jim Burt knocks Joe Montana unconscious as the Giants romp past the San Francisco 49ers 49–3 in an NFC semifinal game.

**Jan. 11, 1987:** With wind gusting through Giants Stadium, the Giants defense stands firm. The 17–0 win over the Washington Redskins puts the Giants into their first Super Bowl.

**Jan. 13, 1991:** The Giants stop the Chicago Bears cold 31–3 in an NFC semifinal game. Again, the Giants defense makes the difference, snagging two interceptions and holding the Bears to 27 yards rushing and no first downs.

# In the Hot Seats at Giants Stadium

The ticket office is bombarded each week with heart-wrenching stories, all designed to gain entrance to the stadium. They don't work. The more than 77,000 seats in Giants Stadium are held by season ticketholders. Another 18,000 names are on a waiting list that will take an estimated 40 years to fulfill. Tickets cost $35-$45 ($350-$450 for the 10-game package) and are occasionally available from New York City ticket agencies (at a much higher price, of course).

• **Good seats:** Giants Stadium boasts no obstructed seats on its three levels and good angles to the field. There isn't a bad seat in the house, even in the lower rows that start 10 feet above the field. The very best seats are on the mezzanine level, particularly in sections 209-213. The lower tier, especially sections 128-134 and 108-114, also affords excellent sightlines; rows 30-35 have the added attraction of being under cover, just as in the mezzanine, but closer to the field. The front rows of upper-tier sections 309-313 and 329-333 have good sightlines, too. The sun hits the north-side stands, which can warm your toes in December but make you squint in September.

 **Scalping:** Stadium management prohibits the resale of tickets, even at face value, on its property. This is not to say no tickets change hands, only that discretion is required. The trade isn't brisk for Jets games, but on Giants game days, scalpers roam, offering tickets for double, sometimes triple, the face value. The state Sports Authority plans a crackdown.

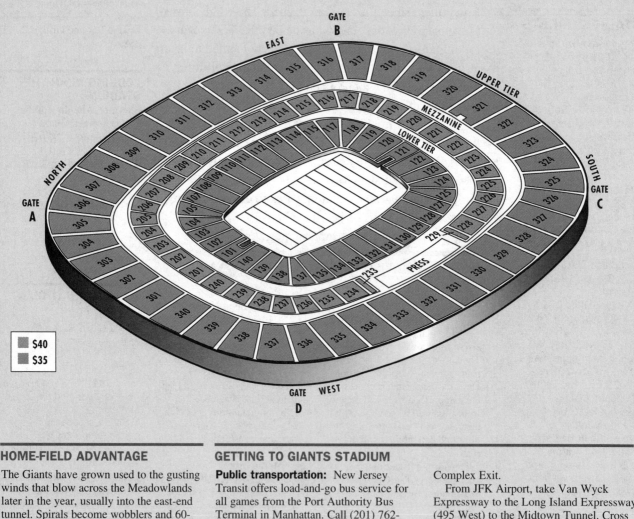

$40
$35

## HOME-FIELD ADVANTAGE

The Giants have grown used to the gusting winds that blow across the Meadowlands later in the year, usually into the east-end tunnel. Spirals become wobblers and 60-yard punts travel 90 yards. The Giants' December home record since 1984 is 16–7.

## GETTING TO GIANTS STADIUM

**Public transportation:** New Jersey Transit offers load-and-go bus service for all games from the Port Authority Bus Terminal in Manhattan. Call (201) 762-5100 for more information.

**By car:** From LaGuardia Airport, take Grand Central Parkway west to Triboro Bridge and follow directions to George Washington Bridge. I-95 to the New Jersey Turnpike. Western spur to the Sports Complex Exit.

From JFK Airport, take Van Wyck Expressway to the Long Island Expressway (495 West) to the Midtown Tunnel. Cross 34th Street and follow signs to the Lincoln Tunnel. Go approximately 4 miles to Route 3 west to the Sports Complex.

From Newark Airport, take the New Jersey Turnpike north to Exit 16W and follow signs to the Sports Complex.

**TICKET INFORMATION**
**Address:** East Rutherford, NJ 07073
**Phone:** (201) 935-8222

**Hours:** Mon.-Fri. 9-4:45.
**Prices:** $40: mezzanine; $35: lower and upper levels.

**Training camp:** Fairleigh Dickinson–Madison University, Florham Park, NJ

TM

## STADIUM STATS

**Location:** East Rutherford, NJ 07073
**Opened:** Oct. 10, 1976
**Surface:** AstroTurf
**Capacity:** 77,121
**Services for fans with disabilities:** Seating available in sections 117–125.

## STADIUM FIRSTS

**Regular-season game:** Sept. 6, 1984, 23–17 loss to the Pittsburgh Steelers.
**Points scored:** 6-yard touchdown reception by Louis Lipps of the Steelers.
**Overtime game:** Nov. 24, 1985, 16–13 over the New England Patriots.
**Playoff game:** Dec. 28, 1985, 26–14 loss to the New England Patriots.

## TEAM NOTEBOOK

**Franchise history:** New York Titans, 1960–1962; New York Jets, 1963–1969 (AFL); New York Jets, 1970–present (NFL).
**Division titles:** 1968, 1969
**Super Bowl appearance:** III, Jan. 12, 1969, 16–7 over the Baltimore Colts.
**Pro Football Hall of Fame:** Weeb Ewbank, 1978; Joe Namath, 1985; Don Maynard, 1987; John Riggins, 1992.
**Retired numbers:** 12, Joe Namath; 13, Don Maynard.

### TICKET INFORMATION
**Address:** Weeb Ewbank Hall, Hofstra University, 1000 Fulton St., Hempstead, NY 11550
**Phone:** (516) 538-7200
**Hours:** Mon.-Fri. 9-5.

**Training camp:** Hofstra University, 1000 Fulton Ave., Hempstead, NY

# Giants Stadium

When the New York Jets departed the Big Apple for the Garden State in 1984, they left behind a dilapidated stadium and second-class citizenship foisted upon them by the New York Mets. What did they get when they crossed the rivers from Queens to Manhattan to alight in East Rutherford, New Jersey? More seats, better parking, a better financial deal and second-class citizenship courtesy of the Stadium's prime tenants, the New York Giants. The Jets try to make the place homey by hanging green coverings and bunting over the (Giants') blue walls, but they failed a few years ago in an attempt to get the New Jersey Sports and Exposition Authority to rename the big cement dish.

Jets fans never will be mistaken for hoity-toity folks attending the opera. They know the game, and make their displeasure known when all is not well. With the Jets, not having had a winning season since 1988, all has not been well in some time. And we're not just talking about boos and chants. At a Monday night game in 1988, with the home team badly trailing Buffalo, some fans set fire to their seats.

By contrast, Giants fans seem positively genteel. Tickets have been in their families longer, and they're more respectful of neighboring patrons. Jets fans tend to be younger and, well, more boisterous. Win or lose, you can expect a hot time at the ballpark when the Jets play.

**$35** **$25**

## HOT TIPS FOR VISITING FANS

### Parking

The cost is $5. And don't worry if you're a little late. The parking personnel are accustomed to sticking latecomers on roadways, grassy dividers and other areas seemingly off-limits, bringing the actual capacity to about 32,000. *(See Giants for traffic, p. 125.)*

### Weather

Bring the Coppertone in September and wear your woolies in December. This is generally a temperate place, but the wintry winds can make a late-afternoon game a thoroughly chilling experience.

### Media bites

**Radio:** All-sports WFAN (660 AM).
**TV:** Regular-season games generally are shown on WNBC (Channel 4).

### Cuisine

The 40 concessions stands, all recently renovated, offer standard fare—hot dogs, pretzels, candy, soda and beer. Nothing exotic, nothing fancy: Big, doughy pretzels are sprinkled with salt—a splash of mustard adds tang—while the dogs are meaty and tasty.

Many fans adjourn afterward to Manny's (201-939-1244), a sports bar and restaurant in nearby Moonachie, to rehash the game. Another popular restaurant not far from the stadium is The Park and Orchard (201-939-9292) in East Rutherford. The Tri-Boro Diner (201-343-7651) in Saddle Brook boasts a huge menu of everything from chef's salad to steaks and chops, and the portions are healthy. Adventurous sorts heading into New York City might like to try Runyon's (212-223-9592) for its sports-savvy patrons or Gallagher's (212-245-5336) for steaks.

### LODGING NEAR THE STADIUM

**Sheraton Meadowlands**
2 Meadowlands Plaza
East Rutherford, NJ 07073
(201) 896-0500
Across the highway from the stadium.

**Meadowlands Hilton**
2 Harmon Plaza
Secaucus, N.J. 07094
(201) 348-6900/(800) 445-8667
1 mile from the stadium.

### GETTING TO GIANTS STADIUM

*(See Giants, p. 126.)*

## HOME-FIELD ADVANTAGE

Wind is a big factor. It tends to swirl and often seems to blow in four directions at once, wreaking havoc on field-goal attempts. Often the ribbons hanging from the goal posts at each end of the field give different indications on the wind direction. Rumor has it that the home team can manipulate the wind by having a gate inside the tunnel behind the end zone raised or lowered, but this urban legend rates somewhere next to the one about Jimmy Hoffa.

## IN THE HOT SEATS

The Jets sell 77,121 tickets for their games, a number that varies slightly depending on how many seats in the suites are sold. Of that total, some 74,000 are season tickets, and the Jets boast an annual renewal average of 96%-97%. The few that don't re-up are generally in the end zone or the upper deck.

A handful of single seats, usually no more than 300-400, go on sale in August at the stadium and at the Jets' training complex in Hempstead, New York. The remainder are allotted for club officials, Jets players and visiting players. The week of a game against an unattractive opponent or a team based far from New York, tickets returned by the visiting club (which is allotted 500) go on sale on Wednesday at the Stadium.

## STADIUM STATS

**Location:** Fifth St., Tempe, AZ 85287
**Opened:** 1958
**Surface:** Grass
**Capacity:** 73,521
**Services for fans with disabilities:** Call the Cardinals ticket office (602-379-0102) for information.

## STADIUM FIRSTS

**Regular-season game:** Sept. 12, 1988, 17–14 loss to the Dallas Cowboys.
**Points scored:** 47-yard field goal by Luis Zendejas of the Cowboys.

## TEAM NOTEBOOK

**Franchise history:** Chicago Cardinals, 1920–1959; St. Louis Cardinals, 1960-1987; Phoenix Cardinals, 1988–1993; Arizona Cardinals, 1994–present.
**Division titles:** 1947, 1948, 1974, 1975.
**Pro Football Hall of Fame:** Ernie Nevers, 1963; Jim Thorpe, 1963; Jimmy Conzelman, 1964; Guy Chamberlin, 1965; John "Paddy" Driscoll, 1965; Charles W. Bidwell, 1967; Ollie Matson, 1972; Larry Wilson, 1978.
**Retired numbers:** 8, Larry Wilson; 77, Stan Mauldin; 88, J.V. Cain; 99, Marshall Goldberg.

# Sun Devil Stadium

The sun always seems to shine on Sun Devil Stadium, the only NFL arena on a college campus. Desert dwellers like to say it's a dry heat, but tell that to the fans who roast in the stands for August preseason games. Temperatures have climbed as high as 122 degrees, and it's worse on the field. Most regular-season games are played in the hottest part of the day—1 P.M. in September and early October, and 2 P.M. the rest of the season.

The sun and the gorgeous setting between two mountain buttes provide most of the heat and color at Sun Devil Stadium. Visiting fans sometimes outnumber Cardinals supporters, especially when the Cowboys come to town. In fact, on those weekends, Interstate 10 in New Mexico and Arizona is filled with Texas license plates. Cowboys fans from West Texas, unable to get tickets to Texas Stadium, drive to Phoenix and pack the stadium, creating a sea of blue that irritates Cardinals players.

Until the team wins, though, the situation is not going to change too much. Phoenix residents, many from elsewhere, are slow to change loyalties—especially the retirees, whose RVs and out-of-state plates are easy to spot in the parking lot. Still, the team slowly is building a following, mostly among the younger set, the most visible proof being "The Wild Cards," a rowdy group in the north end zone who paint their faces and wear red wigs and Cardinals garb. And with the arrival of coach Buddy Ryan, things might really heat up in Sun Devil Stadium before long.

## HOT TIPS FOR VISITING FANS

**Parking**
Even though only 3,500 spaces are around the stadium, parking is ample. Another 10,000 spots are less than a mile from the stadium, and the school band's practice fields are also used. In addition, many fans park in the downtown Tempe area only a few blocks away and walk to the game.

Because there's little highway access, fans should arrive early. Traffic congests on the streets leading to the stadium, particularly on Scottsdale Road from downtown Tempe and on roads from the north. Access will improve in a few years. By the time Super Bowl XXX is played in Tempe, in 1996, the Papago Freeway will have an exit just a few blocks from the stadium.

**Weather**
Fans at Miami's Joe Robbie Stadium might argue, but Sun Devil Stadium is the NFL's best tanning salon. You can catch the best rays in the east stands. Just make sure you bring plenty of sunblock. Stadium officials are well-prepared to handle those who bake too long. The medical staff is the largest in the league: Seven paramedic teams are inside the stadium, a force that includes six physicians and six nurses. The team also provides chilled water throughout the stadium.

Stadium officials have experimented with misting systems, but they are not convinced that it cools the entire stadium.

**Media bites**
**Radio:** KTAR (620 AM—English), KVVA (107.1 FM—Spanish).
**TV:** KTVK (Channel 3, ABC), shows preseason Cardinals games, with former quarterback Neil Lomax as a color commentator. KNXV (Channel 45) is the Fox affiliate.

**Cuisine**
Hot dogs, hamburgers, nachos, pretzels, soft drinks and beer. Fans can purchase only two beers at a time, and no alcohol is sold after halftime.

Outside, there's Macayo's Depot Cantina (602-966-6677) for Mexican. Stan's Metro Deli (602-921-3505) is a favorite of the students. McDuffy's is a sports bar that has off-track betting. Fans also often dine at the Mill Landing (602-966-1700) for seafood, or at the Paradise Bar and Grill (602-829-0606). Fans who don't want to walk the several blocks to Mill Avenue go to nearby Mission Palms Hotel (602-894-1400), site of pregame and postgame parties.

## LODGING NEAR THE STADIUM

**Mesa Pavilion Hilton**
1011 W. Holmes Ave.
Mesa, AZ 85210
(602) 833-5555/(800) 445-8667
8 miles from the stadium.

**The Ritz Carlton Phoenix**
2401 E. Camelback Rd.
Phoenix, AZ 85016
(602) 468-0700/(800) 241-3333
About 10 miles from the stadium.

## THE CARDINALS AT SUN DEVIL STADIUM

**Nov. 13, 1988:** Roy Green catches nine receptions for 176 yards as the Cards beat the New York Giants 24–17.

**Dec. 10, 1988:** Neil Lomax throws for 384 yards in a 23–17 loss to the Philadelphia Eagles.

**Dec. 12, 1992:** Johnny Johnson rushes for 156 yards in a 19–0 win over the Giants.

# IN THE HOT SEATS AT SUN DEVIL STADIUM

Ticket prices were the highest in the league in 1988, the team's first year in Arizona. They averaged $38 a ticket, but the club quickly realized its mistake. Now the average cost is $28—middle of the pack in the NFL—and 40,000 seats are available at $20 a ticket or less. Individual tickets go on sale in mid-July.

Before Ryan came to town, tickets almost always were available on game day, except for the Cowboys. The next-biggest draw is the Chicago Bears, whose fans seem to migrate to the desert each year after the first Midwestern snowstorm. The Cardinals were originally a Chicago team, so the rivalry and fan base remain.

• **Bad seats:** The field was lowered in 1992, so seats are not obstructed: You can sit in the front row and see the entire field. Those in the upper deck get a nice breeze and a good view of the breathtaking sunsets. Only about 27,000 seats have chair backs; the rest are benches. Chair backs can be rented, though, for $2. Nearly 5,000 no-alcohol seats are available, the most in the NFL.

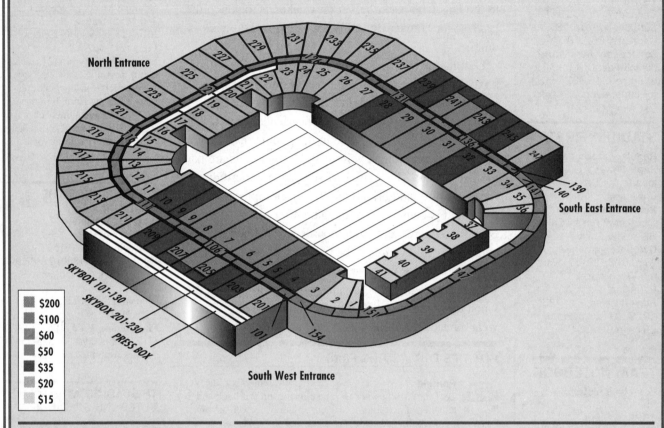

North Entrance

South East Entrance

SKYBOX 101-130
SKYBOX 201-230
PRESS BOX

$200
$100
$60
$50
$35
$20
$15

South West Entrance

## HOME-FIELD ADVANTAGE

The heat can wreak havoc on opposing teams. Just ask the New England Patriots, who melted three years ago when temperatures reached 120 degrees on the sideline. Cardinals coaches don't put thermometers on the visiting sideline but make sure the opposition thinks about the heat. A sign outside one locker room reads: "Make sure you get plenty of fluids." A sign since removed read: "Warning: The Surgeon General reports that exertion coupled with high temperatures can lead to dehydration." The Cardinals also wear white at home so opponents can suffer in darker colors.

## GETTING TO SUN DEVIL STADIUM

**Public transportation:** The system does not run on Sundays. Call (602) 253-5000 for information concerning non-Sunday games.

**By car:** From Sky Harbor International Airport, take 143 north to the 44th Street/Hohokam Expressway exit northbound. Continue to Washington Street and turn right. Washington Street merges with Van Buren Street, which runs across the Salt River bridge before becoming Mill Avenue. Go left off Mill at Fifth Street. The stadium is 3 blocks on the north side of Fifth Street.

**TICKET INFORMATION**
**Address:** 8701 S. Hardy, South Tempe, AZ 85284
**Phone:** (602) 379-0102/(800) 999-1402
**Hours:** Mon.-Fri. 8:30-5.
**Prices:** $200: sections 106 and 134; $100: sections 101-105, 107-111, 129-133 and 135-139; $60: sections 112-128 and 140-154; $50: sections 6-8, 29-31, 205-207 and 241-243; $35: sections 4-5, 9-10, 28, 32, 203-204, 208-209, 239-240 and 244-245; $20: sections 3, 11-27, 33-34, 201-202, 210-238 and 246-247; $15: sections 1-2 and 35-41.

**Training camp:** Northern Arizona University, Flagstaff, AZ

# Veterans Stadium

TM

To Philadelphia's spirited football fans—who have an opinion on everything—Veterans Stadium always has been a huge open-air soapbox. Natives call it, simply, the Vet. Located in south Philadelphia, Veterans Stadium looks a lot like Cincinnati's Riverfront Stadium and Pittsburgh's Three Rivers. There's a hardness, though, about the stadium and an intimidating presence to the fans who pack the Vet on weekends to watch the Eagles—or "Iggles" in Phillytalk—that make a visit unique.

Despite the addition of plush penthouse suites, luxury boxes and fancy elevators, the Vet definitely is showing its age. Neither Big Bird, the unofficial mascot that roams the stands, nor the Eagle cheerleaders can distract a visitor from that fact. Done in the popular earth colors of the '70s, the orange, yellow and brown seats are hard, molded plastic. The AstroTurf surface, often criticized for being dirty and brick-hard, has been replaced several times and is being ripped up again after the 1994 season. New scoreboards and video boards are planned, and every seat will eventually be replaced, but talk of building a stadium for the co-tenant baseball Phillies persists.

Even so, Eagles fans remain a rowdy lot, especially when they lose. Ask any Redskins fan who has dared wear a headdress during his visit.

## HOT TIPS FOR VISITING FANS

**Parking**
Lots start filling with tailgaters about four hours before kickoff. The stadium complex has 10,000 spaces, with another 6,500 in nearby lots. Cost is $5-$10. Wide boulevards and two major expressways help empty lots within an hour. Security at private lots can be a problem. Some fans park along Pattison Avenue and nearby side streets but must arrive a couple of hours early.

**Weather**
Local weather runs the gamut from hot and muggy in September, to gorgeously fresh in October and early November, to damp, wind-blown and sometimes bitterly cold in December. When Leonard Tose owned the Eagles, his helicopter pilot refused to land inside the Vet because of the swirling winds. Fans wear shorts and T-shirts early in the season. But remember, the Vet is near a river on flat land, and temperatures, as well as rain, sleet, and snow can fall unexpectedly in late fall. Wear hoods but don't bring an umbrella—fans behind will let you have it.

**Media bites**
**Radio:** Many fans bring transistor radios to hear long-time WYSP (94.1 FM) announcer Merrill Reese's booming voice describe a touchdown. Sidekick Stan Walters, a former Eagle, is among the NFL's more underrated analysts.
**TV:** Eagles games are telecast on the Fox affiliate, WTXF (Channel 29).

**Cuisine**
In 1986, the stadium added two food courts, behind the 50-yard line (southside) on the 200 and 500 levels, both of which sell cheese steaks, the city's most popular nosh. But for the ultimate cheese steak, try Pat's Steaks (215-339-9872) on your way to the game. Most fans have brunch at home, then bring cheese steaks, hoagies and other sandwiches. Several kinds of beer are sold at stands, but Budweiser remains the most popular; sales stop at halftime .

Few eateries are nearby, although Medora's Mecca (215-336-1655) features delicious Italian food. Also try Celebre's Pizza (215-467-3255). The Stadium Holiday Inn (215-755-9500), part-owned by ex-Eagles quarterback Ron Jaworski, features a Bergey Brunch (named for former Eagles linebacker Bill Bergey), but the real action starts after the game, with patrons stacked five deep at the bar.

## LODGING NEAR THE STADIUM

**Airport Marriott**
4509 Island Ave.
Philadelphia, PA 19153
(215) 365-4150/(800) 228-9290.
4 miles from the stadium.

**Sheraton Society Hill**
1 Dock St.
Philadelphia, PA 19106
(215) 238-6000/(800) 325-3535.
7 miles from the stadium.

## THE EAGLES AT VETERANS STADIUM

**Sept. 23, 1974:** Joe Lavender returns a Dallas Cowboy fumble 96 yards for a touchdown. The Eagles win 13–10.

**Jan. 11, 1981:** Wilbert Montgomery's 194 yards rushing helps the Eagles to a 20–7 victory over the Cowboys and a trip to Super Bowl XV.

**Nov. 10, 1985:** Ron Jaworski throws a 99-yard touchdown to Mike Quick, tying the NFL record for longest touchdown pass. The Eagles beat the Atlanta Falcons 23–17 in overtime.

**Dec. 24, 1989:** The Eagles end the season with a 31–14 win over the Phoenix Cardinals. Reggie White leads the defense to a team-record 62 sacks for the season. Despite two victories over the Giants, the Eagles still wind up second to New York in the NFC East, good for a wild-card berth.

# IN THE HOT SEATS AT VETERANS STADIUM

Win or lose, the Eagles sell more than 55,000 season tickets. Sunday home games are an autumn ritual. Starting in mid-May, 8,000 tickets per game go on sale. Those for Dallas, Washington, Arizona and other traditional rivals are snapped up in a hurry. Each visiting team is allocated tickets (usually several thousand), that, if unsold, are returned late in the week. You might get lucky by calling on Friday before the game.

• **Bad seats:** The worst seats are in the 100 level (sections 100-112, 125 and 152-166) behind the home and visiting benches. Other areas afford decent sightlines, although 700-level seats are far from the field. Some seats in the 300 level are obstructed. The Eagles will lose 1,200 seats (and gain back only 250) when a new disabled-accessible area is constructed in the 300 bleacher area (Gate F).

**Scalping:** Scalpers roam the approach streets and near will-call windows on the concourse between Gates A and H. Typical cost: $75-$85 for the Cowboys, double face value for the Giants games, and $55-$60 for non rivals such as New Orleans and Cleveland. Bargaining is common, arrests are rare.

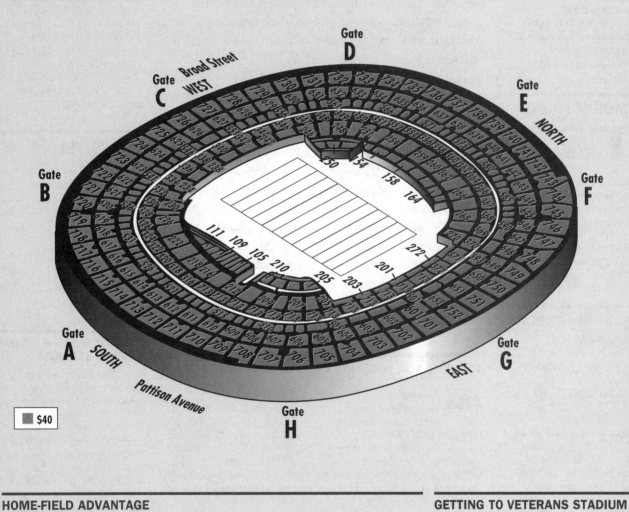

$40

## HOME-FIELD ADVANTAGE

Winds often whip off the nearby Delaware River, creating nightmares for visiting kickers; the turf doesn't help visitors much either. Former Eagles fullback Ronnie Bull once said he could run blindfolded and tell directions by the feel of the synthetic grass. Whatever direction, the Vet's turf is hard and sometimes causes visiting runners to take a pratfall. Full-throated home fans can also intimidate visiting teams, but fickle Eagles rooters can flip-flop. For example, during a 42–3 Monday night loss to the Los Angeles Rams, Eagles fans tossed dog bones onto the field.

## GETTING TO VETERANS STADIUM

**Public transportation:** The Broad Street/Orange Line of the subway stops at the Pattison Avenue exit, across the street from the stadium.

**By car:** From Philadelphia International Airport, I-95 North to the Broad Street exit. Proceed 1 mile past JFK Stadium and the Spectrum. Turn right on Pattison Avenue; Veteran's Stadium is on the left.

**Training camp:** West Chester University, West Chester, PA

**TICKET INFORMATION**
**Address:** 3501 S. Broad St., Philadelphia, PA 19148.
**Phone:** (215) 463-5500 or TicketMaster at

(215) 336-2000.
**Hours:** Mon.-Fri. 9-5.
**Prices:** All seats are $40.

TM

## STADIUM STATS

**Location:** 300 Stadium Circle, Pittsburgh, PA 15212
**Opened:** July 16, 1970
**Surface:** AstroTurf
**Capacity:** 59,600
**Services for fans with disabilities:** Seating available on third level by Gate A and in sections 312-313.

## STADIUM FIRSTS

**Regular-season game:** Sept. 20, 1970, 19–7 loss to the Houston Oilers.
**Points scored:** 22-yard touchdown reception by Jerry LeVias of the Oilers.
**Overtime game:** Sept. 24, '78, 15–9 over the Cleveland Browns.
**Playoff game:** Dec. 23, '72, 13–7 over the Oakland Raiders.

## TEAM NOTEBOOK

**Franchise history:** Pittsburgh Pirates, 1933-39; Pittsburgh Steelers, '40–present.
**Division titles:** 1972, '74, '75, '76, '77, '78, '79, '83, '84, '92.
**Super Bowl appearances:** IX, Jan. 12, 1975, 16–6 over the Minnesota Vikings; X, Jan. 18, '76, 21–17 over the Dallas Cowboys; XIII, Jan. 21, '79, 35–31 over the Dallas Cowboys; XIV, Jan. 20, '80, 31–19 over the Los Angeles Rams.
**Pro Football Hall of Fame:** B. Bell, 1963; A. Rooney, '64; B. Dudley, '66; W. Kiesling, '66; B. Layne, '67; M. Motley, '68; E. Stautner, '69; L. Dawson '87; J. Greene, '87; J.H. Johnson, '87; J. Ham, '88; M. Blount '89; T. Bradshaw '89; F. Harris '90; J. Lambert, '90; C. Noll, '93.

# Three Rivers Stadium

Cozy is not a word most folks would use to describe Three Rivers Stadium, which has the uninspiring concrete-and-steel ambience of those circa-'70 stadiums. But this is Pittsburgh, a town concrete and steel helped build, and somehow the hardnosed Steeler fans and their no-nonsense team match up well with this arena.

Set at the confluence of the Allegheny, Ohio and Monongahela Rivers, Three Rivers Stadium holds fond memories for Steeler fans. The Steelers had been a perennially mediocre squad since their founding as the Pirates in 1933, but the move to Three Rivers in 1970 seemed to signal a turn around. In 1972, anchored by the feared Steel Curtain, the team captured its first division title, and before the decade was over the names Terry Bradshaw, Joe Greene, Jack Ham, Franco Harris and Jack Lambert became synonymous with greatness.

The atmosphere remains highly charged, much as it was during the Steelers' heyday. Banners saluting individual players and the team are draped over the walls, and some fans still wear the team's black-and-gold jerseys with numbers commemorating star players from the glory years, like No. 32 for Franco Harris and No. 56 for Jack Lambert. As the team's success has waned in recent years, more no-shows are obvious, particularly during bad weather. Generally speaking, though, the crowd is pure Pittsburgh, a shot-and-beer kind of town that's not for the faint of heart.

## HOT TIPS FOR VISITING FANS

 **Parking**
There are only about 4,000 spaces, which go for $5, or $125 for season reserved. Several additional lots are located on the North Side in neighborhoods near the stadium. Those who don't want the hassles of last-minute parking should arrive at least three hours prior to kickoff.

Pre- and postgame tailgating is not only permitted but also encouraged. The team suggests arriving by 9 a.m., when the gates open for 1 p.m. games.

**Weather**
Beautiful fall football weather abounds in September and October, when temperatures are in the 60s and 70s. It drops to the 40s and 50s in November, and plunges to who-knows-what by December and January. Dress appropriately.

**Media bites**
**Radio:** Tune in Steelers analyst Myron Cope on the team's flagship station WTAE (1250 AM). His high-pitched, nasal "Pittsburghese" is filled with "Cope-isms," local flavor that will give visitors a taste of what it's like rooting for the hometown team. Cope is the man who popularized the Terrible Towel of the '70s.

**TV:** If the game is sold out, which they usually are, WPXI (NBC) and WTAE (ABC) are the network television affiliates.

**Cuisine**
Try the hamburgers and sausages, which are cooked on a charcoal grill. Primanti Brothers, a well-known local restaurant chain, offers made-to-order sandwiches, and Benkovitz Fish has fresh fish sandwiches. Iron City is the

town's best-known beer and is ideal for washing down a kielbasa sandwich. At night games liquor sales are halted before the game concludes, generally by the end of the third quarter.

Across the river, The Grand Concourse at Station Square (412-261-1717) tops the chow-down list. Also try Ruth's Chris for steaks (412-391-4800), The Carlton (412-391-4099) for American fare or Tambellini's (412-481-1118) for Italian. Froggy's (412-471-3764) offers a pregame brunch followed by bus service to the stadium. Among the top sports bars is the Clark Bar & Grill, located near the stadium.

## LODGING NEAR THE STADIUM

**Westin William Penn**
530 William Penn Place
Pittsburgh, PA 15219
(412) 281-7100/(800) 228-3000
9 blocks from the stadium

**Vista International**
100 Penn Ave.
Pittsburgh, PA 15222
(412) 281-3700/(800) 367-8478
1 mile from the stadium

## THE STEELERS AT THREE RIVERS STADIUM

**Dec. 23, 1972:** In the first playoff game at Three Rivers Stadium, Franco Harris makes his "Immaculate Reception" in the final minute and the Steelers beat the Raiders 13–7.

**Dec. 22, 1974:** The Steelers defeat the Bills 32–14 in the AFC playoffs, on their way to their first Super Bowl victory.

**Jan. 4, 1976:** The Steelers edge the Oakland Raiders 16–10 in the AFC Championship to advance to their second straight Super Bowl.

**Dec. 15, 1985:** Down 21–0 to Buffalo in the second quarter, the Steelers charge back to win 30–24 in their biggest comeback win.

**Dec. 27, 1992:** Barry Foster ties Eric Dickerson's record by rushing for more than 100 yards in his 12th game in one season. The Steelers win 23–13 over the Browns.

# IN THE HOT SEATS AT THREE RIVERS STADIUM

The Steelers have been sold out on a season-ticket basis since 1972. The team withholds a few thousand tickets for every game, which go on sale to the public for $30 in May of each year. Get 'em quick: Typically, they sell out within a few weeks. Mail orders are accepted, starting May 16. On the rare occasion that an opposing team returns a block of its allotted tickets during the season, they are available at the box office on game day.

• **Bad seats:** If you're not sitting between the 30-yard lines, you're a long post pattern from the field, particularly if you're in either end zone. If you have a choice, try to stay away from lower field box seats behind the teams' benches, as they tend to have obstructed views. Seats in the second level and above allow wider viewing.

**Scalping:** Scalping is kept off stadium property, but there are plenty of sellers standing on street corners, mostly in surrounding neighborhoods on the North Side. Prices drop on bad-weather weekends, when tickets are often available for face value.

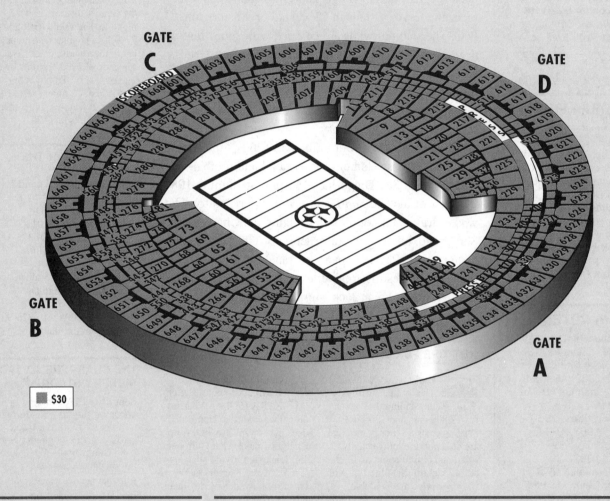

## HOME-FIELD ADVANTAGE

Emerging victorious at Three Rivers Stadium is not an easy proposition, particularly as nasty weather rolls in during the winter months. The Steelers have never posted a losing season at Three Rivers. From 1970 to 1992, the team forged a 133–50 mark (73%) at home.

## GETTING TO THREE RIVERS STADIUM

**Public transportation:** Starting 90 minutes before game time, shuttle buses run along Wood Street in downtown Pittsburgh to the stadium every 10 to 15 minutes. Call (412) 442-2000 for more information.

**By car:** From the east, take the Pennsylvania Turnpike to I-376 West to downtown and the Stadium exit.

From the west, take the Ohio Turnpike to the Pennsylvania Turnpike, then south on I-79 to I-279 South to the Stadium exit.

From the north, take I-79 South to I-279 South to the Stadium exit.

From the south, take 79 North to I-279 North to the Stadium exit.

## TICKET INFORMATION
**Address:** 300 Stadium Circle, Pittsburgh, PA 15212
**Phone:** (412) 323-1200, ext. 205

**Order by mail:** c/o Pittsburgh Steelers, P.O. Box 6763, Pittsburgh, PA 15212
**Hours:** Mon.-Fri. 9-5, plus Sat. 9-12 before home games, and 9-halftime on game days.

**Prices:** $30 every seat.
**Training camp:** St. Vincent College, Latrobe, PA

TM

# San Diego Jack Murphy Stadium

## STADIUM STATS

**Location:** 9449 Friars Rd., San Diego, CA 92108
**Opened:** Aug. 20, 1967
**Surface:** Grass
**Capacity:** 60,836
**Services for fans with disabilities:** Seating available in plaza level sections 17, 25, 31, 43-46 and 57-59.

## STADIUM FIRSTS

**Regular-season game:** Sept. 9, 1967, 28–14 over the Boston Patriots.
**Points scored:** 7-yard touchdown by Paul Lowe of the Chargers.
**Overtime game:** Oct. 12, 1975, 13–10 loss to the Los Angeles Rams.
**Playoff game:** Dec. 29, 1979, 17–14 loss to the Houston Oilers.

## TEAM NOTEBOOK

**Franchise history:** Los Angeles Chargers, 1960; San Diego Chargers, 1961–1969 (AFL); San Diego Chargers, 1970–present.
**Division titles:** 1960, 1961, 1963, 1964, 1965, 1979, 1980, 1981, 1992.
**Pro Football Hall of Fame:** Lance Alworth, 1978; Ron Mix, 1979; Johnny Unitas, 1979; David "Deacon" Jones, 1980; Sid Gillman, 1983; John Mackey, 1992; Dan Fouts, 1993; Larry Little, 1993.
**Retired number:** 14, Dan Fouts.

After some proud decades in the AFL and the NFL, the Chargers went through 10 lean years during the 1980s and early 90s without making the playoffs, but the AFC West championship in 1992 put the Chargers back on top of the San Diego sports scene. Despite their laid-back reputation, San Diego fans enjoy game day with the same fervor as fans in Cleveland or Washington, D.C. The stadium walls are covered with signs, fans are decked out in team colors and some—the Bolt Heads—wear huge foam lightning bolts on their heads. Even though large contingents from colder cities often follow their teams to enjoy the warm weather, they never outcheer the Chargers fans.

Like many arenas built in the late 1960s, "the Murph" is a multipurpose stadium for baseball and football. It was renamed San Diego Jack Murphy Stadium in 1981 in honor of the late *San Diego Union* sports editor who was instrumental not only in bringing the Chargers to San Diego, but also in construction of the stadium and acquiring the Padres expansion franchise. If not one of the more interesting football experiences the league has to offer, game day at Jack Murphy Stadium still is one of the most enjoyable.

## HOT TIPS FOR VISITING FANS

 **Parking**
The lot that surrounds the stadium has room for 17,800 cars and 120 buses. Parking costs $5. For games that are sold out, the lot is usually filled and closed about an hour before kickoff. Satellite lots with shuttle service are available. Many fans arrive early and have tailgate parties while watching the early NFL games on portable TVs. The lot has only four entrances, and traffic is slower as game time nears. After the game, getting out of the lot requires extreme patience.

**Weather**
San Diego has a mild climate, but fans bring sweaters and jackets to afternoon and night games to guard against chilly evenings.

 **Media bites**
**Radio:** All-sports station XTRA (690 AM) carries all games live. Lee Hamilton does play-by-play, while former Chargers players Pat Curran and Jim Laslavic provide analysis.
**TV:** Most Chargers games are telecast on local NBC affiliate KNSD (Channel 39).

**Cuisine**
Concessions stands offer the standard fare of beer, hot dogs, popcorn and nachos. In addition, the stadium offers franchise outlets for Pizza Hut, Rally's Hamburgers and Rubio's fish tacos—a San Diego culinary concoction of fish, cabbage, salsa and lime that's tastier than it sounds. Stands feature espresso, sushi and hand-dipped Häagen-Dazs ice cream.
The Sports Club is on the field level on the closed end zone

side. It offers table seating, food and a bar. A picnic area on the concourse near the scoreboard at the open end provides an area where groups can to hold tent parties before the game; included are tickets, food and a bar.

About 6 miles away downtown is the Gaslamp Quarter, a turn-of-the-century district known for its nightlife. Brewski's (619-231-7700) is a popular restaurant and bar in the Quarter that offers a selection of beers from its own microbrewery. Trophy's Sports Bar, is about 2 miles west of the stadium; it features sports memorabilia and lots of TVs.

## LODGING NEAR THE STADIUM

**Sheraton Harbor Island East and West Towers**
1380 Harbor Island Dr.
San Diego, CA 92101
(619) 291-2900/(800) 325-3535
7 miles from the stadium.

**Marriott Mission Valley**
8757 Rio San Diego Dr.
San Diego, CA 92108
(619) 692-3800/(800) 228-9290
1 mile from the stadium.

## THE CHARGERS AT JACK MURPHY STADIUM

**Sept. 30, 1973:** Johnny Unitas becomes the first quarterback to pass for more than 40,000 yards when he connects with Mike Garrett in a 20–13 loss to the Cincinnati Bengals.

**Dec. 17, 1979:** The Chargers take their first division title in 14 years when they beat the Denver Broncos 17–7.

**Sept. 14, 1980:** Dan Fouts throws a touchdown pass to John Jefferson in overtime to give the Chargers a 30–24 victory over the Raiders.

**Dec. 20, 1982:** The Chargers gain 661 total yards in a 50–34 win over the Cincinnati Bengals.

**Jan. 2, 1993:** Behind Marion Butts' 119 rushing yards, the Chargers beat the Kansas City Chiefs 17–0 in an AFC wild-card game.

# IN THE HOT SEATS AT JACK MURPHY STADIUM

The Chargers sold 48,000 season tickets in 1993 and sold out all eight regular-season home games, though some tickets were available during the week leading up to several games. Also, when the baseball season ends, bleacher seats are added to both end zones, in front of the stadium's permanent seats. These seats, just a few feet from the end zones, are sold on an individual-game basis.

Few tickets are available on game day, though availability depends on the opponent and how the Chargers have been doing on the field. The toughest tickets usually are for AFC West division rivals

Los Angeles Raiders, Kansas City Chiefs, and Denver Broncos. Single-game tickets go on sale in mid-July.

While most of the luxury boxes are leased year-round, a few are available on a game-to-game basis.

• **Bad seats:** The lowest seats on the field level on both sides are too low for fans to see over the players and coaches. That means the seats closest to the field between the 30-yard lines, including some right on the 50, have obstructed views. The team clearly marks all these tickets with obstructed-view warnings. End-zone seats

on the plaza level in the open end have a poor view of the main scoreboard that towers above. Extended plaza seats in the open end zone provide no view of the main scoreboard at all.

**Scalping:** Since it's illegal to resell tickets on stadium grounds, scalpers can be found on Friars Road and Mission Center Drive, which lead to the stadium. Whether or not it's a buyer's market depends on how the Chargers are doing.

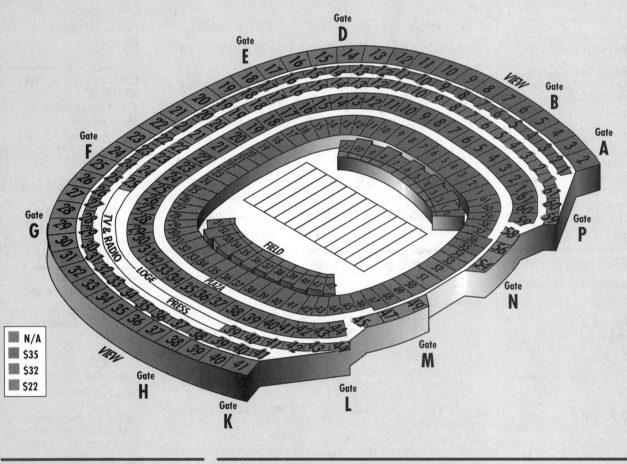

**Legend:**
- N/A
- $35
- $32
- $22

---

## HOME-FIELD ADVANTAGE

Wind and weather are rarely factors, but before the baseball season ends, teams heading toward the closed end of the stadium encounter the dirt of the baseball infield. This can cause problems with footing for runners and kickers. When baseball season ends, the dirt portion is sodded.

## GETTING TO JACK MURPHY STADIUM

**Public transportation:** San Diego Transit offers a Chargers Express directly to the stadium with departures from several locations. Call (619) 233-3004 for more information. North County Transit offers similar service from suburban Oceanside and Escondido. Call (619) 967-2828 for more

information.

**By car:** From Lindbergh Field, Harbor Drive to Grape St. Left on Grape through three traffic lights. Right onto I-5 South to I-163 North, exit east on Friars Road 2 miles to the stadium.

---

**TICKET INFORMATION**
**Address:** P.O. Box 609100, San Diego, CA 92160
**Phone:** (619) 280-2121 or Teleseat at (619) 452-SEAT
**Hours:** Daily 8-5 (offseason, Mon.-Fri. 8-5).

**Prices:** $35: field rows 10 and above, all plaza sections except 49-54, all loge seats, and view sections 1-12, 31-41 and rows 1-4 of sections 13-30; $32: view sections 13-30, end zone plaza sections 49-54 and field rows 1-9; $22: extended plaza

sections 45-50 and rows 27-41 of plaza sections 53-58.

**Training camp:** University of California at San Diego, La Jolla, CA

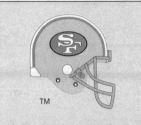

TM

# Candlestick Park

As much as the San Francisco 49ers' tradition is defined by great stars—from Y.A. Tittle to Joe Montana and Jerry Rice—its home stadium is surrounded by an incomparable aura. Candlestick Park is a menacing structure that can give you the chills.

Start with the breathtaking view of San Francisco Bay on the stadium's southeast side. Add the aroma of the popular tailgate parties. Witness hotdog wrappers swirling in the unpredictable wind. Bundle up for typically brisk and damp conditions, and brace for a sea of 49ers-red outerwear in the stands. These are some of the things that make "the Stick" perhaps the NFL's most flavorful venue. Like the Golden Gate Bridge and Fisherman's Wharf, Candlestick Park is a true slice of San Francisco.

Unless you're tailgating, you have no reason to eat before entering the Stick, and it's always wise to bring a jacket, even if its 70 degrees and sunny when you depart for the stadium

All things considered, it's a unique experience—and the quality of football is pretty good, too. Of course, getting a ticket to this taste of the city can be difficult, but if you haven't been to a 49ers game at Candlestick, the experience could be worth the price you have to pay.

such as Anchor Steam, Heineken, Killian's Red and Gordon Biersch. Napa Valley wines are also available.

Your best bet for after the game is downtown San Francisco or North Beach, about 20 minutes away. The Old Clam House (415-826-4880) is nearer the stadium, about 15 minutes away, and is noted for its steamed cherrystone clams and sports-fan clientele. If you're headed toward the South Bay after Sunday afternoon games, Clark's By The Bay (415-367-9222), owned by ex-49ers receiver Dwight Clark, is a good bet.

## STADIUM STATS

**Location:** San Francisco, CA 94124
**Opened:** April 12, 1960
**Surface:** Grass
**Capacity:** 68,491
**Services for fans with disabilities:** Seating available throughout the stadium. Call (415) 468-2249 for information.

## STADIUM FIRSTS

**Regular-season game:** Oct. 10, 1971, 20–13 loss to the Los Angeles Rams.
**Points scored:** 24-yard field goal by Bruce Gossett of the 49ers.
**Overtime game:** Sept. 14, 1980, 24–21 over the St. Louis Cardinals.
**Playoff game:** Dec. 26, 1971, 24–20 over the Washington Redskins.

## TEAM NOTEBOOK

**Franchise history:** San Francisco 49ers, 1946–49 (AAFC); '50–present (NFL).
**Division titles:** 1970, '71, '72, '81, '83, '84, '86, '87, '88, '89, '90, '92.
**Super Bowl appearances:** XVI, Jan. 24, 1982, 26–21 over the Cincinnati Bengals; XIX, Jan. 20, '85, 38–16 over the Miami Dolphins; XXIII, Jan. 22, '89, 20–16 over the Cincinnati Bengals; XXIV, Jan. 28, '90, 55–10 over the Denver Broncos.
**Pro Football Hall of Fame:** L. Nomellini, J. Perry, 1969; H. McElhenny, '70; Y.A. Tittle, '71; O.J. Simpson, '85; J.H. Johnson, '87; B. St. Clair, '90; B. Walsh, '93.
**Retired numbers:** 12, J. Brodie; 34, J. Perry; 37, J. Johnson; 39, H. McElhenny; 70, C. Krueger; 73, L. Nomellini; 87, D. Clark.

## HOT TIPS FOR VISITING FANS

 **Parking**
The stadium lot holds 7,000 cars. Spots cost either $10 or $15, but without prepaid parking tickets, forget about getting into them. Another 10,000 spaces on perimeter roads range from $5 to $10 but many are in unpaved lots. Mud can be a definite factor. The upside to parking lots on the outskirts is quick access in and out of stadium to avoid the often murderous traffic congestion.

Side streets aren't the best idea at night. Spots are extremely limited and a long walk from the stadium. Also, it's a bit risky. Kids in the neighborhoods surrounding the stadium have been known to offer "insurance" for those who dare park.

**Weather**
Big mood swings by Mother Nature are the norm in the Bay Area, so unexpected temperature drops should be expected. During early-season games, the average highs gener-

ally hit the lower 70s and the lows dip to the lower 50s—with a stiff ocean breeze. By the late-season and playoff games, the highs are in the mid-50s and lows in the low 40s. The heaviest periods of rainfall are in December and January.

 **Media bites**
**Radio:** KGO (810 AM).
**TV:** KTVU (Channel 2, Fox); KRON (Channel 4, NBC); KGO (Channel 7, ABC).

 **Cuisine**
No one need go hungry at the Stick—even vegetarians, who can buy veggie burgers, baked potatoes, yogurt, fruit, trail mix and bottled water. Seafood lovers can choose among crab cakes, prawns, gumbo and seafood salad. The Stick also has a number of grill stands featuring hamburgers, specialty sausages and grilled chicken sandwiches.

Candlestick Park offers imported and specialty beers

## LODGING NEAR THE STADIUM

**King George Hotel**
334 Mason St.
San Francisco, CA 94102
(415) 781-5050/(800) 288-6005
About 5 miles from the stadium.

**Westin San Francisco Airport**
One Old Bayshore Highway
Millbrae, CA 94030
(415) 692-3500/(800) 228-3000
About 10 miles from the stadium.

## THE 49ERS AT CANDLESTICK PARK

**Dec. 19, 1971:** The 49ers clinch their second consecutive divisional title, beating the Detroit Lions 31–27 in the last game of their debut season at Candlestick Park.

**Dec. 7, 1980:** Down 35–7 at halftime to the New Orleans Saints, the 49ers make the biggest comeback in NFL history and win 38–35 in overtime.

**Jan. 10, 1982:** Despite six turnovers, the 49ers defeat the Dallas Cowboys 28–27 and advance to their first Super Bowl.

**Dec. 24, 1989:** The 49ers shut out the Chicago Bears 26-0 to close the regular season en route to their fourth victorious Super Bowl appearance.

**Dec. 6, 1992:** Jerry Rice breaks Steve Largent's record for touchdown receptions by making his 101st against the Miami Dolphins. The 49ers win 27–3.

# In the Hot Seats at Candlestick Park

Except for preseason games, it's virtually impossible to purchase a ticket from the 49ers, who have sold out every home game since 1982 and have a waiting list of 17,000 for season tickets.

• **Bad seats:** If your tickets are in the back rows of the lower end zone on the east side, you might get a taste of Candlestick, but you won't see much of the game. Try to avoid tickets for seats in the back rows of odd-numbered sections 1-21 or even-numbered sections 2-8. The upper-reserved seats are pretty good. A few bad seats are in the upper deck—especially in sections 28 and 18, which are obstructed by a protruding press box.

The very best seats are between the 40-yard lines and about 15 to 20 rows up on the east side, opposite the press box. This is the side of the stadium that gets the most extended sunlight and naturally are among the toughest to get. But if you're lucky, you'll sit in odd-numbered sections 43-47.

• **Scalping:** Walking up to the box office

at Candlestick Park and buying a ticket is, well, a baseball thing, so the best bet is to shop around. Experienced patrons say a quick mention at one of the top sports bars in the Bay Area—Ricky's in San Leandro, Pat O'Shea's in downtown San Francisco, the Flatiron in Marin or Kip's in Berkeley—usually produces results. If this fails, scalpers usually can be spotted near the freeway exit ramps. The Golden Rule: If you're willing to pay, no game is impossible to attend.

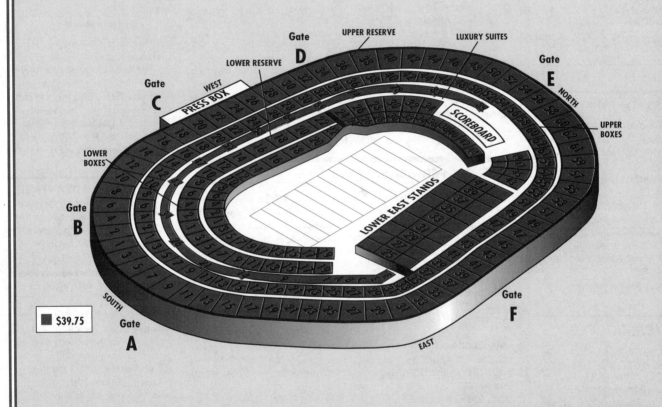

$39.75

## HOME-FIELD ADVANTAGE

The grass field holds water, and while the 49ers have learned to cope with slippery surfaces, visitors can have problems. Wearing the proper shoes is always a major concern.

Then there's the wind, which has a penchant for oddly changing directions during the course of the game. For Joe Montana, getting a feel for the wind in pregame warmups was as much a part of his routine as loosening his arm. The wind is tough on kickers and punters, too. It's no coincidence the 49ers punters and kickers almost never rank among the NFL leaders.

That the 49ers share Candlestick with baseball's Giants gives the football team an advantage down the stretch. Because of baseball season, the 49ers play very few home games in September and early October, so they're often left with a home-heavy schedule in December, when playoff implications become clearer.

These quirks often—but do not always—benefit the 49ers. In the last two NFC title games at Candlestick—with Super Bowl berths at stake—the 49ers lost.

## GETTING TO CANDLESTICK PARK

**Public transportation:** "The Ballpark Express" is available on game day from a number of locations, or take the No. 29 directly to Candlestick. Call (415) 673-6864 for more information.

**By car:** From downtown and the East Bay, take U.S. 101 south to either the Third Street or Candlestick Park exits.

From San Jose, take U.S. 101 north to same exits. The Candlestick Park exit leads to the stadium lots. If you take the Third Street exit, go 3 blocks to Jamestown Avenue. Turn right and continue for 1 mile; the parking lots and stadium are on the left.

**TICKET INFORMATION**
**Address:** San Francisco, CA 94124
**Phone:** (415) 468-2249

**Hours:** Mon.-Fri. 9-5.
**Prices:** All seats $39.75.

**Training camp:** Sierra Community College, Rocklin, CA

TM

# Kingdome

W hen the Kingdome opened on March 27, 1976, it was viewed as the Emerald City's ultimate jewel—a multi-purpose complex that could house an NFL team as well as a Rolling Stones concert. But after weathering 18 Seattle winters, the old gray dome ain't what she used to be—as evidenced by the recent collapse of a roof section.

The latest face lift is a $6 million improvement project intended to correct a situation that prompted one local radio talk show host to dub the Kingdome the "world's largest Chia Pet." The ongoing endeavor will strip the dome's roof to its concrete base and will replace an easily discolored and seemingly always dirty layer of white foam with epoxy.

What the Kingdome does have is location. It sits just north of Interstate 90, the main freeway linking the city to the suburbs east of Lake Washington. And it's just west of Interstate 5, providing easy access from the south and north. It's also just south of downtown, so the Kingdome anchors Seattle's still-growing skyline.

It also helps that Seattle has always been a football town. Fans embraced the Seahawks from Day One, and on game days they arrive early, leave late and scream themselves silly in between. Two players' strikes, the sale of the team and a continuing rebuilding process have helped end the honeymoon, but the love affair burns on.

■ $38 ■ $32 ■ $28 ■ $19

## STADIUM STATS

**Location:** 201 S. King St., Seattle, WA 98104
**Opened:** Aug. 1, 1976
**Surface:** AstroTurf
**Capacity:** 66,000
**Services for fans with disabilities:** Seating available in sections 201, 202, 203, 205, 206, 212, 220, 222, 238 and 240, with more to come in the 100 level.

## STADIUM FIRSTS

**Regular-season game:** Sept. 12, 1976, 30–24 loss to the St. Louis Cardinals.
**Points scored:** 28-yard field goal by Jim Bakken of the Cardinals.
**Overtime game:** Oct. 29, 1978, 20–17 loss to the Denver Broncos.
**Playoff game:** Dec. 24, 1983, 31–7 over the Denver Broncos.

## TEAM NOTES

**Franchise history:** Seattle Seahawks, 1976–present.
**Division title:** 1988
**Pro Football Hall of Fame:** Franco Harris, 1990
**Retired number:** 12, "Fans—the 12th man."

## HOT TIPS FOR VISITING FANS

### Parking
The Kingdome offers 4,000 spaces in three lots, which fill quickly. Another 30,000 spaces are available within a mile of the dome; don't count on finding a freebie on the street unless you plan to arrive several hours before kickoff. Prices at the adjacent lots top out at $10 for the closest ones.

### Media bites
**Radio:** All games are broadcast on KIRO radio (710 AM) and its network.
**TV:** KING (Channel 5), Seattle's NBC affiliate.

### Cuisine
Options include Pizza Hut pizza, frozen yogurt as well as local favorites Ezell's fried chicken and Starbucks coffee and espresso. The concession stands offer microbrews from local breweries. During baseball season, a brew of the game or homestand is offered. Don't let names like Ballard Bitter scare you off.

Instead of tailgating, most fans opt for brunch at one of the many restaurants in Pioneer Square, the area where Seattle grew into a city in the 1890s. Among the most popular are F.X. McRory's (206-623-4800), which features an oyster bar and a great liquor list, and Duke's

(206-622-1092), which has steaks and seafood. A short walk to the northwest of the Kingdome is the waterfront area, which has several outstanding seafood restaurants.

### LODGING NEAR THE STADIUM
**Red Lion Hotel**
18740 Pacific Highway S
Seattle, WA 98188
(206) 433-1881/(800) 547-8010
About 15 miles from the stadium.

**Westin Hotel Seattle**
1900 Fifth Ave.
Seattle, WA 98101
(206) 728-1000/(800) 228-3000
About 2 miles from the stadium.

### GETTING TO THE KINGDOME
**Public transportation:** On game day, a shuttle runs downtown every 10 minutes, starting 90 minutes before kickoff and running as long as it's needed. Many other options are available on public transportation. Call (206) 553-3000 for information.
**By car:** From the north, I-5 South to exit 164. Follow signs to Dearborn Street and the Kingdome. Go right onto Dearborn, then right onto Airport Way after about 5 blocks. At Fourth Avenue South, go right or

left into Kingdome parking.
From the south, I-5 North to exit 163/Spokane Street. Follow Spokane Street off-ramp to Fourth and make a right. Take Fourth south to Royal Brougham Way. Turn left onto Royal Brougham and Kingdome parking is on right.

## HOME-FIELD ADVANTAGE
Opposing teams used to practice with huge speakers blasting crowd noise or rock music to prepare for the painfully loud Kingdome.

## IN THE HOT SEATS
There's a NOW AVAILABLE sign on those once impossible-to-come-by season tickets. Single-game tickets go on sale in early June. Games against the Los Angeles Raiders, the Denver Broncos and the Kansas City Chiefs traditionally sell quickly. Seats on or near the 50-yard line are the best, of course, but any of the 200-level seats—which offer a more intimate atmosphere because of the limited number of rows and overhead television sets—are fine, too.

• **Bad seats:** Because the Kingdome is not a football-only stadium, the 100-level seats nearest the field have a restricted view, and the top-of-domers in the 300 level, especially in the south end zone, make binoculars a must.

**Scalping:** Busy every Sunday on corners around the Kingdome, but recently, there are more sellers than buyers.

# Tampa Stadium

Some places are known for moments when everything went right. Famous touchdown catches. Record-setting runs. Classic playoff games. Tampa Stadium is known for moments when everything went wrong.

The stadium's most notable tenants, the Buccaneers, entered the NFL in 1976 and lost their first 26 games. The Bucs didn't break the streak until the 13th game of their second season, and that happened at New Orleans. The tradition of losing continues to this day. The Bucs have put together an NFL record for futility—11 consecutive seasons with at least 10 losses.

But the problems aren't limited to the Bucs. It was here that a last-second Buffalo field-goal attempt went wide to the right in the New York Giants' 20–19 victory in Super Bowl XXV to begin the Bills' streak of four consecutive Super Bowl defeats. It was here, when Tampa Stadium often hosted preseason NFL games, that Joe Namath suffered one of the knee injuries that cut his career short.

Some locals will tell you the place is cursed. A few years ago, a radio station hired a witch doctor to remove the curse. The witch doctor stood in the parking lot, chanted some magic words and said the Bucs would begin winning. They did win that Sunday, but at the next home game things returned to normal. The Bucs not only lost, they were shut out.

## HOT TIPS FOR VISITING FANS

**Parking**
The stadium's unusual grass parking lots make Tampa popular for tailgating. But most spots close to the stadium are sold for the season. Single-game parking is available for $5 in spots south of Tampa Bay Boulevard. The best bet for single-game visitors, however, may be the lot for Tampa Bay Center, a shopping mall across the street that so far is free.

Traffic backs up on game days. One way to avoid some of the mess is to exit I-275 onto MacDill Avenue, go north approximately 1 mile to Columbus, turn left and follow it to Dale Mabry.

**Weather**
On an average Sunday afternoon in October, the place turns into the world's largest sauna. On special occasions, it throws in lightning.

Before one game in the late '70s, the Bucs' then-public-relations director Bob Best warned officials that forecasters were saying a nasty storm was on its way. Legend has it that an official looked at Best and said, "This is the NFL; we play no matter what the weather." Legend also has it that when the lightning started ripping through the air above Tampa Stadium, a certain official was the first one off the field calling for what turned into a 40-minute delay.

**Media bites**
**Radio:** Gene Deckerhoff and former Buccaneer David Logan are the announcers on WQYK (1010 AM, 99.5 FM).
**TV:** Preseason games are on WTOG (Channel 44) with Jim Kelly and former Cincinnati Bengal Cris Collinsworth are the announcers.

**Cuisine**
You'll find a decent variety—pizza, subs, chicken wings and frozen yogurt. And while fans are not allowed to bring in beverages, stadium officials say you can get a cup of ice at the concessions stand at no cost and fill it at a drinking fountain.

South of the stadium on Dale Mabry are all kinds of fast-food options and chain restaurants. But if you want something more unique and are willing to drive 15 minutes, you can eat Spanish cuisine at the Columbia (813-248-4961), a fixture in historic Ybor City since 1905, or splurge and visit Bern's Steak House (813-251-2421), one of a handful of good restaurants on Howard Avenue.

## LODGING NEAR THE STADIUM

**Hyatt Regency Westshore**
6200 Courtney Campbell Causeway
Tampa, FL 33607
(813) 874-1234/(800) 233-1234
10 miles from the stadium.

**Radisson Bay Harbor Inn**
7700 Courtney Campbell Causeway
Tampa, FL 33607
(813) 281-8900/(800) 333-3333
6 miles from the stadium.

## THE BUCCANEERS AT TAMPA STADIUM

**Dec. 18, 1977:** The Bucs get their first home victory, 17–7 over the St. Louis Cardinals.

**Dec. 16, 1979:** In a driving rainstorm, the Bucs edge the Kansas City Chiefs 3–0 to clinch their first NFC Central Division title. Ricky Bell gains 137 yards.

**Sept. 11, 1980:** A 10–9 win over the Los Angeles Rams avenges a playoff loss the year before.

**Jan. 2, 1983:** Down by 17 at the half, the Bucs, led by quarterback Doug Williams, win in overtime 26–23 over the Chicago Bears to clinch a playoff spot.

**Sept. 13, 1987:** Steve DeBerg throws five touchdown passes as the Bucs trounce the Atlanta Falcons 48–10.

# IN THE HOT SEATS AT TAMPA STADIUM

Unless the Chicago Bears or the Green Bay Packers are in town, you can walk up and buy tickets the day of the game, which stuns visitors from places like Denver and Washington, D.C. With the exception of the glory years—a brief stretch in the late 1970s and early '80s—it has been that way through Buccaneers history. In the last 11 years, the team has sold out 11 games.

For those Chicago games, more than 20,000 Bears' fans—some visitors from up north, some transplanted residents—show up at Tampa Stadium. Before the "Battle of the Bays," thousands of Packers fans gather in the parking lot for a giant tailgate party.

• **Bad seats:** "The Big Sombrero," as ESPN's Chris Berman has dubbed it, is a giant bowl. That's good (no obstructed-view seats) and bad (no obstructed-sun or rain seats). The west side of the stadium falls into the shade in the late afternoon, which is why the locals prefer those seats. The east side stays in the sun throughout the game, which to some visitors is a plus. Some fans like sitting in the south end zone because the players enter and leave the field near those seats. But the Jumbotron scoreboard installed before the last Super Bowl sits behind those seats, so if you want to watch instant replays, go for the north end zone.

 **Scalping:** Late in the season, scalpers practically give away tickets.

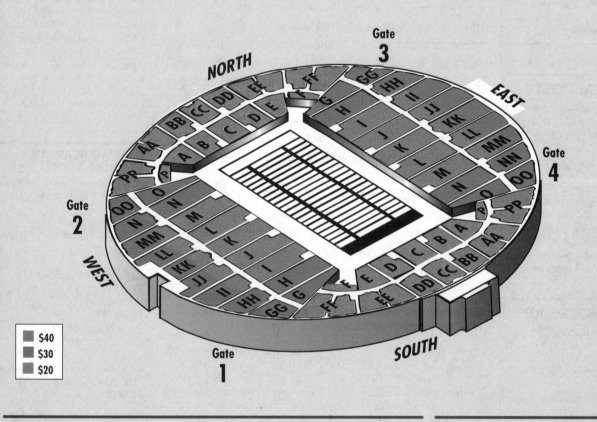

$40
$30
$20

## HOME-FIELD ADVANTAGE

In theory, the Buccaneers should have a home-field edge because of the heat and humidity. They go through training camp in it, they practice in it, they live in it. So when the Chicago Bears or the Green Bay Packers come to visit on a steamy Sunday in October, they should wilt in the fourth quarter, right? So the theory goes. In fact, over the years, the team's coaches have played down the importance of the heat. Ray Perkins went so far as to have the team's bench moved from its traditional west side location, with the sun on their backs, to across the field. Perkins insisted that real men wouldn't be bothered by having the sun in their faces. Of course, by the time he was fired in 1990, Perkins had moved the home bench back to the west. All in all, the Bucs have shown they can blow a fourth-quarter lead at Tampa Stadium just as well as at Soldier Field.

## GETTING TO TAMPA STADIUM

**Public transportation:** The Nos. 7, 11, 32, 36 and 41 buses run to the Tampa Bay Center, which is across the street from the stadium. Call (813) 623-5835 for more information.

**By car:** From St. Petersburg, take I-275 North, across the Howard Franklin Bridge. Go left onto Dale Mabry Highway approximately 1 mile. Stadium is on the right.

From the north, take I-275 South. Go right onto Dale Mabry Highway approximately 1 mile. The stadium is on the right.

**Training camp:** University of Tampa, Tampa, FL

## TICKET INFORMATION
**Address:** Tampa Stadium, 4201 N. Dale Mabry Highway, Tampa, FL 33607
**Phone:** (813) 879-2827 or TicketMaster at (904) 353-3309, (813) 287-8844, or (407) 839-3900.
**Hours:** Mon.-Fri. 9-5, Sat. 9-1.
**Prices:** $40: prime sidelines, rows 1-79; $30: sidelines above row 80; $20: end zones.

TM

## STADIUM STATS

**Location:** 2400 E.
Capitol St. S.E.,
Washington, DC 20003
**Opened:** Oct. 1, 1961
**Surface:** Grass
**Capacity:** 56,454
**Services for fans with
disabilities:** Seating available on levels 2, 3 and 4.

## STADIUM FIRSTS

**Regular-season game:**
Oct. 1, 1961, 24–21 loss
to the New York Giants.
**Points scored:** 17-yard
touchdown reception by
Kyle Rote of the Giants.
**Overtime game:** Nov. 2,
1975, 30–24 over the
Dallas Cowboys.
**Playoff game:** Dec. 24,
1972, 16–3 over the
Green Bay Packers.

## TEAM NOTEBOOK

**Franchise history:**
Boston Braves, 1932;
Boston Redskins, '33–36;
Washington Redskins,
'37–present.
**Division titles:** 1936, '37,
'40, '42, '43, '45, '72,
'82, '83, '84, '87, '91.
**Super Bowl appearances:**
VII, Jan. 14, 1973, 14–7
loss to the Miami
Dolphins; XVII, Jan. 30,
'83, 27–17 over the
Miami Dolphins; XVIII,
Jan. 22, '84, 38–9 loss
to the Los Angeles
Raiders; XXII, Jan. 31,
'88, 42–10 over the
Denver Broncos; XXVI,
Jan. 26, '92, 37–24 over
the Buffalo Bills.
**Pro Football Hall of Fame:**
Baugh, Lambeau, Marshall,
1963; Dudley, '66; Battles,
Millner, '68; Edwards, '69;
Lombardi, '71; Flaherty, '76;
D. Jones, '80; Huff, '82;
Jurgensen, Mitchell, '83;
Taylor, '84; Houston, '86; S.
Jones, '91; Riggins, '92.
**Retired number:** 33,
Baugh.

# RFK Memorial Stadium

Cramped, aging, on the verge of being replaced, Robert F. Kennedy Memorial Stadium nonetheless shakes and shimmies to the incessant drumbeat of Washington Redskins fans' cheers eight Sundays a year. Sure, the crowds have looked a little sparse recently, but don't think that means tickets have suddenly become available for Washington's other sporting passion (aside from politics and rumor-mongering).

The tight squeeze at RFK stems from its cozy confines. At 56,454 seats, it is the second-smallest venue in the NFL. Part of RFK's appeal is that closed-in feeling that allows cheering to reverberate and give the Redskins a true home-field advantage. The end-zone seats are closest to the field, allowing fans to ride visiting quarterbacks when their teams must operate in the shadow of the goal posts.

RFK Stadium lacks many of the modern conveniences. It has no luxury boxes, no premium seating and an open press box cursed by sportswriters. Stadium employees work for the city, not the Redskins, and are known to give civil servants an uncivil reputation.

The club hopes to have a new stadium, seating 78,000, open for the 1996 season. That, however, would move the Redskins from the nation's capital, their home since 1937, to suburban Laurel, Maryland, just 18 miles from Baltimore.

## HOT TIPS FOR VISITING FANS

**Parking**
The Stadium offers 12,500 spaces, which doesn't seem like much but is more than adequate for a venue of this size. About 3,000 of the spaces closest to the entrances are reserved and sold in advance through the Stadium/Armory offices. General parking is $6. Stadium gates open 90 minutes before kickoff, so to ensure parking at a close lot, arrive an extra 90 minutes early. The lots are dimly lighted at night.

**Weather**
Lovely in autumn, cold in winter.

**Media bites**
**Radio:** The Redskins' flagship radio is WTEM (570 AM), with former Redskins Sonny Jurgensen and Sam Huff behind the microphone.
**TV:** Regular-season television will generally be Fox (Channel 5). Coach Norv Turner's weekly show airs on Channel 7.

**Cuisine**
The Stadium food is, well, stadium food, and includes hot dogs, knackwurst and sauerkraut, nachos, French fries, chips, soft pretzels and popcorn. Wine and mixed drinks are available at some concessions locations, as is cappuccino. Available beers are Miller and Budweiser.
The choices improve outside the Stadium. Sophisticated fans party before or after on Capitol Hill—The Hawk and Dove (202-

543-3300) is popular—or in the area around refurbished Union Station, which is on the Metro's Red line. Try The Dubliner for a taste of the brogue. And there's always Georgetown; Irish Times and Mad Hatter's are popular hangouts in that neighborhood.

## LODGING NEAR THE STADIUM

**Loews L'Enfant Plaza**
480 L'Enfant Plaza S.W.
Washington, DC 20024
(202) 484-1000/(800) 235-6397
About 5 miles from the stadium.

**Crystal City Marriott**
1999 Jefferson Davis Highway
Arlington, VA 22202
(703) 413-5500/(800) 228-9290
About 5 miles from the stadium.

## THE REDSKINS AT RFK STADIUM

**Nov. 28, 1965:** Sonny Jurgensen passes for more than 400 yards and three touchdowns, leading the Redskins back from a 21–0 deficit for their greatest comeback ever, 34–31 over the Dallas Cowboys.

**Nov. 27, 1966:** The Redskins wallop the New York Giants 72–41, as the two teams combine to score the most points ever in an NFL game.

**Dec. 31, 1972:** The Redskins beat the defending NFL champion Cowboys 26–3, earning the right to challenge Miami in Super Bowl VII.

**Jan. 15, 1983:** John Riggins' 185 rushing yards lead the way for the Redskins, who cruise past the Minnesota Vikings 21–7 to win a spot in the NFC championship game.

**Jan. 12, 1992:** The Redskins' 41–10 victory over the Detroit Lions in the NFC championship game puts them into their fourth Super Bowl under coach Joe Gibbs and the fifth in the team's history.

**Oct. 12, 1992:** Art Monk catches his 820th pass to become the NFL's all-time leading receiver. The Redskins beat the Denver Broncos 34–3.

# In the Hot Seats at RFK Memorial Stadium

No way. Every home game since the season opener in 1966 has been sold out in advance—every single game, spanning 205 consecutive regular-season games. The waiting list for season tickets runs about 45,000 names, with perhaps a few dozen moving up each year.

• **Good seats:** End zone, if you like to yell at the players and know they can hear you. Mezzanine, for protection from the elements and for sightlines.

• **Bad seats:** The first 10 rows, practically at field level, permit a great view of player necks.

**Ticket scalping:** Since tickets aren't available to the general public, some desperate Redskin fans turn to scalpers or

 ticket brokers. Often tickets can be obtained through advertisements in the local newspapers, but the markup can be two or three times the face value. Games against Dallas, the New York Giants and Philadelphia—all division rivals—are particularly hard to come by and can easily be marked up 300%.

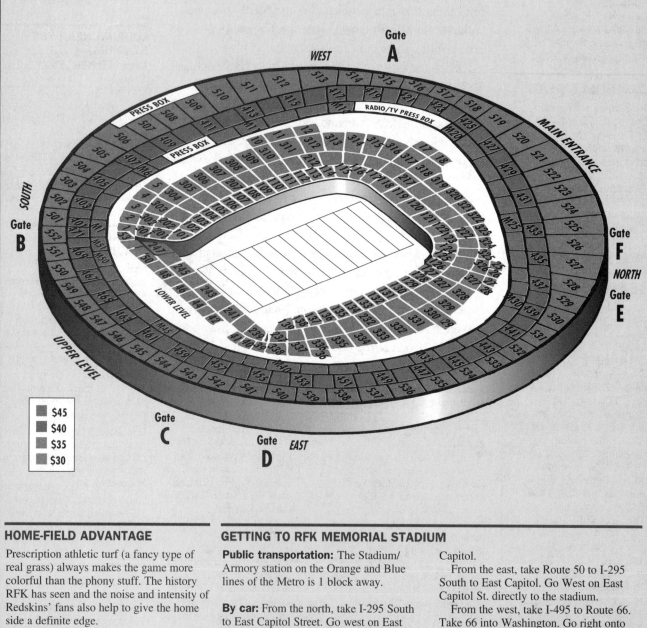

$45
$40
$35
$30

## HOME-FIELD ADVANTAGE

Prescription athletic turf (a fancy type of real grass) always makes the game more colorful than the phony stuff. The history RFK has seen and the noise and intensity of Redskins' fans also help to give the home side a definite edge.

## GETTING TO RFK MEMORIAL STADIUM

**Public transportation:** The Stadium/Armory station on the Orange and Blue lines of the Metro is 1 block away.

**By car:** From the north, take I-295 South to East Capitol Street. Go west on East Capital directly to the stadium.

From the south, take I-395 North to Sixth Street S.E. Go North on Sixth to East

Capitol.

From the east, take Route 50 to I-295 South to East Capitol. Go West on East Capitol St. directly to the stadium.

From the west, take I-495 to Route 66. Take 66 into Washington. Go right onto Independence Avenue and follow Independence to the stadium.

**TICKET INFORMATION**
**Address:** 2400 E. Capitol St. S.E., Washington, DC 20003

**Phone:** (202) 546-2222
**Hours:** Mon.-Fri. 9-5.
**Prices:** $45: mezzanine; $40: 400 level; $35:

200, 300, 500 levels; $30: 100 levels.
**Training camp:** Dickinson College, Carlisle, PA 17013

# BASKETBALL

Courtesy of the Delta Center

## Eastern Conference

## Western Conference

**Atlanta Hawks** ™

## ARENA STATS

**Location:** 100 Techwood Dr. NW, Atlanta, GA 30303
**Opened:** Oct. 15, 1972
**Capacity:** 16,510
**Services for fans with disabilities:** Seating varies, though it is always on the mezzanine level. Seats in first 10 rows available for the visually impaired. Call (404) 681-2100.

## ARENA FIRSTS

**Regular-season game:** Oct. 15, 1972, 109–101 over the New York Knicks.
**Overtime game:** Nov. 7, 1972, 109–107 over the Baltimore Bullets.
**Playoff game:** April 4, 1972, 126–113 loss to the Boston Celtics.

## TEAM NOTEBOOK

**Franchise history:** Buffalo Bisons, 1945–46 (NBL); Tri-Cities Blackhawks, 1946–49 (NBL); Tri-Cities Blackhawks, 1949–51 (NBA); Milwaukee Hawks, 1951–55; St. Louis Hawks, 1955–68; Atlanta Hawks, 1968–present.
**Division titles:** 1956–57, '57–58, '58–59, '59–60, '60–61, '67–68, '69–70, '79–80, '86–87, '93–94.
**Conference titles:** 1956–57, '57–58, '59–60, '60–61.
**NBA championship:** 1957–58.
**Basketball Hall of Fame:** E. Macauley, 1960; A. Phillip, '61; A. Auerbach, '68; B. Pettit, '70; C. Hagan, '77; S. Martin, '81; R. Holzman, '85; B. Houbregs, '86; P. Maravich, '86; C. Lovelette, '87; L. Wilkens, '88; C. Hawkins, '92; W. Bellamy, '93.
**Retired numbers:** 9, B. Pettit; 23, L. Hudson.

# The Omni

One could argue that the Atlanta Hawks deserve more respect than they receive. In 1949, in a prior incarnation as the Tri-Cities Blackhawks, this franchise was one of the original members of the NBA. In their current hometown, however, the Hawks' founding role in the league is not a consideration for fans when they are deciding which team to support. When it comes to local interest, the Hawks take a backseat to the baseball Braves, as well as to the collegians at Georgia Tech. Don't expect an electric, vibrant atmosphere at the Omni when the Hawks play.

There might also be a surprising number of empty seats. The Hawks have not had one season in which their per-game average neared the arena's basketball capacity of 16,510. One local reporter believes part of the explanation for Atlanta's relative indifference to pro basketball lies with the character of the city's population. As in Houston, many people grew up elsewhere, and still follow other teams.

Some cite the downtown address, and the problems people associate with the inner city, as yet another reason why the Hawks have trouble attracting fans, even though the area around the Omni is cosmopolitan and usually quite busy. There has been talk the team will relocate north of Atlanta to an 18,000-seat, yet-to-be built facility, complete with several luxury suites. As negotiations continue between Atlanta and the Hawks to keep the team downtown, plans are for the new arena to open in 1996.

## HOT TIPS FOR VISITING FANS

**Parking**
Given its downtown location, the Omni benefits from being surrounded by parking facilities. There are roughly 300 spaces at the Omni, each costing $7. The CNN Center and World Congress Center offer additional parking; the cost ranges from $7 to $10. The local mass-transit system, MARTA, which has a station next to the Omni, is a favorite way for fans to come downtown.

**Media bites**
**Radio:** WGST (640 AM). **TV:** TBS Sports (national cable) and SportSouth (regional cable). TBS analyst Dick Versace is a former coach of the Indiana Pacers. Mike Glenn, a 10- year NBA veteran and a commentator on TBS' NBA coverage, is also an analyst for SportSouth.

**Cuisine**
Popular items include smoked sausage and chicken wings with sauce. There is also a specialty coffee stand that serves espresso and cappuccino as well as fudge made at the Omni. Two beer stands sell Heineken and Amstel Light, among other brews.

Jocks 'n' Jills (404-688-4225), next to the Omni in the CNN Center, is popular with Hawks fans and NBA personalities after games. A sports bar and grill with nearly 60 television sets, Jocks 'n' Jills is owned in part by former players Doc Rivers, Scott Hastings, Randy Wittman and John Battle. The food court in the lower portion of the CNN Center also features a good variety of fast, convenient places to eat before or after games.

## LODGING NEAR THE ARENA

**Marriott Marquis**
265 Peachtree Center Ave.
Atlanta, GA 30303
(404) 521-0000/(800) 228-9290
½ mile from the stadium.

**Hyatt Regency**
265 Peachtree NE
Atlanta, GA 30303
(404) 577-1234/(800) 233-1234
Less than 3 miles from the stadium.

## THE HAWKS AT THE OMNI

**April 13, 1979:** The Hawks win their first home playoff game in six years, topping Houston 100–91 to advance to the Eastern Conference semifinals.

**Dec. 10, 1986:** Dominique Wilkins scores 57 points against Chicago, an Omni record. The Hawks win 123–95. Four months later, Wilkins ties the record against New Jersey.

**May 7, 1989:** After beating the Bucks in all six meetings during the regular season, the Central Division–champion Hawks fall to Milwaukee 96–92 and are eliminated, three games to two, in the first round of the playoffs.

**Feb. 2, 1993:** Wilkins breaks Bob Pettit's 29-year-old franchise record of 20,880 career points with 31 versus Seattle. The Hawks win 118–109.

**Feb. 2, 1994:** A 118–99 win over Orlando marks Lenny Wilkens' 900th win as a coach, second to Red Auerbach's 938.

**May 8, 1994:** Mookie Blaylock has 18 assists, leading the Hawks to a 102–91 win over Miami in the decisive fifth game of their first-round playoff series.

# IN THE HOT SEATS AT THE OMNI

The Hawks' season-ticket base is approximately 6,000. Tickets for single games are sold starting in early October, but they are consistently available on game nights, mainly for seats in the upper deck. As in the rest of the NBA, games against the league's better teams are the big attraction, as are games against such Southeastern rivals as the Charlotte Hornets and the Orlando Magic.

• **Good seats:** The $20 seats in sections 206-212 and 224-230 at center court in the upper deck offer excellent views for a decent price. If these are unavailable, check out upper-deck sections 213-216 and 231-234.

• **Bad seats:** In terms of comfort and sightlines, the Omni is a pretty good place to watch basketball. Avoid the last several rows of the $10 seats behind the baskets—

sections 201, 217-219, and 235-236—which are far from the floor. Other seats that require a hike are in the last several rows of sections 206-212 and 224-230; they cost $15.

• **Scalping:** There are rarely scalpers outside the Omni, probably because good tickets are usually available at the box office.

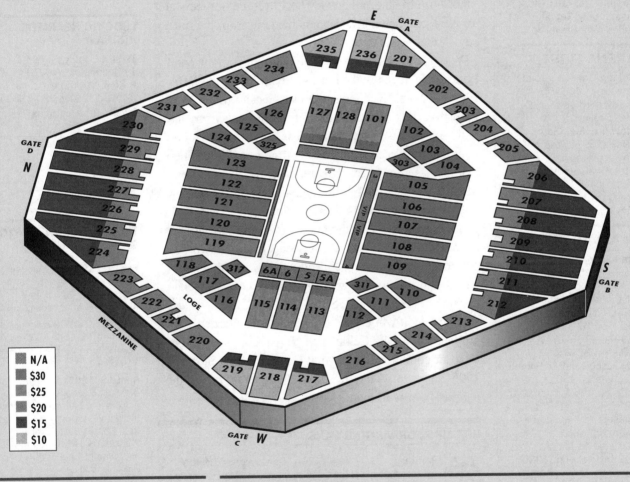

Legend:
- N/A
- $30
- $25
- $20
- $15
- $10

## HOME-COURT ADVANTAGE

With a relatively subdued crowd in a city where pro basketball is not the prime attraction, it might seem as though there is little benefit to the Hawks when they play at home. Nevertheless, this team still posts very respectable home records. Atlanta's 36–5 mark in 1993–94, for instance, was the second-best in the NBA. Maybe the players thrive on the home cooking and extra rest they get when they're not on the road.

## GETTING TO THE OMNI

**Public transportation:** Take MARTA to the Five Points Station and get on a west-bound train. The Omni is the first stop after Five Points.

**By car:** Call (404) 681-2100 for directions to the Omni from anywhere in the Greater Atlanta area.

### TICKET INFORMATION
**Address:** 100 Techwood Dr. N.W., Atlanta, GA 30303
**Phone:** (404) 681-2100 or TicketMaster at (404) 249-6400

**Hours:** Mon.-Fri. 10-5.
**Prices:** $30: middle of sections 101, 113-115, 127-128, sections 102-112, 116-126; $25: sections 101, 113-115, 127 and 128; $20: sections 202-205, 213-216, 220-223, 231-

234, and lower rows in sections 206-212 and 224-230; $15: lower rows in sections 201, 217-219, 235-236, and upper rows in sections 206-212 and 224-230; $10: upper rows of sections 201, 217-219 and 235-236.

# Boston Garden

## ARENA STATS

**Location:** 150 Causeway St., Boston, MA 02114
**Opened:** Nov. 17, 1928
**Capacity:** 14,890
**Services for fans with disabilities:** Seating varies for each game.

## ARENA FIRSTS

**Regular-season game:** Nov. 16, 1946, 55–49 over the Toronto Steamrollers.
**Playoff game:** March 28, 1948, 79–72 loss to the Chicago Stags.
**NBA Finals game:** March 30, 1957, 125–123 overtime loss to the St. Louis Hawks.

## TEAM NOTEBOOK

**Franchise history:** Boston Celtics, 1946–49 (BAA); '49–present (NBA).
**NBA championships:** 1956–'57, '58–59 to '65–66, '67–68, '68–69, '73–74, '75–76, '80–81, '83–84, '85–86.
**Basketball Hall of Fame:** Macauley, 1960; J. Russell, 1964; Auerbach, 1968; Cousy, 1970; B. Russell, 1974; Ramsey, Sharman, 1981; Havlicek, S. Jones, 1983; Heinsohn, 1985; Houbregs, Maravich, 1986; Lovellette, 1987; K.C. Jones, 1988; Bing, 1989; Walton, 1993.
**Retired numbers:** 1, Brown; 2, Auerbach; 3, Johnson; 6, B. Russell; 10, White; 14, Cousy; 15, Heinsohn; 16, Sanders; 17, Havlicek; 18, Cowens and Loscutoff; 19, Nelson; 21, Sharman; 22, Macauley; 23, Ramsey; 24, S. Jones; 25, K.C. Jones; 32, McHale; 33, Bird; 35, Lewis.

The championship banners and retired jerseys, the parquet floor with the dead spots, and the booming ancient organ make this one of the great buildings in NBA history. The Celtics don't believe in gimmicks, mascots, dancers or any other distractions, and only in the past few seasons did they even start having halftime entertainment. When you go to Boston Garden to see a basketball game, the team doesn't feel you need any other form of entertainment. The 19 retired numbers and 16 NBA championship banners hanging from the rafters say all that needs to be said.

You'll find no frills here. The building isn't air-conditioned, which can make it a sweatbox during the NBA Finals in June. Even the scoreboard has no frills. A monstrous box at center court, it has no replay screens and no individual player stats, just the score, the fouls committed by each team and the time remaining. The Garden has a lower-level scoreboard over which fans often drape their coats, eliciting, at least once a game, one of the great Boston Garden public-address announcements: "Will the fans in front of the south scoreboard please remove your coats and sit down?"

Legendary former coach Red Auerbach still attends games and usually sits with Larry Bird, now a special assistant to executive vice president M.L. Carr.

But enjoy it while you can, because the Garden's days are numbered. The Celtics will be playing in new, high-tech, air-conditioned Shawmut Center starting in the 1995–96 season. They're still thinking about taking the parquet floor with them.

## HOT TIPS FOR VISITING FANS

**Parking**
All the nearby parking is private and costly, unless you park in one of the cheaper garages a few blocks away. But Boston gets cold in the winter, and the walk might not be worth it. If you have to drive, take your time leaving because traffic gets congested.

**Media bites**
**Radio:** WEEI (590 AM). **TV:** WSBK (Channel 38), SportsChannel (cable). A replica of the late, legendary announcer Johnny Most's microphone hangs from the rafters with the retired Celtics jerseys, a fitting tribute to one of the greatest, but most biased, announcers of all time. Glenn Ordway, Most's longtime partner, has taken over on the radio. Former Celtics greats Bob Cousy and Tommy Heinsohn team on television.

**Cuisine**
Enjoy the huge pretzels and the plump hot dogs with exceptionally good mustard and buns. The fresh-popped popcorn rivals any movie theater's. Pizzas are baked fresh, and a selection of bottled waters is sold.
The Sports Cafe (617-426-0300) at the Garden will do just fine for after the game. It's at street level and is a good place in which to wait out the crowds;

grab a beer, soft drink or sandwich and rehash the game. You're close enough to downtown to hit one of the great seafood restaurants, such as Legal Seafood (617-864-3400), on the way home. The Cheers bar (617-227-9600) of television fame is inside the Hampshire House hotel in the Copley Square district, about 2 miles from the Garden.

## LODGING NEAR THE ARENA

**Westin Copley Plaza**
10 Huntington Ave.
Boston, MA 02116
(617) 262-9600/(800) 228-3000
2 miles from the arena.

**Marriott Long Wharf**
296 State St.
Boston, MA 02109
(617) 227-0800/(800) 228-9290
1 mile from the arena.

## THE CELTICS AT BOSTON GARDEN

**Feb. 27, 1959:** Bob Cousy dishes out 28 assists as the Celtics score 173 points against the Minneapolis Lakers.

**April 18, 1962:** The Celtics win their fifth NBA title, in overtime against the Los Angeles Lakers, 110–107.

**April 15, 1965:** John Havlicek steals Hal Greer's inbounds pass in the last five seconds of the game, sending the Celtics to a 110–109 win over the Philadelphia 76ers in the deciding game of the Eastern Division final.

**May 10, 1974:** Kareem Abdul-Jabbar of the Milwaukee Bucks hits a 15-foot sky hook with three seconds left to down the Celtics in Game 6 of the NBA Finals.

**April 20, 1986:** Michael Jordan scores an NBA-playoff-record 63 points in a game between the Chicago Bulls and the Celtics. Boston wins in double overtime 131–125.

**May 26, 1987:** In an echo of the Havlicek steal, Larry Bird steals an inbounds pass from Isiah Thomas that leads to a Dennis Johnson basket and a 108–107 win over the Detroit Pistons in the playoffs.

# IN THE HOT SEATS AT BOSTON GARDEN

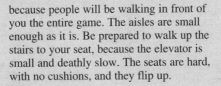

Every game has sold out since Bird arrived in 1979. Built in 1928, this is a small building, seating 14,890. The fans know each other because most have been longtime season ticketholders.

• **Good seats:** Front-row seats opposite the benches are best, but avoid sitting in the first couple of rows on the other side,

because people will be walking in front of you the entire game. The aisles are small enough as it is. Be prepared to walk up the stairs to your seat, because the elevator is small and deathly slow. The seats are hard, with no cushions, and they flip up.

• **Bad seats:** Some obstructed-view seats are sold. That means a pillar is in front of

you. If you don't mind leaning to one side when the ball is at one end of the floor, then go for it.

**Scalping:** Scalping is illegal, but enforcement isn't particularly tough. Scalpers are everywhere around the arena.

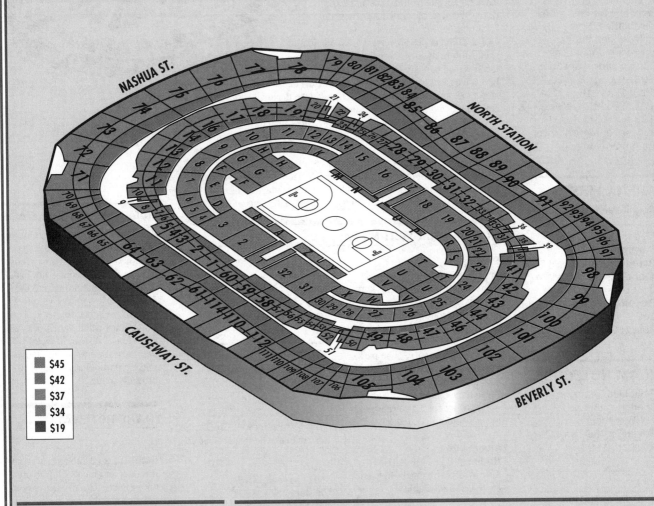

$45
$42
$37
$34
$19

## HOME-COURT ADVANTAGE

The ghosts, the parquet floor, the mystique, Auerbach sitting there smoking his cigar next to Bird, the championship banners, the dead spots on the parquet floor, and the loose rims with the long nets so the rebounds fall straight down instead of bouncing long: all these things make this a tough place for the visiting team to win a game. During the Bird era, home losses were rare, but as the team has declined, so has its home record.

## GETTING TO BOSTON GARDEN

**Public transportation:** Take the Green or Orange MBTA lines to the North Station stop, across the street from the Garden.

**By car:** From the south, follow I-95 North to I-93 toward exit 25 (Causeway Street). Make a left at the bottom of the ramp; the Garden will be to your right.

From the west, take the Massachusetts

Turnpike (Route 90) to Route 93 North to exit 25.

From the north, take I-93 South to Boston, or I-95 South to Route 1 South across the Tobin Bridge. Merge with I-93 South. Take exit 26 (Storrow Drive). Bear right, following signs toward North Station.

**TICKET INFORMATION**
**Address:** 150 Causeway St., Boston, MA 02114

**Phone:** (617) 523-3030 or TicketMaster at (617) 931-2000
**Hours:** Mon.-Fri. 9-5.

**Prices:** $45, $35, $26, $18, $12.

# Charlotte Coliseum

The circular Coliseum is a great place to watch basketball. The Hornets lead the league in attendance, selling out practically every game in this 23,698-seat arena. Owner George Shinn mingles with the crowd, and because so many season tickets are sold, it seems that everyone in the crowd knows everybody else. Fans treat the game like a big family night out and frequently come early for tailgate parties. In a further sign of togetherness, the crowd often actually joins together for a pregame prayer.

The fans and players have a great relationship. Most of the players make their homes in the area, and they are treated like genuine heroes. People here are basketball hungry, and while ACC fans and NBA fans aren't the same animal, the atmosphere can be decidedly collegiate in its enthusiasm and unquestioning support.

But this high-tech arena has attractions other than the fans. The scoreboard has crystal-clear replays, and six other message boards are scattered throughout the arena. SuperHugo, the Hornet's mascot, wears a blue bodysuit with black sunglasses and is a three-time winner of the NBA mascot slam-dunk championship. The Hornets also net a more lucrative accomplishment: their stylish paraphernalia, designed by Alexander Julian, is among the biggest sellers in the league.

Sky ■ $66 ■ $44 ■ $40 ■ $31 ■ $28
$26 ■ $19 ■ $15 ■ $11 ■ $8

## ARENA STATS

**Location:** 1 Hive Dr., Charlotte, NC 28217
**Opened:** Aug. 11, 1988
**Capacity:** 23,698
**Services for fans with disabilities:** Seating available around the perimeter of the upper concourse behind sections 103, 106, 108, 110, 112, 115, 118, 121, 124, 126, 128, 130, 133 and 136, and access to the floor level from rear entrance.

## ARENA FIRSTS

**Regular-season game:** Nov. 4, 1988, 133–93 loss to the Cleveland Cavaliers.
**Overtime game:** April 1, 1989, 124–121 loss to the Portland Trail Blazers.
**Playoff game:** May 3, 1993, 119–89 over the Boston Celtics.

## TEAM NOTEBOOK

**Franchise history:** Charlotte Hornets, 1988–present.
**Rookie of the Year:** Larry Johnson, 1991.

## HOT TIPS FOR VISITING FANS

### Parking
Special roads and exit ramps were built to make getting here as easy as following a sign. Traffic is rerouted on game days to get people in and out as quickly as possible. Still, make sure you arrive early. The parking lot can accommodate 8,000 cars at $3 each, among the lowest in the league. There's an overflow lot for 1,500 more cars, but it's seldom needed.

### Media bites
**Radio:** WBT (1110 AM).
**TV:** WJZY (Channel 46, Cable 8), SportSouth Cable.

### Cuisine
The Crown Club is a 900-seat restaurant with 12 large television monitors. Fourteen permanent concession stands and 10 specialty carts offer food ranging from Carolina barbecue and baked chicken to pizza and baked potatoes. Of course, you can get things like popcorn, candy and peanuts. The NBA recently singled out the Coliseum for having the widest variety of concessions at the lowest prices.

You'll have to drive to any postgame activities, but not far: The arena is only 10 minutes from Executive Park, which has clubs and restaurants and is about 20 minutes from downtown. A popular spot is the All Sports Cafe (704-366-3663) on Fairview Road.

### LODGING NEAR THE ARENA
**Embassy Suites**
480 S. Tryon St.
Charlotte, NC 28217
(704) 527-8400/(800) EMBASSY
Less than a mile from the arena.

**Hyatt**
5501 Carnegie Blvd.
Charlotte, NC 28209
(704) 554-1234/(800) 233-1234
10 miles from the arena.

### GETTING TO CHARLOTTE COLISEUM
**Public transportation:** The Coliseum can't be reached by public transportation.
**By car:** From I-77, take the Tyvola Road exit and follow signs to the Coliseum.

From I-85, get off on Billy Graham Parkway and take the Tyvola Road exit and follow signs to the Coliseum.

## HOME-COURT ADVANTAGE
The fans and the noise can drive opponents crazy. The Hornets have had a winning home record the last three seasons—not bad, considering that going into the 1994–95 season, they've only been in existence for six seasons. Sometimes when the Hornets are on defense, instead of chanting *dee*-fense, *dee*-fense, the fans make a particularly unnerving buzzing sound.

## IN THE HOT SEATS
Not a bad ticket in the house. Each seat is cushioned and comfortable, and the sky boxes are unobtrusive. Usually the only tickets available are the $8 seats high in the end zones, an area in which the sound can get deafening. They're not bad seats, though, especially for the price.

Partitioned areas and elevators aid visitors with disabilities, and the main concourse is wider than normal at 30 feet, so you can easily get to your seat.

**Scalping:** Scalpers get little business, because anyone who has tickets usually holds on to them. Buyers get lucky—people with extra tickets often will gladly sell them at only face value or close to it.

## ARENA STATS

**Location:** 1901 W.
Madison St., Chicago, IL
60612
**Opened:** August 1994
**Capacity:** 21,500
**Services for fans with
disabilities:** Seating available in four 100-level
sections, five 200-level
sections, and 12 300-
level sections.

## TEAM NOTEBOOK

**Franchise history:**
Chicago Bulls, 1966–
present.
**Division titles:** 1974–75,
1990–91, 1991–92,
1992–93.
**Conference titles:**
1990–91, 1991–92,
1992–93.
**NBA championships:**
1990–91, 1991–92,
1992–93.
**Most Valuable Player:**
Michael Jordan,
1987–88, 1990–91,
1991–92.
**Rookie of the Year:**
Michael Jordan,
1984–85.
**Basketball Hall of Fame:**
Nate Thurmond, 1984.
**Retired number:** 4, Jerry
Sloan.

# United Center

The United Center, which opened for the 1994–95 NBA season, is across the street from Chicago Stadium, but it's light years away in history.

The old Stadium had character, from fans leaning over the standing-room-only upper balcony to the hard seats, narrow aisles and down-home charm. The scoreboard was old and outdated, and the players, emerging from the small locker rooms, had to duck to get upstairs to the floor. But no one seemed to mind. The Stadium had mystique, and the kind of atmosphere that comes from moments such as on June 14, 1992, when Michael Jordan—standing on the press table with tears in his eyes, a cigar in his mouth and a bottle of champagne gripped in one hand—hoisted the Bulls' second championship trophy high to the cheering throng. Chicago Stadium's noise was incredible, and when the lights were turned down for the introduction of the Bulls, it was simply electrifying.

The world's greatest basketball player never played a home game in a building with a replay scoreboard. The United Center has one, just part of the new arena's opulence. Its football-bowl shape means even the sections farthest from the floor have good sightlines. The cramped restrooms of the Stadium have gone the way of the eight-track tape, and the 21,500 seats are of the plush, theater-style variety. The city even cleared out about 20 square blocks to try to make the area safer.

While the Blues Brothers, Benny the Bull and the LuvaBulls have moved across the street, Jordan vowed that he loved Chicago Stadium too much to play at the United Center—it's paradoxical, because his popularity and the success of the Bulls under his leadership made construction of the new arena possible. Fans are sure to soon love the new arena as much as Jordan loved the old one. So far, however, he has kept his word: The most that United Center might ever see of Jordan is his bronze statue in the lobby.

## HOT TIPS FOR VISITING FANS

**Parking**
When the Bulls played at Chicago Stadium, parking attendants would start flagging you down 6 blocks from the building, trying to get you to park in their lot. The streets were narrow and bumpy, and that slowed traffic.

The streets have now been widened, and the United Center has taken over most of the parking. These new lots have 25 entry lanes and are well-lighted, clearly marked, fenced and patrolled, so drive right past the lots on Madison. Get to the game early to make sure you get in (club-seat and luxury-box patrons have a guaranteed parking spot included in their ticket price). Street parking is available, but it's risky.

**Media bites**
**Radio:** WMAQ (670 AM—English), WIND (560 AM—Spanish).
**TV:** WGN (Channel 9), SportsChannel (cable). Former Bulls coach Johnny "Red" Kerr, the television analyst, is a show unto himself. Former Bulls center, Tom Boerwinkle, is the radio analyst. He's more subdued than Kerr but still fun.

**Cuisine**
The arena has 46 permanent concessions stands with computerized ordering in each line on the club levels. Themed concessions such as the West Side Deli, Mexican Fiesta, Windy City Grill and Italian Piazza offer a broad range of items that reflect the city's diverse population. Local favorite Old Style leads the list of 25 beers available to chase down the food.

You can buy Bulls and other NBA merchandise at 22 places. The members-only, 285-seat Chicago Stadium Club (a full-service restaurant) and a 100-seat lounge, as well as private function rooms, are also available.

Michael Jordan's Restaurant (312-644-3865) downtown is the obvious place to go. Michael is there most nights he's in town. Red Kerr's is another good spot for sports fans. Planet Hollywood (312-266-7827), the Hard Rock Cafe (312-943-2252) and Ed Debevic's (312-664-1707) are all 15 to 30 minutes away.

## LODGING NEAR THE ARENA

**Westin Hotel**
909 N. Michigan Ave.
Chicago, IL 60611
(312) 943-7200/(800) 228-3000
5½ miles from the arena.

**The Drake**
140 E. Walton St.
Chicago, IL 60611
(312) 787-2200
3½ miles from the arena.

# In the Hot Seats at United Center

This place caters to big spenders, with three levels of private luxury suites (216 in all) and each level is serviced by a private concourse and elevators. The lower-level suites are only 19 rows (18 yards) from the floor. The Club Level Suites are 27 rows up (32 yards). The Penthouse Suites are at the top, above the 300-level seating. In addition to the luxury suites are 3,000 club seats on a private level. The suites, club seats and entire building are sold out for the 1994-95 season.

The 300-level seats will be the easiest to get. If you sit in the high-up-behind-the basket seats, you'll be looking through the backboard, but you'll get used to it. Just get in the building—the experience is worth it. Unlike at the Stadium, there are no standing-room tickets.

**Scalping:** At the Stadium, scalpers would stop cars a mile away, along Madison Street, to offer tickets; that probably won't change. Twice face value has been about the normal markup.

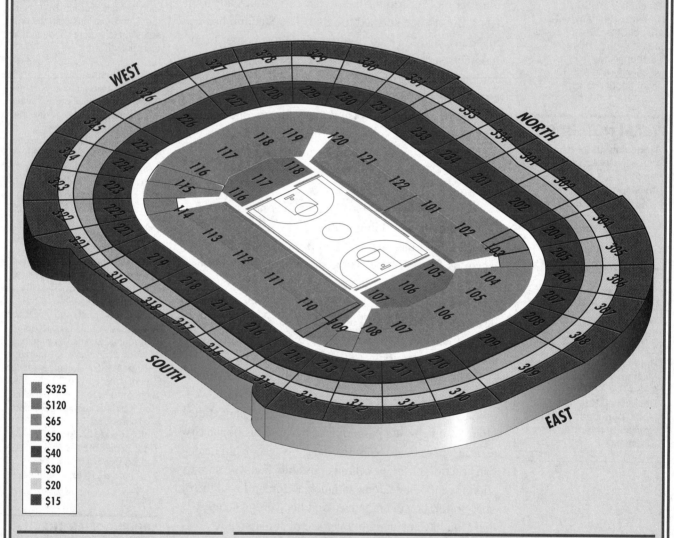

**Price legend:**
- $325
- $120
- $65
- $50
- $40
- $30
- $20
- $15

## HOME-COURT ADVANTAGE

In recent seasons, the Bulls have had one of the best home records in the league. The United Center is a great building, but the Bulls will lose something in atmosphere by leaving Chicago Stadium. It was a unique building that fit the team's character, and only time will tell how the new place will affect the team.

## GETTING TO UNITED CENTER

**Public transportation:** From downtown, take the No. 20 Madison bus westbound or the No. 19 Stadium Express, which runs to the stadium every 10 minutes from 90 minutes before the game until 30 minutes after. For more information, call the CTA at (312) 836-7000.

**By car:** From O'Hare Airport, take I-90 East to exit 28A (Damen Avenue). Take Damen Avenue to Madison Street. The arena will be on the right.

**TICKET INFORMATION**
**Address:** 1901 W. Madison St., Chicago, IL 60612
**Phone:** (312) 455-4000 or TicketMaster at

(312) 559-1212
**Hours:** Mon.-Fri. 12-6.
**Prices:** $65: 100 level, rows 1-11; $50: 100 level, rows 12-19; $40: 200 level, rows 1-

8; $30: 300 level, rows 1-7; $20: 300 level, rows 8-12; $15: 300 level, rows 13-17.

# The Arena at Gateway

Forget all the Cleveland jokes you've heard. Downtown Cleveland is where it's happening, especially if you're a sports fan. While the city gets a bad rap for not being pretty, the Cavaliers' new home is a beautiful building in a beautiful part of town. The Richfield Coliseum was out in the middle of nowhere, but the Arena at Gateway is in the heart of downtown, three blocks from Public Square, in the same complex as the new baseball stadium, Jacobs Field.

The Arena at Gateway is a brand-new, state-of-the-art arena built with the fan in mind. The Richfield Coliseum was too big, with wasted space; the inexpensive seats were too far away, and the sightlines weren't good. That has been corrected, as the best features of all the new arenas were adopted when this facility was constructed.

The Cleveland Lumberjacks hockey team and Cleveland Thunderbolts Arena Football team share the building with the Cavaliers, but it was built for basketball. Besides containing the Cavaliers' practice facility, the Arena has a sports bar with street-level access and a 40- by 100-foot bay window through which you can view downtown Cleveland and the Flats.

■ N/A ■ $48 ■ $35 ■ $30
■ $26 ■ $22 ■ $16 ■ $10

## HOT TIPS FOR VISITING FANS

### Parking
Two on-site garages with 3,300 spaces are connected to the Arena by covered walkways. Because Cleveland gets cold in the winter, pay the little extra (about $3 more) for these spaces. Another 7,000 parking spaces are within a 10-minute walk. On-site parking prices haven't been set, but lots near the Arena range from $3 to $8 for evening parking.

### Media bites
**Radio:** WWWE (1100 AM).
**TV:** WOIO (Channel 19), and SportsChannel Ohio (cable). At 6-11, former Cavs player Jim Chones might be the tallest color man in the league. He's fresh, funny and knowledgeable. Play-by-play man Joe Tait is a legend. He has been the voice of the Cavaliers for 22 seasons. His down-home style is a treat.

### Cuisine
Sammy's at the Arena (216-523-5560) might be one of the best restaurants in town, considering both ambience and location. The 350-seat full-service restaurant, operated by well-known local restaurateurs Denise Fugo and Ralph DiOrio, has a wide variety of meals priced from $5 to $25. Children can have pizza and cookies, while their parents can enjoy a juicy burger and a beer. Low-cal meals are also available.

After the game, a lounge is at street level at the Arena, or head out into Cleveland. John Q's

Public Bar and Grill (216-861-0900), Sweetwater's Cafe (216-696-CAFE) and Snooter's Waterfront Cafe (216-861-6900) are popular.

### LODGING NEAR THE ARENA

**Cleveland Hilton South**
6200 Quarry Lane
Cleveland, OH 44131
(216) 447-1300/(800) 445-8667
10 miles from the stadium.
**Ritz Carlton**
1515 W. Third St.
Cleveland, OH 44113
(216) 623-1300/(800) 241-3333
Next to the stadium.

### GETTING TO THE ARENA AT GATEWAY

**Public transportation:** RTA provides service to Tower City Rapid Station, which has an enclosed walkway to the Arena. Park and Ride services are available. Call (216) 566-5100, ext. 4312, for more information.
**By car:** From the east, take I-90/Route 2 west. Follow signs to downtown, remaining on Route 2 as I -90 curves away to the left. Exit at East Ninth Street and go left to Arena parking.

From the west, take West Shoreway from Lakewood. Continue across the Main Avenue bridge; exit right on West Sixth Street to area parking.

### HOME-COURT ADVANTAGE

Historically in the NBA, teams play well in brand-new buildings. The Cavaliers also have the great advantage of practicing in the same building where they play. The Cavs have been a good home team, winning 83% of their home games since 1991, one of the best home records in the league.

### IN THE HOT SEATS

If close is what you like, this is the building for you, because 60% of the seats are in the lower concourse. The seats are wider and plusher than most places, and the luxury suites are closer to the floor than in any other arena (15 and 30 rows up).

• **Good seats:** Getting tickets will be tough, because much of the building is sold out. If you can get tickets, try to sit opposite the benches and the scorer's table to get a view of the players and the interplay that goes on with the coaches. Corner seats are good in most basketball arenas, something that's especially true here because you're so close to the action.

• **Bad seats:** The building has no bad seats. All the sightlines were done by computer to guarantee the best possible view.

# Reunion Arena

## ARENA STATS

**Location:** 777 Sports St., Dallas, TX 75207
**Opened:** April 28, 1980
**Capacity:** 17,007
**Services for fans with disabilities:** Seating available behind sections 101, 108, 115 and 122.

## ARENA FIRSTS

**Regular-season game:** Oct. 11, 1980, 103–92 over San Antonio.
**Points scored:** Abdul Jeelani, Mavericks.
**Overtime game:** Nov. 28, 1980, 119–117 loss to Denver.
**Playoff game:** April 17, 1984, 88–86 over Seattle.

## TEAM NOTEBOOK

**Franchise history:** Dallas Mavericks, 1980–present.
**Division title:** 1986–87.
**Retired number:** 15, Brad Davis.

---

**TICKET INFORMATION**
**Address:** 777 Sports St., Dallas, TX 75207
**Phone:** (214) 939-2800 or Dillard's at (800) 654-9545
**Hours:** Mon.-Fri. 10-5.

---

In the 1980s, the Mavericks were the hottest sports team in Dallas. They were successful, making the playoffs each year from 1984–88, and immensely popular. As the Cowboys slid into the NFL's cellar, Mavericks games at Reunion Arena became social events at which the big names in Dallas came to see and be seen. Players around the league liked the place, too, for its glamorous, exciting atmosphere and the fast pace of those Maverick teams.

But, as they say, all good things come to an end. Beginning with the 1990–91 season, the franchise slipped from being among the NBA's best to being the league's worst. As the Mavs declined, the Super Bowl–champion Cowboys supplanted them as the kings of Dallas. Many fans, frustrated with the team's poor play, began to stay home, and those who came had little patience. Boos cascaded down from the stands—boos more often directed at the Mavs than the visitors. There remains, perhaps surprisingly, a fairly large reservoir of goodwill and hope about the Mavs, feelings bolstered by changes in management and coaching, plus the presence of such promising young players as Jamal Mashburn and Jim Jackson.

### HOT TIPS FOR VISITING FANS

**Parking**
The arena is surrounded by approximately 6,000 spaces, which cost $5. There is no on-street parking in the area. However, additional parking garages are available downtown and at the nearby Hyatt Regency. Access into and out of the Arena's lots is fairly easy and quick.

**Media bites**
**Radio:** WBAP (820 AM).
**TV:** KTVT (Channel 11) and Home Sports Entertainment (HSE), cable. The Mavs' television announcer is Don Criqui, well-known for his work on the Olympics and on the NFL for CBS and NBC. His partner is Brad Davis, who played 13 seasons for the Mavericks and is the only player in franchise history to have had his number retired.

**Cuisine**
Fans can sample a variety of grilled selections, or burger and hot-dog baskets. Corn dogs, chicken fingers and Pizza Hut pizza are also available. Imported bottled beers, such as Heineken, Molson and Tecate, are also sold.

The Hyatt Regency (214-651-1234) is across the street from the arena and has two popular restaurants. Fausto's Oven (214-651-7144), a bistro-style restaurant, serves such Italian dishes as pesto pizza and the Lonestar Legend, a pizza with jalapeño peppers, smoked chicken and ham. Cafe Esplanade (214-651-7148) is in the hotel's atrium and features Southwestern cuisine.

### LODGING NEAR THE ARENA

**Hyatt Regency Dallas**
300 Reunion St.
Dallas, TX 75207
(214) 651-1234/(800) 233-1234
Across the street from the Arena.

**Loews Anatole Hotel**
2201 Stemmons Freeway
Dallas, TX 75207
(214) 748-1200/(800) 235-6397
About 5 miles from the Arena.

### GETTING TO REUNION ARENA

**Public transportation:** The No. 30 Marsalis bus goes to the Arena. Call (214) 979-2712 for more information.
**By car:** From downtown, take I-35 East north to I-635 West. Exit I-635 at MacArthur Boulevard. Go north on MacArthur to Valley Ranch Parkway and turn right. Take the first left onto Cowboys Parkway; the Arena will be ½ mile up on your left.

■ N/A ■ $24 ■ $19
■ $17 ■ $14 ■ $12

### HOME-COURT ADVANTAGE

Given the team's poor play, fans are often less than rousingly enthusiastic during games, but they can get surprisingly loud if the game is close or the team is doing well. And while the Mavs have become synonymous with basketball futility, they also have a reputation for staging some of the most imaginative halftime shows in the NBA.

### IN THE HOT SEATS

While the Mavericks' poor play is a source of frustration for fans, it's a boon for those seeking tickets. Excellent seats are available for virtually every game.

• **Good seats:** Check out the $24 seats in lower-deck corner sections 106, 110, 120 and 124 for good views. Sightlines from the upper deck are good. Best buys are in upper-deck sections 235-238, 224-227, 215-218 and 204-207. Those corner seats cost only $12 and may be one of the league's best bargains.

• **Bad seats:** If you really want to save money, $5 seats are available at the back of sections 228-234 and 208-214 behind the baskets.

**Scalping:** A local ordinance prohibits ticket scalping on city-owned property, which includes Reunion Arena. The Mavericks and the Dallas police make an effort to enforce this law by occasionally using undercover officers to seek out scalpers.

# McNichols Arena

## ARENA STATS

**Location:** 1635 Clay St., Denver, CO 80204
**Opened:** Aug. 22, 1975
**Capacity:** 17,022
**Services for fans with disabilities:** Seating available in 13 sections on the loge level.

## ARENA FIRSTS

**Regular-season game:** Oct. 25, 1975, 118–101 over the Spirits of St. Louis.
**Overtime game:** Dec. 16, 1977, 117–112 loss to the Washington Bullets.
**Playoff game:** April 20, 1977, 101–100 loss to the Portland Trail Blazers.

## TEAM NOTEBOOK

**Franchise history:** Denver Nuggets, 1967–76 (ABA); Denver Nuggets, 1976–present (NBA)
**Division titles:** 1976–77, 1977–78, 1984–85, 1987–88
**Retired numbers:** 2, Alex English; 33, David Thompson; 40, Byron Beck; 44, Dan Issel.

---

Although Denver has long been associated with recreation and sporting activities, Rocky Mountain fans support their resident pro teams with as much fervor as they attack the ski slopes. The Broncos have sold out for many years, and since their debut in 1993, the Rockies have set records for drawing some of the largest crowds in baseball history. During the 1993–94 season, the Nuggets became a hot item as well, selling out 27 of 41 home games and thereby joining their pro sports brethren as another popular attraction.

McNichols Arena, an oval building on the west side of the South Platte River, opened for basketball in 1975, when the Nuggets were in the ABA. It is immediately adjacent to Mile High Stadium, home of the Broncos and Rockies. In 1987, McNichols underwent a $14 million renovation that included several improvements, such as the installation of a new DiamondVision scoreboard, an improved audio system and closed-circuit television monitors.

This is a young team, which complements the youthful aspect of the city. Watching this dynamic group of players come together has made McNichols a Denver "in" place.

## HOT TIPS FOR VISITING FANS

**Parking**
There are 4,700 parking spaces at McNichols and 3,000 at Mile High Stadium. Prices at either range from $3 to $6. There is some on-street parking in the area.

**Media bites**
**Radio:** KOA (850 AM).
**TV:** KWGN (Channel 2) and Prime Sports Network on cable. Al Albert is the Nuggets' television play-by-play man. Albert began broadcasting Nuggets games in 1975, when they were in the ABA. He left Denver twice to pursue other opportunities but returned in 1989.

**Cuisine**
The Nuggets have made their home unique among NBA arenas by operating three full-service restaurants and a bar, all of which are open to all ticketholders. The Butcher Block serves a selection of hoagies, grilled chicken and beef. Wong Gong's mixes a Chinese decor with alternating buffets ($7.95 per person) of Mexican and Italian foods. The Arena Club opens at 5:30 and offers a buffet for $14.95 per person. Underneath the Arena Club is the Fastbreak Lounge, open at halftime and for up to two hours after the game. Players occasionally stop by after the game.

In addition to providing several restaurant choices inside McNichols, the Nuggets also offer some Denver-area foods at their concession stands. Perhaps the most unusual are a number of buffalo-meat items. Other popular offerings include Greek gyros, quarter-pound hot dogs and a Chicago dog that's topped with peppers, tomatoes, onions and pickles. Imported beers can be found in section 31.

After the game, there's Brooklyn's (303-572-3999), a comfortable bar in a Victorian-style building. Players and Nuggets executives are occasion-al customers. The Wynkoop Brewing Co. is about 10 minutes from McNichols (303-297-2700). This is Colorado's first brew pub, and it is located in a mercantile building that dates from the 19th century. Sample some of the seven homemade beers on tap while enjoying buffalo steak, elk medallions, homemade sausage or a pheasant quesadilla.

## LODGING NEAR THE ARENA

**The Westin Hotel**
1672 Laurence St.
Denver, CO 80202
(303) 572-9100/(800) 228-3000
2 miles from the arena.

**Hyatt Regency**
1750 Walton St.
Denver, CO 80202
(303) 295-1200/(800) 233-1234
3½ miles from the arena.

## THE NUGGETS AT MCNICHOLS ARENA

**Dec. 13, 1983:** Denver and Detroit battle in a triple overtime game that ends 186–184 Pistons. It's the highest-scoring game in NBA history. Kiki Vandeweghe scores 51, Alex English 47.

**May 8, 1986:** Despite English's team playoff record of 50 points, the Nuggets fall to Houston, 126–122, losing the Western Conference semifinals, four games to two.

**May 7, 1994:** The Nuggets stun the SuperSonics 98–94 in overtime at Seattle to eliminate the playoff favorites in the first round. Dikembe Mutombo blocks a record 31 shots in the five-game series in which the Nuggets win the final three games.

**May 15, 1994:** Reggie Williams hits a jumper with 1.9 seconds left to beat the Utah Jazz 83–82. The win keeps the Nuggets alive in the Western Conference semifinals, which they trail three games to one.

**May 19, 1994:** Mutombo and Bryant Stith each make two free throws in the last 30 seconds to give the Nuggets a 94–91 victory over the Jazz, forcing a seventh game.

# In the Hot Seats at McNichols

The Nuggets have a season-ticket base of approximately 10,000. Starting with the 1994–95 season, the team will cap season-ticket sales at 13,000 so at least 4,000 seats will be available for single-game purchases. Single-game tickets go on sale in early October. Any unsold tickets, mostly for seats in the upper deck, are available on game nights, though these are becoming more scarce as the Nuggets' following increases. Tickets for games against the better teams will be very difficult to find.

• **Good seats:** Even though it is some-what older than many NBA facilities, McNichols still offers plenty of good seats. For $20, you can sit in the center balcony area of the upper deck—sections 1, 3, 5, 29, 31, 33, 35, 59, 61 and 63—where the view is very good. Center-court seats in the lower deck are sold to season ticketholders. If you're looking for a bargain, spend $12.50 for seats in the lower two-thirds of upper-deck sections 10, 12, 14, 16, 17, 19, 44, 46, 47, 48, 51 and 53.

• **Bad seats:** The top rows of seats behind the baskets—sections 10, 12, 14, 15, 16, 19, 21, 42, 44, 46-48, 51, and 53—are a long way from center court. However, with the growing popularity of the Nuggets and the increased difficulty of getting good tickets, seats here may be all that's available for selected games.

• **Scalping:** Ticket scalping is illegal in Denver. Nonetheless, scalpers can easily be found, especially for big games, along the way to McNichols from the Mile High Stadium and Arena parking areas.

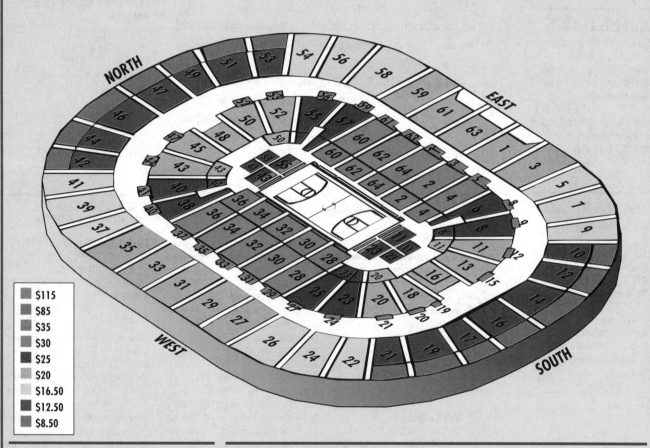

Price legend:
- $115
- $85
- $35
- $30
- $25
- $20
- $16.50
- $12.50
- $8.50

## HOME-COURT ADVANTAGE

Denver's altitude—5,280 feet above sea level—is an advantage the Nuggets seek to exploit. The Nuggets play an uptempo, full-court style at McNichols, particularly in the beginning of each game. The front office also gets into the act, rubbing in the atmospheric advantage by announcing before the opening tipoff, "Welcome to McNichols Arena, 5,280 feet above sea level," and playing upbeat music to accompany the Nuggets' fast-paced basketball.

## GETTING TO McNICHOLS

**Public transportation:** Catch the No. 31 Champa bus on 16th Street and go to 17th Street and Federal. Walk east 2 blocks to the arena. Call (303) 299-6000 for more information.

**By car:** From the east, take Colfax Avenue west to Bryant Street. The Arena will be on the right.

From the west, take Colfax east to Bryant. The Arena will be on the left.

From the north, take U.S. 87 south to the 17th Street exit. The Arena will be on the left.

From the south, take U.S. 87 north to the 17th Street exit. The Arena will be on the left.

## TICKET INFORMATION

**Address:** 1635 Clay St., Denver, CO 80204
**Phone:** (303) 893-3865 or TicketMaster at (303) 290-TIXS

**Hours:** Mon.-Fri. 8:30-5:30.
**Prices:** $ 115: courtside; $85: end courtside; $35: prime loge; $30: center loge; $25: corner loge, end risers; $20: end loge, center balcony; $16.50: corner balcony; $12.50: lower end balcony; $8.50: upper end balcony.

## ARENA STATS

**Location:** 2 Championship Dr., Auburn Hills, MI 48326
**Opened:** Aug. 13, 1988
**Capacity:** 21,454
**Services for fans with disabilities:** Several dozen wheelchair-accessible seats are available. Call (810) 377-0154 for more information.

## ARENA FIRSTS

**Regular-season game:** Nov. 5, 1988, 94–85 over the Charlotte Hornets.
**Overtime game:** Nov. 5, 1988, 94–85 over the Charlotte Hornets.
**Playoff game:** April 28, 1989, 101–91 over the Boston Celtics.
**NBA Finals game:** June 6, 1989, 109–97 over the Los Angeles Lakers.

## TEAM NOTEBOOK

**Franchise history:** Fort Wayne Pistons, 1948–49 (BAA); Fort Wayne Pistons, 1949–57 (NBA); Detroit Pistons, 1957–present.
**Division titles:** 1954–55, 1955–56, 1987–88, 1988–89, 1989–90.
**Conference titles:** 1954–55, 1955–56, 1987–88, 1988–89, 1989–90.
**NBA championships:** 1988–89, 1989–90.
**Rookie of the Year:** Don Meineke, 1952–53; Dave Bing, 1966–67.
**Retired numbers:** 16, Bob Lanier; 21, Dave Bing.

# The Palace of Auburn Hills

As one arrives at the Palace, three things immediately become apparent: First, in an effort to make sure all fans are thinking about the home team, the Pistons broadcast the pregame show over loudspeakers in the parking lot. Second, the arena has a distinctive exterior decoration—adorned with intricately arranged glazed-brick tiles that have a yellow/orange hue. Third, once you enter the building, television monitors bombard you with highlights of recent games, information on upcoming opponents and updates on home-team players.

As striking as all these things are, they don't make up for a bad team. The Detroit Pistons were recently at the top of the basketball world, winning consecutive NBA titles in 1989 and 1990. While the Palace was the center of much celebration then, things have changed here as the team's play has steadily deteriorated.

Following this fall from championship grace, fans tend to be more subdued than they were in the late '80s and early '90s. At least two of them, though, still take pride in their roles as self-appointed cheerleaders: Joe Diroff, a retired schoolteacher, is nicknamed "the Brow" because of his large, bushy eyebrows. During the game, Diroff runs around the arena, hazing the opposing team and leading cheers. While the Brow usually confines his antics to the lower deck, Dancing Ernie is a denizen of the Palace's upper reaches. With his slicked-back hair and modified striptease act, Ernie is hard to miss and, like the Brow, sometimes gets more attention than the game.

## HOT TIPS FOR VISITING FANS

**Parking**
No on-street parking nearby, so you will need to park in the Palace's lot, which has space for 8,200 cars. The price is $5. The Palace sits astride two major roads, I-75 and Route 24. Perhaps because of its location, fans report that traffic moves fairly smoothly before and after the game.

**Media bites**
**Radio:** Pistons Network WWJ (950 AM). Vinnie Johnson, a former Pistons guard, is the color analyst.
**TV:** WKBD (Channel 50) and PRO-AM Sports (PASS) cable.

Kelly Tripucka, a former Pistons forward, is one of the TV commentators. He is joined by George Blaha, an 18-year Pistons veteran who is known for such trademark phrases as "Isiah with the high glasser, and it goes!"

 **Cuisine**
Each of the arena's four corners has its own unique concessions: Mexican Fiesta (nachos, fajitas, margaritas and Mexican beer on tap), Little Italy (meatball subs, wines, Italian sausages), Delicatessen (made-to-order subs, soups in sourdough-bread bowls, gourmet popcorn) and Grill (sausages, chicken, Philly cheese steaks).

Draft beers, including Labatt's, Molson, Stroh's and Frankenmuth Pilsner, a local microbeer, are sold throughout the concourse. A large number of bottled brews, such as Bass, Amstel Light, Karlsberg and Old Detroit, a microbeer, are also available.

If you want a pregame meal, the arena has the Palace Club, which is a restaurant before the game and more of a bar afterward.

Mountain Jacks (810-340-0585), a five-minute drive from the Palace, specializes in steak, prime rib and seafood. Pistons and Detroit Lions players are occasionally customers after the game. Patrick's (810-852-3410) is about 10 minutes from the Palace and features a popular chicken-and-scallop combo, steak and pan-fried chicken.

## LODGING NEAR THE ARENA

**Troy Marriott Detroit**
200 Big Beaver
Troy, MI 48084
(313) 680-9797/(800) 777-4096
8 miles from the arena.

**Auburn Hills Hilton Suites**
2300 Featherstone Rd.
Auburn Hills, MI 48326
(313) 334-2222/(800) HILTONS
3 miles from the arena.

## THE PISTONS AT THE PALACE

**June 8, 1989:** Detroit beats the Los Angeles Lakers 108–105 in Game 2 of the NBA Finals. They end up sweeping the series, four games to none, to win the championship.

**June 3, 1990:** The Pistons beat the Chicago Bulls 93–74 in Game 7 of the Eastern Conference finals to advance to their second NBA Finals.

**March 4, 1992:** Dennis Rodman pulls down 34 rebounds against the Indiana Pacers.

# In the Hot Seats at The Palace of Auburn Hills

Since this is a large arena and the Pistons have been struggling on the court, good seats are usually available. Season tickets go on sale in July; single-game tickets go on sale in the fall.

• **Good seats:** The Palace has a reputation for being an excellent place in which to watch basketball. Not only are the seat locations and sightlines very good, but the plush, theater-style seats are also quite comfortable. It is difficult to find a bad seat, even in the top rows of sections 205, 212, 220 and 226, which are in the corners of the arena. Seats there go for $10.50. Check out the $25 seats in sections 201-202, 214-215 and 229-230, which offer good center-court sightlines from the upper deck; the seats directly above are $19. Another worthwhile buy is a $16.50 seat in section 205-206, 211-212, 220-221 or 225-226; these are the lower rows of the corner sections.

**Scalping:** Illegal, but it still goes on. However, few scalpers are outside the Palace because of its relatively isolated location and the recent fortunes of the club.

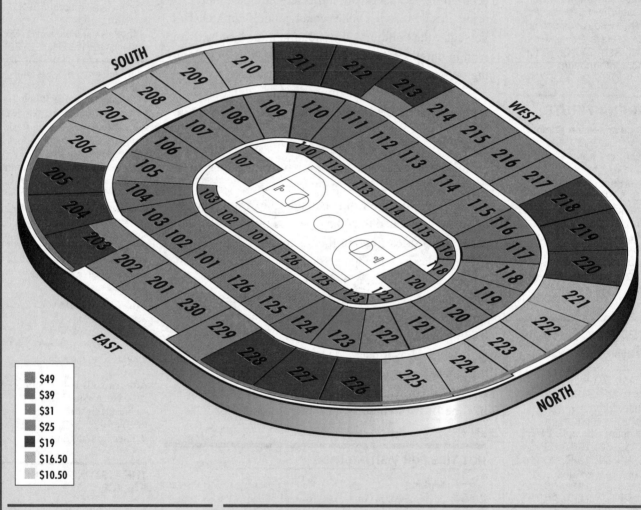

- $49
- $39
- $31
- $25
- $19
- $16.50
- $10.50

## HOME-COURT ADVANTAGE

The Pistons know they need more of an effort to pump up their fans than they did when the team was a championship contender. In an attempt to turn up the decibel level in the Palace, Detroit might soon introduce a team mascot for the first time since the mid-'70s.

## GETTING TO THE PALACE OF AUBURN HILLS

**Public transportation:** You can't reach the Palace by public transportation.

**By car:** From Detroit, take I-75 north. Take exit 81. The arena will be on the right, on Lapeer Street.

---

**TICKET INFORMATION**
**Address:** 2 Championship Dr., Auburn Hills, MI 48326
**Phone:** (810) 377-8600 or TicketMaster at

(810) 645-6666
**Hours:** Mon.-Fri. 10-6, Sat. 10-4, Sun. 10 A.M.-30 minutes after the game.
**Prices:** $49, $39, $31, $25, $19, $16.50,

$10.50

## ARENA STATS

**Location:** 10 Greenway Plaza, The Summit, Houston, TX 77046
**Opened:** Nov. 2, 1975
**Capacity:** 16,279
**Services for fans with disabilities:** Seating available at the top of the 100 level.

## ARENA FIRSTS

**Regular-season game:** Nov. 2, 1975, 104–89 over the Milwaukee Bucks.
**Overtime game:** Jan. 14, 1976, 107–103 loss to the New York Knicks.
**Playoff game:** April 19, 1977, 111–101 loss to the Washington Bullets.
**NBA Finals game:** May 9, 1981, 94–71 loss to the Boston Celtics.

## TEAM NOTEBOOK

**Franchise history:** San Diego Rockets, 1967–71; Houston Rockets 1971–present.
**Division titles:** 1976–77, 1985–86, 1992–93, 1993-94.
**Conference titles:** 1980–81, 1985–86, 1993–94.
**NBA championship:** 1993–94
**Basketball Hall of Fame:** Calvin Murphy, 1993.
**Retired numbers:** 23, Calvin Murphy; 45, Rudy Tomjanovich.

# The Summit

Until they beat the New York Knicks in the 1993–94 NBA Finals, the Rockets were just another of Houston's disappointing sports teams. The Rockets had never won a championship, despite reaching the NBA Finals twice. The Astros and the Oilers also have crushed the expectations of Houston fans in recent years, earning Houston the title "Choke City."

As the 1993–94 NBA playoffs advanced, many Houston fans seemed afraid of the same letdown from the Rockets—a fear they've expressed countless times over the years with empty seats and a fickle affection born of too many trips to the altar with no championship rings to show. Disappointment hung in the air of the Summit, and the city was abuzz over complaints from some Rockets players about a perceived lack of enthusiasm among the fans. The fans still waited to throw in their lot, but once they finally saw the championship trophy in Hakeem Olajuwon's hands, they poured out years of pent-up emotion in a huge victory parade later that week. Now that old heartbreaks have been laid to rest, it's official: Houston definitely loves the Rockets.

The Summit is readily accessible to the waves of Rockets fans who'll now be coming to see their championship team. It's just outside of downtown Houston in an office/hotel complex known as Greenway Plaza. Inside the arena, banners hang from the rafters honoring the only two Rockets to have their jerseys retired—Hall of Famer Calvin Murphy, now a Rockets broadcaster, and Rudy Tomjanovich, the team's head coach. It's only a matter of time before 34, Olajuwon's number, hangs in the Summit, along with the banner that proves Houston no longer deserves the name "Choke City."

## HOT TIPS FOR VISITING FANS

**Parking**
Greenway Plaza has ample parking. A $1 parking charge is added to the price of each game ticket, so no fee is charged for parking in the Rockets' lots. Traffic after the game occasionally moves slowly out of these lots. Several other lots as well as some on-street parking are in the area, and traffic moves faster there.

**Media bites**
**Radio:** KTRH (740 AM—English), KXYZ (1320 AM—Spanish).
**TV:** KTXH (Channel 20) and Home Sports Entertainment (cable). Hall of Famer Calvin Murphy, the Rockets' all-time leading scorer, does color commentary on both cable and broadcast TV.

**Cuisine**
Beginning with the 1994–95 season, fans will benefit from a multimillion-dollar upgrade of the Summit's concessions operation. An addition to the arena near section 108 on the north side of the building will house a 13-stand food court that will feature such varied cuisine as fajitas and Texas-style barbecued brisket and sausage, as well as sushi and margarita bars. Carts serving imported and domestic beers will be stationed in sections 101 and 115 and in the food court.

After the game, stop by Los Andes (713-622-2686), which is occasionally visited by such Rockets luminaries as Hakeem Olajuwon and Otis Thorpe. This glass-roofed restaurant about a block from the Summit specializes in South American cuisine. House of Pies (713-528-3816) is also a short distance from the Summit. Open 24 hours for breakfast, lunch, and dinner, the House is decorated with pictures of celebrity customers and features 40 kinds of pies and cakes.

## LODGING NEAR THE ARENA

**Stouffer Presidente Hotel**
6 Greenway Plaza E.
Houston, TX 77046
(713) 629-1200/(800) 468-3571
Across from the stadium.

**Westin Galleria**
5060 W. Alabama St.
Houston, TX 77056
(713) 960-8100/(800) 228-3500
3 miles from the stadium.

## THE ROCKETS AT THE SUMMIT

**March 18, 1978:** Calvin Murphy sets a Summit record by scoring 57 points in a 106–104 win over the New Jersey Nets.

**May 14, 1981:** The Rockets reach the sixth game of the NBA Finals, but the Boston Celtics take the crown 102–91.

**Feb. 11, 1982:** Moses Malone grabs a record 21 offensive rebounds in a 117–100 win over the Seattle SuperSonics.

**June 5, 1986:** A 111–96 Rockets win over the Celtics tightens the championship series to three games to two. Boston goes on to win the title.

**June 22, 1994:** Led by MVP Hakeem Olajuwon, the Rockets win the NBA title with a 90–84, Game 7 win over the New York Knicks, snaring the first professional sports championship for Houston.

# IN THE HOT SEATS AT THE SUMMIT

Although the Summit opened in 1975, the building shows few signs of age. Sightlines are good, with no obstructed views, and seats are plush, comfortable and no farther than 128 feet from the floor. The Rockets sold out nearly half their games during the 1993-94 season, but their home attendance ranked only 17th in the NBA. During the second round of the 1993-94 playoffs, Game 1 of Houston's series with the Phoenix Suns did not sell out until hours before the opening tap. With the Rockets now a winner, though, fans' inter-

est probably will blast off. All the high-rollers who left their season tickets in the drawer surely will be coming to games, so finding good tickets might no longer be a breeze. Still, this is Houston, a city with a large transient and non-native population. Single-game tickets go on sale in October, and though matchups against marquee teams are sure to go fast, seats against lesser draws won't necessarily move immediately.

• **Good seats:** The $11 seats—in sections

201, 202, 248, 220, 221 and 222—are bargains, and the view is good considering the price. The upper-promenade seats in sections 210-212 and 230-232 cost $23 and are also worth checking out.

 **Scalping:** Scalpers begin approaching fans within several blocks of the Summit. With increased interest in Rockets games, the sidewalk vendors might see the market swing dramatically in their favor for the 1994–95 season.

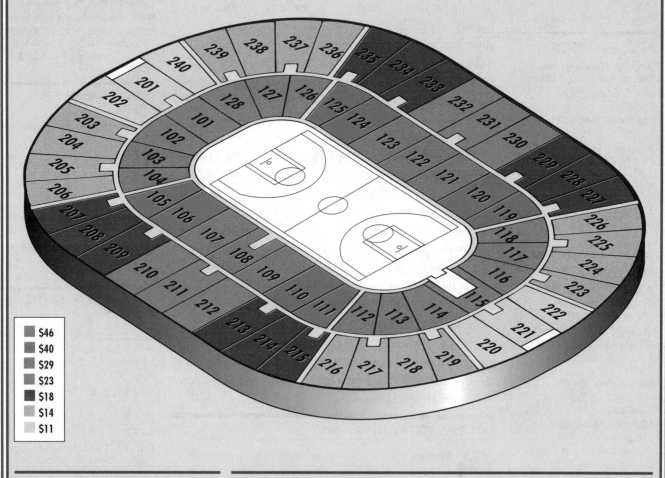

**Price legend:** $46 | $40 | $29 | $23 | $18 | $14 | $11

## HOME-COURT ADVANTAGE

Almost as if they had something to prove to Houston and those fans, the Rockets posted a 35–6 home record during the 1993–94 season, the third-best mark in the NBA. That kind of play and the newly boisterous crowds at the Finals augur well for the Summit to become one of the tougher places to play in the league.

## GETTING TO THE SUMMIT

**Public transportation:** METRO city buses stop just a few blocks from the Summit. Catch either the No. 25 Richmond on Main Street or the No. 53 Westheimer on Walker Street. Call (713) 635-4000 for more information.

**By car:** From Intercontinental Airport in the north, take Will Clayton Parkway east to Highway 59 South. Exit off Highway 59 at Edloe Street. The Summit will be on your right.

From Hobby Airport in the south, take Monroe Road east to I-45 North; go to Highway 59 South, and proceed as above.

### TICKET INFORMATION
**Address:** 10 Greenway Plaza, The Summit, Houston, TX 77046
**Phone:** TicketMaster at (713) 629-3700
**Hours:** Mon.-Sat. 10-6.

**Prices:** $46: Sections 107-109 and 121-123; $40: Sections 105, 106, 110, 111, 119, 120, 124 and 125; $29: Sections 103, 104, 112-113, 117, 118, 126 and 127; $23: Sections 101, 102, 114-116, 128, 210-212 and 230-232; $18: 207-209, 213-215, 227-229 and 233-235; $14: Sections 203-206, 216-219, 223-226 and 236-239; $11: Sections 201, 202, 220-222 and 248.

**Pacers** ™

## ARENA STATS

**Location:** 300 E. Market St., Indianapolis, IN 46204
**Opened:** Sept. 15, 1974
**Capacity:** 16,530
**Services for fans with disabilities:** Seating available in sections 3-22 around the lower concourse; tickets are $2. The restaurant on the seventh floor offers Braille menus.

## ARENA FIRSTS

**Regular-season game:** Oct. 18, 1974, 129–121 loss to the San Antonio Spurs.
**Overtime game:** Oct. 18, 1974, 129–121 loss to San Antonio in double overtime.
**Playoff game:** (ABA) April 10, 1975, 113–103 over San Antonio. (NBA) April 2, 1981, 124–108 loss to the Philadelphia 76ers.

## TEAM NOTEBOOK

**Franchise history:** Indiana Pacers, 1967–76 (ABA); Indiana Pacers, 1976–present.
**Most Valuable Players:** Mel Daniels, 1968–69, 1970–71; George McGinnis, 1974–75 (ABA).
**Rookie of the Year:** Chuck Person, 1986–87.
**Retired numbers:** 30, George McGinnis; 34, Mel Daniels; 35, Roger Brown.

# Market Square Arena

To say that Indiana—where almost everyone follows the Indiana University Hoosiers, and where people have been known to wait in line for hours to see high school hoops—loves basketball is to put it mildly. Despite Indiana's basketball obsession, fans have been somewhat subdued in reacting to the NBA Pacers. The ABA Pacers won three titles between 1967 and 1976, but after the team joined the NBA, fans grew disappointed with a team unable to duplicate past ABA achievements. The Pacers had trouble filling Market Square Arena, let alone igniting the crowds.

And then came 1994. A blazing second half of the season and a rousing performance in the playoffs brought back memories of championship glory. Pacer Mania was born, complete with screaming fans and the loud sounds of Indy cars playing over the arena's speakers. The seats are still empty, but now it's because the faithful are standing and cheering from start to finish. If the young Pacers remain competitive, Market Square will become one of the NBA's loudest, most-frenzied places to watch basketball. As one fan puts it, "You put a winner on the floor, and you'll have Hoosier Hysteria."

$31 $26 $20
$13 $7

## HOT TIPS FOR VISITING FANS

### Parking
Two garages connected to the Arena have spaces for approximately 2,500 cars. The price is $3. Additional lots, with prices ranging from $3 to $5, are in the surrounding neighborhood; on-street parking is limited.

### Media bites
**Radio:** WNDE (1260 AM).
**TV:** WTTV, (Channel 4). Bob Leonard, who coached the Pacers to three ABA titles, is a television broadcaster—as is Clark Kellogg, who played five seasons for Indiana.

### Cuisine
Fans enjoy the jumbo hot dogs, grilled bratwurst and barbecue sandwiches. Mixed-drink stands, which also serve domestic beer, can be found at aisles 3 and 22.

Market Square Gardens, the Arena's sit-down restaurant, opens two hours before game time and closes about an hour after the final buzzer. It has large windows looking down onto center court, so fans can watch the game while they eat.

The Legal Beagle (317-266-0088), 1 block from Market Square and near the city's courthouses, is a popular hangout for fans and players. The restaurant displays pictures and other memorabilia associated with the Indy 500, the ABA and the Pacers. T.G.I.Friday's (317-266-0088) is less than a 10-minute drive from the Arena. Nearly 20 kinds of brews are offered there.

## LODGING NEAR THE ARENA

**The Westin Hotel**
50 S. Capital Ave.
Indianapolis, IN 46204
(317) 262-8100/(800) 228-3000
4 blocks from the arena.

**Hyatt Regency**
1 S. Capital Ave.
Indianapolis, IN 46204
(317) 632-1234/(800) 233-1234
5 blocks from the arena.

## GETTING TO MARKET SQUARE ARENA

**Public transportation:** City bus routes begin and end in downtown Indianapolis, so they all come within 1 block of Market Square Arena. Call Metro Bus for more information at (317) 635-3344.
**By car:** From the east or west, take Washington Street downtown. Stadium will be on the left, between Alabama Street and New Jersey Street.

From the north or south, take I-65 downtown. Exit at Market Street and follow Market 3 blocks west. The Arena will be on the left.

## HOME-COURT ADVANTAGE

This building was transformed in 1994 from an occasionally placid, even staid, venue into a raucous center of local basketball mania. Now, even some fans admit that Market Square Arena is louder during Pacers games than those of the Indiana Hoosiers.

## IN THE HOT SEATS

With its relatively small size, Market Square Arena offers good sightlines and also gives fans the sensation of being close to the action. Size can cause some problems if you're trying to get a ticket. Before 1994, finding Pacers tickets was not a challenge, but it may no longer be a lay-up.

• **Good seats:** Excellent seats are available for $26 on the lower level in the four corners of the court. In the upper deck, check out the $26 and $20 seats at center court, aisles 5-8 and 17-20. Aisles 2-4, 9-11, 14-16 and 20-23, in the corners of the upper deck, offer good views and cost only $13.

• **Bad seats:** For $7, you can sit in the upper deck behind the baskets, aisles 1-2, 11-14 and 23-24, or in the last several rows of the center-court sections. The view is decent, compared to like seats in other arenas, but better seats have been available.

**Scalping:** There are often a fair number of legal scalpers, mostly along the approaches to the Arena. With the team's resurgence, they do not necessarily offer a good bargain.

**ARENA STATS**

**Location:** 3939 S. Figueroa St., Los Angeles, CA 90037
**Capacity:** 15,973
**Services for fans with disabilities:** Seating available at the top of the first loge level; exact placement changes each game.

**ARENA FIRSTS**

**Regular-season game:** Nov. 1, 1984, 107–105 over the New York Knicks.
**Overtime game:** March 3, 1985, 126–122 over the Kansas City Kings.
**Playoff game:** April 28, 1992, 98–88 over the Utah Jazz.

**TEAM NOTEBOOK**

**Franchise history:** Buffalo Braves, 1970–78; San Diego Clippers, 1978–84; Los Angeles Clippers, 1984–present.
**Most Valuable Player:** Bob McAdoo, 1974–75.
**Rookies of the Year:** Bob McAdoo, 1972–73; Ernie DiGregorio, 1973–74; Adrian Dantley, 1976–77; Terry Cummings, 1982–83.

**TICKET INFORMATION**
**Address:** 3939 S. Figueroa St., Los Angeles, CA 90037
**Phone:** (213) 480-3232/(213) 741-0821.
**Hours:** Mon.-Fri. 10-6.

# Memorial Sports Arena

The Clippers are LA's "other" team, taking a back seat to the Lakers in both name recognition and prestige. Unlike their neighbors to the south, the Clippers have never reached the final round of the playoffs, either in their present incarnation or when they were the San Diego Clippers or the Buffalo Braves. Still, this is Los Angeles, and you might spot Arsenio Hall, Raiders owner Al Davis, screenwriter Dan Mazur or Clippers convert Billy Crystal.

The Sports Arena is one of the oldest in the NBA, and the Clippers have talked recently of relocating to a new arena. In 1994–95, they will play several games in Anaheim, ostensibly to expand their fan base. But for now, the Clippers are staying in the arena that, ironically, was the home of the Lakers in 1960–68.

The Arena is well maintained and doesn't show its age. But because the Clippers don't have a fancy, high-tech scoreboard, among other extras, a game here is unique: At a time when most teams compete to see which has the best mascot or electronic presentation, the Clippers stress the action on the court.

## HOT TIPS FOR VISITING FANS

### Parking
Ample spaces are available in lots adjoining the Arena; the price is $7. Some on-street parking is available in the area. Generally, cars move quickly in and out of the lots.

While this is not the best place to take a long walk late at night, the Clippers and the police do a good job with security. The nearby parking lots are well lighted.

### Media bites
**Radio,** KMPC (710 AM).
**TV:** KCOP (Channel 13). Bill Walton, a former Clipper, a member of the Basketball Hall of Fame and an NBC commentator, is a color man on KCOP.

### Cuisine
The Clippers offer a good assortment, ranging from salads, veggie sandwiches and fruit-and-cheese plates, to burritos and Jody Maroni sausages.

The Clipper Club, next to section 2, is a full-service restaurant and popular bar. It opens one hour before the game and stays open approximately 30 minutes after the final buzzer. Occasionally, players stop by.

After the game, head across from the Arena to Julie's Trojan Bar and Grill (213-749-2575), a local institution among USC faithful for more than 50 years. This is a sports bar, decorated with USC memorabilia. Margarita Jones (213-747-4400),

1 block north of the Arena, is a good Mexican restaurant.

### LODGING NEAR THE ARENA

**Los Angeles Hilton and Towers**
930 Wilshire Blvd.
Los Angeles, CA 90017
(213) 629-4321/(800) 445-8667
½ mile from the arena.

**Westin Hotel at Los Angeles Airport**
5400 W. Century Blvd.
Los Angeles, CA 90045
(310) 216-5858/(800) 228-3000
11 miles from the arena.

### GETTING TO MEMORIAL SPORTS ARENA

**Public transportation:** Take the No. 81 bus west to Figueroa Avenue and 39th Street. Walk ½ block to the arena. Call (213) 626-4455 for more information.

**By car:** From the north, take 101 South to 110 South, and exit at Exposition Boulevard. Take a left onto Flower, then a left onto Figueroa.

From the south, take 405 North to 110 North; exit at Martin Luther King Jr. Boulevard. Arena will be on the right.

$275 ■ $140 ■ $110 ■ $45 ■ $41 ■ $38
$31 ■ $24 ■ $21 ■ $18 ■ $14 ■ $10

### HOME-COURT ADVANTAGE

Clippers fans, many of whom are long-suffering and knowledgeable, take a wait-and-see attitude. Still, when they made the playoffs in 1992 and 1993, fans responded and helped create an exciting atmostphere.

### IN THE HOT SEATS

The Clippers have a season-ticket base of approximately 6,000. Tickets for individual games go on sale the first Saturday of October. Unsold seats are sold on game nights. During the 1994–95 season, tickets for games at Anaheim are available through TicketMaster and at the Anaheim box office, but not through the Clippers at the Sports Arena.

• **Good seats:** One distinct benefit of the Clippers over the Lakers is low ticket prices. For a good bargain and a good view, check out the $10 and $14 seats in the middle concourse, sections 1-4, 14-18 and 28A-30. Excellent seats are also available in the middle loge at center court.

• **Bad seats:** Sightlines are generally good, although the seats at the top of the Arena behind the baskets—sections 8, 8A, 9, 23, 23A and 24—seem farther from the floor than comparable seats at newer NBA venues.

**Scalping:** Police have been known to enforce the local ordinance against scalping.

## ARENA STATS

**Location:** 3900 W. Manchester Blvd., Inglewood, CA 90305
**Opened:** Dec. 30, 1967
**Capacity:** 17,505
**Services for fans with disabilities:** Seating available at the top of the loge, in sections 1, 18, 19 and 36.

## ARENA FIRSTS

**Regular-season game:** Dec. 31, 1967, 147–118 over the Houston Rockets.
**Overtime game:** Feb. 17, 1968, 135–134 loss to the Philadelphia 76ers in double overtime.
**Playoff game:** March 24, 1968, 109–101 over the Chicago Bulls.
**NBA Finals game:** April 26, 1968, 127–119 loss to the Boston Celtics.

## TEAM NOTEBOOK

**Franchise history:** Minneapolis Lakers, 1947–48 (NBL); 1948–49 (BAA); 1949–60 (NBA); Los Angeles Lakers, 1960–present.
**Conference titles:** 1948–49, '49–50, '51–52, '52–53, '53–54, '54–55, '58–59, '61–62, '62–63, '64–65, '65–66, '67–68, '68–69, '69–70, '71–72, '72–73, '79–80, '81–82, '82–83, '83–84, '84–85, '86–87, '87–88, '88–89, '90–91.
**NBA championships:** 1948–'49, '49–50, '51–52, '52–53, '53–54, '71–72, '79–80, '81–82, '84–85, '86–87, '87–88.
**Basketball Hall of Fame:** G. Mikan, 1959; B. Sharman, '75; E. Baylor, '76; J. Pollard, '77; W. Chamberlain, P. Newell, '78; J. West, '79; S. Martin, '81.
**Retired numbers:** 13, W. Chamberlain; 22, E. Baylor; 33, K. Abdul-Jabbar; 44, J. West.

# Great Western Forum

This is one of the classiest-looking arenas in the NBA. Aptly named the Forum, the circular building is ringed by white Roman columns. The only problem is that it's in a bad neighborhood. Players have been robbed across the street.

Nonetheless, stars still come out to see the Lakers—the Forum's in Inglewood, but it might as well be in Hollywood. Not as many show up as in the days of Magic Johnson and Kareem Abdul-Jabbar, but Jack Nicholson still has his customary seat a few feet away from the visitors' bench. Dyan Cannon and Arsenio Hall are also diehard regulars, although Hall has been known to sneak across town and catch the Clippers, too. Even the cheerleading dancers, the Laker Girls (Paula Abdul is an alumna), had a movie made about them. The players enter through the rear tunnel, but if you want to star-gaze, arrive early and wait near the canopy at the main entrance to watch the limos drop off the big shots.

The retired jerseys of Wilt Chamberlain, Elgin Baylor, Jerry West, Johnson and Abdul-Jabbar are there to see and, these days, dream about. The relationship between the team and the fans is now strained. The fans used to arrive late and leave early. Now they arrive later, if at all, and leave even earlier. Los Angeles doesn't like losers.

## HOT TIPS FOR VISITING FANS

**Parking**
Don't park on the street. You don't want to be walking around after dark. The closest lots are for preferred seating, but you can park across the street at Hollywood Park or behind the Forum for $6.

This is Los Angeles, everybody drives, and traffic can be murder before and after games. Be patient going home, and leave for the game with time to spare. Traffic patterns change on game days, so make sure you get in the correct lane, because switching lanes is difficult once traffic gets congested.

**Media bites**
**Radio:** KLAC (570 AM), with the legendary Chick Hearn, simulcast on television.
**TV:** KCAL (Channel 9), Prime Ticket cable.

**Cuisine**
Concessions stands are plentiful, and the lines are the most orderly in the league. The usual hot dogs, nachos, popcorn and ice cream are available, as well as mixed drinks, wine and bottled water. Budweiser and a number of imported beers are available.

The place to go is the Forum Club, near the main entrance, but you have to be a season tick-etholder or know somebody. It's like a nightclub after the game, with players and celebs stopping by. You can grab a bite there before the game, too. Tony Roma's (310-674-1679) in Inglewood is good. The Chart House (310-822-4144) and the Black Whale (310-823-9898) in Venice are an easy drive away. Don't plan to walk anywhere; nothing is close enough, or safe enough, to try.

## LODGING NEAR THE ARENA

**Marriott Marina del Rey**
13480 Maxella Ave.
Marina del Rey, CA 90292
(310) 822-8555/(800) 228-9290
5 miles from the arena.

**Ritz-Carlton**
4375 Admiralty Way
Los Angeles, CA 90292
(310) 823-1700/(800) 241-3333
8-10 miles from the arena.

## THE LAKERS AT GREAT WESTERN FORUM

**Feb. 9, 1969:** Wilt Chamberlain sets a Forum record, scoring 66 points against the Phoenix Suns.

**March 19, 1972:** The Lakers trounce the Golden State Warriors 162–99, the largest margin of victory in an NBA game.

**May 7, 1972:** A 114–100 win over the New York Knicks in Game 5 of the NBA Finals gives the Lakers their first championship in Los Angeles.

**Oct. 28, 1973:** Elmore Smith sets an NBA record with 17 blocks against the Portland Trail Blazers.

**June 8, 1982:** The Lakers take Game 6 of the Finals over the Philadelphia 76ers to clinch the championship.

**June 3, 1984:** The first Boston Celtics–Lakers Finals of the Magic Johnson–Larry Bird era comes to Los Angeles. The Lakers beat Boston in Game 3, 137–104.

**June 14, 1987:** The Lakers win Game 6 of the NBA Finals 106–93 over the Celtics to win another title.

**June 19, 1988:** Isiah Thomas of the Detroit Pistons sets an NBA Finals record when he scores 25 points in one quarter. The Lakers win 103–102.

**June 13, 1989:** The Abdul-Jabbar era comes to an end, as the Pistons sweep the Lakers, winning Game 4, 105–97.

**April 15, 1991:** In a game against the Mavericks, Magic Johnson breaks Oscar Robertson's all-time NBA assist record of 9,887.

# IN THE HOT SEATS AT GREAT WESTERN FORUM

The place, big and spread out, looks like it should hold more than 17,505. The seats might seem far from the action, but the farthest is only 170 feet from the playing surface. You can rent binoculars for $5, but be prepared to leave a deposit.

The Lakers have the most expensive tickets in the NBA. Prices are $100, $90 and $62.50 for the best seats; the 128 courtside seats go for $500 a game.

• **Good seats:** The arena has no obstructed-view seats. Each upholstered seat is angled to the center spot on the playing floor. The best seats are on the floor, of course, because you can see the game and the stars better, but they cost big bucks and you have to know someone.

• **Bad seats:** Don't get suckered into buying seats on the end lines, because peo-ple will be walking in front of you all the time. Sit opposite the benches, if possible.

**Scalping:** This used to be the only way to get in, but with the team's playing poorly the past few seasons, tickets are available through normal outlets.

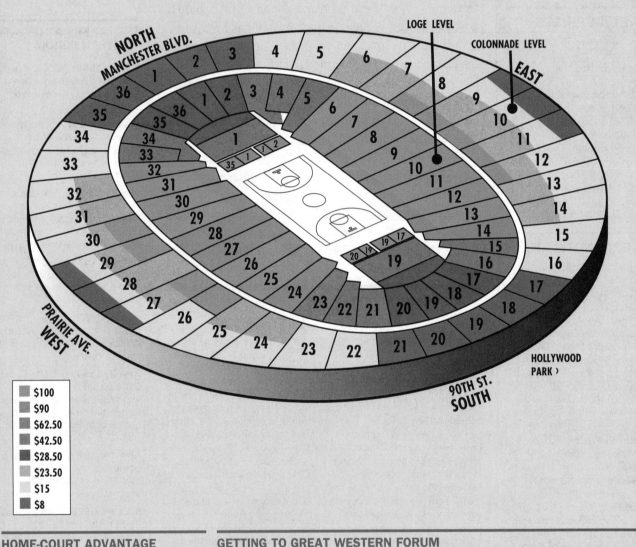

| | |
|---|---|
| ■ | $100 |
| ■ | $90 |
| ■ | $62.50 |
| ■ | $42.50 |
| ■ | $28.50 |
| ■ | $23.50 |
| ■ | $15 |
| ■ | $8 |

## HOME-COURT ADVANTAGE

The stars and the history of the building can be intimidating, and the lifestyle of Hollywood gets opponents in trouble some-times. The clubs, all-night spots and hob-nobbing with celebrities can take a player's legs away.

## GETTING TO GREAT WESTERN FORUM

**Public transportation:** Take the No. 40 bus on South Broadway to Market Manchester. Transfer to an eastbound No. 211 bus. For more information, call (310) 320-9442.

**By car:** From Highway 110, exit at Manchester Boulevard and head west to the Forum. From the San Diego 405 Freeway, exit at Manchester and head east. Also accessible from Highway 105.

**TICKET INFORMATION**
**Address:** 3900 W. Manchester Blvd., Inglewood, CA 90305

**Phone:** (310) 419-DUNK or TicketMaster at (213) 480-3232, (714) 740-2000 or (805) 583-8700

**Hours:** Mon.-Fri. 10-6.
**Prices:** $100, $90, $62.50, $42.50, $28.50, $23.50, $15, $8.50.

# Miami Arena

## ARENA STATS

**Location:** 701 Arena Blvd., Miami, FL 33136
**Opened:** July 8, 1988
**Capacity:** 15,008
**Services for fans with disabilities:** Seating available on the north side of the Arena in the top rows of sections 101, 113, 114, 119, 121 and 126.

## ARENA FIRSTS

**Regular-season game:** Nov. 5, 1988, 111–91 loss to the Los Angeles Clippers.
**Points scored:** Norm Nixon, Los Angeles Clippers.
**Overtime game:** Nov. 18, 1988, 123–117 loss to the Golden State Warriors.
**Playoff game:** April 29, 1992, 119–114 loss to the Chicago Bulls.

## TEAM NOTEBOOK

**Franchise history:** Miami Heat, 1988–present.

## TICKET INFORMATION

**Address:** 701 Arena Blvd., Miami, FL 33136
**Phone:** (305) 577-HEAT.
**Hours:** Mon.-Fri. 10-5.

The Heat might be the most appropriate nickname among all of the NBA's 27 teams. Anyone who spends time in south Florida, especially during the summer, will be convinced. They'll have no trouble spotting the Miami Arena either, which is painted a pastel shade of pink, in harmony with the art-deco architecture for which Miami is known.

Inside, the basketball action is hot and the air blessedly cool. As their franchise improves, Miami fans have warmed to their team. Within the intimate confines of this arena, they can match the noise level of some of the more-established NBA venues, sometimes even without the scoreboard telling them to yell.

Although Heat fans have had a lot to cheer about recently, many have more on their minds than their team's success when they come to Miami Arena. The Arena is located on the edge of a section of Miami known as Overtown, portions of which were rocked by rioting a few years back. Consequently, the team and the city of Miami make a concerted and visible effort to provide security. While some might not feel comfortable taking a postgame stroll through the neighborhood, it should not stop anyone from checking out the Heat.

■ $34　■ $23　■ $17　■ $10.50

## HOT TIPS FOR VISITING FANS

### Parking
Prices at area lots range from $6-$10. Lots in the $5-$6 range tend to be several blocks away. Fans who are concerned about security generally park at the higher-priced lots. Panhandling in the area has been cited by several of the Heat faithful as another reason to park as close to the arena as possible.

### Media bites
**Radio:** WINZ (940 AM-English), WRFM (830 AM-Spanish).
**TV:** WBFA, (Channel 33).

### Cuisine
Miami Arena offers standard fare, but the grilled cheeseburger is particularly recommended. The Arena also serves several distinctive Miami offerings: the Miami Heat tropical drink, made with rum and pina colada mix; potato knishes; kosher hot dogs; Miami Heroes, with ham, cured pork, cheese, pickles and mustard, served grilled on Cuban bread; and *arepas*, deep-fried patties of sweet corn and cheese.

After the game, Bayside Market Place (305-577-3344), a complex of eight restaurants and four bars on 16 waterfront acres, is 5 blocks west of the Arena. Along Biscayne Boulevard, there's the 1800 Club (305-373-1093), where the Heat coaching staff goes after the game to unwind. Jimmy Buffett and Heat players are occasional customers. The menu features traditional items, such as shrimp scampi.

## LODGING NEAR THE ARENA

**Mayfair House**
3000 Florida Ave.
Coconut Grove
Miami, FL 33133
(305) 441-0000/(800) 433-4555
6½ miles from the arena.

**Don Shula's Hotel**
15255 Bull Rd.
Miami, FL 33014
(305) 821-1150
10 miles from the arena.

## GETTING TO MIAMI ARENA

**Public transportation:** Take Metro Rail to Overtown Station, across the street from the Arena. Call (305) 638-6700 for more information.
**By car:** From the airport, take 836 East to the Biscayne Boulevard exit. Make a right at the bottom of the ramp onto Biscayne, and proceed to Northwest 8th Street. Take a right. Miami Arena is 2 blocks, on the left.

## HOME-COURT ADVANTAGE

Engaged, enthusiastic fans, plus the size of the arena, work to enhance and magnify the noise level, especially when there's a sellout. This is especially true against better teams, whom the Heat tend to play well against at home.

## IN THE HOT SEATS

Miami's season-ticket base is between 12,000 and 13,000. All available single-game tickets are put on sale in early October. Any tickets that remain are sold on game nights; although most are for upper-deck seats, there may be scattered singles.

This is one of the smallest arenas in the NBA, and its size translates into a large number of good seats. The $23 seats, located upstairs, offer a good view for the money. Recently, the Heat and the city have discussed building a larger facility. There's also talk of renovation and expansion of the Arena to increase the number of lower-deck seats, suites and luxury boxes, while improving the view.

•**Bad seats:** Though this is a small arena, the seats farthest from the court in the upper deck are a long way from the action.

**Scalping:** The police, with more pressing concerns involving crowds and security, generally seem to leave scalpers alone.

# Bradley Center

The Bradley Center is hard to miss. Located downtown, around the corner from the Mecca, the Bucks' earlier home, and occupying more than a city block, the arena's red-and-pink-granite exterior is visible from several blocks away. Inside are two glass-enclosed atria with columns fashioned from the same granite used for the building's facade.

Although the Bucks' home is impressive, the same cannot be said for what goes on inside. The Bucks have struggled the last several seasons. Milwaukee's poor play and the subdued hometown fans combine to make the experience of going to a game somewhat underwhelming. Even when the decibels rise, the sound seems to get lost.

Although the nonbasketball entertainment at the Bradley Center is not particularly noteworthy either, the local mascot, Bango—a buck with big antlers—is popular. A house band called StreetLife also does its best to get things going during the game. Rather than anticipating the basketball experience of a lifetime, you should expect a quieter kind of NBA evening. The highlight of your visit likely will be the Bradley Center itself, a comfortable, well-built facility.

## HOT TIPS FOR VISITING FANS

### Parking
Although the Bradley Center has no on-site parking, plenty is available in the area, with prices ranging from $4 to $7. Some street parking is available. After games, traffic moves fairly smoothly.

### Media bites
**Radio:** WIMJ (620 AM).
**TV:** WVTV (Channel 18). Jon McGlocklin, one of the original Bucks, is a color analyst on radio and on TV during road games.

### Cuisine
Milwaukee is best known for sausages and beer, both of which are well represented at the Center. Fans also enjoy the pizza, grilled burgers and chicken. Miller products are widely available, as well as local favorites Old Style and Leinenkugel's.

For after the game, Major Goolsby's (414-271-3414) is a block away. This sports bar, popular with fans and players, once was known as the Liquid Locker Room of the NBA. The Water Street Brewery (414-272-1195) is less than three blocks from the Bradley Center. It features eight made-on-the-premises brews, plus more than 20 other beers.

### LODGING NEAR THE ARENA
**Hyatt Regency Milwaukee**
333 W. Kilbourn Ave.
Milwaukee, WI 53203
(414) 276-1234/(800) 233-1234
2 blocks from the arena.

**Wyndham Milwaukee Center**
139 E. Kilbourn Ave.
Milwaukee, WI 53202
(414) 291-4792/(800) 822-4200
4 blocks from the arena.

### GETTING TO BRADLEY CENTER
**Public transportation:** The No. 30 bus stops one block from the arena. Call (414) 344-6711 for more information.
**By car:** From the south, take I-94 North to the Kilbourn/Civic Center exit. Go to the second stoplight and make a left onto North Fourth Street. The Bradley Center is two blocks ahead on the left.

From the north, take I-94 South to the Fourth Street/Civic Center exit, then take Fourth Street to the arena.

From the west, take I-94 East to the Civic Center exit (No. 1H). Take the right fork in the ramp to St. Paul Avenue. Make a left onto North Fourth Street and go six blocks. The arena will be on the left.

## HOME-COURT ADVANTAGE

The Bucks have little or no edge at the Bradley Center. The crowd can be so quiet at times that caustic comments by courtside fans can be heard in much of the lower level. During the 1993-94 season, several players complained about fans' not being enthusiastic enough during games.

## IN THE HOT SEATS

Single-game tickets go on sale in October, but tickets can be purchased on virtually any game night for seats at various locations around the Bradley Center, although most are in the upper tier.

• **Good seats:** Most of the sightlines are good, and the seats are comfortable. Preferred seats are in the lower half of the Center. Check out the $19 seats in sections 400-404, 418-426 and 440-443 of the upper deck's center-court area. Center-court seating near the floor in sections 200-203, 211-217 and 225-227 costs $35, a bargain compared to similar seats at other NBA arenas.

• **Bad seats:** Seats in the upper-deck end zones—sections 431-435 and 409-413—seem more suited to watching hockey than basketball. These seats cost $8 and $11.

 **Scalping:** Scalpers don't have a high profile outside the Center. During the 1992-93 and '93-94 seasons, the Bucks sold out 12 games.

**TIMBERWOLVES** ™

## ARENA STATS

**Location:** Target Center 600 First Ave. N., Minneapolis, MN 55403
**Opened:** Oct. 13, 1990
**Capacity:** 19,006
**Services for fans with disabilities:** Seating available in numerous locations on two levels.

## ARENA FIRSTS

**Regular-season game:** Nov. 2, 1990, 98–85 over the Dallas Mavericks.
**Points scored:** Rolando Blackman of the Mavericks.
**Overtime game:** Feb. 3, 1991, 110–102 over the Philadelphia 76ers, in double overtime.

## TEAM NOTEBOOK

**Franchise history:** Minnesota Timberwolves, 1989–present.

**TICKET INFORMATION**
**Address:** Target Center, 600 First Ave. North, Minneapolis, MN 55403
**Phone:** (612) 673-1313, (612)-673-1645 (group sales) or Ticketmaster at (612) 989-5151.
**Hours:** Mon.-Sat. 9-5.

# Target Center

After the Lakers moved to Los Angeles in 1960, NBA basketball didn't come back to Minneapolis for 27 years. But this could be a short visit. In 1994, the state legislature and NBA commissioner David Stern intervened on separate occasions to keep the Timberwolves in the Twin Cities area, which is already smarting from the loss of its NHL North Stars.

The loss of the Timberwolves would mean more to Minneapolis than just the loss of a basketball team. The Target Center has brought people back downtown to an area known as the Warehouse District, full of artists' studios, restaurants and bars.

Visitors to the Target Center should not be surprised to hear the fans howling like wolves at various points during the game. Minneapolis' version of the noise meter is a "Howl-O'Meter" shown on the large video screen over center court. Given the Timberwolves' record since entering the league, one might think these are howls of pain, but they're really a sign of fans learning to love their team. Only time will tell if Minneapolis fans will lose another sport.

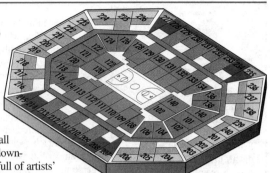

■ N/A ■ $42.50 ■ $29.50 ■ $25
■ $17.50 ■ $13.50 ■ $9.50

## HOT TIPS FOR VISITING FANS

### Parking
Because the Target Center is downtown, plenty of parking is in the area, either on the street or in flat lots. Two city-owned parking garages are connected to the Center by ramps. Parking is $4. Cars move fairly quickly into and out of area lots.

### Media bites
**Radio:** KFAN (1130 AM).
**TV:** KITN (Channel 29) and KARE (Channel 11) both broadcast games. Kevin McHale, the former All-Star forward with the Boston Celtics and an alumnus of the University of Minnesota, is an analyst on the TV broadcasts.

### Cuisine
Among the notable items are the Italian hoagies, steak sandwiches, Italian sausages—and, for a uniquely Minnesota dish, a fried walleye fish sandwich. Fans can also buy fruit and cheese platters and a veggie plate.

Frontrunners, a restaurant and lounge with a sports-bar theme and big-screen TVs, is on the main level, behind sections 101 and 140. Before the game, Frontrunners serves a variety of hot dishes and sandwiches; afterward, it swings into lounge mode.

The Loon Cafe (612-332-8342) is located a block from the arena. The bar/restaurant has a comfortable, old-saloon atmosphere that's perfect for an after-game drink or meal. Rosen's (612-338-1926),

another restaurant/bar, is housed in a former warehouse with high ceilings and hardwood floors. They have excellent pastas and a good selection of beers.

### LODGING NEAR THE ARENA
**Minneapolis Marriott**
30 S. Seventh St.
Minneapolis, MN 55402
(612) 349-4000/(800) 228-9290
2 blocks from the arena.

**Hyatt Regency**
1300 Nicollet Mall
Minneapolis, MN 55403
(612) 370-1234/(800) 233-1234
About 5 blocks from the arena.

### GETTING TO THE TARGET CENTER
**Public transportation:** All buses that go downtown go near the stadium. Call Metro Transit at (612) 349-7000 for information.
**By car:** From the north, take 35W to the Washington Avenue exit. Turn right onto Washington and follow it until First Avenue North. Turn left , and the arena will be in front of you.

From the south, take 35W into downtown. Take the Fifth Avenue downtown exit, then turn left onto Seventh Avenue. Take Seventh to First Avenue North.

From the east or west, take 94 toward downtown, and exit at Fourth Street. Turn right onto First Avenue Center.

## HOME-COURT ADVANTAGE
The Timberwolves have Crunch, a gray wolf mascot, and award-winning video displays to pump up the faithful, and after nearly losing the team to New Orleans, local fans might come to the Target Center in record numbers to show their support for keeping the franchise in Minneapolis.

## IN THE HOT SEATS

Good seats are available for most home games. During the 1993–94 season, the team sold out just four games, down from seven the preceding year. Still, despite this drop and worries about whether the Wolves will stay, interest in basketball remains high in the Twin Cities; the team's home attendance in 1993–94 was the ninth best in the league. The season-ticket base is only about 10,000, though, meaning many tickets are sold on a walk-up basis. Single-game seats go on sale a week or two before the season starts.

• **Good seats:** Virtually all the seats are comfortable and have good views. The top eight rows of sections 206–236 and 216–226 are a good deal at $9.50, considering that the view from here is decent.

**Scalping:** Scalping is illegal in Minneapolis, but some scalpers can be found around the Center. However, you should have no difficulty buying what you want at the box office.

# Brendan Byrne Arena

GATE A
GATE D
GATE B
GATE C

$65 ■ $45 ■ $35 ■ $20
■ $16 ■ $10

Located in the sprawling Meadowlands Sports Complex, which also includes Giants Stadium and a race track, the gleaming white Brendan Byrne Arena can be seen for miles by motorists speeding past on the nearby highway. While Brendan Byrne Arena, Madison Square Garden and their respective basketball tenants share a geographic proximity, that's as far as the similarities go. The Knicks are a big-city team, and the Nets are a creature of the suburbs. Since their first game in the ABA in 1967, the Nets played at four suburban sites on Long Island and in New Jersey before finally moving into their present home in 1981.

Nets fans are divided in their opinions about Brendan Byrne Arena. Some like its atmosphere, which is less hectic than the Garden's, but others say the constant family-oriented, nonbasketball entertainment detracts from the games. The crowd is often fairly quiet; on most nights, Brendan Byrne Arena is a place to enjoy a relaxing evening rather than an intense basketball experience. The exceptions are when the Knicks and many of their fans cross the Hudson River. On those nights, the fans and the two teams, which have a mutual dislike, turn up the heat.

## ARENA STATS

**Location:** East Rutherford, NJ 07073
**Opened:** Nov. 4, 1981
**Capacity:** 20,029
**Services for fans with disabilities:** Seating available in sections 103-105, 111-114, 116-119, 125 and 127-128. Tickets are $35. Call (201) 935-3900 for more information.

## ARENA FIRSTS

**Regular-season game:** Oct. 30, 1981, 103–99 loss to the New York Knicks
**Playoff game:** April 20, 1982, 96–83 loss to the Washington Bullets.

## TEAM NOTEBOOK

**Franchise history:** New Jersey Americans, 1967–68 (ABA); New York Nets, '68–76 (ABA); New York Nets, '76–77 (NBA); New Jersey Nets, '77–present.
**ABA Championships:** 1973–74, '75–76.
**Basketball Hall of Fame:** Julius Erving, 1993.
**Most Valuable Player:** J. Erving 1973–74, '74–75, '75–76 (ABA).
**Rookie of the Year:** B. Taylor, 1973 (ABA); B. Williams, '82; D. Coleman, '91.
**Retired numbers:** 3, D. Petrovic; 4, W. Ladner; 23, J. Williamson; 25, B. Melchionni; 32, J. Erving.

## HOT TIPS FOR VISITING FANS

### Parking
Parking for approximately 4,000 cars is available at the Arena. An additional 25,000 spaces available elsewhere in the Meadowlands. Parking costs $5. The Nets operate free shuttle service to and from the Arena.

### Media bites
**Radio:** WQEW (1560 AM).
**TV:** SportsChannel on cable. Spencer Ross, the Nets' play-by-play cable announcer, has worked for the Jets, the Yankees and the New York Nets of the ABA. Joining him is color analyst Bill Rafftery, a former coach of nearby Seton Hall University who's also an analyst for college basketball games on CBS.

### Cuisine
Local favorites include: Carvel soft ice cream, potato knishes and a Hebrew National hot dog, either plain or with chili and onions. The Arena also has two midcourt, mall-type food areas where you can find hot dogs, burgers, pizza and grilled chicken. Three portable carts stock imported beer, including Molson and Heineken.

After the game, Moonshine Jugs (201-348-1700) in Secaucus and the Jersey Sports Cafe (201-933-3308) in East Rutherford head the list.

### LODGING NEAR THE ARENA
**Embassy Suites Hotel**
455 Plaza Dr.
Secaucus, NJ 07094
(201) 864-7300/(800) 362-2779
2 miles from the arena.

**Sheraton Meadowlands**
2 Meadowlands Plaza
East Rutherford, NJ 07073
(201) 896-0500/(800) 325-3535
½ mile from the arena.

### GETTING TO BRENDAN BYRNE ARENA
**Public transportation:** New Jersey Transit runs load-and-go buses from the Port Authority Bus Terminal in Manhattan. Call (201) 762-5100 for more information.
**By car:** From Manhattan, take the Lincoln Tunnel, then follow Route 3 West directly to the Sports Complex.

From the New Jersey Turnpike, take the western spur to 16W and follow signs to the Sports Complex.

## HOME-COURT ADVANTAGE
The crowd at the Arena is not usually the raucous type that helps win games. When fans get going, it's often with the help of film clips on the video screen. Being the area underdog seems to help them against the Knicks.

## IN THE HOT SEATS

The Nets have become a fairly popular attraction. They sold out 29 of 82 home games during the 1992–93 and 1993–94 seasons, and their attendance was in the middle of the NBA pack. Despite this, good seats should be available at the box office for most games, except against the Knicks.

With the multimillion-dollar provisions of Derrick Coleman's contract beginning to take hold, the team is looking for additional revenue to satisfy obligations to its star forward—look for rising ticket prices. Tickets priced at $16 and $20, though, should not be affected.

• **Bad seats:** This is a fairly large, almost bowl-shaped building more spread-out than other arenas. Most seats are good. Upper-deck seats cost $16, and though they're perfectly acceptable, given the general availability of tickets, you can probably do better if you're willing to pay.

**Scalping:** Very few scalpers are around the Arena, even when the Knicks are in town.

TM

# Madison Square Garden

The reverence attached to Madison Square Garden goes beyond its 26 years at 33rd Street and Seventh Avenue, an honor conferred as much by the Garden's proud lineage as by the many memorable moments this structure has seen. The current MSG is the fourth building so named. The first MSG once housed P.T. Barnum's Hippodrome. The second, built in 1890, was designed by Stanford White, who later was murdered in its roof gardens. In the late '40s and early '50s, college basketball was the real attraction at the third MSG, while pro ball was just an afterthought. But after the point-shaving scandals of the '50s, the Knicks and the NBA began to eclipse college ball in the minds of New Yorkers. The classic 1969–70 Knicks stole the limelight once and for all.

Though MSG has been gussied up in recent years, the memories of those championship teams are still responsible for much of the atmosphere. The high standards to which Knicks fans hold their team derive in large part from those glory years, a comparison which also has burdened the recent strong Knicks teams coached by Pat Riley. Like their city, no other fans can be more unforgiving or more wholeheartedly enthusiastic.

## HOT TIPS FOR VISITING FANS

### Parking

Since the Garden is in midtown Manhattan, many scattered, private lots can be found in the area, averaging $15. Though some of the lots are on side streets and not particularly well-lighted, the neighborhood is active on game nights, so safety is no more a concern than in any other part of midtown. Traffic can move slowly in the streets leading up to the Garden. Plan an extra half-hour or so.

### Media bites

**Radio:** WFAN (660 AM). Former Knick Walt "Clyde" Frazier is the analyst, offering outspoken opinions and colorful patter.

**TV:** MSG Network (cable). Marv Albert has been a Knicks announcer for more than 25 years, as well as doing NBA games on NBC. He's responsible for play-by-play, and John Andriese handles color.

### Cuisine

Given that midtown has no shortage of restaurants, many Knicks fans have a ritual meal at a favorite place and then head to the game. If you decide to rely on the concessions, though, you won't be too badly off. The renovations made to the Garden a few years ago included upgrading the food, which doesn't stray too far beyond the usual arena fare but is tasty nonetheless.

Charley O's (212-630-0343), in the same complex as the Garden at 9 Penn Plaza, is very popular with Knicks fans. The Play-By-Play is another sports bar in the complex; after games, a show that features interviews with players and other famous guests is broadcast from here on the MSG Sports Network.

Champions (212-755-4000) is in the New York Marriott East Side. More than 40 types of beer are available here. A few blocks up, there's P.J. Clarke's, an old time New York bar with lots of cigar smoke and atmosphere.

## THE KNICKS AT MADISON SQUARE GARDEN

**May 8, 1970:** To the surprise of the Los Angeles Lakers, an injured Willis Reed limps onto the court and starts Game 7 of the Finals. Reed hits his first shot and leads the Knicks to an emotional 113–99 win.

**Nov. 18, 1972:** The Knicks come back from an 86–68 deficit by scoring 19 straight points in the last 5 minutes and 11 seconds to beat the Milwaukee Bucks 87–86.

**April 22, 1984:** After scoring 46 points against the Detroit Pistons three nights earlier in Game 2, Bernard King matches that total in Game 3. The Knicks win 120–113.

**May 14, 1992:** Despite spraining his ankle in the third quarter, Patrick Ewing leads the Knicks to a dramatic 100–86 win over the Chicago Bulls, forcing a seventh game in their Eastern Conference final.

**June 2, 1993:** The Knicks fall 97–94 to the Bulls in the pivotal Game 5 of the Eastern Conference final, when Charles Smith is unable to convert on a series of last-second layups.

**June 5, 1994:** Ewing's slam dunk with 27 seconds left gives the Knicks a 94–90 win in Game 7 of their Eastern Conference final over the Indiana Pacers.

# IN THE HOT SEATS AT MADISON SQUARE GARDEN

The Knicks have sold out nearly all of their games since Riley took over the team. Season tickets account for a large number of the seats, but the Knicks put single-game tickets on sale twice a year—once before the season for the first half, and again during the first half for the second half. Tickets go very fast; those calling on the second day might find themselves with slim pickings in terms of available games and seat selection.

• **Bad seats:** The sightlines are generally good, although the nosebleed seats at the top of the Garden, in sections 401-428, are far from the court. The seating area also rises quickly from the floor, making for a steep climb to the upper sections. But even up there, the view can be decent. Throughout most of the Garden, there is not a lot of leg room, so it can get cramped, especially if you are above average size.

 **Scalping:** All along Seventh and Eighth Avenues, between 34th and 31st Streets, though signs warn that it's illegal. With Knicks tickets hard to get, it's definitely a seller's market.

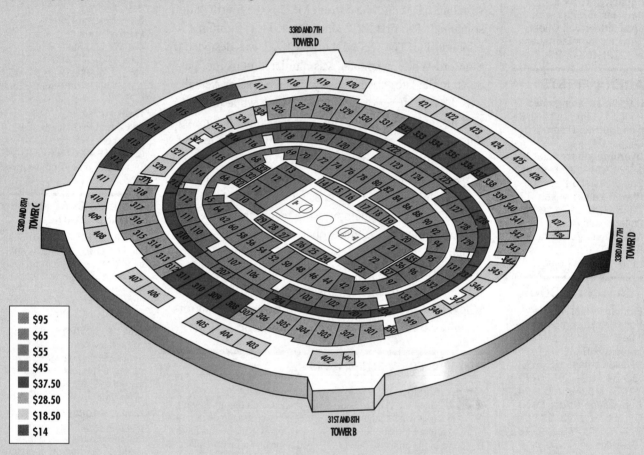

**Price Legend:**
- $95
- $65
- $55
- $45
- $37.50
- $28.50
- $18.50
- $14

## HOME-COURT ADVANTAGE

Even though this is a more upscale, suit-and-tie crowd than you'll see at Rangers games, don't expect quiet stands. Unlike at many other arenas in the league, the scoreboard has to keep up with the crowd. Knicks fans can generate enough electricity and noise to seriously affect the performances of players, many of whom are already a bit starstruck by the famous faces at courtside and the history of this place. A Knicks game at the Garden is not a diverting way to spend an evening; it's an intense and exhilarating experience shared between the fans and their team. Clearly the team responds—they're 69–13 at home since 1992.

## GETTING TO MADISON SQUARE GARDEN

**Public transportation:** Take the B, D, F, Q, N or R train to the 34th Street Station; MSG is 2 blocks west. The A, C, E, 1, 2, 3 and 9 trains all stop at Pennsylvania Station–34th Street, which is directly below MSG.

**By car:** From New Jersey and south, enter Manhattan via the Lincoln Tunnel. Follow signs for downtown and turn left on 34th Street.

From Connecticut and the north, take Route 95 to Route 9A-S. Exit at 34th Street.

**TICKET INFORMATION**
**Address:** 4 Pennsylvania Plaza, N.Y., NY 10001
**Phone:** (212) 465-6741 or TicketMaster at
(212) 307-7171, (201) 507-8900, (516) 888-9000, (609) 665-2500, (914) 454-3388 and (203) 624-0033

**Hours:** Mon.-Sat. 10-6.
**Prices:** $95, $65, $55, $45, $37.50, $28.50, $18.50, $14.

# Oakland Coliseum Arena

Perhaps unbeknownst to many NBA fans, the Golden State Warriors are a hot item in the Bay Area. All their games since 1989 have been sellouts. While such popularity often is reserved for a championship-caliber team, the Warriors have not won a title since 1975, making them a local phenomenon and their ticket sales all the more noteworthy.

Although the Warriors generate a lot of enthusiasm selling tickets, the same does not always hold true inside the Arena. With an exciting team that plays an uptempo, fast-paced game, one might expect the fans to get energized more than they do. When they do get involved, the arena can be an exciting place. The noise seems to be amplified by the building's small size and good acoustics. But then, all too often, the cheering stops and the squeak of sneakers echoes through the house.

The Arena—located in the same complex that contains the Oakland/Alameda County Coliseum, home of the A's—opened in 1966. Only five NBA arenas are older. Depending on your point of view, its age is either a benefit or a drawback. You shouldn't look for a high-tech video screen or fancy luxury boxes, but you can have a great time simply watching NBA basketball, an activity that can seem secondary in many new arenas. With the future in mind, though, the team has discussed moving to a new arena, with San Francisco, San Jose or elsewhere in Oakland or Alameda County a potential site.

## HOT TIPS FOR VISITING FANS

**Parking**
Approximately 10,000 spaces are in the Coliseum Arena's lot, so parking is definitely not a problem. The cost is $6. The area is well-lighted and the team does a good job with security. BART, the local mass-transit train system, has a station within walking distance.

**Media Bites**
**Radio:** KNBR (680 AM-English), KIQI (1010 AM-Spanish).
**TV:** KPIX, (Channel 5); KICU, (Channel 36); and SportsChannel (cable). Steve Albert, another member of the famous Albert broadcasting clan, handles Warriors' play-by-play.

**Cuisine**
Particularly popular are the seven varieties of grilled sausages, including Louisiana hot and Linguia (spicy Portuguese). Pizza, Caesar salad and Oriental chicken salad also are well-liked, as are baked potatoes with a choice of toppings, sourdough-bread bowls filled with clam chowder or chili, Buffalo wings and veggie burgers. Specialty beers, including imports and local microbeers, are sold on tap. The Coliseum Café, a Hofbrau-style cafeteria, is open to ticketholders two hours before the game.
Sam's Hofbrau (510-635-8244) is popular with fans before and after the game. Sam's has a

sports motif, with numerous pictures of past and present Oakland teams and athletes. Nearly 20 beers are on tap, including several microbrews.
Francesco's (510-569-0653) is about a mile from the Coliseum. This family-owned restaurant serves Italian specialties such as linguine with mussels and calamari, trolley sole, swordfish and pesto.

## THE WARRIORS AT OAKLAND COLISEUM ARENA

**March 26, 1974:** Rick Barry scores a career-high 64 points against Portland, leading the Warriors to a 143–120 win.

**May 14, 1975:** The Warriors edge Chicago 83–79 to win the Western Conference final, four games to three. Golden State goes on to win the championship by sweeping Washington in the finals.

**March 30, 1979:** Robert Parish becomes the first Warrior since Nate Thurmond to get 30 points and 30 rebounds in a single game, a 114–98 win over New York.

**Jan. 7, 1984:** The Warriors score a team-record 154 points against San Antonio. Purvis Short sets an NBA high for the season, with 57, in the 154–133 win.

**May 10, 1987:** Eric "Sleepy" Floyd leads the Warriors to a 129–121 victory over the Lakers in Game 4 of the Western Conference semifinals with the year's NBA-playoff-high—51 points. The Lakers take the series, four games to one.

# IN THE HOT SEATS AT OAKLAND COLISEUM

In what has become something of an annual rite of autumn, nearly 13,000 tickets are bought by season ticketholders at the start of the season. The remaining 2,000 or so tickets for individual games are snapped up within hours of going on sale. Although the Warriors often announce on game nights that limited tickets are available, there might not be two seats together; even so, they go fast.

• **Good seats:** The Arena's small size means many good seats for basketball. The Arena was built more like a theater than the typical arena, so rather than a steep incline from the floor, there's more of a gradual climb to the top.

• **Bad seats:** The $9.75 seats are on the north and south sides of the Arena, in end-zone sections 227-231 and 209-213. While there are better seats, given the ticket situation, this is probably what you'll be settling for if you're not a season ticket-holder.

• **Scalping:** Many scalpers frequent the Coliseum, starting about two hours before the game, but they must remain a certain distance from the building.

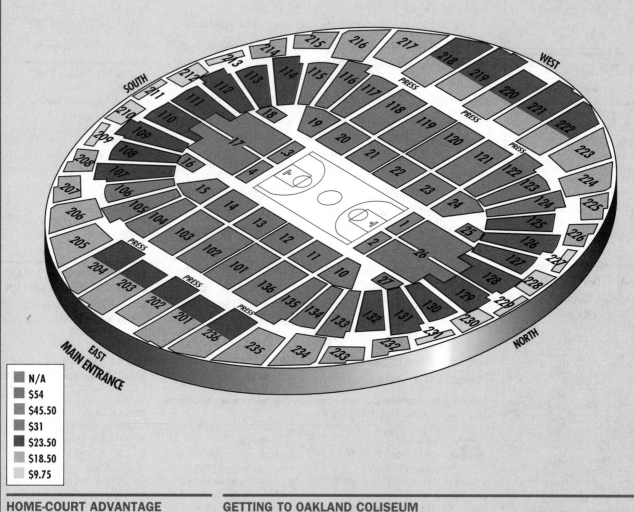

Legend:
- N/A
- $54
- $45.50
- $31
- $23.50
- $18.50
- $9.75

## HOME-COURT ADVANTAGE

On some nights, it can seem the fans actually following the game are outnumbered by those talking business or engaging in other nonbasketball pursuits. During stretches when the Warriors are playing well, of course, everyone pays more attention.

## GETTING TO OAKLAND COLISEUM

**Public transportation:** Take a Fremont BART train (eastbound from downtown San Francisco, southbound from downtown Oakland) to the Coliseum Station. Walk across the overpass and around the south side of the stadium to the Arena. Call (510) 465-2278 for more information.

**By car:** From downtown San Francisco, take I-80 East toward Oakland. Cross the Bay Bridge and take the 580/980 East exit toward Alameda/Downtown Oakland. Follow signs to downtown Oakland and I-880. Go 5 miles on 880 to the 66th Avenue/Oakland Coliseum exit. Cross over the freeway.

## TICKET INFORMATION
**Address:** 7000 Coliseum Way, Oakland, CA 94621
**Phone:** (510) 382-2305 or Bass at (510) 762-2277

**Hours:** Mon.-Fri. 8:30-5.
**Prices:** $54: sections 11-14 and 20-23. $45.50: sections 10, 15, 19, 24, 101-103, 118-121 and 136. $31: sections 16-18, 25-27, 104-106, 115-117, 122-124 and 133-135. $23.50: sections 107-114 and 125-132; lower half of sections 201-204, 218-222 and 236. $18.50: sections 201-208, 214-226 and 232-236. $9.75: sections 209-213 and 227-231.

# Orlando Arena

In the land of Disney, the Orlando Magic go to great lengths to supply fans at the "Orena"—how the locals refer to the Orlando Arena—with as much entertainment and glitz as possible. Between what one reporter described as "nuclear rock music" and the contests, giveaways, prizes and roving magicians, the Orena on game nights can often seem as much a circus tent as a basketball arena. The man behind this extravaganza is general manager Pat Williams, whom one local reporter describes as a "Bill Veeck disciple."

A big part of the off-court "Magic Act" is the mascot, Stuff the Magic Dragon. An energetic entertainer, he is successful at raising the noise level of the crowd. Stuff is joined by a freelance act, a fortysomething gentleman known as the "Fat Guy" for reasons that are apparent.

The other man responsible for the excitement is Shaquille O'Neal. Although some fans have suggested the Magic go too far with all of the nonbasketball amusements, the Orena's vibrant, carnival-like atmosphere seems to match the similar attention paid to Shaq wherever he goes. It is this ambience, coupled with the youthful character of the team, that make this an exciting place for an NBA game.

■ $60 ■ $45 ■ $35 ■ $30 ■ $25
■ $28 ■ $20 ■ $15 ■ $10

## HOT TIPS FOR VISITING FANS

### Parking
There are 4,200 parking spaces within a 1-block radius of Orlando Arena. The charge is $4. Access to the arena is fairly easy. To avoid delays after the game, you can park several blocks away in the downtown area, where there are approximately 6,000 spaces priced from $2 to $4. The team operates a free shuttle from downtown lots to the Arena. Church Street Station, a local entertainment complex, operates a free shuttle to and from the Arena.

### Media bites
**Radio:** WDBO (580 AM).
**TV:** WKCF (Channel 18) and Sunshine Network (cable). Chip Caray, the Magic's television play-by-play man, comes from the well-known broadcasting family.

### Cuisine
Popular items include tacos, burritos, *churros* and assorted Italian fare. A grill serves burgers, fries and chicken. Pizza Hut pizza and Subway sandwiches also are available. Imported and specialty beers including Molson, Sam Adams, Fosters and Heineken are on tap in each of the arena's four corners.

Church Street Station (407-422-2434) is about five minutes from the arena. This entertainment complex contains several restaurants and nightclubs. There is a $15.95 general charge covering admission to the clubs, but Magic fans can get in free by presenting their tickets. Church Street operates its own shuttle, which leaves approximately one hour before the game and departs from the Arena one hour after the final buzzer.

## LODGING NEAR THE ARENA
**Omni International**
400 W. Livingston St.
Orlando, FL 32801
(407) 843-6664/(800) 843-6664
Across the street from the arena.

**Harley Hotel of Orlando**
151 E. Washington St.
Orlando, FL 32801
(407) 841-3220/(800) 321-2323
8 blocks from the arena.

## GETTING TO ORLANDO ARENA
**Public transportation:** A free shuttle runs from various stops to the Arena entrance. Call (407) 841-8240 for more information.
**By car:** From airport, get on Semoran (I-436) and continue 4-5 miles to the East/West Expressway. Go west on the Expressway and connect to I-4; exit I-4 at Amelia Street. Turn left and the Arena is on the left.

## HOME-COURT ADVANTAGE
The decibel increase is magnified by the building's small size, which amplifies the roars from the crowd. The Orlando faithful's cheering has a very definite impact on the players, a young team driven as much by emotion as by talent.

## IN THE HOT SEATS

Since the Magic's debut in 1989, the team has become a hot ticket, selling out every game except two. With a basketball capacity of 15,291, the Arena is one of the smallest facilities in the NBA, but its size creates a certain closeness. This state-of-the-art building also has good sightlines and a large number of comfortable seats.

• **Good seats:** Corner sections, such as 226 and 227, have seats in the F range for $15 that offer good views at a decent price. The $10 seats, the G price, are in the end zones; they're good bargains, but the F seats are better.

**Scalping:** Scalpers can be found around the arena, although not in great numbers. Fans shouldn't expect to bargain down the price of a ticket very much—there are more than enough potential buyers for scalpers to get close to what they're asking.

---

## ARENA STATS
**Location:** 1 Magic Place, Orlando, FL 32801
**Opened:** Jan. 29, 1989
**Capacity:** 15,291
**Services for fans with disabilities:** Seating is available in sections 110–118 and 105–123, with a special entrance on the east side of the building.

## ARENA FIRSTS
**Regular-season game:** Nov. 4, 1989, 111–106 loss to the New Jersey Nets.
**Points scored:** Jerry Reynolds of Orlando.
**Overtime game:** Feb. 14, 1990, 135–129 over the Chicago Bulls.
**Playoff game:** April 28, 1994, 89–88 loss to the Indiana Pacers.

## TEAM NOTEBOOK
**Franchise history:** Orlando Magic, 1989–present.
**Rookie of the Year:** Shaquille O'Neal, 1992–93.

### TICKET INFORMATION
**Address:** 600 W. Amelia St. Orlando, FL 32801
**Phone:** (407) 649-BALL (2255) or TicketMaster at (407) 839-3900
**Hours:** Mon.-Fri. 10-5.

---

# The Spectrum

Philadelphians are well-known for their sports knowledge and their impatience. If the home team is losing, fans make their feelings clear by booing players during the game and venting their disappointment on the city's sports talk-radio programs afterward. Now the 76ers are the team on the hot seat. Fans are frustrated by losing seasons, unpopular trades and an ownership perceived as unresponsive.

This sense of disaffection has permeated the Spectrum. In a city where the Sixers rank fourth among the city's four major-league pro teams in terms of fan interest, poor play translates into a significant drop in support. But even when the team won its last championship, in 1983, the Sixers drew only 646,788 (a franchise record) to the Spectrum. Some ascribe this less-than-overwhelming support not only to lack of interest, but also to the popularity of such local collegiate basketball rivals as Penn, La Salle, Temple, St. Joseph and Villanova.

Fans were further turned off by their team's lengthy negotiations over a new arena, which included an attempt to move to nearby Camden, N.J. This plan, favored by the New Jersey governor, was torpedoed by his successor. Eventually, agreement was reached to build Spectrum 2 down the street from the original, on a site formerly occupied by JFK Stadium. The team hopes to move in for the 1996–97 season.

## HOT TIPS FOR VISITING FANS

**Parking**
Access to the Spectrum is very good, with on-site parking for approximately 10,000 cars at a cost of $4.50 per vehicle. Cars move fairly quickly after the game because the entrance to I-95 is just blocks away. There is also on-street parking next to the naval hospital on the west side of Broad Street, which runs past the Spectrum. However, there have been reports of broken windows in cars parked on this block.

**Media bites**
Radio: WIP (610 AM). TV: WPHL (Channel 17), and SportsChannel (cable). Team statistician Harvey Pollack is famous for his basketball knowledge.

**Cuisine**
Since this is Philadelphia, the Spectrum features such local favorites as pretzels with mustard and cheese steaks. If you want more variety, hot roast-beef and turkey sandwiches are offered while Italian hoagies are sold in the Deli Corner. More than 20 brands of beer are sold, including such popular local brews as Red Bell and Dock Street.

After the game, try Pat's Steaks (215-468-1546) for a slice of true Philly gastronomy. Open 24 hours and offering only counter service with several tables out front, Pat's has been serving up a variety of steak sandwiches since 1930. While the most popular selection is the mushroom cheese steak with onions, you can get pizza steak, steak and peppers, as well as roast pork and sausage. Ask for a "cheese wit," as the locals do, meaning a cheese steak with onions.

Melrose Diner (215-467-6644) is about 10 blocks north of the Spectrum. A favorite late-night haunt of Philadelphians since 1935, many local sports figures, including Dr. J, have been customers over the years.

## LODGING NEAR THE ARENA

**Sheraton Society Hill**
1 Dock St.
Philadelphia, PA 19106
(215) 238-6000/(800) 325-3535
7 miles from the arena.

**Franklin Plaza Hotel**
2 Franklin Plaza
Philadelphia, PA 19103
(215) 448-2942/(800)822-4200
6 miles from the arena.

## THE 76ERS AT THE SPECTRUM

**Jan. 12, 1968:** The 76ers pull down 100 rebounds during a 133–116 win over Baltimore. Wilt Chamberlain has 35.

**Jan. 25, 1970:** Philadelphia and San Diego combine to score 290 points; Philly wins 159–131.

**Nov. 8, 1978:** The 76ers beat New Jersey 137–133 in double overtime, but a protest is upheld and the game is replayed from 5:50 of the third quarter on March 23, 1979. The 76ers win the replay 123–117. In the meantime, Eric Money of the Nets and Harvey Catchings and Ralph Simpson of the 76ers had been involved in a trade, so these three players are possibly the only athletes in pro sports who have played for both teams in the same game.

**Dec. 5, 1979:** Darryl "Chocolate Thunder" Dawkins breaks his second backboard in 22 days, this time against San Antonio.

**May 18, 1983:** Philadelphia takes Game 5 of the Eastern Conference final 115–103 over the Milwaukee Bucks to advance to the championship series. The 76ers then sweep the Lakers to win the title.

# In the Hot Seats at the Spectrum

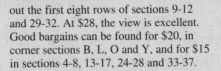

The Spectrum, which opened in 1967, is one of the oldest arenas in the NBA. Perhaps in part because of its age, fans have several complaints, including insufficient lighting and not enough restrooms and concession stands, resulting in long lines for each. The sightlines are generally good.

• **Good seats:** There's little trouble finding good tickets at the box office. Check out the first eight rows of sections 9-12 and 29-32. At $28, the view is excellent. Good bargains can be found for $20, in corner sections B, L, O and Y, and for $15 in sections 4-8, 13-17, 24-28 and 33-37.

• **Bad seats:** Upper-deck sections 41-80 demand a hike up a rather steep incline, and the sightlines aren't too good, either. These seats cost $6.

• **Scalping:** Several scalpers are usually in front of the Spectrum, near the subway station across the street and a block away, near a naval hospital. Scalpers often have a good variety of tickets. Since the Sixers have played poorly lately, sellouts are not an issue and scalpers might be willing to bargain the price down to get rid of the tickets they have.

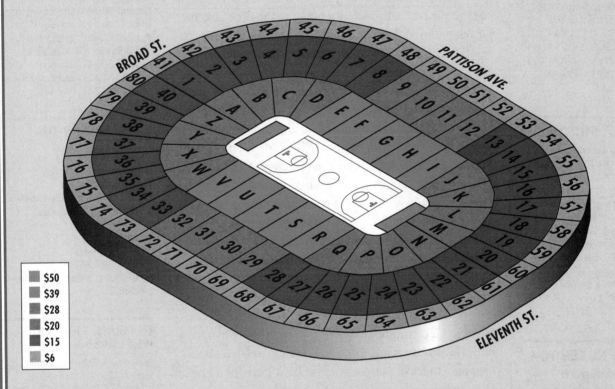

$50
$39
$28
$20
$15
$6

## HOME-COURT ADVANTAGE

Since Philly fans often boo the home team more than the visitors, there's almost an advantage for the visiting team when the Sixers play poorly. Some fans also have little patience for any entertainment-oriented attempts to liven things up when the team is losing. Philadelphia is just a tough town when the locals are not faring well. Fans lament the death of Dave Zinkoff, the team's famous public address announcer, who is honored with a large picture of a microphone hanging from the Spectrum's rafters. His distinctive voice and style—"Now entering the game, Julius Errrrrrrrrrving"—is sorely missed.

## GETTING TO THE SPECTRUM

**Public transportation:** Catch the Broad Street subway at 15th and Market southbound to the last stop, Broad and Pattison. The Spectrum is 1 block away. Call (215) 580-7800 for more information.

**By car:** From the north, take I-95 south to the Broad Street exit. Follow Broad Street to the first light (Zinkoff Boulevard) and turn right. The arena is on the left.

From the south, take I-95 north to the Broad Street exit. Follow Broad Street to the first light (Zinkoff Boulevard) and turn right. The arena is on the left.

From the west, take I-76 east. At Center City, stay to the right and follow signs for New Jersey and the Sports Complex heading toward the Walt Whitman Bridge. Take the Broad Street exit, No. 45 (Sports Complex), and make a right at the bottom of the ramp onto Broad Street. Follow Broad Street (stay to the far left) to Pattison Avenue. Follow Pattison Avenue. The Arena will be on the left.

From the east, take the Walt Whitman Bridge to I-76 west through the tolls. Continue on I-76 west to exit 46B (South 7th Street). Follow ramp and go straight through one traffic light and continue on to Pattison Avenue. Take a right onto Pattison Avenue and follow to 11th Street, the first traffic light. Turn left; the arena is on the right.

## TICKET INFORMATION

**Address:** Veterans Stadium, P.O. Box 25050, Philadelphia, PA 19147
**Phone:** (215) 336-3600 or TicketMaster at (215) 336-2000, (609) 665-2500, (302) 984-2000 or (717) 693-4100
**Hours:** Mon.-Fri. 9-5.
**Prices:** $50: behind the baskets. $39: sections E-I and R-V. $28: sections C, D, J, K, P, Q, W, X, and the lower halves of sections 9-12 and 29-32. $20: sections A, B, L, M, N, O, Y, Z, and the upper halves of sections 9-12 and 29-32. $15: sections 1-8, 13-28, and 33-40. $6: sections 41-80.

# America West Arena

Timing is everything. For the 1992–93 NBA season, the Suns got a new coach in Paul Westphal, a new star in Charles Barkley, and a new building in America West Arena. Even the players voted it the best arena in the league in a 1994 USA TODAY survey.

The Suns hired former player Alvan Adams to tour the finest arenas in the world; the best of their features were incorporated into the Arena's design. Everything is state of the art, built with not only the fans but also the players in mind. Unlike most NBA teams, the Suns practice where they play, in a gym built next to the locker rooms at the arena.

All the seats, even the less-expensive ones, have great sightlines. America West Arena is pretty, too, with the Suns' team colors—purple, orange and copper—everywhere. No expense has been spared on the sound system: The acoustics are superb, so you can clearly hear the public-address announcer, and the music rocks like a concert.

The downtown location is perfect. Crime is low, and plenty of police and security officers help with traffic and directions in and out of the Arena's 11 acres.

Get here early and stroll around. Before game time, bands play outside on the plaza, and Suns fans love to mingle and chat with tourists and visitors before tipoff. Owner Jerry Colangelo's office overlooks the Arena plaza so he can watch the people coming in. Wave to him. He'll wave back. Or, if you are too excited about the game to leave your seat, come back later for a guided tour—it's worth it.

## HOT TIPS FOR VISITING FANS

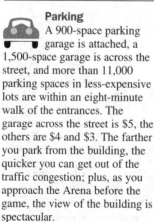

**Parking**
A 900-space parking garage is attached, a 1,500-space garage is across the street, and more than 11,000 parking spaces in less-expensive lots are within an eight-minute walk of the entrances. The garage across the street is $5, the others are $4 and $3. The farther you park from the building, the quicker you can get out of the traffic congestion; plus, as you approach the Arena before the game, the view of the building is spectacular.

**Media bites**
**Radio:** KTAR (620 AM).
**TV:** KUPT (Channel 45) and Dimension Cable (ASPN). All away games are televised on Channel 45 (with the exception of nationally televised games); cable has the home games. The Channel 45 games are simulcast on KTAR.

**Cuisine**
Popcorn, nachos, beer, soda, peanuts, ice cream—all the regular fare—are prepared on site. The service is excellent, too: If you end up buying more food than you can carry, attendants might help you tote it to your seat. The Copper Club is a 10,000-square-foot bar and restaurant with a view of the court on the second concourse level. It serves a buffet on event nights and is open to the public for lunch on weekdays. The first concourse has its own food court, featuring Whataburger, Subway, Pizza Hut and Miss Karen's Frozen Yogurt. It is also open for lunch on weekdays.

The place to go after the game is Majerle's Sports Grill (602-253-0118). Suns star Dan Majerle drops in after every game and mingles, as do most of the players from both teams. It's just up the street at 24 North Second Street, and stays open from 11 to 11 every day. The Arizona Center, at 455 North Third Street, has Sam's Cafe (602-252-3545), Lombardi's (602-257-8323) and Players (602-252-6222) eateries.

## THE SUNS AT AMERICA WEST ARENA

**Dec. 30, 1992:** The Suns stretch their home winning streak to 14 games when they top the Houston Rockets 133–110.

**March 23, 1993:** A brawl erupts during a game against the New York Knicks. Six players are ejected, and $159,500 in fines are levied. The Suns win 121–92.

**April 11, 1993:** The Suns beat the Utah Jazz 112–99, giving them the Pacific Division title.

**May 9, 1993:** After dropping the first two games of the series at home, the Suns come back to beat the Los Angeles Lakers in Game 5 of their playoff series.

**June 5, 1993:** Dan Majerle sets an NBA playoff record with eight three-pointers in an 120–114 win over the Seattle Super-Sonics in the fifth game of the Western Conference final.

# IN THE HOT SEATS AT AMERICA WEST ARENA

The arena seats 19,100 for basketball and has few bad seats. More than 16,000 season tickets have been sold, so getting a ticket can be tough. Try Dillard's ticket system by phone and plan ahead. You can use the on-site ticket office on the main plaza at the northwest entrance, too.

• **Good seats:** Sit opposite the benches, so you can watch the interplay on the sidelines between the coach and the players and see what's going on at the scorer's table. The row of seats on the floor is for the high rollers. The rest of the seats are on risers; you're going to feel close to the action no matter where you sit.

• **Bad seats:** If you can help it, don't sit right behind the basket at any level, because you're often looking through the backboard at a skewed perspective. You don't need to sit at center court, either.

You'll see all you need to see from any corner, as long as you aren't too low.

 **Scalping:** Scalping is legal in Phoenix but can't be done on Arena grounds, so sellers cross the street to do business. The markup is about $20 for a regular-season game. For playoffs and special games, fans pay $50 or more above face value for prime seats.

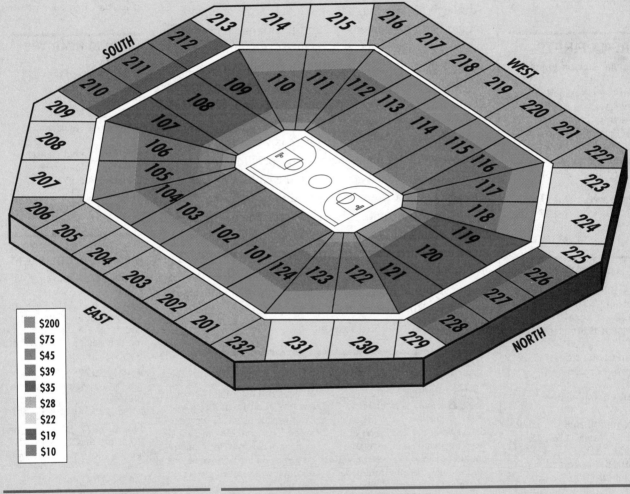

Legend (price levels):
- $200
- $75
- $45
- $39
- $35
- $28
- $22
- $19
- $10

## HOME-COURT ADVANTAGE

The luxury in which the Suns bask can be intimidating to visiting players. The fans are loud and loyal. Even the Suns' front-office personnel are notorious for sitting courtside and riding the refs. The fact that the Suns practice where they play makes a difference as well. They're completely at home here—and what a home! Going into the 1994–95 season, the Suns have won 71 of 82 games in their two seasons here.

## GETTING TO AMERICA WEST ARENA

**Public transportation:** Phoenix transit buses stop ½ block from the arena. The main bus station is across the street. Any bus coming into downtown passes near America West Arena. Call (602) 253-5000 for more information.

**By car:** From the north, take the I-17 Black Canyon Freeway to Washington Street. Go left onto Washington, then left on First Street. The Arena will be on the left.

From the south, take the I-10 Maricopa north to Jefferson Street. Go left onto Jefferson. The Arena will be on the right.

From the east, take the SR 360 Superstition Freeway , to the I-10 Mariciopa, heading north.

From the west, take the I-10 Papago to First Street. Go right onto First Street. The Arena will be on the right.

**TICKET INFORMATION**
**Address:** 201 E. Jefferson St., Phoenix, AZ 85004

**Phone:** (602) 379-SUNS (7867) or Dillard's at (602) 678-2222
**Hours:** Mon.-Fri. 9-5 and during events.

**Prices:** $200, $75, $45, $39, $35, $28, $22, $19, $10.

# Memorial Coliseum

## ARENA STATS

**Location:** 1401 N. Wheeler St., Portland, OR 97232
**Opened:** Oct. 16, 1970
**Capacity:** 12,888
**Services for fans with disabilities:** Seating available in the top rows of sections 5 and 7.

## ARENA FIRSTS

**Regular-season game:** Oct. 16, 1970, 115–112 over the Cleveland Cavaliers.
**Overtime game:** Dec. 20, 1970, 134–132 loss to the Philadelphia 76ers.
**Playoff game:** April 12, 1977, 96–83 over the Chicago Bulls.
**NBA Finals game:** April 29, 1977, 129–107 over the Philadelphia 76ers.

## TEAM NOTEBOOK

**Franchise history:** Portland Trail Blazers, 1970–present.
**Division titles:** 1977–78, 1990–91, 1991–92.
**Conference titles:** 1976–77, 1989–90, 1991–92.
**NBA championship:** 1976–77.
**Basketball Hall of Fame:** Jack Ramsay, 1992; Bill Walton, 1993.
**Retired numbers:** 1, Larry Weinberg (Rod Strickland now wears it with permission from Weinberg); 13, Dave Twardzik; 15, Larry Steele; 20, Maurice Lucas; 32, Bill Walton; 36, Lloyd Neal; 45, Geoff Petrie; 77, Jack Ramsay.

Only seven years after playing their first game, the Portland Trail Blazers won the NBA championship in 1977. "BlazerMania" swept this portion of the Pacific Northwest, and intimate Memorial Coliseum—at 12,888 seats, the smallest in the NBA—became a tough place for visiting teams because of the intense noise.

The Blazers rode this wave of enthusiasm through the '80s into the early '90s. But Portland's failure to win another title has diminished the excitement of area fans. Although it's still tough to find a ticket, the arena no longer has a high-intensity atmosphere; one longtime fan described the noise level in today's Coliseum as "intermittent showers." But it's still a great place to watch a game. Its size makes for good sightlines and an intimate, comfortable atmosphere in which fans can feel more a part of the game.

The time to see the Blazers here is winding down, however. The team and the city are spending $260 million to build a venue across from the Coliseum; the ultra-modern Oregon Arena is expected to open for the 1995–96 season, with full-service restaurants, three levels of seating and loads of comfort-oriented touches. (The cushioned seats, for example, will have more leg room than at the old arena and will be angled according to the sightline of the section they are in.) New arena or old, if the Blazers give the fans something to cheer about, the faithful will respond.

### HOT TIPS FOR VISITING FANS

**Parking**
Plenty is available in the area, with prices in the $10 range. The Blazers also have instituted an innovative shuttle-pass parking system, with free shuttles that run from parking facilities several blocks away to the Coliseum and the Arena. The cost in shuttle areas is $6, and parking/shuttle passes can be purchased in advance with your ticket. Expansion of the shuttle system is planned. Public transportation offers easy access.

**Media bites**
**Radio:** KEX (1190 AM).
**TV:** KGW-TV (Channel 8).
In the past 20 years, Bill Schonley has broadcast more than 2,000 Blazers games on radio and TV.

**Cuisine**
The Coliseum features an outdoor grill that offers burgers and ribs. Kielbasa, hot dogs and freshly made pizza are served inside. Two portable carts sell six to eight brews from local microbreweries. In the new Arena, the selection will be even greater: fans will be able to choose various ethnic items—including Mexican tostadas, Italian breadsticks and pasta in a cup, and Asian dumplings, spring rolls and wok foods—as well as deli-style sandwiches and a fry grill serving chicken, fish and onion rings.

Although the Coliseum has no restaurants, 90 minutes before game time, hamburger and pasta bars open in converted conference rooms at opposite ends of the building's event-floor level. The Oregon Arena will have two full-service lounge/restaurants in an annex built between the new building and the Coliseum.

Jake's Famous Crawfish (503-226-1419), a popular spot with Blazer fans, players and opponents, is about 10 minutes from the arena in a historic building with stained glass and paintings. When Jake's first opened, more than 100 years ago, the crawfish were raised in the basement. Champions American Sports Bar (503-274-2470) is in the Marriott Hotel across from the arena. Visiting teams often stay there, so players are frequent customers.

### LODGING NEAR THE ARENA

**Hotel Vintage Plaza**
422 S.W. Broadway
Portland, OR 97205
(503) 228-1212/(800) 243-0555
4 miles from the arena.

**Red Lion Lloyd Center**
1000 N.E. Multnomah St.
Portland, OR 97232
(503) 281-6111
6 blocks from the arena.

### THE TRAIL BLAZERS AT MEMORIAL COLISEUM

**March 16, 1973:** Geoff Petrie ties a team record with 51 points in a 141–128 win over the Houston Rockets. Petrie had set the original mark two months earlier, also against the Rockets.

**April 5, 1977:** 12,359 watch the Detroit Pistons play the Trail Blazers. It is the last Blazers home game to not sell out.

**June 5, 1977:** Bill Walton has 20 points and 23 rebounds, leading the Trail Blazers over the Philadelphia 76ers 109–107 to win the NBA championship. Walton is named Finals MVP.

**May 19, 1990:** A 108–105 overtime win over San Antonio puts the Blazers into the conference final versus the Phoenix Suns. Terry Porter scores 36 points.

**May 23, 1990:** Down by 18 at the half, Portland makes the second-biggest comeback in NBA playoff history and beats the Suns 108–107 in Game 2 of the conference final.

**Nov. 14, 1992:** Terry Porter sets an NBA record by shooting 7-for-7 from three-point range. He scores 40 points in a 130–116 win over the Golden State Warriors.

# IN THE HOT SEATS AT MEMORIAL COLISEUM

Approximately 95% of the Memorial Coliseum's 12,888 seats are sold to season ticketholders. Remaining tickets for individual games are put on sale two weeks before the season, and are gone by the end of the first day. No tickets are sold at the box office on game night.

For the new Oregon Arena, the Blazers are encouraging fans to buy their seats for six years to be insulated from price increases. This plan also benefits the Blazers since it gives them a relatively large infusion of revenue up front as a hedge against any future drop-off in interest. As with any new arena, however, interest will be high in the first few years after it opens, and tickets will likely become even harder to get on a game-by-game basis.

• **Good seats:** The Blazers have the longest-running streak of consecutive sell-outs in the NBA, surpassing 700, so good seats—any seats—are almost impossible to get. Check out corner sections 4-6, 9-11, 17-19 and 22-24 on the first level. For cen-ter-court, upper-deck seating with excellent views, try sections 51-54, 66-72 and 84-86. Even seats in the upper reaches of the Coliseum are relatively good because of the building's small size.

**Scalping:** The excitement generated by the new stadium should translate into a larger number of scalpers. Buyers shouldn't expect to bargain them down, since demand for tickets will certainly be greater than the supply.

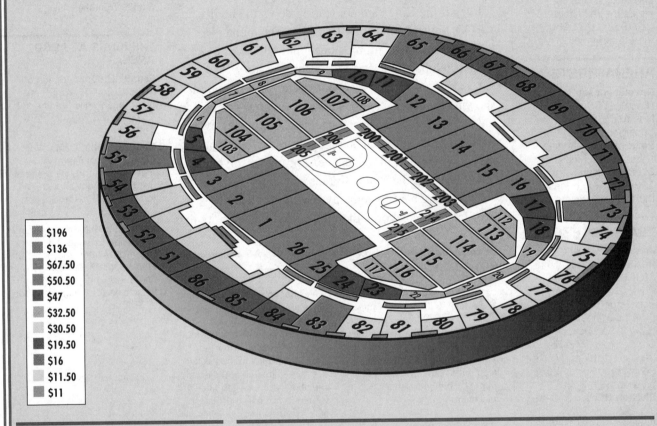

| | |
|---|---|
| ■ | $196 |
| ■ | $136 |
| ■ | $67.50 |
| ■ | $50.50 |
| ■ | $47 |
| ■ | $32.50 |
| □ | $30.50 |
| ■ | $19.50 |
| ■ | $16 |
| □ | $11.50 |
| ■ | $11 |

## HOME-COURT ADVANTAGE

The Blazers' home record has consistently been among the best in the NBA. Even though the fans are not as raucous as they once were, the Coliseum can still get loud if the team is playing well. While the glossy new Oregon Arena might resurrect the electric atmosphere that Portland games once had, some caution that the tremendous investment the Blazers are making in the Arena might not pay off if fans don't believe management is making similarly bold moves to reshape an aging team.

## GETTING TO MEMORIAL COLISEUM

**Public transportation:** No. 1 Greely and Vermont buses go to the Coliseum and Nos. 4, 5, 8, 10, 40, 41 and 77 buses go to the Coliseum Transit Center. Call (503) 238-RIDE for more information.

**By car:** From Portland International Airport, take Airport Drive to I-205 South. Take I-84 into Portland and exit at the Coliseum Exit. Go left onto Broadway 1 block then left onto Williams Avenue and into the parking lot.

## TICKET INFORMATION
**Address:** Memorial Coliseum Box Office, P.O. Box 4448, Portland, OR 97208.

**Phone:** (503) 797-9617
**Hours:** Mon.-Fri. 10-5:30 (phone orders 8:30-5:30).

**Prices:** $196, $136, $67.50, $50.50, $47, $32.50, $30.50, $19.50, $16, $11.50, $11

## ARENA STATS

**Location:** 1 Sports Parkway, Sacramento, CA 95834
**Opened:** Nov. 8, 1988
**Capacity:** 17,014
**Services for fans with disabilities:** Seating varies for each game. Call (916) 928-6900 for more information.

## ARENA FIRSTS

**Regular-season game:** Nov. 8, 1988, 97–75 loss to the Seattle SuperSonics.
**Points scored:** Reggie Theus of the Kings.
**Overtime game:** Dec. 1, 1988, 133–126 loss to the Denver Nuggets.

## TEAM NOTEBOOK

**Franchise history:** Rochester Royals, 1945–48 (NBL); Rochester Royals, '48–49 (BAA); Rochester Royals, '49–57 (NBA); Cincinnati Royals, '57–72; Kansas City-Omaha Kings, '72–75; Kansas City Kings, '75–85; Sacramento Kings, '85–present.
**Division titles:** 1948–49, '51–52, '78–79.
**Conference title:** 1950–51.
**NBA championship:** 1950–51.
**Basketball Hall of Fame:** B. Davies, 1969; J. Lucas, '79; O. Robertson, '79; J. Twyman, '82; N. Archibald, '91.
**Most Valuable Player:** O. Robertson, 1963–64.
**Rookies of the Year:** M. Stokes, 1955–56; O. Robertson, '60–61; J. Lucas, '63–64; P. Ford, '78–79.
**Retired numbers:** 1, N. Archibald; 6, Sixth Man (the fans); 11, B. Davies; 12, M. Stokes; 14, O. Robertson; 27, J. Twyman; 44, S. Lacey.

# ARCO Arena

Sacramento is considered the gateway to California's gold country, and while the city's resident NBA franchise has not struck gold on the court, it certainly has at the box office. Despite no winning seasons since moving from Kansas City in 1985, the Kings have sold out ARCO Arena for every game since it opened in 1988, the third-longest sellout streak in the league, behind Portland's and Boston's. This success is not surprising, considering the Kings are the only game in town in one of the NBA's smallest markets.

Even if the Kings are not tearing down the hoops, ARCO Arena does its best to please. The arena is a large, tan rectangle sitting alone amid 105 acres of largely undeveloped land. Inside, it's another story. As fans enter, they are greeted by countless television monitors showing the Kings' in-house pregame show—unique in the NBA. Once the game starts, the crowd takes over. ARCO has a reputation among players for being one of the loudest arenas in the league, a prime reason being wood floors in the stands so fans can stomp their feet.

Tickets are hard to come by now, and if the Kings ever make the playoffs, they'll be worth much more than their weight in gold.

## HOT TIPS FOR VISITING FANS

**Parking**
ARCO Arena is surrounded by a spacious, well-lighted lot with spaces for 12,000 cars. Cost is $5. The Kings also make an effort to keep traffic moving after the game, keeping waiting time to a minimum.

**Media bites**
**Radio:** KFBK (1530 AM—English), KRCX (1110 AM—Spanish).
**TV:** KFBK, Channel 31.

**Cuisine**
The Kings recently upgraded their concessions. Besides the standard fare, ARCO offers such options as Mexican and Italian cuisine, barbecued beef and the cheddar dog—a fan favorite consisting of a hot dog baked with cheese inside, surrounded by bagel-like dough. ARCO also features a Java City concessionaire that sells specialty coffees.

The Skyline Club, a buffet restaurant in the south corner above sections 202 and 203,

serves hot entrees such as prime rib. The Club opens at 5:30, one hour before the Arena gates open, for fans with a ticket to that night's game. After the game, fans flock to the Locker Room, a nightclub at the north end above sections 214 and 215. Besides a full bar, it offers make-your-own sandwiches for $8. The Locker Room is also open before the game. Players have been known to stop by.

About 15 minutes south is America Live! a multi-entertainment complex containing six nightclubs and two restaurants. The Sports City Cafe (916-447-4600) has a varied menu featuring Louisiana crab cakes, Cornish game hen and an extensive selection of California wines. Next door, the Original Sports Bar not only has the obligatory sports memorabilia and big-screen televisions, but pool tables, a caged basketball court and a video arcade as well. America Live! also includes the Gatlin Brothers Music City Grille (916-447-4500), which showcases local country bands.

## LODGING NEAR THE ARENA

**Hyatt Regency Sacramento**
1209 L St.
Sacramento, CA 95814
(916) 443-1234/(800) 233-1234
10 miles from the arena.

**Courtyard by Marriott-Natomas**
2101 River Plaza Dr.
Sacramento, CA 95833
(916) 922-1120/(800) 443-6000
6 miles from the arena.

## THE KINGS AT ARCO ARENA

**Feb. 9, 1989:** Sacramento makes 16 of 31 from three-point range while beating the Golden State Warriors 142–117.

**Dec. 27, 1989:** Danny Ainge tries for revenge against his former team, but his nine points in overtime are not enough and the Kings fall to the Boston Celtics 115–112.

**Dec. 29, 1992:** The Kings beat the Dallas Mavericks 139–81. Four nights later, they beat the Philadelphia 76ers 154–98, setting a record for the largest back-to-back margins of victory in NBA history.

# IN THE HOT SEATS AT ARCO ARENA

ARCO was built primarily for basket-ball, so the sightlines are excellent no matter where you sit. Although the best seats have already been purchased by season ticketholders, the remaining ones, ranging in price from $20 to $8, are sold on a game-by-game basis.

The season-ticket base is 14,500. Tickets for individual games are sold during the first week of October. Choice games sell out quickly. Remaining tickets can often be had on game night. These are mainly for seats in the upper deck, although you can buy tickets for scattered single seats elsewhere in the arena.

**Scalping:** The paucity of scalpers is due as much to ARCO Arena's isolated location as to the ordinance prohibiting scalping on the grounds. Local fans in search of the best seats usually consult the newspaper for ads offering tickets.

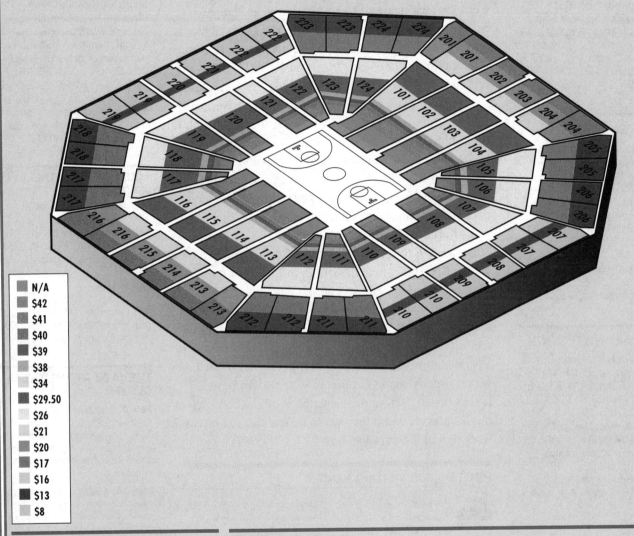

**Legend:**
- N/A
- $42
- $41
- $40
- $39
- $38
- $34
- $29.50
- $26
- $21
- $20
- $17
- $16
- $13
- $8

## HOME-COURT ADVANTAGE

Being a loud and loyal fan base, the Sacramento crowds make their presence felt when the Kings are holding court. The team encourages fans not only with the wooden floor, but also with things like the "Fan-O-Meter" next to the main scoreboard hanging over center court. Its lights are tuned to the amount of noise the fans make, and if the decibels light the Fan-O-Meter all the way to the top, it "explodes" into a multicolored spelling of the team's name.

## GETTING TO ARCO

**Public transportation:** There is no way to reach the Arco Arena on public transportation.

**By car:** From the north or south, I-5 to the Del Paso Road exit. The arena will be visible, so follow signs.

From the east or west, I-80 or U.S. 50 to I-5, then proceed as above.

## TICKET INFORMATION
**Address:** 1 Sports Parkway, Sacramento, CA 95834

**Phone:** (916) 928-6900 or BassCharge at (916) 923-BASS
**Hours:** Mon.-Fri.10-6, Sat. 12-5.

**Prices:** $42, $41, $40, $39, $38, $34, $29.50, $26, $21, $20, $17, $16, $13, $8.

# Delta Center

Salt Lake City is nestled between the Great Salt Lake and its adjacent desert, to the west, and the Wasatch National Forest and Uinta Mountains, to the east. The Utah Jazz are the beneficiaries of the scenic beauty surrounding this community, because they play in the heart of it all. Located in downtown Salt Lake City, the Delta Center is near renowned attractions such as Temple Square and the Mormon Tabernacle. The Delta Center is about 2 blocks from the Salt Palace, the team's first home after it moved from New Orleans in 1979. The Jazz played their home games there until the 1991–92 season.

The Delta Center is a large concrete-and-silver, cube-like structure with plenty of windows; from the front, it looks more like an imposing office building than the home of an NBA team. One way to make sure you're at the home of the Jazz is to look in the parking lot for a distinctive 18-wheel truck, painted with various depictions of Western scenery, owned by Jazz All-Star forward Karl "the Mailman" Malone.

Because of the size of Salt Lake City—the population is about 160,000—and the strong influence of the Mormon religion here, you are less likely to find alcohol-induced rowdyness or obnoxious fan behavior than in other NBA arenas. Still, while the Jazz faithful tend to be less vocal than fans in larger cities, the team has one fan who likes to get very involved. Owner Larry Miller usually sits in the first row, across from his team's bench. Before the game, he is on the court, greeting his players while they warm up and dishing out high fives during the introductions.

## HOT TIPS FOR VISITING FANS

**Parking**
Abundant in the area surrounding the Delta Center, which has no on-site facility. Numerous private lots and garages are available that charge between $3 and $6. Plenty of on-street parking can be found. The surrounding neighborhood is safe, so don't be turned off by strolling to and from the game. A consortium of 17 area businesses offers another parking alternative: They run free shuttle buses from their establishments to the Delta Center. The shuttles begin 90 minutes before the game and continue for approximately one hour afterward. Call Chris Patterson at

Market Street Grill (801-322-4668) for more information.

**Media bites**
**Radio:** KISN (570 AM).
**TV:** KJZZ (Channel 14) and Prime Sports Network on cable.

**Cuisine**
The concessions are run by the Marriott Corporation. Offerings include such brand-name items as Pizza Hut pizza, Russell hand-dipped ice cream and Golden Swirl frozen yogurt, which is sold from four portable carts. On the plaza level in quad one in the western corner of the building, a

food court offers such items as chef and garden salads, baked potatoes with several toppings, and kosher hot dogs.

Squatter's Pub Brewery (801-363-BREW) is only a short distance from the Delta Center. Located in the old Boston Hotel, Squatter's brews its own beer, including six homemade ales. You can watch the brewmasters at work from the restaurant, which serves a diverse menu. D.B. Cooper's (801-532-6105) is a restaurant and nightclub; listen to live jazz, blues or rock while dining on such popular items from the scaled-down menu as Utah smoked trout and fresh fish.

## LODGING NEAR THE ARENA

**Salt Lake City Marriott**
75 W. South Temple
Salt Lake City, UT 84101
(801) 531-0800/(800) 345-4755.
4 blocks from the arena.

**Doubletree**
215 W. South Temple
Salt Lake City, UT 84101
(801) 531-7500/(800) 553-0075.
Across the street from the arena.

## THE JAZZ AT THE DELTA CENTER

**Feb. 3, 1992:** The Jazz play their longest game ever, a 126–123 triple-overtime win against the Chicago Bulls. The game lasts three hours and 11 minutes.

**May 14, 1992:** Utah beats the Seattle SuperSonics 111–100 to advance to its first Western Conference final.

**May 24, 1992:** Karl Malone's 33 points help the Jazz beat the Portland Trail Blazers 121–112 in Game 4, tying the Western Conference final at two games apiece. Portland goes on to win the series, four games to two.

**Feb. 21, 1993:** John Stockton and Karl Malone lead the West to a 135–133 overtime win over the East in the All-Star Game, played at the Delta Center. Stockton and Malone are co-MVPs.

# In the Hot Seats at the Delta Center

Salt Lake City has been quite supportive of its NBA franchise. Since the Delta Center opened, only four games have not sold out. Utah has approximately 14,500 season ticketholders. Single-game tickets are sold during mid-October. During the season, with the exception of a handful of games against Phoenix and Seattle that sell out quickly, remaining tickets are sold one week before the game. All are for upper-deck seating only. Any unsold tickets are available at the box office on game night.

• **Bad seats:** Because the arena was built primarily for basketball, it has good sight-lines. Still, the $9 seats that reach around the top five rows of the corner and end sections are a fair distance from the court.

**Scalping:** Although it's legal in Salt Lake City, the team does not allow scalping on the grounds of the Delta Center. It takes place on the neighborhood streets along the approach to the arena. Some might have lower-deck seats available that they bought from season ticketholders.

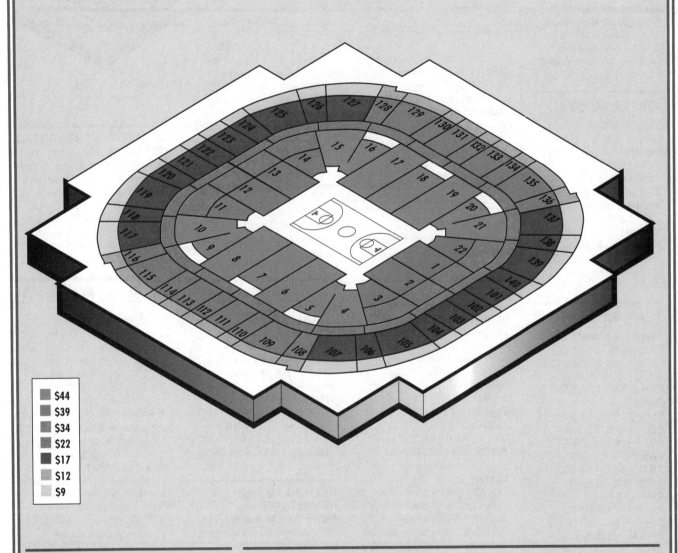

- $44
- $39
- $34
- $22
- $17
- $12
- $9

## HOME-COURT ADVANTAGE

Don't get the idea that just because Jazz fans have a reputation for being better behaved than some of their NBA brethren, they sit on their hands all night. The Jazz keep things lively with exciting play on the court and entertainment provided on a JumboTron scoreboard/video system. The energetic atmosphere has rubbed off on the players, who have won nearly 80% of their home games since the early '90s.

## GETTING TO THE DELTA CENTER

**Public transportation:** UTA buses stop within a block of the Delta Center. Call (801) 287-4636 for more information.

**By car:** From the north or south, take I-15 to the 6th South Street exit. Stay in the right-hand lane. After approximately five blocks, take the Third West Street exit, which will circle and head north on Third West. Follow Third West for about a mile to the arena on your right.

**TICKET INFORMATION**
**Address:** 301 W. South Temple, Salt Lake City, UT 84101
**Phone:** (801) 325-7328 or (801) 355-DUNK

**Hours:** Mon.-Fri. 9-6.
**Prices:** $44, $39, $34, $22, $17, $12, $9.

# Alamodome

## ARENA STATS

**Location:** 100 Montana St., San Antonio, TX 78203
**Opened:** May 15, 1993
**Capacity:** 21,372
**Services for fans with disabilities:** About 300 wheelchair positions are located next to fixed seats for companions.

## ARENA FIRSTS

**Regular-season game:** Nov. 5, 1993, 91–85 over the Golden State Warriors.
**Points scored:** David Robinson of the Spurs.
**Overtime game:** Dec. 8, 1993, 109–107 loss to the Seattle SuperSonics.
**Playoff game:** April 28, 1994, 106–89 over the Utah Jazz.

## TEAM NOTEBOOK

**Franchise history:** Dallas Chaparrals, 1967–70 (ABA); Texas Chaparrals, 1970–71 (ABA); Dallas Chaparrals, 1971–73 (ABA); San Antonio Spurs, 1973–76 (ABA); San Antonio Spurs, 1976–present (NBA).
**Division titles:** 1977–78, 1978–79, 1980–81, 1982–83, 1989–90, 1990–91.
**Rookie of the Year:** David Robinson, 1990.
**Retired numbers:** 13, James Silas; 44, George Gervin.

## TICKET INFORMATION

**Address:** 100 Montana St., San Antonio, TX 78203
**Phone:** (210) 554-7787
**Hours:** Mon.-Fri. 9-5.

San Antonio's rich history is a source of civic pride, and even with NBA basketball, the city misses no opportunity to evoke its storied past: The Spurs, therefore, play in the Alamodome. The original Alamo, only a short distance from the A-Dome, still stands in tribute to the dashing heroes of the frontier. While Davy Crockett and Jim Bowie would have been too short to play pro ball, the Spurs have found an equally colorful team to wage war on the court, led by "the Admiral," David Robinson. Should the energy level lag a bit, the team has another piece of Southwestern heritage on call: Coyote, a Native American trickster figure, stirs up the crowd as the Spurs' mascot.

Viewing the Alamodome from outside, however, the name appears to be a misnomer. Not only (as you might suspect) does the stadium look nothing like the Alamo, it has no conventional dome. Instead, the Spurs' new home features a slightly angled roof that is suspended from cables and attached to four enormous concrete pillars. Inside, the building is equally unusual: Although the Alamodome was built to house the Spurs, it can also host football games. When the Spurs play, the unused sections of the stadium are blocked off by two large blue curtains that hang perpendicular to each other.

## HOT TIPS FOR VISITING FANS

### Parking

The Alamodome has no on-site general parking. However, numerous indoor and outdoor lots, priced from $4 to $7, are nearby; the neighborhood is safe. The most convenient place to park is the Rivercenter Mall garage, across the street. If you have your ticket validated at the mall, you'll get two hours off.

### Media bites

**Radio:** WOAI (1200 AM—English), KCOR (1350 AM—Spanish).
**TV:** KSAT (Channel 12) and KABB (Channel 29).

### Cuisine

The Alamodome features several items from local restaurants, including Whataburger and Rosario's fajitas, tacos and hot-and-spicy nachos. The corn dogs and spicy sausages also are popular. For a healthy nonmeat alternative, try the Caesar salad or the veggie plate.

After the game, head north to the heart of downtown and San Antonio's Riverwalk. Here you will find a large number of good restaurants. Champions Sports Bar (210-226-7171) has 16 TV monitors and two satellite dishes, and serves Tex-Mex food. Rio Cantina (210-226-846) offers patio seating along the river and an extensive menu of well-prepared Mexican dishes. The Zuni

Grill (210-227-0864), next to Rio, serves imaginative Southwestern fare.

### LODGING NEAR THE ARENA

**Airport Hilton**
611 N.W. Loop 410
San Antonio, TX 78216
(210) 340-6060/(800) HILTONS
10 miles from the arena.

**Marriott Riverwalk**
711 E. Riverwalk
San Antonio, TX 78205
(210) 224-4555/(800) 228-9290
Across the bridge from the arena.

### GETTING TO THE ALAMODOME

**Public transportation:** VIA Metropolitan Transit offers transportation options to the Alamodome, including Park & Ride, shuttle service, and VIAtrans service for the mobility impaired. For more information, call VIAinfo at (210) 227-2020.
**By car:** From San Antonio International Airport, take Highway 281 South for approximately 7 miles, exit at Durango, take the turnaround and go south on the access road that runs along the west side of the Dome.

■ N/A ■ $31 ■ $22 ■ $17
■ $10 ■ $8 ■ $5

## HOME-COURT ADVANTAGE

San Antonio fans have responded well to the Alamodome, in part because the Spurs are the only major-league pro sport in town. In 1993–94, the Spurs ranked second in the NBA in attendance, but the Alamodome's size tends to diffuse the noise those fans generate.

## IN THE HOT SEATS

The Spurs season-ticket base is approximately 13,000. Single-game tickets go on sale in early October. Given the arena's size, tickets often are available on game nights for all locations.

• **Good seats:** Because this arena was built with basketball in mind, the vast majority of seats are good ones, certainly better than at HemisFair Arena. When popular opponents come to town and on certain weekends, the Spurs sometimes expand the Alamodome's capacity to 35,000 by opening the upper level. During the 1993–94 season, the upper deck was opened for 10 games. The team plans to increase the number of games with upper-deck seating in sections 301-310 and 336-348 in forthcoming seasons. Upper-deck seats go for only $8 and $5, the latter being arguably the best buy in the NBA.

**Scalping:** Ticket scalping is legal off the Alamodome's grounds. When the top teams play the Spurs, scalpers can readily be found the farther a buyer is from the Dome.

# Tacoma Dome

## ARENA STATS

**Location:** 2727 E. D St., Tacoma, WA 98421
**Opened:** April 21, 1983
**Capacity:** 16,225
**Services for fans with disabilities:** Seating available in sections 2A and 6A-9A.

## TEAM NOTEBOOK

**Franchise history:** Seattle SuperSonics, 1967–present.
**Division title:** 1978–79, 1993–94.
**Conference titles:** 1977–78, 1978–79.
**NBA championship:** 1978–79.
**Basketball Hall of Fame:** Lenny Wilkens, 1988.
**Retired Numbers:** 19, Lenny Wilkens; 32, Fred Brown; 43, Jack Sikma.

A lthough the Seattle SuperSonics aren't playing their home games in Seattle in the 1994–95 season, they are scheduled to return to an enlarged, renovated Seattle Center Coliseum for the 1995–96 season. In the meantime, their home is the Tacoma Dome.

Renovation of the Coliseum, one of the smallest and most outdated buildings in the league, began the day after the Sonics were eliminated from the 1994 playoffs. Capacity of the new facility will be increased and luxury suites will be added. The renovation is expected to take only a year. Because it's on the same site as the old building, much of the old infrastructure can be retained.

The team wanted to remain in Seattle during construction, but the Kingdome—their home a few years ago—was unavailable much of the season, and the Sonics wanted to play all 41 regular-season home games in the same arena. They played at the Tacoma Dome (about 30 miles south) three times during the 1990–91 season when there was a conflict with dates at the Coliseum and the Kingdome.

The downtown Tacoma Dome is well-located and has a unique wooden roof. Built in 1983, it also houses the Tacoma Rockies of the Western Hockey League, was host of the 1987 U.S. Figure Skating Championships, held the NCAA Women's Final Four in 1988 and 1989, and was the venue for hockey, figure skating and gymnastics during the 1990 Goodwill Games. Although Tacoma has vowed to support the team as if it were its own, the club will keep its Seattle name.

The Sonics are pleased that the Coliseum will remain in the Seattle Center, which features an amusement park, museums, a food court, the civic center, the famed Space Needle, ample on-site parking and many good restaurants nearby. It's on the edge of downtown and a couple of blocks from theaters and picturesque Union Bay.

**Cuisine**
The full-service Gallery Restaurant in the Tacoma Dome is open to the public before and after games. The Courtside Club serves season ticketholders, and the 3-pt Club is for the general public. Concessions stands serve the usual hot dogs and popcorn, but many name-brand products like TCBY yogurt and beers from such microbreweries as Red Hook are available.

The attractive, open-air Freight House Mall is next door. Downtown is a half mile away, and restaurant owners are planning a shuttle service to the Tacoma Dome.

## LODGING NEAR THE ARENA

**La Cuerta**
1425 E. 27th St.
Tacoma, WA 98421
(206) 383-5566
¼ mile from the arena.

**Ramada Inn**
2611 E. E St.
Tacoma, WA 98421
(206) 572-7272
About 1 block from the arena.

---

## HOT TIPS FOR VISITING FANS

**Parking**
Tacoma Dome parking is better than at the Seattle Coliseum, with on-site parking for 2,800 cars, nearby private lots and free on-street parking a couple of blocks away. The Stadium lots cost $5; season ticketholders get VIP parking included in their ticket prices. The other lots cost about $2.50.

**Media bites**
**Radio:** KJR (950 AM).
**TV:** KSTW-TV (Channel 11), Cable Prime Sports Network. Kevin Calabro does play-by-play on all 82 radio games and all televised games. The team will have a new color man, because former analyst Wally Walker was named Sonics interim general manager.

# IN THE HOT SEATS AT TACOMA DOME

Seattle fans who want to keep their priority seats for the 1995–96 season must maintain their season tickets while the team is in Tacoma. Sonics season ticketholders who commit themselves to buying 1995–96 season tickets get priority seating at Tacoma Dome.

Because the Tacoma Dome is a large multipurpose building—it seats more than 16,000 for basketball—seats are not the best. But improvements have been made to lure the Sonics. The most expensive floor seats have been put on risers, so you won't have to look at the backs of the heads of the people seated in front of you.

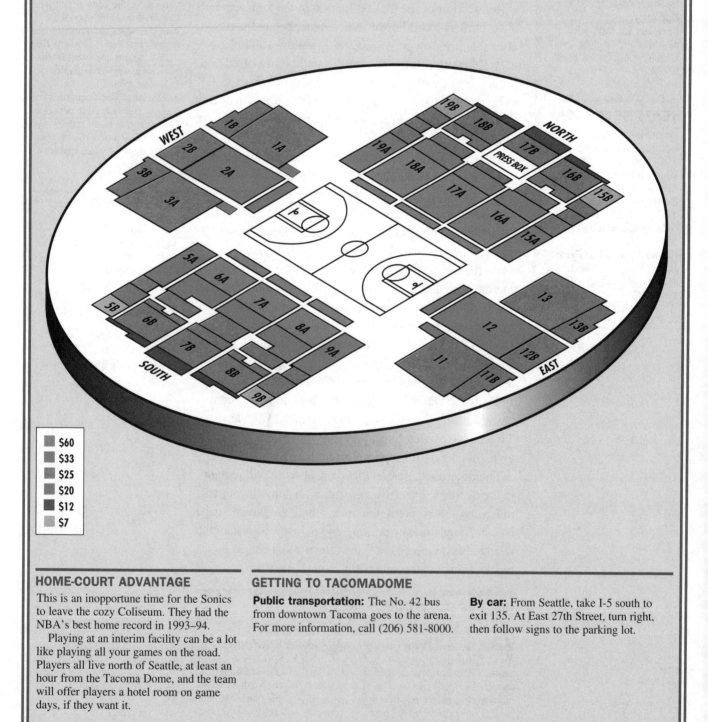

| | |
|---|---|
| ■ | $60 |
| ■ | $33 |
| ■ | $25 |
| ■ | $20 |
| ■ | $12 |
| ■ | $7 |

## HOME-COURT ADVANTAGE

This is an inopportune time for the Sonics to leave the cozy Coliseum. They had the NBA's best home record in 1993–94.

Playing at an interim facility can be a lot like playing all your games on the road. Players all live north of Seattle, at least an hour from the Tacoma Dome, and the team will offer players a hotel room on game days, if they want it.

## GETTING TO TACOMADOME

**Public transportation:** The No. 42 bus from downtown Tacoma goes to the arena. For more information, call (206) 581-8000.

**By car:** From Seattle, take I-5 south to exit 135. At East 27th Street, turn right, then follow signs to the parking lot.

## TICKET INFORMATION
**Address:** 2727 E. D. St., Tacoma, WA 98421

**Phone:** (206) 283-3865 or TicketMaster at (206) 628-0888
**Hours:** Mon.-Fri. 10-5, Sat. 10-2.

**Prices:** $60, $33, $25, $20, $12, $7.

**Bullets** ™

## ARENA STATS

**Location:** 1 Harry S. Truman Dr., Landover, MD 20785
**Opened:** Dec. 2, 1973
**Capacity:** 18,756
**Services for fans with disabilities:** Seating available on the concourse level between the red and blue sections.

## ARENA FIRSTS

**Regular-season game:** Dec. 2, 1973, 98–96 over the Seattle SuperSonics.
**Overtime game:** Nov. 8, 1975, 99–95 loss to the Milwaukee Bucks.
**Playoff game:** March 31, 1974, 98–87 over the New York Knicks.
**NBA Finals game:** May 18, 1975, 101–95 loss to the Golden State Warriors.

## TEAM NOTEBOOK

**Franchise history:** Chicago Packers, 1961–62; Chicago Zephyrs, 1962–63; Baltimore Bullets, 1963–73; Capital Bullets, 1973–74; Washington Bullets, 1974–present.
**Division titles:** 1968–69, 1970–71, 1971–72, 1972–73, 1973–74, 1974–75, 1978–79.
**Conference titles:** 1970–71, 1974–75, 1977–78, 1978–79.
**NBA championship:** 1977–78.
**Basketball Hall of Fame:** Wes Unseld, 1987; Earl Monroe, 1989; Elvin Hayes, 1989.
**Retired Numbers:** 11, Elvin Hayes; 25, Gus Johnson; 41, Wes Unseld.

# USAir Arena

A look at the souvenir apparel worn by residents of Washington, D.C., tells a lot about what a visit to USAir Arena is like. Redskins paraphernalia is followed in popularity by those of the Baltimore Orioles and Georgetown, George Washington and Howard universities. Also seen are a fair number of Washington Capitals T-shirts. But a Bullets hat or T-shirt is the hardest to find. The local NBA team just does not have a loyal following among D.C. sports fans, and USAir Arena is far from a mecca for local sports.

The Arena is on the eastern edge of the Capital Beltway, and many fans express as much frustration with the location of the Bullets' home as they do with the team's lackluster play. USAir Arena has other problems, as well: Besides being one of the dimmer facilities in the NBA, it's not particularly intimate. Given the building's shape, fans not sitting at courtside feel removed from the action. The team has started to explore the possibility of building a downtown arena.

Although Bullets fans are not known for being boisterous, one season ticketholder has a well-deserved reputation around the NBA for being uniquely raucous. Robin Ficker, a local attorney, sits behind the visitors' bench and regularly heckles opposing players. Even though he's ostensibly helping the Bullets, fans quickly tire of his act. In response to complaints about Ficker and other similar individuals, the NBA instituted a rule that if a referee feels a fan is interfering with a team's huddle, he tells the offender to cease and desist. As with a player who gets a second technical foul, the offensive fan can be removed from the building if admonished again.

## HOT TIPS FOR VISITING FANS

**Parking**
USAir Arena is surrounded by a large parking area with spaces for approximately 7,000 cars. The cost is $6. No on-street parking is available. The wait to get out of the lot after the game can be lengthy—all cars must funnel out of one location in order to reach the access road for the Beltway.

**Media bites**
**Radio:** WTEM (570 AM).
**TV:** WDCA (Channel 20), and Home Team Sports on cable. Phil Chenier, who averaged nearly 18 points a game in nine years with the Bullets, including their championship season in 1978, is a commentator on cable broadcasts.

**Cuisine**
Among the most popular items here are the colossal pretzels, twice as large as the standard size, and the kosher hot dogs, which you can get topped with onions, chili, and hot peppers. Freshly made 8-inch pepperoni and cheese pizzas are available too, along with burgers and cheese steaks. A variety of imported bottled beers and cocktails are also sold.

The Showcase Pub and Eatery, open two hours before the game, is a cafeteria-style restaurant. The grilled burgers and onion rings are better than those at the concessions stands, and it has a salad bar. Fans can watch the game on one of several television screens.

Less than five minutes from the Arena is Chadwicks (301-808-0200), part of a local chain that prides itself on having the atmosphere of a neighborhood saloon. Try the crab cakes or Kentucky-style London broil, or design your own burger. Several draft beers are available, including Chadwicks Ale, a microbrew. T.G.I. Friday's (301-345-2503), is about 10 minutes away in Greenbelt. Wash down a plate of blackened-chicken alfredo, ribs or steak with one of the more than 40 types of beer, including Killian's and Foster's on tap. Players are occasional customers at both places.

## LODGING NEAR THE ARENA

**The Greenbelt Marriott**
6400 Ivy Lane
Greenbelt, MD 20770
(301) 441-3700/(800) 228-9290
15 miles from the arena.

**Best Western Capital Beltway**
5910 Princess Garden Parkway
Lanham, MD 20706
(301) 459-1000/(800) 528-1234
5 miles from the arena.

## THE BULLETS AT USAIR ARENA

**April 6, 1975:** Wes Unseld gets 30 rebounds in a 119–103 win over the New Orleans Jazz.

**May 11, 1975:** The Bullets beat the Boston Celtics 98–92, advancing to the championship series against the Golden State Warriors.

**June 4, 1978:** The Bullets win Game 6 of the championship series 117–82 over the Seattle SuperSonics. Three days later Washington clinches the title by topping the Sonics in Seattle.

**Dec. 29, 1990:** Bernard King scores 52 points—a USAir Arena record—as the Bullets crush the Denver Nuggets 161–133. The 161 points also set an Arena record.

# IN THE HOT SEATS AT USAIR ARENA

Despite its drawbacks, USAir Arena has many fine seats. Check out sections 105-109 and 119-123 on the lower level. The center-court view from these seats is excellent, and the price ($27.50) compares favorably to the going rate around the NBA. Sections 203-209, 217 and 219-223 offer good views as well. These seats, at $22, are perhaps the best bargain. Recently, the Bullets have sold out about half of their home games, mostly against the better teams in the league.

• **Bad seats:** The "cheap seats," costing $11, are at the top of the upper-deck center-court sections. Along with seats behind the baskets ($22)—sections 201, 211-216 and 225-228—these can seem far away. Also avoid sections 104, 110, 116 and 124, because you must sit at a relatively awk-ward angle to follow the game.

 **Scalping:** Scalpers begin their approach to fans in the parking lot. But unless those fans are trying to get in to see the Knicks, the Bulls, the Suns or the like, they would probably do just as well at the box office.

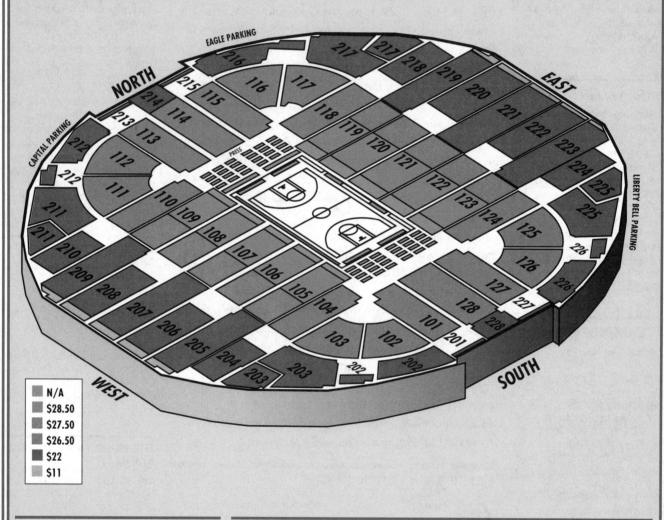

Legend:
- N/A
- $28.50
- $27.50
- $26.50
- $22
- $11

## HOME-COURT ADVANTAGE

Although Washington crowds know their basketball, this does not translate into fervent support. More often than not, fans come to the USAir Arena to see the visiting team from their former hometown or to root for such former local heroes as Patrick Ewing, Dikembe Mutombo and Alonzo Mourning, all of whom played college hoops for Georgetown in this very building.

## GETTING TO USAIR ARENA

**Public transportation:** USAir Arena cannot be reached by public transportation.

**By car:** From downtown Washington, go east on New York Avenue (Route 50). About 5 miles outside of Washington, it intersects with the Capital Beltway. Go south to exit 15A or 17A. The Arena is visible from the highway.

From Baltimore, take the Baltimore-Washington Parkway or I-95 to the Beltway south, to exit 15A or 17A.

## TICKET INFORMATION
**Address:** 1 Harry S. Truman Dr., Landover, MD 20785
**Phone:** (301) NBA-DUNK or TicketMaster at (202) 432-SEAT

**Hours:** Mon.-Fri. 10-5:30.
**Prices:** $28.50: lower halves of sections 105-109 and 119-123; $27.50: upper halves of sections 105-109 and 119-123; $26.50: sections 101-104, 110-118 and 124-128; $22: sections 201-228; $11: last two rows of sections 205-209 and 219-223.

# HOCKEY

By Peter Aaron/ESTO, courtesy Madison Square Garden

## Eastern Conference

## Western Conference

© Mighty Ducks

# The Pond of Anaheim

The Pond might be the Taj Mahal of NHL arenas—or, more properly, the Magic Kingdom. With marble concourses, granite exterior, glass archways and brass fittings, it is the most luxurious and aesthetically pleasing building in the league.

Disney's focus on family-style entertainment is evident at Ducks games. The arena hosted the movie version of the Mighty Ducks before the NHL team hit the ice. Game scenes from *The Mighty Ducks: D2* were shot in the arena in the summer of 1993. Even now, games are as much fun-for-all-ages events as they are hockey showdowns. Pregame, the team's "Wild Wing" mascot drops from the rafters, and fans blow merrily on their duck callers (an average of 2,000 are sold each game) when the Ducks score.

The fans' appreciation can be measured in dollars: The Mighty Ducks have passed the Sharks in merchandise popularity. And though the team doesn't seem to have the star following of the Kings, Michelle Pfeiffer is a regular attendee, as are baseball players Bo Jackson, Tim Wallach and Mark Langston.

■ Club ■ $125 ■ $75 ■ $52.50 ■ $40
■ $28 ■ $23 ■ $20 ■ $18

## ARENA STATS

**Location:** 2695 E. Katella Ave., Anaheim, CA 92803
**Opened:** June 17, 1993
**Capacity:** 17,250
**Services for fans with disabilities:** Seating available in sections 203-204, 211-212, 217-218 and 226-227.

## ARENA FIRSTS

**Regular-season game:** Oct. 8, 1993, 7–2 loss to the Detroit Red Wings.
**Goal:** Aaron Ward of Detroit.
**Overtime game:** Dec. 12, 1993, 2–1 loss to the St. Louis Blues.

## TEAM NOTEBOOK

**Franchise history:** The Mighty Ducks of Anaheim, 1993–present.

## LODGING NEAR THE ARENA

**Anaheim Hilton & Towers**
777 Convention Way
Anaheim, CA 92802
(714) 750-4321/(800) 445-9667
1 block from the arena.

**Embassy Suites Brea**
900 E. Birch St.
Brea, CA 92621
(714) 990-6000/(800) EMBASSY
1 mile from the arena.

## HOT TIPS FOR VISITING FANS

### Parking
Come early and park in the adjacent lots. Because of insufficient parking spaces, several nearby restaurants—Mr. Stox, Catch and Charlie Brown's— offer shuttle service.

### Media bites
**Radio:** KLAC (1350 AM); Charlie Simmer, a member of the Los Angeles Kings' famed "Triple Crown" line, does analysis on radio.
**TV:** KCAL (Channel 9) and Prime Ticket on cable.

### Cuisine
Fish and chips is the most popular item on a tasty and diversified menu. Many varieties of hot dogs are offered and Japanese-style cooking is very popular. You can also get Mexican specialties at the Chili Peppers concession stand. Bottled beers include Tecate, Modelo Especial, and Corona Extra, plus beers from Germany, Canada, Australia, and northern California. The Club level, which you can't access without purchasing a Club seat, has the best selection and four bars. Players tend to go to Catch or El Torito (714-956-4880), a Mexican restaurant chain that has good margaritas. If you don't mind a drive, head to Harry O's (310-545-4444) in Manhattan Beach, a hangout for Kings fans and players. It's owned by former Kings player Billy Harris and is always hopping.

### GETTING TO THE POND
**Public transportation:** A bus stop is in front of the Pond. The city also runs a shuttle from Anaheim Stadium. For more information, call (714) 635-6010.
**By car:** From the north, take Cerritos Avenue to Sunkist Street. Make a left and continue to Douglass Road. Turn right and go approximately a ¼ mile; the stadium will be on your right. From the west, take Ball Road to Cerritos Avenue, then turn right. Follow Cerritos to Sunkist Street, and proceed as above.

From the south, take I-5 north to Katella Avenue. Exit west and follow Katella approximately half a mile. The stadium and parking will be to the right.

From the east, take Katella Avenue west, passing I-5 and Main Street en route. The stadium will be on your right.

### HOME-ICE ADVANTAGE
The team played better on the road than at home, but general manager Jack Ferreira seems to be fashioning a very physical team that should be able to assert itself. All the hoopla surrounding the team's arrival might have distracted players during the first season. The Ducks should be a better home team in years to come. Those duck calls alone should drive opponents batty.

### IN THE HOT SEATS

For the 1994-95 season, any seat might turn out to be a good seat, because the team was anticipating selling out the season before it began. The Ducks planned to hold back about 500 seats to sell on a game-by-game basis. But even those were expected to sell out before the first game.

• **Good seats:** If you have your choice, take the first row in the terrace. That's high enough to give you perspective and close enough to see players sweat.

• **Bad seats:** As in any arena, high in the corner is high in the corner. The row under the press box should be avoided.

**Scalpers:** Because the Mighty Ducks are a hot item, scalping is a cottage industry. When fans exit Highway 57 at Katella Avenue, scalpers are waiting. Other scalpers wander through the parking lot. Scalper prices can start at a 40% markup or higher, depending on the game.

# Boston Garden

B oston Garden is one of hockey's shrines. The rafters are filled with banners attesting to decades of winning tradition by the Celtics and Bruins. This is where Bobby Orr revolutionized the role of NHL defensemen and Phil Esposito became the dominant goal scorer of the 1970s. (You'll find their retired numbers in the rafters, too.) However, the storied history of the building is only part of what makes the Garden so wonderful. The fans, who range from rowdy to wild, and organist John Kiely never fail to pump up the excitement level.

Still, first-time visitors might be taken aback by just how small and old-fashioned the arena is, from the scoreboard to the rock-hard seats, some of which date from the building's opening in November 1928. The Garden has no air conditioning, so fog can form on the ice when it's 60 to 70 degrees outside, and in Game 4 of the 1988 Stanley Cup final, a switch gear blew, causing a blackout. The final had to go back to Edmonton, where the Oilers took the best-of-seven series in five games.

The adjacent Shawmut Center will replace the hallowed rink at the beginning of the 1995–96 season. The arena will have air conditioning, unobstructed views, a video-replay scoreboard and a five-story parking garage. The banners are moving, and the old scoreboard clock will be displayed in the lobby. The rink will be a standard 200 feet by 85 feet. They might be able to take banners next door, but they can't take the history.

---

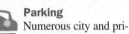

**HOT TIPS FOR VISITING FANS**

**Parking**
Numerous city and private garages surround the Garden. They charge $10. Don't park on the street; meters are for only two hours, and in residential areas, you need a permit.

Traffic can be a nightmare. Boston streets are known for being narrow. The Central Artery, the elevated expressway near the Garden, is one of the busiest roads in the East. If you come very early, you can visit the Garden's Tour and History Center. You start at a mini-museum, which includes Bobby Orr's first contract, then view a video and get a tour of the arena, including the visiting locker room. Admission is $5.50 for adults, $4.50 for seniors and students, and $4 for children 12 and under. The center is open year round from 10 A.M. to 4:30 P.M.

**Media bites**
**Radio:** WEEI (590 AM); Hall of Famer John Bucyk does analysis.

**TV:** WSBK (Channel 38) and NESN (cable); Fred Cusick has done Bruins play-by-play for 41 years, and ex-Bruin Derek Sanderson provides analysis.

**Cuisine**
Sausage-and-pepper sandwiches are the main Boston treat. They are sold in the west food-cart area, which has such diverse offerings as knackwurst and fried dough. Of traditional arena fare, the soft pretzels, hot dogs and nachos are great. Beer on tap is Miller Lite, Coors and Budweiser, but imported draught is available. Because food areas are split and lines are long, getting all you need in one intermission is

sometimes a problem.

After the game, many Bruins fans head to North Station's Sports Cafe (617-723-6664), which has two crowded, noisy bars and five TVs. Bruins players often pop in. Also recommended is The Harp (617-742-1010), an upscale Irish spot across the street. A 20-minute wait can be expected after a game. Bruins or visiting players often come by.

## THE BRUINS AT BOSTON GARDEN

**March 28, 1929:** In their inaugural season at the Garden, the Bruins win 2–0 in Game 1 of the best-of-three Stanley Cup finals against the New York Rangers. The next night, the Bruins beat the Rangers in New York for the title.

**Dec. 12, 1933:** Bruin Eddie Shore blindsides Ace Bailey of the Toronto Maple Leafs, ending Bailey's career.

**Jan. 21, 1945:** The Bruins crush the Rangers 14–3, the most decisive home win in team history.

**April 2, 1969:** Phil Esposito scores four goals and two assists as the Bruins beat the Maple Leafs 10–0 in a quarterfinal game. The 10 goals are a Boston playoff record, as are Esposito's six points.

**May 10, 1970:** A 4–3 overtime win against the St. Louis Blues gives the Bruins a four-game sweep and the Stanley Cup.

**May 15, 1990:** Petr Klima of Edmonton scores 55 minutes, 13 seconds into overtime, giving the Oilers a 3–2 win over the Bruins in Game 1 of the Stanley Cup finals.

# In the Hot Seats at Boston Garden

Boston Garden's overhanging balcony and steep upper-end sections ensure that no seat is too far from the ice. But overhangs caused by the balcony and the luxury boxes create 1,200 obstructed-view seats. These are the least expensive tickets. Obstructions range from having to crane your neck to see the scoreboard to sitting behind a pole. Under the balcony, TV monitors are provided. The Bruins play to 98% capacity, and if seats are available, they are usually the obstructed ones. The Bruins put all tickets on sale in September.

• **Good seats:** The first rows of the balcony provide the best view. They're fairly close but are high enough to see plays developing.

• **Bad seats:** The lower section isn't that great. If you sit too low, the glass can distort your view. If you sit too far back, you're under the balcony.

• **Moving down:** Tickets are checked. But if someone holding a ticket for a lower-level seat doesn't show up by the first intermission, ushers occasionally will let you move down.

**Scalping:** Scalpers can be found on Causeway Street; prices are in the $50-$200 range.

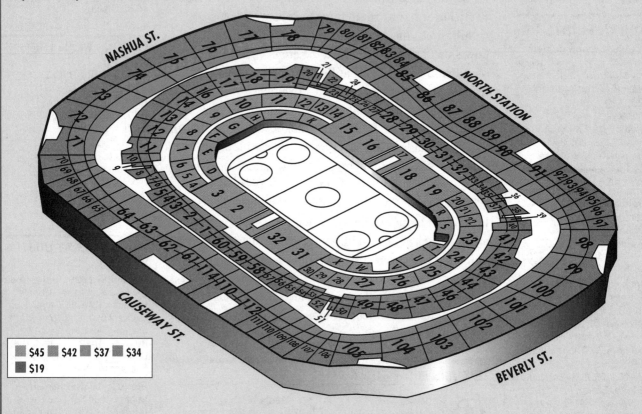

$45  $42  $37  $34
$19

## HOME-ICE ADVANTAGE

The Bruins have had a winning record for each of the past 27 seasons, the longest current streak in pro sports. During that period, they are 698-149-148 at home. Why? Boston Garden has the smallest ice surface in the NHL. It's 191 feet by 83 feet, instead of the NHL-mandated 200 by 85. The 9 feet are chopped off at center ice, so that makes it easier for rushing defensemen or defensemen good at outlet passes. The Bruins have had defensemen who excelled at both—Bobby Orr and Ray Bourque. The 2 feet lost in width makes a difference in the corners, and today's "muckers" take advantage. Also important are the fans, as loud as any in sports.

## GETTING TO BOSTON GARDEN

**Public transportation:** The Green and Orange lines of the MBTA, also known as the "T," stop at North Station. On the Green Line, only the C (North Station) and E (Lechmere) trains stop there. The North Station train terminal serves the northern suburbs, but on some lines, the last train leaves before the end of the game. Call (617) 722-3200 for more information.

**By car:** Call (617) 227-3200 for recorded directions.
From the south, follow I-95 North to I-93 toward exit 25 (Causeway Street). Make a left at the bottom of the ramp. The Garden will be immediately on the right.
From the west, take Massachusetts Turnpike (Route 90) to I-93 North to exit 25.
From the north, take I-93 South to Boston, or take I-95 South to Route 1 South, cross the Tobin Bridge, and merge onto I-93 South. Take exit 26 (Storrow Drive). Bear right and follow signs toward North Station. At the stop sign, make a left onto Lamancy Way. At the first traffic light, make a left onto Causeway Street. The Garden is ¼ mile on the left.

**TICKET INFORMATION**
**Address:** 150 Causeway St., Boston, MA 02114

**Phone:** (617) 227-3200 or TicketMaster at (617) 931-3100
**Hours:** Mon.-Sat. 11-7, Sun. and holidays 1-7.

**Prices:** $45 $42, $37, $34, $19.

# Memorial Auditorium

The coldest walk in all of hockey is said to be the one between the parking lot and Memorial Auditorium in Buffalo. Located downtown, just blocks from the shores of Lake Erie, "the Aud" sees all the alarming weather this city is known for: sudden lake-effect blizzards, biting winds and mounds and mounds of snow.

But the Aud is worth the trip for a nostalgic visit to what hockey buildings used to be like. And don't delay—the Aud will be replaced by a larger, luxury-box-filled arena a couple blocks away in the middle of the 1995–96 season.

Built in 1940, the Aud isn't terribly attractive from the outside. Tucked almost underneath the New York State Thruway, it's a gray-granite, governmental-design building—and a brown roof does little to enhance the image. But inside, the Aud has much of the charm of the Forum in Montreal and Maple Leaf Gardens, places where hockey is king.

With a smaller-than-normal ice surface, Sabres games have long been known as rock-'em-sock-'em affairs. The fans—maybe as much to stay warm as anything—tend toward wild, rowdy behavior, especially on Friday nights, the usual home night for Buffalo.

That spirit could be lost when the Sabres move to the Crossroads Arena, just 2 blocks farther down Main Street. Sales of corporate boxes and premium seating will foot the bill for the new building, and the local blue-collar fans who have supported the team since its inception in 1970 are already feeling squeezed out.

pers and onions on a roll. The concessions stands serve Busch, but small beer-only stands offer Molson Canadian, Molson Ice and O'Keefe for the same price as the Busch.

Plenty of choices after the game are within walking distance. The new hot spot is Jim Kelly's Sport City Grill (716-849-1200), just 4 blocks down Main Street. It's like walking into a sports museum. Also try Garcia's Irish Pub, opposite the Aud. The pub is sometimes a postgame hangout for players.

## ARENA STATS

**Location:** 140 Main St., Buffalo, NY 14202
**Opened:** Oct. 14, 1940
**Capacity:** 16,284
**Services for fans with disabilities:** Seating available in Red and Orange sections.

## ARENA FIRSTS

**Regular-season game:** Oct. 15, 1970, 3–0 loss to the Montreal Canadiens.
**Overtime game:** Feb. 17, 1984, 5–4 over the Minnesota North Stars.
**Playoff game:** April 7, 1973, 5–2 loss to the Montreal Canadiens.
**Stanley Cup finals game:** May 20, 1975, 5–4 over the Philadelphia Flyers in overtime.

## TEAM NOTEBOOK

**Franchise history:** Buffalo Sabres, 1970–present.
**Rookies of the Year:** Gil Perreault 1971–72; Tom Barrasso 1983–84.
**Hockey Hall of Fame:** Tim Horton, 1977; Marcel Pronovost, 1978; Punch Imlach, 1984; Gil Perreault, 1990; Scotty Bowman, 1991; Seymour H. Knox III, 1993.
**Retired number:** 11, Gil Perreault.

## LODGING NEAR THE ARENA

**Buffalo Hyatt Regency**
2 Fountain Plaza
Buffalo, NY 14202
(716) 856-1234/(800) 233-1234
4 blocks from the arena.

**Buffalo Hilton**
120 Church St.
Buffalo, NY 14202
(716) 845-5100/(800) HILTONS
2 blocks from the arena.

## THE SABRES AT THE AUD

**April 22, 1975:** Buffalo wins a playoff series for the first time by defeating the Chicago Blackhawks 3–1, taking the series four games to one.

**May 20, 1975:** Warm weather caused fog to form during Stanley Cup final. A bat also dropped in. It was killed by Buffalo's Jim Lorentz.

**Dec. 21, 1975:** The Sabres score 14 goals and 26 assists, setting an NHL record with 40 total points during a 14–2 rout of the Washington Capitals.

**March 19, 1981:** The Sabres score an NHL-record nine goals in one period as they trounce the Toronto Maple Leafs 14–4.

**Feb. 6, 1986:** Dave Andreychuk scores five goals against the Boston Bruins in an 8–6 victory.

**April 27, 1994:** Dave Hannan ends the sixth-longest game in NHL history with a goal at 5:47 of the fourth overtime as the Sabres beat the New Jersey Devils 1–0, tying their playoff series at three games apiece. The game lasts six hours and 12 minutes.

## HOT TIPS FOR VISITING FANS

**Parking**
The Aud lot is just a block and a half from the arena, toward Lake Erie. It's fairly big, and the price is no worse than any others in the area. Get in before 6:30 (for 7:30 games), and you should be fine; try a little later, and there's a line. Still, there's plenty of smaller lots usually $5 within a 10-block radius. The one-way streets (and having Main Street closed to traffic) can make it tough to circle around looking for the ideal spot—the best bet is just to get in one and walk.

**Media bites**
**Radio:** WGR (550 AM). Former Sabres player Larry Playfair does color commentary.

**TV:** WUTV (Channel 29), the Fox affiliate, broadcasts away games.

**Cuisine**
For the most part, the stands offer the usual fare of hot dogs, popcorn and nachos. If you want something peculiar to Buffalo, try "beef on weck," roast beef on kümmelweck (a crusty roll) with horseradish. In the main seating area, on the concourse behind upper Gold/Red section 16-18-20, is a small stand selling the sandwiches, though the sign says BEEF ON WICK. Just off the main lobby is a small lounge with a bar and beer garden, where they have another taste treat: grilled bologna sandwiches with pep-

# IN THE HOT SEATS AT MEMORIAL AUDITORIUM

Though it's a smaller building, getting into the Aud hasn't been that tough. Friday games—especially against glamour opponents—are toughest, but always check in at the Aud box office.

• **Good seats:** The two sections closest to the ice, the gold and red seats, are the same price. So, if you're going to pay the price, you might as well sit in the reds. No posts obstruct the view, so any seat in the reds is going to be good. But most of the golds and reds along the sides belong to season ticketholders.

Best bets are the lower blues, cheaper than the golds or reds. Try to get a seat in the 10 side sections (sections 14-22 on the Main Street side and 15-23 on the Pearl Street side): They're much more accessible by portal and aisles—so you don't have to walk over people already seated. The only downside is that you're sitting in wooden chairs rather than padded, theater-style seats. The balcony—especially on the sides—is also a great deal. It hangs over the blue seats, and if you're in the lower five rows or so, you feel like you're right on top of the ice.

• **Bad seats:** The upper blue seats—especially the last three rows. The balcony overhang cuts off the scoreboards and most of the atmosphere. The balcony is at least $4 cheaper and a better seat.

• **Moving down:** Getting into the golds is hard, but ushers don't check tickets much for the other sections. For the most part, the crowd has arrived by the middle of the first period, so if you spy empty seats, try moving in the first intermission.

**Scalping:** Most often found on the corner of Main and Terrace.

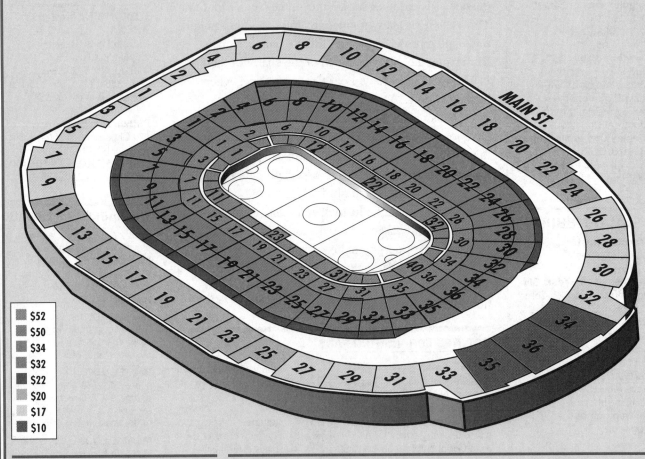

| | |
|---|---|
| ■ | $52 |
| ■ | $50 |
| ■ | $34 |
| ■ | $32 |
| ■ | $22 |
| ■ | $20 |
| ■ | $17 |
| ■ | $10 |

## HOME-ICE ADVANTAGE

One thing about Sabres games: The local fans usually go home happy. The Aud's ice surface measures 193 feet by 84 feet; it's 7 feet shorter and 1 foot narrower than NHL standards, so the Sabres have built their team strong to take advantage of the smaller rink.

## GETTING TO MEMORIAL AUDITORIUM

**Public transportation:** The No. 8 Main light rail transit goes directly to the arena. Metro buses also stop at the arena. Call (716) 855-7211 for more information.

**By car:** Take New York State Thruway to the Buffalo exit, then Route 33 west into the city. Exit at Oak Street. Go right onto Swan Street, left onto Washington Street. The Aud is on the right.

## TICKET INFORMATION
**Address:** 140 Main St., Buffalo, NY 14202
**Phone:** No phone orders to the Aud, so call TicketMaster at (716) 852-5000, (716) 232-1900 or (800) 755-5589
**Hours:** Mon.-Sat. 10-9, Sun. 10-6.
**Prices:** $52: gold; $50: red; $34: lower blue prime; $32: lower blue; $22: upper blue; $20: orange prime; $17: orange corner; $10: orange south.

# Olympic Saddledome

## ARENA STATS

**Location:** Olympic Way, Calgary, AL, Canada T2P 3B9
**Opened:** Oct. 15, 1983
**Capacity:** 20,230
**Services for fans with disabilities:** Seating available in the Main Concourse.

## ARENA FIRSTS

**Regular-season game:** Oct. 15, 1983, 4–3 loss to the Edmonton Oilers.
**Playoff game:** April 4, 1984, 5–3 over the Vancouver Canucks.
**Stanley Cup finals game:** May 16, 1986, 5–3 over the Montreal Canadiens.

## TEAM NOTEBOOK

**Franchise history:** Atlanta Flames, 1972–80; Calgary Flames, 1980–present.
**Stanley Cup:** 1988–89
**Rookies of the Year/Calder:** Eric Vail, 1974–75; Willi Plett, 1976–77; Gary Suter, 1985–86; Joe Nieuwendyk, 1987–88; Sergei Makarov, 1989–90.
**Hockey Hall of Fame:** Glenn Hall, 1975; Lanny McDonald, 1992; Guy Lapointe, 1993.
**Retired number:** 9, Lanny McDonald.

## TICKET INFORMATION

**Address:** P.O. Box 1540, Station "M," Calgary, AL, Canada T2P 3B9
**Phone:** (403) 261-0475 or (403) 270-6700.
**Hours:** Mon.-Fri. 9-5.

---

The thing that sets the Olympic Saddledome apart from other arenas constructed in the early 1980s is its original purpose, which was to host the 1988 Winter Olympics. It was the first building in North America designed to accommodate the larger, international-sized ice surface. Accordingly, the first 13 rows of seats are perched on risers that can be pulled back in the manner of bleacher seats in a high school gymnasium.

The saddle-style design of the roof was borrowed from the USAir Arena in Washington, D.C., but it works in Calgary because of the city's Western heritage. Designers attached 6,000 acoustic tiles to the concrete roof panels, providing excellent concert sound. The downside is that the tiles muffle crowd noise in what already is arguably the quietest building in the league. Unless the signboard prompts fans to make noise, it generally doesn't happen spontaneously. The team's mascot, Harvey the Hound, is the only other added attraction.

The building is undergoing a renovation that will add more luxury boxes, improved food, a wider concourse and a replay scoreboard.

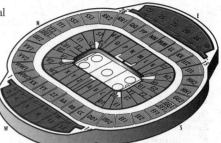

■ $48 ■ $36 ■ $30
■ $25 ■ $19

## HOT TIPS FOR VISITING FANS

### Parking
The Saddledome isn't the only venue on the Stampede Grounds, so if there's another event, parking can be difficult. Only 2,500 spaces are on the Stampede Grounds and they go for C$3.50.

Residents of Victoria Park will allow you to park on their lawns or in their driveways for about C$3. Two large lots off Olympic Way fill up quickly once the Stampede Grounds is full.

### Media bites
**Radio:** CFR (660 AM).
**TV:** CITC (Channel 7).

### Cuisine
Pretty stock stuff, though one gourmet delight added for the 1994 playoffs was homemade sausage from Spolumbo's deli, a local favorite. The best food is served in the Saddleroom Restaurant (403-261-0573), which provides a wide range of reasonably priced entrees for anyone who can get in.

Dusty's Saloon, a cowboy bar roughly 3 blocks from the Saddledome, attracts out-of-town coaches and players. The more trendy hangouts are Stinky's, a sports bar, and Hy's (403-263-2222) which has good steaks. If players aren't at Dusty's, they are probably at Hy's.

### GETTING TO THE SADDLEDOME
**Public transportation:** LRT

stops at Stampede Park, just across the street from the Saddledome. The C train offers service from University of Calgary to the arena door. Call (403) 262-1000 for more information.
**By car:** From Highway 1, take Center Street south. Go left onto Ninth Avenue, then right onto First Street. S.E. and left onto 12th Avenue. Go right onto Olympic Way, directly to the Saddledome.

### LODGING NEAR THE ARENA
**Westin**
320 Fourth Ave. S.W.
Calgary, AL
Canada T2P 2S6
(403) 266-1611/(800) 228-3000
½ mile from the arena.

**Palliser**
133 Ninth Ave. SW
Calgary, AL
Canada T2P 2M3
(403) 262-1234/(800) 441-1414
Less than a mile from the arena.

### HOME-ICE ADVANTAGE
In 14 years in Calgary, the Flames have never had a losing home record. Altitude might be one factor. Many times, a team will come in a day early, schedule permitting, to get used to the altitude, which is about 3,000 feet above sea level.

### IN THE HOT SEATS

Despite their quiet crowds, the Flames usually run one-two with the Detroit Red Wings in NHL attendance. Apart from a handful of single tickets available at the box office for most games, every seat in the two lower bowls is sold on a season-ticket basis.

Tickets for the upper loges go on sale at the start of each month.

• **Good seats:** There are virtually no bad seats in the two lower bowls. Sections A, M, N and Z are the most popular.

Oddly enough, row 26—the first row of the second tier—is the priciest seat in the house, at C$48. That's a hefty premium to pay, considering that two rows back, you're paying only C$25 for virtually the same view.

• **Bad seats:** In the summer of 1987, just before the Olympics, a third tier of seats was added, the so-called upper loges. Seeing a game from there is like watching a table-hockey game.

**Scalping:** The price—and availability—varies from night to night. The Toronto Maple Leafs and the Montreal Canadiens are the two top draws. It's illegal to sell anything on the Stampede Grounds, so generally scalpers get warned off by security before the police step in.

---

# United Center

A fter 65 years as the Madhouse on Madison Street, the fabled Chicago Stadium has become the Memory of Madison Street, falling victim to old age and progress. Across the street stands the $175 million United Center, the home away from home for Blackhawks (and Bulls) fans for many decades to come.

About 2½ times larger, United Center provides the best of the new while carrying on some of the Stadium's traditions. The building's exterior design borrows heavily from 1920s architecture, making it appear older and more homey than most modern arenas. Inside, the seats are wide and comfortable. Sightlines, sometimes nonexistent from the Stadium's mezzanine and second balcony, are outstanding, with no obstructions. Hockey fans will be glad to know that the sound from the Stadium's stately Barton organ has been painstakingly re-created, a process that took more than a year. Notes from the original organ had to be recorded and then used as the basis for creating the sound of the new Allen organ. In addition, sound absorbers and deflectors have been installed to help re-create and amplify the roar of noise that made the Stadium famous.

■ $75 ■ $60 ■ $50
■ $35 ■ $25 ■ $15

## ARENA STATS

**Location:** 1901 W. Madison St., Chicago, IL 60612
**Opened:** August 1994
**Capacity:** 20,500
**Services for fans with disabilities:** Seating available in sections 104, 108, 115, 119, 204, 213, 217, 221, 230, 302, 304, 307, 310, 313, 317, 318, 322, 324, 327, 330 and 333.

## TEAM NOTEBOOK

**Franchise history:** Chicago Blackhawks, 1926–present.
**Stanley Cups:** 1933–34, '37–38, '60–61.
**Most Valuable Players/Hart:** M. Bentley, 1945–46; Rollins, '53–54; Hull, '64–65, '65–66; Mikita, '66–67, '67–68.
**Rookies of the Year/Calder:** Karakas, 1935–36; Dahlstrom, '37–38; Litzenberger, '54–55; Hay, '59–60; T. Esposito, '69–70; Larmer, '82–83; Belfour, '90–91.
**Hockey Hall of Fame:** Gardiner, Morenz, 1945; MacKay, '52; Hay, Irvin, Keats, Lehman, '58; Denneny, '59; Boucher, '60; Norris, '62; McLaughlin, '63; D. Bentley, Seibert, Stewart, '64; Mosienko, '65; M. Bentley, Brimsek, Lindsay, '66; Abel, '69; Dye, Gadsby, '70; A. Wirtz, '71; Burch, Coulter, Ivan, '74; Hall, Pilote, '75; B. Wirtz, '76; Orr, '79; Lumley, '80; Stanley, '81; Hull, Mikita, '83; P. Esposito, '84; Mariucci, Olmstead, Pilous, '85; T. Esposito, '88; Poile, '90; Smith, '91.
**Retired numbers:** 1, Hall; 9, Hull; 21, Mikita; 35, T. Esposito.

## HOT TIPS FOR VISITING FANS

### Parking
Up to 5,500 official parking spots are within a 4-block area. Prices are $10 for regular spots, $12 for premium. A number of lower-priced lots nearby hold approximately 2,000 cars, but almost none are patrolled, so the likelihood of vandalism and break-ins is high. Street parking is forbidden in a 4-block radius.

### Media bites
**Radio:** WMVP (1000 AM).
**TV:** SportsChannel for road games.

### Cuisine
Chicagoans love to eat. With that in mind, United Center has a considerably larger menu than at Chicago Stadium. In addition to the usual hot dogs and nachos, themed concessionaires abound, which offer deli sandwiches, Mexican and Italian specialties and grilled meats. To wash down all that food, the United Center offers 25 different beers. After the game, try Cheli's Chili Bar (312-455-1237), which is owned by Hawks defenseman Chris Chelios and offers 20 kinds of chili. Another hangout is Hawkeyes (312-226-3951), a sports bar with many Blackhawks players among its clientele.

### GETTING TO THE UNITED CENTER
**Public transportation:** The No. 19 Stadium Express bus operates every 10 minutes from 1½ hours before each game until half an hour after. For more information, call (312) 836-7800.
**By car:** From O'Hare Airport, take 90 East to the Madison Street exit. Turn right on Madison, and follow it for about a mile. The United Center will be on the right.

### LODGING NEAR THE ARENA
**The Drake**
140 E. Walton St.
Chicago, IL 60611
(312) 787-2200
5 miles from the arena.

**Westin**
909 N. Michigan Ave.
Chicago, IL 60611
(312) 943-7200/(800) 228-3000
5 miles from the arena.

### HOME-ICE ADVANTAGE
For at least the first few games in their new home, the Blackhawks are likely to be on a par with opponents. The Hawks will need time to learn the nuances and bounces off the dasher boards and to become familiar with an ice surface that is about 9 feet longer than in the old rink. One thing that's sure to cheer both Hawks and visitors—leaving behind the hordes of roaches that lived in both Stadium locker rooms.

## IN THE HOT SEATS

Some 20,500 seats are available for hockey, nearly 2,000 more than at Chicago Stadium. The team will continue offering some single-game tickets on either the day before a game or on game days, but selection will be limited, and most seats likely will be in the upper reaches of the new arena.

• **Good seats:** If you can get one, the 3,000 club seats offer private parking, waitress service and an attached computer keypad through which you can place food orders from your seat.

• **Moving down:** Crowd-control personnel positioned at the entrance to each seating section inspect every ticket. If you manage to sneak past and are caught, you'll be politely asked once to go back to your original seat. If you are caught again, you'll be evicted.

 **Ticket scalping:** Scalpers are around out front, and their prices are high. United Center officials promise a sharp crackdown this year on scalpers and buyers. Police aren't as plentiful in the 2 to 4 blocks surrounding the arena, but that area also brings with it the potential for crime.

**TICKET INFORMATION**
**Address:** 1901 W. Madison St., Chicago, IL 60612
**Phone:** (312) 943-7000 or (312) 455-7000.
**Hours:** Mon.-Sat. 10-6.

# Reunion Arena

Don't be fooled into thinking Dallas isn't a hockey town. Though the Stars have been here only since 1993, minor-league teams here and in Fort Worth had already introduced some Dallas fans to the game, and they quickly came to understand NHL hockey. Forward Russ Courtnall said that at first, fans cheered only the physical aspects of the game, but as the first season wore on, they began appreciating good breakout passes and other subtle plays that seasoned fans notice. The hockey team is carving out a niche in the Dallas sports market.

Don't get too attached to Reunion, though. The Arena opened in April 1980 and is already considered out of date because it lacks luxury suites. Another major problem is the decibel level. All arenas play loud music, but the sound in Reunion is so loud that occasionally players can't hear their coach's instructions, even when they are standing right next to him. Nonetheless, it will be a sad day for fans when the Arena is replaced. It has some of the best sightlines in the NHL and is an intimate place in which to watch a game.

■ $100 ■ $70 ■ $60 ■ $50 ■ $38
■ $30 ■ $28 ■ $25 ■ $12

## HOT TIPS FOR VISITING FANS

### Parking
Plenty of parking (costing $5) is adjacent to the stadium, including a five-level, 2,100-space parking structure. Downtown traffic can be very hectic close to game time, so give yourself some extra time or walk if you're at a downtown hotel.

### Media bites
**Radio:** KLIF (570 AM).
**TV:** KTVT (Channel 11), KTXA (Channel 21) and Home Sports Entertainment on cable. Mike Fornes, a two-time Emmy winner, is the announcer of choice. His play-by-play is simulcast on radio and TV.

### Cuisine
Though you can get chili, you won't find any other Texas treats in the concession stands. The more popular items are frozen yogurt and nachos. Miller, Budweiser and Coors Light are available on tap and you can also get bottled Heineken and Molson or chardonnay, white zinfandel and wine coolers. If you get a Stars Club seat (a few are available on a single game basis), you have access to the private Stars Club outside the Arena, which has a fully stocked bar, sandwiches, snacks and a pregame buffet. Given the downtown location, fans have plenty of nightspots from which to choose after the game. Many opposing teams stay at the Hyatt, across the street. Some fans head there, but many head to West End Marketplace,

Dallas' version of Boston's Faneuil Hall. The cities, most popular sports bars are Humperdinks on Greenville, Randy White's restaurant, Slap Shot's and Christie's. Because Stars players live 20 to 30 miles from the Arena, if they congregate, it's usually at the Stars Club.

## GETTING TO REUNION ARENA
**Public transportation:** The No. 30 Marsalis bus goes to the arena. Call (214) 979-2712 for more information.
**By car:** From DFW Airport, take the South Airport exit, and go East on Highway 183 to I-35E South. Get off at the Reunion Boulevard exit and follow signs to the Arena.

## LODGING NEAR THE ARENA
**Hyatt Regency**
300 Reunion Blvd.
Dallas, TX 75207
(214) 651-1234/(800) 233-1234
Across the street from the arena.

**Holiday Inn**
1933 Main St.
Dallas, TX 75201
(214) 741-7700/(800) 465-4329
7 blocks from the arena.

## HOME-ICE ADVANTAGE
The Stars went an impressive 23-12-7 at home in their first season in Dallas, an improvement from the previous season (18-17-7) in Bloomington. The main reason is fan support. Because the NBA Mavericks have played so poorly recently, Dallas fans were hungry for a winner to root for during the winter, and the Stars came through, going 10-1-7 in their first 18 home games.

## IN THE HOT SEATS

The Stars sold out 21 of 40 games in 1993–94, including 15 of their last 16. But tickets to most of those games were available until a day or two before the contest.

• **Bad seats:** This is one of the best arenas in which to watch a game; only the seats near the glass should be avoided.

• **Moving down:** Reunion Arena attendants seem less than vigilant. Some will stop you, but others seem to recognize squatters rights if a seat is empty. But the Stars are becoming too hot a ticket for moving down to be much of an option.

**Scalping:** Scalpers are found on the corner closest to Reunion Tower.

# Joe Louis Arena

## ARENA STATS

**Location:** 600 Civic Center Dr., Detroit, MI 48226
**Opened:** Dec. 12, 1979
**Capacity:** 18,227
**Services for fans with disabilities:** 200 seats available in the concourse level.

## ARENA FIRSTS

**Regular-season game:** Dec. 27, 1979, 3–2 loss to the St. Louis Blues.
**Goal:** Brian Sutter of the Blues.
**Playoff game:** April 7, '84, 4–3 loss to the Blues.

## TEAM NOTEBOOK

**Franchise history:** Detroit Cougars, 1926–30; Detroit Falcons, '30–32; Detroit Red Wings, '32–present.
**Stanley Cups:** 1935–36, '36–37, '42–43, '49–50, '51–52, '53–54, '54–55.
**Hockey Hall of Fame:** Connell, Foyston, Frederickson, Hay, Keats, Norris Sr., '58; Adams, Thompson, '59; Walker, '60; Conacher, '61; J. D. Norris, '62; Goodfellow, Seibert, '63; Stewart, '64; S. Howe, Barry, '65; Lindsay, '66; Abel, Kelly, B. Norris, '69; Gadsby, '70; Sawchuk, Weiland, '71; Holmes, G. Howe, '72; Harvey, '73; Ivan, Voss, '74; Hall, '75; Quackenbush, '76; Delvecchio, '77; Bathgate, Provonost, '78; Lumley, '80; Bucyk, Mahovlich, '81; Ullman, '82; Lynch, '85; Boivin, '86; Giacomin, Ziegler Jr., '87; Park, '88; Lewis, Sittler, '89; Martyn, '91; Dionne, '92.
**Retired numbers:** 1, Sawchuck; 6, Aurie; 7, Lindsay; 9, G. Howe; 10, Delvecchio.

The Red Wings haven't won the Stanley Cup since 1955, but their fans may be among the most loyal in the world. Until Tampa Bay passed them last season, the Red Wings were the NHL leader in attendance for seven straight seasons. When the team is playing well, the building rocks with excitement.

The arena was dubbed the "Joe Louis Warehouse" when it first opened in 1979 because of its vast, stark look, but when Mike and Marian Ilitch bought the team in 1982, they immediately spruced up the building. The spacious concourse is not only extremely colorful, with hockey artwork decorating the walls, but also fan-friendly; there is room to maneuver around those who are standing in line for pizza and suds. Though Joe Louis Arena hasn't known an NHL championship, the Red Wings' seven Stanley Cup banners hang from the rafters, as do recent divisional title banners and the retired numbers of Gordie Howe, Larry Aurie, Alex Delvecchio, Ted Lindsay and Terry Sawchuk. Only Howe graced Joe Louis ice and that was as a Hartford Whaler in 1980.

Rock music and a dancing puck on the scoreboard get some people dancing in the aisles during timeouts, but the Red Wings' most eagerly anticipated tradition is the throwing of an octopus on the ice during the playoffs. This unusual ritual began when only four NHL teams made the playoffs, and the eight legs symbolized the eight victories needed to win the Stanley Cup. Because 16-legged creatures are rare, an octopus is still sneaked in now. Attendants are booed if they use a shovel to remove the octopus and wildly applauded if they use their bare hands.

## HOT TIPS FOR VISITING FANS

**Parking**
If you don't know your way around Detroit, park in the lots adjacent to the arena. The Joe Louis parking structure, on Jefferson Avenue, is less than 50 yards from a main entrance. It's easily accessible from the Lodge Freeway (U.S. 10); the exit off the Lodge is marked as JOE LOUIS PARKING. A ramp leads you right into the parking structure on the second level, which is well lighted and safe. Some street parking is available on Fort Street, running parallel to Jefferson, but most knowledgeable fans consider that risky.

**Media bites:**
**Radio:** WJR (760 AM); For a treat, take a radio and earplugs with you to the game and listen to the call of Hall of Fame announcer Bruce Martyn, who is in his 30th season broadcasting Red Wings games.
**TV:** WKBD (Channel 50), PASS (Pro-Am Sports Service) and pay-per-view's Special Order Sports.

**Cuisine**
Since Red Wings owner Mike Ilitch made his fortune with the Little Caesars chain, pizza is clearly the top item on the Detroit menu. The Coney Island stand offers kielbasa, bratwurst and other sausages. A sub shop offers all sorts of sandwiches, and a turkey stand offers turkey salads. Fresh fruit, ice cream and frozen yogurt are also sold. The beer selection is wide, including Miller, Stroh's, Molson, Labatt's and Lowenbrau on tap or in bottles. Lines move quickly.

After a Red Wings game, many fans head to Nemo's Saloon at the Westin Renaissance Center or Galligan's on Jefferson, across from the Ren Cen. Players also often gather at Galligan's. Fans coming in by car can start the night at Andrews on the Corner or at Dunleavy's, both on Joseph Campau Avenue, and take advantage of the bus service to and from Joe Louis Arena. Other fans cross the bridge into Windsor, Ontario, to have a drink at former NHL coach Don Cherry's bar.

## LODGING NEAR THE ARENA

**Omni Detroit**
333 E. Jefferson Ave.
Detroit, MI 48226
(313) 222-7700/(800) 843-6664
3 blocks from the arena.

**Westin Hotel**
Renaissance Center
Detroit, MI 48243
(313) 568-8000/(800) 228-3000
½ mile from the arena.

## THE RED WINGS AT JOE LOUIS ARENA

**Feb. 11, 1982:** The Red Wings score two goals on penalty shots; Tom Gradin and Ivan Hlinka are the shooters, and Gilles Gilbert of the Vancouver Canucks is the goalie.

**Dec. 23, 1987:** Bob Probert racks up an NHL-record eight penalties, as the Buffalo Sabres beat the Red Wings 5–2.

**April 12, 1991:** Detroit is called for 33 penalties in a game against the St. Louis Blues, tying an NHL record, and the team sets a record with 152 penalty minutes.

**March 24, 1992:** Pittsburgh Penguins great Mario Lemieux scores his 1,000th point, but the Red Wings win 4–3.

# In the Hot Seats at Joe Louis Arena

Order your tickets early, or be prepared to sit well above the ice. The Red Wings have sold out 167 of their last 168 home games and have had crowds of 19,000 or more in 314 of their last 316 games. The best seats are in the lower bowl, and they are all owned by season ticketholders. The only way to find a lower-bowl ticket is to pay $75 or more through a private ticket service. Several are listed in Detroit newspapers. Though most offer some very good seats, fans should exercise caution, because not all are equally reputable. One of the best seats for Red Wings games isn't a seat at all. Standing-room tickets allow patrons to stand in the aisle above the lower bowl. One word of warning: If you purchase a standing-room ticket, you had better be first in line when the door opens. The sprint to secure prime standing spots often resembles the Oklahoma land rush.

• **Bad seats:** Built in 1979 with the fan in mind, the arena has no obstructed views. However, the higher lettered rows in the upper bowl are a long way from the ice. If you have to choose among a group of higher seats, most Joe Louis fans will tell you to avoid behind the net, because it's difficult to see what's happening at the other end. If you're a Red Wings fan and have to be at one end of the arena, choose the east side because Detroit shoots for two periods at that end.

• **Moving down:** All lower-bowl seats are sold for each game, and no-shows are rare. Finding a lower seat unoccupied doesn't happen very often.

 **Scalping:** The resale of tickets, even at face value, is illegal in Detroit. However, several people buy and sell tickets near the Joe Louis parking structure.

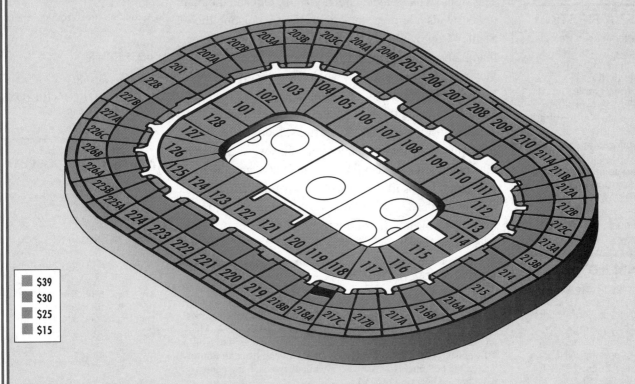

$39
$30
$25
$15

## HOME-ICE ADVANTAGE

Though Joe Louis doesn't have the reputation of a Chicago Stadium or a Madison Square Garden in ability to intimidate opposing teams, home ice has been good to the Red Wings. They have eight consecutive winning seasons there, which includes 1989–90, when they didn't make the playoffs. The Red Wings were still 20-14-6 in Joe Louis in that season. But even the most loyal of fans can sometimes turn, as shown in 1993–94 when they booed goaltender Tim Cheveldae to the point that the Red Wings were forced to trade him.

## GETTING TO JOE LOUIS ARENA

**Public transportation:** A Detroit People Mover station is at the arena and a bus stop is at Cobo Hall, which is adjacent to the arena. Call (313) 933-1300 for more information.

**By car:** From the south, go north on I-75 to the exit for U.S. 10. Exit southbound onto U.S. 10 and head south for 1 mile. Take the Joe Louis exit, which will lead to the Arena.

From the north, go south on I-75 until it meets I-375 South. Exit onto I-375 South and continue to the Jefferson Avenue exit. Go west on Jefferson Avenue for 1½ miles; the Arena will be on the left.

**TICKET INFORMATION**
**Address:** 600 Civic Center Dr., Detroit, MI 48226
**Phone:** TicketMaster at (810) 645-6666

**Hours:** Mon.-Fri. 10-6.
**Prices:** $39: Sections 101-128 (rows 1-18) and 201-228 (row 1); $30: sections 201-228 (rows 2-12); $25: sections 201-228 (rows 13-21); $15: sections 201-228 (rows 22-27).

# Northlands Coliseum

The good news is that this building boasts not a single obstructed-view or bad-angle seat. The bad news is that the Coliseum is to hockey what Riverfront, Three Rivers and Veterans stadiums are to baseball. Functional? Extremely. Lovable? No. The building looks like a hubcap on the prairie when viewed from a plane. But if the seats and cement don't inspire first-time visitors to pull out their cameras, the memorabilia signifying the great feats that have occurred within these walls most certainly will.

Though he left in 1988, the Coliseum is still known as The House That Wayne Gretzky Built. Outside the main doors stands a bronze statue with No. 99 hoisting the Stanley Cup overhead. From the rafters hang no fewer than 22 banners, including five denoting Stanley Cup victories won in a building where Gretzky, Mark Messier, Paul Coffey, Grant Fuhr, Glenn Anderson and Jari Kurri played the best hockey of their careers.

Like most western Canadian rinks, though, this arena is as quiet as a library. Edmonton's fans were spoiled by the countless Gretzkian feats of the 1980s, and the more pedestrian teams in the '90s often have had a tough time raising the dead. Owner Peter Pocklington plans to refurbish the Coliseum, if not the team, in hopes of drawing back some fans.

## HOT TIPS FOR VISITING FANS

**Parking**
Stadium parking is C$3.50, or you can pay an extra buck for closer parking off Capilano Freeway on the east side of the building. No cheaper neighborhood parking is nearby; even if you find an on-street spot, the savings are not worth the walk in January. On cold winter nights, wise fans find heated underground parking downtown (about C$6) and take the Light Rail Transit subway. The LRT Coliseum stop is above ground, so you'll still need a warm coat, but the subway certainly beats a long, windy postgame walk to your ice-cold vehicle in the arena parking lot. If you are driving, avoid the Capilano Freeway exit south of 118th Avenue. It can be backed up a long way.

**Media bites**
**Radio:** CFCW (790 AM).
**TV:** CFRN (Channel 2).

Radio play-by-play announcer Rod Phillips has called games since 1972 in the WHA. Many locals hit the mute button on their TVs and listen to Phillips while they watch the game.

**Cuisine**
On average, the food is unsurprising. The hard ice-cream cones are excellent, and the popcorn is above average, but otherwise, your best bet is a steak at Coliseum Steak and Pizza (403-474-1640) before the game; it's 2 minutes west on 118th Avenue and was frequented by Gretzky and Messier in their Oilers days. If you're determined to eat in the arena, the best variety is on the lower-level concourse. Molson beer and wine coolers are also available. The concessions are expected to be upgraded substantially.

After the game, the LRT rider gets a good deal, with several good options by stops downtown, but not much near the rink. Sherlock Holmes Pub, about a block from the Central Station LRT drop, is favored by fans for a postgame pint. The players frequent Barry T's. It's not a relaxing setting, but it's great for singles.

## THE OILERS AT THE NORTHLANDS COLISEUM

**Feb. 15, 1980:** Wayne Gretzky ties an NHL record with seven assists in an 8–2 win against the Washington Capitals.

**Feb. 18, 1981:** Gretzky scores four goals in one period, tying an NHL record, in a 9–2 win against the St. Louis Blues.

**May 19, 1984:** The Oilers beat the New York Islanders 5–2 to clinch their first Stanley Cup.

**Dec. 19, 1984:** Gretzky scores his 1,000th point in a 7–3 win against the Los Angeles Kings.

**May 30, 1985:** An 8–3 victory over the Philadelphia Flyers gives Edmonton its second consecutive NHL championship.

**May 20, 1987:** Jari Kurri scores at 6:50 of overtime in Game 2 of the Stanley Cup finals against the Flyers. The Oilers win the game 3–2 and take the series, four games to three.

**March 1, 1988:** Gretzky becomes the NHL's all-time assist leader, with 1,050, in a 5–3 win over the Kings.

**Oct. 15, 1989:** Gretzky returns to Northlands Coliseum with his new team, the Kings, and becomes the NHL's all-time scoring leader with a goal at 19:07 of the third period. His 1,851 points move him past Gordie Howe.

# IN THE HOT SEATS AT NORTHLANDS COLISEUM

If ever a buyer's market for hockey tickets existed, this is it. The Oilers sold out only three games in the 1993–94 season. The only tough tickets are for Montreal's annual Christmas season visit and the two Maple Leafs games. Los Angeles is also a favorite opponent, but with three visits a year, you should have no trouble getting a seat.

• **Good seats:** All seats are decent values. The budget-conscious should try the first four or five rows of the colonade, rather than the executive seats. The low blues are excellent seats—particularly the first row, where you have no "leaners"

obstructing your view.

• **Bad seats:** As with most arenas, if you sit up close to the ice, the glass can distort your view. The C$12 seats are very high up.

• **Moving down:** This town has little traffic, which means people who buy red seats (mostly wealthy season ticketholders) are either in their seats by the 10-minute mark, or they're not coming. The "expansion seat boogie" works especially well on cold mid-week nights from December to February, when many older folks with good seats opt to stay home and watch the game on TV. Buy a C$12 seat and pick out

a pair of open reds after the 15-minute mark of the first period. Grab those seats right at the start of the first intermission when ushers aren't guarding the aisles, and be sitting there when people arrive for the second period. You'll get some stares, but only until the puck drops.

**Scalping:** With so few sellouts, scalpers don't make a great living. They are outside the Coliseum for every game, however, on the south side of the building by the subway exit, and on the pedestrian bridge over 118th Avenue.

*Seating chart legend:*

| | |
|---|---|
| ■ | C$50 |
| ■ | C$45 |
| ■ | C$35 |
| ■ | C$30 |
| ■ | C$25 |
| ■ | C$20 |
| ■ | C$15 |
| ■ | C$12 |

## HOME-ICE ADVANTAGE

Little home-ice advantage remains at the Coliseum, where visiting teams used to be happy to escape with their jockstraps. With the Oilers weakened by the selloff of all the team's stars, they have become an easy mark in recent years for teams making the Edmonton-Calgary swing through Alberta. Points are hard to come by in Calgary, so visiting teams bear down here to avoid a provincial sweep.

Fans are purists, so they're more intent on watching a game they deeply understand than disturbing their concentration with clapping. No sirens, spotlights or

foghorns going on here, and almost no signage either, except for the families of visiting players from Alberta, British Columbia and Saskatchewan.

One note: Crowds have dwindled as the local hatred for owner Pocklington has grown, but the team with the NHL's youngest players typically responds to a rare sellout and an opposing uniform they don't see too often, like a Boston or Montreal jersey. The most fun you'll have here is a Saturday night game against the Canadiens or the Maple Leafs.

## GETTING TO NORTHLANDS

**Public transportation:** Light Rail Transit stops at the Coliseum, as do the Nos. 5, 11, 18, 20, 23, 28 and 70 buses. Call (403) 421-4636 for more information.

**By car:** From the Municipal Airport, take 118th Avenue 3 miles straight into the city. It runs right past the Coliseum.

From Route 16, the Yellowhead Trail, take 82nd Street south. Turn left onto 118th Avenue.

## TICKET INFORMATION
**Address:** 7424 118th Ave., Edmonton, AB, Canada T5B 4M9
**Phone:** (403) 471-2191 or TicketMaster at

(403) 451-8000.
**Hours:** Mon.-Fri. 9-5.
**Prices:** $50: gold; $45: silver; $35: executive; $30: executive terrace; $25: terrace;

$20: side colonade; $15: end colonade; $12: gallery.

# Miami Arena

Fog at the Boston Garden. Puddles at New York Rangers games. So how, you ask, does a south Florida hockey team have some of the best ice in the NHL? Director of operations Preston Williams credits the combination of two Zambonis, a water-treatment system, training of the staff at an ice school in Canada and the fact the ice surface stays down almost season-round. Or perhaps it's because the building is kept very cold. Game-time temperatures dip into the 50s, even high up in the arena. No matter the cold air, the atmosphere inside the arena is hot.

Miami Arena opened in 1988 but was not used for hockey until the Panthers began play in 1993. The Panthers tend to pack most of the 14,700 available seats. Most of the fans are hockey-starved, transplanted Northerners; plenty of young families are also in attendance, as are groups of high school girls hoping for a glimpse of their favorite player.

Having come from elsewhere, the fans know hockey and are fanatical about their new team. And the Panthers came through for them in 1993–94, compiling the best record ever of any first-year NHL team. The Panthers also accommodate newcomers to the game, providing a pamphlet on hockey rules. This pamphlet is available at the Guest Relations booths, near sections 237 and 217.

■ $55 ■ $38 ■ $25 ■ $20 ■ $17

## ARENA STATS

**Location:** 701 Arena Blvd., Miami, FL 33136
**Opened:** July 13, 1988
**Capacity:** 14,700
**Services for fans with disabilities:** Seating available in all price ranges in sections 101, 113, 114, 119 and 121.

## ARENA FIRSTS

**Regular-season game:** Oct. 12, 1993, 2–1 loss to the Penguins.
**Goal:** Martin Straka of the Penguins.
**Regular-season win:** Oct. 14, 1993, 5–4 over the Ottawa Senators.
**Overtime game:** Oct. 17, 1993, 3–3 tie with the Tampa Bay Lightning.

## TEAM NOTEBOOK

**Franchise history:** Florida Panthers, 1993–present.

## TICKET INFORMATION

**Address:** 701 Arena Blvd., Miami, FL 33136
**Phone:** (305) 530-4435 or TicketMaster at (800) GO-PANTH. In Dade County, (305) 358-5885; in Broward County, (305) 523-3309; in Palm Beach, (407) 966-3309
**Hours:** Mon.-Fri. 10-4.

## LODGING NEAR THE ARENA

**Doral Ocean Resort**
4833 Collins Ave.
Miami, FL 33140
(305) 532-3600/(800) 22-DORAL
8 miles from the arena.

**Sonesta**
350 Ocean Dr.
Key Biscayne, FL 33149
(305) 361-2021/(800) 766-3782
10 miles from the arena.

## HOT TIPS FOR VISITING FANS

### Parking
The closest lots, across the street, cost $10. Lots 1 block away cost $5. For the extravagant, valet parking is available for $12. Most fans park in the $5 lots. Security guards are positioned around the arena and the parking lots. A limited number of metered street spaces are available around the outside of the $5 lots; the meters are off at night, but the neighborhood, on the edge of Overtown, can be risky at that time.

### Media bites
**Radio:** WQAM (560 AM—English). WCMQ (1210 AM—Spanish).
**TV:** Sunshine Network and occasionally WBFS (Channel 33). Denis Potvin and Jeff Rimer are on the mikes.

### Cuisine
The food is only average, but the selection is remarkable—especially the liquor. Frozen-drink stands are spread throughout the concourse, offering everything from piña coladas to mixed drinks and draft beer. Food stands offer the typical stadium fare, but the stands near section 232 also offer pizza, hero sandwiches, shrimp or wings, and fries and Polish sausage.

Popular bars in nearby Bayside include Houlihan's, Hooter's and the Hard Rock Cafe. Or if you're going north of Miami, try the Penalty Box (305-565-6658) in Fort Lauderdale. Owned by Rosie Paiement, former NHL right wing and brother of ex-NHL player Wilf Paiement, it's a hockey fan's heaven. Rosie organizes bus trips for each game. The cost is $40, and reservations should be made at least a week in advance.

### GETTING TO MIAMI ARENA
**Public transportation:** The Overtown Metrorail stop is just across the street from the arena. Call (305) 638-6700 for more information.
**By car:** From the airport, take 836 east to Biscayne Boulevard. Exit right at the bottom of the ramp onto Biscayne Blvd. Proceed to Northwest 8th Street and make a right. The Arena is 2 blocks on the left.

From Miami Beach, take I-395 west to the Biscayne Boulevard Exit. Go left onto Biscayne Boulevard and south 3 blocks to Northeast 8th. Right onto Northeast 8th for 3 blocks. Stadium is on the left.

## HOME-ICE ADVANTAGE
Good ice can be a disadvantage for a clutch-and-grab team such as the Panthers. The team's biggest advantage is fan noise, which seems louder because of a low roof.

## IN THE HOT SEATS

The lower-bowl seats are filled with season ticketholders and are not available on an individual-game basis. The Panther Pack seats, which go on sale for $8 at 10 a.m. on the day of the game, usually sell out quickly. Individual seats may also be available for the mezzanine and the reserved section.

• **Good seats:** The Panther Pack seats offer a good view. Whichever of the other upper sections you prefer, the best view is between the blue lines, in sections 230-232 and 210-212. Sections 210-212 also afford a view of the player benches.

• **Bad seats:** In the lower bowl, the first 10 rows are partially blocked by the glass and have reduced vision of the boards and corners.

**Scalping:** The city does an effective job of preventing scalping, which is illegal.

# Hartford Civic Center Coliseum

## ARENA STATS

**Location:** 242 Trumbull St., Hartford, CT 06103
**Opened:** Jan. 11, 1975
**Capacity:** 15,635
**Services for fans with disabilities:** Seating available in the last two rows of sections 101, 106, 107, 112, 113, 118, 119 and 124. For more information, call (203) 249-7528 or TTY (203) 549-7706.

## ARENA FIRSTS

**Regular-season games:** Jan. 11, 1975, 4–3 over the San Diego Mariners in overtime (WHA); Oct. 11, 1979, 4–1 loss to the Minnesota North Stars (NHL).
**Overtime games:** Jan. 11, 1975, 4–3 over the San Diego Mariners (WHA); Nov. 26, 1983, 4–3 over the New York Rangers (NHL).
**Playoff game:** April 11, 1980, 4–3 overtime loss to the Montreal Canadiens (NHL).

## TEAM NOTEBOOK

**Franchise history:** New England Whalers, 1972–79 (WHA); Hartford Whalers, 1979–present (NHL).
**Retired numbers:** 2, Rick Ley; 9, Gordie Howe; 19, John McKenzie.

**TICKET INFORMATION**
**Address:** 242 Trumbull St., Hartford, CT 06103
**Phone:** (203) 727-8101 or TicketMaster at (203) 525-4500
**Hours:** Mon.-Sat. 10-6 (Mon.-Fri. 10-6 in the off season).

The Hartford Civic Center is located inside a mall—appropriate, since the Whalers are shopping for an identity. The team has moved around, starting in Boston in 1972 as the World Hockey Association's New England Whalers, then to Springfield, Mass., in 1974, then to the new Civic Center in Hartford in 1975, back to Springfield for two years (the arena's roof collapsed during a 1978 snowstorm) and finally to the National Hockey League in 1979. The team had a good WHA history, but its NHL tenure has been undistinguished. The Whalers also play in a state where University of Connecticut basketball is king.

All this and a poor economy leave a lot of empty seats at the Civic Center. Attendance averages 10,500 at the 15,635-seat arena. Businessmen and children are noticeably scarce.

Inside, the arena provides good sightlines and its center-ice scoreboard/video screen has excellent resolution and can be seen from all angles. Nothing else stands out about the arena. If the Whalers are playing well, the arena can be exciting. If not, the place can be dreary.

## HOT TIPS FOR VISITING FANS

### Parking
Lots beneath the Civic Center and at the Sheraton-Hartford have spaces for $6. City lots farther from the arena can go as low as $3, but the walk can get cold.

### Media bites
**Radio:** WTIC (1080 AM).
**TV:** SportsChannel New England. Longtime NHL goaltender Gerry Cheevers does analysis on TV.

### Cuisine
Prices are low, but so are the quality and variety, and lines are long. The Carvel ice cream is very popular. If you have extra money, the Coliseum Club offers a buffet dinner before the game and tickets for two at a price of $100. Reservations are required.

Several bars in the neighborhoods are open after the game, but going to the mall establishments is more convenient. The mall has more than 70 restaurants and shops, plus the Sheraton-Hartford hotel. Recommended restaurants: Chuck's Steak House (203-241-9100), Margarita's (203-724-3331) and Gaetano's (203-249-1629).

### LODGING NEAR THE ARENA
**Sheraton Centre**
315 Trumbull St.
Hartford, CT 06103
(203) 728-5151/(800) 325-3535
Adjacent to the arena.

**Goodwin Hotel**
1 Haynes St.
Hartford, CT 06103
(203) 246-7500/(800) 922-5006
Across the street from the arena.

### GETTING TO HARTFORD CIVIC CENTER COLISEUM
**Public transportation:** Shuttle buses from commuter lots downtown are available. Call (203) 728-6637 for more information.
**By car:** From the north or south, 91 to Trumbull Street, exit 32B. Civic Center is five lights ahead.

From the east, take I-84 West to Main Street, exit 50. Go right past the Holiday Inn, then go left at traffic light onto Main Street. At the second traffic light, go right onto Church Street. Civic Center is at the next intersection.

From the west, take I-84 East to Ann/High Street. Go right onto High Street and, at the first light, left onto Church Street. Civic Center is at the next intersection.

### HOME-ICE ADVANTAGE
Not much of one. The Whalers are only slightly better than .500 in their history at home, and in recent years, they're well below that. The place can get noisy when it's full, but that doesn't happen often.

**VIP ■ $42 ■ $34**
**■ $29 ■ $25 ■ $19**

## IN THE HOT SEATS

Tickets go on sale in August, but with a small season-ticket base and an average attendance of 10,500, you can usually get tickets in all price ranges on game day.

• **Good seats:** Even with the empty seats, same-day discounted tickets aren't offered. Most of the 100 level seats go to season ticketholders. The 200-level seats offer the best combination of view and price. The steepness of the 300 level makes it ideal for watching plays develop.

• **Bad seats:** The lowest seats in the 100-level often have views distorted by the glass and/or blind spots, particularly if you're sitting in the bottom five rows behind the nets. In the bottom 10 rows of the 200 and 300 levels, railings or fans–who are allowed to move about during play–can obstruct your view. Rows AA through GG in the 300 level require a hike of up to 60 stairs.

• **Moving down:** Don't bother. Ushers are instructed to check all tickets.

**Scalping:** Because of the empty seats, there is little need, except when the Bruins or the Rangers are the opponent and huge convoys of their fans make the trip. The Whalers post guards to discourage scalping.

# Great Western Forum

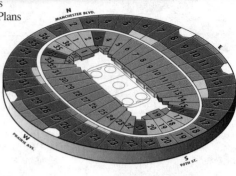

■ N/A ■ $80 ■ $70 ■ $50 ■ $45
■ $38 ■ $24 ■ $22 ■ $11

## ARENA STATS

**Location:** 3900 W. Manchester Blvd., Inglewood, CA 90305
**Opened:** Dec. 30, 1967
**Capacity:** 16,005
**Services for fans with disabilities:** Seating available in the main concourse.

## ARENA FIRSTS

**Regular-season game:** Dec. 30, 1967, 2–0 loss to the Philadelphia Flyers.
**Overtime game:** Oct. 5, 1983, 3–3 tie with the Minnesota North Stars.
**Playoff game:** April 4, 1968, 2–1 over the Minnesota North Stars.
**Stanley Cup finals game:** June 5, 1993, 4–3 overtime loss to the Montreal Canadiens.

## TEAM NOTEBOOK

**Franchise history:** Los Angeles Kings, 1967–present.
**Most Valuable Player/Hart:** Wayne Gretzky, 1988–89.
**Rookie of the Year/Calder:** Luc Robitaille, 1987.
**Retired numbers:** 16, Marcel Dionne; 30, Rogatien Vachon.

### TICKET INFORMATION

**Address:** 3900 W. Manchester Blvd., Inglewood, CA 90305
**Phone:** (310) 673-6003 or TicketMaster at (213) 480-3232, (714) 740-2000, (619) 278-8497 or (805) 583-8700
**Hours:** Mon.-Fri. 9-5:30.

The Great Western Forum, which opened in 1967, is on its last legs even as the Kings started to thrive. Plans are under way to build a modern arena with sky boxes aplenty. But, as is usually the case when comparing old stadiums to new ones, the Forum's small size is a plus for fans, most of whom are reasonably close to the ice. The greatest lure, though, is the presence of Wayne Gretzky, the NHL's all-time leading scorer and the most recognized name in the sport's history. The retired numbers of Rogie Vachon and Marcel Dionne adorn the walls in honor of their service in the 1970s, yet many in southern California didn't know the team existed until owner Bruce McNall acquired Gretzky in 1988.

Since Gretzky's arrival and the Kings' 1992–93 appearance in the Stanley Cup finals, as many stars are in the stands as are on the ice. Just as Jack Nicholson and other Hollywood luminaries ringed the court during the Lakers' showtime years, the stars have joined the ranks of Kings regulars. Even former president Ronald Reagan has attended playoff games. The concourse area is more cramped than one would like, but if you wander around the building through the glitter dresses and Armani suits, it's clear that Kings games are now Hollywood happenings.

## HOT TIPS FOR VISITING FANS

### Parking
The lots surrounding the Forum are the safest. Overflow parking goes across the street to Hollywood Park, which some fans say is easier to exit. Both lots charge $6. After the game, traffic controllers keep the cars moving, so you can get out of the lots quicker than you get in. Don't park on the side streets; they're permit-only.

### Media bites
**Radio:** XTRA (690 AM).
**TV:** Prime Ticket Cable Network and KTLA (Channel 5). Bob Miller is in his 22nd season as "the Voice of the Kings." If he sounds familiar, it's because he provided voiceovers in *The Mighty Ducks* and *The Mighty Ducks: D2*.

### Cuisine
You'll find more along the lines of basic hot dogs and cheeseburgers than California specialties, but burritos are available. You can get carved roast-beef sandwiches and salads at the Whistle Stop Restaurant, a stand-up deli. Of the concession-stand food, fans seem to like the chicken sandwiches best. Domestic beers are Miller, Budweiser and Coors. Heineken and Molson are also on tap, and there's an imported bottled-beer stand. For wine and mixed drinks, the Whistle Stop offers a fully stocked bar.

Other than fans and players who stay after the game at the private Forum Club, most fans leave Inglewood for postgame partying. Much of the hockey crowd, including players, heads to Harry O's (310-545-4444) in Manhattan Beach. Owned by former Kings player Billy Harris, this sports bar is always hopping and usually jam-packed. To dine, players and fans seem to like Jerry's Deli (310-821-6626) in Marina Del Rey.

## GETTING TO THE GREAT WESTERN FORUM

**Public transportation:** Take the No. 40 bus to Market Manchester. Transfer to an eastbound No. 211. For information, call (310) 320-9442.
**By car:** From Highway 105, exit at Prairie Avenue and head north for a few blocks to the Forum.

## LODGING NEAR THE ARENA

**Marriott Airport**
5855 W. Century Blvd.
Los Angeles, CA 90045
(310) 641-5700/(800) 228-9290.
8 miles from the arena.

**Radisson Hotel**
1400 Parkview Ave.
Manhattan Beach, CA 90267
(310) 546-7511/(800) 333-3333.
8 miles from the arena.

## HOME-ICE ADVANTAGE

Though the crowd isn't as hostile as in other arenas, opposing teams don't seem to play well at the Forum. Maybe it's the time change, or perhaps it's because teams are usually in the midst of a long road trip when they hit L.A. Or maybe the players are thinking more about golf than hockey in L.A.

## IN THE HOT SEATS

Though the Kings sold out 32 of 41 home games in 1993–94, most weren't sellouts until the last minute. Fifteen minutes before game time, a few tickets are usually left; most are for excellent seats because the $24 and $11 tickets tend to sell before the $80 and $45 tickets. By the way, those $11 tickets are decent seats.

- **Bad seats:** Some seats high in the corner are located as much as 170 feet from the ice. If you sit next to the glass, it's rather difficult to see what's happening along the boards on your side.

- **Moving down:** Back in the PG days (pre-Gretzky), you could buy the cheapest ticket and sit anywhere in the building, but those days are long gone. Ushers are particularly vigilant in patrolling the areas where higher-profile season ticketholders sit. They will know if you don't belong.

**Scalping:** Ticket availability is such that most don't need to resort to scalpers.

# Montreal Forum

## ARENA STATS

**Location:** 2313 Ste. Catherine St., Montreal, PQ, Canada H3H 1N2
**Opened:** 1924
**Capacity:** 17,959
**Services for fans with disabilities:** Seating in lower level.

## ARENA FIRSTS

**Regular-season game:** Nov. 29, 1924, 7–1 over the Toronto St. Pats.
**Playoff game:** March 26, 1930, 2–2 tie with the Chicago Blackhawks in triple overtime.
**Stanley Cup finals game:** April 3, 1930, 4–3 over the Boston Bruins.

## TEAM NOTEBOOK

**Franchise history:** Club de Hockey Canadien 1909–10, '16–17; Club Athlétique Canadien, '10–16 (NHA); Montreal Canadiens, (NHL) '17–present.
**Stanley Cups:** 1915–16, '23–24, '29–30, '30–31, '43–44, '45–46, '52–53, '55–56 to '59–60, '64–65, '65–66, '67–68, '68–69, '70–71, '72–73, '75–76 to '78–79, '85–86, '92–93.
**Hockey Hall of Fame:** Morenz, Vezina, '45; Joliat, Northey, '47; Lalonde, Malone, '50; Cleghorn, Gardiner, Raymond, '58; Mantha, Selke, '60; Hall, Hainsworth, M. Richard, '61; Laviolette, O'Brien, Pitre, '62; Dandurand, Gorman, '63; Durnan, B. Siebert, '64; Blake, Bouchard, Lach, Reardon, '66; T. Johnson, '70; Beliveau, Geoffrion, '72; Harvey, Molson, '73; Moore, '74; Cattarinich, '77; Plante, Pollock, '78; H. Richard, '79; Worsley, '80; Mahovlich, '81; Cournoyer, '82; Dryden, '83; Lemaire, '84; Olmstead, '85; Savard, '86; Laperriere, '87; Lafleur, O'Connor, '88; Bowman, '91; Gainey, '92; Lapointe, Shutt, '93.

---

T he Montreal Forum, arguably the most famous hockey arena in the world, is in its final days. Barring construction delays on the new arena, 1994–95 will be the final full season in the 70-year-old building. The move to the new arena, at Windsor Station in downtown Montreal, is planned for midseason 1995–96. Officially it's unnamed, but locals are calling it the New Forum.

It'll be difficult to bid adieu to the old Forum. Eleven Cup-clinching games were played here. You can feel the history in the building, and the club ties the past to the present beautifully. Walk the third-level concourse and you'll find large mosaic displays of every Canadiens team. On the first level, Canadiens Hall of Famers are honored with plaques. Illuminated photos of current players and the Molson's Cup also are on display. Even the escalators, when lighted, look like crossed hockey sticks.

The crowd at Canadiens games is a mixture of corporate "visitors" and die-hard hockey fans. Until the playoffs, you won't see the folks in the lower-level red seats getting too wild. But if you look beyond the corporate seats, you'll find a knowledgeable and demanding hockey crowd. Fans tend to arrive late and become more intense as the game goes on. They expect excellence and let the team know when it falls short.

## HOT TIPS FOR VISITING FANS

**Parking**
No parking is available at the arena, but a number of lots and garages are nearby. Near the rink, expect to pay C$11 As you get farther away, the price drops. Garages aren't always clearly marked. Crowds are generally late-arriving, so you shouldn't have trouble finding a place unless you hit the rush.

**Media bites**
**Radio:** In English, Hall of Famer Dick Irvin handles play-by-play on CJAD (800 AM) and CBMT (Channel 6). Games in French are broadcast on CBF (690 AM).
**TV:** CBFT (Channel 2), CBMT (Channel 6) and RDS (cable).

**Cuisine**
The fare is quite pedestrian for a city known for its culinary excellence. One exception is the hot dogs—they're grilled, and the rolls are toasted. Montreal's specialty, smoked meat, is served on sandwiches, and pizza, ice cream and Tim Horton's doughnuts are also available. The club is owned by the Molson Brewery, so don't expect to find other brands. But Molson is a first-class Canadian beer, and the Forum stocks 11 different varieties.

Your choices for dinner after the game are relatively slim in the immediate area. A few fast-food and sit-down restaurants are on Ste. Catherine. The mall across Atwater Street offers several options. Crescent Street—about a 10- to 12-block walk toward downtown—has several fine restaurants, ranging from the distinguished Les Halles (514-844-2328) to the Hard Rock Cafe (514-987-1420). For deli fare, try Dunn's (514-866-4377) downtown. Keep in mind that many of the nicer spots require gentlemen to wear jackets.

## LODGING NEAR THE ARENA

**Bonaventure Hilton**
1 Place Bonaventure
Montreal, PQ
Canada H5A 1E4
(514) 878-2332/(800) 445-8667
About 1½ miles from the arena.

**Le Chateau Champlain**
1050 W. Legeuche-Tiere
Montreal, PQ
Canada H3B 4C9
(514) 878-9000/(800) 441-1414
About 2 miles from the arena.

## THE CANADIENS AT THE FORUM

**April 3, 1930:** Howie Morenz scores the game-winning goal as Montreal defeats the Boston Bruins 4–3, taking their third Stanley Cup championship, their first at the Forum.

**Jan. 28, 1937:** Morenz breaks his leg in a game against the Chicago Blackhawks. He dies on March 8, and the funeral service is held at the Forum on March 11.

**Nov. 8, 1942:** The Canadiens beat the New York Rangers 10–2, and Maurice Richard scores his first NHL goal, beating goalie Steve Buzinski.

**Dec. 16, 1950:** Jean Beliveau and Bernie Geoffrion make their NHL debuts in a 1–1 tie with the Rangers.

**Oct. 19, 1957:** Richard becomes the first NHL player to score 500 goals when he beats Blackhawks goalie Glenn Hall at 15:52 of the first period in a 3–1 Canadiens win.

**May 1, 1965:** Beliveau scores the game-winning goal only 14 seconds into the first period, as the Canadiens beat the Blackhawks 4–0 and take their ninth Stanley Cup at the Forum, their 13th cup overall.

**May 21, 1979:** Montreal beats the Rangers 4–1 to clinch its fourth consecutive Stanley Cup and 10th at home.

**June 9, 1993:** The Canadiens beat the Los Angeles Kings 4–1 to clinch their 24th Stanley Cup.

# IN THE HOT SEATS AT MONTREAL FORUM

Tickets are hard to get, but not impossible. Most of the arena is sold out on a season-ticket basis. About 1,200 seats and 1,700 standing-room tickets are available on an individual-game basis, but most are gone as soon as they go on sale. The club designates one day in late August (for games in the first half of the season) and another in early December (second-half games) for sale of individual-game tickets. As the time nears, call the club and get the date. Orders are limited to a maximum of four tickets a game for four games.

Standing-room tickets (C$12) are a little more available, but because they're sold in advance, you should get to the Forum early. Doors open one hour before faceoff (1½ hours before playoff games), and SRO fans sprint to the prime standing spots on the blue line behind the red and white sections. Balconies on each end of the ice hold about 300 seats each, and they're very popular with the non-season-ticket crowd. If you can get one of the lower rows, the seats aren't bad. The new arena will seat 21,260 (no standing), and club owners want to increase the number of tickets available on an individual-game basis, so the ticket situation should improve.

• **Bad seats:** You might find your view of the scoreboard or clock partially obscured in the upper rows of the balcony, and the standing-room area gets very crowded, particularly up top. But take what you can get. The Forum is an excellent place to watch hockey, so no seat (or non-seat) is terrible.

**Scalping:** Scalpers set up shop on Ste. Catherine outside the Forum and command significant markups.

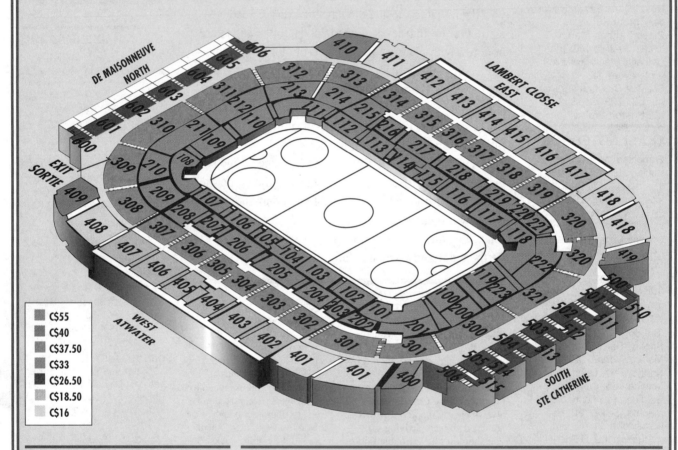

- ■ C$55
- ■ C$40
- ■ C$37.50
- ■ C$33
- ■ C$26.50
- ■ C$18.50
- ■ C$16

## HOME-ICE ADVANTAGE

The Forum has some of the better ice in the NHL, so to take advantage, the Canadiens traditionally have built their team with speed and finesse. The "Flying Frenchmen" tradition and style is generally preferred by the fans. However, the last couple of years, the Habs (short for Les Habitants) have been more of a blue-collar team, relying on defense and the goaltending of star Patrick Roy. Both formulas work. The Canadiens have a home winning percentage of .740.

## GETTING TO MONTREAL FORUM

**Public transportation:** The Atwater Stop of the MUTC Subway is at the Forum. Buses also serve the Forum. Call (514) 288-6287 for more information.

**By car:** From the south, take route 15 north to route 10 west. Follow route 10 across the Champlain Bridge, where it turns into route 15. This road will take you to route 720 north. After about 2 miles, follow signs to the Forum.

From the west, take route 401 in Ontario which becomes route 20 in Quebec. Follow this road into Montreal, where it becomes route 720. From route 720, follow signs to the Forum.

## TICKET INFORMATION
**Address:** 2313 Ste. Catherine St., Montreal, PQ, Canada H3H 1N2

**Phone:** (514) 932-2582 or Admission at (514) 790-1245.
**Hours:** Mon.-Fri. 10-6.

**Prices:** C$55, C$40, C$37.50, C$33, C$26.50, C$18.50, C$16, C$12.

# Brendan Byrne Arena

## ARENA STATS

**Location:** East Rutherford, NJ 07073
**Opened:** Nov. 4, 1981
**Capacity:** 19,040
**Services for fans with disabilities:** Seating available on the concourse and in lower lobby. Call (201) 935-3900 for information.

## ARENA FIRSTS

**Regular-season game:** Oct. 5, 1982, 3–3 tie with the Pittsburgh Penguins.
**Goal:** Don Lever of the Devils.
**Overtime game:** Nov. 12, 1983, 4–3 loss to the Calgary Flames.
**Playoff game:** April 9, 1988, 3–0 over the New York Islanders.

## TEAM NOTEBOOK

**Franchise history:** Kansas City Scouts, 1974–76; Colorado Rockies, 1976–82; New Jersey Devils, 1982–present.
**Rookie of the year/Calder Trophy:** Martin Brodeur, 1994.

## TICKET INFORMATION

**Address:** East Rutherford, NJ 07073.
**Phone:** (201) 935-3900 or TicketMaster at (201) 507-8900, (212) 307-7171, (914) 454-3388 or (516) 888-9000
**Hours:** Mon.-Fri. 9-6, Sat. 10-6, Sun. 12-5.

## LODGING NEAR THE ARENA

**Sheraton Meadowlands**
Two Meadowlands Plaza
East Rutherford, NJ 07073
(201) 896-0500/(800) 325-2525
½ mile from the arena.

**Meadowlands Hilton**
2 Harmon Plaza
Secaucus, NJ 07094
(201) 348-6900/(800) HILTONS
1 mile from the arena.

L ooking east from the Meadowlands' Byrne Arena parking lot, you can see the tops of the Empire State Building and the World Trade Center. Though New York City is 6 miles away, it still manages to overshadow much of what happens in East Rutherford, N.J.

One of the better-kept secrets in the NHL, the hockey/basketball venue at the Meadowlands Sports Complex is a sight to behold. The arena is named after the former New Jersey governor who helped push through the Meadowlands complex and joined with owner John McMullen in moving the Colorado Rockies franchise from Denver. Finished in 1981, it features many of the amenities that NHL teams push for nowadays: concourse-level luxury boxes, wide concourses, plentiful concession stands and state-of-the-art scoreboards. The stadium's most impressive aspect, though, is its size. To get its true impact, arrive early and walk into the seating area when it's mostly empty—you'll feel like you're inside a canyon.

The franchise, although plopped down in an area of one-time Rangers fans, is building support as the team improves. The secret is getting out. So, if you're in New York, make the journey through the Lincoln Tunnel. It's well worth the trip.

**■ $35 ■ $30 ■ $26 ■ $14**

## HOT TIPS FOR VISITING FANS

### Parking
You're stuck with the stadium lot, which costs $5. If you park on the access roads, you might get ticketed or towed. Make sure you arrive early because the Arena lots have only 4,500 spaces. Overflow parking is at Giants Stadium, which is a hike. If you need to get on the turnpike when you leave, park in the front or back and work your way to the northeast corner. That puts you right at the on ramp.

### Media Bites
**Radio:** WABC (770 AM). Sherry Ross is the first woman to do analysis for an NHL team.
**TV:** SportsChannel.

### Cuisine
Pretty much standard stadium fare. The Hebrew National hot dogs are better than the ones in the regular concession stands. The jumbo pretzels are a good buy at $1.75. The rest of the food is so-so. Budweiser and Miller are offered on tap, and Heineken, Beck's and Molson are available at portable stands. Other portable stands offer wine or mixed drinks.

After the game, most of your choices are in Secaucus. Several players go to the Houlihan's there. Other fan hangouts are Moonshine Jugs (201-348-1700) and the Jersey Sports Cafe (201-933-3308). Devils fan-club members often congregate afterward at Rutt's Hut, a hot-dog-and-beer joint in Clifton.

### GETTING TO BRENDAN BYRNE ARENA
**Public transportation:** New Jersey Transit offers load-and-go bus service from the Port Authority Terminal in Manhattan. Call (201) 762-5100 for more information.
**By car:** From the Lincoln Tunnel, take Route 3 West directly to the Sports Complex. Northbound on the New Jersey Turnpike, take the western spur to 16W and follow signs to Sports Complex.

Southbound on the Garden State Parkway, leave the Parkway at exit 163 and follow Route 17 South to Paterson Plank Road east to the Sports Complex.

### HOME-ICE ADVANTAGE
The arena's biggest advantage is its proximity to New York. The New York media concentrate on the Rangers and Islanders, allowing the Devils to operate in relative obscurity, which has allowed them to steadily improve.

## IN THE HOT SEATS

With the luxury boxes on the concourse level and no other overhangs, there isn't a bad seat in the house. Seats are generally available in all sections. Warning: Rangers-Devils games and late-season Saturday matinees sell out, so order early for those.

• **Bad seats:** Just a few minor annoyances. Down low, the folding chairs on the metal risers are not as comfortable as the chairs bolted into the cement risers. In sections 203 (5-10), 204 (rows 6 and 7), 226 (6 and 7), and 227 (5 and 6), a railing cuts across your view of the goal. Noisy rooms of machinery sit at the top of sections 207, 217, 228 and 238, but you'll quickly get used to the sound. The building is very cold, so bring a jacket if you're sitting down low.

• **Moving down:** Possible in the upper section, but wait until the second period.

 **Scalping:** Management is very strict. Those who work anywhere except Gate D, where management can monitor them, can be threatened with prosecution. A few scalpers can be found at Gate D and they generally offer tickets at face value, more if the Rangers are the opponent. They'll also buy your extra tickets, but not at face value.

# Nassau Veterans Memorial Coliseum

The view of the ice from Nassau Coliseum's section 329 takes you under the New York Islanders' four Stanley Cup banners and over a lot of empty seats. Just as the Islanders' play turned ordinary when the team grew old, the Coliseum, which opened in 1972, is showing signs of age. The color scheme—or what passes as one—makes the arena look darker. Seats added over the years have obstructions. The sound system—or clock radio, as one fan calls it—is so-so in most seats and unintelligible from the upper section. Crowds can be sparse, and fans are tough on the team. Also, the arena is pretty much accessible only by car. In a metropolitan area that boasts hockey at Madison Square Garden and the Meadowlands, the Coliseum comes in third.

But that's not to say going to a game isn't fun. The Islanders shut out the lights for pregame announcements, play the James Bond theme and then turn on the lights when the team bursts onto the ice. P.A. announcer Rich Kahn is great, particularly when he says "Pierre Turrrrr-geon," and the fans can shout as loud as any in the league. And if you can get a ticket to a Rangers-Islanders game, by all means go. With about a 50-50 ratio of fans, the back and forth in the stands can be as exciting as the action on the ice.

The Islanders have talked of asking Nassau County for renovations, but no formal request has been made. In the meantime, don't go to the game expecting to relive the magic of the 1980s.

## HOT TIPS FOR VISITING FANS

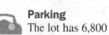

**Parking**
The lot has 6,800 spaces, and on a night with a sparse crowd, that's more than enough. But arrive early, just in case. The price is a reasonable $4.50. Roads from the parking lot to Hempstead Turnpike back up after the game. If you work your way to the west exit and leave by Earle Overton Boulevard, you'll have easier access to Hempstead Turnpike and Meadowbrook Parkway.

**Media bites**
**Radio:** WPAT (930 AM).
**TV:** SportsChannel. Play-by-play announcer Jiggs McDonald has often been used on national broadcasts.

**Cuisine**
The food is so-so. Your best bets are the Hebrew National hot dogs (they taste better after the first intermission) and the French-bread pizza. A Pizza Hut Express is scheduled to open in 1994. The chicken sandwiches are OK. The on-tap beers are Budweiser and Miller, and you also can get Heineken and Beck's. Bottled water sells for $2. Mixed drinks, beer and wine are also available at the downstairs bars.
Mulcahy's in Wantagh drops

the cover charge (which runs up to $7) on Friday and Saturday nights if you have an Islanders ticket stub. The bar has eight giant screens, 50 monitors and occasionally features prominent entertainment acts. Most of the section 329 fans go to the T.G.I. Friday's in Uniondale.

# IN THE HOT SEATS AT NASSAU VETERANS MEMORIAL COLISEUM

With an average attendance of 12,191 in a 16,297-seat arena, seats are available in all price ranges. The lower bowl is your best bet if you're willing to pay. The glass doesn't interfere too much with your vision, but it's better to sit a little higher. The best deal is the 200 level. The 300 level is good, too, except up high. If you want the higher, less expensive seats and want to be able to see the scoreboard, sit in sections 328-339. If you're looking for some off-ice entertainment, sit in or next to section 329, but the rowdy fans there warn that you shouldn't bring the kids.

• **Bad seats:** The upper two rows are horrendous: there is little shoulder room; luxury boxes cut off your view of the scoreboard above row N in sections other than 328-339, and in section 319, above row P, part of your view of the ice is cut off. TV monitors are provided in obstructed sections.

• **Moving down:** The ushers check tickets and are very serious about not letting anyone sneak down. Ushers sit on the stairways during play, and to get to the 100 level, you'll have to walk over them.

Moving down is possible in the 300 level, but wait until the second period.

**Scalping:** A few operate in the main parking lot, south of the arena. Because of the infrequent sellouts, it's not worth their while. It's illegal in Uniondale to sell tickets for more than face value, so if you're selling extras, be advised that that's all you'll get.

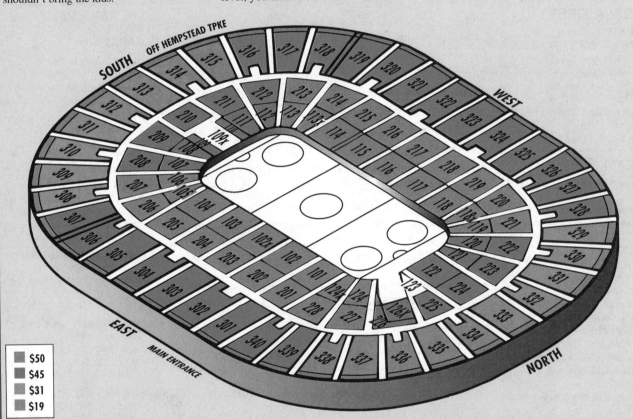

Legend:
- $50
- $45
- $31
- $19

## HOME-ICE ADVANTAGE

Three reasons for the Islanders' home-ice advantage. The fans: When things are going well, the fans are among the loudest in the league. New York bragging rights: With two rivals in the metropolitan region, the Islanders carry the banner for the city's eastern suburbs. The playoff mystique: The Islanders save their best for the playoffs, particularly when their backs are against the wall.

## GETTING TO NASSAU VETERANS MEMORIAL COLISEUM

**Public transportation:** Take the Long Island Railroad to Hempstead Station. Walk 1 block to the Hempstead Bus Terminal. The N70, N71, and N72 buses will drop you off on the Hempstead Turnpike opposite Nassau Coliseum. Call (516) 222-1000 for bus information.

**By car:** From Connecticut and Northern New York state, take I-95 to Throgs Neck Expressway. Cross Throgs Neck Bridge and continue about 3 miles to the Long Island Expressway East (I-495). Take the LIE about 7 miles to exit 38 (Northern State Parkway East). Go south to exit 31A (Meadowbrook Parkway South), then to exit M4 (Nassau Coliseum).

From Manhattan: take the Midtown Tunnel to the LIE East and follow same directions as above.

## TICKET INFORMATION
**Address:** Uniondale, NY 11553
**Phone:** (800) 882-ISLE (4753) or TicketMaster at (516) 888-9000 or (212) 307-7171

**Hours:** Mon.-Sat. 10:45-5:30.
**Prices:** $50: sections 101-106, 113-119, 124, 201-207, 213-221, 227-228; $45: sections 107-112, 120-123, 208-212, 222-226, 301-307, 318-328 and 339-340; $31: sections 308-317 and 329-338; $19: last four rows of sections 301-340.

## ARENA STATS

**Location:** 4 Pennsylvania Plaza, New York, N.Y. 10001
**Opened:** Feb. 11, 1968
**Capacity:** 18,200
**Services for fans with disabilities:** Seating available in the 200 sections.

## ARENA FIRSTS

**Regular-season game:** Feb. 18, 1968, 3–1 over the Philadelphia Flyers.
**Playoff game:** April 4, 1968, 3–1 over the Chicago Blackhawks.
**Stanley Cup finals game:** May 4, 1972, 5–2 over the Boston Bruins.

## TEAM NOTEBOOK

**Franchise history:** New York Rangers, 1928–present
**Stanley Cups:** 1927–28, '32–33, '39–40, '93–94
**MVP/Hart:** O'Connor, 1947–48, Rayner, '49–50, Bathgate, '58–59, Messier, '91–92.
**Rookies of the Year/Calder :** MacDonald, 1939–40; Warwick, '41–42; Laprade, '45–46; Lund, '48–49; Worsley, '52–53; Henry, '53–54; Vickers, '72–73; Leetch, '88–89.
**Hockey Hall of Fame:** Morenz, L. Patrick, 1945; Cook, '52; Boucher, Johnson, '58; O. Siebert, '61; E. Siebert, '63; D. Bentley, '64; M. Bentley, Pratt, '66; Colville, '67; Hextall, '69; Gadsby, '70; Geoffrion, '72; Harvey, Rayner, '73; Coulter, '74; Bathgate, '78; Howell, '79; Patrick, Worsley, '80; Gilbert, '82; P. Esposito, '84; Ratelle, '85; Giacomin, '87; Lafleur, O'Connor, Park, '88; Smith, '91; Dionne, '92; Laprade, '93.
**Retired numbers:** 1, Giacomin; 7, Gilbert.

# Madison Square Garden

Madison Square Garden is New York—big, loud, jam-packed and proud. In keeping with the city's vertical landscape, even the ice surface is five stories above the street.

A visit to the circular Garden will stir your senses. One of the loudest arenas outside Chicago, the 18,000-plus fans match the volume of the fabulous sound system.

Self-proclaimed "true" Rangers fans sit in the upper tier, once known as the blue seats before a 1991 renovation changed them to teal. Rhythmic "Let's go, Rangers" chants cascade down from that level as well as rude comments about opposing players.

This crowd is loyal (witness the 1975 standing ovation for returning goaltender Eddie Giacomin), totally unforgiving (as when former Islanders star Denis Potvin was booed unmercifully at a recent Heroes of Hockey game), and proud, especially so now, since the Rangers finally brought home the Stanley Cup in 1994. The only question now is how will the fans handle a new Stanley Cup banner after so many decades without?

## HOT TIPS FOR VISITING FANS

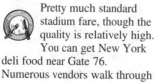

**Parking**
Lots can be found around the area and average about $15. The neighborhood surrounding the Garden is bustling, and the Garden itself is above Penn Station, one of New York's commuter hubs, so it's well-traveled and generally safe. Traffic down Seventh Avenue and on crosstown streets can be knotty before games, so give yourself extra time.

**Media bites**
**Radio:** WFAN (660 AM), WEVD (1050 AM) and WXPS (107.1 FM).
**TV:** MSG Network. Former Rangers goaltender John Davidson does analysis.

**Cuisine**
Pretty much standard stadium fare, though the quality is relatively high. You can get New York deli food near Gate 76. Numerous vendors walk through the lower-level seats, which keeps down the lines at the food courts. Beer-only stands have the same effect. The End Court bar, which offers mixed drinks, is near Gate 64. No food courts in the upper level.

Some nearby postgame hangouts are Penn Bar, Blarney Rock and Hickey's. Charley O's is in the Penn Plaza complex, as is the Play-By-Play, which hosts a show on the MSG Network after games. For Italian, try Carmine's (212-221-3800) or Dock's (212-986-8080) on the east side for seafood. Up Third Avenue from Dock's, there's P.J. Clarke's, the perfect bar for an after-game drink and cigar.

## LODGING NEAR THE ARENA

**Best Western Hotel Pennsylvania**
401 W. 33rd St.
New York, NY 10001
(212) 736-5000/(800) 233-8585

Across the street from the arena.

**Essex House**
36 Central Park South
New York, NY 10019
(212) 371-4000/(800) 221-4982
A little more than a mile from the arena.

## THE RANGERS AT MADISON SQUARE GARDEN

**Nov. 21, 1971:** The Rangers score the most goals in team history when they beat the California Golden Seals 12–1.

**May 4, 1972:** The Rangers win their first Stanley Cup finals game at this Madison Square Garden, beating the Boston Bruins 5–2.

**April 8, 1982:** Mikko Leinonen gets an NHL-playoff-record six assists as the Rangers beat the Philadelphia Flyers 7–3 in the first round of the playoffs.

**Feb. 23, 1983:** Mark Pavelich ties a team record when he scores five goals against the Hartford Whalers in an 11–3 win.

**April 13, 1985:** Tim Kerr of the Philadelphia Flyers sets an NHL-playoff record with four goals in the second period of a 6–5 win over the Rangers.

**April 16, 1992:** The Rangers beat the Pittsburgh Penguins 7–1, clinching the President's Trophy for the league's best record.

**May 27, 1994:** Stéphane Matteau scores in the second overtime to give the Rangers a 2–1 win over the New Jersey Devils in Game 7 of the Eastern Conference finals.

**June 14, 1994:** Mark Messier scores the winning goal as the Rangers beat the Vancouver Canucks 3–2 in Game 7 of the Stanley Cup finals, giving New York its first Cup since 1940.

# IN THE HOT SEATS AT MADISON SQUARE GARDEN

Sightlines are generally good. An eight-sided center-suspended scoreboard has four television screens that follow all the action and show any view that might be obstructed. The best seats are down low, but these tend to be corporate seats and are rarely available. Frequent sellouts, particularly with how well the Rangers played in the 1993–94 season, mean you have to plan ahead.

• **Bad seats:** The arena has three interior concourses in the lower tier. If you're sitting in the first two rows behind each of these, your view will be blocked on occasion by passing fans and vendors. If you're sitting behind the goal in the 300 level, the net closest to you is hard to see. If you sit in section 406, next to the broadcast booth, a good chunk of your view is cut off.

• **Moving down:** Don't bother. With aver-age attendance of 18,000 in an 18,200-seat arena, empty seats are rare.

**Scalping:** Plenty of scalpers are around the arena, and with the law of supply and demand, it's a seller's market. But as with most scalpers, buyers who wait until the game starts, find that prices go down dramatically.

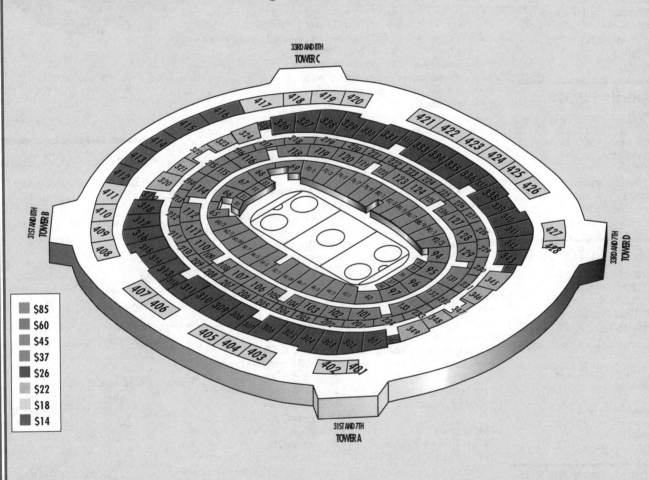

**Legend:**
- $85
- $60
- $45
- $37
- $26
- $22
- $18
- $14

## HOME-ICE ADVANTAGE

Though it has improved in recent years, the ice at MSG has been ranked by players as the worst in the NHL. The Garden has about 320 events a year, and the ice is made on game day. This leads to poor skating conditions and bouncing pucks. And the Rangers, who skate there 41 games a year, get the advantage, particularly over Canadian teams used to good ice.

The Rangers also say their fans are worth a goal a game. Besides being a little intimidating and occasionally rude, Rangers fans are very knowledgeable. A good pass will start them cheering. The large season-ticket base brings camaraderie in the stands and a strong identification with the team. This is evident against the suburban Islanders and Devils. The Rangers are .670 against them at home.

## GETTING TO MSG

**Public transportation:** Take the B, D, F or Q train to the 34th Street Station; MSG is 2 blocks west. Or take an A,C, E, 1, 2, 3 or 9 train to Pennsylvania Station–34th Street, which is directly below MSG.

**By car:** From New Jersey and the south, enter Manhattan via the Lincoln Tunnel. Follow signs for downtown and turn left on 34th Street.

From Connecticut and the north, follow Route 95 to Route 9A-S. Exit at 34th Street.

---

**TICKET INFORMATION**
**Ticket Office:** 4 Pennsylvania Plaza, New York, NY 10001

**Phone:** (212) 465-6040 or TicketMaster (212)307-7171
**Hours:** Mon.-Sat., 10-8; Sun., 11-7

**Prices:** $85, $60, $45, $37, $26, $22, $18, $14.

---

# Ottawa Civic Centre

The Ottawa Senators' home opener in 1992 ended the NHL's longest victory drought at 58 years. Welcome to the Ottawa Civic Centre, a new 27-year-old arena that's part of a football stadium and hosts a struggling third-year franchise with eight Stanley Cup banners and a retired number. All these contradictions exist because when Ottawa was awarded an expansion franchise, it adopted the name of the successful team that ceased play in 1934.

Needing a temporary arena, management chose the Civic Centre, home of the Ottawa 67s junior team and part of Lansdowne Park football stadium. Too small for NHL hockey, the stadium required a massive renovation, including replacing every seat, that was finished a half-hour before the opening.

The Senators say their job now is for the team to get the fans going. As with most fans in Canada, they're knowledgeable—and quiet. The Senators invite various entertainers to rile the fans up and have a mascot—Spartacat, the lion.

A more serious bit of inspiration is the banner honoring Frank Finnigan, who scored the winning goal in 1927 for the old Senators' last Stanley Cup. He helped to bring NHL hockey back to Ottawa, but died in 1991, before the Senators resumed play. The team retired his number on opening night.

CS85 ◼ CS70 ◼ CS55 ◼ CS44
CS32 ◼ CS26 ◼ CS27.50 ◼ CS24

## HOT TIPS FOR VISITING FANS

### Parking
The stadium lot costs C$11 and can be difficult to exit after a game. A small C$10 lot across Bank Street provides an easier exit. The neighborhood is nice, and some fans park on residential streets. City parking restrictions generally end at 7 P.M. Hurley's Sports Coliseum, a bar at 1500 Bank Street, offers free shuttle-bus service. Buses leave a half-hour before the game. Ask the bartender for a ticket.

### Media bites
**Radio:** CFRA (580 AM—English) and CJRC (1150 AM—French).
**TV:** CHRO (Channel 6), and CGOH (Channel 7).

### Cuisine
A wide selection. The pastries, which range from $3 to $3.50, are highly recommended. Other specialties are the smoked-meat sandwiches and jalapeño sausages. *Poutine*—fries with cheese and gravy—is an acquired taste. Molson draft sells for $3.75. The large number of vendor carts keeps the lines manageable, though walking through the concourse can take time.

If you took a shuttle bus from Hurley's, it's a nice place to hang out after the game. Players often go to eat at Capone's (613-828-8366), an Italian restaurant in the city's west end. The younger players go to Le Bistro, across the river in Hull, Quebec. Ottawa's main strip of bars is on Elgin Street.

### GETTING TO OTTAWA CIVIC CENTRE
**Public transportation:** Buses stop in front of the Civic Centre. Call (613) 741-6440 for more information.
**By car:** From the U.S., cross at Ogdensburg, New York, and go north on Highway 16 for approximately 50 miles. At the Ottawa city limits, Highway 16 changes into Prince of Wales Drive. At Preston Street, Prince of Wales changes into Queen Elizabeth Driveway. Enter Lansdowne Park off Queen Elizabeth.

### HOME-ICE ADVANTAGE
The Senators might have a Roman logo, but the Civic Centre is no lion's den. Various aspects of the arena—below-average ice surface, sharper corners and close-in fans—could provide an edge, but Ottawa doesn't yet have a team that can take advantage of them.

## IN THE HOT SEATS

With 8,200 season ticketholders in a 10,585-seat stadium, availability can be a problem. Tickets for the second half of the season go on sale in mid-December. Sections 1-12 offer at-your-seat service, but these are taken up by season ticketholders. Standing room is available in that section for less than half the price. If these are unavailable, try to get a seat in the lower bowl or mid-bowl. No alcohol is allowed in parts of sections 16, 23 and 27.

• **Bad seats:** Above row MM, the luxury boxes cut off your view of the scoreboard. Small scoreboards are provided. If you like to keep track of shots, the shot counter isn't visible up high in sections 16-23. This upper section also can feel claustrophobic because insulated pipes and girders are over you, but there's no danger of banging your head if you stand up.

• **Moving down:** Don't even think about it. Management is strict, and frankly, there aren't a lot of empty seats. Fans are allowed down to watch warmups.

**Scalping:** Illegal scalpers can be found along the Bank Street entrances. For a Montreal Canadiens or Toronto Maple Leafs game, scalpers can command $400 a ticket.

# The Spectrum

Rocky Balboa's statue seems appropriate for the home of the Broad Street Bullies. And while the Spectrum is a shrine to those Stanley Cup years, the arena doesn't honor the fisticuffs. Rather, it honors the underdog spirit that allowed the Philadelphia Flyers to become one of the most successful expansion franchises.

In addition to the Rocky statue, there are statues of the scoring of a key Flyers goal and of good-luck charm Kate Smith. A Wall of Fame inside details the arena's history. When you come to the Spectrum, you feel like you're part of the Flyers family, one of the main reasons that Flyers fans are among the most loyal, knowledgeable and demanding in the league, though the relationship has been strained by the team's recent slide.

The arena is not as impressive as the atmosphere. It's your basic three-level stadium. In contrast to the name "Spectrum," the seats are all one color: red. It has a nice scoreboard but lacks luxury boxes and other amenities of newer stadiums. But the Flyers promise wonderful things for Spectrum 2, which is scheduled to be built next door and is supposed to open in 1996.

## ARENA STATS

**Location:** Pattison Place, Philadelphia, PA 19148
**Opened:** Sept. 30, 1967
**Capacity:** 17,380
**Services for fans with disabilities:** Seating available throughout the stadium, but primarily in section C. Locations vary for each game. Call (215) 336-3600 for more information.

## ARENA FIRSTS

**Regular-season game:** Oct. 19, 1967, 1–0 over the Pittsburgh Penguins.
**Overtime game:** Nov. 20, 1983, 6–5 over the Pittsburgh Penguins.
**Playoff game:** April 4, 1968, 1–0 loss to the St. Louis Blues.
**Stanley Cup finals game:** May 12, 1974, 4–1 over the Boston Bruins.

## TEAM NOTEBOOK

**Franchise history:** Philadelphia Flyers, 1967–present.
**Stanley Cups:** 1973–74, 1974–75.
**Most Valuable Players/Hart:** Bobby Clarke, 1972–73, 1974–75, 1975–76
**Hockey Hall of Fame:** Bernie Parent, 1984; Bobby Clarke, 1987; Ed Snider, 1988; Bill Barber, 1990; Keith Allen, 1992.
**Retired numbers:** 1, Bernie Parent; 4, Barry Ashbee; 7, Bill Barber; 16, Bobby Clarke.

## HOT TIPS FOR VISITING FANS

**Parking**
Two main lots are on the south side of Pattison Avenue. Sometimes the Veterans Stadium lot across the street is available, but that costs more. If you arrive early, street parking is available on Pattison Avenue east of the stadium or west of Broad Street. Avoid the small neighborhood just north of Veterans Stadium, where residents are eager to call tow trucks.

If the Phillies or the Eagles are at home, traffic will be a nightmare.

**Media bites**
**Radio:** WIP (610 AM).
**TV:** Prism and SportsChannel Philadelphia (mostly home games); WPHL (Channel 17), away games. Play-by-play announcer Gene Hart has been with the team—on TV and/or radio—since its inception in 1967.

**Cuisine**
Plenty of Philadelphia delicacies are available. Soft pretzels might seem traditional, but the city is famous for them. Eat them with mustard. Hoagies can be found at several stands, or try the cheese steak smothered with fried onions. The traditional stadium fare also is good.

The Spectrum is in a light-industrial/warehouse district, so there isn't much to do there after the game. Sometimes players go to the bar at the Coliseum in Voorhees, New Jersey, their practice facility. The Philly Legends sports bar is a few blocks away, in the Holiday Inn. Partially owned by former Eagles quarterback Ron Jaworski, it draws more of a Phillies and Eagles crowd, but there is Flyers memorabilia on the walls. The atmosphere is loud, and the crowd is young. Philadelphia's major nightclub district is on South Street, south of downtown.

## LODGING NEAR THE ARENA
**Holiday Inn**
10th Packer Ave.
Philadelphia, PA 19148
(215) 755-9500
2 blocks from the arena.

**Sheraton Society Hill**
1 Dock St.
Philadelphia, PA 19106
(800) 325-3535
4 miles from the arena.

## THE FLYERS AT THE SPECTRUM

**March 1, 1968:** A blizzard tears a hole in the Spectrum roof, forcing the team to play the rest of the season on the road.

**May 19, 1974:** A goal by Rick MacLeish gives the Flyers a 1–0 win over the Boston Bruins in Game 6 of the Stanley Cup finals. Philadelphia wins the series, four games to two, becoming the first expansion team to take the Cup.

**May 13, 1975:** Kate Smith continues her streak of good luck for the Flyers. After hearing her sing "God Bless America," the Flyers beat the New York Islanders 4–1 and advance to their second consecutive Stanley Cup finals.

**Jan. 11, 1976:** The Flyers defeat the visiting Soviet Army team 4–1, the first NHL team to do so.

**April 1, 1976:** Reggie Leach becomes the second NHL player to score 60 goals in one season.

**Dec. 11, 1978:** Tom Bladon sets an NHL record for the most points by a defenseman in one game with four goals and four assists. The Flyers beat the Cleveland Barons 11–1.

**Oct. 14, 1979:** A 4–2 win over the Toronto Maple Leafs starts a streak of 35 consecutive games without a loss for the Flyers.

**Nov. 15, 1984:** Bobby Clarke's number 16 is retired and the Flyers improve their record to 55-9-2 in games in which Kate Smith's recording of "God Bless America" is played beforehand.

**Dec. 8, 1987:** Ron Hextall becomes the first goalie in NHL history to shoot the puck directly into the opposing net. The Flyers beat Boston 5–2.

# IN THE HOT SEATS AT THE SPECTRUM

If you want two seats together, make sure you order early because the 17,380-seat Spectrum averages 99% capacity. Seats in the lower bowl are difficult to get, but some single seats might be available even if you order late. The second level is moderately priced for hockey, and the sightlines are good. Most out-of-towners end up in the second and third levels. When the rival Washington Capitals or New York Rangers are in town, security posts more officers in sections with out-of-town fans.

• **Bad seats:** The obstructed-view seats are behind the stairwells leading to the upper balconies. Locals tend to chuckle when disconcerted visitors realize how bad their seats are. In the corners, you can barely see from the blue line in. These discounted seats are sold only at the stadium and are essentially a ticket into the building.

• **Moving down:** Fans are allowed in the lower section to watch practice. But don't bother staying—ushers will know you're a stranger. If you have an obstructed-view seat, wander a little in the first period and keep your eyes peeled. Even in a sellout, there are empty seats up high. Grab one at the start of the second period.

 **Scalping:** The Flyers used to broadcast that scalpers' tickets might be forged or stolen. Also, police officers are posted in the parking lot near the rear entrance to the Spectrum. Still, you can find scalpers near the subway station.

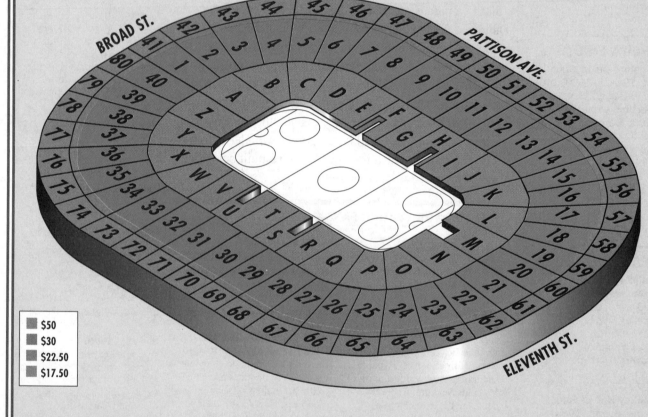

$50
$30
$22.50
$17.50

## HOME-ICE ADVANTAGE

God bless Kate Smith. The Flyers first played Kate Smith's version of "God Bless America" on Dec. 11, 1969. The Flyers won that game and kept winning when it was played. She sang the song live three times, including the Flyers' Stanley Cup–clinching victory against the Bruins in 1974. In 1975, her last appearance, the Islanders tried to bribe her with a bouquet of flowers, but they still lost. The duo of Smith and the Flyers have an astounding 62-13-3 record.

## GETTING TO THE SPECTRUM

**Public transportation:** Take the Broad Street subway from 15th and Market southbound to Broad and Patterson. The Spectrum is 1 block away. Call (215) 580-7800 for more information.

**By car:** From the north, take I-95 South to the Broad Street exit. Follow Broad to Zinkoff Boulevard and turn right.

From the south, take I-95 north to the Broad Street exit and proceed as above.

From the west, take I-76 east. At Century City, follow signs for the Sports Complex. Take the Broad Street exit, No. 45. Go right onto Broad. Stay left to Pattison Avenue.

From the east, take Whitman Bridge to I-76 west, to exit 46B, South 7th Street. Go through one traffic light to Pattison Avenue. Go right onto Pattison to the first traffic light, and then left onto 11th Street.

## TICKET INFORMATION

**Ticket office:** Pattison Place, Philadelphia, PA 19148

**Phone:** TicketMaster at (215) 336-2000, (609) 665-2500 or (302) 984-2000.
**Hours:** Mon.-Fri. 9-6, Sat. 10-4:30.

**Prices:** $50: sections A-Z; $30: sections 1-40; $22.50: upper rows of sections 1-40; $17.50: sections 41-80.

# Pittsburgh Civic Arena

## ARENA STATS

**Location:** 300 Auditorium Place, Pittsburgh, PA 15219
**Opened:** Sept. 17, 1961
**Capacity:** 17,537
**Services for fans with disabilities:** Seating available in sections B5 and B11. Special arrangements can also be made before the game by calling (412) 642-1892.

## ARENA FIRSTS

**Regular-season game:** Oct. 11, 1967, 2–1 loss to the Montreal Canadiens.
**Overtime game:** Oct. 12, 1983, 4–3 loss to the Winnipeg Jets.
**Playoff game:** April 23, 1970, 3–2 over the St. Louis Blues.
**Stanley Cup finals game:** May 15, 1991, 5–4 over the Minnesota North Stars.

## TEAM NOTEBOOK

**Franchise history:** Pittsburgh Penguins, 1967–present.
**Stanley Cups:** 1990–91, 1991–92.
**Most Valuable Player/Hart:** Mario Lemieux, 1987–88, 1992–93.
**Rookie of the Year/Calder:** Mario Lemieux, 1984–85.
**Hockey Hall of Fame:** Andy Bathgate, 1978; Leo Boivin, 1986; Scotty Bowman, 1991; Bob Johnson, 1992.
**Retired number:** 21, Michel Briere.

The round home of the Pittsburgh Penguins is cold and forbidding, hunched halfway up The Hill like an artifact from the Arctic. That's why fans call the Civic Arena the Igloo. But the locals take a lot of pride in the building. The roof was built in 1961 of 2,950 tons of Pittsburgh stainless steel, something not so plentiful today. It's one of the few retractable roofs that actually works well even if it isn't opened very often, and never for hockey games. The best aspect of the roof, though, is that it has no interior supports, which means there are very few obstructed-view seats in the Arena.

The Arena was designed for use by the Civic Light Opera, and the conditions of a $1 million grant from Edgar J. Kaufman required the retractable roof so the CLO could play *en plein air*. Unfortunately, when the roof was opened, the sound blew out, so the CLO and the symphony moved on to better concert halls, leaving the Igloo to the Penguins, who came in 1967.

In the early days, fans often were heard to grumble that the AHL Hornets, the league-champion team whom the Pens supplanted, were better than the Penguins, but you don't hear such grumbling now. In fact, some would say you don't hear much of anything in the Arena now that the Pens are playing well, and going to hockey games has become the thing to do in Pittsburgh. A lot of suits and ties are seen in the Arena these days, and the crowd isn't as rollicking as it once was. Some might even call it dull, but that tends to be the price of success, even in the home of Pittsburgh steel.

## HOT TIPS FOR VISITING FANS

**Parking**
The cost is $6 to park in one of the five Arena lots, but the two closest to the Arena are permit-only parking for season ticketholders. Arrive 45 minutes early to get a spot in one of the other three; of those, the East Lot, above the Arena, offers the speediest exit. Parking at nearby Chatham Center and St. Francis Central Hospital is also $6. Limited street parking is available a few blocks away on Forbes Avenue, and there's lot parking on the campus of Duquesne University.

**Media bites**
**Radio:** WTAE (1250 AM) and WVPY (96.6 FM).
**TV:** KBL (cable), KDKA (Channel 2), and Penvision (pay-per-view).

**Cuisine**
Nothing to die for, but nothing will kill you. Actually, the nachos are quite tasty, and the vendors are generous with the hot peppers. The rest of the culinary options are your basic arena food. No Pittsburgh specialties are available, except for beer: locally brewed Iron City and I.C. Light are sold, as well as Budweiser, Molson, Miller and Coors.

Afterward, many people pour down The Hill to a strip of bars and restaurants on Forbes Avenue: Souper Bowl (412-471-0416), Loafers Restaurant & Bar (412-391-4087) and Corleone's Pizza (412-281-8181). Clientele ranges from blue collar to BMW.

Equally close to the Arena but a little more upper crust are the Ruddy Duck in the Ramada Inn (412-281-3825), Hugo's Rotisserie in the Hyatt (412-471-1234) and Anthony's (412-261-2215) on Fifth Avenue.

## LODGING NEAR THE ARENA

**Ramada Inn**
1 Bigelow Sq.
Pittsburgh, PA 15219
(412) 281-5800/(800) 228-2828
1 block from the arena.

**Hyatt**
1 Chatham Center
112 Washington Place
Pittsburgh, PA 15219
(412) 471-1234/(800) 233-1234
Across the street from arena.

## THE PENGUINS AT THE CIVIC ARENA

**Nov. 22, 1972:** The Penguins score five goals during two minutes and seven seconds of a 10–4 rout of the St. Louis Blues, the fastest five goals by one team in NHL history.

**Dec. 31, 1988:** Mario Lemieux becomes the first NHL player to score a goal in each of the five possible ways during a single game: even handed, shorthanded, power play, penalty shot and, as time ran out, into an empty net.

**April 25, 1989:** Mario Lemieux scores five goals, four of them in one period, as the Penguins win Game 5 of the division final against the Philadelphia Flyers 10–7. The five goals ties an NHL playoff record.

**May 11, 1991:** The Penguins down the Boston Bruins 5–3 to advance to their first Stanley Cup finals. Pittsburgh goes on to beat the Minnesota North Stars, four games to two, for the title.

**May 26, 1992:** The Penguins defeat the Blackhawks 5–4 in the first game of the Stanley Cup finals. Pittsburgh sweeps the series for its second consecutive title.

# IN THE HOT SEATS AT PITTSBURGH CIVIC ARENA

Tickets go on sale in September and sell well, but not particularly quickly. Sellouts are not as common now as in the early '90s. Tickets available on game day usually are for section F and D seats.

• **Good seats:** The only poles are those supporting the super boxes and the press box; the seats behind those poles, in sections D-25 and D-7, go for just $22.50. The best seats for your money probably are the 3,000 spots in the two E-level balconies. The balconies are at the ends of the

ice, so you don't need to twist and turn to follow the action. Section A, close behind the glass and the penalty boxes, is considered choice, since you can hear the players. But you're paying $47 to sit behind Plexiglas.

• **Bad seats:** Unless you can't afford anything else, skip the limited-view seats in D-7 and D-25. Section F, is very high both in altitude and price considering its location. Fans can't see the scoreboard from the last few rows of section C

because the balconies block the view.

• **Moving down:** Fans say the ushers will move you down for a couple of bucks.

**Scalping:** Scalpers can be found within two blocks of the Arena, and their prices are not outrageous. Even for sellouts or playoffs, tickets often are available for only $10 or $15 above face value.

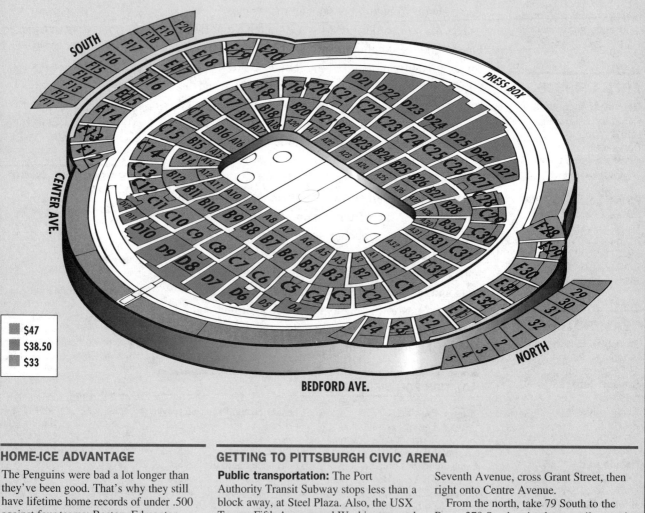

## HOME-ICE ADVANTAGE

The Penguins were bad a lot longer than they've been good. That's why they still have lifetime home records of under .500 against four teams: Boston, Edmonton, Montreal and the New York Rangers.

The fan factor is negligible. As the team got better, the crowds got larger but less boisterous. Still, Vince Lascheid is one of the wittiest organists in professional sports.

## GETTING TO PITTSBURGH CIVIC ARENA

**Public transportation:** The Port Authority Transit Subway stops less than a block away, at Steel Plaza. Also, the USX Tower, Fifth Avenue and Washington, and St. Francis Central Hospital bus stops are within 1 block of the Civic Arena. Call (412) 442-2000 for more information.

**By car:** From the south, take 279 North through the Fort Pitt Tunnel to Liberty Avenue. Go right off Liberty Avenue onto

Seventh Avenue, cross Grant Street, then right onto Centre Avenue.

From the north, take 79 South to the Route 279 South exit, about a mile past the Wexford Exit. Follow 279 South over Veterans Bridge to the Sixth Street exit. Go left at the light onto Bigelow Boulevard.

---

**TICKET INFORMATION**
**Address:** 300 Auditorium Place, Pittsburgh, PA 15219

**Phone:** (412) 642-1985/(412) 333-SEATS
**Hours:** Mon.-Fri. 8:30-5:30.
**Prices:** $47: A, B, C levels; $38.50: D level;

$33: E and F levels; $22.50: scattered limited-view seats.

# Colisée de Québec

■ C$56.25 ■ C$54.25 ■ C$42.50 ■ C$37.50 ■ C$34.50
■ C$31.75 ■ C$31.25 ■ C$22.50 ■ C$17.25

If Yankee Stadium is the House That Ruth Built, then the Colisée is the House That Jean Built. Hall of Famer Jean Beliveau, le Gros Bill, started his career in Quebec City, first at the junior level and then in the Senior League. He filled the Colisée at a time when the building was struggling to establish its viability before he left to lead the Montreal Canadiens to 10 Stanley Cups. Quebec City traces its hockey heritage even farther back, though, to when the Quebec Bulldogs won the Cup in 1911–12 and 1912–13.

In some Canadian arenas, French is spoken over the loudspeakers, but there's no English translation here. More than 95% of Quebec City's inhabitants are French-speaking. The exclusive use of French isn't the only thing that makes the Colisée distinctive. Compared to other NHL arenas, crowds are quiet, but this hides the fans' intensity.

To see the fans at their most intense, come whenever La Bataille de Québec (the Battle of Québec) is waged between the Nordiques and their hated rivals, the Canadiens. This is a war of opposites between Montreal, the business hub and cosmopolitan metropolis, and Quebec City, the much smaller provincial capital. Though the fleur-de-lys of Quebec has had its dramatic triumphs over the *Sainte Flanelle*, or "holy flannel," uniforms of the Canadiens, it's still Montreal with the historic edge, which also adds fire to the rivalry.

## HOT TIPS FOR VISITING FANS

### Parking
4,500 spots at C$5 are on the Colisée grounds and in the adjoining race track and exposition grounds. A number of businesses, especially on the north side of the Colisée, offer parking for C$2 or C$3. You also can park on the numerous side streets if you get there early.

### Media bites
**Radio:** CJRP (1060 AM).
**TV:** Television Quatre-Saisons (Channel 2) and Cable 13.

### Cuisine
The Colisée reputedly has the best hot dogs in the league. The weiners are steam heated, but what sets these hot dogs apart are the buns. They're toasted in a waffle press. While at the Colisée, you also can sample a Québec specialty called *poutine*: French fries with cheese curds melted into the fries with gravy. The house beer is O'Keefe.

After the game, take boulevard Hamel right off the south-side parking lot and head west to La Cage aux Sports (418-872-3000). The food is good and inexpensive, with everything from chicken wings to shrimp. If you want to catch up with the players, try the Dagobert, a popular downtown disco on Grande Allée.

### GETTING TO THE ARENA
**Public transportation:** Buses stop in front of the arena, and the city runs a special on game nights. Call (418) 627-2511 for more information.
**By car:** From downtown, Highway 40 to route Soumonde, or boulevard Laurentienne to route Soumonde and follow to the arena.

### LODGING NEAR THE ARENA
**Hotel Normandin**
4700 boulevard Pierre Bertrand
Quebec City, PQ
Canada G2J 1A4
(418) 622-1611/(800) 463-6721
6 ¼ miles from the arena.

**Hotel Le Dauphin**
400 rue Marais
Quebec City, PQ
Canada G1M 3R1
(418) 688-3888/(800) 668-5911
6 ¼ miles from the arena.

### HOME-ICE ADVANTAGE
Nordiques fans know their hockey, and they're very demanding. They're quick to boo the home team when it's playing sloppy hockey, and they've been known to cheer wildly and sarcastically for the visiting team when the Nords are being blown out.

### IN THE HOT SEATS

With a season-ticket base of 10,200, seats are readily available for most games, especially in the corner blues and the upper decks.

• **Good seats:** The most avid Nordiques fans swear by seats in the upper decks. These diehards will tell you that's where you'll feel the enthusiasm. The sightlines are great, and for the money they're hard to beat.

Les Galeries Populaires are a good buy for families on a limited budget.

• **Bad seats:** The view of the ice surface is partially blocked in rows G-I in sections 7, 8, 11, 12, 15 and 16 in the upper mezzanine. Fans won't be able to see the clock from most seats in the top rows of the east and west mezzanine seats because the upper decks drop down over them. And if you're in the last row, you won't be able to see the far boards if you stand up. All of these obstructed-view seats (132 in all) are sold for $16.

• **Moving down:** A number of seats in the reds often go unused. Fans can spot these and take them if they're discreet.

• **Scalping:** They hang around the lane next to the ticket office at the southwest corner of the Colisée starting at midafternoon on game day.

## ARENA STATS

**Location:** Corner of 14th St. and Clark Ave., St. Louis, MO 63102
**Opened:** October 1994
**Capacity:** 18,500
**Services for fans with disabilities:** Seating available throughout the arena.

## TEAM NOTEBOOK

**Franchise history:** St. Louis Blues, 1967–present.
**Most Valuable Player/Hart:** Brett Hull, 1990–91.
**Hockey Hall of Fame:** Doug Harvey, 1973; Dickie Moore, 1974; Glenn Hall, 1975; Jacques Plante, 1978; Joseph Lynn Patrick, 1980; Emile Francis, 1982; Dan Kelly, 1989.
**Retired numbers:** 3, Bob Gassoff; 8, Barclay Plager; 11, Brian Sutter; 24, Bernie Federko.

### TICKET INFORMATION
**Address:** 100 N. Broadway, Suite 820, St. Louis, MO 63102
**Phone:** (314) 781-5300
**Hours:** Mon.-Sun. 10-6.

## LODGING NEAR THE ARENA

**Hyatt**
1820 Market St.
St. Louis, MO 63103
(314) 231-1234/(800) HILTONS
2 blocks from the arena.

**Hampton Inn**
2211 Market St.
St. Louis, MO 63103
(314) 241-3200/(800) 426-7866
5 blocks from the arena.

# Kiel Center

Needing to replace aging St. Louis Arena, developers and city officials put into practice Missouri's motto as the Show Me state. The plan: build an ultra modern arena that continued the revitalization of downtown at a manageable cost.

The result: the new $135 million Kiel Center. Built on the site of the renowned Kiel Auditorium, on the south side of downtown next to the historic Kiel Opera House, the 664,000-square-foot, 18,500-seat arena promises to pick up for hockey's Blues where St. Louis Arena, opened in 1929, left off. Rather than being a multipurpose building first and a hockey arena second, Kiel Center is a hockey facility that accommodates other purposes. A $3.5 million video scoreboard with animation and replay capability hangs over center ice. The arena's neutral colors, plants and artsy neon signs might seem more fitting for California than Missouri, but St. Louis Arena's noise level, trademark Budweiser song and foghorn after goals will all be part of the Blues games at Kiel Center.

Even though it tries to preserve some familiar aspects, the Kiel Center borrows from other arenas. Kiel Center president Jud Perkins visited more than 40 arenas in the last seven years, so you'll note similarities to The Pond of Anaheim, Boston Garden, Market Square Arena and Calgary's Olympic Saddledome. The next step for the Kiel Center is to build its own tradition for the Blues.

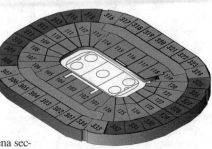

■ N/A ■ $55 ■ $45 ■ $37 ■ $30

## HOT TIPS FOR VISITING FANS

### Parking
More than 6,000 parking spaces are available within a 3-block radius, including a 1,240-space parking garage that adjoins the arena. Prices range from $5-$10. You can park on nearby streets, but some consider the neighborhood more than 3 or 4 blocks away to be risky.

### Media bites
**Radio:** KMOX (1120 AM).
**TV:** KPLR (Channel 11).

### Cuisine
The richest food—in calories and cost—is in the Club Restaurant, which is open to people in luxury suites and club seats. It offers a huge buffet, with different selections daily, including New York strip loin and prime rib.

On the concourse is the usual selection of hot dogs, nachos and pretzels. The Kiel Grill booth offers chicken wings, French fries, hamburgers and steak sandwiches. Other specialty booths include Taste of the Hill (named after a predominantly Italian section of St. Louis), St. Louis–style Food, the Italian Deli and Sweets And Such for desserts. Kiel Center sits in the shadow of an Anheuser-Busch brewery, so Budweiser and Bud Light are offered, but there's also a wide selection of imported beers, such as Corona, Molson and Heineken.

Your best bet after the game is

to visit Union Station, a former railroad terminal that has been converted into a mall. Another place expected to be a new fan hangout is Maggie O'Brien's, at 2000 Market Street.

## GETTING TO KIEL CENTER
**Public transportation:** A MetroLink station is directly south of the Kiel Center at 14th Street and Clark Avenue. For more information on MetroLink service, call (314) 231-2345. The city's Bi-State bus system also has service to the Center; call (314) 231-2345 for more information.
**By car:** From the west, take I-44 east, exit at Jefferson Avenue and proceed north. Turn right at Chouteau Avenue, then left at 18th Street, and follow signs.

From the south, take I-55 north, then take the Downtown Exit to Memorial Drive. From Memorial Drive, turn left at Market Street, then left at Tucker. At Clark Avenue, turn left or right.

From the north, take I-70 east. Then take the Memorial Drive Exit to Market Street. Proceed west on Market Street to 16th Street and make a left.

From the east, take I-64 west to the Ninth Street Exit. Turn left on Clark Avenue and proceed to the arena.

## HOME-ICE ADVANTAGE
St. Louis Arena used to be one of the most fearsome places for visiting teams to play in. While St. Louis's domination has slipped in recent years, a new home very easily could make the Blues king of the Kiel. They might struggle for the first few games, getting to know the nuances and bounces off their new dasher boards and getting familiar with the ice at Kiel Center. But the foghorn can rattle opposing players, and the fans are very supportive of the team.

## IN THE HOT SEATS

With the Blues having a season-ticket base of 14,000 and playing at 98.4% capacity, tickets can be hard to come by, particularly with fan interest in the new building.

Designers increased the angle between seats so fans will have a higher plane of seating, giving an overhang type of view.

• **Good seats:** The best seats, if you can get them, are the 1,640 premium club-level (center mezzanine) seats, which offer seat-side food and beverage service.

• **Bad seats:** The Kiel Center has no obstructed views, but as with any arena, if you sit too close to the glass, your view of parts of the ice can be distorted.

**Scalping:** Scalping is illegal. The city was hard on scalpers at St. Louis Arena and will crack down on them at the Kiel Center.

# San Jose Arena

TM

## ARENA STATS

**Location:** 525 W. Santa Clara St., San Jose, CA 95113
**Opened:** Sept. 8, 1993
**Capacity:** 17,190
**Services for fans with disabilities:** Seating available in sections 102, 213, 217 and 218, and in front of sections 104-112.

## ARENA FIRSTS

**Regular-season game:** Oct. 14, 1993, 2–1 loss to the Calgary Flames.
**Goal:** Kip Miller, San Jose.
**Overtime game:** Oct. 16, 1993, 1–1 tie with the Boston Bruins.
**Playoff game:** April 22, 1994, 3–2 loss to the Detroit Red Wings.

## TEAM NOTEBOOK

**Franchise history:** San Jose Sharks, 1991–present.

Nary a discouraging word escapes the lips of Sharks fans when they talk about their Men of Teal and the San Jose Arena, which stands a few blocks west of downtown San Jose on Santa Clara Street. Indeed, in their first season in the arena, the Sharks played to 96.5% capacity, selling out most games. This happened despite pricey tickets (up to $71), concessions and parking ($10).

Fans who brave the prices are treated to an enjoyable experience. It starts with a breathtaking entrance, which leads into a 60-foot glass-enclosed, terrazzo-tiled cathedral lobby. The sound system cranks out 70,000 watts through 32 speaker clusters. Seats are comfortable, with good leg room and cup holders, and sightlines are excellent. Even at the highest seats, the circular, state-of-the-art replay scoreboard guarantees a great view.

And make sure you get to the game on time—the Sharks provide one of the greatest openings in the NHL. The players skate through the fog-belching mouth of a 17-foot shark's head, complete with glowing red eyes. It's enough to raise the noise to feeding-frenzy level.

If the Sharks' play continues to match the popularity of their logo merchandise and the fervent support of their fans, the Arena will become one of the most treacherous places for visiting teams to swim in and one of the best places in which to watch a hockey game.

## HOT TIPS FOR VISITING FANS

**Parking**
Of the 1,750 spaces in two Arena lots, many are immediately west and are reserved by suite and club-seat holders. Late-arriving or early-leaving fans should pay the $10 and park close. Almost 7,000 more spaces are available in private and city lots within half a mile. Downtown, you can park for as little as $3 and catch a free shuttle bus. Free parking is available west of the railroad tracks on the west side of the arena. The neighborhoods are safe, but beware of "permit only" residential areas. The fine if you are caught is $51.

**Media bites**
**Radio:** KFRC (610 AM), or KLIV (1590 AM) and KKHI (1550 AM) when conflicts with A's games on KFRC. **TV:** KICU (Channel 36), KGO (Channel 7) and SportsChannel.

**Cuisine**
The fare is expensive, but the 22 point-of-sale stands offer plenty of variety. Try TCBY yogurt, Häagen-Dazs ice cream, Mexican food, small pizzas, Sausage Haus or Gretel's Bakery. The tequila chicken sandwich is particularly yummy, but it's available only in The Club, accessible to those with the $71, $61 or suite tickets. If your taste in beer runs to something more exotic than Miller Genuine Draft, head to Beers of the World kiosks. Specialty drinks include margaritas, chardonnay and a house white wine.

Scott's Bar and Grill (408-971-1700) downtown offers a seafood menu; visiting players, many of whom stay at the nearby Hyatt Regency or Hilton, stop by for one entree—the shark.

After games, Henry's, two blocks down a side street from the Arena and tucked under the superstructure of Highway 87, is packed with Sharks fans. If you're looking for a little less talk and more action, head for San Jose Live, upstairs in the pavilion across First Street from the Hyatt. The centerpiece is a 20-foot-plus basketball cage, plus 13 pool tables, dart boards, fussball and table-hockey games. The heart of San Jose's burgeoning night club scene is only a few blocks away from the Arena, in a few blocks of South First and Second streets.

## LODGING NEAR THE ARENA

**DeAnza Hotel**
233 W. Santa Clara St.
San Jose, CA 95113
(408) 286-1000/(800) 843-3700
3 blocks from the arena.

**Hilton**
300 Almaden Blvd.
San Jose, CA 95110
(408) 287-2100/(800) HILTONS
1 mile from the arena.

## THE SHARKS AT SAN JOSE ARENA

**March 20, 1994:** Wayne Gretzky reaches Gordie Howe's mark of 801 goals when he ties the game between the Los Angeles Kings and the Sharks at 6–6.

**March 29, 1994:** Sergei Makarov scores the Sharks' first penalty-shot goal as they beat the Winnipeg Jets 9–4.

**April 23, 1994:** Goalie Arturs Irbe has a pass stolen from him behind the net, resulting in a Detroit Red Wings goal, but the Sharks rally and win 4–3 to tie their playoff series at two games each.

**April 26, 1994:** The Sharks take Game 5 against the Red Wings, to gain a 3–2 lead in their series.

**May 10, 1994:** Sergei Makarov notches four points as the Sharks beat the Toronto Maple Leafs 5–2, taking a 3–2 edge in their Western Conference semifinal series.

# IN THE HOT SEATS AT SAN JOSE ARENA

While tickets could be purchased within 48 hours of a game during the 1993–94 season, the team's success means getting a ticket will be more difficult this season. The season-ticket base was expected to increase to 13,000-14,000. Single-game tickets for the remaining 3,000-4,000 seats were scheduled to go on sale in October, but unlike last season, team officials were considering holding back a block of tickets for each game. Most tickets available would be high or in the corners.

• **Good seats:** Every seat gives an unimpaired view of the playing area. Try the $44 seats in sections 101 and 115; they are the top six or seven rows of the lower level, between the blue lines, and are high enough to see all the action, strategies and angles. For value, try the $30 seats.

Be aware that by being only a couple of rows higher, you might be able to save $11 or more a seat. For example: The first row of the second level is $44, but the second row is $30, or $26 at the ends.

 **Scalping:** Even though most games in 1993–94 were sellouts, the last tickets usually don't go until game day. Look for scalpers plying their trade discreetly along Santa Clara Street in the 2 blocks between downtown and the Arena.

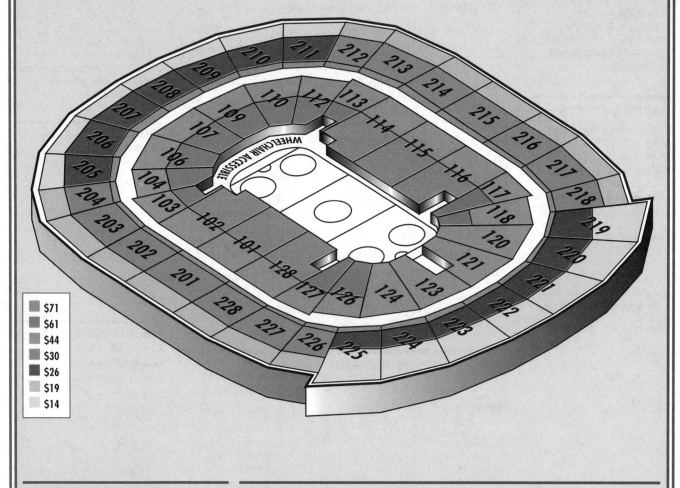

$71
$61
$44
$30
$26
$19
$14

## HOME-ICE ADVANTAGE

With each score or near score, the teal-clad fans erupt in a frenzy and do their group chomp, arms acting like jaws and fingers like teeth. The Sharks and their first-year Arena fans melded in a building-shaking, Fan Appreciation Night, mutual lovefest after the final regular-season game in 1994, and the noise continued through the Sharks' surprising run through the playoffs. There are no signs that it will let up in the near future.

## GETTING TO SAN JOSE ARENA

**Public transportation:** From San Francisco, take Amtrak/CalTrail to Cahill Station, across the street from the arena. Call (800) 660-4287 for more information. In San Jose, Light Rail goes to the Santa Clara Street Station downtown; 15-minute walk along Santa Clara Street gets you to the Arena. Also, shuttles run to and from the Arena during Sharks games. For more information about Light Rail and buses, call (408) 321-2300.

**By car:** From San Francisco and the north, take 101 south to the Guadalupe Parkway (Route 87). Exit right onto Park Avenue approximately 3 blocks to Autumn Street. Go right on Autumn Street for about 2 blocks. Arena is on the left.

From the south, take Route 87 north to San Jose. Exit at Santa Clara Street, turn left and follow Santa Clara approximately 2 blocks. Arena is on the right.

**TICKET INFORMATION**
**Address:** 525 W. Santa Clara St., San Jose, CA 95113
**Phone:** (408) 999-5765 or Bass Tickets at

(408) 998-BASS, (510) 762-BASS, (707) 546-BASS, (916) 923-BASS, (209) 226-BASS, (209) 952-BASS, or (800) 225-BASS.
**Hours:** Mon.-Fri. 9:30-5:30, Sat. 9:30-1.

**Prices:** $71: sideline club seats; $61: end/corner club seats; $44: lower reserved and first two rows upper rim; $30, $26, $19, $14: upper reserved.

## ARENA STATS

**Location:** 1 Stadium Dr., St. Petersburg, FL 33705
**Opened:** March 3, 1990
**Capacity:** 28,000
**Services for fans with disabilities:** Seating available throughout the arena, but mostly around the first level. Call (813) 229-8800 for information.

## ARENA FIRSTS

**Regular-season game:** Oct. 7, 1992, 7–3 over the Chicago Blackhawks.
**Goal:** Chris Kontos of Tampa Bay.
**Overtime game:** Jan. 24, 1993, 2–2 tie with the Minnesota North Stars.

## TEAM NOTEBOOK

**Franchise history:** Tampa Bay Lightning, 1992–present.

## TICKET INFORMATION

**Address:** 501 E. Kennedy Blvd., Suite 175, Tampa, FL 33602 or 1 Stadium Dr., St. Petersburg, FL 33705
**Phone:** (813) 229-8800 or (813) 896-2658, or TicketMaster at (813) 287-8844 in Tampa, (813) 898-2100 in St. Petersburg, (407) 839-3900 in central Florida and (904) 353-3309/(813) 825-3120 in northern Florida
**Hours:** Mon.-Fri. 9-6.

## LODGING NEAR THE ARENA

**Hilton**
333 First St. S
St. Petersburg, FL 33701
(813) 894-5000/(800) HILTON
16 blocks from the arena.

**Stouffer Vinoy Resort**
501 Fifth Ave. N.E.
St. Petersburgh, FL 33701
(813) 894-1000/(800) HOTELS1
2 miles from the arena.

# ThunderDome

The Tampa Bay Lightning were looking for a bigger temporary home after playing a year at Tampa's tiny Expo Hall. St. Petersburg's Suncoast Dome was seeking a tenant after being jilted by baseball teams. But what started as a marriage of convenience has become a success story, in terms of attendance and technology.

Ice, dasher boards and revised seating had to be fitted in the renamed ThunderDome. Modifications were made to the lighting and sound systems. A heating, ventilation and air-conditioning system had to be added to maintain the ice. The cooling system was the biggest test. In an early exhibition game, the ice melted, but project coordinators said the system was intended as a portable one. In the new, more powerful system, the pipes are buried and better insulated.

The flashiest new attraction is the $1.5 million, eight-sided, center-ice Supervideo screen.

Tampa Bay fans love their new team and its new home. Attendance in the Lightning's first year at the 28,000-seat ThunderDome averaged more than 21,000, including an NHL-record 27,227 in the home opener. The team has decided its permanent home, to be built in Tampa, will have more than 20,000 seats. Until that arena is finished, however, the ThunderDome's field of dreams will continue to be coated with ice.

■ $50 ■ $34.50 ■ $28.50 ■ $25
■ $19.50 ■ $15 ☐ $12 ■ $8

## HOT TIPS FOR VISITING FANS

### Parking
The neighborhood around the ThunderDome isn't the greatest, so you might want to pay the extra money ($8 vs. $6) and park in the stadium lot; arrive an hour early because spots fill quickly. Many lots around the ThunderDome are not well-lighted. Another option is to park in the free lots in downtown St. Petersburg and take a shuttle. It has five stops and runs from an hour before each game to an hour after the game.

### Media bites
**Radio:** WFNS (910 AM).
**TV:** Home games are shown on the Sunshine Network; selected road games are on WTOG (Channel 44).

### Cuisine
Many fans flock to the concessions stand run by the Olive Garden, an Italian-restaurant chain. At other stands, you'll find your basic arena food. Budweiser and Labatt's are offered on tap. If you're sitting in the Club section, you can get food delivered to your seat.

After the game, walk across the street to Ferg's Sports Bar (813-360-9558). You can get big pitchers of beer and a decent lineup of food. But get there early—it fills up. If you're looking to go to the beach, try the

Hurricane (813-822-4562). It offers grouper sandwiches, late-night jazz and a breathtaking view of the Sunshine Skyway Bridge from the rooftop.

### GETTING TO THE THUNDERDOME
**Public transportation:**
Numerous buses pass near the arena, including the No. 18, which stops right at it. Call (813) 530-9911 for more information.
**By car:** From the north, take I-275 going south. The Thunder-Dome is clearly visible from the highway. Take the Thunder-Dome exit off I-275 and follow signs to the stadium.

From the south, I-275 north to the ThunderDome exit. Follow signs to the stadium.

### HOME-ICE ADVANTAGE
The huge crowds and the soft ice can create an edge for the Lightning. But the young team is still building, and hasn't yet really taken advantage of these.

An intense rivalry is developing with the fellow expansion team Florida Panthers, owned by Marlins owner H. Wayne Huizenga. Many in the Tampa Bay area believe he is the reason there is no baseball at the ThunderDome. As payback, the out-of-town scoreboard refers to the Panthers as Miami instead of Florida.

## IN THE HOT SEATS

Single-game sales start in September; order early for games against the Florida Panthers, the Los Angeles Kings and the New York Rangers. For most other games, about 10,000 seats are available near game time, mostly in the upper level. Club level has a waiting list.

• **Good seats:** Your best bet is along the Club levels or the D section, which has lots of leg room, a sensational view of the Supervideo and a perfect angle to the action. Even the bleacher and general admission seats offer decent views.

• **Bad seats:** The risers for the A-section seats don't have enough of a slope, so if a tall person sits in front of you, it's hard to see.

 **Scalping:** Not much need, but if you want to find a scalper, look on First Avenue South and Ninth Street North. The markup for premium games is generally $8-$10 above face value, more if the Panthers are the opponent.

# Maple Leaf Gardens

## ARENA STATS

**Location:** 60 Carlton St., Toronto, ON, Canada M5B 1L1
**Opened:** Nov. 12, 1931
**Capacity:** 15,642
**Services for fans with disabilities:** Seating in the gold sections.

## ARENA FIRSTS

**Regular-season game:** Nov. 12, 1931, 3–1 loss to the Chicago Blackhawks.
**Playoff game:** March 29, '31, 6–0 over the Blackhawks.
**Stanley Cup finals game:** April 9, '32, 6–4 over the New York Rangers.

## TEAM NOTEBOOK

**Franchise history:** Toronto Maple Leafs, 1926–present.
**Stanley Cups:** 1931–32, '41–42, '44–45, '46–47, '47–48, '48–49, '50–51, '61–62, '62–63, '63–64, '66–67.
**Hockey Hall of Fame:** Hewitt, 1947; Clancy, Irvin, Smythe, '58; Selke, '60; Apps, Conacher, Day, Hainsworth, '61; Schriner, '62; Hewitt, Horner, S. Howe, '65; M. Bentley, Kennedy, Pratt, Primeau, '66; Broda, '67; Dye, '70; Jackson, Kelly, Sawchuck, '71; Carl Voss, '73; Moore, Nighbor, '74; Armstrong Bailey, Drillon, Pilote, '75; Bower, '76; Ballard, Horton, '77; Bathgate, Bickell, Plante, Pronovost, '78; Lumley, '80; Mahovlich, Stanley, '81; Ullman, '82; Imlach, Parent, '84; Olmstead, Pilous, '85; Keon, '86; Sittler, '89; Flaman '90; Pulford, '91; Mathers, McDonald '92.
**Retired numbers:** 5, Barilko; 6, Bailey.

---

Walking down Carlton Street in downtown Toronto, there's little to tell you that you're approaching a hockey shrine. You pass the Pizza Hut, the Days Inn—then, suddenly, there's a small building made of yellow brick with a marquee above the doors. That's Maple Leaf Gardens.

But it's exactly that, well, nondescriptness that makes Maple Leaf Gardens arguably the most hallowed building in all of hockey. Indeed, once the Montreal Canadiens, Boston Bruins and Chicago Blackhawks move into their new buildings by the end of 1995, it will be the last remaining building used from the days of the "Original Six."

For hockey fans—especially Canadians—the Gardens represents the last example of a bygone era, a time when going to an NHL game meant dressing up in your Sunday best. Toronto tourism executives say they receive more requests for directions to the Gardens than any other site in the city.

The Gardens has changed little since it was built in 1931. It is a place of reverence for many people—they're the ones wandering around each of the concourses, staring at the old pictures of past Maple Leafs teams and great moments in Leafs history. For them, this isn't just a stadium, it's a monument to hockey.

## HOT TIPS FOR VISITING FANS

**Parking**
Since the Gardens is in downtown Toronto, a number of small lots are around. Generally, any within about a five-block radius of the building charge C$20 for game parking. The farther away you get, the cheaper parking is, down to about C$5 near the lake, but that's a good half-hour walk up Yonge Street from the Gardens.

**Media bites**
**Radio:** FAN (1430 AM).
**TV:** Global CBC.

**Cuisine**
Mostly standard arena fare, but the prices aren't bad. Nearly both sides of each concourse are concessions stands. The hot dogs are a great value. The all-beef frank is about nine inches long, grilled in front of you, and served on a poppy-seed bun. It almost qualifies as a sausage—though there are those, too. A Canadian hockey tradition is a meat sandwich on rye; there are three stands where the beef is hand-carved.

Not long ago, beer wasn't available at Maple Leaf Gardens. Now you can get Molson Canadian Light and a nonalcoholic offering.

A favorite Canadian postgame snack is beer and doughnuts. Don't ask. For the doughnuts, go to Tim Horton's—it seems like there's one on every street corner. For the beer, head just a few steps away to Yonge Street.

Two Maple Leafs fan hangouts are on Carlton Street: P.M.Toronto and M.L.-Gardoonies. Another choice is the bar at the Days Inn next to the Gardens—surprisingly, it rocks with hockey fans, most of whom didn't want to pay scalpers' prices. Also, Wayne Gretzky has a restaurant near

SkyDome, though, of course, he's usually off playing with the Kings.

## LODGING NEAR THE ARENA

**Days Inn**
30 Carlton St.
Toronto, ON
Canada M5B 1L1
(416) 977-6655/(800) AAA-DAYS
Adjacent to the arena.

**Howard Johnson Plaza Hotel Downtown**
475 Yonge St.
Toronto, ON
Canada M4B 1L1
(416) 924-0611
Behind the arena.

## THE MAPLE LEAFS AT THE GARDEN

**April 9, 1932:** Led by Ace Bailey, King Clancy and Harvey "Busher" Jackson, the Maple Leafs take their first Stanley Cup by beating the New York Rangers 6–4.

**Nov. 1, 1946:** A new sport edges into the spotlight—the first NBA game is played in Maple Leafs Gardens. The New York Knickerbockers defeat the Toronto Huskies 68–66.

**April 16, 1949:** A 3–1 victory over the Detroit Red Wings gives Toronto the Stanley Cup, its fourth in five years.

**April 18, 1963:** Dave Keon ties an NHL record with two short-handed goals in Game 5 of the Stanley Cup finals. The goals prove to be the margin of victory, as the Maple Leafs win the game 3–1 over the Red Wings and take their second consecutive Cup.

**Feb. 7, 1976:** Darryl Sittler sets an NHL record with a total of 10 points—six goals and four assists—leading the Maple Leafs to an 11–4 win over the Boston Bruins. The six goals is also a team record.

**Oct. 15, 1983:** Toronto and the Chicago Blackhawks explode for five goals during one minute and 24 seconds of the second period. Three belong to the Hawks and two are Toronto's, but the Leafs go on to win 10–8.

# IN THE HOT SEATS AT MAPLE LEAF GARDENS

The size of Maple Leaf Gardens limits the seating choices available. The Maple Leafs, who have a season-ticket base of 13,000, put all remaining tickets on sale during the first week of October. It's best to order then, because they tend to go quickly. Games against Montreal or one-time visitors with marquee players, such as Pittsburgh, sell out. For other games, you can sometimes get gray seats, the highest level, on game nights.

• **Good seats:** Any of the middle five sections in the red and green seats probably are better deals than at many other

rinks, given the exchange rate. The ends are fun; the steepness of the seats gives you the feeling you're almost hanging from the wall. But during play you have to sit forward—a bar in front of each seat (so you don't pitch forward on the person in front) blocks part of the near zone if you sit back.

• **Bad seats:** The end sections in all color groups could cause a stiff neck. Because the seats were built facing forward, when you sit straight up, you're actually looking at the seats beyond the end of the rink. The grays are a long way from the action, and

in the top two rows you can only see the very bottom of the scoreboard.

In some places, standing room can be the best deal in the house. But not here. Only 124 tickets are available, and you have a reserved standing place that's completely cut off from the action.

 **Scalping:** If the Leafs are doing well, it's the toughest ticket in town. Scalpers are tough; they get top dollar, and there's little room for negotiation. Fans are sometimes approached by scalpers as they walk up Carlton from Yonge Street.

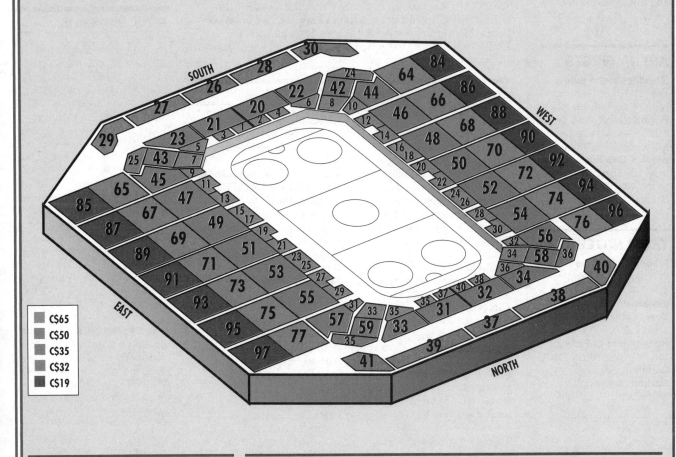

| | |
|---|---|
| ■ | C$65 |
| ■ | C$50 |
| ■ | C$35 |
| ■ | C$32 |
| ■ | C$19 |

## HOME–ICE ADVANTAGE

Torontonians tend to be a little conservative, and Leafs fans are certainly the same. Surprisingly, when the Canadiens come to town, there are almost more red sweaters in the building than blue. The big rival these days is the Detroit Red Wings—also an Original Six team, but a rivalry forced more by the conference setup. Still, the Leafs-Wings battles of the '40s for the Stanley Cup are legendary.

## GETTING TO MAPLE LEAF GARDENS

**Public transportation:** The College Station subway stops at the corner of Yonge and Carlton. The Carlton streetcar stops directly in front of the stadium. Call (416) 393-4636 for more information.

**By car:** From the airport and Niagara Falls, take 427 south to QEW East. Take the Jarvis Street exit north to Carlton Street. Turn left. The Gardens will be on the left.

**TICKET INFORMATION**
**Address:** 60 Carlton St., Toronto, ON Canada M5B 1L1

**Phone:** (416) 977-1641
**Hours:** Mon.-Thur. 9-5, Fri. 9-12:30.
**Prices:** C$65: gold; C$50: red; C$35: blue.

C$32: green; C$19: gray.

# Pacific Coliseum

Though Vancouver is one of North America's younger cities, it has a long history of progressive hockey arenas. Around 1915, as they were toiling in the Pacific Coast League, the Vancouver Millionaires played in the Denman Street Arena, the first building in western Canada to have artificial ice. In 1968, Vancouver again became the envy of other hockey towns when the Pacific Coliseum opened and the Vancouver Canucks of the Western Hockey League moved in. Instead of being designed in a rectangular shape, the new arena was circular, leaving every seat with a good view of the ice.

Vancouver's knowledgeable fans are louder than typical Canadian rooters but less boisterous than U.S. fans. The crowd is polite and well behaved. Now that the Canucks have stars Pavel Bure, Trevor Linden and Kirk McLean, and are playing well enough to reach Game 7 of the Stanley Cup finals, fans feel they've been rewarded for their loyalty.

The Canucks have decided to construct a new building downtown. General Motors Place is scheduled to be ready for the start of the 1995–96 season. This $100 million, 20,000-seat arena, like its innovative predecessors, promises to be a showcase.

■ C$63.25 ■ C$54.50 ■ C$38.50 ■ C$29

## HOT TIPS FOR VISITING FANS

### Parking
With 5,000 spaces costing C$5, parking is easy to find on the PNE grounds. On streets, cars must have a "resident" decal, or they're apt to be ticketed or towed. If you want to park on residential streets, some home owners will let you park in their driveway for C$15-C$20.

### Media bites
**Radio:** CKNW (980 AM).
**TV:** BCTV (Channel 11) and TSN (Channel 30).

### Cuisine
With many British descendants in the area, the fish and chips and chicken and chips are fan favorites. Otherwise, only typical arena food is found on the main concourses. Your best bet is to go to a building attached to the Coliseum that has an open-air barbecue. As with most arenas in Canada, Molson is the dominant beer, but Vancouver fans like the locally produced Kokanee.

During the week, Kits on Broadway (604-736-5811) is a good place in which to grab a quick bite and a drink. On the weekend, Richard's on Richard (604-687-6794) is "the" place to see and be seen in Vancouver, though the dress is a little more formal than at Kits. The Big Bam Boo Club (604-733-2220), on the other hand, caters to a funkier crowd. Double Overtime Sports Grill (604-683-7060), Malone's

(604-684-9977) and the Shark Club Bar & Grill (604-687-4275) are geared toward sports fans.

### GETTING TO PACIFIC COLISEUM
**Public transportation:** B.C. Transit buses stop at the corner of Hastings and Renfrew. Call (604) 264-5000 for information.
**By car:** Go east on Hastings Street to Renfrew Street. The arena is on the corner.

### LODGING NEAR THE ARENA
**Atrium Inn**
2889 E. Hastings St.
Vancouver, BC
Canada V5K 3N7
(604) 254-1000
Across the street from the arena.

**Best Western Exhibition Park**
3475 E. Hastings St.
Vancouver, BC
Canada  V5K 2A5
(604) 294-4751/(800) 528-1234
2 blocks from the arena.

### HOME-ICE ADVANTAGE
The Pacific Coliseum is not usually a lively place, but many feel that the fans and their towels carried the Canucks through the playoffs and into the Stanley Cup finals in 1993–94. The downside is that when the crowd is dead, the team tends to play the same way.

## IN THE HOT SEATS

The Canucks typically play to a 92% or 93% capacity, but the trip to the Stanley Cup finals is expected to increase that. Still, with a season-ticket base of 10,300, you generally can get tickets. Individual-game tickets go on sale in late September, and you usually can get a ticket close to game day.

• **Good seats:** The higher rows in the numbered sections will take you farthest from the game, but they are also the least expensive. Unfortunately, there aren't many bargains. The best deal going is with Safeway grocery stores, which sell tickets for the upper blues for C$20.

• **Bad seats:** Hockey is a game of reflexes, and you should be prepared to use yours if you are sitting in the lettered sections A-C, L-P, or Y-Z. These are the corner and end sections, and though the view is fine, this is also the perfect spot to be found by a flying puck. The glass that goes around the boards is higher than that of some other buildings, especially along the sides of the rink.

• **Moving down:** You can move from one numbered seat to another, but getting by the usher into a lettered section from a numbered section might be a different story.

**Scalping:** Scalpers take up positions on the sidewalk outside the front doors or across Renfrew, but not on the grounds.

# STADIUM STATS

**Location:** 1 Harry S. Truman Dr., Landover, MD 20785
**Opened:** Dec. 2, 1973
**Capacity:** 18,130
**Services for fans with disabilities:** Seating available on the concourse level between the red and blue sections.

# ARENA FIRSTS

**Regular-season game:** Dec. 15, 1974, 1–1 tie with the Los Angeles Kings.
**Goal:** Yvon Labre of the Capitals.
**Overtime game:** Oct. 8, 1983, 8–7 loss to the New York Islanders.
**Playoff game:** April 9, 1983, 6–2 loss to the New York Islanders.

# TEAM NOTEBOOK

**Franchise history:** Washington Capitals, 1974–present.
**Retired number:** 7, Yvon Labre.

**TICKET INFORMATION**
**Address:** 1 Harry S. Truman, Dr., Landover, MD 20785
**Phone:** (301) 386-7000 or TicketMaster at (202) 432-SEAT
**Hours:** Daily 10-5.

# USAir Arena

Located just off the Capital Beltway in Prince George's County, Maryland, the potato-chip-shaped USAir Arena (for 19 years the Capital Centre) is a lot like the hockey team that plays there: not very flashy, no star attractions, just good enough to get the job done. Inadequate lighting adds to the problem, making the Arena dreary. Because of the Capitals' traditional slow starts and playoff disappointments, fans tend to sit on their hands early in the season. When a game isn't going well, they can be deadly quiet and have to be egged on by a noise meter. Sometimes, they are even outshouted by large contingents of out-of-town fans. USAir Arena hopes to take off with help from sponsorship money. Abe Pollin, who owns the arena as well as the Capitals and the NBA's Washington Bullets, has agreed to put the $1 million a year received from USAir into improving the building, particularly in the concourse area. Still, there's talk of relocating the Caps in downtown Washington, D.C.

■ $45 ■ $41 ■ $38
■ $35 ■ $28 ■ $12

## HOT TIPS FOR VISITING FANS

### Parking
You're stuck with the stadium lot, which costs $6. About a dozen spots are available on Largo Drive, off the Central Avenue exit, but you'll have to come early. If you're coming in the Central Avenue entrance, make sure to arrive early and stay to the left, or you'll get directed into a large auxiliary lot that takes forever to exit.

### Media bites
**Radio:** WMAL (630 AM). Play-by-play announcer Ron Weber has never missed a Capitals game.
**TV:** WDCA, (Channel 20) and Home Team Sports.

### Cuisine
Pretty much the standard fare, most of it on the expensive side. Beside the usual offerings, the stand near Portal 2 offers sausages. The Showcase Pub and Eatery has a wider variety of food, milk for the kids and mixed drinks for the adults.

The favorite postgame hangout is Chadwick's (301-808-0200), a quarter-mile from the arena at the Hampton Inn. It offers casual dining in a cozy atmosphere. Players sometimes show up. The Penalty Box, a sports bar in Alexandria, shows hockey games.

## GETTING TO USAIR ARENA
**Public transportation:** The arena can't be reached using public transportation.
**By car:** From downtown, take New York Avenue to Route 50. Take the Beltway (I-95) south to exit 17A or 15A.

From Baltimore, take Baltimore-Washington Parkway or I-95 to the Beltway, then south to exit 17A or 15A.

## LODGING NEAR THE ARENA
**Hampton Inn**
9421 Largo Dr. W
Landover, MD 20785
(301) 499-4600
Less than ¼ mile from the arena.

**Holiday Inn–USAir Arena**
9100 Basil Ct.
Landover, MD 20785
(301) 773-0700
2 miles from the arena.

## HOME-ICE ADVANTAGE
After Rod Langway arrived in 1982–83 and the team began making the playoffs, the Capitals became tough at home. Only in one season, 1989–90, did they struggle even a bit (19-18-3). In 1985–86, they were an astounding 30-8-2.

The fans can be disturbingly quiet, especially early in the season when Redskins and Orioles fever afflicts them, but when football season is over and the Capitals begin their traditional January run to the playoffs, they really get into the game.

## IN THE HOT SEATS

Easy to come by, especially early in the season, when Washington fans still are distracted by football.

The best seats are in sections 222 and 209, which allow views of the whole ice and all scoreboards. Avoid row D: no legroom. If you're a fan of the opponent, sit in the $28 seats. Fans of Eastern Conference rivals, particularly of the Rangers, Penguins and the Flyers, show up in droves.

• **Bad seats:** With a few exceptions, sightlines are good and the Telscreen shows any action that is obscured. However, unless you sit in the corners, you'll find the Telscreen blocks your view of either the out-of-town scoreboards or the shot counter. If you're sitting in sections 106 and 108, you'll be watching the game on TV if the action is in the far end. Make sure you're either in the very front or at least eight rows up. In the second level, particularly in the corners, railings can obstruct your view in rows AA through CC.

• **Moving down:** Possible within the upper level. Wait until the second period to move down.

 **Scalping:** Though there is little need to buy a scalped ticket, scalpers abound. They gather around the footbridge leading from the auxiliary parking lot and near the Stars and Stripes entrance.

# Winnipeg Arena

## ARENA STATS

**Location:** 15-1230 Maroons Rd., Winnipeg, MB, Canada R3G 0L5
**Opened:** 1954
**Capacity:** 15,393
**Services for fans with disabilities:** Seating available throughout the stadium. Call (204) 780-7328 for more information.

## ARENA FIRSTS

**Regular-season game:** Oct. 14, 1979, 4–2 over the Colorado Rockies (NHL).
**Goal:** Morris Lukowich of the Jets.
**Overtime game:** Oct. 12, 1983, 4–3 over the Pittsburgh Penguins (NHL).
**Playoff game:** April 7, 1982, 4–3 loss to the St. Louis Blues (NHL).

## TEAM NOTEBOOK

**Franchise history:** Winnipeg Jets, 1972–79 (WHA); Winnipeg Jets, 1979–present (NHL).
**Hall of Fame:** Bobby Hull 1983
**Retired number:** 9, Bobby Hull

---

**TICKET INFORMATION**
**Address:** 15-1230 Maroons Rd., Winnipeg, MB, Canada R3G 0L5
**Phone:** (204) 780-7328
**Hours:** Mon.-Sat. 9:30-5:30.

---

Although Winnipeg Arena opened in 1954, it wasn't until 1972, when Bobby Hull received a check for $1 million from the fledgling World Hockey Association's Winnipeg Jets, that it began its glory days. Two Europeans, Anders Hedberg and Ulf Nilsson, joined the Jets soon after and, with Hull, formed one of the most exciting lines in hockey. The trio led Winnipeg to three Avco Cups, and the entire city came down with a serious case of hockey fever.

The Jets entered the NHL in 1979. While the team has never since come close to recapturing those memorable early years, Winnipeg still has the fever, fed over the years by great moments such as Serge Savard's last game, a number of Canada vs. Russia games and lots of junior hockey. The winter temperatures in Winnipeg often drop to 30 below zero, yet the building fills to capacity with fans who never know for sure if their cars are going to start after the game.

As hockey has grown here, so has the Arena. With more and more people wanting to see the Jets, the building's roof was raised in 1979.

■ C$50 ■ C$36 ■ C$30
■ C$25 ■ C$20 ■ C$12

## HOT TIPS FOR VISITING FANS

### Parking
Ample parking is available. Expect to pay C$5. Behind the arena is the Polo Park shopping center. Nights when the mall is closed, you can park in the lot for free; otherwise the charge is C$5. Call the mall (204-784-2500) on the day of the game for more information. Across St. James Street are a number of stores that also let you park, for C$5.

### Media bites
**Radio:** CJOB (680 AM).
**TV:** The Jets haven't had much luck with television. Sometimes CKY (Channel 5) or CKND (Channel 12) will have broadcasts. TSN (Channel 14) or CBC (Channel 2) sometimes will show national games.

### Cuisine
Groan. The food is generally awful and unimaginative, so eat before the game or prepare to be satisfied with hot dogs, popcorn, peanuts and soft drinks.

After the game, try Grapes (204-783-3485), a popular place with fans and players. If you are looking for something more lively, the Palomino Club (204-772-0454) usually hops as well. On the weekend, you might head down to the market-square area of downtown to check out The Bank (204-943-2582) or Wise Guys (204-956-2333).

### GETTING TO WINNIPEG ARENA
**Public transportation:** Winnipeg Transit buses stop in front of the arena. Call (204) 986-5700 for more information.
**By car:** From the airport, take Route 90 to Ellice Avenue and turn left. Go 1 block to St. James Street. Turn right. The arena is ahead.

### LODGING NEAR THE ARENA
**Polo Park**
1405 St. Matthews Ave.
Winnipeg, MB
Canada R3G 0L5
(204) 775-8791/(800) 665-0033
Across the street from the arena.

**Country Hospitality Suites Inn**
730 King Edward St.
Winnipeg, MB
Canada R3G 0L5
(204) 783-6900/(800) 456-4000
2 miles from the arena.

### HOME-ICE ADVANTAGE
Although the Jets have yet to make a dent in the Stanley Cup history books, fans in Winnipeg are a proud bunch. Come playoffs, the intensity goes up a notch.

The Original Six teams still have fans in Winnipeg, so when they visit, expect to see plenty of the opposition's sweaters around.

## IN THE HOT SEATS

Winnipeg Arena offers good sightlines from just about any seat in the house.

The leg room is limited in the upper deck, and if you are sitting on the east side (sections 36-44), you can't see the score clock because the press box is in the way. Television monitors that show the score are provided. The good news is that the upper decks offer an excellent view of the ice. The cost is C$20 to sit in end sections 36, 44, 45 and 53; because of the view, these might be the best value in the building. Anywhere else in the upper deck is C$25.

• **Bad seats:** The worst buys are in the high north end. These cost C$30 but are farther from the action than seats in the corners or sides that go for C$25. Also, seats that are low in sections 4-6 or 21-24 are behind the nets and at the perfect height for dodging flying pucks.

• **Moving down:** You might not find many good seats empty, but if you do, moving down is usually not a problem if you wait until at least midway through the first period.

 **Scalping:** A number of people sell tickets on the sidewalks in front of the arena. It's not legal, but the police don't bother with arrests.